BOSS-BUSTERS
& SIN HOUNDS

BOSS-BUSTERS & SIN HOUNDS

Kansas City and Its Star

HARRY HASKELL

UNIVERSITY OF MISSOURI PRESS
COLUMBIA AND LONDON

Library of Congress Cataloging-in-Publication Data

Haskell, Harry.
    Boss-busters and sin hounds : Kansas City and its Star /
Harry Haskell.
        p.   cm.
    Summary: "Haskell tells the tale of the Kansas City Star's rise
and decline, taking readers into the city room and executive offices
of one of the most respected American newspapers. This story
includes Kansas City notables such as Tom Pendergast, J. C. Nichols,
Frank Walsh, William Rockhill Nelson, Henry J. Haskell and
Roy A. Roberts"—Provided by publisher.
    Includes bibliographical references and index.
    ISBN 978-0-8262-1769-1 (alk. paper)
    1. Kansas City Star (Kansas City, Mo. : 1885)—History.
I. Title.
    PN4899.K4S74 2007
    071.781'39—dc22
                                                    2007022277

Designer: Kristie Lee
Typesetter: The Composing Room of Michigan, Inc.
Printer and binder: The Maple-Vail Book Manufacturing Group
Typefaces: Adobe Caslon, Engravers MT, Copperplate

"News is as hard to hold as quicksilver, and it fades more rapidly than any morning glory. But, for all that, it is the best yardstick we have to hold up against the growth and decay of human lives and human ideas. It is a sounding board, employed by ordinary well-meaning newspaper men, on which the love-calls and the prayers, the whines of meanness and the trumpets of glory, receive their test. It is cheap and worthless stuff, and it is the sinews of history."

—Stanley Walker

For my father and mother

CONTENTS

PREFACE

———————◆———————

Hurricane Katrina's devastation of New Orleans in 2005 elicited outrage over the George W. Bush administration's apparent callousness and the staggering incompetence of the federal and state relief effort. Significantly, however, no hue and cry for fundamental governmental reform was raised in the wake of this largely preventable human tragedy. Yet just over a century earlier, a similarly catastrophic storm that laid waste to Galveston, Texas, sparked a coast-to-coast movement for nonpartisan commission government and helped propel the progressives' ambitious reform agenda to the forefront of the nation's consciousness.

At the time of the great Galveston hurricane, in 1900, Missouri and Kansas ranked among the most progressive states in the Union. Notwithstanding sharp differences in demographic makeup and historical experience, both were prime testing grounds for innovations ranging from the initiative and referendum and public ownership of utilities to laws regulating child and female labor and the country's first municipally funded welfare agency. Today, the Sunflower State is better known as a stronghold of Christian fundamentalism than as a laboratory for social and political experiment, while the Show Me State is linked in the public mind with such high-profile neoconservatives as former United States Attorney General John Ashcroft and Governor Matthew Blunt.

What accounts for this dramatic about-face? Where are the "insurgent" reformers of yesteryear, the intrepid idealists who stormed the citadel of officialdom and instigated a far-reaching reexamination of America's social contract? Not, to judge from recent history, in the statehouses of the once proudly progressive Midwest. Nor are many insurgencies evidently afoot in the boardrooms of newspapers that in times past crusaded for change, held corrupt officials and malefactors of great wealth accountable to the people, and in the process crucially helped to define not just who Americans were as a nation but who we could and should be.

The pages that follow tell the story of one great newspaper and of the compelling "power of purpose" it exerted during what might be called the long Progressive Era, stretching from the birth pangs of the reform movement in the late 1800s to its death of terminal complacency in the 1950s. For the better part of those six or seven changeful decades, the *Kansas City Star* was among the most respected and influential daily newspapers in the English-speaking world. Its voice, the authentic voice of middle America, resonated far and wide, not just in Kansas City and its immediate environs but the length and breadth of the great Missouri River Valley, from sea to shining sea, and even, to a degree now almost unthinkable, far beyond American shores.

The *Star*'s story is unique and uniquely colorful, as any story must be that features such bigger-than-life personalities as William Rockhill Nelson, Teddy Roosevelt, William Allen White, Frank Walsh, Sinclair Lewis, Tom Pendergast, Harry Truman, and Roy Roberts. At the same time it is a deeply and characteristically American story, equal parts high drama and low farce, a story of rags and riches, God and Mammon, sin and redemption, vaunting ambition and cynical deceit, lofty promises and gutter politics. The parallels with recent American history—disillusionment with liberal reform, the hijacking of the GOP by the far right, the inexorably widening gap between haves and have-nots, the attack on civil liberties, the country's go-it-alone attitude toward the rest of the world—are as alarming as they are instructive.

Whether one views the news media as part of the solution or part of the problem, there is much to be learned from the faith, optimism, and resilience that informed the progressive journalism of the twentieth century. Even in this age of soundbites and blogs, podcasts and satellite TV, the free press remains as fundamental to the American way of life as free-market capitalism, religious toleration, and representative government. The romance of the gumshoe reporter, licensed to go where angels fear to tread and, as my journalist grandfather used to say, cry woe to those who are at ease in Zion, endures even as the public's confidence in the traditional news media sinks to new depths. Irreverent, irrepressible, and oftentimes irresponsible, the news media play a complex role in our democracy, acting as both mentors and monitors, cheerleaders and gadflies, detached observers of the status quo and committed catalysts for reform.

If print newspapers are an endangered species in the twenty-first century, outmoded by the very electronic media they are belatedly trying to embrace, news junkies have never had it so good. Americans of the future are likelier to suffer from a surfeit than from a dearth of information. Yet today's ethereal Internet "communities" have little in common with the real-life bricks-and-mortar communities that newspapers, big and small, have served since time immemorial. Nor is it clear that so-called grassroots journalism, modeled on the consumer-generated content of the Wikipedia, can provide the critical judgment exercised by experienced editors trained to sift through the news of the day and help readers make sense of the world's daunting incoherence. The digital age has given us the ability to customize our daily intake of information and commentary, but the long-term social cost of screening out news that individuals consider irrelevant or distasteful remains to be reckoned.

Few, I suspect, would rush to turn back the clock to a time when it was said that "the *Star* is Kansas City and Kansas City is the *Star*." But we may yet think again. If there is a more powerful engine for community building and civic renewal than a strong local newspaper, it has yet to be invented. For news, like politics, is fundamentally local. News is not only, in Stanley Walker's memorable phrase, the "sinews of history"; it is also the tie that binds our body politic, that makes the many one, that empowers the individual even as it stirs the masses. Whatever forms newspapers may take in the future, it is hard to see how society can continue to progress without them.

BOSS-BUSTERS
& SIN HOUNDS

PROLOGUE

———◆———

A Puritan in River City

In July of 1896, the summer the Democratic Party burst at the seams and ran the free-silver firebrand William Jennings Bryan for president, a slender, intense young man from rural Ohio came to Kansas City to make his name and, God willing, a livelihood to support his family of impecunious missionaries.

Henry Joseph Haskell—Harry to his friends—had twenty dollars in his pocket and a freshly minted degree from Oberlin College. Amiable and quick-witted, with a worldliness that belied his boyish features, he was bent on becoming a fiction writer in the mold of Richard Harding Davis. He had already made a start by selling one or two stories to *Munsey's* mass-market magazine. Meanwhile, he reckoned, newspaper work was as good a way as any to earn a living. When a classmate from Kansas City invited him to come down and size up his prospects, he wasted no time in setting out for the "wild & wooly west."[1]

As his train steamed toward the big bend where the Missouri River swings east toward St. Louis, Haskell caught his first glimpse of the ill-kempt metropolis known far and wide as the "Pittsburgh of the West." On his right hand, in the flat bottomland straddling the Missouri-Kansas border, rose the smelters, grain elevators, packinghouses, mills, and factories that proclaimed the bustling city a center of trade, commerce, and industry. Farther west, near where the Kansas, or Kaw, River emptied into the Mighty Mo, he espied the spot where Lewis and Clark had encamped on the return leg of their voyage of discovery. Dead ahead sprawled the West Bottoms, a gritty industrial dis-

1

Union Depot in the mid-1890s. Alighting from their trains, visitors caught an unforgettable glimpse of the river city's splendor as well as its squalor.

trict hatched by railroad tracks, as teeming with humanity and vice as any unruly seaport.

The train slowly snaked through the iron cage of Octave Chanute's celebrated Hannibal Bridge. The first permanent span over the Missouri, it had lured the railroads to Kansas City in the 1870s and provided a vital economic lifeline to the upper Midwest. Steamboats, wharves, and squatters' tents jostled for space beside its massive limestone piers. The bluffs south of the river were slowly being whittled away to accommodate the city's mushrooming business district, but the earth movers had spared the imposing promontory that overlooked the confluence of the rivers. Once home to the elite, Quality Hill had lapsed into genteel decay and wooden shanties clung forlornly to its skirts, an eyesore soon to be swept away in an audacious gentrification project that would make Kansas City the talk of the nation.

Emerging from the ornate Victorian depot, Haskell stepped out onto Union Avenue, a dusty, cobblestone-paved thoroughfare lined with "saloons, curio shops, news stands, cigar stands, and everything to attract the tourists and get some of their money." Delivery wagons hauling kegs of beer and freshly slaughtered carcasses wove in and out among horse-drawn cabs and wary pedestrians. Iron-rimmed wheels and Clydesdales' heavy hooves filled the air with their din. The sweet stench of the stockyards mingled with the all-pervading smoke and soot. "Little flecks of greasy smut" stuck to clothing and lodged in nooks and crannies. A row of spindly trellises lofted cable cars and streetcars, cousins to Pittsburgh's trademark inclines, up the rocky slope to the "city on the hill." Every car line ended in open farmland, where developers confidently predicted thriving communities soon would sprout, and at all hours the rails "could be heard cooing in the distance like the hum of a bumblebee."[2]

The raw-edged cityscape put Haskell in mind of his childhood in Bulgaria, where in 1862 his parents had established one of the region's first Protestant evangelical missions. Life in the remote mountain hamlet of Samokov, thirty-five miles southeast of Sofia, was bucolic but primitive and often treacherous. Excursions to outlying villages were made on foot or horseback under the ever-present threat of attack from wolves, highwaymen, and marauding Turkish militia. Packed off to Ohio to prepare for college, young Harry had dutifully signed the volunteer pledge, planning to follow his older brother and sister in their parents' missionary footsteps. But four years of Oberlin's liberal education persuaded him that his true calling lay elsewhere.

For callow idealists like Haskell, burning to set the sinful world to rights, newspapering beckoned as a kind of secular mission. And Kansas City on the eve of the twentieth century was ripe for a great awakening. "A smutty and religious town," the writer Edward Dahlberg recalled his childhood home, whose inhabitants—numbering some 160,000 by the time Haskell arrived—were "wild about Christian Science, vice and lots of penance." A frontier town that boasted more than twice as many saloons and gaming houses as churches, where Jesse James's farmhouse was a local landmark and the proud citizenry took the outlaw's orphaned son to its bosom. To William Allen White, who arrived five years earlier to cut his teeth in metropolitan journalism, Kansas City resembled nothing so much as an "overgrown country town," its manners and appearance "consciously citified, like a country jake in his first store clothes."[3]

At the junction of Ninth, Main, and Delaware streets that marked the heart of downtown, a correspondent for *Harper's Weekly* watched a cavalcade of America pass before his eyes—"cow-boys fresh from the cattle trails, railway laborers just in from the grade, breathless business men from the buildings roundabout, well-groomed tourists from the East, farmers from down the river, immigrants from all parts of Europe, the typical English tourist with wide-check suit and plaid travelling cap, and various other kinds of people that one meets oftenest in some central railway point like Kansas City."[4] Together, the railroads and rivers made Kansas City a cosmopolitan crossroads, gave it its brash, buoyant, transient spirit. Not by a long stretch a world city, as its more fanciful boosters proclaimed, it was manifestly a city on the move—and on the make. To the twenty-two-year-old pilgrim from Ohio, it seemed a land of promise, a city of the future.

Haskell quickly landed a job as a reporter on the *Kansas City World*, a plucky but cash-starved daily that "had been taken over by the banks on two or three occasions, only to be temporarily rescued by some minor capitalist, whose hopes outran his capacities as publisher." With the presidential campaign in full swing, the town was abuzz with news of Bryan's dramatic come-from-behind victory at the Democratic convention in Chicago. The "silver-tongued" Nebraskan had surged past Missouri's "Silver Dick" Bland on the fifth ballot, thrilling the nation's downtrodden and dispossessed with his legendary "Cross of Gold" speech. Sound-money Democrats wrung their hands in consternation. The platform adopted in Chicago not only meant "national repudiation and spoliation" but was "an open door to revolution," thundered Henry Watterson of the *Louisville Courier-Journal*. The *Kansas City Star*, owned and edited by Watterson's chum William Rockhill Nelson, denounced the "treachery" of the party bosses in denying a third nomination to Grover Cleveland, "the only leader produced by the Democracy since Tilden who has been able to command the confidence of the people."[5]

If the great divide in national politics was paved with silver and gold, blue and gray distinguished the opposing camps in local affairs. Missourians, their professed allegiance to the Stars and Stripes notwithstanding, held the old South and its extinct "catfish" aristocracy in tender regard. Memories of bushwhackers, border wars, and tyrannical Union generals were slow to die among loyalists of the lost cause. George Creel, Haskell's fellow cub reporter on the *World* and later Woodrow Wilson's wartime propaganda chief, recalled the self-styled "colonels" of the Confederacy, "living in a past that they refused to put behind them," who peopled the town of Independence during his childhood. The old-timers "rocked on every front porch, held forth in the courthouse yard on summer afternoons, delivered all the Fourth of July orations."[6] Even Haskell, a Yankee born and bred, felt a lump rise in his throat when he covered the funeral of General Joseph Shelby and watched the Confederate hero's horse pass by with his empty boots reversed in the stirrups.

Old battle lines marched through the city's newsrooms as well. The morning *Journal*, founded before the Civil War, remained as ever the staid and venerable voice of moderate Republicanism. Long edited by a dignified, erudite alumnus of the Grand Army of the Republic, Robert T. Van Horn, it had lately come under the control of an up-and-coming railroad attorney, presaging a change in tone if not in policy. The *Times*, struggling to stay afloat in the crowded morning field, waved the banner of southern Democracy, though somewhat less effectually than in its heyday under the robustly partisan editorship of the late Morrison Munford. The *World* had joined the fray in 1894 as an "independent" evening paper and, despite its chronic financial woes, showed sufficient spark to catch the eye of E. W. Scripps, who soon would annex it to his journalistic empire. A succession of editors made a valiant bid to establish the *World* as the river city's flagship of progressive reform, but their efforts were too little and too late. Nelson had already staked his claim.

Sixteen years old in 1896, the evening *Star* had sprinted to a circulation of sixty thousand, leaving its closest competitor in the dust. In newsrooms for miles around, ambitious young men bided their time, hoping for an entrée to Nelson's eye-catching new plant at the corner of Eleventh and Grand. Everyone, it appeared, aspired to be a "*Star* man," but it didn't take Haskell long to discover that nobody on the paper "ever died, resigned, or was fired." Some grew weary of waiting and struck out to run their own newspapers. Creel briefly tested the waters in New York before returning in 1899 to launch a weekly journal of opinion and society. Progressive in politics and literary in character, the original Kansas City *Independent* modeled itself faithfully on the *Star*. But Creel realized it was futile to compete with the Nelson paper, which even at that early date "came close to being Holy Writ in Kansas and Western Missouri."[7]

Eastern Missouri was dominated, then as later, by Joseph Pulitzer's formidable *St. Louis Post-Dispatch*. For fortune had bestowed on the Show Me State two of the nation's great progressive newspapers, proud emblems of the rival cities' world-class political corruption. Nelson and Pulitzer had set out to prove that newspapers could thrive by serving the common good, rather than the narrow interests of an individual or a political party. Philosophically, the two lords of the press were soul mates; it was in the practice of "public-service" journalism that they parted ways. Nelson's *Star* was first and foremost a family newspaper, sober and repressed in its typography, though renowned for its stylish writing and fearless editorial policy. It was, Haskell assured his devoutly religious brother, "a clean sheet" that "excludes the disgusting & revolting from its columns."[8] The *Post-Dispatch*, by contrast, bore a strong family resemblance to its sister paper, Pulitzer's racy *New York World*, which was fast becoming a byword for sensationalism and populist crusading.

The "yellow" journalism that sprouted in the journalistic hothouse of New

York ripened to maturity during the Spanish-American War. Waged within easy reach of New York newsrooms, the Caribbean conflict tested the mettle of reporters and soldiers alike. As the ruinously costly competition between the *World* and William Randolph Hearst's *New York Journal* heated up, the *Star* virtuously resisted the jingoistic stampede. But gleaning grains of truth in the torrent of wartime dispatches, commentaries, and official bulletins was no easy task. Nelson's editors, few of whom had traveled abroad, reacted diplomatically to the sinking of the American battleship *Maine* on February 16, 1898. "It is to be earnestly hoped that investigation will reveal the purely accidental nature of the catastrophe," the paper editorialized. "The United States does not desire war, and Spain certainly should not." Nelson himself felt duty-bound to caution the *Star*'s readers against believing everything they read in newspapers.

> It should be constantly kept in mind that the known facts of the Maine disaster are few and that conjecture and opinion are the basis of most of the matter printed upon the subject which is now engrossing the attention of the American people. Added to this, it must be admitted, is the fact that sensationalists and "fakers" are given boundless opportunity by circumstances such as these and much that is recklessly perverted and shamelessly invented is offered the reading public by authority of certain conspicuous newspapers which seem to have extraordinary facilities for getting the facts, but which in this case, have already sent forth stories that were afterward demonstrated to be spurious. It is necessary for every well-meaning newspaper to print everything that has the semblance of truthfulness and trust to developments, day by day, to sift the facts from the rubbish of prejudice and sensationalism. The public should bear these things in mind and read with discrimination and with due consideration to the trustworthiness of the sources to which the various accounts are accredited.[9]

Not that the *Star* was shy about blowing its own horn. Even an inland newspaper with coffers considerably smaller than Pulitzer's and Hearst's could afford to splurge in a national emergency. Just before the war, Nelson had sent a correspondent to Cuba to investigate conditions in the Spanish concentration camps. Albert Miller's harrowing reports prompted the publisher to dispatch, with appropriate fanfare, a trainload of food and clothing to the starving internees. In Washington, Miller later scored another scoop—or so the *Star* claimed—in breaking the news of President McKinley's ultimatum to Spain hours before other papers picked up the story. On another memorable occasion General Nelson A. Miles, interviewed in Puerto Rico by the paper's special correspondent, hotly denounced the War Department's incompetence and accused officials in Washington of undermining his command. Nelson ran the story without flinching, but his editors hung on tenterhooks until Miles reached New York and confirmed the *Star's* exposé of the juicy scandal.

"It was the sort of war that all wars ought to be but never can be again," Haskell reminisced decades later, "a series of easy victories for the forces of righteousness with little loss of life and a lot of spectacular incidents." Nine days before the *Maine* plunged into the mud of Havana harbor, he strode proudly into Nelson's newsroom as the *Star's* new assistant telegraph editor. As he marked up the wire copy that flowed in from the four corners of the earth, Haskell reflected that he had been preparing for this work all his life. He had seen more of the world than most men his age and knew that there was more to it than was dreamed of in the austere fundamentalist theology of his forebears. At Oberlin he had become an ardent convert to Henry George's radical single-tax doctrine. Although he identified himself as a Congregationalist, his soul was stirred by a freethinking impulse that would eventually steer him into the broad lap of the Unitarian Church. In drama his adventurous tastes ran to Shaw and Ibsen, in philosophy to Dewey and Russell. The world of ideas was his home; nothing pleased him more than a sharp-witted intellectual debate. His cardinal virtue, in Creel's estimation, was his "steadfastness, a sense of direction and certainties based on principle." Nelson, with a keen appreciation for the market value of knowledge, singled out his young recruit as "the first walking dictionary I ever knew."[10]

Scholarly and soft-spoken, Haskell stood out like a purebred show dog among the rough-and-ready news hounds kenneled in newsrooms throughout the West. The *Star's* editorial writers were a different breed altogether—poets, historians, essayists, playwrights, philosophers. Instinctively, Haskell gravitated toward these "gentle, intelligent, fine-tempered men of ideals and high visions."[11] Before long he began moonlighting for the editorial desk. Too modest to approach the chief editorial writer directly, he would wait for the epicene Alexander Butts to go out for lunch, then steal into his office and deposit his literary offerings on the desk. As a rule, they appeared in the next day's paper word for word as he had written them.

Haskell's big break came in the spring of 1900. An officer in the U.S. Army engineering corps had been convicted of fraud in connection with a harbor-dredging project at Savannah, Georgia. Captain Oberlin Carter, a highly cultivated man with an unblemished military and scientific record, protested his innocence to no avail and was sentenced to five years in the federal peniten-

The *Star's* junior editorial writer, Henry J. Haskell (right), in the office he shared with Richard Lindsay (left) and D. Austin Latchaw. "I do hope to help a little in the building of Kansas City," he wrote his parents.

tiary at Leavenworth, Kansas. The drama of a distinguished patriot fighting to clear his name was the kind of edifying human interest story that Nelson loved to read in his paper. Haskell wangled the coveted assignment to interview the prisoner. On the hour-long train ride from Kansas City to Leavenworth, he became convinced of Carter's innocence and, "under the stress of sincere feeling," filed a long, emotionally charged account of the "closing of the outside world" on the hapless officer.[12]

Notoriously parsimonious with praise, Nelson said nothing about the story at the time. Only later did Haskell learn through the office grapevine that the "Old Man" had his eye on him. That summer, when one of the senior editorial writers died, Nelson and Butts gave him the nod. The salary of $22.50 a week, with the vague prospect of a raise after he made good, was less than he felt he deserved. On the other hand, he reasoned, writing editorials for the *Star* would enable him "to exert quite a bit of influence" in the community.[13] Now at last he could propose to his college sweetheart, exchange his cramped bachelor's flat for a rented bungalow, and take his place in smart society.

Soon, happily married and residing in an upscale neighborhood a few blocks from the paper, Haskell was squarely on the path to middle-class respectability in a middle-sized city in middle America. Jobs in New York and Denver had tempted him in the past, but now working for the *Star* seemed the answer to all his dreams. It was so much more fulfilling, so much more *consequential,* than being a short-story writer, or even a missionary. Yet chafe as he might at his parents' Old Testament beliefs, Haskell strove to live up to their lofty ideals. "You have always done everything possible for me," he wrote in thanking them for a wedding gift. "I'd like to amount to something some day just so that you might be sure all your care hadn't been wasted. I do hope to help a little in the building of Kansas City."[14]

Thus did the future editor of the *Kansas City Star* apprentice himself to William Rockhill Nelson, master builder of newspapers and cities.

PART 1

BARON BILL

William Rockhill Nelson in his favorite photograph.

CHAPTER 1

---◆---

The Daily W. R. Nelson

Long before he started publishing newspapers, William Rockhill Nelson was a successful builder of roads, bridges, and houses. So it's not surprising that his conception of journalism was in the most literal sense constructive. "Anybody can print the news," he once told an interviewer, "but the *Star* tries to build things up. That is what a newspaper is for."[1]

Nature fitted Nelson superbly for the part he was destined to play. With his short, bandy legs and massive torso tapering to a frosty, tousled peak, he was likened variously to a snow-capped volcano, a venerable Buddha, and an overstuffed baby pig. William Allen White described him in midlife as "a great hulking two-hundred-sixty pounder, six feet tall, smooth-shaven, with a hard, dominating mouth and a mean jaw, high brow, and wonderful eyes, jade in color, which opened with wide frank cordiality or squinted like the lightning of Job." Stand-up collars, which Nelson had permanently sewn to his linen shirts to spare himself the strain of reaching behind his back, encased his bulldog neck. His deep, rumbling voice "rattled like artillery" when he grew agitated—which, White observed, was a frequent occurrence.[2]

No topic brought out the editor's big guns like the manifest destiny of Kansas City and the Missouri River Valley. Nelson and other potentates of

> *"I am publishing the Daily W. R. Nelson. If people don't like my paper they can buy another."*
>
> —William Rockhill Nelson

the Fourth Estate took it for granted that what was good for them was good for their fellow citizens, and vice versa. An early-day *Star* editorial writer was simply stating the obvious when he commented that "the *Star's* prosperity is so closely allied with the growth and progress of Kansas City that its principal aim is to promote the welfare of this community in all its material and municipal relations." So closely identified were the city and its leading paper, Oswald Garrison Villard wrote, that it was virtually impossible to determine "whether the *Star* made Kansas City famous or Kansas City the *Star*, or even to try to figure out just how much each has contributed to the development of the other."[3]

In journalism's hall of fame, Nelson occupies a niche beside such legendary figures as Horace Greeley, Charles Dana, Henry Watterson, and Joseph Pulitzer. Yet he discounted his own genius, attributing the *Star's* phenomenal success to the fact that it was published in what he called, with unabashed hyperbole, "the greatest newspaper field of its population on the globe."[4] As a staging point for the overland trails leading to Santa Fe, California, and Oregon, the Kansas City area had been a magnet for traders, pioneers, adventurers, and entrepreneurs since the days of Lewis and Clark. Over the thirty-five years of Nelson's residency, from 1880 to 1915, the city's population grew more than fivefold, making it the largest metropolis between St. Louis and San Francisco. The *Star's* field was great indeed, extending from Missouri to Colorado and from Iowa to Texas. Kansas, where the "Daily W. R. Nelson" reigned supreme, was a breeding ground for agitators, radicals, cranks, and other troublemakers—the kind of misfits who kept things perpetually stirred up and whom Nelson, by his own account a natural insurgent, admired and emulated.

Gilded Age Kansas City was awash in money, much of it eastern capital attracted by the town's strategic location, abundant natural resources, and wide-open business culture. William Gilpin of Independence, a charter member of the local booster club, went so far as to predict that the next great "world city" would arise somewhere in the vicinity of the Kawsmouth. "Centropolis," as he optimistically christened his prairie utopia, was still a pipe-dream when it appeared on a map drawn in 1859, nestled between the nine-year-old City of Kansas, the county seat of Independence to the east, and the bustling hamlet of Westport to the south.[5] Two decades later a group of developers, bankrolled by British investors, laid out a real-life Centropolis in the valley of the Blue River, hard by the brand-new factory towns of Manchester, Sheffield, and Leeds. These anglicized industrial suburbs, no less than the sooty smokestacks standing sentinel above the Missouri River bottoms, attested the city's irrepressible urge to rise above its cow-town origins.

By the mid-1880s Kansas City was riding the crest of a giddy real estate boom that exceeded even Gilpin's wildest dreams. Properties rose exponentially in value, sometimes changing hands two or three times in a single day. Fortunes were made and squandered overnight. At the crest of the bubble, in 1887, sales of local real estate totaled a jaw-dropping $88 million. Sharks, speculators, and "dollar swappers" with money to burn swarmed into the city. A newcomer from the East marveled to see armies of workmen "cutting down hills, filling up gorges, erecting buildings worthy of Wall Street next door to a pasture, carrying the cable lines out into forests where wild game still wandered."[6] The upstart metropolis soon found itself vying with St. Louis and Chicago as the hub of a sprawling commercial empire. Hard-headed businessmen drew up plans for a railway from Kansas City to the Gulf of Mexico that would link America's breadbasket with the Pacific coast of South America.

The great era of city building was at hand. That it was also the golden age of American journalism was no coincidence. Newspapers and cities across the land sprang up side by side, flourishing and floundering together amid the social upheavals of the late nineteenth and early twentieth centuries. Rampant urbanization hastened the demise of the old-style "personal" journalism associated with the generation of Greeley and Dana, as newspapers transformed themselves from organs of proprietary opinion and political propaganda into more or less faithful mirrors of the melting-pot communities they served. The so-called New Journalism, as practiced by the likes of Pulitzer and Nelson, was predicated on the assumption that the public, given the necessary information, would naturally act in its own interests. As Nelson put it, "You can always trust the people to do what is best when they know what is best."[7]

To be sure, Nelson and Pulitzer seldom passed up an opportunity to tell readers what was best for them. That, too, was what a newspaper was for. Hard-pressed wage-earners, Nelson reasoned, had little time or energy to look after even their most vital interests. It was the "peculiar privilege, if not obligation" of the "free progressive, vigilant, vigorous newspaper" to "survey the whole field and act for the whole community." Pulitzer evinced a similarly paternalistic attitude when he glorified the humble journalist as "the lookout on the bridge of the ship of state," a far-seeing leader who "brings all classes, all professions together, and teaches them to act in concert on the basis of their common citizenship." In this light, what one admirer described as Nelson's "government by newspaper" was not simply an expression of the hunger for power and prestige that had launched countless press lords on political careers. It was also an unselfish response to the intractable social and political problems brought on by the Industrial Revolution, problems that most municipalities had scarcely begun to address, much less solve.[8]

At its best, the progressive New Journalism served as a counterweight to the laissez-faire commercialism that threatened to turn American cities into ungovernable patchworks of special interests and privilege. At its worst, it speeded the breakdown of the polity by trying to be all things to all people, substituting a titillating smorgasbord of news and features for a genuinely communitarian vision of city life. If the new urban marketplaces were coming more and more to resemble private businesses, newspapers had never been anything else. The object of a newspaper, Charles Dudley Warner of the *Hartford Courant* pointed out in 1881, "is to make money for its owner. Whatever motive may be given for starting a newspaper, expectation of profit by it is the real one." This home truth was hardly news to Nelson, insist as he might that "income and revenue must be an incident rather than a purpose" for a paper's existence. Nor did it jar with Pulitzer's dictum that the more profitable a newspaper was, the better it could "stand loss for the sake of principle and conviction."[9]

In affirming their faith in the profit motive, the reform-minded practitioners of the New Journalism seemed to suggest that public and private interests were, if not consistently harmonious, at least fundamentally compatible. That proposition would be put to the test as American society struggled to reinvent itself in the Progressive Era.

Nelson might have been referring to himself when he declared that the *Star* was "independent but not neutral." Iron-willed and refractory from boyhood, he remained a free spirit to his dying breath. "I never enjoyed being bossed," he admitted in a rare moment of introspection. "It was my disposition to feel that nobody had any rights over me."[10] The University of Notre Dame, where his father had consigned the unruly youngster for disciplining, sent him packing after four semesters of studious hell-raising, and Nelson returned home determined never again to answer to authority higher than his own.

Isaac DeGroff Nelson, a man of means and influence in Fort Wayne, Indiana, welcomed his prodigal son back to the fold and secured for him a respectable position as deputy clerk in the county circuit court. Nelson settled down to read law, passed the bar, and for a time seemed content to pursue a legal career. But restlessness soon got the better of him. When his grandfa-

Nelson as an up-and-coming contractor in Indiana: the bad boy makes good.

ther and namesake, William Rockhill, gained control of twelve hundred acres of prime suburban real estate, he invited young William to help plan and construct a new subdivision known as Rockhill Additions. The experience instilled an enthusiasm for the building trade that marked Nelson for good. In later years he would say that although newspapering had been his life, he had always considered building houses to be "the greatest fun in the world."[11]

At an age when most of his contemporaries were apprenticing in a profession, Nelson was running his own construction firm. He already had a practical knowledge of building materials, engineering, architecture, contracting, and real estate; soon his father taught him the rudiments of agriculture and livestock breeding as well. Having profitably sat out the Civil War in Indiana, Nelson felt the itch to branch out and took to speculating in commodities. In the late 1860s, when land in the South was cheap and cotton prices were high, he and a friend bought a plantation off the coast of Georgia and a general store in Savannah. For once his luck failed him. Cotton prices plummeted, Nelson retreated to Indiana, and his partner defaulted, saddling him with a mountain of debt. Paying it off ate up most of the fortune (variously estimated at between $100,000 and $200,000) that he had amassed in the construction business. Nelson shrugged this calamity off as a trifling setback. "Lack of self-confidence was never one of my failings," he remarked to a colleague. "I don't suppose I ever lost a minute's sleep over the affair. I knew I was going to win in the end."[12]

Nelson's education in both newspapers and politics began at home. Isaac Nelson, a lifelong Democrat, had owned the *Fort Wayne Sentinel* for a brief period around the time his second son was born in 1841. Upon returning to Indiana, William struck up a friendship with the local Democratic chieftain who had lately taken control of the paper. Nelson *fils* scraped together enough money to acquire a small joint interest in the *Sentinel,* and together the two men used it to boom Samuel Tilden for president in 1876. The reformist governor of New York recognized Nelson as a kindred soul and recruited him to help manage his campaign, observing that he appeared to be "the only Democrat in Indiana" who was "not a candidate for the presidency."[13] Like Dana and Watterson, Tilden's foremost journalistic allies, Nelson was bitterly disillusioned when conservative southern Democrats "stole" the nomination for Rutherford B. Hayes. In 1880, the Democrats having failed to renominate Tilden, he bolted the party, becoming a lifelong mugwump and scourge of reactionary "Bourbonism."

In a lesser mortal, such inconstancy might have been mistaken for opportunism. Nelson, characteristically, made a virtue of his political irregularity. It freed him to make common cause, as whim and circumstance dictated, with men of all stripes and convictions, from venal party bosses to boss-busting reformers, without forsaking his progressive principles. A born pragmatist, Nelson was leery of ideologies and platforms. He reserved the right to change his mind on any issue without prior notice, the better to keep opponents off balance—and also, it sometimes seemed, employees in their places. "This is the way I feel now," he liked to taunt his editors. "To-morrow I may look at it differently, and if I do I don't know that any of you fellows need remind me of it."[14] Come election time, the *Star* more often than not found itself crossing party lines or straddling fences, although the latter was not a posture that Nelson could maintain for any considerable length of time. The rebel in him coexisted with an almost adolescent propensity for hero worship. Once he made up his mind about a man, he brooked no carping or second-guesses.

In 1879 Nelson still harbored hopes of inducing Tilden to throw his hat into the presidential ring again. Political calculations may have played a part in his decision to purchase his father's old paper that February in partnership with a veteran Fort Wayne newsman named Samuel Morss. Or perhaps, as Morss told the story, Nelson was simply "in the right mood" to take up "a different line of business" after a bridge he had built in Iowa was washed away in a storm and the owners reneged on their contract.[15] Over the next eighteen months, the avowedly "independent Democratic" *Sentinel* fought the good fight for political reform, well-built roads, modern waterworks, and other municipal improvements. But the editors' exhortations fell on deaf ears. Fort Wayne, they concluded, was hopelessly hidebound and parochial. Casting about for a field worthier of their talents, they investigated such up-and-coming localities as St. Louis, Brooklyn, and Seattle before fixing their sights on Kansas City. That neither Nelson nor Morss had ever set foot in Missouri was of no account. Like thousands of other young men who heeded Greeley's call to go west, they were spurred on by a sense of manifest destiny, a starry-eyed, almost mystical faith in the future, and a very down-to-earth desire to get rich quick.

Arriving at Kansas City's new Union Depot in early August 1880, the thirty-nine-year-old Nelson was a picture of health and confidence: portly, baby-faced, clean-shaven, his hair already thinning and gray as iron. Morss, his junior by nearly a dozen years, was slight of build and, as would shortly become apparent, constitutionally far from robust. With his bushy side-whiskers and pince-nez spectacles, he looked more like a mild-mannered bank clerk than a hard-boiled newsman. The partners took rooms in the Pacific House Hotel at Fourth and Delaware, in what passed for the central business district. With the three thousand dollars realized from the sale of the *Sentinel,* they rented a second-floor office next door, rounded up a skeleton staff, and set out to canvas the town. By the time the first edition rolled off the hand-fed flatbed press a month or so later, the *Evening Star* boasted some three thousand subscribers, proof positive, the editors proclaimed, that Kansas City had "a better demand for a good cheap evening paper than any other city in the country."[16]

Evening newspapers were still a novelty in the 1880s and prosperous morning dailies saw no reason to take them too seriously. "Twinkle, twinkle, little Star, bright and gossipy you are," patronized the *Kansas City Times* in a saucy jingle penned by its versifying managing editor, Eugene Field. Flattered by the attention, the Hoosiers rolled up their shirtsleeves and got down to work, Morss supervising the news-gathering operation while Nelson tended the paper's business affairs. (Inability to fathom the mysteries of a balance sheet never impeded his God-given talent for making money.) Bachelors both, the

Star's proprietors put in long hours that left little time for socializing or recreation. Nelson, in particular, seemed to be suffering from something akin to culture shock. "Temperamentally he did not belong with the hell-roaring crowd that was dominant in the town," wrote Henry Haskell. "While he occasionally played poker with his fellow citizens, those associated with him noticed a certain aloofness. He did not quite know where he did belong. He was still trying to find himself."[17]

Nelson was content to let his partner establish the paper's "bright and gossipy" voice. He set no store by his literary ability and wrote little or nothing for publication, employing professional wordsmiths to flesh out the barebones ideas he was forever scribbling on scraps of paper and discarded envelopes. In the journalistic fashion of the day, only a favored few were accorded the privilege of bylines in the *Star*. Nelson, for his part, cultivated what White termed "a sort of elaborate anonymity." Long after he had become rich and famous, the editor could walk the city streets without fear of being recognized, like a monarch venturing incognito among his subjects. That was the way he liked it. If Nelson didn't fit into his new surroundings, they would have to be made to fit him. Kansas City was still young and malleable enough to be molded into the kind of community he visualized, a city built in his own expansive self-image. "I was going to live here, wasn't I?" he demanded. "Well, if I ever expected to get anywhere with my paper Kansas City had to be made into a place that somebody besides a few dollar swappers would want to live in."[18]

The prospect that greeted Nelson and Morss was unpromising, to say the least. "In wet weather the town-site was a sea of mud and in dry weather a desert of dust," a contemporary recalled. Hogs roamed freely through the streets, which were mostly unpaved, and rough wooden planks served as sidewalks. The gas supply was feeble and erratic; the era of electric light was still a year away. Rickety, mule-drawn streetcars provided the only public transport and the foul taste of the city water, piped all but untreated from the Kaw River, "made whiskey-drinking a virtue." Simmering beneath the thin upper crust of frontier gentility was a motley stew of "renegade Indians, demoralized soldiers, unreformed bushwhackers, and border ruffians, thieves, and thugs imported from anywhere, professional train-robbers of home growth, and all kinds of wrecks of the Civil War." Haskell characterized the city as "a community of go-getters with a houn' dawg background. The go-getter spirit kept it on its toes fighting for railroads, fighting for trade. The houn' dawg tradition left it satisfied to be stuck in the mud."[19]

Extricating Kansas City from the mire would have to wait. The editors' first order of business was to articulate a bold, forward-looking agenda that would

Looking east on Ninth Street from Delaware, 1880, a stone's throw from the first *Star* office. The city streets were a "sea of mud" in wet weather, a "desert of dust" in dry.

set the *Star* apart from the city's four established English-language dailies. In their maiden issue, which hit the streets on September 18, 1880, Morss and Nelson pledged to provide "a cheap afternoon newspaper, of the highest class," one that was "absolutely independent in politics, entirely disconnected from the rings and cliques of all descriptions, and wholly free to labor for the interests of the people, and to wage warfare upon corrupt and extravagant tax eaters, of all parties." The *Star* would be entertaining, spicy, readable, and, above all, cheap and concise, enabling "intelligent" readers to keep abreast of current events "with the minimum expenditure of time and money." Its four tightly packed pages would digest the news of the day without forcing readers to slog through "long speeches and sermons, ponderous editorials, and prosy, tedious dissertations upon dry subjects." In sum, the *Star* would "devote its best energies to aiding the work of building up the material and moral interests of Kansas City, and developing the great Missouri Valley, of which this is the metropolis."

Such highfalutin promises were boilerplate, snake oil being no scarcer in journalism than in politics. But Nelson and Morss soon proved that they were sincere in their desire to promote the city's "material and moral interests" as well as their own. The formula they had worked out in Fort Wayne would serve them well: a price of two cents an issue (the competing Kansas City dailies sold for five), political independence coupled with a commitment to popular reform, and an unswerving focus on local news (Morss's specialty) and civic boosterism. In league with the *St. Louis Post-Dispatch,* which Pulitzer had picked up at a fire sale a couple of years earlier, the *Star* soon sallied forth on a crusade against government corruption, election fraud, illicit lotteries, saloon keepers, tax dodgers, and robber barons. Readers on both sides of the state welcomed the newspapers' campaign for clean air and water, safe and well-maintained streets and bridges, and modern sanitation. In what White described as the perpetual conflict between "property and men," Nelson and Pulitzer instinctively sided with their fellows.[20]

Nevertheless, in billing itself as "a paper for the people," the *Star* begged an essential question. Although Nelson prided himself on being a Jeffersonian democrat, at heart he remained an elitist, a bootstrap social climber who accepted nature's aristocracy as a fact of life. (There is some evidence that Morss, whose origins were humbler than Nelson's, held more plebeian views. But his influence on the paper effectively ended when he left Kansas City under mysterious circumstances about eighteen months after the *Star*'s founding.) Nelson's journalistic model would be the high-class *Boston Transcript,* whose prestige rested on a slender base of some thirty thousand "serious-minded" subscribers. "I do not want the *Star* to be a *Transcript,*" Nelson would tell his staff in later years, "for the latter does not seek any circulation that is not of its kind, and I want all kinds, but I for sure want the *Star* to have the necessary 30,000. We can get along without the baseball extras, the wasted papers in the street cars, the Board of Trade and Stock Yards circulation but the loss of those 30,000 serious-minded readers would mean the *Star*'s finish and so long as those readers are held, so long will the *Star* be Kansas City's leading paper."[21]

Nelson's broad-gauged appeal produced results. By 1891 the *Star* counted people of "all classes and conditions"—"Republicans, Democrats, Prohibitionists, [Farmers'] Alliance men, white men and black men, Catholics, Protestants and free thinkers, native Americans and naturalized foreigners, business men and professional men"—among its forty-four thousand subscribers. But Nelson valued respectability more than demographic diversity. Nothing illustrated the contrast between him and Pulitzer more clearly than their attitude toward circulation. While the *Post-Dispatch* and the *New York World* courted readers with ever more luridly sensational fare, Nelson steadfastly refused to move down market. In one of his more Pollyannaish precepts, no doubt polished for posterity, he admonished his employees that "the great newspaper should be the welcome visitor in every house because of its cheer. It should be a family friend and adviser, and the carrier's coming should always be eagerly looked for by every member." A more characteristic aphorism attributed to Nelson captures the authentic voice of the burly bon vivant who partook of food and drink in liberal measure: "God's great gift to man is appetite. Put nothing in the paper that will destroy it."[22]

The quest for appetizing reading matter inspired one of Nelson's most successful innovations. The early *Star* could ill afford a large reporting staff or costly telegraph tolls. Searching for a substitute for hard news, Nelson hit on the not-so-new idea of reprinting feature material from other newspapers, magazines, and books. Most publishers, however, used reprint as filler; Nelson made the "exchange desk" the pride of the *Star.* "That reprint idea just fitted the picture for me, hard up as I was, and I hoped it would fit for our readers, and it did," he explained. In time, the exchange department staff would rival that of the city desk and reprint, much of it painstakingly condensed and rewritten, would account for as much as a third of the *Star*'s editorial content. On a given day, readers might open their newspapers to find a serialized novella by Balzac or Thackeray, a timely background piece on a franchise dispute in Cleveland, and an essay on daily life in medieval England. Nelson, who was widely read despite his truncated education, liked to remind his editors that "Plato and Carlyle and Emerson might be just as good correspondents as the fellows who are sending the other papers reports of dog fights in San Francisco."[23] It was all part and parcel of his grand strategy of catering to the masses while cultivating the "best people."

From its inception, the *Star* was part schoolmaster and part court jester, part civic cheerleader and part crusader for good government and wholesome living. If it spoke for no identifiable political party or school of thought, that was largely because Nelson himself subscribed to no recognized philosophy of politics, journalism, or indeed life. In his outsized passions and prejudices, he exemplified "the attitudes, tastes, and manners of the country squire of an older America." Self-interest, fortified by Jeffersonian individualism, was the prevailing strain in his character. "A man of high ideals, honest, courageous, independent, devoted to the advancement of great causes, he was at the same time intensely selfish and ruthless in having his own way." More altruistic in principle than in practice, Nelson extended a helping hand to the needy but resented demands on his generosity. Sympathetic to the workingman's plight, he disdained anyone who put himself out for hire, observing that "any man worth more than $5,000 a year" should be in business for himself.[24] The better world he sought was one in which virtue and industry were their own reward, and equality of opportunity translated naturally into social and economic justice. Only later in life, as experience tempered his libertarian instincts, would he come to believe that individual initiative and free-market capitalism were insufficient to safeguard the "material and moral interests" of the common people who looked to the *Star* for leadership.

In staking out its dual role as "mentor and monitor" of the boisterous, ill-mannered boomtown, the *Star* incurred a special obligation to practice what it preached.[25] Its pronouncements carried the more weight in that they emanated from the paper's own manifest decorum, decency, and good taste. Like Pulitzer, Nelson understood that the acquisition of power and influence in the newspaper business was largely a numbers game. But whereas Pulitzer counted his mass readership in the hundreds of thousands, Nelson honed in on a relatively small group of movers, shakers, and taste makers. Kansas City in the late 1800s was rapidly approaching maturity. It needed what every growing city needed—population, investment, and clean, progressive government. Above all, it needed respectability. The *Star* would teach White's "country jake" to think, look, and behave like a gentleman.

Nelson's refusal to duck a fight was as much part of the gentleman's code as it was of the frontiersman's. Contrarian to the core, he acknowledged that he was "inclined to believe in raising the devil on principle." This cantankerous streak precipitated a confrontation with the local traction monopoly soon after his arrival in Kansas City. The streetcar company's president, an Irishman "of strong will and powerful physique," had friends high up in the business world.[26] Among them were the directors of the Armour bank, the city's leading commercial lender. Nelson offended these men at his peril; as the

Star's circulation shot up, he would soon be forced to apply to the bank for a loan to increase his press capacity. But such practical concerns didn't deter him from arguing that Kansas Citians deserved far better service and equipment than "Boss" Thomas Corrigan had seen fit to provide. In due course, a majority on the City Council came around to Nelson's view that extending the company's exclusive franchise was contrary to the public interest and opened the door to competitors.

Admirers would often cite the battle to nullify the "streetcar influence" in municipal affairs as evidence of the editor's incorruptible integrity. By Nelson's own account, his motives were less exemplary. "I have no more courage than the rest of them," he confessed to White. "But I saw those damned scoundrels putting all kinds of pressure on the mayor—from all the so-called respectable and business element—to tie the people up in a knot, and I had faith that the people would not stand it, and then," he laughed, "you know all the other papers were in the scheme, and there was too much competition in that line—so I took the chance."[27] The disarming disclaimer was vintage Nelson. Whatever tactical skirmish he happened to be waging at the moment, he never lost sight of his long-term objective: to set himself up as the tribune of the people and supreme arbiter of civic virtue.

The *Star's* war of attrition against the Metropolitan Street Railway would become its longest-running but by no means most successful crusade. A tally Nelson ordered toward the end of his life revealed that since 1880 the paper had published a grand total of some twenty-five hundred columns on the subject of streetcars and cable cars. Yet in 1914 voters approved a franchise concession that Nelson had fought with all the firepower in his editorial arsenal. Even sympathetic observers complained that the *Star's* relentless persecution of the Corrigan interests smacked of overkill. Ed Howe, the celebrated Atchison editor known as the "Sage of Potato Hill," speculated that Nelson's grand obsession was sparked less by public spirit than by the ill will the Met had fomented against him over the years. Charles Gleed, proprietor of the probusiness *Kansas City Journal,* charged that Nelson "made magnificent use of the street car facilities of the town to further his own schemes for land development"; when the Met management "would not or could not do what he wanted done," he let them have it. Corrigan's version of the story was that Nelson tried to blackmail him into advertising in the *Star* and declared war on the company when he refused to play along.[28]

All of these allegations are plausible and each, as Nelson would have been the first to admit, contained a nugget of truth. His motives were seldom pure. Besides, in his words, "hitting back" was "damned human." From his youth as a self-styled "bad boy" at Notre Dame, he had cast himself as a scrapper who thumbed his nose at authority and refused to concede defeat. It was his conceit that, in the long haul, the "Daily W. R. Nelson" never lost a fight either. *Star* reporters and editorial writers had standing orders to hammer away at the proprietor's pet issues day after day, week after week, from every conceivable angle, until, as Nelson put it, the desired results would be attained without anyone remembering who had started the campaign. "The public doesn't yearn to have its opinion guided and instructed," he said. "It wants to get the news and to be entertained. Such instruction as we have to impart must be made a secondary matter. If we can sneak up behind a man when he isn't looking and instruct him, all well and good. But if he gets the idea that our main purpose is to edify him, he runs so fast that we never can catch him."[29]

The policy of sneaking up on readers in preference to beating them over the heads occasionally made it necessary for Nelson to rein in some of his more prolix writers, especially on the editorial page. "I don't want the *Star*'s editorials to be a lot of literary essays," he insisted. "I want to get things done." His most succinct statement of editorial practice, written a few months before his death, revealed a decidedly mixed attitude toward editorial writers as a class. "We have felt that the old fashioned sort of editorial writer who sits at his desk and does nothing but grind out opinions can be no factor in affairs, and therefore we have tried to get away from that sort of thing on the *Star*. For instance, a man is assigned to the subject of the Municipal Water Plant for Kansas City, Kansas, and he writes both the news and the editorial comment on the news. In this way he can write with real knowledge of the situation. The same way we wish our City Hall reporter to turn in editorial comment on City Hall news. As you see, the scheme does not permit us to develop professional editorial writers."[30]

Successful editorial writers knew their place in Nelson's scheme of things. Haskell, who directed the *Star*'s editorial page for more than forty years, held that editorials should express the "personality" of the newspaper—meaning, of course, the personality of its autocratic proprietor—rather than promote an activist agenda. He shared Nelson's view that the editorial page was an extension of the news columns, a forum primarily for news and ideas rather than opinions. The editorial writer "should be the ideal reporter, on the watch constantly to report new ideas of importance to the public that may not come to it in any other way." This was closer to Nelson's and Pulitzer's ideal than the tub-thumping editorial pages of Greeley and Dana, which everyone agreed had seen their day. Anyhow, Nelson was never quite comfortable with men on

The *Star*'s "local room" around 1900. Nelson considered reporters like A. B. Macdonald (front) the big toads in the journalistic puddle.

his payroll expressing independent opinions. Still less did he approve of the editorialist's penchant for splitting hairs, deeming evenhandedness a vice. "People say there are two sides to everything," he announced at an editorial conference one day. "There's only one side and that's our side."[31]

Nelson's ambivalence toward editorial writers was counterbalanced by an extravagant regard for reporters. When a correspondent for *Collier's* interviewed him for a series on American newspapers, he took the opportunity to affirm one of the basic tenets of the New Journalism: "It's the news columns that do the business—mostly. But don't quote me," he added with a twinkle in his eye. "The boys that write our editorials wouldn't like it." In a speech to journalism students at the University of Missouri, he stopped just short of pronouncing editorial writers expendable. "We could get on pretty well without our various sorts of editors. But we should go to smash if we had no reporters," he said. The reporter was the "essential man on the newspaper." In addition to demonstrating initiative, imagination, and a "nose for news," he must be "a good citizen, in all that that term implies. He must be honest; he must be sincere. He must be against shams and frauds. His heart must be right. Mere smartness will never give permanent success."[32]

"*Star* men"—whether reporters, editors, or editorial writers—were never allowed to forget that they were Nelson's personal representatives and owed their allegiance to him. "My staff know exactly my ideas and they carry them out fearlessly and fully," he bragged to a visitor in 1896. Everyone in his employ was charged with a "continuous assignment" to look after "the permanent things, both great and small, with which the *Star* is engaged." Reporters were dispatched around the country, and sometimes overseas, to write about ideas and programs that Nelson wanted Kansas City to adopt. He was known to turn writers loose for months, or even years, to investigate subjects that had captured his fancy. One cub, assigned to write a series of articles on the social impact of the Industrial Revolution, in desperation invented a fictional old-timer and "put in his mouth a series of more or less naive reflections on how times had changed." The nebulous project "died of inanition" after a few months, the reporter recalled, but no word of reproach ever reached his ear.[33] Impervious to failure himself, Nelson could overlook almost any shortcoming so long as his employees subscribed to the *Star*'s greater "purposes." Since those purposes were for the most part uncommonly enlightened and progressive, most of his staff cheerfully marched to his drum, though not without frequent sniggering behind the Old Man's back.

Much as he detested sharing the limelight, Nelson didn't hesitate to surround himself with men who were his journalistic and intellectual superiors. Ironically, most of his top editors were dyed-in-the-wool Republicans who gagged at his adulation for Grover Cleveland and slipped heretical editorials in under his nose whenever they could get away with it. The ringleader of this mischievous conspiracy was James Runnion, a glum, sober-sided pal of Nelson's from Notre Dame who succeeded Morss as second in command. While Nelson was abroad in 1896, Runnion took it upon himself to suggest in print that William McKinley might not be altogether unfit to hold the nation's highest office. This backhanded endorsement nearly precipitated a breach with Nelson, who abominated the conservative Republican candidate as much as he did the radical William Jennings Bryan. But Runnion was indispensable and knew it. He had had a stellar career in Chicago as a journalist and playwright before coming to Kansas City. When Nelson incorporated the Star Company in 1889, he made Runnion his junior partner and paid him fifty dollars a week—higher than any other salary on the books, including Nelson's own.

If Runnion served as a balance wheel to stabilize Nelson's impulsive gyrations, managing editor Thomas W. Johnston brought to the paper a touch of the poet. A fastidious stylist who "loved writing for its own sake and played with a news page as a sculptor plays with the chisel on his block," Johnston was instrumental in establishing the *Star*'s literary reputation and imbuing the news columns with what White called "a certain gay cynicism." As Nelson's chief talent scout, he nurtured such celebrities as William Allen White and Alfred Henry Lewis, whose fame rested on the short stories they wrote for the *Star* in the early 1890s. White's exuberantly folksy style packed a deceptive punch; Johnston said he could "conceal more dynamite in three or four innocent lines" than any writer he knew.[34] His articles often carried bylines, as did Lewis's popular "Old Cattleman" tales and muckraking "Kicker" columns—a sure sign of Nelson's favor. Yet after a few months both men developed wanderlust and quit the *Star*, Lewis to become Washington correspondent for the *Kansas City Times*, White to win celebrity on his own terms as editor of the *Emporia Gazette*.

Enterprising reporters like White and Lewis would always be the big men on the newspaper as far as Nelson was concerned. Yet for all his impatience with "professional editorial writers," he regarded the editorial page as the heart and soul of the paper. After Runnion died in 1897, he entrusted its direction to Alexander Butts, a kindly, gregarious bachelor well known in Kansas as a newspaper paragrapher. Butts considered himself a "born exhorter" and in later years wrote weekly sermons for the paper. His gift for forming friendships at all echelons of society helped offset Nelson's aloofness and propensity for making enemies. Another Kansas notable was Noble Lovely Prentis, whose high-flown prose graced the *Star*'s editorial page in the 1890s. The author of numerous books on travel and history, he had served in the Union army in the Civil War and was said to know something about every subject under the sun. White described Prentis and Butts as "self-made newspapermen of the old school, writers by ear rather than by note."[35] Together, the three men helped make the *Star* the most influential paper in the Sunflower State from the 1890s long into the twentieth century.

Man for man, the *Star*'s staff could hold its own by comparison with any newspaper in America. Nelson liked to tell how, on a hunch, he hired a teenage immigrant named August Seested and quickly made him the paper's business manager, a position he would hold for some four decades. Although Nelson rewarded loyalty, he didn't believe in enticing people with fat salaries. As a rule, he paid his employees just enough to keep them from getting itchy feet, out of a sincerely held conviction that "the surest way to ruin a good newspaperman is to put some money in his pocket."[36] Reporters were forever grousing about their stingy wages and a few discontents, emboldened by White's example, left in search of greener pastures. Most, however, accepted Nelson's terms because of the *Star's* missionary spirit and the cherished freedom to speak their minds—as long as they didn't stray too far from the Word according to Baron Bill.

Absorbed in his own affairs, Nelson paid little attention to other newspapers and declined to measure himself against his peers. The *Star,* he said, was edited not for his fellow publishers but for the ordinary men and women who subscribed to it for a paltry dime a week. Although he prided himself on being a self-made newspaperman, it would be nearer the truth to call him a journalistic magpie who took whatever he needed from those around him. Samuel Morss unquestionably taught him a good deal during the three years they worked side by side in Fort Wayne and Kansas City. But Nelson could never bring himself to give his more experienced partner due credit. After Morss sold his interest in the business and returned to Indiana in early 1882, ostensibly because of poor health, he was all but blotted out of the *Star's* history. For decades rumors persisted that Nelson had run him out of town, even though the two men remained friends. In all likelihood, Morss had simply come to realize that Nelson was incapable of serving as anything but captain of his own ship.

One of the few pieces of practical advice that Nelson freely acknowledged originated with the editor of the *Indianapolis News.* On the eve of his departure for Kansas City, John Holliday counseled, "Until you get established, blow your own bugle. Don't be modest about telling them what a good paper you are giving them."[37] Never one to hide his light under a bushel, Nelson blew his horn both loud and shrill. In its early years, the *Star* experimented with self-promotion disguised as charity (free meals and circus passes for newsboys), as public service (prizes for planting trees in western Kansas), and as entertainment (contests in mystery writing and pigeon shooting). Nelson drew the line at the kind of sensational stunts and advertising gimmicks that Pulitzer and Hearst went in for. But there was no call for them anyway. By the mid-1890s the *Star* boasted more than twice the combined circulation of all the other Kansas City dailies. This claim, backed up by a panel of business and professional men chosen by Seested, was better than any promotion money could buy. More valuable than the bragging rights it earned for the *Star* was the right to raise advertising rates to a level commensurate with its market share.

If Nelson had any journalistic mentor, it was his old friend Henry Watterson of the *Louisville Courier-Journal.* The two men had been thrown together by Tilden's ill-starred 1876 campaign, in which the Kentuckian had played a key role as adviser and strategist. A white-maned scion of the Old South, Watterson embodied the best in the southern liberal tradition. The twin pillars of his Democratic faith were free trade and reconciliation between North and South. Following his lead, Nelson embraced free trade as his lifelong cause, and it was largely to spread the gospel of tariff reform, as preached by his revered Grover Cleveland, that he launched a weekly farm edition of the *Star* in 1891. It was an inspired move, for the *Weekly Star* proved not only a steady money maker but also an effective vehicle for projecting the *Star*'s power throughout the far-flung hinterland that Nelson regarded as his domain by divine right.

In Watterson's vivid phrase, Nelson was the "rural rooster" whose wake-up call generated much of the energy for progressive reform in the sparsely populated but politically consequential states of the Midwest and West. In Washington's corridors of power, however, "Marse Henry's" feisty, folksy voice resonated far more strongly than Nelson's. The son of a U.S. congressman, he was once elected in Tennessee to serve out the term of a deceased Democratic representative. In 1901 Nelson facetiously (or so one presumes) proposed Watterson as a candidate for president, lauding him in the *Star* as "a thorough patriot and as staunch and fine an American as has ever been born on the soil of the Republic." In a letter to Watterson, Nelson described himself as "a Democrat who never votes the Democratic ticket." He depended on Watterson, he wrote, "to keep my Democracy in trim," adding that "when I have been in the Democratic ranks I have followed you devotedly, looking on you as my real guide, philosopher and friend."[38]

Like Nelson, Watterson believed that the ideal newspaper was not only honest and fearless but "amiable and unpretentious; speaking the language and wearing the habiliments of the people." His contention that the modern journalist had supplanted the novelist and dramatist as an observer of society was reflected in the *Star*'s emphasis on human interest stories and serialized literature. To the resolutely forward-looking Nelson, however, Watterson's definition of a successful paper as one that provided a faithful history of yesterday was incomplete. More to his taste was Pulitzer's ringing statement of journalistic principle: "The newspaper that is true to its highest mission will concern itself with the things that *ought to happen tomorrow*, or next month, or next year, and will seek to make what ought to be come to pass. . . . The highest mission of the press is to *render public service.*"[39]

Pulitzer and Nelson shared a passion for journalistic activism and public

service. Near contemporaries, they were both self-made men who surrounded themselves with unusually able staffs and fiercely guarded their independence. Yet in other respects they were polar opposites. Nelson, warm-
blooded and down to earth, is unlikely to have taken to the reclusive, highly
strung German. Pulitzer's yacht was his only real home, whereas Nelson built
one mainly for show. Shuttling from port to port, firing off telegrams to his
editors on the *World*, Pulitzer was rarely in town when Nelson visited New
York. And he never returned to Missouri after 1888, having turned his back
on St. Louis five years earlier with a terse directive to the *Post-Dispatch*'s editors to leave him alone and follow their own judgment.[40] Nelson, by contrast,
was distinctly reluctant to delegate authority, and the thought of moving away
from Kansas City seems never to have crossed his mind.

Given their differences in style and temperament, and the traditional rivalry between Kansas City and St. Louis, it's not surprising, perhaps, that Nelson and Pulitzer had little or nothing to do with each other. More puzzling is
Nelson's relationship—or lack of one—with Victor Lawson, the widely admired proprietor of the *Chicago Daily News*, the paper to which the *Star* was
most often compared. Like Nelson, Lawson pursued a successful career in
business before taking up journalism in the 1870s. The *Daily News* was one
of the original popular penny papers, independent and progressive in politics,
strong on local news, saucy but "clean," and immensely profitable. Contemporary observers and historians alike routinely bracketed it with the *Star*.
Lawson and his partner, Melville Stone, later general manager of the Associated Press, knew Nelson personally and thought highly of him. Yet no correspondence with the *Star*'s editor survives in either man's private papers. Nor
is there any evidence that Nelson consciously patterned the *Star* on the older
Daily News.

No doubt Nelson's image as a self-starter was tailored to his psychological
needs. He had always cast himself as a pioneer and rebel. Such influences as
he admitted to having absorbed were largely negative rather than positive. He
felt just as strongly about what he wanted his paper *not* to be as about what
it should be. In his eyes, William Randolph Hearst was a byword for cheap
sensationalism. "Hearst may edit all the other newspapers," he once told a
group of publishers, "but he isn't going to edit the *Kansas City Star*." E. W.
Scripps's genuinely progressive politics were more compatible with Nelson's
than Hearst's pseudo-populism, but Scripps too was suspect on account of his
chain-building methods. Although he was proprietor of the *Kansas City World*
for a decade, Scripps seems to have avoided all contact with his redoubtable
competitor. Late in life, he came to rue his role in ushering in the age of cor-

porate journalism. Nelson may have had Scripps and Hearst in mind when he declared that he was no mere "merchant in newspapers," but instead had dedicated the *Star* to "advancing the interests of Kansas City."[41]

If Pulitzer, Hearst, and Scripps exerted an incomparably greater influence on the newspaper profession than Nelson, it was partly because they saw their "field" as the whole United States rather than just the territory surrounding the Missouri River Valley. Moreover, the innovative journalistic methods and strategies they adopted were almost universally applicable. What Nelson accomplished, by contrast, was in many respects unique not only to Kansas City but also to the early Progressive Era. Just as the "Daily W. R. Nelson" was an extension of its proprietor, so Kansas City was, in a very real sense, the *Star* writ large. To a degree seldom approached in any other American community, Nelson's newspaper defined Kansas City's self-image and physical development, set the public agenda, and created a potent and enduring civic mythology.

Estimates of when the *Star* pulled out in front of the pack vary. By the early 1890s it was recognized as setting the pace in Kansas City journalism, as measured by both circulation and prestige. Patronizing references to the "Twilight Twinkler" had given way to respectful allusions to the "money making evening illuminary." The *Star* had proved itself a match for all comers. In 1886 a group of Detroit newspapermen led by Willis Abbot, future editor of the *Christian Science Monitor,* purchased the *Kansas City News* and challenged the *Star* head to head in the evening market. Three years later, bruised and chastened, Abbot fled to Chicago, leaving his "journalistic scalp in the possession of Colonel Nelson."[42] Ed Howe and others went down to similarly ignominious defeats as Nelson made good on his promise to put the *Star* "beyond competition." Within a decade of its founding the paper was returning a solid operating profit; by the turn of the century its position was well-nigh unassailable.

Charles Austin Bates, a journalism expert who visited Kansas City in 1897, rated the *Star* "one of America's four greatest evening newspapers." It combined, he wrote, the "fearlessness of editorial policy" that characterized the *New York Evening Post,* the "incomparable home circulation" of the *Washington Star,* and the "popular circulation and pulling power" of the *Chicago Daily News.* Everyone Bates interviewed agreed that Nelson's paper was a gilt-edged advertising medium. A few merchants considered the *Star*'s rates—higher than those charged by some of the Chicago dailies—extortionate and mounted a feeble boycott. But Nelson laughed them off, bragging that he had been known to "throw out several columns of advertising to make room for reading matter" without giving it a second thought. Business manager Gus Seested had had the foresight not to put too many eggs in the real estate basket in the booming 1880s, as other papers did. Instead, he convinced the managers of the new department stores to sign long-term, self-renewing contracts that obligated them to purchase space in the paper every day. This policy, it would be said, carried the *Star* through the financial storms of the eighties and nineties. By maximizing ad revenue and skimping on salaries, Nelson earned the wherewithal to spend liberally on news. In 1896, Bates reported, the *Star* wired more copy from the Chicago Democratic convention than any other paper in the United States.[43]

With Seested peering over his shoulder, Nelson devised an unbeatable business strategy compounded of prudence and daring. From the outset, he borrowed heavily and plowed most of his earnings back into the newspaper. He responded to competition by plunging deeper into debt, confident that by improving the efficiency of the operation and the quality of the product he would ultimately come out ahead. As other papers rose and fell by the wayside, the *Star* marched from strength to strength, occupying quarters of ever-increasing grandeur and pretension. In 1889 Nelson erected an ornate neoclassical building at Eighth and Wyandotte, said to be the first in the country designed specifically for a newspaper, at a reported cost of $125,000. Five years later the *Star* moved into a still more ostentatious Beaux Arts–style office at the northeast corner of Eleventh and Grand, a prime location across from Bullene's swank department store, thereby ensuring that the "best people" could admire Nelson's new presses through the street-level plate-glass windows. The editor installed himself and Seested in regally appointed offices on the upper floor. The new *Star* building was meant to impress, and impress it did, both inside and out. Howe likened the calm, cloistered atmosphere to that of a bank:

> When a man walks into the office of the *Kansas City Star,* a boy in uniform walks up to him, and asks whom he wants to see. If the visitor gives a name, the boy takes a book from his pocket, glances into it, and, in a dignified manner, tells the person at what hour the person in question can be seen. A boy ushers the visitor into the presence of the person asked for, and waits for the conversation to close, when the boy shows him directly out of the building. If the oldest subscriber should go into the *Star* office to loaf, and "josh" with the editor, he would freeze to death before he got out of the building. The *Star* office is a place to do busi-

The palatial *Star* building at Eleventh and Grand, designed by Henry Van Brunt, with its street-level plate-glass windows. "Many a business house could learn a valuable lesson from the *Star*," said rival publisher Ed Howe.

ness. The employes [*sic*] are paid to work, and there is no sign of idle talk. This is business as it should be. Many a business house could learn a valuable lesson from the *Star*.[44]

Those who assumed that Seested was the financial wizard behind the *Star*'s phenomenal success were only partly right. It's true that Nelson knew little about accounting, and cared less. But he had Midas's touch when it came to turning goodwill into gold. All the same, his fellow businessmen never seemed to know quite where they stood with Nelson. They were torn between regarding him as one of their own and as a menace to their inalienable right to the unfettered pursuit of wealth. Get-rich-quick types who had come to Kansas City to make their fortunes and push on to the next venture instinctively mistrusted a stay-at-home maverick who let money flow through his fingers and equated his own interests with those of the community. To them, Haskell wrote, Nelson seemed "the incarnation of an alien outlook on life."[45]

One prominent skeptic was Kersey Coates, a respected merchant and city father who, in the late 1860s, had built a mansard-roofed Opera House at Tenth and Broadway, across from the Coates House hotel. The second-floor auditorium was said to boast the largest stage west of the Mississippi. By the early eighties, however, the stately wood-and-brick structure had deteriorated into a firetrap. The *Star,* eager to establish its crusading credentials, demanded that the Opera House be upgraded as an urgent matter of public safety. Assuming he was being set up for blackmail, Coates sat back and waited for the customary demand for advertising. Instead, the *Star* ramped up its criticism. At length, or so the story goes, Coates understood what manner of man he was dealing with. He apologized to Nelson in person, spent forty-five thousand dollars fixing the theater up, and even stood surety on a loan that Nelson obtained from the Armour bank to purchase a new press.

Running an independent newspaper, Nelson was learning, required not only honesty and courage but also diplomacy and willingness to compromise. As the proprietor of a growing business, he couldn't afford to get on the wrong side of too many people in town, particularly the "best people" on whose good opinion the *Star*'s prestige and prosperity depended. At same time, he couldn't afford to ignore legitimate news, even if it meant stepping on sensitive toes. In later years, he liked to tell the story of a brawl on a downtown street corner involving a jilted husband and a prominent merchant with whom his wife was having an affair. The businessman sent his lawyer to the *Star* to offer a thousand dollars in advertising for keeping the incident out of the paper. Nelson swallowed hard and showed the emissary the door. "That thousand dollars looked mighty big to me," he admitted. "But of course I knew that a newspaper that suppresses news commits suicide. So I told him I would like the contract, but we were going to print the story, and he hinted I was an unpractical person and went away."[46]

Anecdotes of a similar nature, some almost surely apocryphal or freely embellished, proliferated over the years. Though Nelson never courted publicity, he relished the idolatry that his reputation for fearlessness inspired in his awestruck underlings. It pleased him to be seen as a rugged iconoclast, an outsider who didn't quite fit in, even as he maneuvered himself into position as a consummate insider. Like most of Nelson's performances, it was a brilliant improvisation, for he enjoyed being an enigma to others almost as much as he detested examining his own motives. "It was awful," White commiserated. "To be a gentleman; to be a mugwump; to refuse honest money for a peccadillo about professional ethics; to devote more space to Henry James than to Jesse in Jesse's home town, and still to be a big, laughing, fat, good-natured, rollicking, haw-hawing person, who loved a drink, a steak, a story, and a fight— strong men shuddered and turned away from the spectacle. They couldn't be sure whether he was crazy or they were!"[47]

The ideal editor, Nelson theorized, "should own no property, he should have no wife, no child; he should have no home, preferably living in a hotel; he should possess nothing except his newspaper; he should not mingle with people and should make no friends; have absolutely no financial or social interest in his community."[48] Nelson himself was too practical, or perhaps too self-indulgent, to observe such a monastic regimen. On the road to affluence and power, he violated his idealistic precepts in every particular.

The injunction against marriage was the first to go. A year or so after arriving in Kansas City, Nelson fell in love, apparently for the first time in his life, with the daughter of a well-to-do physician from Champaign, Illinois. Ida Houston was plain, placid, dull, and rich. No one was so tactless as to suggest that Nelson married her for her money, but her sizable dowry—rumored to be as much as fifty thousand dollars—undoubtedly helped keep the *Star* afloat in the early years when it was still subsisting hand to mouth. After the birth of their daughter, Laura, in 1883, the couple began climbing the social ladder, moving from a modest rooming house on the fringe of Quality Hill into the homey but somewhat frowsy Coates House. (Kersey Coates, Nelson affectionately observed, could do anything better than anybody else except run a hotel.) Gingerly emerging from his shell, Nelson joined the downtown Kansas City Club and, a few years later, the suburban Country Club. Although William Allen White praised Nelson as one of the few publishers he had ever known "who did not yield to the lure of the country club," Nelson felt he had earned the right to sit at the high table with the social elite.[49]

Unlike most of his peers, Nelson wasn't a man of property—yet. It was probably lack of liquid capital rather than caution that had dampened his enthusiasm for Kansas City's real estate spree of the mid-1880s. Old-timers recalled that whenever he showed signs of succumbing to the temptation, Seested restrained him by threatening to quit. But the builder in Nelson wouldn't lie still; he hankered after a piece of the action, however small. Soon he found what he was looking for—a dilapidated farmstead on ten gently rolling acres overlooking Brush Creek, a couple of miles south of the city limits. The acquisition of this isolated parcel in 1886 made Nelson both the butt of jokes and a figure of controversy. After he induced the water company to extend a pipeline to his new property, paying a premium for the service, crit-

Ida and Laura Nelson around 1884.

ics accused him of abusing the power of his newspaper. Nonsense, the editor shot back. No one had any right to criticize him for spending in Kansas City the money he had earned there.

How much money the *Star* was making by the early 1890s was anybody's guess. Enough, evidently, to pay for trips abroad, expensive private schools for Laura, and a country house that Nelson's opponents would one day deride as a "baronial castle." Oak Hall, like the *Star,* was a long-range project. Over the years, in the course of numerous remodelings, it came to epitomize the editor's ideal of a residence for the best class, combining European-flavored design with indigenous materials such as limestone and pine. (The quarter-sawn oak paneling and timbers that gave the house its name were an afterthought, acquired from friends in Indiana.) Nelson himself apparently drew up the plans and hired a succession of "name" architects to, as he put it, keep him from "going wrong." Monumentally self-assured in every other aspect of his life, he evinced the timid conservatism of a parvenu in matters of taste. "I never would build a house unless I had authority for it at least a century old," he explained. "You never can tell whether some new style is good. But if a house has stood a century and still is good, you can be pretty sure of it."[50]

In late middle age, Nelson was enjoying the creature comforts of the landed gentry to the hilt. "I admit that I am fond of the good things of life and that I propose to provide them for myself and my family to the extent that my income justifies," he declared in an open letter to his critics in the *Star*. People usually addressed him to his face as Colonel Nelson, the honorific title attesting both his social prominence and his undoubted skill as a campaign strategist. (Nelson had never served in the military, White explained, he just "looked coloneliferous.") The development of Oak Hall gave rise to a less flattering sobriquet: the "Baron of Brush Creek." Ensconced in his estate, with its parklike grounds and array of outbuildings, the editor was a sitting target for satirists who accused him of aping Old World customs. Brann, the self-styled Texas "iconoclast," wrote that "all of his servants are English and wear side-wheel whiskers; he docks the tails of his horses to make them resemble English cobs; he turns up his twousahs—paid for by the widow and water-works—whenever it's raining in Lunnon."[51] Brann's information was faulty—Ida Houston was not a widow and the money Nelson borrowed from the water company in 1882 had long since been repaid with interest—but his irreverent jab nonetheless hit home.

In due course, Baron Bill's real estate interests and social aspirations threw him together with the dean of the local architectural fraternity. Henry Van Brunt, a blue-blooded Bostonian with a weak chin, droopy mustache, and a general "air of impatient arrogance," came to Kansas City in 1887 to design stations for the Union Pacific railroad.[52] His impressive portfolio of commissions for Harvard and the Brahmins of Beacon Hill inspired Nelson to think big. The two men moved in the same moneyed circles and had similarly eclectic tastes, which in Van Brunt's case ranged from Gothic Revival to Queen Anne classicism. Hired to design the *Star*'s new headquarters in 1894, the architect produced an Italianate Renaissance–style *palazzo* crowned by a balustraded loggia. (Haskell, who went to work there in 1898, discerned elements of Lorenzo the Magnificent in Nelson's complex personality.) A couple of years earlier, Van Brunt's firm had received the coveted commission for the Electricity Building at the Chicago World's Fair. In an influential essay entitled "The Columbian Exposition and Modern Civilization," he extolled the Beaux Arts style as the answer to the hopes and aspirations of up-and-coming communities like Kansas City.

> The Exposition will furnish to our people an object lesson of a magnitude, scope, and significance such as has not been seen elsewhere. They will for the first time be made conscious of the duties, as yet unfulfilled, which they themselves owe to the civilization of the century. They will learn from the lessons of this wonderful pageant that they have not as yet taken their proper place in the world; that there is something far better worth doing than the mere acquiring and spending of wealth; that the works of their hands, their products, their manufactures, are not necessarily the best in the world; that their finer arts are in nearly every respect deficient in finish and in aim . . . . Such a realization by such a people will bear fruit, not in the apathy of mortification and defeat, but in that condition of noble discontent which carries with it its own speedy correction. . . . The low routines of life will be broken by a spirit of reform. New shoots will be grafted on the homely but vigorous stock; and the fruitage should have a larger and more vigorous growth, if there is any virtue left in that native force of character which is making a family of commonwealths in the wild prairies of the West.[53]

Van Brunt's flowery prose might have sent the *Star*'s copyeditors reaching for their pruning shears. The sentiment behind it, however, was music to Nelson's ears. Van Brunt's exalted vision of the White City, with its "uniform and ceremonious style," at once emblematic of civic reform and spiritual renewal, neatly dovetailed with the editor's private interests—interests which were, as always, inseparable from his public agenda.[54] The impetus behind the Chicago fair furnished the vital spark for Nelson's greatest and most enduring campaign: a sprawling system of parks and boulevards that would once and for all transform the mud-bathed frontier metropolis into a world city.

CHAPTER 2

❖

City Beautiful

Standing atop a knoll in Kansas City's Penn Valley Park, Henry Schott heaved a sigh of satisfaction. In the vale at his feet, hundreds of dilapidated structures had been cleared away, the old cellar holes and cisterns filled with topsoil. A man-made lake had been dredged to trap the freshets and streams that cascaded through the rugged ravine with every downpour. Along the water's verge ran a gently curving carriageway, studded with graceful lampposts. Schott, a senior *Star* editor, painted an idyllic picture for readers of *World's Work* magazine: "To-day a lake shines in the sun where the ramshackle houses lay deepest. The slopes are covered with grass, and smooth white roads, circling about vine-grown cliffs, are lost in groves of trees deceptive in their appearance of maturity. Children romp on the terraces and nurse girls gossip in the shade on the broad stone steps."

> *"Beauty has always paid better than any other commodity, and always will."*
>
> —Daniel H. Burnham

In the distance, smart couples promenaded through West Terrace Park, where dressed-stone retaining walls and graded drives were slowly transforming the ragged bluffs into an elegant podium for Quality Hill. Nowhere had the landscaper's hand wrought greater wonders than on the broad double-roadway that served as the centerpiece of the city's embryonic network of boulevards and parks. Only yesterday, it seemed, the corridor between Independence Avenue and Twelfth Street had been "covered largely with cabins and shanties occupied mainly by Negroes." Now, Schott gushed, "the shacks have given way to fountains and gardens. A pergola, that with its garlands and canopies of green appears as if decorated for a feast day, stands where were ramshackle houses, barns, and sheds. The pickaninnies have disappeared with their homes, and apartment houses of the best type have come to the Paseo."[1]

In the eyes of Schott's employer, William Rockhill Nelson, these verdant vistas were the hallmarks of an orderly, efficient, progressive metropolis. The urban parkscape taking shape before his eyes that crisp autumn day in 1905 represented the culmination of a plan hatched a dozen years earlier by an improbable coalition of activists—barons of industry, prosperous businessmen, political bosses, newspapermen, lawyers, professionals from all walks of life. About most things they disagreed vehemently, and often violently. But as the nineteenth century drew to a close, they were briefly united by a vision of the city of the future that beckoned just over the horizon.

George Kessler was in a testy mood as he escorted Schott around the city's newest park. Stocky and restlessly energetic, with a trim mustache and rimless glasses that accentuated his resemblance to Theodore Roosevelt, Kessler was proud, capable, and more than a little vain. Of late, he had begun to feel slighted by his comrades in the City Beautiful movement. Some of them had hinted, tactlessly, that Frederick Law Olmsted deserved credit for Kansas City's vaunted metamorphosis from cow town to modern metropolis. Kessler acknowledged his debt to the pioneering landscape designer, but facts were facts. "Not long after I came West," he informed the *Star* man, Nelson "asked me to submit plans for the improvement of the West Bluff. I climbed into the tower of the Union Depot and made my sketches. Those drawings were the first work done on the park system of Kansas City."[2]

Born and trained in Germany, Kessler united the soul of an artist with a head for business, a combination the *Star*'s proprietor found irresistible. When and how the two men met is uncertain. Kessler's statements on the subject were few and invariably vague, and any early correspondence he may have had with Nelson has vanished. Baron Bill's friends maintained that he discovered Kessler, while Kessler's son testified that the landscaper wangled an introduction to the editor through a mutual newspaper acquaintance. Whatever the truth, the twenty-seven-year-old Kessler's confident aplomb won Nelson over, and by the early 1890s they were working hand in glove.

Arriving in Kansas City two years after Nelson, in 1882, Kessler had made his mark by refurbishing a railroad excursion park in suburban Merriam,

Oak Hall as seen from the north, about 1890: a fairy-tale castle for the "Baron of Brush Creek."

Kansas. Soon private clients began clamoring for his services, among them Samuel Jarvis and Roland Conklin, partners in a prestigious mortgage banking firm with offices in Kansas City, New York, and London. In 1886 they formed a syndicate to develop a high-class subdivision on the eastern edge of Westport. Kessler had the engineering expertise as well as the European cachet the bankers were looking for. Engaged to spruce up an awkwardly situated ravine, he created a tastefully unobtrusive sunken park that helped induce financiers, stockyards officials, and other nobs to relocate to the Hyde Park neighborhood.

Nelson, whose newly acquired country estate lay a mile or so south of Hyde Park, had ample opportunity to admire Kessler's handiwork. The publisher's farmhouse was a weekend cottage at first, a rustic retreat from the heat and dust of the city. But within months he broke ground for a more pretentious residence. With its cone-capped turrets, round-arched doorways, and red-tiled roof, Oak Hall might have been mistaken for a storybook Norman castle. By 1889 the *Star* was in the black and the Baron was ready to occupy his new abode. With six-year-old Laura in tow, the Nelsons forsook their downtown apartment and moved to the wilds of Brush Creek.

No sooner had he settled in than the country squire started badgering the Westport City Council to pave the dirt road that marked the western boundary of his estate. It was along this course, the future Warwick Boulevard, that

Nelson rode downtown every day in a horse-drawn buggy. By way of farm fields and orchards, his commute took him past the stately mansions of Hyde Park, where Kessler had turned the offensive gully into a naturalistic playground in the best Olmsted manner. Farther north, the editor's route skirted Penn Street ravine, still defaced by tumbledown shanties and rickety boardwalks. To a man of Nelson's refined sensibility, the blasted landscape of "Vinegar Hill" was an intolerable affront.

Nelson wasn't the only land-hungry newsman who had his eye on Kessler. Charles Grasty, wunderkind of the *Kansas City Times* and Nelson's boon companion, craved a piece of the real estate action as well. A man of boyish charm, with a rubicund face and a reputation as a Don Juan, the future editor of the *Baltimore Sun* had a financial stake in Hyde Park and other Jarvis and Conklin developments on the east side. Morrison Munford had named Grasty managing editor of the *Times* in 1883, at age twenty, and he was credited with making the paper a beacon of southern Democracy. Unfortunately, neither man's journalistic acumen availed when the bottom abruptly fell out of the market in mid-1888 and the supply of ready money that had fueled their speculations dried up. "One day, every man you met had thousands; the next, it would have required a search warrant to find a fifty-dollar bill," a fellow scribe recalled.[3]

Reading the handwriting on the wall, Grasty hastily decamped in the summer of 1890, trailing rumors of adulteries "of a grossly levantine and brutal nature."[4] Making port in Baltimore, he presently gained control of the *Evening News* and turned it into a veritable facsimile of Nelson's crusading *Star*. When a friend sought help in improving a parcel of land near the city, Grasty induced Jarvis and Conklin to capitalize the venture. They were joined by another Kansas City refugee, Edward H. Bouton, who had also been hit hard by the market crash and was eager to escape the clutches of his creditors. Bouton, in turn, put Kessler on the payroll as the project's "topographical and landscape engineer."

The Roland Park Company was incorporated on July 30, 1891. Much written about and widely imitated, the Baltimore development would be the progenitor of countless garden suburbs and planned residential communities around the country. Thanks to his friendship with Grasty and Kessler, Nelson kept close tabs on its progress. So too, in the not very distant future, would a young Kansas City real estate genius named J. C. Nichols.

Eighteen eighty-one was an auspicious year for proponents of municipal improvements in Kansas City. Twice that April the Missouri River surged over its banks and inundated the low-lying industrial district. Train service was suspended for ten days, to the chagrin of railroad officials who had recently doubled the capacity of the gaudy terminal on Union Avenue. Around the corner, on St. Louis Avenue, a jovial, powerfully built foundry worker named Jim Pendergast bought a hotel cum saloon that soon became a popular hangout for the day-laborers and down-and-outers of the hardscrabble West Bottoms. Meanwhile, across the state line in the Argentine district, a thirty-year-old mining engineer lately arrived from Colorado secured a controlling interest in the city's largest smelter. His name was August Meyer.

By rights, Nelson should have shunned Meyer and Pendergast like the plague. The former represented an industry notorious for its robber barons and cutthroat labor policies, the latter lowlife saloons and corrupt, boss-ridden politics. But both were forceful, practical men and, in their own spheres, men of vision. Nelson needed their help as he meticulously laid the groundwork for his urban beautification crusade in the late 1880s.

Under its existing charter, the city lacked statutory authority to spend taxpayers' money on parks. An enabling law was drafted at Nelson's expense, only to die in legislative committee in Jefferson City. The measure was resubmitted, shot down by the courts, redrafted, and ultimately passed into law. Nelson commissioned Kessler to work up preliminary landscaping plans. He hired engineers to study parkways and boulevards around the country, and assigned reporters to write about the parks movement in Chicago, Minneapolis, St. Louis, New York, Washington, Baltimore, and elsewhere. Courtesy of the *Star*, it was said, the people of Kansas City "had parks and boulevards for dinner every night."[5]

Nelson was in high dudgeon, a force of nature, relentless and unstoppable. Clean elections, public ownership of utilities, and the other items on the reformers' lengthy docket were all worthy causes. Naturally, the *Star* got behind them. But the campaign for physical improvements was something the veteran contractor could really sink his teeth into. The swashbuckling fight for parks and boulevards would lay to rest Kansas City's tawdry past as a dollar swapper's paradise. Waged in print and on the ground, it would be the defining crusade of the editor's life. "Forever driven by the devils within him—or the angels—to smash and build," Nelson the master builder was also a destroyer.[6] His City Beautiful would rise on the ashes of the old order.

In 1889 Kansas Citians got a new home-rule charter and with it their first Board of Park Commissioners. The necessity for such a body had been brought home when a visiting expert had the effrontery to point out that only one large American city, Pittsburgh, maintained fewer parks in proportion to its population than Kansas City. Local boosters waxed indignant. To be compared to the Steel City in terms of industrial prowess was one thing; to be pilloried for failing to provide civilized amenities was another. Even businessmen who had hitherto been deaf to pleas for parks now sat up and listened. "Make Kansas City a good place to live in," the motto of the new Commercial Club, served notice on the absentee landlords and eastern speculators who had made a killing in the real estate boom and were now sitting on their nest eggs.

Nelson was champing at the bit. As soon as he freed up a little cash, he began scouting around for property to buy and improve. A tract on the fashionable northeast side had caught his eye in the early 1880s, but he balked at the inflated price and walked away.[7] In later years the publisher would speak of his decision to turn south as if it were preordained. But manifest destiny had less to do with it than cool calculation and good timing. Land in Westport, outside the city limits, was comparatively cheap. Moreover, Nelson never liked being part of a crowd. He envied the lebensraum his father enjoyed on the outskirts of Fort Wayne. When a downtown merchant complained that the city's southerly drift had to be checked or their businesses would be ruined, Nelson boomed, "Not at all. You couldn't stop it if you tried. Why try to hold back the ocean? I will not do a thing to stop it. I could not and nobody else could. But why not get in line with the town's growth?"[8]

Whether Nelson was being shrewd or merely disingenuous, neither he nor anyone else could have predicted with certainty where Kansas City's future boundaries would lie. In 1885 the city limits had been pushed south to Thirty-first Street (then called Springfield) and east to Cleveland. But the tide had yet to turn; most of the real estate action was still taking place on the east side, where one freewheeling developer, Willard Winner, controlled more than twelve hundred acres. Characteristically, though, Nelson had a plan up his sleeve. He didn't have the resources to finance it yet, but his newspaper was prospering, his credit was good, and he had the most precious asset of all: unbounded confidence in his own judgment and abilities. If he said Kansas City was going to move south, then move it would—and he would show the way.

Shortly before purchasing his Brush Creek getaway, Nelson erected a cluster of one-story rental homes on the south side of Springfield, just east of Grand. Little more than efficiency apartments, the narrow "shotgun" houses were so cramped that to save space bathtubs were placed in the kitchens and disguised by removable tabletops. Officially, the tiny enclave was known as DeGroff Place, after Nelson's paternal grandfather, but its popularity with bargain-hunting newlyweds earned it the nickname Bride's Row.[9]

From its front stoops, the new landlord surveyed the scattered settlements sprouting up in and beyond the Blue River valley. In 1887 an investment company announced plans to improve 1,269 acres northeast of Independence with an extensive network of boulevards and parks, but the real estate crash put paid to such grandiose schemes. By the early nineties Winner and most of his fellow east-end tycoons had run out of cash and property earmarked for upscale residential neighborhoods was being sold on the cheap to African Americans displaced by gentrification elsewhere in the city. Even those pillars of the mercantile establishment, Jarvis and Conklin, found themselves dangerously overextended as property values plummeted. In the summer of 1891 they foreclosed on a $100,000 mortgage taken out by the hapless Morrison Munford of the *Times*. (The venerable newspaperman would die months later, broke and broken-spirited.) One day Jarvis ran into Nelson at the Kansas City Club and offered to sell him the morning paper on bargain-basement terms.[10] But Nelson wasn't interested in buying the *Times* at any price just then. He had better things to do with his money.

Earlier that year the editor and his wife had deeded a triangular slice of land just west of Oak Hall to the town of Westport. It was slated for an extension of the future Warwick Boulevard, which Nelson envisioned as the major west-side thoroughfare to downtown Kansas City.[11] When the Park Board refused to play ball, Nelson lined ten blocks of the roadway with elm trees at his own expense. The pieces of his puzzle were slowly falling into place. East-side development was at a standstill. The venture capital that had flooded the city in the 1880s had dried up. Real estate was a bargain. Those who had husbanded their resources during the bubble had the field to themselves. Patiently and methodically, Nelson set about augmenting his landholdings in Westport. When his elderly father visited him in 1890, Oak Hall already presented an impressively baronial aspect. By the time he met Kessler a year or so later, the City Beautiful was taking tangible shape in his mind.

Nelson pursued that vision, as he pursued everything he desired, with a single-minded concentration bordering on obsession. He exasperated his managing editor by assigning the *Star*'s ace reporter and literary celebrity, Alfred Henry Lewis, to the parks-and-boulevards beat on a full-time basis. "That's it," T. W. Johnston exploded to Lewis when the order came down from on high. "I only wish he was responsible for the getting out of that rag. But no, I'm to do that! And when I get a man I can use to advantage, he must needs have him to write up his infernal parks and boulevards. If I were to get a Hans Christian Anderson [*sic*], who could write the best fairy story in the world, it wouldn't be a week before he'd want him to write a fairy story with a park for the plot and a boulevard for the hero."[12]

Nelson's schemes were hardly the stuff of fairy tales, though they were rich-
ly stocked with heroes and villains. The latter, in this instance, were the landed gentry who were content to sit back idly and watch their property portfo-
lios appreciate in value. The *Star* consigned them to membership in the
"Hammer and Padlock Club," signifying their determination to beat down the
forces of progress and keep their wealth under lock and key. Such standpatters were anathema to Nelson. He preferred the company of risk takers like
Grasty, who put their money and ideas on the line, and entrepreneurs like
Arthur Stilwell, the charismatic builder and promoter of railroads from
Kansas City to the Gulf Coast. Unlike the Roland Park Company, however,
Nelson's plans weren't dependent on outside capital. He would realize them
on his own—with a little help from his friends.

After the Missouri Supreme Court struck down Kansas City's park law on
a technicality in January 1891, park advocates pinned their hopes on amend-
ing the two-year-old city charter. In the run-up to the charter election, August Meyer made a carefully pitched appeal to his colleagues in the Commercial Club. He pointed out that the real estate frenzy of the past decade had
"suddenly transformed a village into a city." Cities needed parks and boulevards in order to draw the "very best class of people." Such amenities, while
costly, had always been profitable investments, since adjacent property typically rose enough in value to pay for them in a few years. "A beautiful city will
always attract men who have money," Meyer told his audience. "They will
want to invest their money in a city that is progressive and well governed. They
will want to have homes in a city of that kind. They will want to establish business enterprises here."[13]

Meyer's mercantilist argument carried the day, and in early 1892 voters approved the charter amendments by a five-to-one margin, removing the legal
shackles that had hobbled the original Park Board. A reconstituted Board of
Park Commissioners took office on March 5, with Meyer in the president's
chair. A multimillionaire nature lover who dabbled profitably in real estate, he
was a fountain of energy—trim, athletic, and gregarious, with deep-set eyes,
close-cropped hair, and an aquiline nose. Horseback riding was his favorite
recreation. He loved to roam the hills south and east of the city, assessing the
lay of the land. On one such outing his eye would be caught by a piece of property Nelson owned near Oak Hall, in what was known as the Southmoreland
neighborhood. The smelting magnate was thinking of moving away from Independence Avenue and building a new mansion with elaborate grounds laid
out by their mutual friend George Kessler.

The other members of the carefully balanced board represented the various constituencies parks advocates needed to woo and win over. Louis Hammerslough, a German Jew, had sold his lucrative retail clothing business several years earlier and embarked on a second career as proprietor of the *Kansas City Globe*. William C. Glass owned one of the city's largest wholesale liquor companies and traded in real estate on the side. Adriance Van Brunt (no relation to Nelson's friend Henry) was a well-connected architect who designed homes for bigwigs in Hyde Park and elsewhere. All three were men of consequence in the community. But only one other commissioner, Simeon B. Armour, stood on an equal footing with Meyer in the business world.

The patriarch of the city's stockyards aristocracy, Armour shunned the limelight, living modestly in a large but unpretentious frame house at 1216 Broadway. Kansas City's Armour meatpacking plant was the second largest in the country after the family's Chicago operation, headed by Simeon's brother, Philip Danforth Armour. The Kansas City plant sprawled over fifteen acres of river bottomland on the state line, not far from the belching smokestacks of Meyer's Argentine smelter. Days after taking his seat on the board, Simeon would receive a telegram from Chicago giving the green light for a further expansion aimed at turning the Kansas City plant into the world's largest meatpacking operation.[14]

While Meyer enjoyed a reputation for treating his employees decently, Armour's concept of labor relations was decidedly old-school. In response to the industrial unrest of the 1890s, he imported unskilled workers from southern and central Europe as strikebreakers, housing them in the squalid slum known as the "Patch" hard by his packing plant. Armour was as tough as a branding iron. Under grilling by a U.S. Senate committee in 1889, he had swept aside allegations that the "beef trust" was an illegal combine and haughtily refused to answer questions put to him by the formidable Senator George Graham Vest of Missouri.[15] Such a man was unlikely to be cowed by mere city councilors.

The park commissioners quickly swung into action. Having secured Kessler's services as "secretary" for one hundred dollars a month, they proceeded to call in Olmsted's landscape firm for consultation. Kessler was incensed but wisely held his tongue. His name, after all, presumably would be on the final plans. In the event, Olmsted was abroad, taking a much-needed break from his nerve-racking work on the Chicago World's Fair. His partner, Henry S. Codman, arranged to come to Kansas City in April 1892 and offer his advice to the commissioners in Olmsted's place. But Codman's perfunctory five-page report contained little of substance beyond what Kessler and

Meyer had already observed for themselves. His principal recommendation was that the board set aside at least one "great rural park," in order to "bring some of the advantages of the country into the city." Meyer vetoed this idea, partly because he doubted the board could muster the necessary political support and partly because he considered smaller neighborhood parks better value for the city's money. Codman further urged the board not to acquire land west of Agnes Avenue on the river bluffs, arguing that it would be cut off from parkland on the east and overlook an unsightly industrial district. At the same time, he proposed that the future North Terrace Park be connected to the riverfront, "with its ample possibilities in boating and other aquatic sports."[16] Each of these suggestions the board likewise saw fit to disregard.

Considering how little practical help Meyer and his colleagues gleaned from the document, one wonders why they deemed it necessary to bring Codman in at all. The answer, surely, is that they needed the endorsement of the country's foremost landscape firm to win the support of the City Council and business community. This purpose having been served, Codman's report was, it seems, simply filed away.

Kessler, in any case, was already formulating a plan of his own. In May 1892, his preliminary sketches of the West Bluffs fresh in mind, he sat down in his office at 602 Wyandotte and drafted an eight-page prospectus for a city-wide system of parks and boulevards. "Perhaps few owners of realty," he wrote in flowing longhand, "appreciate the fact that much of their property is unproductive because our city is spoken of as a good city for business but no place to live in." To counter this unfavorable reputation, Kessler proposed to create a chain of modestly scaled parks linked by broad, tree-lined boulevards. Inner-city green spaces would serve as small "oases in a desert of houses," while a belt of larger outlying parks was designed, in the best Olmsted tradition, to "bring within the city the charms of country scenes and clean fresh air."

Kessler brought his vision down to earth by sketching an imaginary tour along a greenway extending east from downtown along what he called "Eleventh St. Boulevard." Beyond Prospect Avenue, the traveler turned north to the river bluffs, pausing to admire the "vistas through the trees as though pictures set in frames of foliage." Thence the route swung south through the Blue River valley to a "south park" located somewhere in the Brush Creek valley. After continuing toward Westport, the tourist completed his circuit via a west-side boulevard leading back into the business district. Eleventh Street Boulevard would pass through the heart of downtown (and, perhaps not coincidentally, the new *Star* office that Nelson would soon erect at Eleventh and Grand). The rest of the system was to be suburban or rural in character, isolated from "the active business life of the city."[17]

Landscape engineer George Kessler (lower left) and friends in one of his naturalistic city parks, savoring "the charms of country scenes and clean fresh air."

Kessler's plan was both practical and compelling, but in the spring of 1892 it was still far from reality. Under the new charter, the Park Board was empowered only to condemn land for park purposes. It remained unclear how the real estate, to say nothing of any improvements, was to be paid for. Over the ensuing months, the parks forces marshaled their arguments with care.

Council members were discreetly lobbied. Delbert Haff, the board's resourceful attorney, set to work on the necessary legal and financial framework. Meyer dispatched a committee to investigate parks and park laws in Chicago,
Boston, Baltimore, Washington, Brooklyn, New York, Buffalo, and St. Louis,
while he himself "spent at least three hours a day in looking over the city and
vicinity" on foot and horseback.[18]

At length, the board's indefatigable president prevailed on Olmsted to
grace the city with his presence. On October 14 the *Star* reported that the "famous landscape engineer" had arrived the previous evening and was lodging
at the Coates House. Suffering from debilitating "neuralgia and toothache,"
Olmsted was conserving his strength to cope with last-minute crises at the
Chicago fair.[19] His imprimatur was nonetheless crucial to Meyer's plans. According to both the *Star* and the *Times,* he accompanied the park commissioners on a tour of the city on October 15. Yet none of the local papers ran
an interview with the ailing dignitary. Indeed, there were no follow-up stories
of any kind. The long-awaited visit would remain shrouded in mystery. Was
Olmsted too indisposed to speak to reporters? Or could it be that he failed to
provide the unequivocal endorsement the board expected from him?

Months later, Meyer would recall that Olmsted had been "particularly
pleased" with the board's plans for North Terrace Park, commenting blandly
that "here was an opportunity to produce something characteristic and beautiful that any city might be proud of."[20] Like a pope dispensing benedictions,
the great man seems to have stayed just long enough to see the sights and bestow an innocuous blessing. Small wonder Kessler bridled at the suggestion
that Olmsted, not he, was the father of Kansas City's parks and boulevards.

Another year of negotiating and wrangling would elapse before the Park
Board's master plan was ready to be unveiled. The final proposals were largely consonant with those embodied in Kessler's draft, with one notable exception: Eleventh Street Boulevard, which Kessler conceived as "the key to the
whole system," had quietly been scrapped as a major east-west artery in favor
of Independence Avenue and Seventh Street. Partly because of business opposition to downtown land-taking, the central business district had been by-
passed and the whole system effectively reoriented along a north-south axis.
As the principal east-side boulevard, the Paseo became the de facto backbone
of the system, linking the well-to-do neighborhoods on the river bluffs with
the still largely undeveloped districts east and south of the city proper.

The lengthy report the board submitted to Mayor W. S. Cowherd on October 2, 1893, would come to be regarded as a classic of American urban plan-

ning.[21] A collaboration between Meyer and Kessler, it reflected both Olmsted's naturalistic manner and the neoclassical formalism of Baron Haussmann and other European city planners. Meyer, mindful of the need to enlist public support, highlighted the system's benefits for all. Parks and boulevards would attract talented entrepreneurs, "that class to whose experience, ability and means the building up of a city is always largely due." But cities also had a responsibility to provide "a reasonable modicum of rational enjoyment and recreation" for the working classes. Echoing a familiar Nelsonian theme, Meyer drew a parallel between physical and spiritual well-being. The daily grind of commerce, no less than the overcrowding of tenements, stifled both body and soul.

That moral uplift and civic progress were natural byproducts of rising property values was the cornerstone of Meyer's philosophy. The city, he wrote in language foreshadowing that of latter-day zoning regulations, should "encourage the fullest use and the highest possible development and improvement of all lands." In its first four decades, Kansas City had spread out higgledy-piggledy, without benefit of a comprehensive plan. The baleful effects of unregulated development could still be mitigated, if not erased, by setting aside the choicest real estate for residential neighborhoods and reserving less desirable land for parks, roadways, industry, and infrastructure. In that way, Meyer argued, "values of lands within the city will reach a level in harmony with the uses to which the lands are best suited, and those uses having been definitely established, values, instead of being variable and uncertain, will become fixed."

Here was the nub of the argument. Investors had been thrown off balance by the wild gyrations of the 1880s real estate market, which had rewarded speculation and discouraged long-term planning. Stability was Meyer's watchword. If only his fellow citizens had awakened "fifteen or twenty years ago," he lamented, "a plan might have been adopted that would have made this one of the most beautiful cities in the world." Regrettably, however, Kansas City "did not then promise the future that we all now believe is in store for her." In the report's most quoted passage, Meyer predicted that a well-designed network of boulevards and parks, sensitively adapted to the natural terrain, would "give a permanent residence character to certain sections of the city" and "determine and fix for a long time to come, if not permanently, the best and most valuable residence property." Almost as an afterthought, he added that the Park Board's proposals would preserve established neighborhoods by checking the already pronounced "tendency to spread out and to build residences in the suburbs."

In light of Meyer's imminent move to outlying Westport, the latter statement is open to a somewhat cynical interpretation. It can hardly have been
accidental that he and Kessler both paid special attention to the "topographical enigma" of the southern suburbs. The gently tilting plateau extending beyond the city limits from Springfield to the Brush Creek valley, Meyer wrote,
was pockmarked with settlements that appeared to have been "sown by the
whirlwind." In imposing a "gridiron system of streets" over this "irregular territory," poorly planned development had given it an "appearance of ragged-
ness" that was "all but indescribable." He went on to warn that "if on the South
Side future growth should continue as it has begun, our city would in that direction be composed of alternating patches of good and poor residence localities."

Meyer and Kessler had no more intention of allowing this to happen than
did the Baron of Brush Creek.

The Park Board's report ignited a firestorm of controversy when the City
Council took it up on October 12. In a debate characterized by raw demagoguery, class animosity, and ad hominem attacks on both Meyer and Nelson,
one point elicited general agreement: the system would be a drain on the city's
treasury for years, if not decades, to come. Even supposing the requisite political will could be summoned, statutory limits on the city's indebtedness
would have to be raised or some other means devised to finance the improvements. This would have been a tall order in the best of times. In late 1893 the
nation was in the grips of a panic-induced depression that would soon bring
the park movement to a crashing halt across the country. Meyer and his colleagues hoped Kansas City would be an exception, pointing out that the construction of parks and boulevards would provide employment and stimulate
the local economy. This was good enough for Alderman Jim Pendergast, who
cast the deciding vote in the lower house's five-to-four acceptance of the report. Many of his constituents lived in the dirt-poor neighborhoods of the river bottoms, and a public-works project that promised more "jobs for the boys"
appealed to the Democratic chieftain's sense of civic spirit.

While the pros and cons of the plan were being aired in council chambers
and courtrooms, Kessler kept busy preparing questionnaires for property owners, drafting model ordinances, and escorting aldermen around the route of
his proposed boulevards. Nelson, meanwhile, had his hands full with the move
into the elegant new newspaper plant that Henry Van Brunt had designed for
him at Eleventh and Grand and the long-anticipated debut of the *Star*'s Sunday edition. Simultaneously, the editor's campaign for municipal ownership of

the waterworks was coming to a head as well. The $3.1 million price tag posed a seemingly insoluble problem, since there wasn't enough money in the city's depression-depleted treasury to pay for both parks and waterworks. The situation called for creative financing and Park Board attorney Delbert Haff obliged by proposing a system of tax certificates based on special-assessment districts—in effect, a value-added tax on rising property values—as a fiscally prudent and politically painless way to fund the construction program.

The two measures were put to the voters at a special election set for June 6, 1895. Though confident of victory, Nelson was taking no chances. Letters to the editor were planted in the *Star*. Articles enumerating the social, economic, and health benefits of parks were reprinted from other newspapers and magazines. Local promoters of the plan received lavish publicity. On a more practical level, Baron Bill cut a deal with Hugh McGowan, a prominent member of the notorious Democratic "combine" that dominated local politics. A "rough-neck Irish police commissioner who had fought his way up from the ranks in politics," McGowan took pride in ensuring that city elections were at least tolerably free of fraud and corruption.[22] Beneath their bad-boy exteriors, he and the publisher were kindred spirits. A Missouri commissioner to the Chicago World's Fair, McGowan had fallen under the spell of the White City. As the *Star*'s campaign intensified, he called on the editor at his new office to discuss the forthcoming charter election.

"Colonel," said he, "you seem to feel strongly about this amendment." Nelson allowed as it was "the biggest thing that has been before Kansas City in years."

"Well," the commissioner came back, "if you want it you can have it. But it will take a little money for the workers."[23]

McGowan delivered the goods: almost before the grease on his palm had worn off, the charter amendments had passed by a lopsided margin of nearly six to one. Nelson never forgot the favor. Two years later, the asphalt company McGowan represented would receive the contract to pave Warwick Boulevard near Oak Hall.

Although a key battle had been won, the fate of the parks-and-boulevards system still hung in the balance. "The land speculators were the hard core of the opposition," Henry Haskell wrote. "When the boom broke they were left holding the sack. Their consuming ambition thereafter was to see that taxes were held down until they could get out from under."[24] Businessmen, for their part, took a dim view of Haff's special assessments, which they not unreasonably regarded as a radical income-redistribution scheme inspired by Henry

George's single-tax heresy. George's intent, however, was to break up socially undesirable concentrations of wealth and population. Meyer, Nelson, and Kessler, as would soon become clear, had a very different endgame in mind.

Meyer's contention that the system would forestall suburban flight was, alas, largely a smokescreen. By the early 1890s smart money was already flowing south. Indeed, Nelson and other forward-looking developers were banking on it. It seems likely that, far from stabilizing older neighborhoods, the dramatic appreciation of land values—which alone made a citywide network of parks and boulevards possible—actually encouraged many homeowners to sell out and move to less expensive areas. By one estimate, moreover, assessments on property owners in the city's park districts prolonged the depression by siphoning $25 million out of the real estate market over the next dozen years.[25] To their credit, the park commissioners had never suggested that taxpayers wouldn't feel the pinch. They had simply maintained that the burden on the economy was sustainable and, in the long run, beneficial for the city as a whole.

These intricate economic arguments masked a host of motives, some openly acknowledged, others implied or barely hinted at. In order to attract and hold desirable middle-class residents, Kansas City needed to eliminate, or at any rate sweep under the carpet, the most unsavory aspects of modern urban life. No one could object to making the city cleaner, healthier, and more beautiful. The question was, whose ox would be gored in the process? Who would speak for the hapless "pickaninnies" whose homes stood in the way of the Paseo, the displaced denizens of Vinegar Hill, or the shanty dwellers clinging for life on the tumbledown West Bluffs? When poor folk were shunted aside in the name of beautification, no provision was made for rehousing them. The Park Board, Meyer and Kessler felt obliged to remind their fellow citizens, was not a welfare agency, and condemnation, then as later, proved a blunt and pitiless instrument for addressing the endemic problems of poverty and blight.

Neither "shiftless" African Americans nor "wild-eyed" radicals had more than a marginal place in the idealized polity of the City Beautiful. Although the Midwest was a nexus of populist agitation in the 1890s, it was not the "condition of noble discontent" that Henry Van Brunt found so salutary and hopeful, but something far rawer and more ominous. Such disquieting social trends accentuated the park movement's pronounced antiurban bias. As Meyer wrote in the board's report, "Life in cities is an unnatural life. It has a tendency to stunt physical and moral growth." Henry George, too, saw cities as incubators of poverty, vice, and iniquity. The overriding concern he held in common with Meyer and Kessler was to disperse the inner-city population,

The West Bluffs, before and after beautification. Parks and boulevards, George Kessler and August Meyer argued, would attract the "very best class of people" to the growing city.

to let air and light into overcrowded districts. (Reformers described parks as cities' "lungs.") This goal is hard to reconcile with Meyer's prediction that parks and boulevards would somehow preserve existing neighborhoods. In fact, as time would show, they had precisely the opposite effect. Meyer was not just wrong, he was spectacularly, fundamentally wrong.

Park advocates got it right in one important respect, however. In facilitating an exodus from the central city, the board's plan struck at the very heart of the Democratic machine's power. In years to come, Kessler would implicitly admit that this had been on the City Beautiful reformers' unspoken agenda all along. Looking back in 1917, he contended that "in sharp contrast to the feeling of sectionalism and consequent antagonism of one section to another within a city existing in some communities, the boulevards and parkways of Kansas City have accomplished the real purpose outlined by Mr. Meyer in the first report, namely, the tying together of all sections and the uniting of Kansas City as a whole into a community whose purposes and actions are for the benefit of the city as a whole at all times."[26] In the boss-busters' lexicon, this was coded language for loosening the stranglehold the Democratic satraps had long exercised from their headquarters in the river wards.

Little of this was immediately apparent in the euphoric aftermath of the 1895 charter election, however. It took Pendergast, McGowan, and up-and-coming boss Joseph Shannon some time to comprehend that they had been outflanked by the wily Baron Bill and the parks brigade.

Nelson skipped the victory celebration, having sailed to Europe in February 1895 for an extended stay with his wife and daughter. He had traveled abroad once before, in the early nineties, but that brief taste of Old World culture had merely whetted his appetite. Now he was going to do it right. He would take the grand tour, domiciling his family in Paris and exploring other countries on the side. While Laura was in school, Nelson passed the time with comrades like McGowan, Henry Watterson, and Samuel Morss. His apartment near the Arc de Triomphe afforded an excellent view of Haussmann's boulevards, through which he roamed at leisure in a horse-drawn landau, attended by an English coachman and footman. Far from Kansas City's madding crowds, Nelson learned to read (though not to speak) French, accompanied Ida to houses of haute couture, and cultivated his taste in fine art and food. On an excursion to Florence, he commissioned copies of Old Master paintings and sculpture for a new gallery he was planning back home.

The Nelson who came back to Kansas City twenty months later was domesticated, "fond of the good things of life," and solicitous of his family, particularly his daughter, on whom he doted. "Whether he realized it or not," Haskell wrote, "he returned from Europe more than ever a spiritual alien to the go-getter and houn' dawg atmosphere that still pervaded Main Street, Walnut Street, Grand Avenue and the packing centers of the West Bottoms."[27] Next door to Oak Hall, Meyer had moved into his twenty-six-room Queen Anne–style mansion, designed by Van Brunt's firm, with its tastefully understated "oriental" garden laid out by Kessler. Nelson fraternized with Meyer and their fellow social registrants at the city's most exclusive clubs. As publisher of one of the greatest newspapers in America, and undisputed king of Kansas City's journalistic mountain, he had finally arrived.

Resuming his command in the autumn of 1896, Nelson orchestrated the *Star*'s campaign against the "mossbacks" and "knockers" who were contesting the city's condemnation proceedings in North Terrace and West Terrace parks. The gala opening of Swope Park that June had serendipitously provided the "large rural scenic park" that Codman had recommended. Nelson seldom ventured so far afield, however, having his own private park just outside his front door. Oak Hall had become grander with each successive addition, until it more than ever resembled an English "country house." Nelson told friends he wanted it to feel like a "home" rather than a "palace" or "public institution." Withal, it was a home fit for a king, a cross between Versailles and a British gentlemen's club. The publisher personally supervised the appointments, selecting everything from massive antique furniture and oriental rugs to china, silver, and linen. The manse provided a worthy setting for his personal art collection, which would eventually include paintings by Reynolds, Corot, Troyon, Monet, Constable, Gainsborough, Ribera, and a portrait of Nelson by William Merritt Chase.[28]

Not surprisingly, Nelson treated the collection of pseudo–Old Masters he was donating to the city, at 110 West Ninth Street, as an extension of his private domain, engaging his house architect, Van Brunt, to decorate the galleries and even dictating the opening hours. "Well, this seems to rub some of the lard off of Kansas City," a young art lover exclaimed at an opening reception in early 1897. The "new" Nelson was in his element, circulating among the invited guests as they oohed and aahed over reproductions of Raphael's *Sistine Madonna* and Botticelli's *Spring* and plaster casts of the *Venus de Milo* and *Apollo Belvedere*. The editor had recovered his composure after blowing up at a *Times* man who had had the impertinence to ask how much the artworks cost. The words were hardly out of the reporter's mouth before Nelson slammed his fist down on his desk, almost upsetting an inkwell. "That's nobody's damn business but mine," the proud possessor thundered. "I bought and paid for these things with my own money, and I am not going to tell any-body how much I spent. I am doing this because I think it will be a good thing for our town, and the cost has nothing to do with it."[29]

Rich as he was, Nelson couldn't afford to stock his Western Gallery of Art with *real* Old Masters. Nor did he pretend to be a connoisseur. He was, how-ever, becoming admirably proficient in the arts of noblesse oblige.

On a roll, Nelson ratcheted up his real estate activity as the end of the cen-tury approached. The four cramped rowhouses he had built in the mid-1880s had been just the beginning. In 1897 he purchased a tract of land bordered by Thirtieth and Springfield, Oak and McGee. There he erected a dozen sub-stantial dwellings on alternating lots, leaving extra space between, and rented them to employees and friends. DeGroff Way (not to be confused with near-by DeGroff Place) occupied a hillside overlooking the hallowed grounds of the Civil War–era Union Cemetery. The two-story houses, with their deep, south-fronting verandas, recalled the well-proportioned cottages that French settlers built along the Mississippi River before the West was won.[30]

Anticipating that the city limits would soon be pushed south to Forty-ninth Street, Nelson was already hatching bigger plans in the vicinity of Oak Hall. One day businessman U. S. Epperson called on the editor at home and caught an earful. Bursting with enthusiasm, Nelson "brought out a prelimi-nary sketch some four or five feet square," indicating the roads, home sites, landscaping, and other improvements he planned to make in what he called the Rockhill district. Epperson quickly calculated how much all this would cost and commented that it would be cheaper to have the plans made into a landscape painting to hang on the wall. Nelson's face fell as he rolled the sketch back up. The trouble with most men, he muttered, was that they didn't "allow their imagination and mentality full range," while the few who did were generally "prevented from going forward from lack of confidence." If the Park Board didn't have the gumption and foresight to carry out his plans, Nelson declared, he would build the boulevards himself.[31]

In 1898 the Missouri Supreme Court upheld the validity of the city's con-demnation proceedings. This was the board's cue. Land for the first section of the Paseo was cleared by April and work on other parts of the system got un-der way in earnest. As the Oak Hall neighborhood became increasingly sub-urbanized, Nelson began looking around for a farm where he could raise the purebred shorthorn cattle that had been his late father's pride and joy. Present-ly he found a 160-acre spread near what is now Eighty-fifth and Wornall, just south of his friend Kirk Armour's cattle ranch. The old farmhouse, formerly

Rock Hill Boulevard, Kansas City.

An idealized view of William R. Nelson's Rockhill development is shown in this early twentieth-century postcard. The publisher's mansion is visible through the trees.

owned by relatives of frontiersman Daniel Boone, was fitted out with Nelson's trademark deep porches, a massive stone fireplace in the living room, and an attic large enough to accommodate a billiard table and a dance floor for Laura and her teenage friends.[32] Closer to home, Nelson bought an antebellum brick house in Westport as a wedding present for his managing editor and, on an adjacent lot, put up a new wood-frame building to house the exclusive Miss Barstow's School, where Laura was enrolled.

By the turn of the century, the Hammer and Padlock Club had all but conceded defeat, but things were still moving too slowly for Nelson's taste. Making good on his promise to Epperson, he set an example for the city by constructing a boulevard to his own exacting specifications. Even Kessler could scarcely have improved on Rockhill Road, with its picturesque limestone bridge spanning Brush Creek and a companion right of way, bowered by a double row of shade trees, for the car line that the Metropolitan Street Railway Company obligingly extended to the publisher's property. In a news story announcing the project, the *Star* echoed the wistful tone of the Park Board's 1893 report: "Kansas City might have been beautiful if the first builders had accepted nature's picturesque streets, avenues, and boulevards." The new road would "furnish the beginning of the new way of building Kansas City, in the newest part of Kansas City, where the trees and grades and slopes and views will not be ruthlessly destroyed."[33]

Nelson's model thoroughfare was hardly the "beginning" of anything, of course. All over the city, crews were hard at work under Kessler's watchful eye, grading and paving streets and planting trees and shrubs by the tens of thousands. But Nelson was determined to present himself in new light—not simply as the park movement's publicist in chief but as a master builder in his own right. This ambition didn't go down well with Democratic Mayor James A. Reed, who was equally determined to honor his campaign pledge to lower taxes and rein in the free-spending Park Board. When Reed moved to stock the board with his own appointees, August Meyer took it as a signal to step down. "We have all been to some extent gifted with poetic vision," he wrote to Kessler in the spring of 1901, "and I think have been capable of developing in our own minds a fair combination of the aesthetic and business features of the park business. . . . [I]t has been a most difficult task for our old Park Board to stand firm by its convictions as to the public needs, and at the same time not to overburden those who had to stand the cost. I have the conviction that we have all tried to do our duty, and it will always be a great source of satisfaction to me to look upon the days of co-operation with all of you, whose aims have been high and whose motives have always been pure."[34]

Sadly, Meyer would not live to see those high aims come to fruition. After his death in 1905, the city erected a monument in his memory at Tenth and the Paseo. Facing the graceful, stair-stepped pergola that descended toward Kessler's sunken tapestry garden, Daniel Chester French's dignified bas relief paid tribute to the imaginative businessman who had

> planned and toiled
> That dwellers in this place
> Might ever freely taste the
> Sweet delights of nature.

Weeks after Meyer penned his poignant valedictory, a pair of University of Kansas undergraduates worked their way across the Atlantic on a cattle boat and spent the summer seeing the sights of Europe. For Jesse Clyde Nichols, who had scarcely been off the farm in Olathe, Kansas, this budget version of the grand tour was a once-in-a-lifetime experience. He was impressed by the way European houses and cities, respectful of their surroundings, were built to last, so unlike the formless, quick-sprouting cities of America. Above all, he admired England's tidy suburban districts, where, as he wrote in an article for his hometown paper, "every home is surrounded by parks or beautiful lawns and flower gardens" and "whenever possible, a road runs around a hill instead of over it."[35]

With his bland, unflinching gaze, firmly drawn mouth, and receding hairline, the precocious twenty-one-year-old already projected the image of a successful businessman. Bright and industrious, Nichols inspired confidence in everyone he met. Following a postgraduate year at Harvard, where he studied the economic theory of real estate development, he returned to Kansas City and went into business with a couple of fraternity brothers. They bought some land in Kansas City, Kansas, put up a hundred or more modest frame houses, and sold them on easy terms to working-class families. In April 1905 Nichols and his partners offered their first house and lot for sale on the Missouri side. Bismark Place, ten scruffy acres on a hillside south of Brush Creek, lay just outside the newly extended city limits. Originally platted in the 1880s, the nucleus of the future Country Club district was a wasteland of derelict farm fields, quarries, rubbish dumps, and truck gardens. Undaunted, Nichols built a cottage for himself and his wife and "knuckled down to selling lots."[36] Most days found the young entrepreneur working alongside his crews as they graded streets, dug drainage ditches and septic systems, and laid down plank sidewalks. He met prospective customers at the end of the Rockhill streetcar line and ferried them to Bismark Place in his horse-drawn buggy.

Lacking water lines, sewers, gas, and electricity, Bismark Place was hardly prime real estate. But it had one incalculable advantage: it lay just across the valley from Nelson's Rockhill development.

From his simple homestead, Nichols enjoyed a splendid view of the editor's castle and the beehive of construction activity around it. By 1904 Nelson had assembled a parcel of some 275 acres and broken ground for his first large-scale subdivision. Over the next half-dozen years, a hundred or so unpretentious stone-and-wood homes would spring up in the shadow of Oak Hall. Framed with two-by-six boards instead of the standard two-by-fours, and bedecked with porches for sleeping and socializing on sultry midwestern nights, they were as sturdy and inviting as the homes Nichols had seen in Europe. Nelson regarded cheap construction as false economy and insisted that his houses be "as good fifty years from now as they are to-day."[37] More to the point, he meant his homes to last because they were his monuments. Building houses was his hobby and he could afford to indulge himself. The Rockhill houses were said to have been built to his designs, though that may be too grand a term for what were surely no more than sketch plans that his resourceful jack-of-all-trades and construction foreman, Pete Larson, fleshed out on site. Nelson's architectural repertoire was limited to two or three basic patterns, but his houses were attractively proportioned, situated on lots of ample dimensions, and altogether more desirable than most residences in the city's older, more densely settled neighborhoods.

Rockhill was different in another way as well: virtually none of the "Nelson houses" was for sale. Why anyone would want to buy a home when he could rent a perfectly good one was a mystery to Baron Bill. He saw nothing untoward about flaunting his position as a landlord while the *Star* trumpeted the virtues of home ownership. Besides, Nelson prided himself on being a good provider. He spared no expense in adorning streets and home lots with plants from his own nursery, quarrying limestone locally for the low-slung stone fences, and importing exotic squirrels to enhance the countrified setting. One resident—who, like many of his neighbors, was both Nelson's tenant and his employee—described Rockhill in the breathless tone of a garden catalogue:

> There were miles of rock walls, bordering newly paved streets; miles of crimson rambler roses stretching into the distance like gorgeous banners. Back of the rose bushes, rows and clumps of spirea made cascades of white in their period of blooming. Scattered informally, were bushes and groups of Japonica, dressed in deep red, in their turn, vying with weigela in the colorful progression of springtime. Upshoots of yucca made white splashes against the dominant green of everything. Endless rows of elm saplings along the sidewalks gave only a hint of their stature and spread in the years to come.[38]

The Rockhill Realty and Improvement Company, capitalized at $200,000, had been incorporated on January 6, 1902. Of the initial issue of two thousand shares, Nelson held all but two. His nominal partners were Gus Seested, the *Star*'s indispensable business manager, and an "editorial secretary" named Clark H. Smith.[39] Seested kept the books for his boss's expanding newspaper and real estate operations, in addition to monitoring the not inconsiderable costs of upgrading Oak Hall. (The latter was the one aspect of his financial affairs about which the publisher preferred to be kept in the dark.) Unschooled as an accountant, Seested entered figures in a fastidious hand that disguised the arcane idiosyncracies of his bookkeeping. As Nelson's business concerns proliferated, the flow of cash in and out of various accounts became almost impossible to trace, so that one can only guess how much of his wealth was generated by real estate and how much by the *Star*.

However closely intertwined Nelson's two lines of business were, there was no doubt which came first. In 1901 he sold his newly improved cattle ranch to pay down the $140,000 purchase price of the floundering *Kansas City Times*. Much as he loved playing the gentleman farmer, he coveted the *Times*'s morning Associated Press franchise even more. In explaining the decision to a colleague, he reached for an architectural metaphor: "When one of my competitors adds a new set of steps to his house I want to put on a new front porch. The *Times* is our new front porch." Several months later, when the "paper trust" abruptly raised the price of newsprint, Nelson made a snap decision to build his own mill in the East Bottoms. The experiment in self-sufficiency would last less than a decade. Faced with building a second plant in Canada to ensure a supply of wood pulp, Nelson mothballed the paper mill as impulsively as he had erected it.[40] A more conventional businessman might have hesitated to tie up capital for such a meager return, but financial considerations were beside the point. Nelson had proved that he couldn't be held hostage.

Similarly unorthodox thinking lay behind the editor's purchase, soon after the turn of the century, of two farmsteads abutting Rockhill on the south side of Brush Creek. Although he had no plans to put houses there in the immediate future, he didn't let the land sit idle. After shelling out a small fortune for one of the farms, Nelson "put a grading and quarrying crew on it for nearly five years," Pete Larson recalled. "The land had a lot of deep gulleys, but along the south side was far above grade because of cuts made for both Troost avenue and Fifty-first street. We would grade off the clay formation to the rock layer, then blast out the rock, resuming the grading when we again reached clay or shale. In this way the farm finally became an even slope, all regardless of cost."[41]

Once satisfied with the lay of the land, Nelson planted trees along Rockhill Road all the way to Fifty-second and Oak. From there his informal allée continued west for another mile or so, past J. C. Nichols's middle-class oasis to the golf links and polo fields of the Kansas City Country Club. The latter occupied the site of present-day Loose Park, on land leased from Nichols's business partner, Hugh Ward. Both Nichols and Nelson highlighted the exclusive club in their real estate ads. Eager to show that he wasn't just another fly-by-night speculator, Nichols stretched the truth and promoted Bismark Place as part of the Rockhill district.[42] The master builder and the young tyro were playing the same game.

Forty years later, Nichols recalled tantalizingly few details of his introduction to the great man. Early in his career, he wrote in an unpublished memoir,

William Rockhill Nelson, that bluff, hearty owner and editor of the *Kansas City Star,* began to take an interest in our efforts and to my great surprise sent for me. Our properties were just southwest of Oak Hall, his luxurious home, and the Rockhill area of homes he was building at that time. He was an ardent believer in better residential areas, and better planned cities. He encouraged me greatly by telling me that anything would be better than the use of the land made by the pre–Civil War owners. However, much to my dismay, we nearly lost his friendship when he learned that we had had the audacity to name our second subdivision "Rockhill Park." We had a hard time convincing him that we had not known that "Rockhill" was his middle name.[43]

For Baron Bill to summon Nichols merely to offer encouragement sounds distinctly out of character. More likely, he wanted to take a closer look at the young upstart who had brazenly invaded his territory and exploited his family name. Nichols lost no time in capitalizing on his new acquaintance. According to family legend, he decided to make amends for his faux pas by paying the Nelsons a formal social call. One Sunday, he and his wife presented themselves at Oak Hall, where the butler "graciously showed them into the foyer" and took Nichols's calling card. Minutes later, he returned to announce that Nelson wasn't receiving visitors. Acting on impulse, "young J. C. took Jessie firmly by the arm, pressed past the butler, and headed directly to Nelson's library, where he spent the next hour and a half getting properly acquainted."[44]

This calculated effrontery seems to have produced the desired effect, for Nichols continued to use the Rockhill name in a series of new subdivisions. Nelson's indignation, if such it was, soon gave way to pleasure at the young developer's flattering imitation. Perhaps, he reasoned, there was more to be gained by working with Nichols than by resisting him. After all, the twenty-seven acres on the northern boundary of the Country Club district that Nichols and his backers had recently acquired, as a hedge against industrial development in the Mill Creek valley, would serve equally well as a buffer for Nelson's residential enclave.

Nichols and Nelson embraced each other as allies, just as Kessler and Nelson had years before. It's easy to imagine the boyishly enthusiastic newspaperman and the smooth-talking developer poring over a map on Nelson's library table, excitedly laying out the city of the future. Unlike Epperson, Nichols intuitively grasped the practicality of Nelson's vision. That the future belonged to entrepreneurs like him must have been clear to the publisher, for he was an astute judge of men. Nichols represented a new breed; his character, values, and capabilities had yet to be fully tested. But he was a self-made man, a man of the soil, a dreamer. Nelson could hardly fail to see in him a reflection of the callow twenty-year-old who had served as his grandfather's apprentice developer in Indiana more than half a century earlier.

Yet for all their affinity, the two men differed profoundly in temperament and life experience. Nelson had been expelled from Notre Dame for unruliness, whereas Nichols graduated at the top of his University of Kansas class. Nelson learned everything he knew on the job, while Nichols studied real estate development at Harvard. By nature, Nelson was an absolute monarch, Nichols a chairman of the board. Both, however, understood that Kansas City's unfolding parks-and-boulevards system was a city plan in all but name. They felt secure investing south of the city limits because the 1893 plan, and its subsequent elaborations, guaranteed that others would follow. As a blueprint for development, the Park Board report had taken most of the guesswork, and much of the risk, out of the real estate game.

The name of the game was permanence. Obsessed with avoiding the boom-and-bust cycles of the past, Nelson and Nichols condemned real estate speculation as tantamount to robbery. While Nelson sought to "immutably establish" Rockhill as a "residence district of high class," Nichols advertised that anyone who bought property in his Country Club development could rest assured that it would "permanently remain Kansas City's best residential district." Both men took their cues from Meyer and Kessler's assertion that parks and boulevards would "fix for a long time to come, if not permanently, the best and most valuable residence property" in the city.[45] This was an effective sales pitch, appealing as it did to both pocketbook and posterity, and the payoff was not long in coming. Affluent families soon began emigrating from decaying older neighborhoods that had supposedly been "stabilized." As early as 1904 Nelson could boast that Southmoreland was home to Meyer, members of the Armour and Cudahy families, and a nephew of John Deere, as well as a number of big-shot lawyers and grain merchants.[46] Nichols too was building relationships that would prove crucial to his success, forging alliances with businessmen such as Frank Crowell, Herbert Hall, and Edwin Shields; Charles W. and J. Ogden Armour, scions of the Chicago meatpacking dynasty; banker and Democratic powerbroker William T. Kemper; and, not least, Tom Pendergast, heir apparent to his brother Jim's throne in the First Ward.

To say that this was not Nelson's crowd would be an understatement. In fact, some of the editor's most cordial enemies were lining up behind Nichols. But Nelson didn't judge the developer by the company he kept. A man on his way up in the world, he understood, had to take help where he found it.

Hadn't he himself once borrowed $7,500 from the same water company that the *Star* later fought tooth and nail? Hadn't he made common cause with Jim Pendergast and Hugh McGowan, whose bossism he felt obliged to condemn in print? And wasn't Kirk Armour, public face of the hated "beef trust," one of his bosom friends?

Nelson invested when and where he chose, heedless of short-term returns, secure in the knowledge that the money at risk was his own. Nichols, by contrast, was compelled to weigh every investment or expenditure—invariably involving other people's money—against its long-term profitability. That he actually owned little of the land he was developing served merely to reinforce his natural caution. "Buy low, sell high" was his cardinal rule. Nichols had no firsthand memories of the 1880s real estate bubble, but he had absorbed its lessons just the same. Nelson, in his autocratic impulsiveness, embodied the virtues and vices of an older buccaneering merchant class. Nichols represented the ascendancy of conservative, commercial values over the unbridled capitalism that had shaped Kansas City in its first half-century.

By 1907 Nichols's position was stable enough to insulate him from the financial gales that were once again buffeting the country. When Hugh Ward and he collaborated to convert part of Ward's family farm into the tony Sunset Hill subdivision, they brought Kessler in to give it the requisite touch of class. Nichols's business grew by leaps and bounds, and in 1908 he announced that he and his partners had no less than a thousand acres under development. Although a far cry from Willard Winner's holdings at the height of the boom two decades earlier, this was nearly four times as large as Nelson's Rockhill, and it put Nichols in a league of his own.

Flush with success, the developer built a commodious new house for his growing family at 48 East Fifty-second Street. Faced with limestone, it centered on a thirty-foot-long living room with oak paneling and a broad stone fireplace that wouldn't have looked out of place in Oak Hall. While not quite baronial, it was a suitably impressive residence for an ambitious twenty-eight-year-old who had just been made a director of the Commerce Trust Company, with access to an $800,000 line of credit and an office in the bank's lavishly appointed new headquarters downtown.

Nichols was clearly "the real thing," as Nelson liked to say. It was time to confer his official blessing. In a fulsome interview that ran in the *Times* in July 1909, the up-and-coming "real estate operator" was singled out for exemplifying Kansas City's can-do spirit at its best. "Where he got his insight into the development of real estate is somewhat of a mystery," the paper observed.

J. C. Nichols officiates at the dedication of a park in his Armour Hills subdivision, with the president of the home owners' association by his side. By nature, Nichols was a chairman of the board, Nelson an absolute monarch.

"Nichols says it's simply a matter of hustle and watching carefully the growth of the city. However that may be, he became a real estate operator with 1½ million dollars behind him to spend in the development of 1,000 acres of land in the same time that it would take the average man to reach the position of confidential clerk in a rental agency." Baron Bill was saluting Nichols as his peer—no mere wage earner, but an independent man of property. The editor could hardly have made it plainer that he looked upon Nichols as his designated successor at the helm of the City Beautiful brigade.

Both Nichols's Country Club and Nelson's Rockhill implicitly accepted the social hierarchy enshrined in the Park Board's 1893 plan: a Parisian-style network of "grand boulevards" lined with showy mansions, interfilled with streets and neighborhoods of more modest character. Bismark Place had conformed to the traditional rectilinear grid, with lots measuring forty to fifty feet in width. But beginning in 1907, Nichols adopted more naturalistic layouts and varying frontages capable of accommodating larger, more expensive homes. Even so, blocks and neighborhoods within individual Nichols subdivisions remained stratified both economically (as determined by minimum home-building-cost requirements) and aesthetically (as determined by architectural designs). Nichols's City Beautiful was one in which people knew their place and gravitated naturally toward their own kind and class.

Nelson's social attitudes were more complex. As a newspaperman, he decried class consciousness and special privilege without fear or favor. As a developer, he believed in preserving the time-honored social distinctions. That portion of Rockhill for which he was most directly responsible—the area south of Forty-seventh Street—clearly reflects the editor's view of a well-ordered society. There the disposition of lots was strictly class-hierarchical. Lining the main thoroughfare (and thus facing the grounds of Oak Hall) were the largest houses, reminiscent of those Nelson had constructed on DeGroff Way. They were mainly reserved for *Star* editors and executives. Behind them, on Houston Street, stood the homey bungalows of "Honeymooners' Row." The Pierce Street houses, one block farther south and the last to be built, were smaller still, though their deep backyards, extending the full width of the block, compensated for the narrowness of the lots.

Nelson's sprawling abode stood above and apart, on a broad expanse of tree-studded lawn, dwarfing the architect-designed mansions to the east and west that constituted the most exclusive section of Rockhill. As Oak Hall grew ever more solidly imposing, a close associate of the editor remarked, "people said not inappropriately that he was a feudal lord living among his tenantry."[47] Nelson resented any intrusions on his pastoral idyll and, like any feudal lord, took pains to secure the boundaries of his fiefdom. The Nichols developments afforded protection on the west and south, as did the cluster of fine homes in Hyde Park and Janssen Place to the north. In 1902 the Park Board extended Gillham Road along an old creek bed that delineated the eastern edge of Rockhill, thus creating a natural barrier between Nelson's development and the lower-middle-class district closer to Troost Avenue. Whether the park commissioners constructed the new boulevard "simply to keep the editor off their backs or to elaborate on Kessler's rather spartan initial plan is not clear," according to one student of the park system.[48] Either way, the board played into Nelson's hands.

In their campaign to bring residents of the "best class" to Kansas City, Nelson and Nichols relied on what a later, more image-conscious age would euphemistically call "public-private partnerships." Kessler, his feet firmly planted in both worlds, played a key role as the developers' accomplice and go-between. Yet Kessler's relations with Nelson had grown increasingly strained since he opened an office in St. Louis in 1903 to oversee the landscaping of the Louisiana Purchase Exposition. When Henry Schott interviewed him two years later, Kessler freely acknowledged the editor's part in instigating his work on the West Bluffs. Despite the fame and fortune that had flowed from that project, however, Kansas City had never given him the recognition he felt he deserved. Too often, writers and public officials carelessly credited Nelson—or, worse, Olmsted—as the city's master beautifier. In an effort to set the record straight, Kessler had begun claiming full credit for the parks and boulevards, asserting in a booster tract issued by the Commercial Club that he alone had "designed and supervised the improvements as they exist today."[49]

Nichols's rising fortunes gave Kessler a convenient excuse to transfer his faltering allegiance. As early as 1906 he was doing business with a number of the developer's principal backers. A year later he and Nichols began working together on plans for Sunset Hill, and possibly Rockhill Place as well. Both subdivisions would be distinguished by Kessler's trademark curvilinear streets and naturalistic landscaping. Around the same time, Nichols and Ward invited him to lay out a new south-side boulevard intended to replace the Paseo as the city's most prestigious address. Because its route lay outside the city proper, the Park Board was enjoined from funding the project itself, but the commissioners gladly accepted the new double-roadway as a gift from the Nichols Company. Subsequently, Nichols cajoled the board into extending Ward Parkway south to Gregory Boulevard and north to the new Mill Creek Parkway (also on his property), giving Country Club residents direct access to the older boulevards that led downtown.

Nelson could hardly have done better himself. How much Nichols picked up from his mentor can only be surmised, but he was clearly learning to manipulate public improvements to his own advantage. His collaboration with Kessler had entered a new and more open phase. Nichols solicited the land-

scaper's help in persuading the Park Board to connect Ward Parkway with
Mill Creek Parkway, and city workers, at Kessler's behest, were detailed to
plant trees along streets in Sunset Hill. When Meyer Boulevard was being laid
out, on the city's far south side, Kessler's staff furnished detailed specifications
for curbs, sidewalks, and streets on adjacent Nichols property. On another occasion, Nichols caught wind of plans for an east-side addition to the boulevard system and remonstrated with Kessler, arguing that Sunset Hill deserved
priority. Kessler reassured him that the project in question would have no impact on the Park Board's long-range plans for the Country Club district.[50]
However dismayed Kessler may have been by the slow deterioration of the
Paseo, his masterpiece of engineering and design, he recognized that the city's
center of gravity and wealth was shifting inexorably to the west and south.

What Nichols coyly described to Kessler as his "somewhat delicate situation with the city" made such conflicts of interest understandable, if not un-
avoidable.[51] Unlike Nelson, however, Nichols was seldom called to account
for working the system. People tended to believe the best of him and the worst
of Nelson, partly because Nichols never made enemies if he could help it,
whereas Baron Bill collected them like trophies. Nichols's Teflon image arose,
too, from his special status as a "progressive" businessman in a community that
was striving to put on a new face politically as well as physically. In the progressive utopia, cities would be run like businesses and the Chamber of Commerce would be for all intents and purposes a branch of municipal government. Besides, conflict of interest was in the eye of the beholder. For who was
to say just where the public interest left off and private interest began?

Working both jointly and severally, Nelson, Nichols, and Kessler produced
a master plan for a kind of city the world had never known before. The Country Club district, with its well-maintained roads and car-friendly shopping
centers, would become the archetypal "automobile suburb." Kessler hardly
could have foreseen the impact of the motor car when he plotted Kansas City's
original boulevards. But it's symptomatic of his genius that the 1893 Park
Board plan, formulated in the horse-and-buggy era and brought to fruition in
the automobile age, made the transition with little or no modification. The
new boulevards that Kessler and Nichols laid out in the Country Club district
tied seamlessly into the existing system. If Ward Parkway was not conceived
as a series of small linear parks, like the Paseo, it was because it was never intended for active recreation, much less civic or ceremonial functions. Rather,
it served as a neutral backdrop for a suburban life that was increasingly focused on the private sphere—on the sleek, self-contained automobiles that

whisked up-to-date Kansas Citians from door to door and the hidden back-yards that Nichols preferred to Nelson's sociable front porches.

The City Beautiful that Kessler, Meyer, and Nelson envisioned was explicitly urban in character. The 1893 report distinguished between villages, where homes, shops, and factories were jumbled together in picturesque disarray, and well-ordered cities in which residential neighborhoods were clearly defined and businesses would naturally seek out "establishments of the same character." Nichols's Country Club, contrariwise, was explicitly inspired by the villages he had visited in England in 1901. As such, it was inherently antiurban. Put another way, Nichols set out to create a kind of village within the city. While advocating comprehensive urban planning for Kansas City as a whole, he provided for the well-to-do in a separate enclave, with the Country Club Plaza as its own downtown. Ironically, after going to extraordinary lengths to link his development to the boulevards that served the old central business district, Nichols gave Country Club residents every reason to avoid going there.

Nelson and Nichols each traveled to Europe at a formative time in his life, but the lessons they absorbed there engendered antithetical attitudes toward the urban environment. Nichols caught his first glimpse of the Old World from the deck of a cattle boat, explored it on a bicycle, and slept in hostels and country inns. Nelson sailed in first-class staterooms, lived in style in the center of Paris, and toured France and Italy in plush, horse-drawn carriages. Such disparate experiences naturally induced widely differing visions of civic order. Nelson saw it as emanating from a benevolent autocrat, while Nichols returned from Europe an apostle of the middle class and the free market. Nichols considered bourgeois home owners the ultimate guarantors of civic virtue; Nelson preached home ownership for the masses, but in practice preferred to be lord of the manor.

Nichols's civic ideal found its fullest expression in the Country Club district's extensive network of home owners' associations, which sponsored such community-building activities as Christmas caroling, social clubs, and lawn contests. The associations served as Nichols's eyes and ears, helping ensure that homes and yards were well maintained and reminding residents of such neighborly courtesies as closing garage doors and reporting clogged sewers. Participation, voluntary at first, was soon made compulsory, a civic obligation that conscientious Country Clubbers took as seriously as churchgoing or Rotary work. Although these paternalistic groups had no counterparts in Rockhill, Nelson in his way was just as persnickety as Nichols. Using the newspaper as a megaphone, he was forever soapboxing about planting bulbs, keeping grass mowed, making houses cyclone-proof, providing adequate ventilation, and generally poking his nose into other people's domestic affairs.

Eventually, Nichols came to the conclusion that home owners' associations, though useful for inculcating civics lessons, had no real teeth. The City Beautiful movement, for all its high-blown rhetoric, had failed to combat urban blight, offering "merely vague hopes that tree-lined boulevards and parks would establish a neighborhood 'tone' which everyone would respect." Nichols couldn't bank on hope. It would be years before his highly leveraged developments turned a profit. Meanwhile, he had to find a way of protecting their book value, preferably increasing it. A man's home, to Nichols, was more than a castle; it was a sacred investment too valuable to entrust to "the private and selfish interest of the real estate speculator."[52] Deed restrictions, which he had begun filing on new Country Club subdivisions as early as 1907, put the force of law behind his campaign for neighborhood beautification and stability.

Nichols Company covenants covered everything from lot sizes and setbacks to house colors and architectural styles. Initially, restrictions were imposed for a fixed time period, which home owners could extend by a simple majority vote. But in 1914 Nichols pioneered the use of self-renewing restrictions that remained in force in perpetuity unless a majority of residents voted *against* them. "Our object," he explained, "was to provide proper residential environments, excluding every unwholesome and unattractive influence, then preserve those environments by proper restrictions." Nichols didn't need to specify what he meant by "unwholesome and unattractive" influences. By near-universal consent, they included both African Americans and Jews. Although Jews weren't legally barred from owning homes in Nichols developments, as late as 1917 only five Jewish families lived in the district, all as a result of resales.[53] Nor, at first, were racially restrictive covenants deemed necessary in a southern-leaning city where blacks "knew their place."

Yet the absence of black faces (except, to be sure, as laborers or domestic servants) in the manicured precincts of the Country Club and Rockhill was no accident. Roland Park, the model for Nichols's development, had been one of the earliest communities in the country to adopt racial covenants, and by 1910 Baltimore had legalized residential segregation with the enthusiastic support of Charles Grasty's *Sun*. It may have been through Grasty that Nichols struck up a friendship with Edward Bouton, the former Kansas Citian who steered Roland Park through its first few decades.[54] Following Bouton's example, Nichols explicitly excluded blacks from the Country Club district no later than 1914. That this was not merely a concession to prevailing social mores, as in the case of Jews, is suggested by the fact that Nichols continued to favor racially restrictive covenants even after the U.S. Supreme Court declared them unconstitutional in 1948.[55]

Racial segregation in the Country Club and Rockhill magnified the tendency, whether intentional or incidental, of the parks-and-boulevards system to ghettoize African Americans on the city's east side. Although Kansas City wouldn't adopt formal zoning until 1923, the plan the Park Board proposed thirty years earlier clearly implied a gradual redistribution of urban and suburban neighborhoods into residential, commercial, and industrial zones. Meyer and Kessler never used the word *race,* but racial zoning was a natural consequence of their stated intention to establish, once and for all, "the best and most valuable residence property" in the city. Troost Avenue, long a mixed area of stately homes and middle-class bungalows, would become the de facto dividing line between whites and blacks, haves and have-nots. The irreversible decline of the Paseo, now extended all the way to Swope Parkway, would leave Swope Park, the crown jewel of the city's Olmstedian "emerald necklace," increasingly cut off from the city's more affluent population.[56]

Whether the creators of the parks-and-boulevards system consciously willed this black-white split into existence is debatable. Their underlying prejudice, however, would retrospectively become clear when Delbert Haff, the former Park Board attorney turned "civic housecleaner" in the 1920s, proposed that the white establishment fund the development of a separate but notionally equal "Country Club district" for the city's African American residents. To Haff, Nelson, Nichols, and many other civic leaders, segregation of the races, like segregation of economic classes, was both a fact of life and an essential means of defusing "sectarian" conflict. The old city, with its congested mishmash of ethnic groups and industrialized squalor, was indelibly associated in their minds with social strife and boss politics. The new metropolis—the glittering City Beautiful of salubrious hills and vales, winding boulevards, and spacious, well-appointed homes—was the showplace of progressive ideas. Even Kessler admitted that, far from stemming urban sprawl, the parks-and-boulevards movement had scattered Kansas City's population over a vast area, the consequent "wide distribution of all classes" having all but eliminated the "problem of congestion."[57]

By the time he wrote those words in 1910, Kessler was firmly in the Nichols camp. Unlike Nelson, Nichols was a builder not merely of houses and cities but of "communities." Mesmerized by Daniel Burnham's 1909 city plan for Chicago, which aimed to transform the Windy City into an aristocratic, Beaux Arts–style "metropolis for businessmen," Kansas City's iconic developer was peddling a prepackaged lifestyle and a set of ethical and aesthetic

values that came with it. Like Burnham and Kessler, Nichols viewed city beautification not as a luxury or a mere badge of maturity, but as at once a moral
imperative and a hard-nosed business proposition. Kansas City's multimillion-
dollar system of parks and boulevards, Kessler boasted, had proved itself a
"paying investment in every sense of the word." The "mossbacks" and doubting Thomases had been proved wrong. "Beauty always pays in the end,"
Nichols would later observe, echoing words Burnham had uttered some three
decades before.[58]

As Nichols and Nelson constructed their interlocking versions of the City
Beautiful, the Commercial Club took to advertising the grown-up cow town
as "America's most beautiful city." A recommended itinerary for visitors with
time to kill between trains guided tourists through the Rockhill and Country
Club districts by way of landscapes beautified by parks and boulevards.[59] It
was almost exactly the same route along which Kessler had led his imaginary
visitor in his 1892 prospectus for the system. Henceforth, Rockhill and Country Club, Nelson and Nichols, would be forever linked in civic mythology and
in the highways and byways of Kessler's entropic city.

By 1910 the flurry of construction in Rockhill was abating and the first
phase of Nelson's development was all but finished. That fall, the editor acquired a son-in-law—and a new business partner. Irwin Kirkwood, a native
of Baltimore, had moved to Kansas City five years earlier to work for a prestigious real estate company. Soon afterwards he met Laura Nelson at the Missouri Hunt and Polo Club and, to her parents' chagrin, proceeded to introduce her to a "fast, horsey crowd who drank and gambled."[60] Nelson didn't
bother to hide his feeling that Kirkwood was a black sheep, and quite possibly an adventurer. But Laura, sheltered and pampered from childhood, had
inherited her father's headstrong ways, and that November she and Kirkwood
were quietly married in New York's Trinity Church.

After the newlyweds returned from their honeymoon in Paris, Nelson signaled his forgiveness—and his determination to keep Kirkwood on a short
leash—by building them a home next door to Oak Hall and either giving or
loaning his son-in-law $150,000 to set himself up in business. A year later the
two men formed the N-K Realty Company, Nelson owning 1,498 shares and
Kirkwood and the ever-faithful Pete Larson one apiece.[61] With Baron Bill
holding the purse strings, Kirkwood turned his attention to his father-in-law's
undeveloped property south of Brush Creek and east of Nichols's Country
Club. The two young realtors were a study in contrasts. Kirkwood, the scion
of an old Maryland family, came from money but had little of his own. In

Kansas City he quickly gained a reputation as a dandy and man about town. Nichols, one year Kirkwood's junior, was a thrifty, hard-working farm boy. He would be a pro at everything he turned his hand to, from real estate to politics, while Kirkwood would remain a dilettante. Nichols could fend for him-self; Kirkwood had to be cosseted. Nelson was disappointed in Laura's choice but accepted the necessity of subsidizing his son-in-law as an investment in her future.

The editor had reached a turning point. The *Star*, led by his handpicked "helpers," was going stronger than ever and many of his progressive reforms were in place. But Meyer's death in 1905 had marked the end of the coalition that had waged the great campaign for parks and boulevards. Nelson consoled himself by diverting his energies to national politics, cementing his friendships with President Theodore Roosevelt and Secretary of War William Howard Taft. In 1907 he built a big house on Boston's North Shore, ostensibly to escape from Kansas City's torrid summers, but transparently to be closer to the action. His Magnolia "cottage" was a virtual replica of the first home he had built in Rockhill, as Oak Hall's guest house, and its elaborate gardens recalled those Kessler had created on the Paseo.

Kessler, too, had been distancing himself from Kansas City. Fed up with the fickleness of the Park Board and the shenanigans of local politicians, he had pulled up stakes and moved his internationally known design firm to St. Louis. There he sulked in his tent, lobbing occasional potshots at Nelson and other ingrates he had left behind. Although he continued to serve as consultant to the Park Board, Kessler was spending as little time as possible in Kansas City. His current project, a civic center and plaza south of the new railroad terminal to be situated in the valley of O.K. Creek, had been on the planning boards for a decade and seemed unlikely to materialize anytime soon.

Meanwhile, the *Star* had moved into a new building at Eighteenth and Grand designed by the well-connected Chicago architect who had recently won the commission for the train station. Jarvis Hunt, prone to Beaux Arts pomposity, proposed an "ornate marble building with plenty of columns" for the newspaper plant. Nelson, however, envisioned something plainer and browbeat Hunt into producing a restrained essay in neo-Renaissance architecture, the sole extravagance being its intricate "tapestry" brickwork.[62] Ground for the new building was broken in November 1909 and thirteen months later it was ready for occupancy. In its utilitarian majesty, the *Star*'s contribution to the City Beautiful symbolized both the power of the press and the magnetic pull of the high-toned residential developments that were transforming the old trailhead depot of Westport beyond recognition. Nelson had turned his back

The *Star*'s plant at Eighteenth and Grand, shortly after it opened in 1911. Nelson's utilitarian offering to the City Beautiful was designed by Jarvis Hunt, architect of the new Union Station.

on the mighty river that encapsulated so much of Kansas City's colorful past. His nose, as always, was to the front. The *Star* now faced south, toward the future. Soon the rest of the city would too.

By the time the *Star*'s new presses rolled for the first time in January 1911, steam shovels and dynamite crews were swarming like ants over the future site of Union Station. Excavation had been under way since August and Hunt was growing impatient. Flamboyant and imperious, he chafed at the endless bickering over design details and budgets that had delayed construction of his masterwork. "You've got $50 million worth of parks and boulevards and $50 million worth of terminals," he fumed, inflating the figures for emphasis. "You ought to be howling." Kessler, whose plans for the station plaza had encountered similar foot dragging, reminded city officials that "there is no reason in the world why we should bear with the new depot being ugly merely because it is useful."[63] What Hunt and Kessler had in mind was a far cry from the small patch of greenery railroad executives wanted to plant in front of their terminal. The architect and engineer proposed to incorporate the station park into a civic center worthy of a worldly metropolis, a cluster of grand Beaux Arts–style buildings arrayed around a formal semicircular plaza.

The *Kansas City Journal*, echoing the sentiments of many downtown business leaders, pooh-poohed the plan as the "pet enterprise of the biggest political boss of the city." Even Baron Bill endorsed the Hunt-Kessler scheme with something less than his usual gung-ho enthusiasm, possibly sensing the mounting resistance to his benevolent rule. Another controversy flared up over a related proposal to flatten the notorious Main Street "hump" in front of the station plaza entrance and widen the roadway to boulevard dimensions. Businessmen who initially supported the road project—after all, bigger mountains had been moved to make way for downtown shops and office buildings in the not-so-distant past—balked when they learned how much it would cost. The *Post* alleged that the scheme to "shut off Main street as a business thoroughfare" and reroute traffic to Grand Avenue would enrich Nelson and his cronies, a charge not easily dismissed out of hand in light of Seested's and Kirkwood's substantial real estate interests in the vicinity of the train station.[64]

However many nests stood to be feathered by the civic center scheme, it unquestionably dovetailed with Nelson's plans in one important respect. Ever since his Parisian sabbatical in 1895–1896, the editor had been toying with the idea of affixing his name to an art museum that would put Kansas City on the cultural map. The faux masterpieces displayed in his Western Gallery of Art had never been more than a glorified teaching collection, and in any case the gallery had already outgrown its second home in the new Public Library. When a reclusive heiress named Mary Atkins bequeathed $300,000 for a municipal art museum in 1911, Nelson suddenly lost interest in reproductions and began focusing on the real thing. With the Atkins money on the table, he no longer needed to worry about a museum edifice. His legacy, instead, would be to fill it with the best art money could buy.

This noble resolve, which Nelson kept close to his vest for the time being, naturally whetted his interest in the civic center. While his own bricks-and-mortar project climbed skyward, course by course, at Eighteenth and Grand, he and Hunt spent long hours closeted together, reviewing the architect's ambitious plans for the complex of city offices and cultural buildings. This was Nelson's final answer to the merchant who, years before, had sounded the alarm about an exodus from downtown. The editor hadn't just climbed on the bandwagon; he was in the driver's seat. Confident that the city was at last growing his way, he had his own desk placed in the southeast corner of the *Star*'s newsroom, the better to watch the new train station slowly rise from the mud.

Even then, Nelson wasn't quite finished building. The would-be countryman treated himself to one last fling. In October 1912 he purchased a tract of open land near Grain Valley, a few miles east of downtown, and turned it into a model farm of the sort popular with his fellow plutocrats in the East. Near one boundary of the four-hundred-acre expanse he built a modest one-level farmhouse surrounded by a white picket fence. Cattle grazed in the surrounding pastures, waiting to be crossbred with stock imported from England, the land of Nelson's forebears. An all-weather road, built at public expense, conveyed the editor from the leafy precincts of Oak Hall to his new rural estate. Sni-a-Bar Farms eventually grew to 1,750 acres and Nelson stipulated in a codicil to his will that it be maintained as a working farm for thirty years after his death.

Cattle and culture: this, then, is what Nelson's epic crusade to make Kansas City a fit place to live came down to at last. The crusty old Hoosier had sunk his feet into the black midwestern soil, while his spirit soared aloft with the angels and saints of the Old Masters. In afterlife, the Baron of Brush Creek, his sins mostly forgotten, would himself become a patron saint of his adopted city. In his apotheosis, cow town and City Beautiful, commerce and art, would be providentially reconciled.

By the time Union Station was dedicated in October 1914, Nelson knew he didn't have long to live. That summer he had canceled a trip to Europe and vacationed in Colorado instead. Hunt's monumental civic center was a dead letter; not for another decade would the Liberty Memorial arise on the hill above the cavernous depot. The towering stone column and its "eternal" flame would remain a lonely beacon, commemorating not just the nation's war dead but the City Beautiful that might have been. In time, the art gallery and other components of the stillborn Beaux Arts ensemble would be resurrected in the Brush Creek valley, forming a suburban cultural center most conveniently accessible to Rockhill and Country Club residents. Orphaned, Union Station would remain behind as testament to the aesthetic reformers' unfulfilled dreams.

If, as Kessler asserted, the underlying goal of the parks-and-boulevards campaign had been to bind the city together both physically and socially, anybody could see that something had gone sorely amiss. By late 1914 the system as originally projected was essentially complete. Some ninety miles of roadways and two thousand acres of parks had been constructed at a cost to the citizenry of more than $14.7 million. Yet the city remained as divided as ever. Fault lines of class, race, and politics had deepened in the two decades it had taken to carry the Park Board's plan to fruition. The board itself had lost all semblance of independence and was firmly under the thumb of machine politicians. The Paseo, grandest of Kessler's grand boulevards, and the once solidly white, middle-class neighborhoods of the north and east sides were slowly mutating in ways that comfortably middle-class progressives found deeply unsettling. To many, it appeared that the road to the City Beautiful had detoured into a cul de sac.

CHAPTER 3

❖

Progressive Decade

Kansas Citians greeted the twentieth century in a manner befitting the self-styled "central city of the West." Convention Hall, a stone-and-steel phoenix risen miraculously from the ashes of its predecessor at Thirteenth and Central, was thronged with local glitterati. Under ordinary circumstances, many of them would never have been seen together under the same roof. But it was no ordinary occasion that had lured fifteen thousand people out that frosty New Year's Eve of 1900. The Century Ball was at once a coming-of-age party and the grandest orgy of self-congratulation the fifty-year-old city had ever seen.

> *"You are a Progressive. Your nose is to the front. The past doesn't interest you."*
>
> —William Rockhill Nelson to Theodore Roosevelt

A breathtaking display of ten thousand incandescent lights, surpassing even the Edisonian marvels of Electric Park, shone down on dancers gliding across the floor in historical costumes. Masses of evergreens, enough to fill fifteen railroad flatcars, swung in garlands from the soaring trusses overhead and festooned bleachers and balconies. In box 47 sat the *Star*'s owner, making one of his rare public appearances, his wife and teenage daughter by his side.[1] Many of the patrons who had bought their boxes at auction had partaken of William Rockhill Nelson's hospitality—he was known for setting an elegant table and kept one of the best wine cellars in town. To most of the revelers, however, he was just a name, hated or revered in equal measure.

In the next box sat Kirk Armour, head of the powerful meatpacking family's business concerns in Kansas City. The summer before he and Nelson had scoured the English countryside in search of breeding stock for the herds of prize-winning cattle that grazed on their farms south of the city. Armour's town house, a $125,000 château occupying a full city block in the exclusive Hyde Park neighborhood, rivaled Oak Hall in opulence. A dignified six-footer, fond of horseback riding and golf, Armour had a superb physique but a fatally weak heart. Nelson would be at his bedside when he died ten months later.

Familiar faces, old and young, friend and foe, met the editor's gaze at every turn. August Meyer, his neighbor and confederate in the parks-and-boulevards campaign, had recently sold his Argentine smelter to the Guggenheim trust, reaping a $12 million windfall.[2] Rector Cameron Mann of Grace Church, Nelson's closest friend among the clergy, would deliver the eulogy at his funeral fifteen years later. Gardiner Lathrop, the city's leading corporate attorney, had a mansion near Oak Hall and socialized regularly with the Nelsons. Former city attorney Frank Walsh, a rising star in Democratic politics, would become the editor's personal lawyer and confidant. Newspaperman Hal Gaylord would sell his debt-ridden *Kansas City Times* to Nelson within the year, cementing the *Star*'s near monopoly.

James Reed, elected mayor the previous spring over the *Star*'s fierce opposition, was dancing with his wife on the floor below. So was former Missouri governor T. T. Crittenden, a "Bourbon" Democrat whose son would be elected mayor in 1908 and unaccountably champion one of Nelson's most cherished reforms. Closer by, in box 54, sat Governor Lon V. Stephens. A month earlier the hot-headed Democratic incumbent had penned an open letter to the *Kansas City World* vilifying Nelson as a "slimy serpent" who "hangs upon the neck of Kansas City like a millstone."[3] Unperturbed, Baron Bill nodded toward banker W. T. Kemper, like Reed a fast-rising ally of "Goat" boss Jim Pendergast.

For this one evening, at least, the lions were lying down with the lambs.

That the Century Ball was taking place at all was cause for jubilation. In April the city's new Convention Hall had gone up in flames, just weeks before Democratic stalwarts were scheduled to arrive for their national convention. Nelson's friend U. S. Epperson, a wealthy packinghouse manager, had spearheaded a crash effort to rally "Kansas City spirit, Kansas City pluck and Kansas City money" in resurrecting the auditorium.[4] With crews working around the clock, the "ninety-day wonder" was ready in the nick of time to receive the out-of-town delegates and journalists.

As far as Nelson was concerned, Convention Hall's dramatic rebirth was more newsworthy by far than the lackluster presidential contest. His beloved Democratic Party was a lost cause, shanghaied by William Jennings Bryan and the prairie populists. Bryan's opponent, William McKinley, had done little to inspire confidence in his four years in office. Besides, the rock-ribbed Republican protectionist was anathema to Nelson, an ardent free-trader whose litmus test for a candidate was, and always would be, a commitment to substantive tariff reform. So dispiriting did the editor find the prospect of a rematch between McKinley and Bryan that the *Star* sat back and invoked a plague on both their houses.

When McKinley won a second term that fall, however, Nelson accepted the people's verdict with surprising equanimity. By then Baron Bill was feeling more charitable toward the chief executive. A few weeks earlier he had met Theodore Roosevelt and seen in him the salvation of the Grand Old Party.

Mark Sullivan, one of the original journalistic muckrakers, testified that "the liberal and progressive movement which arose in the Middle West" in the first decade of the twentieth century "centered largely around the *Kansas City Star* and the other forces of public opinion which took their leadership from the *Star*."[5] The progressive movement, like Nelson himself, defies tidy categorization. Each was an amalgam of disparate and often discordant impulses, simultaneously harking back to a libertarian paradise of independent small landholders and anticipating the highly urbanized, nationalistic state of the later twentieth century. Nelson had too much blue blood in his veins to place his faith unreservedly in popular democracy. At the same time, he was too much a man of the people to believe that a self-perpetuating political elite could be trusted with the delicate task of governance.

William Allen White of the *Emporia Gazette,* who came as close as anyone to being Nelson's journalistic alter ego, described his youthful self as a "jellied broth of Hamiltonian socialism and Jefferson[ian] anarchy."[6] White cut his political teeth as a conservative critic of "Sockless" Jerry Simpson and other members of the *Star*'s radical "alfalfa contingent," whom he famously debunked in his 1896 editorial "What's the Matter with Kansas?" But America's quintessential small-town editor was out of step with his fellow Kansans. Overwhelmingly agrarian and devastated by the economic turmoil of the 1890s, they turned to the radical programs of the Populist Party, the Farmers' Alliance, and the Socialist-Labor Party. The Sunflower State, home to a phenomenally successful socialist newspaper called the *Appeal to Reason,* was the epicenter of a populist earthquake that would rattle the nation to its core, while traditionally Democratic (and slaveholding) Missouri incubated reforms that would eventually be adopted nationwide under the aegis of mainstream progressives like Roosevelt and Robert La Follette.

Radical dissenters and reactionary "standpatters" maintained a crude balance of power on both sides of the state line, a situation agreeable to conservative plutocrats like Philip D. Armour. "We are all feeling better this morning," the Chicago packer wrote to his nephew, Kirk, in Kansas City after McKinley's victory in the fall of 1896. "The election has gone about as we expected, although we are a little bit disappointed over losing Nebraska. We are not much disappointed over Kansas, as we learned to know what was the matter with Kansas long ago, and I guess long-haired populism is so deeply seated there, that it will take some time to eradicate it, as it does to get some of these Southern States out of their Democratic rut. In fact," Armour added, "the only thing that can be said against your city is that it is too uncomfortably near to both Kansas and Missouri."[7]

Nelson, too, had begun to wonder what the matter was with Kansas and Missouri. For two decades he had been telling the citizenry how to clean up their acts, but no one seemed to be listening. As the 1890s drew to a close, with little to show for the *Star*'s good-government crusade, he was inclined to agree with White that the pernicious influence of money and entrenched party bosses was the root of all evil in public life. Suspicion gave way to certitude when the machine installed Reed in the mayor's office in the spring of 1900. That calamity, followed by the conflagration of Convention Hall and the uninspiring Bryan-McKinley contest, convinced the editor that the two-party system had to be torn down and rebuilt from the ground up. Nelson would do his share of the demolition and construction work. All he needed was a reform politician, preferably one of national stature, who was big and brave enough to break the mold.

Roosevelt and Nelson hit it off from the start. At the end of September 1900, the vice presidential candidate delivered a stump speech at Convention Hall, regaling a crowd of some twenty thousand for three-quarters of an hour with a rousing account of his fight, as governor of New York, to bring down the Tammany Hall "ice trust." Next day the Rough Rider paid a courtesy call on the *Star*'s publisher at Oak Hall in the company of Governor Curtis Guild of Massachusetts and Albert Beveridge, the first-term senator from Nelson's home state of Indiana. While they waited for their host, Roosevelt ran his finger along the spines on Nelson's well-stocked bookshelves, picking out the ancient Greek classics. "I always ask for them in a man's library," he explained to one of the editor's associates.[8]

Theodore Roosevelt and
William R. Nelson in an
unposed snapshot. The
Star hailed the Rough
Rider as a "fine, strong and
symmetrical American."

Formalities duly observed, the four men pulled up their chairs and got down to business. The two-party system, all agreed, was rotten through and through. But Americans were inured to it, Roosevelt contended. Besides, no man could have an effective voice in public affairs without a party organization to back him up. Nelson countered that a public-spirited newspaper could accomplish more by preserving its independence. A daily paper, he argued, "was different from an individual in two respects. It always had an audience, and it never was a candidate for office. So it could be more influential in getting done the things it approved if it stood outside of parties and helped whatever officials were trying to put into effect the policies it stood for."[9]

Although Roosevelt wasn't convinced, he was impressed by Nelson's vehemence. On board the train to Nebraska the next day, he dictated a warm note to his new friend: "How I do wish I could spend the next week in your library instead of upon this infernal campaigning trip!" The *Star* responded in kind, declaring the Republican candidate not merely "wholesome" but "abstemious," "athletic," and "robust and intense at every point." There was, the paper declared, "no better sample of a fine, strong and symmetrical American in public life to-day than Theodore Roosevelt."[10]

Roosevelt's presence on the ticket as a counterweight to the staunchly probusiness McKinley buoyed Nelson when the Republicans sailed back into office that November. Even before the election, the *Star* had forecast that Roosevelt would be his party's presidential nominee in 1904. Although the Commercial Club rolled out the red carpet for McKinley's visit in the spring of 1901, it was no secret that Kansas City was a hotbed of Roosevelt sentiment. That July, a small-time Republican operative named E. Mont Reily formed what he claimed was the nation's first "Roosevelt 1904 Club," a venture that enjoyed Nelson's tacit support. It was an auspicious start to Reily's career as a presidential prognosticator, which would culminate in his early-bird promotion of Warren Harding's candidacy in 1920.

In the event, Roosevelt's fans didn't have long to wait. On September 6, 1901, McKinley was felled by an assassin's bullet in Buffalo and died eight days later. An Italian theater musician identified as "the leader of a considerable band of Anarchists in Kansas City" was swiftly arrested in New Mexico on the strength of evidence that he had been overheard talking about a presidential assassination attempt several months earlier.[11] Although it was later established that Leon Czolgosz had acted alone, the revelation of unpatriotic tendencies in their midst troubled the town's prosperous burghers, who prided themselves on living in one of the country's most peaceable and "all-American" cities.

With unceremonious dispatch, the *Star* hailed the "caprice of fortune" that had summoned Roosevelt "to take the higher place, with nearly four years ahead of him." Nelson dashed off a telegram to the new president, pledging his paper's steadfast support.[12] All of a sudden, the future looked several shades brighter.

Roosevelt had been in office barely two weeks when a short dispatch about the kidnapping of an American missionary appeared on the *Star*'s front page. Ellen Stone was reportedly being held in "an almost inaccessible mountain defile" somewhere in western Turkey by a band of "brigands" who demanded the astronomical sum of $110,000 for her release. (Subsequent reports added, almost incidentally, that a young Bulgarian woman, several months pregnant, had been abducted at the same time.) In violating two of the nation's most sacred ideals, virginal womanhood and Christian piety, the kidnappers aroused what one diplomat called "the chivalric and outraged feeling of the American people."[13]

The "Miss Stone affair" would go down in history as America's first modern hostage crisis. To contemporaries, it marked the first full-blown international crisis of Roosevelt's fledgling presidency. The kidnappers, it transpired, were no ordinary bandits but political revolutionaries sworn to free Macedonia from Ottoman oppression. Tied to the liberation struggle against the infidel Turk, the seemingly trivial incident took on global significance. Within weeks the area around the remote Bulgarian hamlet of Samokov, where Miss Stone was stationed, was crawling with journalistic bloodhounds on the scent of a meaty story. By early October, Pulitzer's *New York World* and Hearst's *New York Journal* had agents on the scene, cash in hand, vying to secure exclusive rights to the captives' story.

Henry Haskell followed the wire reports avidly. The *Star*'s freshman editorial writer knew that region of Bulgaria intimately, having spent three years there as a schoolboy. Miss Stone, an extremely proper and rather formidable Bostonian, was a friend and colleague of his parents at the Samokov missionary station. Moreover—although this detail wasn't reported for some time—the abductors had delivered the ransom note to his older sister, Mary, under highly dramatic circumstances in the dead of night. Haskell's father had hand-carried the note to the American representative in Constantinople, and both he and his elder son, Edward, of the American mission in Salonica, would be embroiled in the protracted negotiations for the women's release.

Both the U.S. government and the American Board of Commissioners of Foreign Missions in Boston showed every indication of desiring to wash their hands of the affair. A spokesman for the evangelical body pointed out that kidnappings were an occupational hazard in the lawless Balkans. If the ransom were to be paid, he said, "missionaries would never be safe from capture." The State Department announced that although it regrettably had neither the funds nor the statutory authority to meet the brigands' demands, it would "do everything within its legal power to relieve the situation." Roosevelt was equally standoffish, advising a subordinate merely to "urge upon Congress as strongly as possible to appropriate money to repay the missionaries in the event of its proving impossible to get from the Turkish or other Government the repayment."[14] The president's gut instinct was to show the Turks and Bulgarians (it wasn't clear which government was involved) who was boss by ordering American gunboats through the Dardanelles. Fortunately, cooler heads prevailed and Roosevelt resigned himself to sullen impotence.

Frustrated by this high-level stonewalling, Miss Stone's family appealed directly to the American public and received more than sixty thousand dollars in contributions. The kidnappers, monitoring press reports of the fund-raising campaign from their mountain hideaway, lay low and took advantage of the free publicity for their cause. As the crisis dragged on through the fall and early winter, the hostages were shunted around the countryside—still, as far as could be determined, dressed only in summer clothing—ineffectually pursued by squads of Bulgarian and Turkish soldiers, sundry spies of uncertain allegiance, and a posse of increasingly distraught missionaries.

While the *Star* maintained a dignified objectivity, the *St. Louis Post-Dispatch* played the story for all it was worth, embroidering the facts as necessary when "hard" news wasn't forthcoming. As Pulitzer's editors in New York ramped up their competition with the *Journal,* a missionary official in Boston took it upon himself to grant the *World* exclusive rights to Miss Stone's story in consideration of a fifteen-hundred-dollar "donation" to the Samokov mission. Not to be outdone, the *Journal* published a lurid account of Mary Haskell's midnight face-off with the brigands' emissary, who was said to have brandished a gun and threatened to "blow her brains" out if she revealed his identity.[15]

As diplomats groped for a solution to the impasse, missionaries and correspondents circled warily around each other in a shadow-game of cat and mouse. "Our greatest terror is from the newspaper men," Edward Haskell wrote conspiratorially to a colleague. "If we can keep them off our track for a fortnight more I have strong hopes that the release will have been effected." Finally, in late January 1902, the ransom money was delivered, and three weeks later the hostages were freed, unharmed. In the end, neither Pulitzer nor Hearst won his exclusive. At the eleventh hour, Sam McClure, the muckraking magazine editor, swanned in and trumped the free-spending moguls by reaching Miss Stone first and buying her story for five thousand dollars. Back in the United States, the celebrated "Bible lady" took in thousands more for a series of lectures on the chautauqua circuit, while her former colleagues tut-tutted over her unseemly "eagerness to exploit her sufferings for commercial purposes."[16]

The Miss Stone affair had been an eye-opener for all concerned. The Protestant missionaries, popularly believed to be guileless and unworldly, had shown themselves masters of realpolitik and tough-minded negotiation. Roosevelt and his advisers had learned a sobering lesson about the limits of America's newfound power, the danger of gunboat diplomacy, and the crucial importance of good foreign intelligence. For members of the Fourth Estate, the denouement to the crisis was either a vindication or a condemnation—depending on one's point of view—of checkbook journalism and sensationalism.

For Haskell, the episode had a more personal significance. Not so long ago he had published fictional potboilers, seething with pious indignation, about the stereotypical evil Turk. The hostages' ordeal had shown that no one side in such a dispute possessed a monopoly on right or righteousness. If journalism was a secular mission, then newsmen would be well advised to emulate the religious missionaries whose insight and discretion had delivered the captives from harm. There was no substitute for balanced, objective reporting grounded in firsthand observation and a sure grasp of history. Yellow journalism didn't pay. In the final analysis, it wasn't Pulitzer's and Hearst's wads of cash but McClure's gumshoe resourcefulness that clinched the deal for Miss Stone's story.

Nelson's interest in the story, as in most news from abroad, was short-lived. Nevertheless, it was becoming clear to him that America's expanding world role in the Roosevelt era made Haskell's international perspective and expertise invaluable.

In the spring of 1902 McClure sent his managing editor, Lincoln Steffens, around the country to investigate the progress of municipal reform. "He went as far as Kansas City, Missouri," the magazine publisher recorded, "and in the office of the *Star,* a newspaper singularly well conducted by an editor and staff of unusual quality, he learned of the extraordinary work of Folk in St. Louis. He went to St. Louis and on his own initiative prepared an article on the revelations brought at the trials that Folk had carried on against grafters."[17]

Joseph W. Folk—nicknamed "Holy Joe" because of his habit of quoting scripture in the courtroom—was the dour, fire-breathing public prosecutor of St. Louis. Elected in 1900 with the support of Democratic boss Ed Butler, he subsequently turned on the machine with the stern fury of a moral crusader. By the summer of 1902, he had brought indictments against Butler and a host of other city officials and business leaders. Steffens, in collaboration with the *Post-Dispatch*'s city editor, wrote two damning exposés of the boodle and fraud that flourished in the cesspool of St. Louis politics. Other cities offered more muck for his rake and his *McClure's* articles, serialized in the *Star* and dozens of other papers, soon made Steffens a household name. Nelson's only complaint was that he failed to inscribe Kansas City in his honor role of civic corruption.

Steffens's *Shame of the Cities* transformed Folk into a national figure as well. In the 1904 gubernatorial election, Folk's clarion call for "civic righteousness" propelled him to victory over a St. Louis businessman allied with the Republican machine. As governor, Folk championed such progressive causes as honesty in government, Sunday saloon closings, police reform, and antitrust legislation. Reelected two years later, he burnished his credentials by securing passage of a raft of measures dear to reformers' hearts. But Folk's sparkling political career fizzled out after he left the governor's mansion in 1908 to run unsuccessfully for the U.S. Senate. The state party organization turned its back on him and even four years later President Wilson considered him too radical for a cabinet appointment. A political pariah, Folk moved to Washington as chief counsel of the Interstate Commerce Commission and wound up back in private law practice, sharing an office with another veteran of Missouri's progressive crusades, Francis Patrick Walsh.

A big, athletic, wavy-haired Irishman, Frank Walsh exuded boyish vitality coupled with the warmth and charisma that Folk so conspicuously lacked. Nelson adored him like a wayward son, much as the editor's own father had treated him, and accorded the lawyer the same uncritical acceptance the *Star* extended to Roosevelt. In old age the editor told a mutual acquaintance that he had known Walsh "intimately since his boyhood," but this can't be right, as Walsh didn't move to Kansas City until he was in his early twenties.[18] Still, the affectionate reference points up the special quality of the two men's friendship, reaching as it did across a treacherous political divide, Walsh's unsavory ties to Democratic bosses and railroad lobbyists, and Nelson's ill-concealed contempt for the legal profession.

It was Walsh's activist conception of the law, his impatience with hairsplitting and temporizing, that endeared him most to Baron Bill. "If you want the city to undertake something that isn't exactly contemplated by the charter and the constitution and such foolishness, most lawyers spend all their time telling you how it can't possibly be done," the editor remarked. "Frank always says, 'All right, I believe we can find a way to do that.'" Walsh once demonstrated his resourcefulness in a colorful libel trial involving the city's Pendergast-controlled police department. When an informer whose testimony was crucial to the *Star's* defense vanished under highly suspicious circumstances, Walsh tracked him down in Dallas and took his deposition. But the possibility that the stool pigeon might sing a different tune on the witness stand called for extra precautions. Walsh promptly arranged for him to be spirited away to South America, whereupon the prosecution rested its case.[19]

Always happy to deploy his oratory in the service of underdogs and progressive causes, Walsh rose to prominence as an ambitious trial lawyer, a brilliant assistant city counselor, and a peerless practitioner of Democratic politics. But conventional success left him unfulfilled and in 1900 Walsh renounced his lucrative corporate work to become, in his words, "a free lance in the legal profession." As a self-styled people's attorney, he would spend the rest of his life defending socialists, anarchists, syndicalists, and outcasts of every description. One of his early clients was Jesse James, Jr., whose acquittal on charges of train robbery Walsh won by tugging shamelessly on the jurors' heartstrings, thereby scoring his first victory against then city prosecutor James Reed. Over the years, he and the "Stormy Petrel" would square off in the courtroom on many memorable occasions. Walsh's career as Reed's chief antagonist—he liked to tell friends that Reed put his eight children through college—secured his niche in the *Star*'s pantheon and encouraged Nelson to overlook his dalliance with the hated Democratic boss Joe Shannon.

Like Nelson, Walsh sported a deep-seated streak of political nonconformity. Despite his affiliation with Shannon's "Rabbit" faction, he maintained cordial relations with the Pendergast "Goats." At the Democratic state convention in July 1902, he issued a personal declaration of independence by ramming through a platform plank denouncing corporate contributions to party campaign funds. Overnight, Walsh became a force to be reckoned with in national Democratic circles and, somewhat incongruously, the darling of the reformers clustered at the feet of Nelson and Folk.

As Walsh saw it, Roosevelt's 1904 presidential campaign, generously funded by Armours, Morgans, and other "malefactors of great wealth," conclusively demonstrated the corrosive influence of money in politics. Nelson, however, was in one of his euphoric moods and positive that the country was at last in good hands. The *Star* pulled out all the stops, proclaiming that Roosevelt had "shown a knowledge of Western conditions and a sympathy with Western ideas unequaled by any president since Lincoln." That fall, Roosevelt carried the state by a slim majority, outdrawing the undistinguished Democratic nominee, Judge Alton B. Parker, by 321,449 to 296,312. Not since Reconstruction had Missourians voted Republican in a presidential contest. In a famous cartoon for the *Chicago Tribune,* John McCutcheon personified the Show Me State as a "mysterious stranger," attired in the fancy black dress of a southern grandee, forsaking the "solid South" and taking his place in a long column of Republican states.[20]

For Kansas City's machine Democrats, 1904 was a year of unmitigated disaster. The rising tide of reform threatened to undermine the very foundation of politics as they knew it. Republican Jay Neff had walked off with the prize in the spring mayoral contest and virtually every Democrat had been swept out of office. Even Jim Pendergast's kid brother, Tom, had been denied a second term as county marshal. Having fought each other to a draw in the donnybrooks of the 1890s, Pendergast and Shannon had recently agreed to a "fifty-fifty compromise" on party patronage; now there would be less of it than ever to pass around. Shannon accepted his party's ignominious defeat philosophically. "I did not find a Republican who was for Parker," he told a *Star* reporter after the fall election, "but I found many Democrats who were for Roosevelt. Inquiry usually developed the fact that they were people who are satisfied with present conditions. They were small merchants who had made some money in the last two or three years, or workingmen who have been busy, most of the time."[21]

To Nelson's delight, mugwumpery enjoyed bipartisan appeal. Herbert Hadley, the state's new Republican attorney general, showed every sign of being as intrepidly progressive as Folk. A background in corporate law had instilled in him a healthy skepticism about big business, and within weeks of taking office he instituted antitrust proceedings against Standard Oil, charging that the mammoth combine had illegally monopolized the Missouri market by secretly gaining control of two nominal competitors. In a bravura display of "militant progressivism," Hadley marched into Washington and New York to beard the corporate lions in their dens. Under threat of subpoena, John D. Rockefeller, Sr. ducked for cover and remained in hiding for weeks. The *Star,* condemning Standard Oil's "schemes of predatory aggrandizement," pressed Hadley to "go after him and keep at it."[22] When Rockefeller finally surfaced and haughtily consented to be interviewed at home, the attorney general retorted that he already had all the evidence he needed, but if and when he should require the oilman's testimony, he would set his own terms.

The national press depicted the epicene, Roman-nosed Hadley as a plucky David battling the corporate Goliath. The truth was somewhat less romantic. Hadley was no crusading trustbuster in the Roosevelt mold but a cautiously progressive Republican possessed of a brilliant legal mind and a well-developed sense of fair play. It was his carefully crafted legal argument, rather than his bird-dog tenacity, that laid the groundwork for the federal government's successful breakup of Standard Oil's monopoly in 1911. Missouri voters found Hadley's legal activism more to their liking than Folk's moralistic crusading and elected him governor in 1908 by the largest majority in the state's history. Although neither Folk nor Hadley made much headway against bossism in Kansas City and St. Louis, they brought the issue of municipal cor-

Henry J. Haskell, the *Star*'s city editor, interviews reformist Mayor Henry Beardsley in 1906. "A big city can stand only a limited amount of that kind of reform in one dose," quipped Democratic boss Joe Shannon.

ruption to the fore and helped make Missouri a showplace of progressive legislation, from government regulation of business and municipal ownership of utilities to penal reform and child welfare.

In Kansas City, Mayor Neff and his successor, Henry Beardsley, made efficiency the keynote of their moderately progressive Republican administrations. A new city charter, tepidly supported by the *Star* but enthusiastically approved by voters in 1908, streamlined city government and made it marginally more responsive to the citizenry. But a backlash was already developing. When Beardsley was ousted that spring by Democrat T. T. Crittenden, Jr., Shannon was ready as always with a pithy analysis. "The so-called liberal element saw in Beardsley the representation of reform ideas," he advised the *Star*, "and a big city can stand only a limited amount of that kind of reform in one dose. The Democrats made an aggressive campaign while the Republican campaign was generally of the genteel order." It was a mistake that Nelson wouldn't make again. "I've tried to be gentle and diplomatic," the editor reflected, "but I've never done well in my stocking feet."[23]

Nelson was pushing seventy and his patience with the fits-and-starts pace of progressive reform was wearing thin. Nudged by Walsh, he had begun moving to the left on social issues and even allowed his writers to comment favorably on Russia's October Revolution in 1905. "The injustices and evils that modern industrial development have brought upon the United States are not to be compared with those existing in Russia. The American people are enlightened and are schooled in self-government. They have a long history of dearly-won freedom. Their grand dukes of business are not half so strongly intrenched as the members of the Russian royal family. In view of recent events in Russia, who can doubt that when the American people become aroused they will right existing wrongs as thoroughly and as speedily as the Russians have abolished their political evils?"

This thinly veiled call for a workers' insurrection was one of many excerpts from the *Star* reprinted approvingly in the *Appeal to Reason,* the unofficial house organ of the socialist movement.[24] Its founder, J. A. Wayland, had met the radical labor organizer Mother Jones in Kansas City and, with her assistance, launched the paper out of a small downtown office in 1895. Two years later, Wayland moved the *Appeal* to the rural county seat of Girard, in southeastern Kansas, and applied himself to replicating the circulation-building techniques that Nelson and Pulitzer had used with such success. By the turn of the century, the socialist weekly had a hundred thousand subscribers scattered around the country, a figure that would rise to nearly half a million by 1910—more than three times the circulation of the daily *Star.*

Nelson's opinion of the radical gadfly in his journalistic backyard is unrecorded and there is no evidence that he and Wayland ever met. But in its formative years the *Appeal* welcomed the *Star* as a fellow traveler on the path to socialist enlightenment. Fred Warren, who signed on as Wayland's managing editor in 1904, imbued the *Appeal* with an aggressive, muckraking spirit that made the mainstream press sit up and listen. In the wake of Charles Edward Russell's exposé of the "beef trust," he invited a little-known fiction writer named Upton Sinclair to investigate sanitation and working conditions in the big meatpacking plants. Hoping to dramatize the issue for the masses, Warren sent Sinclair to Chicago late that fall with instructions to write an "Uncle Tom's Cabin of the wage slaves."[25] Sinclair rose to the challenge and the first installment of *The Jungle* ran in the *Appeal* on February 25, 1905.

The timing of Sinclair's literary bombshell was perfect. Just four days earlier, the federal Justice Department had launched a full-scale investigation of the meatpacking industry's alleged violations of the Sherman Antitrust Act. Subpoenas had been served on 185 witnesses in Kansas City and elsewhere. The *Star* accused J. Ogden Armour and his fellow beef trusters of abusing their power "in oppressing the people, in killing competition, in ruining men of smaller capital." Criminal charges should be lodged against industry executives, the paper argued, because "the trusts will never respect the laws designed to regulate them until representatives of the trusts are put in prison for violating these laws."[26] As Sinclair raced to finish his manuscript by September, government lawyers gathered a mass of incriminating testimony and evidence against the packers. On December 15 a federal grand jury in Kansas City indicted employees of four major packing houses, including Armour, for accepting illegal rebates from the railroads.

Roosevelt was in a ticklish position. Meatpackers had been major contributors to his 1904 presidential campaign. Furthermore, he detested Sinclair's radical politics and resented being backed into a corner by Warren's *Appeal*, which he denounced as a "vituperative organ of pornography, anarchy and bloodshed."[27] Not until *The Jungle* appeared in book form, early in 1906, and became an overnight bestseller did he reluctantly order a wider-ranging inquiry. Even then he sat on the official report until Sinclair forced his hand by revealing its conclusions in the *New York Times*. In the wake of a second and equally damning probe, Congress passed the landmark Meat Inspection Act and the Pure Food and Drug Act, for both of which Roosevelt shamelessly claimed credit.

Nelson, too, was capable of turning a blind eye to monopolistic practices when personal friendship was involved. One beneficiary of his indulgence was August Meyer, the multimillionaire president of Consolidated Kansas City Smelting and Refining, who died two weeks before the Kansas City grand jury returned the indictments against the packers. In a letter written a decade earlier to Charles Francis Adams, a Boston financier with extensive interests in Kansas City, Meyer suggested it might be wise for his company "to combine with other works, and, by eliminating competition, to bring about better margins"—a policy that, if implemented, clearly would have violated the Sherman Act's injunction against restraint of trade. When Meyer sold the smelter in 1899 and became a director of the powerful Guggenheim trust, which controlled 80 percent of U.S. lead production, the *Star* took the opportunity to praise him for having, in effect, fattened the calf for slaughter.[28]

On the other hand, Nelson's soft spot for the senior Armours did little to slake his fury against the Metropolitan Street Railway Company (on whose board they served) and other "franchise grabbers." The *Star*'s decades-long campaign to eradicate the "streetcar influence" in city affairs came to a head in 1909, when the Met demanded long-term franchise concessions. The ensuing fracas turned personal relations topsy-turvy. Fred Bonfils and Harry Tammen, the "Katzenjammer Kids" of yellow journalism, purchased the *Kansas City Post* that fall in silent partnership with J. Ogden Armour, transformed it into a mirror image of their profitably scandalous *Denver Post,* and joined battle with Baron Bill on the Met's behalf. Meanwhile, Walsh—who was close to Tammen and Bonfils and had formerly been the Met's attorney—sided with the *Star* against the company. Met president Bernard Corrigan charged that Nelson and his "hired stump speaker" had "tried in every conceivable way to incite the employees of the Metropolitan to organize a strike."[29] Opponents countered that workers at the Armour packing plant had been strong-armed into supporting the franchise. The *Star* and its allies eventually won that battle, but the "traction trust" survived to fight—and ultimately prevail—another day.

Closer to home was the sensitive issue of monopoly in the newspaper industry itself. As Hearst, Scripps, Munsey, and other press lords expanded their empires, the *Star* raised the alarm about creeping concentration of ownership. At the same time Nelson, as a director of the powerful Associated Press, was lending his name to an organization that effectively made each of its member papers "a monopolist of the world's news in its immediate locality." Nelson had fought hard to grab the morning and afternoon Associated Press franchises in Kansas City, and both he and his successors used their influence on the board to deny the wire agency's service to competing newspapers and buttress the *Star*'s dominant position. To a fellow publisher who observed that he had created a pretty tight monopoly in Kansas City, Nelson replied disarmingly, "The only monopoly I recognize as legitimate is the monopoly of excellence. As long as we give people more for their money than they can buy anywhere else on earth, why shouldn't they take the *Star*?"[30]

Why indeed? The question became almost academic after the *Star* gobbled up the *Kansas City Times* in 1901 and instituted a round-the-clock news cycle. Since then, Nelson and his hard-driving business manager, Gus Seested, had felt justified in charging premium "combination" rates that effectively compelled advertisers to purchase space in both the morning and afternoon papers. Those who protested or advertised in other newspapers were penalized by losing their position or being banished from the *Star* altogether. This bald-faced infraction of the spirit of the Sherman Act showed how far Baron Bill was willing to go to crush his competitors. Decades after his death, when the *Star* became a textbook case of newspaper monopoly, federal antitrust investigators would trace the illegal practices back to the old trustbuster's doorstep.

Nelson's attitude toward the trusts was complicated, contingent, and often convoluted. For all their bellicose rhetoric, neither he nor Roosevelt was implacably hostile to big business. They simply insisted that it play by the rules on a reasonably level field. Both men were often forced, by temperament or circumstance, to improvise their morality. At once admiring and wary of what he called Roosevelt's "lawless mind," the editor refused to be shackled by legalistic constraints or the puny bonds of consistency.[31] Nelson embraced men like Sinclair and Steffens, whom Roosevelt considered pests. The socialist bugbear held no terror for him; it was not the radicals but the reactionaries who posed the greater threat to the progressive revolution.

Despite Roosevelt's lack of discernible progress in the all-important matter of reducing trade barriers, Nelson continued to regard him as fundamentally progressive. The president's public disavowal of third-term aspirations in 1904 struck the editor as "unnecessary and ill advised," but he considered Roosevelt bound to honor his pledge.[32] As the lame duck encountered mounting resistance from Republican standpatters in his second term, Nelson grew increasingly anxious to settle the question of a suitable successor. Several administration stalwarts were presumed to be in the running, including Secretary of State Elihu Root, Treasury Secretary George Cortelyou, and—Nelson's odds-on favorite—Secretary of War William Howard Taft. Roosevelt's reluctance to bestow his support on one man or another puzzled Nelson even more than his unaccountable lack of enthusiasm for lower tariffs.

Tension between the friends boiled over in the late summer of 1906. Nelson, who had gone to Carlsbad, Germany, in search of a "cure" for his bulging waistline, received word that Roosevelt was placating the protectionists. With heavy heart, he cabled his editors in Kansas City to hold the equivocating president's feet to the fire. At the same time, he sent Roosevelt an unambiguous warning. "With some concessions on the tariff question I believe that in 1908 Taft can beat Bryan, but [I] am not nearly so sure of that as I am that neither he nor any other republican candidate on a stand pat platform can carry a sufficient number of electors in the states west of the Allegheny mountains to make a decent sized picnic party." When Roosevelt indignantly insisted that he had been misquoted, Nelson continued to berate him for undermining Taft's cautiously progressive position on tariff reform. "What I now fear most is that the situation will give such confidence to the radicals in the republican party that Taft will not be acceptable and his nomination turned down. So then, is no one in sight but Taft or Root, excepting always yourself, who would be acceptable to me and hundreds of thousands of others?"[33]

In fact, Nelson had already made up his mind that Taft was the best man to run against perennial Democratic candidate William Jennings Bryan in 1908. The amiable, absentminded secretary was almost as popular with the Washington press corps as his gregarious chief. Built like a large furry animal (he reminded William Allen White of a "great New Foundland dog"), Taft had ingratiated himself with the three-hundred-pound publisher by the apparently innocent device of sharing his dietary regime. In June 1906 Nelson gently prodded the Ohioan to run for president, joking that "while it is ordinarily accepted that the race is to the lean man"—an allusion to Root, perhaps—"this time I think it is necessary to enter a portly gentleman."[34]

By the following summer, Roosevelt was ready to come down off the fence. Or so he assured the Star's Washington correspondent, Richard Lindsay. "Why, Dick," he exclaimed, "I would walk on my hands from here to the capitol to nominate Taft!" At more or less the same time, Roosevelt told his private secretary that Root was his man. According to William Loeb, it was only after Root declined to run that the president gave the nod to Taft.[35] Though heartened by Roosevelt's apparent conversion, Nelson sensed he was having second thoughts about his election-night promise not to run in 1908. The editor was disturbed by a report that Republican delegates from southern states were being pledged to Roosevelt, on the tacit understanding that they would be released to Taft at the convention. This bit of chicanery was attributed to Frank Hitchcock, one of Roosevelt's key political advisers.

Outraged, Nelson stormed into Washington in early December to have it out with the president. According to Roosevelt's aide Archie Butt, the two short-fused dynamos "nearly came to blows" in the executive office. Pounding his fist on the table ("a normal procedure under the circumstances," Haskell dryly observed), Baron Bill insisted that if Roosevelt "did not reiterate his position as to a third term he would be credited with hypocrisy, if not downright duplicity." In that case, Nelson intimated, he might be compelled to throw his considerable avoirdupois behind a Democratic candidate. "Here, how about this? You said you did not intend to run again and we all know you meant it. Hence we are all out working for Taft. Now comes this talk again. Settle it once and for all. Hurry now! Don't let any grass grow under your feet!"[36]

Roosevelt, unused to being read the riot act and reportedly "furious" with Nelson for doubting his word, grudgingly issued a terse statement to the Associated Press reiterating his 1904 pledge. No one was more relieved by the president's "second renunciation" than his unprepossessing secretary of war. Writing on Christmas Day, Taft thanked Nelson for his "most efficient aid at a time when aid was most necessary." His altercation with Roosevelt had "cleared the political atmosphere somewhat" and allowed Taft's "smothered boom to rise again to respectable proportions."[37] Such abject gratitude might have seemed disingenuous in another man, but Taft's modesty was transparently sincere. Sedentary and nonconfrontational by nature, and having no burning desire to be the nation's commander in chief, he inevitably suffered by comparison with the ambitious, dynamic Roosevelt. Deep down, Taft coveted only one office—that of chief justice of the U.S. Supreme Court.

Nevertheless, Taft had let himself be convinced that he was Roosevelt's rightful heir. By the time Republican delegates and newsmen descended on Chicago in mid-June, his nomination was a foregone conclusion and speculation shifted to his choice of running mate. Nelson and others backed Governor A. B. Cummins of Iowa, a favorite among western progressives, while the eastern wing of the party rallied behind James Sherman of New York, a conservative nonentity known for his "sunny" disposition. Caught in a no-win situation, Taft took political cover and refrained from expressing a preference, but Nelson continued to press his case. Cummins's nomination, he wrote to the secretary, "would give the greatest sort of encouragement to your friends in the West" by showing "that the party is absolutely on the dead level on the tariff and other progressive planks. What is wanted is a running mate to help lick Bryan, not one to please Reactionaries."[38] Taft, however, was less concerned with pleasing his friends in the West than with currying favor among eastern Republicans, and quietly acquiesced when the delegates awarded second place on the ticket to Sherman.

Lindsay looked on the bright side, pointing out "that if the other fellows had got the president and the platform and we had got only the vice president we would have thought we hadn't got a thing." But his employer was in no mood for consolation. The day before the crucial vice presidential vote, Nelson had buttonholed Charles P. Taft in the lobby of Chicago's Annex Hotel and demanded that he help block Sherman's nomination. According to press reports, the editor harangued the secretary's half-brother "in a tone loud enough for a hundred to hear" and threatened to bolt if the New Yorker was nominated. Nelson later blamed a certain "professional Republican politician" for eavesdropping and jumping to the wrong conclusion. But the fact that he waited a full month to refute the reports suggests he was secretly pleased to have put the wind up Taft.[39]

By midsummer Nelson saw all too plainly that his "new hero" had feet of

William Howard Taft tees off at Hot Springs, Virginia, in 1908. When newsmen pressed him to campaign more vigorously, Taft "only laughed, and went on playing golf."

clay. Yet both men were determined to make the best of a bad situation. As the campaign shifted into high gear, the *Star*'s endorsements grew less fulsome, stressing Taft's steadiness and dependability instead of his dubious Rooseveltian virtues. In private, Nelson continued to press him to "emphasize tariff revision about to the limit that you feel the party will stand." If the secretary felt unable to say what his western friends wanted to hear, the editor hinted broadly, he had better say nothing at all. It was "much more important" that Taft "rest and play golf and ride horseback and that sort of thing from now till November" than it was to "make speeches."[40] Taft was only too glad to take Nelson's advice and spent most of the summer golfing with political cronies in Hot Springs, Virginia.

Lindsay, no duffer on the links himself, often joined Taft's foursomes in the line of duty. But as the summer wore on, he and O. K. Davis of the *New York Times* became increasingly alarmed by the candidate's complacency. When the newsmen urged him to formulate "a definite line of action" for the campaign, Taft "only laughed, and went on playing golf." Roosevelt, meanwhile, was acting more forcefully presidential than ever, lobbying over the heads of an increasingly ornery Congress for judicial reform and other measures. But he knew his time was up. Ray Stannard Baker of the *American Magazine* found him resigned, almost rueful early that fall. To Baker's suggestion that the people might still be clamoring for him in 1912, the president replied with arresting candor: "Revolutions don't go backwards. New issues are coming up. I see them. People are going to discuss economic questions more and more: the tariff, currency, banks. They are hard questions, and I am not deeply interested in them; my problems are moral problems, and my teaching has been plain morality."[41]

It had slowly dawned on Nelson that Taft was no more committed to meaningful tariff reform than Roosevelt. Indeed, in his acceptance speech he had gone out of his way to reject the Democratic doctrine of tariff "for revenue only"—a policy the *Star* had consistently supported for years—in favor of traditional Republican protectionism. This was a bitter pill for Nelson to swallow and he gamely tried to convince himself that Taft's real policies could be read between the lines. "You can't condense the 'keynote' of the campaign into a thousand words even if Moses did reduce the account of the creation to six hundred," he jested. It was natural for Taft to emphasize "views with which the East is most in sympathy—for the East is going to elect you. But it would delight us of the West if our convictions—and prejudices—should be treated with as much consideration as possible."[42]

When this approach showed no signs of bucking up Taft's sagging progressivism, Nelson changed tack and appealed to his political instincts.

> The truth is, you don't need to worry about the conservatives. They must support you whatever happens. Where have they got to go? They can't possibly turn to Bryan and his quack remedies, including free silver. They can't even be indifferent. Too much is at stake in a business way. You are their only salvation. I am firmly convinced that the thing to do— the only safe and prudent thing to do—is to force the fighting on as radical lines as you can stand for. There is no need to emphasize your conservatism. That you are sane and fair is everywhere taken for granted. But

it will help a lot to keep aggressively to the front the progressive things you stand for. Of course that is what the West is looking for. But I believe it is what is needed in the East as well.[43]

Taft's mixed message somehow got through to the voters and he trounced Bryan in November by a two-to-one electoral margin. Nelson was under no illusion that it represented a victory for progressivism, but he took heart from the election of solidly progressive Republicans to the governorships of Missouri and Kansas at the same time the Sunflower State sent his friends Joseph Bristow to the U.S. Senate and Victor Murdock to the House of Representatives in Topeka.

Fatigued by his unaccustomed exertions, Taft looked forward to returning to Hot Springs with his pal Lindsay. "Can't you send that bald-headed rooster on here to do strictly newspaper work?" he wired Nelson after the election. The editor obligingly instructed his correspondent to report for duty with his golf sticks. But a few days later an old kidney ailment flared up and Lindsay returned to Washington, gravely ill. The president-elect was coming off the green when an aide handed him a telegram from Nelson. The forty-three-year-old Lindsay had died on November 30. "Oh, no, no. It can't be," Taft groaned, visibly distraught. "Why, only last Thursday I saw him in his room here at the hotel. Poor old Dick."[44]

At a critical juncture, Nelson had lost the man who had been his eyes and ears in Washington for half a dozen years. Few in the capital press corps could match Lindsay's contacts, sources, and political instincts. Nelson could hardly hope to find an equally experienced and well-connected political reporter to replace him. But he could appoint a correspondent who understood the issues that mattered to the *Star* and its readers, and whose personal loyalty to the proprietor was beyond question. Looking around the newsroom, he found his man in the *Star*'s erudite, soft-spoken city editor.

Henry Haskell's stock had been rising ever since he first caught the publisher's eye nearly a decade earlier. Although Nelson liked to say that the reporter was the "big toad" in the journalistic "puddle," he respected editorial writers who knew better than to indulge in "literary essays" and selected them with care. Haskell's promotion to the editorial page at the tender age of twenty-six was a sign that Nelson was looking to the future. As the United States began to flex its muscles beyond its shores, it was useful to have an editorial writer who could comment authoritatively on the Boxer Rebellion in China,

guide the average reader through the thickets of world trade and economic issues, and provide historical perspective on international incidents like the kidnapping of Ellen Stone.

Promoted to city editor in 1905, Haskell was a far cry from the popular image of the crusty newsroom dictator. Courteous and unflappable, he left any
chewing out that needed doing to his assistant, Charles Dillon, whose sharp
"Irish tongue" stung cub reporters and veterans alike. More schoolmaster than
drill sergeant, Haskell treated even the most routine assignment as a lesson in
journalistic decorum and precise literary usage. No one better exemplified
Nelson's dictum that a *Star* man should be a gentleman first and foremost.
Haskell was a scholar too, contributing thoughtful essays on such topics as the
problem of evil and the economic interpretation of history to the *Outlook* and
the *Independent,* high-toned magazines with close ties to his parents' Protestant missionary movement.

Haskell's salary as city editor—sixty dollars a month, twice as much as he
had drawn as an editorial writer—made him a privileged member of the
Fourth Estate. Slipping effortlessly into his managerial role, he moved with
his wife and their three-year-old son into one of the first Nelson-built houses
in Rockhill. As a charter member of the prestigious Knife and Fork Club, he
rubbed shoulders with the city's business and professional elite and met many
of the public figures with whom he would later come into contact in Washington. He didn't hope to fill Lindsay's shoes as a presidential confidant, nor
was it expected of him. Nelson wanted a first-class newsman to represent the
Star in the nation's capital, to be sure, but above all he wanted a man who
would be a friend to his friends, a diplomat who never strayed beyond the letter of his instructions, and a servant who knew his master's mind inside out.

In 1908 Haskell had spent the first of several summers with Nelson at the
editor's seaside "cottage" near Gloucester, Massachusetts. In their leisurely
conversations about life, journalism, and politics, interspersed with excursions
around New England, Haskell got his first taste of the high life and the heady
power associated with it. Exhibiting the proper mixture of deference and independence of judgment, he soon made himself as indispensable to Nelson in
Washington as Lindsay had been. Bristow, one of the freshman "insurgents"
of the congressional class of 1909, praised him to the editor as "honest and intelligent and sincere in his efforts to help" the progressive cause. To one of
Nelson's familiars, the Kansas senator described Haskell as "one of the finest
young fellows I have ever met. He is so conscientious and upright that I have
become very much attached to him. He is more lenient in his judgment of the
President than I am, and has more hope for the future."[45]

Haskell had good reason to be hopeful. He knew, as only a handful of others on the paper did, that Nelson had recently written a new will. Under its terms, the *Star* on his death would come under the control of a group of employee trustees. Haskell was being groomed to take his place in the tight little directorate that would ensure the paper remained true to its founder's vision. Unlike Pulitzer, Nelson had no sons to carry on his life's work. In any case, flesh and blood meant less to him than principles, steadiness, and dependability. "I would rather have a less brilliant man, if I am surer of his loyalty," he said.[46] Beguiled as he was by flamboyant personalities like Lindsay and White, it was—for the moment, at least—in less scintillating men like Haskell, Gus Seested, and Ralph Stout that he placed his trust.

At this particular juncture, local politics was of more immediate concern to Nelson than Washington affairs. Henry Beardsley's defeat in the spring 1908 mayoral election presaged a return of the spoilsmen to City Hall. Democratic candidate T. T. Crittenden, Jr. portrayed the reform-minded Republican as Nelson's puppet, pledging that "when I am mayor the business of the city will be done in the city hall and not in the *Star* office." So confident had the *Star* been of Beardsley's reelection that no one thought to prepare a sketch of his victorious opponent for the next day's paper.[47] Once in office, however, Crittenden confounded his critics by assisting at the birth of Kansas City's signature contribution to the progressive movement.

The Board of Public Welfare, the first municipally funded welfare agency in the country, was the mongrel brainchild of a German businessman, a Russian social worker, and an Irish lawyer. William Volker, millionaire philanthropist and purveyor of home furnishings, was modest, retiring, devoutly Protestant, and conservatively libertarian in politics. Jacob Billikopf, liberal, Jewish, apolitical, was bright, ambitious, and intent on raising the standards of his profession. Frank Walsh, street-smart and gregarious, paraded his radicalism and Catholicism and relished the rough-and-tumble of Democratic politics. This interdenominational trio liked to call each other "coreligionists," the religion they shared being, of course, progressivism.

When Billikopf arrived in January 1907, Kansas City was poised on the cusp between complacency and reform. As superintendent of the United Jewish Charities, he worked in the small community of eastern European Jews concentrated on the increasingly impoverished east side. This immigrant population was part of a larger community of need—white and black, native-born and "hyphenated" American—that the fast-growing city had swept aside. Social activists like Walsh, progressive businessmen like Volker and Alfred Ben-

jamin, and liberal religious leaders like Charles Ferguson of All Souls Unitarian Church embraced the energetic young social worker. Billikopf soon struck
up a friendship with Haskell, who had taken spiritual refuge in Ferguson's
church, and for the next decade would call the newspaperman's home his own.
Through Haskell, he gained access both to gentile society and to the *Star*.

Progressivism Kansas City style had recently been discovered by the national press. That fall, Walsh and Ferguson met in New York with the famed
muckraker Ida Tarbell and her boss, Ray Stannard Baker. Tarbell, the clergyman excitedly reported, was impressed by "Kansas City's vigorous progress
along both commercial and intellectual lines" and proposed to write about it
in the *American Magazine* as part of a series of articles on the "creative and
constructive forces" at work in various American cities. Meanwhile, a home-
grown publicity machine run by the Commercial Club's dapper, droopy-eyed
secretary, E. M. Clendening, advertised that Kansas Citians prided themselves
on making "liberal provision for the unfortunate," a euphemism for the unco-
ordinated patchwork of some three dozen private charitable and religious
groups that attended to the needs of disadvantaged citizens.[48]

Such puffery counted for little in the festering slums of the Bowery and the
gritty mill towns of the Blue River valley, which had been hard hit by the lingering effects of the 1907 "Roosevelt depression." When Mayor Crittenden
appointed a committee to investigate unemployment relief, Volker and his fellow commissioners recommended that the city create an independent, nonpartisan welfare board with broad powers to undertake "aggressive, systematic preventive work."[49] In April 1910 an ordinance was passed by the City
Council with the support of Crittenden. Under Volker's low-key leadership,
the new agency combined a traditional emphasis on self-help with a forward-
looking commitment to activist government. Aiming to wean its clients off
public assistance as quickly, efficiently, and inexpensively as possible, the welfare board provided a minimum of direct financial aid and concentrated on offering access to loans, jobs, housing, and free legal and financial advice. These
services were supplemented by factory inspections, monitoring of private
charities, supervision of dance halls and movie theaters, and a "scientific" survey of social conditions around the city.

Volker, Walsh, and Billikopf had sat on an earlier commission charged with
overhauling the city's antiquated system of pardons and paroles. In one of its
first actions, the welfare board mothballed the old workhouse at Twentieth
and Vine streets, a forbidding, castlelike stone pile notorious for overcrowding and filth. The *Star* backed plans to replace it with a new municipal farm
and Nelson assigned Haskell to organize a print campaign for the requisite

McClure Flats about 1911, with the new *Star* headquarters in the background.
Nelson assigned editorial writer William Allen White to clean up the notorious slum
in the early 1890s; two decades later little had changed.

bond issue. In due course, a tract of land was acquired ten miles southeast of
the city, where the ubiquitous George Kessler laid out flower and vegetable
gardens designed to inculcate a work ethic and sense of beauty in the inmates.
Modern and efficient, the farm was a showcase for City Beautiful principles
as well as penal reform. Its quarries supplied crushed stone for the city's boulevards and the entire operation was conducted on business lines, prisoners
earning fifty cents a day toward paying off their fines.

From the welfare reformers' perspective, the parks-and-boulevards system
constituted nothing so much as a massive slum-clearance project. As attorney
for both the city's tenement commission and the welfare board, Walsh had
seen more than enough of the squalid housing in neighborhoods untouched
by the beautification bonanza. A 1912 Board of Public Welfare report painted a harrowing picture of homes without gas or running water, unsanitary
privies that bred typhus, and vermin-infested rooming houses. At the same
time, the report noted, material conditions had improved markedly for the industrious and relatively affluent, "few cities in the United States" having "better housing for the middle class and for a large part of the working class."

Thanks to the welfare agency, the *Star* intoned, "the family of small means" was now "able to share in the advantages of the city's progress." Thus were the disparate strands of social and aesthetic reform woven together in the middle-class progressives' uplifting rhetoric.[50]

In truth, the reformers rallied around the Board of Public Welfare presented anything but a unified front. Some stressed honesty and efficiency in government, others beautification of buildings and landscapes, still others improvement of conditions among the poor. Many social activists criticized parks and boulevards as expensive luxuries that benefited mainly the already well to do. For its part, the City Beautiful crowd was content to leave welfare work to the private sector. Kessler lobbied hard for playgrounds in his parks but complained sourly when "expensive directors and sociological workers" were hired to supervise the children who used them.[51] Kansas City's elite Civic League focused almost exclusively on monitoring elections for fairness and pressing for businesslike administrative reforms in city government.

Even as the Commercial Club trumpeted the welfare board's accomplishments, the fragile consensus that had brought the agency into existence was unraveling. Democratic politicians pressured Billikopf and fellow social worker Leroy Halbert to steer patronage to the machine. The City Council, jealous of its prerogatives, blocked appropriations for the board, compelling Volker to dig deeper and deeper into his own pocket for funding. The acrimonious bickering over money and personnel finally resulted in Halbert's being forced out of his job shortly after a disillusioned Billikopf had quit to lead a campaign for Jewish war relief in New York. By 1918 the Board of Public Welfare would be effectively dead.

The heyday of progressive reform in Kansas City lasted little more than a decade. In later years, Billikopf would reminisce to Volker about the days "when you and I and several associates labored together in unity and harmony in behalf of those less fortunate than ourselves." That unity had been weakened, and ultimately torn apart, by the shifting currents of politics and civic reform. People and programs came and went, Billikopf reflected. Only Nelson's "Twilight Twinkler" remained fixed in the firmament, dependable as a lodestar, steadfast in what George Creel called its "power of purpose."[52]

Try as he might to remain on the sidelines during the 1908 campaign, Roosevelt couldn't help making news. In the waning months of his administration, he was challenged not only by the resurgent conservative wing of his own party, led by Speaker of the House Joe Cannon, but also by restive reformers on the left. In Joseph Pulitzer's eyes, the president had broken faith with his liberal supporters by accepting money from the likes of J. Ogden Armour and J. P. Morgan four years earlier. Roosevelt's "real weakness and vulnerability," he told an editorial writer on his *New York World,* lay "in his jingoism, blatant militarism, unconstitutionalism, in the personal Government he has substituted for that of law, in what Nelson very well termed, his lawless mind."[53] Once again, the two editors found themselves basically in harmony but marching to different drummers. For Nelson, Roosevelt's "lawless mind" was a badge of courage and independence; for Pulitzer, it evinced the rottenness at the heart of the American political system.

On the eve of the election, the *World* exposed a scandal involving financing for the Panama Canal. Both Roosevelt's brother-in-law and Taft's half-brother, it was alleged, had illegally profited from the deal through insider knowledge. Although the president himself was not directly implicated, his judgment and integrity had been impugned. Roosevelt's response was swift and decisive. "I do not know anything about the law of criminal libel, but I should dearly like to have it invoked about Pulitzer," he wrote to Henry Stimson, U.S. attorney for the southern district of New York and a rising star in the Republican Party. Pulitzer, the president went on, was "one of these creatures of the gutter of such unspeakable degradation that to him even eminence on a dunghill seems enviable." In a message to Congress, Roosevelt denounced the *World*'s exposé as "a string of infamous libels" and pronounced it "a high national duty" to bring the publisher to justice.[54]

Pulitzer, in turn, defiantly accused the president of asserting "the doctrine of lese majesty" and vowed that the *World* would never be muzzled. As tempers flared, the *Star* attempted to put the dispute between its two allies into perspective. "It may be true that the President has taken this matter somewhat seriously," the paper commented. At the same time, "Mr. Roosevelt may exaggerate the impression that these slanders have made on the people. It would take something more than newspapers having reputations for unscrupulous attacks, especially along political lines, to make the country waver one jot in its faith in the President or in the essential honesty of any transaction that has had his supervision."[55] Torn between friendship and professional solidarity, Nelson fudged. The issue, the *Star* lamely suggested, was not one of legality or ethics, let alone freedom of the press, but of simple trust in an exemplary public servant.

In February 1909 a grand jury in Washington, D.C., indicted Pulitzer and several others for libel. Since the defendants resided outside the court's jurisdiction, however, they were technically beyond the arm of the law. Frustrated, Roosevelt ordered Stimson to prosecute the publisher by other means, declaring that it had always been his policy to "reach the head man," whether the offender was a "big financier, a big politician, or a big newspaperman."[56] The administration pursued its libel case all the way to the U.S. Supreme Court, which ruled unanimously in Pulitzer's favor in January 1911. Papers from coast to coast hailed the decision as a landmark victory against government censorship. Ten months later Pulitzer died, his laurels as journalistic crusader intact. In a rare public comment on a colleague, Nelson eulogized him as "the leading journalist of his day, the pioneer in modernizing the newspaper. It was his discovery that newspapers must be entertaining. His energy, ability, and originality in applying this idea brought unprecedented success to the *World* and made a lasting impression on journalism. Even newspapers that believed his methods extreme could not escape being profoundly influenced by them. Blind and ill as he was much of his life, he was a tremendous factor in American affairs."[57]

Was it simple jealousy that prevented Nelson from acknowledging Pulitzer's greatness as a moral force in the progressive crusade? Or was the *Star*'s publisher, all but blind himself and bloodied in many a losing battle, unconsciously composing his own epitaph? Baron Bill had been called many things in his time, some flattering, some libelous, a few unprintable. At this point in his life, he desired above all to be called "a tremendous factor in American affairs."

As Taft counted down the days to his inauguration, Nelson and Roosevelt conducted a ritual courting dance. "It is quite worth while to have a real President of the United States," the editor wired when Roosevelt intervened to settle a controversy concerning the Kaw River in January 1909. To which the president replied, "It is even better worth while to have a real editor of just the right kind of paper." Whether Taft had it in him to be "a real President" remained to be seen. Nelson had found him in high spirits before Christmas, when he called on the secretary in Washington. "Didn't we whip them!" Taft exclaimed with a hearty chuckle. Why, the Republicans had even carried traditionally Democratic Missouri. "But not by much!" Nelson couldn't resist taunting. Taft parried the blow with a jovial riposte: "We're no hogs!"[58]

Beneath the lighthearted banter, Nelson was apprehensive. Back home in Kansas City, he wrote Taft that he was "a good deal concerned over the prospects for a carefully considered and sincere revision of the tariff" and urged him to take the ball away from the House Ways and Means Committee, which he regarded as "a committee of Stand Patters by instinct and habit." Taft was in a bind. He knew tariff reform was Nelson's idée fixe and, as always, was eager to oblige a friend. But he wasn't convinced that wholesale revision of tariff schedules was either necessary or desirable. In any case, as long as conservative Republicans remained in control of congressional committee assignments, the president had little room to maneuver. Taft replied noncommittally, assuring Nelson that he remained firmly opposed to the protectionist hard-liners and promising to set up a permanent tariff commission, in the fullness of time, to remove the issue from politics altogether.[59]

Another disappointment soon followed. Justifying his decision to stock his cabinet with corporate lawyers, Taft told Nelson that whereas Roosevelt's function had been "to preach a crusade against certain evils," it was now his job "to put that reform into legal execution." Taft's lack of guile had always endeared him to Nelson. But to imply that he was a practical man of action while Roosevelt—now rusticating on safari in darkest Africa, the better to keep his tongue in check—was an idealistic windbag strained the editor's credulity. In May, his forbearance exhausted, Nelson descended on the White House to insist that Taft make good on his campaign pledge to press for modest, targeted revisions in tariff rates. The president's perfunctory response was to call on Congress to take the matter up expeditiously. In a special session that summer, the House passed a mildly progressive bill that Taft felt he could safely sign. When the legislation reached the Senate, however, Republican leader Nelson Aldrich of Rhode Island caved in to a determined cabal of eastern protectionists and western proponents of a high tariff on cattle hides. Senator Bristow called the deal "deceptive, dishonest," and "corrupt"; Nelson branded it sheer "extortion."[60]

Ignoring the progressives' demands that he denounce Aldrich, Taft showed no inclination to wield his big stick. Relaxing at his new summer getaway on Boston's North Shore, a short hop from Magnolia, he was spending all his spare time on the golf course, doing his best to put the tariff fracas out of mind. Nelson made one last attempt to sway him on a neighborly Fourth of July visit. The "great free trader," Archie Butt reported to his sister, came "to assure the President that the entire West" was against the tariff bill.[61] Affable as ever, Taft heard the editor out, then proceeded to sign the compromise legislation that emerged from the joint congressional committee. Nelson kept his distance the rest of the summer. "I haven't tried to see the President since he came North, because I couldn't see that a conversation at this time would be especially agreeable," he told William Allen White in August. "I got along fairly well in spite of the dead cats and tin cans that came in the direction of the revisionists with no protests from the White House, until the bill came to be signed and the dinner given to the framers. There wasn't a man around the

President at that time who had been for him for the nomination. All of his associates were from the crowd that fought him before the Chicago convention. That got on my nerves."[62]

By now, even Taft could see that he and Nelson were on a collision course. The inevitable crash finally occurred when the president visited the small town of Winona, Minnesota, to lend a hand in the reelection campaign of a Republican congressman who had supported the Payne-Aldrich tariff. In a speech on September 17, Taft praised the legislation as "the best tariff bill that the Republican party ever passed." Butt wrote to his sister that the president's ill-considered remarks "had a very bad effect throughout the West," which was putting it mildly. For Nelson, the Winona speech marked the final triumph of experience over hope. "Mr. Taft assumes that by signing the bill the tariff issue has been disposed of for some years. So far as the west is concerned this is an utterly fallacious assumption," the *Star* editorialized. Hadn't Taft himself led the Republican Party "out of the standpat rut and placed it before the country as a tariff revision party"? For the president now to declare that party unity was paramount and that progressive congressmen had been wrong to oppose Payne-Aldrich was utterly "amazing." After all, "Mr. Taft was accepted and elected as a progressive, not as a reactionary."[63]

Nelson manifested his displeasure in a more concrete way by banishing Taft from the gallery of progressive heroes displayed on one wall of the *Star* office. "Ralph," he called to his managing editor the day after the speech, "didn't we have a picture of Cleveland?" Yes, Ralph Stout replied, the portrait of Nelson's Democratic idol should be somewhere around the building. He reminded the publisher that he had taken it down a year or so earlier, around the time of Taft's election, and replaced it with the new president's likeness. "Find it!" barked Baron Bill. After much scurrying about, Cleveland's picture was duly located. Nelson pointed to the vacant place on the wall behind his desk, next to Roosevelt and Tilden. "Hang it up there," he ordered, "and put that other one away somewhere."[64]

Afterwards, Nelson would blame himself for "misunderstanding" Taft's tariff policy, confessing that his "affection and enthusiasm" had led him to "read into" the president's mind "purposes that were not there." The two men continued to see each other socially, clapping each other on the shoulders and exchanging pleasantries as if nothing had come between them. But Taft knew he could no longer count on Nelson's support, and later that year his advisers put out a feeler about buying the *Kansas City Journal* and making it an administration organ. Nelson was further disillusioned by the controversy that erupted when Interior Secretary Richard Ballinger, one of Taft's probusiness privy council, sacked a subordinate for blowing the whistle on his plan to expedite the sale of a hundred thousand acres of western public land that the Roosevelt administration had sequestered from development. Outraged by what the *Star* called a "looting of the national domain by the privilege grabbers," Forest Service chief Gifford Pinchot mounted a whispering campaign against his boss.[65] When Taft, who sincerely believed that some of his predecessor's conservation policies were unwise and possibly unconstitutional, fired Pinchot for insubordination in January 1910, he forfeited his last vestige of progressive support.

In Magnolia that August, a group of reporters spotted Nelson as he was leaving to pay his respects to Taft and asked if he thought the embattled president could be reelected. "Now, boys," the editor responded with a disarming grin, "you mustn't ask me foolish questions." What, the reporters pressed, was the significance of the recent Republican upsets in Kansas and Iowa? "Simply that the Republican party hasn't kept its pledges, particularly with regard to the tariff. You just watch Kansas and you will see what the rest of the country will do," opined the Sage of Brush Creek. "The Republicans imagine that the war is still on and they are standing on the past glory of the party. . . . The next House of Representatives will be either Democratic or else controlled by the Insurgents." And Roosevelt—was it possible that he could stage a comeback in 1912? "Come back?" Nelson roared. "Why he'd sweep the country."[66]

As Nelson and Taft shot the breeze in Massachusetts, Roosevelt was campaigning his way across the West in a halfhearted bid to shore up Republican solidarity. Home from his self-imposed exile, he joined Pinchot, William Borah, and other progressive notables in late August at the annual Frontier Day festivities in Cheyenne, Wyoming. Nelson had been urging him to run again for months. "So far as all present indications go there isn't going to be a tide setting toward Oyster Bay in 1912. It's going to be a torrent and a torrent that no man on earth can withstand," he had written to Roosevelt in London. Before the 1908 convention, the editor said,

> Taft always insisted he had no qualifications for the job. We thought differently. But he was right and we were wrong. The American people want an executive in the President's office, not a judge who hears arguments on all sides and finally gives his opinion on a technicality. The President must carry the big stick and be ready to fight. But when you come to think of it, you never saw Taft fighting with his nose all bloody and one eye hanging down on his cheek, and his front teeth knocked out. The

newspapers have dealt with Taft with the greatest gentleness. But he thinks he has been very badly treated and goes about sobbing over it publicly. A cry baby won't do.[67]

Nelson floated the idea of a third-party candidacy when he saw Roosevelt in New York in mid-July. Neither of the two major parties, in his view, was big enough, politically or ideologically, for a man of Roosevelt's stature. "My hope," he wrote, "is that eventually there may be formed a party of the Square Deal—national in scope—with a live leader and held together by belief in a principle and not by the hope of spoils which keeps the present parties together." Rumors as to Roosevelt's intentions flew thick and fast all summer. Taft, golfing at the aptly named Myopia Club in Beverly, Massachusetts, noted them but was not unduly perturbed. Meanwhile, Roosevelt was holding court in Oyster Bay, testing the political waters and behaving more like a candidate every day. Writing to Nelson on August 24, he left little doubt that the die was already cast. "From my personal standpoint, I am sorry that the 'Old Guard' have put themselves in such shape that I shall have to go in and try to smash them. I think defeat is inevitable anyhow here in New York, and this makes me loath to assume the responsibility. But I don't see how I can avoid taking the lead in this fight as the situation is now."[68]

Roosevelt was straining to portray himself as a reluctant warrior. In actuality, both he and Nelson were spoiling for a fight. One week later, the Rough Rider threw down the gauntlet in a gesture pregnant with symbolism. The occasion was the dedication of a state park in Osawatomie, Kansas, honoring John Brown. Roosevelt seized the opportunity to associate himself with the implacable abolitionist who had spilled proslavery blood there fifty-four years earlier. As his train chugged across the prairie from Denver, thousands of farmers and their families lined the tracks in the drenching rain, cheering ecstatically and craning weather-beaten necks for a glimpse of their hero. "There is no longer the least question as to how the Western country regards the Colonel," observed the *New York Times*. "He is not only their idol; he is their Moses as well." Aboard the train, a cadre of reporters and politicians was "bubbling over with enthusiasm," while Roosevelt himself, Henry Haskell noticed, remained sober and self-composed, his nose often buried in a book of moral philosophy.[69]

At Osawatomie, Roosevelt was driven through fields black with mud to the hallowed battleground, where a makeshift platform had been erected in a grove of elm and hickory trees. Alighting from the car, he had to fight his way through "solid ranks of men and women"—crowd estimates varied from fifteen to thirty thousand—who "seemed intent only on getting near enough to touch him." Many were too far away to hear his distinctive high-pitched voice, but seemed content to be in the presence of the five-foot-ten-inch bundle of energy whom Kansas governor Walter Stubbs introduced as "the greatest man in the world."

Every word in Roosevelt's ninety-minute address was chosen with care. Ghost-written by Pinchot and White, it was by turns conciliatory and confrontational, radical and reassuring, hortatory and reflective. Recalling the "furious popular passion" that had split the young nation asunder half a century before, Roosevelt asserted that "the attitude of the West," so forcefully articulated by Brown and Lincoln, had reunited a people who were now "struggling in peace as well as in war for the uplift of their common country." The chief aims of the contemporary struggle were "equality of opportunity" and "the destruction of special privilege." The "men who possess more than they have earned" stood pitted against the "men who have earned more than they possess." Then Roosevelt lunged into the attack. "We must drive the special interest out of politics," he fairly screamed. "The Constitution guarantees protection to property, and we must make that promise good. But it does not give the right of suffrage to any corporation. The true friend of property, the true conservative, is he who insists that property shall be the servant, and not the master, of the commonwealth, and who insists that the creature of man's making shall be the servant, and not the master, of the man who made it. The citizens of the United States must effectively control the mighty commercial forces which they have themselves called into being. There can be no effective control of corporations while their political activity remains."[70]

One by one, Roosevelt recapped the major themes of his presidency: corporate accountability, conservation of natural resources, a strong army and navy, the protection of human over property rights. Echoing the platform adopted by the Kansas progressives, he called for a graduated tax on income and inheritances, a workmen's compensation law, regulation of child and female labor, direct primaries, and vigorous prosecution of corrupt public officials. Such reforms, he recognized, unavoidably implied "a far more active governmental interference with social and economic conditions in this country than we have yet had." It was no longer enough to "stand for fair play under the present rules of the game"; the rules themselves had to be changed. It devolved upon the president, as "steward of the public welfare," to lead the country away from "sordid and selfish materialism" toward a "New Nationalism" under which local and sectional interests would be subordinated to the common good.

At one point Roosevelt departed from his prepared text to take an impromptu stab at the hapless incumbent. "A broken promise is bad anywhere, but it is worst in the field of politics," he declared, clearly alluding to Taft's tariff treachery. "No man in public life should be content to make a pledge on the stump that after his election he doesn't keep. If he makes a pledge and doesn't keep it, hunt him out of public life." The crowd, scenting blood, bayed its approval.

The next day, fifty thousand Kansas Citians braved a downpour to greet Roosevelt en route from Union Depot to the Baltimore Hotel. Tailoring his message to a more conservative urban audience, he portrayed himself not as a fire-breathing populist but as a levelheaded, civic-minded reformer. When a group of newspapermen at a Commercial Club luncheon improvised a ditty characterizing him as "an insurgent through and through," Roosevelt called out jovially, "Just change that word 'Insurgent' to 'Progressive,' and it's all right." Later, Roosevelt invited Herbert Hadley up to his hotel room and urged the popular Missouri governor to help organize a new political party. As Hadley recollected their conversation, he replied that a party was "a matter of growth, of tradition, and of historical associations inherited from generation to generation." Men didn't simply "throw off old political associations and put on new ones as they would put off an old or put on a new suit of clothes." He himself wasn't prepared to bolt the GOP and trusted the former president wouldn't do anything rash.[71]

After Roosevelt left town, Nelson offered the presumptive candidate another piece of political advice. It had occurred to him that the opposition would "constantly be prodding" and "lying about" Roosevelt in hopes of provoking him to defend himself. That he must never do, the editor cautioned. "It is always a bad policy in my opinion to get to talking about the past. You are a Progressive. Your nose is to the front. The past doesn't interest you."[72] In response, Roosevelt unbuttoned himself to his old friend in a long letter, ruminating on the future of the Republican Party and candidly assessing his chances for recapturing the White House. Opponents of reform, he wrote, would rather see corrupt political bosses

stay in power than see the Republican Party victorious if it is to represent the principles that were set forth in my speeches at Osawatomie and Kansas City. So I cannot tell what the result will be. It may be that I shall be beaten at the Convention: and if I win at the Convention the probabilities are that we shall be beaten at the polls; and in either case, I shall

Theodore Roosevelt and Governor Herbert Hadley of Missouri in Kansas City, the day after the former president's bridge-burning speech at Osawatomie, Kansas: progressives or insurgents?

be attacked with jeering derision for a defeat which will undoubtedly be in part due to the fact that people are at the moment frightened at my having taken in clear-cut fashion a position to which nevertheless they must themselves inevitably come, and partly to the fact that I shall pay the penalty for the misdeeds of the Republican Party at Washington and Albany, for which I am not only not responsible, but which I am doing my best to remedy.[73]

That November, while he was in New York to attend his daughter's wedding, Nelson called on Roosevelt in his office at the *Outlook* magazine. Speaking afterwards to reporters who wanted to know what he thought about the recent and upcoming elections—for by now Nelson was a newsmaker himself—the editor artfully dodged the question. "The west understands Roosevelt and it understands that he is not merely the leader of the Republican party—he is the leader of the American people. The parties are breaking up and under the influence of the old party ties, it may take two years, it may take four, it may take six for the people to come together in the fight for their own rights, but when it does come there won't be anything to it. Nineteen hundred and twelve for Roosevelt? It's too early to discuss that and there are too many cross currents in the political stream. The trouble is that people don't realize that that is the last thing that Roosevelt is worrying about."[74]

But Roosevelt *was* thinking about 1912. So were his supporters, their faith in the political process unexpectedly restored by his electrifying call to arms at Osawatomie. Progressives, Republican and Democrat alike, were already breaking ranks and migrating toward what White recognized as Roosevelt's "undeclared third party."[75] Nelson had been waiting for the old party organizations to self-destruct ever since the Tilden debacle of 1876. The veteran mugwump was girding for battle. His last and greatest campaign was about to begin.

CHAPTER 4

◆

Insurgents

The Roosevelt and Taft forces converged on the 1912 Republican convention determined to fight to the finish. Inside Chicago's cavernous Coliseum the battle lines were sharply drawn, the atmosphere hair-trigger tense. A phalanx of armed police guarded the speaker's platform and the railings were sheathed with barbed wire to deter protesters. "The bitterness of the conflict" between progressives and conservatives "had reached a die-in-the-ditch feeling," recalled Wichita newspaper editor Henry J. Allen.[1] Ostensibly, the major bone of contention was procedural—a dispute over several hundred delegates whose seats were claimed by the rival pretenders to the Republican throne. In fact, it was a battle for the soul of the GOP and the future of the progressive movement.

> *"An insurgent is a Progressive who is exceeding the speed limit."*
>
> —Theodore Roosevelt

William Rockhill Nelson had set up camp in the Congress Hotel, where he commanded his small battalion of journalist-conscripts into the progressive army. Enervated by the sweltering June heat, he spent long hours ensconced in a large chair by a window opening onto Lake Michigan. Nevertheless, the crafty campaigner stayed in close touch with Allen, Herbert Hadley, and Roosevelt's other floor managers. Although showing his age, the seventy-one-year-old publisher remained a masterful figure and the progressives made no significant move without his advice and consent. Nelson's devotion to the cause was unquestioning and unquestioned. Had he not forsaken the balmy breezes of Boston's North Shore to witness what he believed, with every fiber of his failing body, would be the Armageddon of the reactionaries?

Hadley, Missouri's reformist governor, had worked hard to hold the state delegation in line behind Roosevelt. A Republican loyalist, he worried that either Taft or Senator Robert La Follette, standard-bearer of the western progressives, would drive moderate voters into the arms of the Democrats. If Roosevelt was the convention's rough-riding hero, Hadley was its knight in shining armor. "Slim and lithe as a movie actor" in William Allen White's admiring eyes, he had a "kindly, resonant voice" and a "firm and determined" manner that made him the "gallery idol."[2] But Hadley's air of cool command was deceptive. Suffering from the early stages of tuberculosis, he was running a high temperature and would soon be forced to retire from politics.

Over the next five days, the governor was foremost among the compromise candidates whose names emerged from the frenzied backroom brokering. In the middle of the raucous delegate debate, the auditorium erupted in a spontaneous chant of "We want Hadley, we want Hadley!" The convention "went wild," his wife recorded in her diary. Hadley "had risen to read a report on something when they began to cheer, to clap, to throw up their hats, to march and carry their banners and it lasted 40 or 50 minutes until a woman in the gallery, Mrs. Davis, unfurled a picture of Roosevelt and began to lead cheering of her own for Roosevelt. Then the crowd seemed to remember that Roosevelt was their candidate and that it was for *him* they had come there, *and* the cheering was turned to him."[3] Allen, surveying the demonstration from the floor, noted that a number of well-known Taft supporters were shouting wildly for the governor in a transparent attempt to divide and conquer their opponents.

Ironically, Taft and Roosevelt had each considered inviting Hadley to be his running mate. Whether first or second on the ticket, the clean-cut, self-effacing hero of the Standard Oil fight was deemed acceptable to conservatives and progressives alike. Moreover, a candidate from the Show Me State would help pull in the Missouri vote if, as expected, Speaker of the House Champ Clark of Bowling Green, north of St. Louis, brought home the Democratic nomination in July. When Nelson broached the subject, Roosevelt replied evasively that although Hadley "would be a most admirable running mate," he preferred to keep his options open. Hadley tartly rebuffed a group of Taft delegates who sounded him out about a draft, saying that he had no "ambition to drive a hearse." For his part, the president made it clear that under no circumstances would he step aside in favor of Hadley or anyone else.[4]

Roosevelt was playing hard to get, a tactic that combined political advantage with the appearance of principled statesmanship. After his bridge-burning Osawatomie speech in 1910, he had assured Hadley in Kansas City of his determination to reform the Republican Party from within. Although he denied any intention of seeking another nomination, he told the governor that he "would also be opposed to seeing such a result prevented through the manipulation of politicians opposed to [his] nomination, if a clear majority of the party desired it." Allen, however, testified that Roosevelt told *him* that Hadley would make a "splendid president" and that he was prepared to support the Missourian provided the delegate rolls were "purged" in Chicago. This meant, as Allen understood it, that "if the Taft men desired to nominate Hadley, they would have to admit delegates whom the credentials committee had discarded and who, if restored to the convention, would constitute a majority committed to Roosevelt."[5] In effect, Roosevelt agreed to support Hadley only on condition that he himself was guaranteed the nomination.

By week's end, it was clear that Republican conservatives, led by convention chairman Elihu Root, would have their way in the credentials committee. On Friday night, Allen, White, Kansas governor Walter Stubbs, and other progressive die-hards huddled to plot the "most effective exit" from their predicament. As Allen recalled, it was Nelson who suggested that the surest way of making their voices heard was to abstain from the final delegate vote. The following day, Allen delivered a bellicose statement in Roosevelt's name, charging Root and his associates of fraudulently "overriding the will of the rank and file of the party." Now it was the reformers' turn to stand pat. "We do not bolt. We merely insist that you, not we, are making the record. And we refuse to be bound by it. We have fought with you five days for a square deal. We fight no more, we plead no longer. We shall sit in protest, and the people who sent us here shall judge us." As fistfights broke out on the floor, the renegades staged a dignified "silent protest," each answering "present, but not voting" when his name was called.[6] With Taft's delegates in the overwhelming majority, his victory was a foregone conclusion.

Nelson was just as keen as Roosevelt to split the GOP down the middle. But for strategic reasons he had opposed calling on Roosevelt's unseated delegates to reconstitute themselves as a rump convention. Now, with Taft's nomination in the bag, the editor took heart from a hastily issued summons to a late-night parley of disaffected progressives in Chicago's Orchestra Hall. This was the moment he had been waiting for. A "virtual third party" no longer, the Republican insurgents were ready to declare their independence. Roosevelt's men urged Nelson to attend the meeting and take his place on stage beside the other ringleaders of the insurgency, but he demurred. "If I go," he explained, "they would see I'm old and half blind. If I don't appear, perhaps they will think I'm a dashing young blade."[7]

That Saturday, the insurgents—for so they called themselves, brandishing their enemies' term of derision—planted the seed of the new party that promised to revolutionize American politics. "It was nearing midnight when the Roosevelt delegates reached Orchestra Hall from the Coliseum," recalled Ralph Stout, Nelson's burly managing editor. "Singing crusaders packed the hall. Men, reluctant to cast the die, peeped in and went away. Others walked boldly down the aisle so all might see." The cabal lasted into the small hours of Sunday morning, and by the time the rebels scattered to their beds, dog-tired but exhilarated, all knew there could be no turning back. The party of Lincoln had been laid to rest; a new political era was dawning. It was "a time of deep travail for many a statesman," Stout soberly observed.[8]

Some held back even then. Kansas senator Joseph Bristow skipped the Orchestra Hall meeting. White, busy writing his convention wrap-up, didn't hear about the revolution until it was a fait accompli. When Governor Stubbs contrived to be summoned back to Topeka on urgent business, Nelson froze him in his tracks. "So you are going to run away from us, are you!" he bellowed. Baron Bill "left his mouth open for the unspoken God damn, just looking at Stubbs. Stubbs stayed," White recalled. Hadley, too, refused to bolt and insisted on placing Missouri's delegation on record for Roosevelt, a decision he would later regret. Nelson had no patience for such dithering. "Our boys fancy there is some regret on part of Missouri gentlemen who hurried from Chicago to stay regular and are now hearing things. We think they'll have to come across," he wired Roosevelt after the convention.[9]

The newborn was formally christened the National Progressive Party, though as yet it could scarcely be called a party, let alone national. Pledging that he was with Roosevelt "tooth and nail to the limit and to the finish," Nelson dispatched Henry Haskell, now his chief editorial writer, to New York to report on the candidate's hastily formulated platform. From his Massachusetts retreat, a buoyant Nelson assured Roosevelt that Missourians were signing up in droves. "Hadley is edging up cautiously toward third party and I predict he will join in time," he wired to Oyster Bay. "Haskell just told me of his visit with you. We all feel mighty fine and believe Chicago outcome was best possible."[10]

On July 8 Nelson joined representatives of thirty-nine other states in calling for a national Progressive convention to be held in Chicago in early August. The fledgling party had a charismatic leader, a handful of well-heeled

backers, and legions of willing workers, but the laborious process of nominating full slates of candidates and placing them on the ballot in all the states had
scarcely begun. With Missouri's convention set for the end of July, the editor
broke his vow of political abstinence and agreed to serve as state party chairman. There was no time to lose. Nelson was too old to wait patiently for the
millennium. For him, Roosevelt and the Progressive Party represented the
last, best chance of a lifetime.

Nelson hurled all the resources at his command into the Bull Moose campaign: his influential newspaper, his underpaid but fiercely loyal minions, his
bulging pocketbook, and his brute, indomitable strength. Stout was commissioned as the editor's field marshal, his subalterns received their marching orders, and a platoon of *Star* men fanned out over the state, missionaries of the
new political faith, while Nelson called the shots from his war room in New
England. "Everything was done in his name," Stout wrote. "He gave *carte
blanche* for its use by his lieutenants. But he kept in daily touch with every
move. Often twenty telegrams a day passed between the home office and his
cottage by the sea."[11] To Roosevelt in Oyster Bay, Nelson issued upbeat reports at regular intervals:

> It may look as if I had been down here at Magnolia enjoying myself
> and neglecting my job in Missouri. But the fact is I have been represented
> by some real workers. The *Star* staff has been neglecting the business of
> publishing a newspaper this summer, and has been scattered over Mis-
> souri organizing the Progressive Party. We have sent men into the bulk
> of the counties of the state . . . . As a result of this work we have an or-
> ganization in pretty nearly every one of the 115 counties . . . . Mr. Stout,
> our managing editor, who has been in charge of the work, has been sur-
> prised at the extent of the sentiment. Wilson isn't developing strength in
> the state at present. The schoolmaster doesn't appeal to the ordinary plug
> citizen. We have hoped that we might work out a plan by which we could
> get Hadley's cooperation, in which case we would have a fighting chance
> to carry the state. But we haven't arrived at one yet.[12]

The governor, clinging to the forlorn hope that the GOP could again be
the party of meaningful reform, offered himself as an honest broker between
the feuding factions. Armed with a peace proposal, he ventured to Kansas City
in mid-July and reported to Roosevelt that Nelson and Stout were receptive
to his "plan of placing the Republican electors upon both tickets, with the
agreement that they should vote for that candidate for President upon whose
ticket they received the most votes." His strategy, Hadley explained to White,

was "to keep the Progressives and the progressive Republicans close enough together so that eventually we can join together and work effectively in one organization."[13]

Reconciling upper- and lower-case progressives, however, was easier said than done. Although progressive sentiment ran strong in Kansas City and St. Louis, the state Republican organization remained securely in the hands of party regulars, who had done handstands to cast themselves in a progressive light in the run-up to the summer conventions. A release put out by the Republican State Press Bureau asserted that "every real Republican is a progressive. But some Republicans mistake petulant protest for progress. Real progress comes from real purpose—a purpose to make things better by patient endeavor rather than by hasty protest."[14] The message was clear: Only "real" Republicans like Taft and Hadley were worthy of the name "progressives"; Roosevelt and his fellow insurgents were mere protesters.

Since his earliest days in office, Roosevelt had presented himself as a moderate progressive in the East and a radical insurgent in the West. So effective had this double-act been that few of his closest friends—perhaps not even Roosevelt himself—felt sure of his core political identity. The personality split was accentuated by Roosevelt's long and bitter contest with La Follette for leadership of the Republican Party's progressive wing. La Follette's National Progressive League, although just over a year old in 1912, had already made substantial inroads among Roosevelt's supporters in the Midwest and West. As governor of Wisconsin, "Fighting Bob" had made his state a laboratory for progressive reform and his eponymous weekly paper was a mouthpiece for the Rough Rider's increasingly outspoken critics.

To Roosevelt and his patrician supporters, the brainy, mop-maned La Follette posed nearly as great a menace to the Republic as loony left-wingers like Bryan. Still, it was nip and tuck which of them would lead the progressive charge in the fall presidential election. White, Victor Murdock, and others put money on both horses, paying lip service to La Follette's insurgency while prodding Roosevelt to enter the race. Nelson, too, was hedging his bets. Writing to Haskell in September 1911, he counseled prudence and forbearance. "Of course we have to say of LaFollette that he is a good man and does *not* weight 250 pounds. Until we get our bearings we ought to shy when we come to the dangerous places in the road. We can give the news though, be amiable with Taft and say pleasant things of our friends including LaFollette."[15]

For some time Haskell's editorial page went on saying pleasant things about the Wisconsin senator without actually committing the *Star* to his candidacy. Nelson's wait-and-see policy paid off when the fallout from La Follette's anticapitalist rant at a magazine publishers' dinner in Philadelphia derailed his presidential train in February 1912. The editor's interest in him, tepid at best, cooled markedly thereafter. "We have all been greatly disappointed in LaFollette," he wrote to Roosevelt. "His course has shown that he isn't the big, disinterested progressive we thought him."[16] Within days of La Follette's fatal gaffe, Hadley, Stubbs, and the governors of five other states signed a round-robin letter urging Roosevelt to declare his candidacy, and by the end of the month the Rough Rider had officially thrown his hat into the ring.

Hadley's apostasy fortified Baron Bill's faith that the Progressives would run away with the prize in the Missouri primaries. Dismissing the very real threat posed by the Taft forces, he blithely informed Roosevelt in March that "a few men met without any authority in a small room in a hotel behind locked doors on Saturday and elected a 'contesting delegation' to Chicago. Of course the game they are working all through Missouri is plain enough. But it is so raw that the national committee won't dare stand for it in Chicago." Roosevelt was equally scornful of the "fake contesting delegations" that Missouri's Republican leaders, anxious to avoid an open schism, planned to send to the convention. The conservatives, he said, had shown that "if they cannot murder the progressive movement, they wish to see the Republican party commit suicide."[17]

In the aftermath of the Chicago revolt, Republican regulars took pains to avoid antagonizing the Star's powerful editor unnecessarily. But Nelson, buoyed by the Progressive stampede, looked forward confidently to seeing Taft thrashed at the polls in November. "You may have noticed that there is no rejoicing on the part of the reactionaries," he crowed to Roosevelt. "They don't even claim that they have you down and out in their usual vein. Instead, they are leaning up against the ropes, gasping for breath, thankful that they barely escaped a knockout, and wondering what is going to happen to them in the next round."[18]

In deference to Nelson, Missouri Progressives held their convention in Kansas City at the end of July. In a telegram to the delegates, Roosevelt reiterated his uncompromising stand against the "two old political machines," both of which were "inefficient" and "corrupt." Through Haskell, visiting him at Oyster Bay, the Progressive candidate issued a more temperate statement for popular consumption. "Tell the Progressives of Missouri—yes, and of Kansas, too—that I was prepared for the Progressive sentiment in the West. But tell them I was not prepared for it in the East. Yet we are getting reports from New York, New Jersey, Connecticut and Massachusetts that are fully as astonishing as our reports from the Progressive West. . . . And we must remember that we haven't got started yet. When we get well going—. Well, just tell the Progressives of the West that we shall wake the other fellows up—and that we are going to sweep things."[19]

The Kansas City convention was the *Star*'s show from gavel to gavel. "T.J. Murphy, a *Star* reporter, was in the chair of the national committeeman, representing the 'Baron,'" reported an outstate newspaper. Political writer Fred Trigg "acted as chairman" of the convention, while "other reporters for the Nelson papers controlled the admission tickets" and "directed" its "general progress." Managing editor Stout had emceed a preconvention pep rally at the Coates House hotel, in an attempt to "manufacture enthusiasm" among the delegates.[20] A revival-meeting atmosphere pervaded the Shubert Theatre, with a St. Louis delegate leading the obligatory rendition of Roosevelt's theme song, "Follow, Follow, We Will Follow Teddy." The convention closed with a mass recitation of the Lord's Prayer, after which a band struck up "God Be with You Till We Meet Again."

Stout, Murphy, Trigg, and other *Star* men had been canvassing the state for the past several weeks. If they had any doubts that Roosevelt was the Moses destined to lead the Progressives to the Promised Land, they knew better than to share them with their true-believing employer. Where, after all, had journalistic objectivity gotten one of their colleagues? Sent to assess Roosevelt's support in the Missouri hinterland, a cocky cub named Roy Roberts brought back word that Nelson's favorite was running well behind both Taft and Wilson. The publisher promptly found another reporter to tell him what he wanted to hear. But Nelson's displeasure was short-lived. After Roberts's predictions were borne out in the fall election, he was rewarded with a posting to Washington, distinguishing himself as an ace political reporter, presidential counselor, and, ultimately, Nelson's successor.

The Show Me State was in the spotlight again when Democrats convened in Baltimore in early July. On the sidelines, nursing his wounds, was the gaunt figure of "Holy Joe" Folk, who had been itching to come in from the political wilderness since vacating the Missouri governor's mansion in 1909. State party leaders had given him what he thought was an ironclad guarantee of support for a favorite-son presidential bid, but at the eleventh hour Champ Clark, the powerful and self-promoting Speaker of the House, double-crossed him. In consequence, the convention had unfolded as a contest between Governor Woodrow Wilson of New Jersey, the outsider favored by the party's liberal wing, and Clark, a savvy insider who was widely regarded as a tool of Tammany Hall and Wall Street.

The *Star*'s editor (seated at high table, in front of bunting) presides at a postelection Progressive Party dinner in Kansas City's Convention Hall, November 26, 1912. Nelson boasted that "the *Star* never loses."

Roosevelt was rooting for Clark, reasoning that Wilson, if nominated, would probably be elected. Prior to the convention, Nelson had shown the Progressive candidate a ludicrously boastful memoir the Speaker had written in the course of a previous campaign. "We ought to have a barrel of fun with it," the editor chortled. "My idea is to print it in fac-simile. But when? Probably not until immediately after the Democratic convention. I would hate to put anything in the way of Champ's nomination, for I regard him as the easiest man in the country for you to beat." Roosevelt, who was not above a bit of good, clean skullduggery himself, advised his trigger-happy friend that "such ammunition should not be fired until the enemy is within range."[21] Reluctantly, Nelson backed off. The *Kansas City Post*, meanwhile, whipped up a little mischief of its own. Bonfils and Tammen figured they could get a rise out of their competitor by attacking Roosevelt. When the *Star* obligingly lashed out at Clark, the *Post*'s proprietors put an elderly animal on display at the paper's headquarters wearing a sign that identified it as "Nelson's goat."

Clark, too, had a bestial moniker—"the Lion of Democracy"—and held a lion-sized lead going into the Baltimore convention. To Kansas City's own James Reed, elevated to senatorial rank in 1910, went the privilege of placing Clark's name in nomination. Reed's Missouri colleague, Senator William Stone, was playing the odds, discreetly brokering Wilson's nomination while serving as Clark's floor manager. Wilson gained steadily from the moment balloting began, and the scales tipped dramatically when William Jennings Bryan, who had come to Baltimore instructed to vote for Clark, unexpectedly shifted his support to the governor. The forty-sixth ballot finally put Wilson over the top.

Roosevelt recognized that Wilson was the strongest candidate the Democrats could have put up against either him or Taft. His nomination would divide the progressive vote and probably cost Roosevelt the election. But Roosevelt was determined to see it through, come what may. "I have counted the cost," he confided to Haskell. "While conditions may change completely by November, it looks at this time as if we were going into a forlorn hope. I know what men will say if we are defeated. I know what my share of the responsibility will be. But no one need pity me the morning after the election, no matter what the result may be. My reward is going to come in having a hand in a fight worth making."[22]

Nelson pronounced himself well satisfied with the outcome of the convention, signaling as it did the ascendancy of the insurgent element in both major parties. Wilson was too professorial for the editor's taste, but he had a first-rate head on his shoulders and his heart was in the right place. Nelson had had his eye on him ever since Wilson came to Kansas City in 1905 as president of Princeton University. The next time he visited, in the spring of 1911, he was a coming man in the Democratic Party and image makers were hard at work transforming the ivory-tower intellectual into a folksy, shirt-sleeve politician. Seated in a rocking chair, Wilson gazed out benignly from the Star's front page above a caption that read, "Plain speaking is a habit I learned in the class room." The accompanying interview praised New Jersey's reform governor as a "new type of public man . . . the 'scholar in politics,' but not a visionary, a dilettante, or a pedagogue."[23]

Wilson revealed a feistier side in a speech to the Commercial Club, not hesitating to invoke the dreaded "r" word. Party lines were breaking down, he observed, and men in both parties were "going in the same direction toward the progressive or radical ideas." The country couldn't afford not to move forward. "If you get up and say, 'All progressives who wish to go ahead stand on this side, and all standpatters who never dare do anything without finding out what their grandmothers would do stand on that side,' I know where the most of American citizens will stand," Wilson declared. "It will be with the men who want to do things. That I conceive to be the creed of the radicals. I don't think any man in Kansas City is afraid of the radicals." Few in the white-collar crowd would have described themselves as radicals, but by the time he sat down many would have been ashamed to be called anything but progressive.

Speaking at the Coates House later that day, Wilson described progressives as people who "look facts in the face and meet them," while reactionaries had "no stomach for facts" and buried their heads in the sand. Both parties were inevitably "breaking away from the past" because "the life of America is not the life it was twenty years ago. We have changed our economic conditions from top to bottom and with our economic conditions has changed also the organization of our life. The old party formulas do not fit the present problems." Conservatives were in for a rude awakening if they failed to change the way business was conducted. "There isn't one of you who doesn't know that the methods of corporations are wrong," Wilson told the lawyers in the audience. "You know the inside of the machinery and you know what kind of laws would regulate these concerns. But if you sit by and criticise, it won't be long until the people will destroy the corporation."[24]

Roosevelt himself couldn't have said it better. In some respects, Nelson had to admit, Wilson was more consistently and reliably progressive than Roosevelt ever had been or was ever likely to be. The editor couldn't quite bring himself around to White's agnostic view that "it made no great difference" which of the two men won the presidency in 1912. But the governor had impressed him more favorably than any Democrat since his revered Grover Cleveland. "Everybody is talking about Woodrow Wilson," he bubbled to Henry Watterson in Louisville. "If he keeps on as well as he has been doing I don't see how he could fight the *Star* off and keep it from supporting him for President. If Wilson were running right now he couldn't be beaten."[25]

That fall, Nelson traveled to Oyster Bay expressly to warn the former president that the *Star* might be compelled to back Wilson in the next election. He meant it as a challenge, but for the time being Roosevelt wasn't rising to the bait.

So long as Roosevelt bided his time, waiting to be drafted by public acclamation, Nelson had little choice but to keep his options open. The more he saw of Wilson, the more he liked him. Men whose opinions he respected— White, George Creel, Frank Walsh—admired Wilson too. At the same time, Nelson was bound and determined to keep Roosevelt's increasingly unconvincing noncandidacy alive. In mid-February 1912, with La Follette all but out of the running after his disastrous tirade in Philadelphia, a group of Roosevelt's key boosters held a strategy meeting in Oyster Bay. Nelson emerged from the conclave in high spirits. "Roosevelt cannot stop the nomination coming to him and he will be the next President of the United States," he assured a reporter for the *New York Sun*. Roosevelt was no radical but a conservative, the editor said, "and I have told the multi-millionaires to their faces they will be crying for him before this thing is over." En route to Kansas City, Nelson informed the *Philadelphia Bulletin* that he anticipated a "battle royal" between Roosevelt and Taft for leadership of the Republican Party. "I say with the firmest conviction that with Taft on the Republican ticket and Woodrow Wilson on the Democratic, the former would not get an electoral vote west of the Mississippi River."[26]

To Nelson, Taft's ill-gotten victory in Chicago came not as a disappointment but as a relief. At last the Progressives were free to strike out on their own. In his view, the new party urgently needed to distinguish itself from the progressive wings of the two major parties and could best do so by staking out a position even farther to the left. Near the end of July, he laid his cards on the table in a six-page letter calculated to light a fire under Roosevelt. It outlined two reforms—Nelson called them "hobbies"—that he wanted the Progressive Party to embrace in the interest of driving "the money out of the voting booth and out of the court house": free justice and public financing of elections. Roosevelt responded warily that he agreed with the editor "in principle." He had long maintained that the state should bear the expenses of holding elections and was disposed to believe it should provide free justice for its citizens as well. But the idea of government funding for lawyers' fees and trial costs was "such a radical one that I do not know how it would be greeted, and it is something we shall have to fight for later."[27]

Nelson was disappointed but not surprised. Roosevelt was understandably gun-shy after being shot down by Republican conservatives that spring, when he advocated popular recall of judges and judicial decisions in a speech at Columbus, Ohio. A few days later, Nelson had run into O. K. Davis at the *Star*'s Washington bureau and asked what he thought of the candidate's proposal. When the *New York Times* man said he thought judicial recall was too radical a measure for the American people to accept, Nelson exploded, "My boy, I'm for Roosevelt, first, last, and all the time. I'm for him right or wrong. I won't admit, even to myself, that I don't like anything he does. The way to fight is to fight, and, by God, we're in a fight now. This is going to be a fight to the finish, and every man in this country has got to get on one side or the other. My side is with Roosevelt. Where are you going to stand?"[28]

No trace of either Nelson's or Roosevelt's "radical" ideas was discernible in the platform the Progressives eventually adopted. The party's ballyhooed "Contract with the People" would be a litany of progressive standbys—direct primaries, woman suffrage, restrictions on campaign contributions, civil service reform, a nonpartisan tariff commission, workmen's compensation, unemployment insurance, and so on. According to White, who sat on the platform committee, Roosevelt seemed "ready to approve anything that any responsible Progressive brought to him in sincerity." The resulting laundry list served less as a coherent program of reform than as an all-purpose justification for Roosevelt's wild-card candidacy. Abandoning his bid to radicalize the party, Nelson fell back on hero worship. Haskell was astounded to hear him confess that he never even took the trouble to read the Progressive platform. "By God," thundered the Baron, "Roosevelt is platform enough to me!"[29]

The Progressives opened their convention on August 5 in Chicago's Coliseum, where the Republican old guard had reaffirmed its faith in Taft barely a month before. Smoothly scripted, the event made up in fervor what it lacked in suspense. Roosevelt and his running mate, Governor Hiram Johnson of California, were nominated without opposition or debate. Nelson sent a telegram from Magnolia that chairman Albert Beveridge read aloud to the fourteen thousand delegates and observers. "Lord, how I wish I were with you. What a great day, the launching of a party of imagination, hope and prospects. We can afford to give the other fellows their memories and disappointments. The past has no interest for us. The future is our fruit. . . . The Lord is surely with us. He has given us the men as well as the opportunity." A ripple of excitement ran through the clean-cut, well-mannered crowd, which struck one observer as resembling a "convention of Sunday School Superintendents."[30]

The next day Roosevelt, declaring himself "as strong as a bull moose," held his devotees rapt with a spellbinding "confession of faith." Calling upon those who had "come together to spend and be spent in the endless crusade against wrong" to arm themselves for "the never-ending fight for the good of mankind," he reprised his stirring war cry: "We stand at Armageddon, and we battle for the Lord." To Haskell, Roosevelt's words breathed "the spirit of Plymouth Rock and Jamestown" and were "one with the Declaration of Independence." The Progressives' social contract, he told the *Star*'s readers, was a document worthy of the Founding Fathers, "transcribed in words of direct, living fire" straight from the "consciences," "intellects," and "hearts" of the American people. To the managing editor of the *Appeal to Reason*, it was plain that the Progressives had effectively coopted the radical left. "I sat within twenty feet of Roosevelt and there were times when I could have shut my eyes and readily believed that I was listening to a Socialist soap boxer! My prediction that Roosevelt would steal our platform bodily has been fulfilled," Fred Warren wrote to Socialist candidate Eugene Debs.[31]

In Massachusetts, Nelson breezily waved questions about Taft aside when he received a reporter from the *Boston Herald* at his summer home. "The President and I are still friends and will continue so. I admire him heartily as a man and a friend. Now let's not talk about the President, for I will not criticize my friend." Nelson didn't "venture opinions," the awestruck interviewer remarked, he shot "them off like a nitro-glycerine blast." The *Star*'s owner was "inclined to believe" that the Progressive Party would "run like a prairie fire." In any case, the only real contest would be between Roosevelt and Wilson. "The Republican party has gone as the Whig party went. It has finished its work and is done. It has no purpose or reason for existing. Neither has the Democratic party, so far as that is concerned."[32]

Haskell, mingling with the delegates in Chicago, portrayed the convention as a manifestation of a great popular movement that was poised to wrest control from professional politicians and vested interests.

> At Chicago six weeks ago the convention was a battle field. There was an irrepressible conflict between the forces of the past and those of the future. The cynical spirit that asked, "What's the use of considering the merits of these contests? haven't we got the committee?" finally triumphed, and the bosses, the special agents of privilege, were left in charge of the wreckage of a once great party. At Baltimore the convention was dominated by politicians of the old school. But the men who sat silent at Chicago and an aroused public sentiment forced the concession of Woodrow Wilson's nomination from bosses who hoped to capitalize his popularity to strengthen their own hold on the organization. At the convention just closed for the first time the people took charge, made a platform embodying a great program for social betterment and named their trusted leaders to head the movement.[33]

The pure, visionary politics of the City Beautiful on the Hill had supplanted the old-time politics of corrupt bosses and smoke-filled back rooms. Recalled O. K. Davis, "Old newspaper men, hardened by many years of expe-

The army of Progressive Party faithful in Chicago's Coliseum, August 6, 1912: the pure, visionary politics of the City Beautiful on the Hill.

rience, made cynical and skeptical by constant contact with human deceit and insincerity, came to scoff, and went away filled with wonder and amazement, to write such things of a political convention as they had never dreamed." As both observers of and participants in the crusade, Haskell and his fellow scribes believed they had witnessed a transcendental event. "Those who had experienced it felt for the rest of their lives that they had been to the mountain and looked from Pisgah into the Promised Land," a later historian would write. "Nothing would ever touch them so deeply again."[34]

In the end, the race was not even close. Wilson swept Missouri with 330,746 votes to Taft's 207,821 and Roosevelt's 124,371. Despite the *Star's* valiant efforts, the Democratic ticket carried Kansas City by an overwhelming margin. Nationwide, Wilson's plurality of more than six million votes assured him a clean sweep of the electoral college. Nevertheless, Nelson professed satisfaction with Roosevelt's 27 percent of the popular vote and eighty-eight electoral votes. "It is magnificent even to lose with such a leader," he telegraphed to his friend on election night. Within days, Nelson sent Henry Allen to Washington as the *Star's* special correspondent to keep an eye on things in the capital. To Henry Watterson he wrote that he was "bearing up well" under the Democratic victory after the only election he could recall in years "when everybody was pretty well satisfied."[35]

Even the Socialists had cause to celebrate. Debs had garnered more than nine hundred thousand votes nationwide and the *Appeal to Reason*, with nearly half a million readers, was at the zenith of its fortunes. But the insurgents couldn't rest easy yet. Immediately after the election, Taft's Justice Department moved against Debs, Warren, and J. A. Wayland in connection with the *Appeal*'s hard-hitting exposé of corruption and brutality at Leavenworth Penitentiary. The reactionaries' parting shot was more than Wayland could bear. On November 10 the founder of the *Appeal* committed suicide in Gerard, Kansas, leaving behind a note that read: "The struggle under the capitalist system isn't worth the effort. Let it pass."[36]

The *Star*, too, was on its guard. Warning that Bourbon Democrats would do their best to sabotage Wilson's reforms, it quoted Frank Walsh as saying: "If the reactionary wing of the Democratic Party in Congress tries to prevent him from carrying out the policies the American people expect of him there will be the same split in the party that has just sent the Republican party to its grave. And, as in that case, it will be the progressive Democracy that remains above ground." Nelson claimed Walsh as a Progressive in all but name. All of Kansas City, the *Star* declared, had "come to depend on" the irrepressible Irish lawyer as one of its "constructive forces." It was regrettable that Walsh had chosen not to stand for governor in 1912, but he had done so for the best of reasons. "What we need for this time more than lawmakers and law governors is agitators," he told the *Star*. "An agitator is a man who won't stand for lies because they are old. The danger to an agitator is that he may get an office. Office holding and the itch for office have spoiled more good men than all other things combined."[37]

These sentiments hadn't restrained Walsh from helping put a notably unprogressive Democrat in the Kansas City mayor's office in the spring 1912 election, when the Pendergast Goats and Shannon Rabbits conspired to unseat the reform-minded Republican incumbent, Darius Brown. The contest was a milestone on Tom Pendergast's route from hard-working superintendent of streets to all-powerful machine boss. Carrying 245 pounds on his five-foot-nine-inch frame, Alderman Tom had a gravelly voice and piercing gray eyes that flickered from empathy to anger in a flash. Shorn of his youthful Bismarck moustache, the balding Pendergast could pass for a prosperous, middle-aged businessman. That, as a matter of fact, was how he liked to think of himself. His business was politics and he practiced it gregariously, reaching across the aisle to Republicans like Conrad Mann, the driving force behind the Chamber of Commerce (the old Commercial Club), and party strongman Tom Marks. At the same time, he displayed commendable openmindedness in cooperating with reform Democrats like Walsh, whose law partner, James Aylward, would become Tom's right-hand man.

It was all part of Pendergast's grand plan to beat the progressives at their own game. Kansas City was home to more than a quarter-million people, including growing numbers of foreign-born Germans, Russians, Irish, Italians, Swedes, and other ethnic groups. Although the *Star* claimed to be read in virtually every household—its paid circulation was roughly 150,000, far in excess of the number of dwellings—the city was no longer governable by the tight-knit aristocracy that looked to the newspaper for leadership. While Nelson focused ever more intently on reaching the thirty thousand "best" readers, Pendergast concentrated on the communities of immigrants and first-generation Americans. His political base was the First and Second Wards, where the new arrivals mostly settled. Boss Shannon's lay farther to the south, in the comparatively affluent Ninth Ward.

Dissatisfied with the "fifty-fifty compromise" on party patronage that Shannon had worked out with Jim, Tom Pendergast set out to displace his rival once and for all. In 1911 he threw the first of his annual Christmas dinners for hard-luck cases on the north side as a memorial to his late brother. Dispensing charity and favors had always been part of the Pendergast business plan, of course, but Tom's innovation of branching out into social work brought the machine into direct competition with the city's Board of Public Welfare. The new line proved such an effective recruiting device that the 1912 election resulted in a Democratic landslide. Henry Jost, an assistant city prosecutor, left the good Mr. Brown in the dust.

In a shrewd move, Jost rewarded Walsh for his support by naming him to head the city's Civil Service Board. In addition to being a staunch Democrat and friend of the workingman, Walsh was an independent-minded reformer known to be in Nelson's good book. The *Star* praised his appointment as "a blow to the spoilsmen," and so it was, for a time.[38] An outspoken opponent of partisanship in municipal affairs, Walsh had tenaciously insulated the welfare board from political pressure as its unpaid attorney. Before long, however, Jost and Pendergast began muscling in on his turf, eyeing the hundred or so jobs at the board's disposal. Jacob Billikopf and Dante Barton, the lone radical on the *Star*'s editorial staff, warned that the agency's independence was at stake. Walsh sympathized, but by the fall of 1912 his hands were full with other matters.

That summer, Walsh received a telegram asking him to come to New Jersey and meet Governor Wilson. Daisy Harriman, a wealthy union supporter, hoped that the lawyer's national reputation and political pull in Missouri would help Wilson capture the crucial labor vote in the fall election. Walsh, she recalled, came away from the get-acquainted session "convinced that Mr. Wilson's progressiveness was more progressive than" Roosevelt's and promptly offered his services to the party. At Wilson's invitation, he moved to New York that September to head up the Democratic National Committee's new "social center bureau," a network of public forums where voters could meet to discuss political and social issues. It was a short-term assignment, meant to last only through the election. But Walsh had bigger ideas. The bureau, he told the *Star*, was only the first step on the road to lasting "social and industrial justice" in the United States.[39] Wilson had bigger ideas too—and Walsh would be part of them.

In March 1911 Joseph Pulitzer II stopped off in Kansas City on his way west and inspected the *Star*'s brand-new office building at Eighteenth and Grand. As one of the heirs apparent to the Pulitzer kingdom—he would take charge of the *St. Louis Post-Dispatch* after his father's death that October—he received red-carpet treatment and an audience with the proprietor. Nelson's policy of boosting Kansas City impressed the future press lord favorably. "His paper fairly bristles with civic pride, in strong contrast (as has often been pointed out to me) with the sharply critical and dissatisfied tone of the P-D," he wrote to Pulitzer *père*. Nelson informed his visitor that while he and his colleagues liked nothing better than a rip-roaring crusade, "we don't stick our nose into every corner dog fight."[40]

By picking his fights carefully and generally siding with the angels, Nelson had built the *Star* into one of the country's most profitable and respected dailies. Charles Grasty of the *Baltimore Sun* rated it "the best newspaper in America" and attributed its success to the editor's chronic dissatisfaction. Nelson refused to "allow a speck of dry rot to appear in the *Star* office" and never felt the paper was "as good as it ought to be," wrote his old friend. Will Irwin, who surveyed the American press for *Collier's* in 1910, found Nelson's property "so fortified, so stable, that it almost defies competition."[41] Irwin was referring to financial stability, but the *Star*'s journalistic position was equally impregnable. Known far and wide as a writer's paper, it owed its reputation for literary excellence to T. W. Johnston, Jr., a tall, ramrod-backed, Olympian figure known as "Icicle" to the reporters who cowered under him. A fastidious dresser who parted his hair in the middle, Johnston traveled extensively, read broadly, and drank to excess. Long after he succumbed to alcoholism and stopped coming into the office for more than a few hours a day, he remained the editor's pet and the subject of office legend. Not until early 1913 would Nelson finally pension him off with a golden handshake in the form of a fifty-thousand-dollar trust fund.

This episode caused the editor "great travail of spirit," but once a thing was done he seldom looked back. The older Nelson got, the more open he became to fresh blood and ideas. After Johnston's involuntary retirement, he would formalize Haskell's proximity in the line of succession by awarding him Johnston's old title of associate editor. More than a promotion, it was a public sign of the trust and affection Nelson felt for his chief editorial writer. At the same time, he had come to rely more and more on Dante Barton, the "socialist with a sour face and a warm heart" who escorted Irwin around the office and introduced him to the publisher.[42] To Haskell's dismay, Nelson seemed to approve of the radical views that Barton often expressed in his impassioned editorials. Haskell regarded his colleague as an unhealthy influence on the publisher. And beside Barton stood *his* bosom friend Frank Walsh, the son Nelson never had, his indispensable attorney, fixer, political emissary, and social conscience.

Walsh and Nelson had many things in common, one of them being a lack of due reverence for the judiciary, a similarity that came to light early in 1913, when a routine item in the *Star* about a local divorce trial nearly landed the publisher in jail. The story, though slightly garbled, plainly implied that the divorcée's ex-husband had been ordered to pay her lawyers' fees before she herself received any alimony. The *Star* properly criticized this "important ruling in favor of the divorce lawyers." The only difficulty was that Judge Joseph A. Guthrie had made no such ruling. Accordingly, he pronounced that the *Star* had defamed the court and cited both Nelson and his reporter for contempt. Baron Bill summoned the reporter and calmly inquired whether the article was substantially accurate. Assured that it was, he slammed a fleshy hand down on his desk and announced to the whole newsroom, "Then we will fight the writ!" Not only would the *Star* issue no retraction or apology, the proprietor himself would make a rare courtroom appearance.[43]

That, however, was as far as Nelson was prepared to go in making a public spectacle of himself. Although the *Star* printed thousands of words about the trial, he declined to take the stand in his own defense and rebuffed the Associated Press's request for a statement, wisely referring all questions to his attorney. There was never any doubt as to who would defend him. Walsh, the editor said, was "the only lawyer in town with the nerve and wit to fit exactly

SCENES IN JUDGE GUTHRIE'S COURT WHEN
NELSON WAS FOUND GUILTY OF CONTEMPT

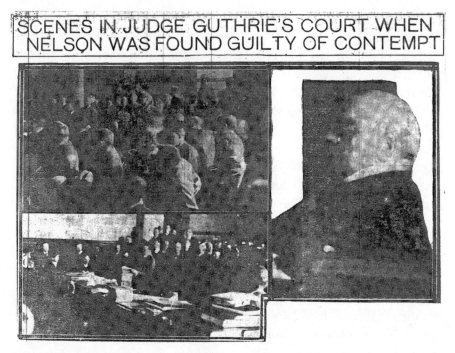

A *Kansas City Post* photographer caught a rare glimpse of Nelson (right) and attorney Frank P. Walsh (at podium, lower left) in Judge Guthrie's courtroom in early 1913: the "Old Lion of American journalism" confronts his accusers.

into my side of the case."[44] Unfortunately, Walsh was tied up in a sensational murder trial, defending the physician accused of murdering the reclusive philanthropist Thomas Swope. But it so happened that a member of the jury had suddenly been taken ill and the trial had been postponed, leaving Walsh free to take Judge Guthrie on.

The courtroom was packed on the day of the trial and all eyes were on Nelson. "Give 'em hell," he whispered audibly to his lead counsel. "I don't care what happens. . . . If they put me in jail I'll stay there till the ants carry me out through the keyhole." Walsh repeatedly moved to enter evidence in his client's defense, and each time the prosecution's objections were sustained. When Guthrie delivered himself of a lengthy and uncharacteristically eloquent opinion, Walsh smelled a rat. His partner stole behind the bench and confirmed that the judge was reading from a typescript. Bouncing to his feet, Walsh requested that the record show the judgment had been written in advance. For once, his motion was not denied. "The decision was in the breast of this court," Judge Guthrie freely admitted, "and it was as easy for this court to prepare its opinion at one time as another."[45]

The prosecuting attorney demanded that the judge impose an exemplary punishment. "For this defendant, a fine would be a farce. It would be like saying to him: 'Contribute a postage stamp to the public treasury and go on your way, printing all the mendacious articles you please.'" Guthrie sentenced Nelson to a symbolic day in jail and ordered him taken into custody forthwith. "Can't you wait until I get my hat? I won't run off," Nelson protested as the deputy sheriff seized his arm.[46] Thinking quickly, Walsh requested a ten-minute stay so he could run upstairs and obtain a writ of habeas corpus from the appeals court. Guthrie refused. Further ill-natured sparring ensued, until the judge grudgingly relented. The writ was duly issued and the editor released.

The national press gleefully pounced on the story of Nelson's run-in with the law. "Lock up the Old Lion of American journalism? Nonsense! There isn't a jail in Missouri big enough to hold him," thundered Grasty's *Baltimore Sun*. The *Post-Dispatch* condemned Judge Guthrie's contempt citation as "an outrageous exercise of arbitrary power" intended to muzzle the free press and shield the courts from public criticism. A "leading Socialist" who wrote to the *Star* to express support for Nelson had similar concerns. "What will happen to a small paper that tells the truth if Judge Guthrie can punish the *Star*? I believe that not only Kansas Citians, but every person in the United States should take up the fight." A letter from a seven-year-old Platte City girl gave the editor special pleasure: "My mamma read about the way those men tried to treat you, and then she waved the paper over her head and said, Hurrah for Mr. Walsh; and I asked who was Mr. Walsh, and what was the matter with him, and mamma said he was the fine Irish lawyer that stood up in front of you and made them leave you alone. So I say hurray for Mr. Walsh too, and hurrah for you, and hurrah for the *Star*, and I just hope you beat them good."[47]

Nelson decided he quite enjoyed his high-profile martyrdom and made himself conspicuous at the Associated Press's annual spring meeting in New York. A journalist friend reported to Walsh that "the Baron of Brush Creek was in our midst all week" and "got no end of notoriety because of his skirmish with Judge Guthrie. He was photographed and sketched and cartooned and biographied. Gus Seested was along and he too came in for a share of the spotlight. Only thing that made me peevish was that in the printed stories no word was said about the Baron's able and efficient chief counsel who alone was responsible for keeping the old pirate out of jail."[48]

On May 1 the Missouri Supreme Court ruled unanimously that Nelson was indeed guilty of contempt but threw out his sentence on the grounds that Judge Guthrie had violated his due process rights. Two months later, Walsh submitted a two-thousand-dollar bill for services rendered to the *Star*'s business manager. Seested coolly replied that he couldn't pay the invoice until it was approved by Nelson, who was recuperating from his ordeal in Massachusetts. In the meantime, the attorney might want to reconsider his "rather stiff" fee. "Maybe I am wrong about it but I feel Mr. Nelson will be disappointed when he receives this bill," Seested wrote, adding, "It is only due to my friendship for you that I hesitate to send the bill on to Mr. Nelson in its present state."[49] Walsh, aware that Seested and his colleagues resented his intimacy with their boss, apparently chose to ignore the warning.

Nelson's courtroom adventure added fuel to his campaign for free justice, confirming his belief that American justice was not only not free but not equal. As he explained to an interviewer while his appeal was pending, "A poor owner of a legal right gives a $5 fee to a $5 lawyer. A rich defender of a legal wrong gives a $5000 fee to a $5000 lawyer. The scales of a purchased justice tip to the wrong side."[50] This lopsided inequality had been revealed in Judge Guthrie's courtroom, though not in quite the way Nelson meant. Demonstrably in the wrong, he had paid his lawyer a rich man's fee to get him off on a technicality. If anyone else had been in the dock, Nelson might have called it not a victory for freedom of the press but a perversion of justice.

Nelson continued to support the Progressive Party, with both his paper and his purse, long after he had concluded that its moment had passed. Roosevelt, meanwhile, was once again lying low, writing his autobiography, contributing articles to the *Outlook*, and attempting to disassociate himself from what he viewed as a failed revolution. True to form, he was planning another trip abroad, this time to Brazil, to explore the unmapped River of Doubt. Whatever doubts he may have had about his immediate political future were concealed behind a screen of calculated ambiguity. On the eve of his departure in early October 1913, he assured supporters at New York's Roof Garden restaurant that he would "never abandon the principles to which we Progressives have pledged ourselves."[51] But Roosevelt's devotion to principles wasn't the issue; how much longer he would be content to remain the party's titular head was.

The day before Roosevelt and his entourage departed for South America, President Wilson signed into law a sweeping new tariff bill that significantly lowered duties across the board and added many items to the duty-free list; the anticipated loss of revenue would be offset by a controversial new income tax. Nelson welcomed the legislation, but Roosevelt considered it no better than the protectionist Payne-Aldrich bill it replaced. In a heated exchange of letters the previous summer, Nelson had reminded his candidate that they had almost come to a parting of the ways over the tariff question seven years earlier. The Progressives who had rejected the Underwood Tariff, he argued, had effectively voted to perpetuate the existing system of special privileges. He accused Roosevelt of parroting "the Taft argument which we all denounced a year or two ago." Distressed by their spat, Nelson told White that he couldn't "help feeling that the attitude of the Progressive congressmen is threatening the future of the party, for it not only is allying them with the standpat Republicans, but it also is putting them in the position before the country of playing politics."[52]

Although the tariff dispute didn't undermine the Progressive Party, as Nelson feared, his support for the bill cost him the services of his celebrity Washington correspondent. During the House debate, Henry Allen had filed a series of articles pointing out what he called the "jokers" in the Underwood bill. This outburst of unorthodoxy had elicited numerous telegrams from the home office forcefully reminding him of the *Star*'s unalterable policy. After the paper criticized the fourteen "standpat Progressives" who voted with the Republicans against the bill, Allen chucked it in and returned to Wichita. Wilson, he grumbled to White, had demonstrated "all the cock-sureness of a free trade theorist. He is honest, just as you say he is, and not entitled to any particular credit for being so. God made him that way. Neither is it a thing for us to get excited about. I do not counsel any system of attacking Wilson; but I do believe the hour for rapturous praise of him from Progressives is over, until we have seen how his free trade theories work out."[53]

At the end of August 1913, with Congress deliberating over tariff reform and a far-reaching overhaul of the banking system, Wilson's right-hand man brought the American ambassador to Germany to call on the *Star*'s publisher at his seaside house in Magnolia. "It pleases Col. Nelson to have me take members of the administration to meet him," Edward House recorded in his diary, "and in turn he is influencing Progressive senators to support both the Tariff and Currency Bills."[54] Nelson was neither too proud nor too independent to be flattered by House's attentions. With Roosevelt out of office, and soon to be halfway around the globe, he sat back and allowed himself to be courted by the new resident of the White House.

All summer long, House waged a quietly determined campaign to win Nelson's confidence. With his legislative program hanging in the balance, Wilson sorely needed the support of western progressives. Vacationing at Beverly, just down the coast from Nelson's "Willowbank," the presidential adviser made a point of dropping by casually as often as two or three times a week, sometimes alone, sometimes in the company of Washington bigwigs such as Treasury Secretary William McAdoo, Attorney General James McReynolds, and special counsel T. W. Gregory, who was heading the government's investigation into the New Haven Railroad.

House was an old hand at political matchmaking, having built a patronage machine that controlled the state house back home in Texas for more than a decade. He genuinely enjoyed Nelson's company, finding the aging editor "still full of fire and humor." A short, balding, weak-chinned man, House was a good listener and the soul of discretion. As he and Nelson relaxed on the veranda overlooking Lobster Cove, trading political small-talk and reminiscences, House would pull a letter out of his pocket from time to time and read excerpts to his host. Under pretense of dispensing privileged information, he avoided sensitive or controversial topics.[55] When Nelson disparaged William Jennings Bryan, Wilson's pacifist secretary of state, House held his tongue and heard him out. He had bigger fish to fry with the "old gentleman."

As House's unobtrusive wooing continued through the fall and winter, the *Star*'s attitude toward Wilson warmed perceptibly. A front-page editorial published in early November compared him to Roosevelt as a fighter for social justice. Two days later a letter to the editor, signed "Would Like to Be a Democrat," elevated Wilson and Roosevelt to positions alongside Nelson's revered Tilden and Cleveland. Both articles were "dictated by the Colonel himself" according to Walsh, who sent clippings to House with Nelson's blessing. House declared himself highly gratified by these tokens of journalistic esteem. "It is delightful to know that a man of Colonel Nelson's wide influence thinks of the President as he does," he wrote to Walsh. "I hope sometime to bring the two together and if Colonel Nelson should ever come East I hope that you will see that I am informed."[56]

Nelson and Wilson never did meet face to face, for the sun was already setting on the editor's day as an active political campaigner. But he told Walsh that "we are all tickled to death over the President and the Administration generally," adding, "Everything is lovely." Everything did seem to be going Nelson's way that winter. When Wilson signed the Federal Reserve Act just before Christmas, the *Star* went all out, declaring that the president had proved himself a "great leader" and an "effective statesman" in overcoming the entrenched opposition to both currency and tariff reform. The "Taft myth" had turned into the "Wilson actuality."[57]

By early January, Nelson judged the time was ripe to broach the subject he had been building up to: landing one of the new Federal Reserve banks for

Kansas City. In a letter to House, he boasted that few cities "outside the million population class"—not excepting St. Louis—could support "a newspaper that costs anything like as much as the *Star.*" As the "capital" of a vast inland trading territory, Kansas City was the logical site for a regional bank. Moreover, Nelson hinted, it would be politically advantageous for a progressive president to see that a bank was located in a region that was "the natural center of interest in progressive policies." Nelson's tone was light-hearted— at one point he joked that Secretary McAdoo should be thrown into the Missouri River if he failed to steer the reserve bank to Kansas City—but his intent was earnest.[58] Kansas City, he knew, could no longer depend on population increase alone to fuel its engine of economic growth. In order for the *Star* to retain its regional hegemony and overwhelming advantages as an advertising medium, the city would have to carve out an unassailable position as a commercial and financial hub.

In March 1914, with the deadline for allocating the regional banks fast approaching, Nelson made his final pitch. He dispatched Walsh to call on House in Washington, armed with a superfluous letter of introduction. "The easiest job in the world has been assigned to my particular friend Mr. Frank P. Walsh. He is to bring back with him the Kansas City reserve bank. But for all that it is such a simple matter, and for all that he usually gets what he goes after, Frank tells me that he is going to ask your counsel and help." Several days later, the editor received a "guarded message" relayed through Walsh, followed by a note from House assuring him that "unless some change is made, you will have your desires."[59] Soon thereafter the Treasury Department announced that both Kansas City and St. Louis had won the lottery, making Missouri the only state in the Union with two Federal Reserve banks. For Nelson, victory tasted all the sweeter for having been won on Walsh's coattails.

Nelson's "particular friend" needed no introduction to Washington officialdom in the spring of 1914. The flamboyant chairman of the United States Commission on Industrial Relations was a household name. Walsh's nomination for the post had shown that Wilson was serious in his desire to address the systemic injustices of unchecked capitalism. The country was in a parlous state. Militants on the left were challenging the labor movement's old-line leaders. Escalating industrial strife threatened to cripple the nation's economy and spark open class warfare. With Socialists in the mayors' offices in more than fifty American cities, even conservative business leaders had urged Wilson to take action before it was too late.

Walsh's work at the Bureau for Social Centers had not gone unnoticed in the upper echelons of the administration, and his vision of expanding the bureau into a permanent vehicle for achieving social and industrial justice suggested that he was just the man Wilson was looking for—a courtroom lawyer with impeccable progressive credentials, keen political instincts, a highly evolved social philosophy, and plenty of guts. Reformers on the far left of the political spectrum found Walsh equally attractive. No less an authority than Emma Goldman considered him "the most vital person" she met in Kansas City during the labor battles of the early 1900s. Walsh, she wrote, "could always be depended upon to aid an unpopular cause. By nature he was a fighter, his sympathies were with the persecuted."[60]

Labor and capital were more or less equally represented on the nine-member Industrial Relations Commission. While conscious of his role as mediator, chairman Walsh left no doubt as to whose side he was on. "We can't amend the Constitution," he told Dante Barton of the *Star*, "but we can put men in the courts who will be for the rights of man rather than for the wrongs of property. We can put a progressive sentiment behind the laws so strong that the judges, from the lowest to the highest courts, will be afraid to overthrow the people's will." George Creel, writing in *Collier's*, praised Walsh as the sort of man who "could put teeth in a Canton-flannel dog." Interviewed at his law office in Kansas City, Walsh assured Creel that the commission wasn't a stalking-horse for socialism. "It *is* a tremendous forward step, yet, when one stops to think, it is only what the Government has been doing for crops and animals the last quarter of a century. Considering the time and money spent on cattle diseases and the boll weevil, it isn't such a radical thing to search for the germs of social hate and the causes of human discontent and unhappiness, is it?"[61]

Creel soon moved to Washington as a member of the commission's high-powered research staff. Barton, too, expressed a wish to join Walsh's "group of conspirators against the peace and dignity of things as they are," asking the chairman to "put in an extra pinch of dynamite" for him.[62] The incendiary nature of the commission's inquiry became clear as it shuttled from coast to coast, taking testimony from labor leaders, captains of industry, academic experts, and ordinary men and women. Over the next year and a half, more than seven hundred witnesses would take the stand, ranging from "Big Bill" Haywood, Morris Hillquit, and Samuel Gompers to Andrew Carnegie, Henry Ford, and George Perkins. This long-running political road show proved as mesmerizing to Americans of the Progressive Era as the McCarthy and Watergate hearings would to their descendants. Walsh combined the roles of prosecutor and father confessor. Boundlessly energetic, by turns courteous and hectoring, he held center stage at the commission's public hearings and maneuvered behind the scenes to maintain a precarious consensus.

Riveting as they were, the proceedings might have remained a sideshow of Wilson's hectically productive first term had events not played into Walsh's hands. In April 1914, barely six months after the Senate confirmed his appointment, a strike at a Rockefeller-owned coal mine in Ludlow, Colorado, erupted in appalling violence. Some two dozen men, women, and children were killed when state troopers, acting in concert with private militia, stormed a tent city occupied by the strikers' families. The "Ludlow Massacre" dramatized the hazardous and degrading conditions in the mining camps more vividly than any testimony the commission had so far heard. Creel dashed to the scene, denounced those responsible for the tragedy as "traitors to the people" and "accessories to the murder of babes," and urgently wired Walsh to investigate.[63]

In December 1914 the full commission finally repaired to Colorado for two weeks of hearings. Walsh recognized it as a golden opportunity to galvanize public opinion, telling his colleagues that if the sessions went well, they would "stamp our commission all over with success." The hearings went very well indeed, unearthing a mine of evidence of corporate culpability and ruthlessness. Walsh was shaken by the harrowing accounts of the miners' plight. Before leaving Denver, he took a parting shot at the villains in a nationally syndicated newspaper article titled "No Santa at the Mines."[64] (The mine operators countered by belatedly distributing Christmas candy to three thousand miners' children.) Then he hastened back to New York to preside over the next round of hearings, at which the commission would take testimony from John D. Rockefeller, Jr.

It had been less than a decade since the senior Rockefeller's unforgettable run-in with Walsh's fellow Missourian in the landmark Standard Oil case. Herbert Hadley's intrepid pursuit of the fugitive tycoon, and Rockefeller's ignominious defeat at the hands of federal antitrust prosecutors, had stained the family escutcheon. Junior proved himself more adept at public relations than his father. He strode confidently into the hearing room in New York's City Hall, approaching the tribunal with disarming deference. Spying Mother Jones in the crowd, he stuck out his hand and invited the legendary labor organizer to his office, saying, "There are so many things on which you can enlighten me." Polite but unshakable, Rockefeller denied any knowledge of conditions on or under the ground at his company's mines. He was deeply distressed, as anyone must be, by the reports he had read in the newspapers.

But company directors, he insisted, were responsible only for financial affairs. He himself hadn't so much as set foot in Colorado for ten years.[65]

Rockefeller's plea of ignorance, coupled with his convincing show of magnanimity and contrition, worked like a charm. Even Mother Jones, who had been jailed and held incommunicado during the Ludlow strike, was seized by an irresistible urge to forgive. To Walsh, however, the performance smacked of an elaborate sham. He had seen too much of corporate malfeasance to swallow Rockefeller's story whole. While he and the increasingly irate oil magnate traded insults in the press, Walsh set his detectives to work. In the spring of 1915, they hit pay dirt. Letters and company records subpoenaed by the commission proved beyond reasonable doubt not only that Rockefeller had been fully aware of what mine operators in Colorado were doing in his name, but that he had unreservedly approved the strong-arm tactics used against the strikers.

Walsh made the incriminating documents public at a press conference in Kansas City on April 23. Although several commissioners feared that the investigation was turning into a personal vendetta, they had no choice but to haul Rockefeller back in for a second grilling. This time Walsh took off his gloves. Displaying his formidable inquisitorial skills, he bore down relentlessly on the slight, boyish-looking plutocrat. To critics who chided him for bullying the likable witness, Walsh retorted that the commission had been created to investigate the causes of labor unrest, not to serve as an impartial court of law. "I am sure you will not think it boastful when I say that I turned the young man inside out, and left him without a single justification for anything that took place in Colorado," he wrote to Barton, adding that he had naturally had to "get a little rough at times" in the interest of revealing the truth.[66]

Walsh vowed that the commission's final report to Congress would not sit on a shelf gathering dust. But by the time it came out, in late summer of 1915, the European conflict was monopolizing newspaper headlines. Suddenly, social and industrial justice seemed of less pressing importance than "war preparedness." Walsh and his colleagues hadn't even been able to agree among themselves. Bitterly divided, they compromised by issuing three separate reports. The "majority" or "staff" report—which Walsh again saw fit to release in the *Star*'s hospitable backyard—endorsed a raft of legislation long championed by progressives, Single Taxers, and other reformers, including a steeply graded inheritance tax, a vigorous crack-down on monopolists, a tax on nonproductive land, and a guaranteed right to collective bargaining. The commission was unanimous in its view that American workers had been denied their fair share of the wealth generated by the nation's expanding economy

Organized labor lionized Frank Walsh for exposing John D. Rockefeller, Jr.'s complicity in the 1914 Ludlow Massacre. John Lawson, head of the United Mine Workers, represents the victims of the tragedy in this cartoon from the *Machinists' Monthly Journal.*

over the past quarter-century. Even agriculture, the cornerstone of the Jeffersonian republic, had been taken over by a form of "industrial feudalism." These conditions, if unrelieved, would lead either to "active revolt" or to "sullen hatred" between haves and have-nots. Either way, the commissioners warned, the widening gap between rich and poor posed a grave threat to American democracy.[67]

The Industrial Relations Commission had given Americans an unprecedented snapshot of their society, plumbing its heart of darkness and illuminating its unfulfilled promise. Frank Walsh, scourge of Missouri's corrupt Democracy, defender of the weak and oppressed, friend of Joe Shannon and Tom Pendergast, of Emma Goldman and Jacob Billikopf, of Harry Tammen and William Rockhill Nelson, had given the performance of a lifetime. The *Star*'s "fighting idealist" had argued the case for far-reaching reform more compellingly than any newspaper or politician. Commissioner Daisy Harriman refused to sign the majority report, deeming it irresponsibly radical, but her husband considered the commission's eleven volumes of testimony nothing less than "the comédie humaine of America." The drama that had played itself out under Walsh's direction "had to be staged," he told her, "and your unjudicial chairman was just the impresario that was needed."[68]

In late 1913, while the commission was preparing to hold its first public hearings, Walsh returned to Kansas City to lend a hand in Nelson's campaign for nonpartisan city government. The day after Christmas, he told three hundred members of the elite City Club that, regardless of their party affiliations, it was their civic duty to nominate a ticket pledged to "commission" government in the forthcoming municipal election. The *Star* was backing the nominally nonpartisan ticket headed by the former Republican mayor fondly known to Senator James Reed as "Darius Disastrous Brown." Reed, spokesman for the Pendergast interests, charged that the reform ticket had been "born in the *Star* office," with Nelson as "its father and its mother and its wet nurse." That spring, when Democrat Henry Jost trounced Brown by ten thousand votes, nearly doubling the margin of his victory two years earlier, Nelson consoled himself by reflecting that many voters had scratched the Democratic and Republican party-line tickets. "Commission government is right. Nonpartisan city government is right. In the end they must win," the *Star* proclaimed in a front-page editorial.[69]

With plans for government reform back on hold, Baron Bill shifted his attention to another pet cause. The Metropolitan Street Railway, whose bid for a forty-two-year franchise had been rejected at the polls in 1909, was back again with a more modest request for a thirty-year extension. The directors took the precaution of hiring Nelson's friend and Rockhill neighbor Frank Hagerman to represent the company. In a lengthy exchange of letters later published in the *Star*, the attorney argued, pleaded, and negotiated with the editor, to no avail.[70] Nelson had no taste for compromise. After more than thirty years of battling the Corrigan traction dynasty, he wasn't about to lay down his arms.

So exercised did Nelson get over the Met's latest "franchise grab" that he stayed home from Magnolia that summer to lead the fight in person. This time, however, Walsh wasn't at his side, having joined party bosses Tom Pendergast and Tom Marks in a bipartisan effort to grant the Met's wishes. Both sides dug into their bags of dirty tricks. Profranchise forces put out a Yiddish-language circular bizarrely alleging that Baron Bill's opposition was part of a plot to make himself "czar" of Kansas City and expel its Jewish population. The *Star* published a series of blatantly racist stories accusing the Corrigan interests of crudely attempting to buy the black vote. In the increasingly ugly fracas, franchise opponents found it expedient to call on one or two men from Nelson's "son-of-a-bitch" list for assistance. The editor acquiesced stoically, muttering, "The bed is getting damned lousy but I guess we will have to sleep in it."[71] In July 1914 the people rendered their verdict, decisively approving the franchise.

Exhausted, Nelson withdrew to Colorado Springs for a belated family vacation. He and his wife revisited old haunts in a chauffeur-driven touring car. Smarting from his recent rebuffs at the polls, the seventy-three-year-old editor sensed that his long insurgency was entering its final phase. The outbreak of war in Europe could mean only one thing: the world he had known, railed against, and battled to reform was falling apart. He scarcely knew whether to cheer or weep. He and his fellow progressives had eagerly awaited the twilight of the old gods, but now it was nigh they feared what the new dawn might bring. William Allen White, who was summering at his cabin in Estes Park when Archduke Ferdinand was assassinated, instinctively realized that the looming crisis would nip America's reform movement in the bud.

Nelson's nose-to-the-front optimism never quite deserted him, however. A. B. Macdonald, the veteran reporter who accompanied him to Colorado, recalled that the editor "had an inexhaustible store of anecdotes and good stories, and his soul overflowed with cheerfulness and laughter." The old campaigner spoke affectionately about the men on the *Star* "force" and declared that "as long as he lived the *Star* would keep on fighting for the right things, regardless of all." That summer, prohibition was at the top of his agenda. "If they will bring me one man, just one, that whisky has ever benefited," he told Macdonald, "I will give up my fight against it; and they can have the whole country to search in for that one man."[72] The editor was preaching to the converted. A ruddy-cheeked, owl-eyed Canadian of Scots descent, Macdonald had forsaken his Baptist upbringing to take up the boozy life of an investigative reporter. But despite his penchant for poker and luridly sensational crime stories, he remained at heart a prudish man for whom alcohol quickly lost its appeal. In the summer of 1914, he and Nelson were transforming themselves from confirmed teetotalers to ardent prohibitionists.

As the guns of August exploded across the Atlantic, Nelson took aim at the "brewers, saloon keepers and rum sellers" back home in Jackson County. Egged on by Macdonald and Ralph Stout, he instructed his "sob and sorrow writers" to break out their "most destructive war implements" in the battle to make the county dry. The "whiskey crowd," he reminded his lieutenants, had always been the *Star*'s "active and vicious enemies. We must smash them." He "would rather win the fight against booze than have all the millions of all the brewers on earth." After a hard-fought (but, by Kansas City standards, singularly tame) election, the dries declared victory. The *Star* crowed that it had been "a case of the saloon against the home—and the home won." Flushed with euphoria, Nelson telegraphed his editors: "God moves in a mysterious way His wonders to perform. How much brighter the political sky than two weeks ago."[73]

As his personal day of judgment drew near, Nelson took solace in the thought that God was in heaven, even if all wasn't quite right in the world. Never a conventionally religious man, he was clearly undergoing a spiritual awakening. When Helen Keller called at the *Star* office in the spring of 1914, the normally thick-skinned editor was overcome with emotion. "My dear little Angel," he addressed the blind woman in a letter, "when you visited here I couldn't help feeling distressed over the way the Creator had treated you. But after your visit and after reading your article I have been reconciled. As the old hymn says, 'God moves in a mysterious way, his wonders to perform,' and there seems no way for great good to be accomplished except through great suffering."[74]

The article that triggered Nelson's effusion appeared on the front page of the *Star* on April 28. "A Plea from Helen Keller" started in the upper right-hand corner, traditionally reserved for the day's lead story. The subject of her bold appeal was venereal disease, a major cause of blindness in children. "It has been known for more than twenty-five years that this disease is preventable. But this knowledge has been kept almost exclusively as the possession of physicians," Keller wrote. Abandoning the clinical language of the social worker, she called for Victorian inhibitions to be cast aside in the name of progress and enlightenment. "We must all emancipate ourselves from the shackles of authority. We must look at life for ourselves, look at it honestly, fearlessly, compassionately. Only when we so look at life shall we take the first step towards our salvation. Not by hiding the ignorance, the selfishness, the unholy passions, the inhumanity of man to man, can we bring about our social deliverance."

Several editors had turned Keller away before Nelson invited her to break the taboo surrounding venereal disease in his "family" newspaper. There was, Keller later recalled, "an obstinate silence concerning those social evils throughout the country, and a young woman was not supposed to speak openly on the subject. Therefore when I tried to have an article printed about venereal disease and methods of preventing blindness, it was rejected. I called on Col. Nelson, the editor of the 'Kansas City Star' and pleaded with him to do what he could for the keeping of the light in babies' eyes. His abrupt, rugged individuality awed me, but to my surprise he wept as I pictured to him the tragedy which condemned countless little ones to lifelong darkness simply because unpleasant truths were shunned. He ordered my article to be published in the 'Star,' and the movement began which disseminates the knowledge that saves."[75]

Calling Keller "the sweetest, finest, noblest spirit in the world," Nelson wrote, with uncharacteristic humility, "When I think of what you have accomplished and then of what I had accomplished at your age—and for that matter in the course of quite a long life—I feel absolutely ashamed of myself."

But Keller was no sweetly inoffensive angel of mercy. As Nelson well knew, she was also an avenging angel, a fiery crusader for women's rights with close ties to the radical wing of the labor movement. A card-carrying Socialist, she had vigorously protested Fred Warren's conviction in 1909 on charges of sending defamatory material through the mail. In a letter printed in both the *Appeal to Reason* and George Creel's *Independent,* she defended Warren in language that must have warmed the cockles of Nelson's heart. "One need not be a Socialist to realize the significance, the gravity, not of Mr. Warren's offense, but of the offense of the judges against the constitution, and against democratic rights. . . . It has been my duty, my life-work, to study physical blindness, its causes and its prevention. . . . What surgery of politics, what antiseptic of common sense and right thinking shall be applied to cure the blindness of our judges and to prevent the blindness of the people who are the court of last resort?"[76]

Far from being put off by Keller's political views, Nelson found them inspirational. For years he had been confounding the conventional wisdom about the conservatism of the rich by becoming increasingly liberal. Although his political thinking was far too undisciplined to make doctrinal socialism attractive, he realized that the progressive insurgents had more in common with the Socialists than with any other established political party. After the 1912 election, the *Star* noted with apparent equanimity that the Socialist vote in Jackson County, in line with a nationwide trend, was nearly double that of four years earlier. Victor Berger, the defeated Socialist congressman from Wisconsin, was singled out for his "patriotism," "fine character," and "fidelity to the principles he believed in." Barton's low-key campaign to win his boss's heart and mind was paying off. No longer did the *Star* disparage socialism as a heresy promulgated by delusional populists. It was a respectable political philosophy that deserved a fair hearing. "If socialism is not all good, but there is that in it which will help to a better adjustment of society, then that good in it should be seized by society," the paper argued.[77]

Such sentiments were distinctly unpopular in a city beset by spreading social unrest and labor strife. As Socialists and union organizers, anarchists and Wobblies, assorted radicals and other undesirables moved in, the authorities swiftly clamped down. By the spring of 1914, the new "model" municipal farm was overflowing with IWW men and women who had fallen afoul of draconian vagrancy laws or had the temerity to protest the harsh penalties meted out by the courts for disturbing the peace. In this volatile environment, Nelson unhesitatingly threw the *Star*'s pages open to unorthodox, unsettling, and often radical points of view.

One day in the summer of 1914, a young Russian man who taught Hebrew at Temple B'nai Jehudah called on Haskell in the newsroom. Isaac Don Levine proposed to write "a series of homespun pieces" for the *Star* "on life in the United States as seen by an immigrant." Haskell liked the idea and decided to give the novice newsman a chance. Over the next few weeks, Levine's fictionalized "Letters from an Immigrant" received prominent play in the paper. Casting himself as an Old Country rube coming to terms with a sophisticated alien culture, Levine marveled at the city's modern amenities, from skyscrapers, motion pictures, cheap newspapers, and home mortgages to tree-lined boulevards, well-equipped schools, efficient mail service, and free public libraries. But these wonders of American civilization didn't blind him to the dark side of paradise as represented by political bosses, quack doctors, lynchings, saloons, vice, and labor strife.[78]

In Levine's chatty "letters" to the home country, the *Star* hit upon a clever device to air radical opinions without appearing to endorse them. Levine warned that "the clamor of the masses" was "getting louder and louder" owing to the "high cost of living." Americans were reluctant to admit that industrial unrest was "not a result of immigration, but of unspeakable conditions" in factories and plants. They had yet to learn that labor strife was "not a local issue but an international one" and that "the social system of mankind" was destined to undergo a "great change" in the not-too-distant future. Four years after Kansas Citians created the Board of Public Welfare, "the younger generation in this great democratic republic" showed little interest in "social and humanitarian problems," Levine observed. On the other hand, labor unions, municipal ownership of utilities, and other reforms proved that the "seeds of socialism" were being planted "under the legal protectorship of the government" even while "the climax of capitalism is reached in many branches of industry."[79]

To Levine (who would later metamorphose into a shrill anticommunist), Kansas City on the eve of World War I seemed a veritable hotbed of radicalism. When Eugene Debs came to town in the fall of 1914, Levine looked on as the "fiery socialist evangelist" practically "brought the roof down with his forceful denunciation of the iniquities of capitalism." A few months later he heard the anarchist Alexander Berkman give a dryly academic "lecture on surplus value and a critique of the Marxist cult of statism." But it took more than soapbox revolutionaries to distract Kansas Citians from the *Star*'s temperance crusade and the "cold war" between Nelson and Pendergast, Levine found. In any case, "all the kings and rulers of Europe were remote shadows in Kansas City as compared with the glorified figure of Teddy Roosevelt, who, as leader

Theodore Roosevelt (back seat, left) and Irwin Kirkwood parked in front of Oak Hall, September 1914. As the Progressive Party languished, Roosevelt and Nelson came to a parting of the ways.

of the Bull Moose movement, cut a Napoleonic pattern in the minds of the populace."[80]

Nelson and Roosevelt met for the last time in September 1914. Two years after their quixotic stand at "Armageddon," the Progressives were fighting for their very survival as a political force. Roosevelt had reluctantly agreed to make one more campaign swing in aid of the party's candidates in the Midwest. On the hustings the Bull Moose was his old, electrifying self, but between speeches he often seemed moody and withdrawn. Driving from Wichita to Hutchison, Kansas, in Irwin Kirkwood's open touring car, he sat in the back seat singing softly to himself and tapping out the rhythm with his hand on the side of the car. Lost in thought, he hardly missed a beat when the chauffeur slammed on the brakes at a partially obscured grade crossing, narrowly averting a fatal collision with a speeding train.[81]

Back in Kansas City, Nelson laid on a supper for his old comrade at Oak Hall. According to one witness, Roosevelt "was in high spirits and the flow of conversation, intimate and of infinite variety, lasted for hours." But the spirit of auld lang syne couldn't disguise the wedge that time and politics had driven between the two men. Unbeknownst to his guest, Nelson had recently instructed his managing editor to put out the word that the *Star* would "always avail itself of the wagon going the farthest its way, whether driven by Roosevelt or Wilson." A few weeks earlier the editor had privately reassured Roosevelt that although the *Star* was "getting on fairly well" with the new Democratic administration, he continued to hope that "things will work around so that either in 1916 or 1920 there will be just two parties—the Progressive and Conservative—and that we can still be carrying your flag."[82]

Roosevelt, however, had other plans for retaking the White House. For some time he had been trimming his sails, sidling up to the Republicans, and mending fences with his old friends on Wall Street. Not long after his visit to Oak Hall, he signaled his intention to abandon the Progressives' slowly sinking ship. In a long, self-serving letter to William Allen White, but meant for Nelson's eyes as well, he reflected that the new party had failed to capture the voters' imagination. It was obvious that

> the bulk of our people are heartily tired of me and that as far as making political speeches or taking part in any more party activities is concerned, my duty for the time being is to obey the directions of the New Bedford whaling captain when he told his mate that all he wanted from him was "silence; and damn little of that!" From the night of election two years ago I have felt that the chances were overwhelming against the permanence of the Progressive party. . . . When we failed to establish ourselves at the very outset as the second party, it became overwhelmingly probable that politics would soon sink back into the conditions that had been normal for the previous half century, that is, into a two-party system, the Republicans and the Democrats alternating in the first and second place. Under such circumstances it was likely that we would keep only the man of high principle and good reasoning power and the cranks. The men in between left us.[83]

The "wave of reform" that Roosevelt claimed to have set in motion in his first term had crested and spent itself. "While I was President, we had succeeded in keeping it as a sane and constructive movement. From the time I ceased being President, it went every which way. It was quite impossible that a movement in which LaFollette occupied a prominent place should not in the long run alienate and disgust decent men. The insurgents in Congress were good for nothing except to insurge." Although Roosevelt judged that the country was "sick and tired of reform," he told White that he remained optimistic. "The people are sure to wake up in the end. Our cause will eventually triumph, even although under other leaders and under another name. And personally I shall, if only in the ranks, fight for everyone of our principles as long as I live."[84]

Nelson received a copy of the letter from White just before Thanksgiving. He had few illusions left where Roosevelt was concerned and took his defection in stride. Calling Haskell to his desk, he dictated an equable reply to be relayed through White. Nelson's "general idea," Haskell paraphrased,

> is that T.R. has faced the situation frankly and as it is. He has a sort of hunch that what Roosevelt says about himself applies to the *Star* as well, and that what people expect of it is civility and darn little of that. So for the present he is going to try to restrain the *Star* from having opinions on all sorts of political subjects although he recognizes that his restraints do not always last as long as he expects them to in the first place. He quite agrees that the country is in a reactionary mood and that it is getting to the point where it resents advice of all sorts and wants a rest. He is inclined to think that Wilson recognizes this fact and is trying to put the soft pedal on but he rather feels that Wilson is one of these restless men and won't succeed in being quiet very long.[85]

Nelson was no more successful at muting himself. Even now that his body was racked with chronic pain and he could barely make anyone out at twenty paces, he stepped up his agitation for free justice, state-run charities, unemployment relief, a citywide polling place to ensure clean elections, and other radical innovations. Dissatisfied with the piecemeal reforms the progressives had achieved at the state and local levels, he insisted that modern industrial problems demanded action by the federal government and stopped just shy of calling for the kind of welfare state that the *Star*, with its traditional emphasis on individual freedom and responsibility, had long resisted. Tragedies like the Ludlow Massacre had brought the fundamental inequities of the capitalist system into sharp relief. "I am never afraid that the men on top of the mine cannot take care of themselves," the editor said. "My concern is for the men at the bottom of the mine, digging the coal."[86]

Long before the onset of his final illness, Nelson had been methodically putting his affairs in order and trying to decide what to do with the *Star* after his death. Seested, with whom he often discussed the matter, received the impression that Nelson thought the paper could not continue without him. In any case, Nelson envisioned another kind of immortality for himself, something along the lines Andrew Carnegie had achieved with his lavish bequests for public libraries. Although he wasn't in Carnegie's league as a plutocrat, his comparatively modest fortune of five or ten millions would go a long way in Kansas City. He assigned his staff to research the wills of wealthy men around the country. Meanwhile, behind their backs, he was rewriting his own testament in a way that his close associates would come to regard as a betrayal.

On April 16, 1914, the *Star*'s owner filed a new will in the Jackson County Courthouse. Under its terms—known at the time only to his attorney, Frank Rozzelle, his wife, daughter, and a handful of intimates—virtually his entire estate would one day go toward purchasing works of art for a yet-to-be-built public gallery. Nelson provided munificently for Ida and Laura, leaving the newspaper in trust to them for the rest of their lives, and more modestly for other members of his immediate family. But neither his faithful "helpers" at the *Star* nor his long-time domestic servants received so much as a penny. After the deaths of his wife and daughter, the *Star* was to be sold outright to the highest bidder. Nelson took pains to ensure that the contents of the new will remained secret, having it witnessed by two loyal retainers: Pete Larson, his veteran estate manager, and editorial secretary Percy W. Smith.

It hadn't always been thus. Sometime before 1908, Nelson had drawn up another will that reflected a very different attitude. In it he had left the *Star* in trust to his employees and designated staff trustees to run it after his death. This was consistent with his often-stated belief that the *Star*, as a public trust, was not his private property to dispose of however he chose. What prompted his change of heart can only be conjectured. As late as the summer of 1914, he told A. B. Macdonald of his hope that the *Star* would still be "a militant, fighting force in the community" a century hence. Yet that winter Gus Seested came away from the editor's sickbed convinced that Nelson would have suspended publication on the day of his death without remorse if he could have found any other way to support his family.[87]

Speculation about Nelson's motives in establishing the art gallery that bears his name would continue for decades. The official version, enshrined in accounts ultimately traceable to Stout, Haskell, and their associates, was that he had intended to leave his estate for art ever since his life-altering European sabbatical of 1895–1896. This may be true—after all, one of the first things Nelson did when he got back from Paris was to open a gallery of high-art reproductions—but it still doesn't explain why he waited until 1914 to change his will. The proximate cause of that decision almost certainly lies closer at hand. And when one unravels the warp of Nelson's life that winter and spring, one name stands out like a brightly colored thread: Frank Walsh.

More than a "particular friend," the irrepressible impresario of the Commission on Industrial Relations had become the editor's moral compass, his envoy to Colonel House and President Wilson, the steady arm he grasped when Roosevelt faltered. Nelson had always admired Walsh's agile legal mind, the "nerve and wit" that had spared him the indignity of a jail sentence. On such a vital matter as his will, he would surely have sought his old lawyer's advice. The firm of Rozzelle and Walsh was no more, but the former partners remained friends. Had Nelson wanted to put their three heads together, he had any number of opportunities, including Walsh's visit to Kansas City in December 1913. Walsh's speech to the City Club dwelled mostly on Nelson's good works and was not, as he admitted to Billikopf, "intended to tell the audience too much about Commission Government."[88] Why Walsh should have chosen to eulogize Baron Bill as a public benefactor on that particular occasion is unclear—unless, that is, he knew something his listeners didn't.

The evidence that Walsh persuaded Nelson to change his will is purely circumstantial. What is not in doubt is that the men who had been led to believe that they would inherit the paper after Nelson's death felt bitterly disappointed and held Walsh in some way accountable. They didn't merely disapprove of Walsh's politics; they resented the way he had insinuated himself into their employer's trust and affection. Haskell felt his disinheritance personally as well as professionally. His relationship with his missionary father, who died in March 1914, had been respectful but physically and emotionally distant. In many ways, he felt closer to his capricious, paternalistic boss, and Nelson reciprocated. In the summer of 1914, Nelson sent his associate editor some token of appreciation—a "certificate of usefulness" he called it—for coordinating the *Star*'s commission government campaign. When Haskell protested that he didn't deserve it, Nelson replied in words that came straight from the heart: "It has always been the policy of the *Star* to cut out love and affection and divide with those who know how to make a newspaper. Not that love and affection is wanting and it is mighty fine when one finds in a good friend a splended [*sic*] man."[89]

All that summer in Colorado, which would be his last, the editor was in an uncharacteristically nostalgic frame of mind. To Macdonald, his traveling companion, he reminisced about the men on the *Star* with open affection. "You can't find their equal in all America. There is not a man among them for whom I have not a high personal regard." The irony of Nelson's mellowness wasn't lost on Macdonald, who had once quit the *Star* out of frustration at Nelson's niggardly wages. Was the old man growing sentimental with age? Or was he, perhaps subconsciously, making amends for cutting Macdonald and his colleagues out of his will? Not even his closest acquaintances could read his thoughts. "I happened to know Mr. Nelson fairly well in his later years," recalled Haskell. "But I never was really acquainted with him. Nobody was. He was always a well of undiscovered possibilities. Even to himself he must have remained a good deal of a mystery."[90]

For Haskell and his associates, Nelson's last will and testament would be the central mystery of his life. Why would this journalistic genius risk letting his great creation fall into the hands of an unsympathetic outsider? Why hadn't he emulated Joseph Pulitzer, who left two vigorously liberal newspapers and a school of journalism as his monuments? His lieutenants were willing and able to soldier on. Hadn't they been fighting Nelson's battles for thirty-five years, fleshing out his ideas, spreading his gospel, covering the town so thoroughly that it was said if something hadn't been reported in the *Star*, it hadn't happened?

Casting about for clues, they came up with contradictory explanations for his behavior. The Old Man had gone senile toward the end of his life. Pain had clouded his judgment. He was no longer responsible for his actions. His sound progressivism had run amok and exposed him to dangerously radical influences. He was selfish at heart and couldn't bear the thought of anyone else running, much less owning, his newspaper. He didn't believe in free lunches; no one should gain profit or credit from an enterprise that he hadn't started from scratch. He was opposed in principle to hereditary wealth and wanted the fortune he had amassed to be returned to the people. His achievements as a "city builder" were at least as important as his journalistic legacy. He had intended to endow an art gallery for the city for years; the only question was how.

One equally plausible solution to the riddle was never mentioned, perhaps because it cut uncomfortably close to the bone: Nelson didn't trust his would-be successors to carry the newspaper forward in the direction he had set in the last years of his life. They were too cautious, too conservative, too conventional in their outlooks. Seested's business acumen had been crucial to the paper's success, but he and Ralph Stout had never been idea men. Nor, Nelson confided to Haskell, had T. W. Johnston, even before he took to drink. Haskell himself was a first-rate journalist and a "splended man" but, alas, not one of nature's insurgents. As for Irwin Kirkwood, he was hardly the kind of man Nelson would have chosen to publish a real estate journal, let alone the *Star*. The more advanced the editor's social and political attitudes became, the more isolated he felt from the men who worked under him. Could it be that Nelson's final will represented not a breach of faith *with* his employees, after all, but a loss of faith *in* them?

By late fall of 1914 Nelson was visibly failing. Tiring easily, he reduced his working hours and stopped staying late on Saturday nights to see the paper to bed. Associates noticed him pacing the floor beside his big desk in the corner of the newsroom. Often he seemed to be rubbing his side, though he complained of nothing more serious than indigestion. It was some time before doctors diagnosed the problem as liver disease—often brought on, ironically, by excessive drinking.

As winter set in, Nelson bowed to the inevitable and stayed home altogether. He had telephones installed around Oak Hall and bombarded his staff with "suggestions" for articles and editorials. But although his mind remained sharp and his voice still boomed imperiously, his massive body was wasting away. In early March, an attack of uremic poisoning sent him into a coma. He hung on for five more weeks, fading in and out of consciousness, while messages from well-wishers flooded in. Nelson was touched but not mollified. "Those messages of sympathy and appreciation have been fine," he whispered one night to his son-in-law. "But remind the men at the office of one thing. The interests that are against Kansas City are still in control. The fight on them mustn't let up, no matter if they do say nice things about me."[91]

At last, Nelson took matters into his own hands and ordered his doctors to cut off the saline solution that had been keeping death at bay. After lingering for five days, unconscious, he gave up the ghost at two in the morning on April 13, 1915. Frank Walsh was in Chicago when he heard the news. In a telegram to the *Star*, he saluted Nelson's "grand fight" for the "weak and oppressed everywhere," pointedly adding that "those of us who knew him best may be solaced by the fact that we did understand and appreciate him to the utmost while he lived."[92] With that shot across the bow, Walsh adjourned the Industrial Relations Commission and hurried to Kansas City for the funeral.

PART 2

INTERREGNUM

Irwin Kirkwood and
Laura Nelson Kirkwood.

CHAPTER 5

---◆---

Bully Pulpits

Never had William Rockhill Nelson looked more serenely baronial than on the day of his funeral, as his body lay in state in Oak Hall's dark-paneled library. Cascading banks of flowers, climbing nearly to the ceiling, engulfed the coffin. President Wilson sent a wreath of white carnations. A hoard of mourners overflowed the big house and spilled out onto the grounds, where trees and shrubs were "just budding into seasonal life." Thousands of men, women, and children, "bankers and barbers and newsboys, judges and laborers and the three hundred members of the Commercial Club," had come to pay their last respects to the "big boss" and "newspaper dictator."[1] After seventy-four turbulent years, his spirit was finally at rest.

April 16, 1915, a Friday, was warm and sunny. The *Star* put out its final edition at noon, then shut down for the rest of the day. Employees had had a private viewing of the casket that morning. Eight men from various departments of the paper had been chosen to serve as pallbearers alongside Pete Larson and Ben Bondeson, Nelson's long-time domestics. Throughout the city, flags flew at half-staff on stores, offices, and government buildings. Schools were dismissed at midday and

> *"Nelson's greatest victories, like the millenniums he was constantly expecting to come marching at his orders, were always just around the next corner. He never transcended his insurgency."*
>
> —Henry J. Haskell

children lined the streets to catch a glimpse of the cortège. The Board of Trade and Livestock Exchange suspended operations in observance of the funeral, as did banks, courts, and post offices. Even the Metropolitan Street Railway, Nelson's nemesis, brought its cars to a halt for five minutes when the service began at 2:30.

Bishop Cameron Mann had returned from Florida to deliver the eulogy. The former rector of Grace Church recalled his departed friend as "in the radical sense of the words, democrat and republican, insisting on personal rights and civic responsibility. He was an American of reddest blood, with a consuming zeal to make this splendid city where he dwelt a full realization of the American ideal." Other tributes streamed in from great and small, and the *Star* printed them all. Theodore Roosevelt hailed the editor as "one of the foremost citizens of the United States, one of the men whom our republic could least afford to spare." In the lower house of the City Council, Speaker Miles Bulger, the scrappy "Little Czar" of the Second Ward, introduced a resolution lauding Baron Bill as "a great soldier" who "never hauled down his colors or recognized that the day was lost."[2]

As usual, the *Star* reserved the last word for itself—some fifteen thousand words, to be more precise. Nelson's obituary consumed two full pages of the April 13 edition. Autocratic to the last, the famously publicity-shy editor had made sure it said no less—and no more—than he wanted it to say. Mostly written by Ralph Stout, Henry Haskell, and A. B. Macdonald, the editor's death notice had been set in type weeks earlier and brought to Oak Hall for Nelson's approval. In the emotion of the hour, few readers noticed how much the newsmen had discreetly omitted or the pains they had taken to explain away their chief's eccentric "hobbies" and other all-too-human foibles.

Frank Walsh wasn't taken in. He who had been one of Nelson's most trusted friends and agents, who had kept him out of jail and helped open his eyes to the plight of the underclass, received barely a passing mention in the official account of the editor's life. The new regime at the *Star* seemed determined to place Nelson on a pedestal and selectively draw a veil over his past. Walsh was equally resolved to fix him in the public mind as a bona fide radical. Nine days after the funeral, he helped organize a public memorial service at the Grand Opera House. One after another, speakers recalled Nelson's work on behalf of the poor and oppressed, his fight to root out ugliness and injustice, his valor as a man of action and vision. Walsh, speaking last, sounded a more personal note, his deep, resonant voice carrying easily through the hushed auditorium.

For a third of a century I knew him. I knew his early struggles; I knew him in his day of triumph. He was a man massive of intellect, gigantic in form, a man cast in all things in a great mold, possessing as the center of his being the soul of a poet and the brain of an artist. Yet in the expression of that spirit, whether as the great editor, the business man, the master builder, there was the modesty of his great democracy, the simplicity of a child, the courage and the heart of a lion. . . . What was the central idea that stood out in the columns of the *Star*? The idea of the destruction of slavish adherence to party, the unshackling of the mind so that a free state could meet its destiny. That central idea was voiced in a cry and protest against special privilege, against private greed. . . . At all times he was for the rights of the poor, for the weak against the strong. . . . Mr. Nelson was a great business man, but not in the sense that the ordinary business man might view it. . . . His life and his accomplishments are a stern rebuke to the cruelty and immorality that lie hidden behind that conventional expression, "business is business." . . . We have laid him to rest. Already there is fading into forgetfulness those blurring details that sometimes obscured and overcast the goal for which the battle was fought, and we are coming to read his life as a great completed book. The solace that is ours as we reflect upon his loss is that we who really knew him in his life knew him in all the greatness that was his.[3]

The calculated affront wasn't lost on Walsh's fellow members of the Commercial Club, many of whom took a dim view of his populist grandstanding on the Industrial Relations Commission. Nor were the *Star*'s executives amused by his appropriation of Nelson's legacy. Walsh was nothing but an interloper, an opportunist who had manipulated the aging editor for his own purposes. Now that Nelson was gone, they were free to subject him to the "silent treatment" the *Star* reserved for a select group of public enemies. Soon, Walsh's name would all but disappear from the pages of the hometown paper that had once sung his praises so freely.

The aversion was mutual. Walsh had long since made up his mind about Nelson's successors. Able journalists to a man, they lacked their master's burning desire to set the world to rights, if need be by subverting the existing order. He had seen this coming. As Nelson's failing eyesight and strength made him increasingly dependent, the men in his inner circle had not only read aloud to him but drafted, typed, and edited his letters and memos. Sitting behind his big desk in a corner of the newsroom, jealously protected by the palace guard of Gus Seested and Ralph Stout, he had become an ever more remote and isolated figure. A web of myth and idolatry had enshrouded him long before his mortal remains were laid to rest in Mount Washington Cemetery.

The *Star*'s new high command consisted of men who had long served under Nelson. Managing editor Ralph Stout had been with the paper since 1893. City editor George Longan and associate editor Henry Haskell, director of the editorial page, had thirty-two years' seniority between them. Gus Seested was universally recognized as the office supremo. On staff since 1881, the business manager had been Nelson's right-hand man and confidant as long as anyone could remember. His power derived partly from his intimacy with the Nelson family and partly from his unrivaled knowledge of the newspaper's operation. Nelson and he had long observed the conventional wall between the business and editorial departments by keeping offices in separate rooms. But with the move to the new plant at Eighteenth and Grand, Seested had occupied a desk adjacent to Nelson's in the wide-open newsroom. The deference induced by this conspicuous proximity to the throne was reinforced by Seested's reserved, somewhat Machiavellian personality. Hovering over Nelson's sickbed, he had been privy to discussions of the editor's will and his feverish frettings about the *Star*'s future. The rest of the staff sensed obscurely that their fate was in his hands.

As trustees of the Nelson estate, Ida Nelson and Laura Nelson Kirkwood were now the *Star*'s legal proprietors. Nelson's widow had never shown any discernible interest in the paper, but Laura made no secret of her desire to take an active part in its management. To her father's underpaid editors, who had watched her grow up in the lap of luxury, with frequent trips to Europe and an expensive finishing school in the East, she was still a "poor little rich girl" who had rashly married a man her parents disapproved of. Despite her profession that the *Star* was a sacred trust, nothing in Laura's pampered past encouraged them to believe that she would ever treat it as more than a plaything. Why should she, after all, considering that she and her mother were each drawing five thousand dollars a month from the estate, as much as top executives earned in a full year under Nelson?[4]

In any case, the newspaper was almost exclusively a man's world. If any member of the Nelson family belonged in the newsroom, it was Irwin Kirkwood, Laura's debonair, polo-playing husband. He had achieved a modest success in real estate and made himself useful around the paper, but old-timers dismissed him as a spendthrift playboy whom Nelson had been forced to rescue from near penury. Laura and Ida, however, made Kirkwood their special representative and awarded him a private office at Eighteenth and Grand. His reported salary of thirty thousand a year was matched only by Seested's.[5]

No expression of ritual fealty to the founder's memory, however, could disguise the fact that the *Star* was no longer the "Daily W. R. Nelson." What it was, what it could be, depended not just on the top managers but on Ida and Laura's willingness to continue investing in the paper against the dread day when it would be converted into cold cash to pay for Nelson's "great dream of democracy." In a funk, the executives unburdened themselves to White. In hindsight, some felt, they would have been smart to follow his example, buy a small-town newspaper, and set themselves up as their own bosses. Twenty years earlier, when White had left the *Star*, a journeyman journalist could still afford a property like the *Emporia Gazette*. But times had changed. Now, only a rich man could aspire to own a newspaper. They had no choice but to stay.

Haskell, Nelson's deposed heir apparent in the newsroom, was torn. He had risen through the ranks faster than he had ever dreamed possible and achieved his ambition to "help a little in the building of Kansas City" many times over. Yet it was uncertain how long the *Star* could preserve its integrity and independence under the threat of the auction block. Haskell seems to have felt sanguine enough about his prospects to turn down an invitation to join the editorial staff of the prestigious *New York Evening Post*. The future looked less bright to his colleague Dante Barton. Under Nelson, Barton had felt free to press his socialist agenda, but the editor's death had cast both him and the paper adrift. Chafing at the conservatism of Seested and the other top brass, Barton had been talking with Walsh about a job in Washington, where his talents and political inclinations would be better appreciated.

Walsh, too, was ready for a new assignment. The Industrial Relations Commission wrapped up its work in August 1915 and the chairman returned to Kansas City at the end of the month to release a strongly worded report calling on Americans "to use every means of agitation, all avenues of education and every department and function of Government to eliminate the injustices exposed by this commission." After two years on center stage, Walsh was looking forward to a break. "Having been so very noisy lately," he wrote to a friend, "I feel it is time for me to subside."[6] But subsiding was no more in Walsh's nature than in Nelson's. Even as the commission was submitting its findings to Congress, he was laying the groundwork for a private organization to push for implementation of its controversial recommendations. His neglected law practice was in need of attention, and every day the mail brought appeals for help and requests to speak on behalf of various causes. As if that wasn't enough to keep him busy, Walsh was about to realize his life-long dream of publishing a newspaper.

On October 15, 1915, the *Kansas City Post* announced that the fifty-one-year-old attorney had "assumed sole direction" of its "editorial, news and business policies." Only a few months earlier, the Bonfils and Tammen paper had accused Walsh of being Nelson's puppet. The new publisher, however, was prepared to let bygones be bygones. He and the *Post*'s freewheeling proprietors were really "birds of a feather," Harry Tammen suggested in a letter confirming his appointment. "Some of the superior people of Kansas City, or at least they say that they are superior, assume that you lack character and a lot of other things," Tammen wrote. "The same is assumed about us." But, he added, "I believe and know that God put the most venemous [sic] reptile on earth and sanctions its life."[7]

To the "superior people" at the *Star*, Tammen and Bonfils were the lowest of the low and the *Post*, with its screaming headlines, red-face type, and bombastic editorials, represented yellow journalism at its most contemptible. Yet Walsh's national celebrity, and his willingness to plow profits from his lucrative law practice into the paper, made him a prize catch. He was under no illusion that "Bon and Tam" shared his passion for social justice, but as long as they didn't tie his hands, he was happy. "The *Post* will be Walsh and Walsh will be the *Post*," he assured an acquaintance, with a Nelsonian flourish. "I have an absolutely free hand under my agreement. I have an interest in the paper and under the arrangement am the permanent publisher of it forever. It will be the freest, well financed paper that ever existed in the United States. I know just how tough the battle will be here but I have gone into it heart and soul and I am satisfied that we will gain the field."[8]

Seested and his colleagues didn't take Walsh's bravado too seriously, but to play it safe they placed an order for new linotype machines and enough presses to boost the *Star*'s printing capacity by half. Walsh recognized that the *Post* was no match for the *Star* in terms of economic clout. Bon and Tam had shown no inclination to upgrade the paper's ramshackle plant and the *Star* had a vise-lock on local advertising dollars. Instead, Walsh was gambling that an infusion of bold, progressive leadership would give Nelson's successors a run for their money. "The great newspaper up above has lost its strong hand and clear brain," he told a friend, "and notwithstanding the splendid ability of many of the men upon it, there is, and under the will of Mr. Nelson can be, no head to the concern."[9]

Try as he might to emulate Nelson's "personal" journalism, Walsh's hyperactive style as editor couldn't have been more different. Refusing to be chained to his desk, he was constantly on the go and in the public eye—traveling, lawyering, speechifying, writing for magazines, and advocating for scores of liberal causes and organizations. With his old friend Jacob Billikopf, he lobbied hard for Louis Brandeis's confirmation as the first Jewish justice of the U.S. Supreme Court. It was rumored that he would use his *Post* editorship as a springboard for political office, possibly challenging Jim Reed for his Senate seat. But Walsh, like Nelson, prized his independence too highly to take up politics as a profession. He confined himself to sending word to Wilson through Colonel House that he was at the president's "disposal at all times" and remained "eager for an opportunity to serve" the administration.[10]

While awaiting a call from the White House, the *Post*'s publisher moonlighted as chairman of the Committee on Industrial Relations, a political action group set up by organized labor in the fall of 1915 to put teeth into the congressional commission's reports. Dante Barton, demoralized by the *Star*'s apparent lurch to the right, seized the chance to jump ship and put his talents to use in the committee's Washington headquarters. At the same time, he began writing a book about industrial democracy, with Walsh as his nominal coauthor. Barton embraced his new work with a gusto he hadn't felt for months. No one had asked him to leave the *Star* in so many words, but his left-wing views were increasingly unwelcome on the editorial page. White agreed with Haskell's diagnosis that he had been seduced by the simplistic nostrums of socialist quacks.

> I note what you say about Dante Barton, and I consider all that has happened to Frank Walsh, and it comes to me that the reason why labor, often is led by cheap skates, is not that the men who lead labor are cheap skates before they begin as labor leaders; but it is because of the psychology of the game. They see certain definite, and sometimes tremendous wrongs; to right them, they lose their moral bearings. These men do not track intellectually along the lines of ethics, as the race has worn those lines deep and smooth and certain. So these men, taking short cuts, to what seems [*sic*] to be highly desired ends, get off the rails, run wild, see red and act like hell. Murder, lying, arson, forgery, deception of all kinds—the whole calendar of crimes against man and against property may follow this psychological break down, and the man who has it does not realize how ineffective he is in his combat.[11]

Whether or not Barton and Walsh had lost their moral bearings, they had indubitably lost their patience with well-meaning reformers who placed the rights of property ahead of the rights of men. In early May 1916 Walsh abruptly resigned after less than seven months at the helm of the *Post*. Running the paper, he explained to a friend, had "demanded all of my time, to the elimination of everything else that I wished to do in the world." Will Marion Reedy, the famed progressive editor in St. Louis, put it more bluntly. "Mr. Walsh was a good editor, but he did not edit much. His time was too much taken up in oratorical advocacy of social and economic reforms. An editor must edit and he must be there as the news comes in and bat out its interpretation hot to the public. Mr. Walsh could not do this and tread the rostrum too. No editor can."[12]

A letter from a Kansas City businessman, preserved in Walsh's papers at the New York Public Library, suggests another motive for severing his connection with the *Post*. "I sincerely hope that your plans do not go awry and that you will obtain control of the *Kansas City Star* and stand for the fundamental ideas of humanity, because you can accomplish so much more with that paper than you are now doing." The subtext is tantalizing. Not content with filling Nelson's shoes, did Walsh aspire to fill his office chair as well? Clearly, *something* was afoot. That summer, Walsh's friend Jake Sheppard, a socialist attorney from Fort Scott, Kansas, made separate overtures to Colonel House and Eugene Debs concerning the establishment of "a great Free Press in America." Walsh deemed the project so important that he sent Sheppard all the way to New Hampshire to hand-deliver a letter to Wilson's adviser. In the meantime, Walsh himself traveled to Denver to discuss a new joint venture of some sort with his erstwhile employers. Tammen's follow-up is cryptic but suggestive: "Am glad all that was done matched and am certain that no combination can get away with our combined forces."[13]

The inference that Walsh was lining up backers to buy the *Star* from Nelson's estate is corroborated by other evidence. The *Appeal to Reason* had been floundering since J. A. Wayland's suicide in 1912 and the subsequent departures of "fighting editor" Fred Warren and Eugene Debs. The labor movement needed a robust journalistic voice to take its place, just as Wilson needed influential allies in the press to support his bid for a second term. In the summer of 1916 Walsh campaigned extensively for the Democratic president while keeping his lines open to Debs and the Socialist Party. His track record as an articulate champion of labor, loyal friend of the administration, and, latterly, two-fisted newspaperman gave him unique stature in the progressive socialist-democratic movement. In his own eyes, and conceivably in those of

Debs and House as well, he was the ideal man to lead the *Star* back to its rightful place as a fearless defender of the "weak and oppressed."

Walsh and his opponents at Eighteenth and Grand were playing for higher stakes than the ownership of a newspaper. The prize they coveted was Nelson's intangible legacy. Whoever emerged as his legitimate heir would have an authority that reached far beyond the *Star* newsroom. The many constructive roles Nelson had played in his life—road builder, city builder, newspaper builder—had finally been bundled together in a single word: *insurgent.* His transformation from "progressive" to "insurgent" owed as much to Walsh as to any man alive. Perhaps the greatest part of Nelson's genius, greater even than running the newspaper, lay in his ability to hold the city's fractious progressive coalition together. No individual or group of reformers could ever duplicate his "government by newspaper" in a balkanized community of more than 280,000 souls. Harmonizing their discordant interests required the skills of a new kind of "master broker." Walsh, who had long since transferred his base of operations to the East, was no longer eligible for the part. The mantle fell instead on the broad, prize-fighter shoulders of Thomas Joseph Pendergast.

Less than three weeks after Nelson's funeral, Pendergast gave up his seat on the City Council and returned to private life. Joining the southward exodus, he had sold his modest home on West Thirteenth Street, in the run-down First Ward, and taken up residence in the Country Club district. His new home, a solid, stone-sided affair, stood just around the corner from the house J. C. Nichols was building for himself. (Ironically, the Pendergast abode was designed by Frederick Gunn, one of several architects Nelson had hired to work on Oak Hall.) The Democratic boss's sudden embrace of upward mobility set tongues wagging. Some went so far as to suggest that he was turning over a new leaf, putting the honky-tonks and brothels of Twelfth Street and Old Town behind him. The chief Goat himself offered a more straightforward explanation for quitting the council. "I moved into my new home at Fifty-fourth and Wyandotte streets and I could not represent my ward and not live there very well, so I resigned. There could be no other reason."[14]

A devoted family man, Boss Tom saw no reason to deny himself the creature comforts enjoyed by other well-to-do Kansas Citians. But retiring from public life was the farthest thing from his mind. Like any politician worth his salt, he was keeping up with the times. Nichols, with his "one thousand acres protected" from blight and well-organized associations of home owner vigilantes, was the face of the future. Over the years, he and Pendergast would forge a mutually advantageous working relationship. Nichols gave Pendergast respectability, while Pendergast provided the political connections Nichols needed to achieve his ambition of making the Country Club the city's most desirable neighborhood, "a region of clean and proper living," as a promotional booklet described it, where "the home-owner and his family might find *permanence* in neighborhood society, in school, in church, in community interest, in high citizenship."[15]

Nichols was something of a master broker himself. Certainly, his assiduous cultivation of Nelson had paid off in spades. Nichols vigorously promoted such pet projects of the editor as the civic center near the Union Station; in turn the newspaper not only publicized but patronized his developments. Haskell and other *Star* executives moved out of Rockhill into the Country Club district, assuming prominent roles in Nichols-sponsored home owners' associations. It didn't take long for Pendergast to discover that he, too, could play that game. As his Democratic machine put down roots in the newer residence wards on the south side, it set up a network of neighborhood political clubs to provide recreation and social services for its genteel, middle-class constituents. A busy schedule of bridge parties, teas, dances, picnics, and bowling matches helped build a cadre of grateful voters whose support for the machine could be counted on at election time.

As Pendergast settled into his new life as a prosperous businessman—his concerns included several contracting and construction firms and a wholesale liquor company—he prepared to renew his struggle with Joe Shannon. The rival bosses had buried the hatchet in 1914 in the common cause of quashing the *Star*'s commission government initiative. But the death of their mutual enemy had revived their antagonism. The February 1916 city primary would pit Shannon's ally, popular two-time incumbent mayor Henry Jost, against Pendergast's candidate, R. Emmett O'Malley. Boss Tom had a soft spot for the compliant Democratic councilman. A couple of years earlier, he and Senator Reed had exerted themselves on behalf of O'Malley's bid for the Kansas City postmastership, a patronage gold mine, but their efforts had been thwarted after Nelson confidentially informed Colonel House that O'Malley was "a typical cheap politician identified with a rotten machine."[16] That setback made the Goat leader keener than ever to place O'Malley in the mayor's office.

There was joy in Rabbitville when Jost dealt O'Malley a sharp defeat in the Democratic primary. But Shannon's victory was pyrrhic. Pendergast promptly announced that he couldn't in good conscience support a Jost ticket, thereby splitting the Democratic vote and throwing the advantage to George Edwards, a conservative, probusiness Republican. The *Star* weighed in on the side of Edwards's nominally bipartisan "New Rule Ticket," while the newly invigorated *Post* waged a no-holds-barred battle for Jost's reelection. Editor Walsh himself contributed a hundred dollars to Jost's campaign chest and flailed the *Star* for encouraging Pendergast to break ranks. Nelson, he implied, never would have stooped to such despicable tactics. "The *Star*'s trickery and trading and the greed of its managers has [*sic*] forced it to follow where it used to lead. It defiles everything it touches. Its greed is its creed," thundered the *Post.*[17]

Not since the swashbuckling free-for-alls of the 1890s had Kansas Citians witnessed such a luridly exciting mayoral contest, with Goats and Rabbits indulging in a veritable orgy of dirty tricks. When Pendergast hired thugs and police stooges to work the polls, the *Post* charged that criminal elements had run amok in the north end and were intimidating voters with revolvers and blackjacks. The *Star*, always happy to apportion blame evenhandedly between the bosses, accused Shannon and his cronies of suborning the police, threatening opposition election officials with arrest, inciting "anarchy, bribery, [and] thuggery," and in general using "every form of demagoguery and deceit his active mind could invent."[18] Predictably, this spirited internecine feud set off a Republican landslide that swept Edwards into office.

The first municipal election of the post-Nelson era finished off the Democrats' "fifty-fifty compromise" and, as would shortly become apparent, hastened Pendergast's ascendancy. For some time, nevertheless, Shannon continued to contest the party leadership with Boss Tom. One prominent casualty of the dispute was the Board of Public Welfare, the jewel in the city's progressive crown. Walsh's move to Washington had left the agency vulnerable to political pressure at the very time Pendergast was launching his counterattack on the Rabbits. Both Democratic factions had a vested interest in restoring the machine's power as the city's principal dispenser of charity and patronage. Over the next several years, politicians virtually gutted the highly regarded welfare board under the guise of cost cutting. Jacob Billikopf had thwarted Mayor Jost's bid to dismiss Leroy Halbert, the brilliant head social worker, by threatening to resign in 1915. But in the end the machine-dominated City Council simply eliminated Halbert's position and with it the last vestige of the board's independence.

Such brazen maneuvers took the wind out of the progressives' sails. Adrift in the political doldrums, and lacking a recognized leader, the movement badly needed a successful campaign to energize its base. Kansas Citians had demonstrated their resistance to reform by repeatedly voting down proposals to take partisan politics out of local government. When Mayor Edwards appointed a citizens' board to draft a new charter providing for commission government, Nelson's dream seemed on the verge of coming true. In October 1916, however, a competing plan for city-manager government emerged and won the *Star's* support. The campaign for charter reform collapsed in acrimony and confusion. Opposed by the Edwards administration, the Pendergast organization, and a cross-section of progressives, the city-manager plan was decisively rejected at the polls the following March. Sadder but wiser, the reformers withdrew to fight another day.

With reformers and machine pols bickering among themselves, the city's once-mighty engine of progress first stalled, then shifted into reverse. Presidential politics was in a similar holding pattern. Once again, the 1916 election pitted the progressive Wilson against a conservative Republican. And once again the Bull Moose was the joker in the deck. Far from keeping quiet, as he had promised White and Nelson in the fall of 1914, Roosevelt had issued a string of vituperative and increasingly personal attacks on Wilson. In this smear campaign he was ably assisted by his old friend General Leonard Wood, former Army chief of staff, who had thumbed his nose at the president by agitating for universal military training at a time when Wilson was claiming credit for keeping the country out of war. Trapped between warmongers, pacifists, and isolationists, Wilson campaigned to shore up America's defenses as the surest way of insulating it from the European conflict. "This month should not go by without something decisive being done by the people of the United States by way of preparation of the arms of self-vindication and defense," he lectured a crowd in Kansas City's Convention Hall on February 2. It was America's "noble part" in the conflict to "stand steady, to stand cool, to keep alive all the wholesome processes of peace."[19]

The rudimentary state of the nation's defenses made Wilson's policy of strict neutrality prudent as well as popular. Roosevelt, however, denounced it as a badge of weakness. He knew he was swimming against the tide but deemed it his patriotic duty to speak out against the Democratic administration, just as he had against the Republican standpatters. Even so, Roosevelt appeared reluctant to challenge Wilson for the presidency when William Allen White met him in Kansas City that spring. "I was not sure then that he should make the sacrifice and run," the editor recalled, "for we agreed, he and I, that Wilson would probably be re-elected and his candidacy would be a sacrifice hit. Again he declared that he did not want to be a martyr, that he might fizzle out as a perennial third-party candidate." Roosevelt "had no desire for

A standing-room-only crowd in Convention Hall listens to Woodrow Wilson's war-preparedness speech on February 2, 1916. The banner behind the speaker's platform reads "Our President."

posthumous glory," he assured White. "He wanted to be a vital part of his times. At parting, as I left the room, he said: 'No, White, I just mustn't do it. As things look now, it would be more than the Progressives ought to ask of me!'"[20]

Whatever his private misgivings, in public Roosevelt continued to act and speak like a candidate hot on the campaign trail. Throughout the spring, Roosevelt hammered away at his tried-and-true themes of patriotism and war preparedness in a series of speeches around the Midwest, culminating in a Memorial Day appearance in Kansas City which the *Star*, in a paroxysm of praise, compared favorably to Pericles' legendary oration "over the first slain of the Peloponnesian war."[21]

Eight days later, Progressives and Republicans convened simultaneously in Chicago in a symbolic bid to lasso the ornery Bull Moose back into their respective corrals. Peace brokers in both parties hoped to put together a harmony ticket and had their eyes on Charles Evans Hughes, the well-respected associate justice of the Supreme Court. Roosevelt, accustomed to being lionized at political gatherings, was miffed by this turn of events but realized he held a weaker hand than at the 1912 Republican convention. In publicly distancing himself from both parties, he had alienated many of his fans and reduced himself to playing the role of spoiler. Knowing that his only chance of beating Wilson lay in uniting Republicans and Progressives behind him, he continued to hope, with little apparent justification, that he, not Hughes, would be the consensus choice.

Representatives of the two parties huddled long hours in search of compromise, but it soon became clear that nothing short of a cataclysm would induce conservatives to support the apostate Roosevelt. When Republican delegates brought Hughes's name forward, Progressives responded by pushing their man's nomination through on a voice vote. For a brief, tantalizing moment, history seemed about to repeat itself. Then Roosevelt pulled another surprise. White recalled the pall that fell over the convention when his letter of renunciation was read out. The silence gave way to "a roar of rage . . . the cry of a broken heart such as no convention had ever uttered in this land before." Oswald Garrison Villard of the *Nation* had a more cynical reaction. "Around me men of the frontier type could not keep back their tears at this self-revelation of their idol's selfishness, the smashing of their illusions about their peerless leader. Then the Colonel went back to the 'thieves and robbers' he had so ardently denounced from 1912 to 1915, and the Progressive party was betrayed and slain."[22]

Deprived of its reflexive first choice, the *Star* hastily bestowed its blessing not on Wilson—who would surely have been Nelson's pick—but on Hughes. Like Roosevelt, the bearded, genial justice had been a notable reform governor of New York. But there the resemblance stopped. An uninspiring speaker who seemed anxious to offend no one, Hughes was a sorry stand-in for the old Rough Rider and seemed genuinely bewildered by White's advice that he reach out to disaffected Progressives. "What are the Progressive issues?" he asked the Emporia editor in Colorado that August. "I have been out of politics now so long that I am not familiar with it. Just how should I express my sympathy with the Progressive movement?"[23]

Hughes's cluelessness and Roosevelt's recusal left Wilson's claim to leadership of the movement unchallenged. Many Progressives were reeling from their erstwhile favorite's metamorphosis into a Hun-bashing chauvinist—"a regular Gyp the Blood," Walsh called him, and the enemy of "every man who would stand for human rights." Roosevelt's bellicose presence on the campaign trail continually threatened to embarrass the GOP candidate, who, like Wilson, was doing his best to toe the thin line between preparedness and warmongering. "I couldn't write anything about this campaign to save my soul," White confessed to Haskell. "I don't know what I believe myself and I have had no courage to tell other people what they should believe." The American electorate, it seemed, was equally ambivalent. Wilson held onto the presidency by a paper-thin majority of six hundred thousand popular and twenty-three electoral votes. White believed he was reelected because, when push came to shove, the progressive heartland refused to back a conservative Republican against a liberal Democrat. How much longer the Midwest would remain solidly progressive was anybody's guess. As war fever spread, the Brahmin historian Henry Adams lamented to a British friend that "our old world is dead. The huge polypus waiting to pop over us is what we call the Middle West, which corresponds to your middle class. It has a stomach but no nervous centre,—no brains."[24]

In some respects, the *Star*'s gung-ho coverage of the war did suggest that its brains had sunk to its gut. Within days of Nelson's death, the paper published an inflammatory—and, it proved, completely unsubstantiated—report of Japanese gunboats lurking off the coast of Mexico. Arthur Krock, the *Louisville Courier-Journal*'s Washington correspondent, gloated over the gaffe to his boss, Henry Watterson. "I give thanks to the fact that I am [such] a 'bear' when it comes to sensational news that I was not guilty of—shall I say the 'bull'?" he wrote to Nelson's old comrade in arms. With the restive Bull Moose snorting at its back, the *Star* took an increasingly hawkish line that came naturally to its senior executives. Stout, emulating Roosevelt, railed against the "pacifists and hyphenated enemies on our own soil" and saw that they got what was coming to them in the *Star*'s news columns. Seested ranted against Germany and itched for the United States to declare war. Kirkwood, dissuaded by his colleagues from enlisting on account of Laura's frail health, declared in frustration that "the most unfortunate man in the world today is he who for some reason cannot carry a gun."[25]

Although such jingoism was foreign to Haskell's essentially analytical temperament, he too had come to question whether Wilson was capable of providing the strong, forward-looking leadership the country needed. "He reminds me of the bull that paws the earth and snorts and rushes madly at the fence to tear it down. When he reaches it he sniffs a moment and then goes to eating grass," he wrote to White.[26] Haskell's brother and sister had been deeply involved as missionaries in the bloody Balkan conflicts of 1912–1913. He understood the causes and likely consequences of the Great War as well as any of his colleagues. But as chief editorial writer he was responsible only for commenting on the European situation, not planning and directing the *Star*'s news coverage. In the short term, at least, there was little he could do to counter his colleagues' lack of interest in foreign affairs, an attitude vividly illustrated by an incident that had occurred the summer before Nelson died.

The *Star*'s night telegraph editor was vacationing in Paris when hostilities broke out. Elated by the prospect of covering "the greatest story of a lifetime," E. B. "Ruby" Garnett cabled home for instructions and waited impatiently to be ordered to the front. When Stout wired back that the office wanted nothing more than feature stories and suggested he save money by filing them by surface mail, Garnett could hardly believe his eyes. "Here was I, the *Star*'s telegraph editor, within a hundred miles of the battle front at the beginning of a war—and all my newspaper wanted from me was features by mail. That was Ralph Stout's judgment. I knew that intuitively. There had been no conference with Mr. Nelson; no turning the matter over in any conference. . . . No, just a thrifty managing editor, so vitally concerned with the affairs of Kansas City and the states of Missouri and Kansas, that he saw little good in having a staff man covering a war in Europe." Garnett furiously shredded the cablegram and booked passage home.[27]

From Stout's seat in the newsroom, the local temperance campaign that Nelson was directing from Colorado that August automatically took precedence over a perplexing conflict in a distant corner of the world. The *Star* had never had a full-time foreign correspondent, finding the news provided by wire services and occasional "special writers" sufficient to satisfy its readers' limited interest in the world beyond the Missouri River Valley. (Nelson's attitude toward foreign news was characteristically practical: "I'd like to read it, but there are so few of me.") As Europe burst into flames, however, that attitude began to change. Charles Grasty, forced out of the editorship of the *Baltimore Sun* in a dispute with the paper's owners, went overseas early in the war as a correspondent for the *Star* and the Associated Press. After the United States entered the conflict, Stout sent one of his battle-hardened police reporters to France to chronicle "life in the trenches" for the folks back home. Otto P. Higgins, a "big, bear-like man" given to gambling and bibulous conviviality, would achieve notoriety as Kansas City's corrupt police chief in the 1930s.[28] To supplement his workmanlike reportage, the *Star* arranged for special front-line dispatches from local celebrities Henry Allen of the *Wichita Beacon* and novel-writing minister Burris Jenkins, who toured the war zone on relief missions.

As waves of American doughboys slowly tipped the balance in favor of the Allies, the *Star* positioned itself in the vanguard of the war effort. In June 1917, two months after the declaration of war, Kirkwood ran into Roosevelt on a westbound train out of New York. They discussed Roosevelt's proposal to muster a division and lead it to France. Kirkwood had been looking forward to serving under his command, but Wilson had icily rebuffed Roosevelt in what many saw as a gesture of petty vindictiveness. Now Kirkwood had another idea: Would Roosevelt consider writing special editorials on the war for the *Star*, along the lines of the articles he had been contributing to the *Metropolitan* magazine? Roosevelt accepted on the spot. "Such a proposition would not tempt me from many newspapers," he told Kirkwood. "In fact I know of no others except the *Kansas City Star* and the *Philadelphia North American* from which I would consider it. The *Star* particularly appeals to me as being printed in the heart of the great progressive Middle Western country, and because, too, of my love and affection for Colonel Nelson."[29]

On September 4 the *Star* proudly announced that Nelson's hero had joined the staff with the honorary rank of associate editor. For Roosevelt, contemplating another run for the presidency in 1920, Kirkwood's promise of editorial freedom was no doubt a more important consideration than the princely salary of twenty-five thousand dollars a year. Late that month, in Kansas City to deliver an address as part of "Old Glory Week," Roosevelt slipped away from the flag-waving throngs and reported for duty in the newsroom. "The cub reporter will now begin work," he announced, striding briskly to his assigned desk. While star-struck editors and reporters tried to concentrate on their own work, Roosevelt picked up a pencil and, "with much scratching and interlining," dashed off an editorial for page one of the next morning's paper. "Bismarck announced that his policy for Germany was one of blood and iron," he wrote in his barely legible scrawl. "The men who now guide, and for some decades have guided, German international policy have added gold as the third weapon in Germany's armory."[30]

Stout beamed as he scanned the sheets of newsprint before stuffing them into the pneumatic tubes to be whisked to the composing room. Roosevelt still carried a big stick, but he wasn't walking softly any more. The editorial seethed with red-hot indignation. It was outrageous, the ex-president wrote, that Germany's former ambassador in Washington had been permitted to hand out bribes to domestic dissidents. The Wilson administration should have broken relations with the Reich long ago. Now that America had finally entered the war, open dissent could no longer be tolerated. Everyone caught "playing the pro-German game" should be presumed guilty until proved innocent. "The pacifist, the man who wishes a peace without victory, the supporter of Senator La Follette or Senator Stone, the man who in any way now aids Germany, may be honest; but he stands cheek by jowl with hired traitors, and he is serving the cause of the malignant and unscrupulous enemies of his country."[31]

It was one thing to criticize the senators from Wisconsin and Missouri, who had made themselves fair game by voting against Congress's declaration of war. But Roosevelt's barely concealed attack on President Wilson, who had led the nation into war under the slogan "peace without victory," was a more serious matter. Was the author of this intemperate diatribe the same Roosevelt who had stolen the Socialists' thunder in Chicago a mere five years earlier? For that matter, could the *Star* be the same newspaper that, shortly before Nelson's death, had published an editorial cartoon placing Wilson alongside Jefferson, Madison, and Monroe in a portrait gallery of "great Virginians"? In an interview with the trade journal *Editor and Publisher,* Laura Kirkwood defended Roosevelt's arrangement with the *Star* as wholly "in line with my father's ideals."[32] To many outside the paper, however, the signed editorials appeared to be disturbingly out of line.

The Wilson administration's fumbling attempts to put the country on a war footing provided plenty of grist for Roosevelt's mill. After making several trips to Washington to investigate the situation in the spring of 1917, a gloomy Haskell wrote to White that "there is nobody to hook things up and produce team work except the President and he doesn't work very hard on the job. One day I was there he spent the morning golfing with Mrs. W., went to a McAdoo wedding in the afternoon and to the theater at night. That isn't the sort of spirit that puts ginger into a great organization." Armed with information leaked by disaffected military officers, Haskell and Washington correspondent Roy Roberts gathered evidence to back Roosevelt's allegation that the War Department was training soldiers bound for France with "broomsticks" instead of rifles. As the columnist savaged the administration for incompetence and inefficiency, Navy Secretary Josephus Daniels wrote in his diary: "T. R. at large, writing and speaking in disparagement of America's preparation for war, is helping Germany more than the little fellows who are being arrested and giving aid and comfort to the enemy. Can *Kansas City Star,* containing his allusions to soldiers training with broom-sticks, be excluded from the mails along with other papers spreading what is construed as seditious?" Ominously, Daniels added that "B".—Postmaster General Albert Burleson— had assured him he was having the paper "read carefully and would not hesitate to act."[33]

For the time being, the threat to the *Star* remained implicit. If any of the paper's executives knew about the government's surveillance, they showed no sign of being intimidated. To the contrary, Stout egged Roosevelt on, dismissing his concern that he was causing trouble for the paper. "To be entirely frank," the managing editor wrote in mid-December, "I think you have been speaking rather softly of late. You have never worn gum shoes and you never

can. You have got to be your own self. We want you to write what you think
and we will print it. There is just one danger in this—and that is a danger the
Star has always been under, with Colonel Nelson and since,—of giving our
readers the idea we are a common scold. We ought to criticize when we can
do it constructively. We ought to do everything we possibly can to win the
war: praise when praise is merited, criticize when criticism is just and will advance the country's interests."[34]

Scolding, however, is what Roosevelt did best. He used his new bully pulpit in the *Star* to lob potshots at Socialists, Bolsheviks, Wobblies, pacifists, and
sundry other "internationalists" bent on making peace prematurely instead of
fighting until Germany was "beaten to her knees." Patriotism, as Roosevelt
saw it, was an all-or-nothing proposition. Americans of German extraction
had a special obligation to prove their allegiance to the Stars and Stripes.
"There can be no such thing as a fifty-fifty loyalty between America and Germany. Either a man is whole-hearted in his support of America and her allies, and in his hostility to Germany and her allies, or he is not loyal to America at all. In such case he should be at once interned or sent out of the country."
Henceforth, Roosevelt declared, English exclusively should be taught and
used in American primary schools. Any immigrant who failed to learn English within five years should be deported and foreign-language newspapers
should be proscribed. In a stunning perversion of the Progressives' battle cry,
he declared that "a square deal for all Americans means relentless attack on all
men in this country who are not straight-out Americans and nothing else."[35]

As Roosevelt ranted, papers in other cities—which received his editorials
free of charge—reported that reader interest was slumping. Worse, from the
Star's perspective, they seemed to be having no effect on the Wilson administration's policies. Something needed to be done, the managers decided.
Haskell was duly dispatched "as an emissary to the colonel to get him to di-
vert his single track mind from criticisms of Wilson to more general and constructive suggestions of how the war might be conducted more effectively."
The *Star*'s resident intellectual outlined some sample articles and carried them
to Roosevelt in New York, explaining "as diplomatically as possible that there
were a good many aspects of the war that the West was interested in but which
probably had not come to his attention." The columnist listened politely and
thanked his visitor for the suggestions, whereupon Haskell returned to Kansas
City and awaited the outcome of his mission. When the next telegram arrived
from Oyster Bay, he found that Roosevelt had "used our four suggested editorials all right. He compressed them into one editorial and then started on
broomstick preparedness again."[36]

Haskell's exasperation wasn't shared by Stout, who felt that his Johnny One Note was conducting a campaign in the best Nelsonian tradition by "pounding continually on a few things, dressing each article in different language, but keeping to the front all the time the central idea."[37] Tediously and tendentiously repetitive as they were, Roosevelt's illiberal screeds were precisely what Stout and Kirkwood had bargained for.

A month after Roosevelt made his debut in the *Star*, a brash, eighteen-year-old Chicagoan breezed into the newsroom. Fresh out of high school, Ernest Hemingway had come to Kansas City to visit his aunt and uncle, and it was their acquaintance with Haskell that won him a berth in city editor George Longan's prize stable of reporters. Although Hemingway wouldn't stay long enough to make much of an impression on Haskell or anybody else, the *Star* left a lasting mark on him. In later years he liked to say that the paper's no-nonsense style sheet, emphasizing straightforward sentences "with the sting of a well pruned switch," was a formative influence on his bare-bones prose.[38] How much the future author of *A Farewell to Arms* and *The Sun Also Rises* may have ingested by reading the vividly evocative battlefront dispatches of Jenkins and Allen, to say nothing of Roosevelt's tub-thumping editorials, is a matter of conjecture.

Bursting with youthful machismo, Hemingway took naturally to the cult of masculinity that flourished at the post-Nelson *Star* in time of war. Stout, beneath his graying, phlegmatic exterior, still exhibited the athleticism that had made him Nelson's favorite "bouncer." Kirkwood, too, exuded virility, with his movie star's good looks and equestrian flair. Nelson's disdained son-in-law had earned the respect of newsroom veterans by applying for service in the Army officers reserve corps. "Darn fine spirit," Haskell burbled when he told White the news. "He is the real stuff and a wonderful asset to this newspaper."[39] Like Kirkwood, Hemingway craved a piece of the action, and after spending six months chasing ambulances and shadowing policemen on Kansas City's mean streets, he quit the *Star* to join the Red Cross ambulance corps in Italy. Apparently, no one thought of asking him to file dispatches from Europe.

The Kansas City that Hemingway briefly experienced was hell-bent for war. The *Star* had set the pace in the first Liberty Bond drive, in the fall of 1917, by buying a hundred thousand dollars' worth of bonds and reselling them to employees on interest-free installments. With heavyweights like banker W. T. Kemper and developer J. C. Nichols spearheading the campaign, prominent citizens were under the gun to buy bonds or risk being publicly pilloried in the *Star*'s shame-list of holdouts. Under its new management, the paper unabashedly realigned itself with the conservative business interests that Nelson had kept at arm's length. Gone were the stirring editorials defending the rights of the poor and oppressed. Instead of clamoring for industrial justice, the paper judiciously called for impartial arbitration of labor disputes.

Star executives had good practical reasons for trimming their sails. Although the paper continued to generate healthy profits, it was neither financially nor editorially independent in the way it had been while Nelson was footing the bills. The trust had effectively converted it into a cash machine. It was commonly supposed that Seested and Stout played it safe by routinely suppressing stories that might offend advertisers, businessmen, or other influential people. One reporter told Upton Sinclair of his discovery that a cartel of local packinghouses was meeting every week to fix meat prices. He bribed a porter to reveal the conspirators' names and smuggle him into the Armour Building at Fifth and Delaware. Dashing back to the office "in a fever of excitement," he marched up to Stout's desk and told the managing editor what he had overheard from his hiding place. After conferring with Seested, Stout decided the story was too hot to handle. "I guess we won't print any more meat trust stories for a while," he informed the speechless reporter.[40]

An upsurge of wartime labor unrest put the new regime's principles to the test. Long-simmering tensions came to a boil in the spring of 1918, when Kansas City was virtually shut down by an acrimonious general strike that made headlines from coast to coast and battered its carefully crafted image as a harmonious, homogenous community. The trouble started when unorganized laundry workers walked off their jobs in February. Independent washerwomen, mostly African American, joined commercial laundresses and male truck drivers in demanding higher wages and an eight-hour workday. The dispute quickly turned violent. Police struggled to restore order as rampaging strikers torched bundles of laundry and pelted streetcars with stones. Sent to investigate a mob that had gathered at Fourteenth and Euclid, Hemingway stumbled upon a scene of mayhem straight out of a European battlefield. When a stray missile hit and wounded a policeman, the cub reporter obligingly pointed the culprit out, only to be set upon by the angry throng himself. Taking to his heels, Hemingway escaped on a passing streetcar and fled back to the office to file his story.

As the protest gathered momentum, men and women in unionized industries—restaurants, breweries, movie theaters, streetcars—went out in solidarity with the laundry workers. Week after bloody week, as many as twenty-five

Armed militia guard a streetcar during Kansas City's violent general strike of 1918. The Employers' Association, backed by the *Star*, vowed to hold the line against "unscrupulous Unionism."

thousand strikers waged pitched battles in the streets with scabs and armed thugs deployed by the powerful Employers' Association. One sympathetic witness described the strikers as being in a "tense sacrificial mood" after enduring weeks of provocation by "a low class of strike breaking gun men" who had "deliberately created disorder" by "insulting and beating women strikers and shooting promiscuously into crowds." Police brutality was rampant. Laundry owners, backed by the Chamber of Commerce, refused to talk with the strikers or even submit the dispute to arbitration.[41] A public hearing called to air their grievances was canceled when the Muehlebach Hotel barred its doors to black workers.

Burris Jenkins, recently returned from war-torn Europe, called on both sides to sit down at the negotiating table. "Remember," the minister intoned from his pulpit, "there is no difficulty so great that willing men cannot straighten it out. And if you are not willing men, I must brand you as traitors to your country." Meanwhile, a number of Jenkins's fellow clergymen demonstrated their patriotism by preaching anti-union sermons helpfully prepared and distributed by the Employers' Association. Its leaders had shown they meant business by amassing a hefty war chest (reported to contain a million dollars), a private security force, and a corps of mercenary strikebreakers. In the midst of the protest, the association took out a large ad in the *Star* urging all "decent citizens" to rise up against "unscrupulous Unionism." Surely, Kansas Citians would not watch idly as their city became "conspicuous as a hotbed for enemy propaganda," "disgraced and discredited at what perhaps is the most critical period in the history of the world."[42]

The employers' scare tactics prompted the governor of Missouri to intervene. When National Guardsmen failed to enforce peace in the streets, the association prevailed on federal officials to threaten the strikers with prosecution for undermining the war effort. American Federation of Labor president Samuel Gompers, an ally of the Wilson administration, dispatched a representative to Kansas City to bring local labor leaders to heel. This well-orchestrated campaign of intimidation, calumny, and coercion ultimately yielded a compromise settlement: Laundry owners agreed to raise workers' wages, while the Employers' Association pledged to take no reprisals against strikers. The *Star* declared it a victory for arbitration, but the fragile truce would not hold for long.

Although Frank Walsh kept tabs on the crisis in Kansas City through informants in the labor movement, he showed little inclination to become actively involved. In any case, his hands were effectively tied, for in the spring of 1918 he was taking up new duties in Washington as cochairman of the National War Labor Board. Charged with arbitrating labor disputes in industries deemed vital to the war effort, the board had little real power and compliance with its recommendations depended largely on the goodwill of labor and management. Walsh was back on the stage that he had dominated so compellingly as head of the Commission on Industrial Relations. This time, though, he shared billing with an unlikely costar: none other than the arch-standpatter himself, William Howard Taft.

Since vacating the White House five years earlier, the former president had been teaching law at Yale and stumping the country on behalf of a postwar "League of Nations" to keep the peace. He had accepted his new assignment with strong misgivings, deeming his Democratic counterpart "radical and unsound," an image that Walsh had done little to dispel in his recent high-profile fight to improve working conditions in the railroad and meatpacking industries.[43] The Kansas Citian was equally wary of Taft, whom he viewed as little more than an apologist for powerful employers and reactionary moneyed interests.

To their mutual astonishment, however, the two lawyers got along famously. At their joint behest, the Labor Board unanimously adopted a set of basic principles, including workers' right to unionize and bargain collectively, a living wage, and equal pay for women. Taft soon began pushing for pro-labor measures that took even Walsh aback. When the former president urged Wilson to order streetcar companies in Kansas City and elsewhere to raise fares in order to fund a substantial wage increase for employees, Walsh questioned whether the chief executive had the necessary legal authority. "You are making me a conservative!" he exclaimed during a board meeting. Commending Taft's open-mindedness in abandoning "the time-honored dicta of Adam Smith," Walsh pressed him to spread the word. "If you succeed in telling the truth to the Republican party, you will be the greatest benefactor of the age. And this, even though they do not hearken unto it."[44]

Walsh himself would never quite despair of telling the truth to his fellow Democrats, but by the fall of 1918 he was growing increasingly alarmed by Wilson's authoritarian tendencies. Immediately after the armistice, he resigned from the Labor Board on the familiar pretext of returning to his law practice. Press reports suggested that he had bigger projects in mind and wanted a free hand to pursue them. Over the ensuing months, he watched in dismay as many of the pathbreaking settlements the board had brokered came unstuck, reversing labor's dramatic wartime gains. When Kansas City streetcar workers struck again that December, the government brought its full weight down on the employers' side. A friend wrote that there was talk of bringing Walsh and Taft in as arbitrators, but he doubted anything would come of it "as I think the street car company would be afraid to trust a decision from you." Six months later the strike was broken and organized labor was in retreat across the country. Walsh, who had already moved on to his next campaign, for Irish independence, grumbled that the Labor Board had "degenerated into a mere false hope for labor."[45]

Socialists, too, had seen public opinion swing decisively against them since the party's unprecedented showing in 1912. No one was more aware of this than Rose Pastor Stokes, a petite Russian immigrant who worked as a cigar maker in Cleveland before her fairy-tale marriage to the "millionaire socialist" J. G. Phelps Stokes. "Rose of the Ghetto," as she was known in the slums of New York, was a leading light of the socialist sisterhood. Moved by the plight of Kansas City's downtrodden laundry workers, she accepted an invitation to address a women's club at the Baltimore Hotel in March 1918. The club's president was an admirer and felt that her unorthodox views deserved a hearing. In the event, both Stokes and her five hundred listeners got more than they bargained for. Warning that she wasn't going to say what many of them wanted to hear, she defended the Socialist Party's stand against "industrial serfdom," praised revolutionary Russia as the workers' best hope for deliverance from wage slavery, and recanted her earlier support for the war. "Surely there is not a capitalist, or a well informed person, in the world today who believes that this war is being fought to make the world safe for democracy. It is being fought to make the world safe for capital," Stokes declared.[46]

Hisses and murmurs of "traitor," "disgrace" buzzed around the ballroom. Several diners headed for the doors before the speech was over. An unnamed "officer of America's fighting forces" informed the *Star* that he considered Stokes's remarks more "disloyal" than the propaganda disseminated by the IWW. The club's president first defended the speaker then turned against her. "In view of Mrs. Stokes's denunciation of profiteers," the *Star* commented snidely, "it might be said that there are persons who have a notion that a lecturer who receives $300 for the sort of an address that Mrs. Stokes made Saturday night, is somewhat familiar with profiteering herself."[47]

Claiming that the *Star* had "garbled and twisted" her words beyond recognition, Stokes spoke to a reporter two days after the dinner with the intention of setting the record straight. This time she was quoted as saying that she did not "oppose the war, or its prosecution, in any sense." She saw no way it could end "except by the defeat of Germany" and believed that "the government of the United States should have the unqualified support of every citizen in its war aims." This pushed Stokes over the top. On her way out of town, she mailed the *Star* a salty rebuttal, asserting that the headline over the interview, "Mrs. Stokes for Government and Against War at the Same Time," grossly misrepresented her views. "I made no such statement, and I believe no such thing. No government which is *for* the profiteers can also be *for* the people, and I am for the people, while the government is for the profiteers. I expect my working class point of view to receive no sympathy from your paper, but I do expect that the traditional courtesy of publication by the newspapers of a signed statement of correction, which even our most Bourbon papers grant, will be extended to this statement by yours."[48]

Ralph Stout received Stokes's disclaimer in the afternoon post and gave orders that it be printed in full the next morning. The original letter, which the managing editor considered "disloyal" and possibly incriminating, he forwarded to the U.S. district attorney. Later that week, federal marshals arrested Stokes in the Ozarks hamlet of Willow Springs and charged her with violating the nine-month-old Espionage Act. Driven back to Kansas City under guard, she was questioned and released on ten thousand dollars' bail. One month later, she was indicted for encouraging "insubordination, disloyalty, mutiny and refusal of duty" in the country's armed forces.

The *Star*'s reaction was swift and jubilant. "If Mrs. Stokes were a good American (which she is not) and wanted to exercise her right of free speech to point out how America could make better progress in winning the war she would find plenty of good Americans to help defend her rights if the police attempted to invade them. But constructive criticism actuated by patriotic motives is one thing, and destructive criticism actuated by hostility to the government and opposition to the war is quite another." Had the editorial writer forgotten that the *Star* itself had been sharply critical of the Wilson administration's conduct of the war and identified profiteering as a major problem? The issue would hit front pages later that year when Edward Deeds, head of wartime aircraft production, was nearly court-martialed for releasing misleading figures and acting on inside information. Privately, Haskell surmised that the Dayton industrialist had awarded a big order to his old company because "everybody else was getting rich out of government contracts" and "he saw no reason why they shouldn't." Haskell's investigations in Washington convinced him that "business men generally seem to regard the war as an opportunity to get theirs—and they get."[49]

The fine line between the *Star*'s purportedly "patriotic motives" and Stokes's "hostility to the government" would be the decisive factor in her trial. To lead her defense, Stokes chose Seymour Stedman, a prominent Chicago attorney with close ties to the socialist movement. (She told a friend that she preferred "to lose with a socialist and take my ten-year sentence, than to win with a capitalist representative and go scot free.") The prosecution was in the hands of District Attorney Francis Wilson, a freckle-faced former state senator from Platte City who would be Tom Pendergast's short-lived candidate for governor in 1932. A dyed-in-the-wool Democrat, Wilson had little in common politically with Judge Arbra Van Valkenburgh, a Taft appointee whose judgments were reputed to be as "unchangeable as the laws of the Medes and Persians."[50] But they saw eye to eye on the issues raised by Stokes's case, which, it turned out, had remarkably little to do with the letter she had so impetuously mailed to the editor of the *Star*.

Van Valkenburgh made his sympathies plain from the outset of the four-day trial. Whether Stokes had physically obstructed recruitment in the armed forces was immaterial, he ruled. All the government needed to prove was that she had voiced opposition to administration policies. Waving Stedman's objections aside, he allowed Wilson to introduce irrelevant and inflammatory testimony and listened approvingly as the district attorney branded Stokes "the most vicious German propagandist in the United States of America now at large." Stout, the lead prosecution witness, testified that he had sent Stokes's letter to the authorities, on his own initiative, because he "felt it was a matter the government should have." When Stedman's cross-examination elicited the damaging admission that the *Star* had distributed the allegedly "disloyal" document to tens of thousands of readers, the judge reminded the jury that Stokes had appealed to the managing editor's "chivalry and courtesy" in demanding that her correction be published.[51]

On May 23 an all-male jury of Missouri farmers pronounced Stokes guilty as charged and nine days later Van Valkenburgh sentenced her to ten years in the Missouri State Penitentiary at Jefferson City. Republican William Borah of Idaho gallantly rose to her defense on the Senate floor, accusing the Wilson administration of ignoring the problem of profiteering and declaring—under cover of congressional immunity—that he too was "for the people where the Government is for the profiteers." In New York, Roosevelt's secretary received a call from a reader suggesting that he "commend Mrs. Stokes for her work in the uplift of the poor but condemn her for her utterances against the Government."[52] But Roosevelt was on the rampage against the proposed Sedition Act and had made it clear that he believed the Espionage Act already on the books applied to everyone except himself. Besides, he could hardly condemn Stokes for saying what he had said on more than one occasion.

It was left to Eugene Debs to point this inconvenient truth out in an impassioned plea on behalf of his socialist comrade. "I want to say that if Rose Pastor Stokes is guilty, so am I," he told a crowd in Canton, Ohio, on June 16. "If she should be sent to the penitentiary for ten years, so ought I. What did she say? She said that a government could not serve both the profiteers and the employees of the profiteers. Roosevelt has said a thousand times more in his paper, the *Kansas City Star*. He would do everything possible to discredit Wilson's administration in order to give his party credit." The socialist leader got his wish when the Justice Department indicted him under the Espionage Act as well. Stedman took on his defense but admitted to Stokes that he had little hope of success. "Debs expects a conviction, he will take back nothing, qualify nothing. Only attacking appeals to him and that is the only thing left to do." Stokes refused to hold her tongue while awaiting the outcome of her own appeal, asserting that "I will not buy my freedom by paying with silence."[53] At Debs's trial in Cleveland that September, she was arrested for applauding during Stedman's opening statement and held Debs's hand as his ten-year sentence was read out.

Stokes's conviction would finally be reversed in 1920. The appeals court, while commending Judge Van Valkenburgh for his "rich and inspiring expressions of patriotism and of the nobility of our aims in the war," ruled that "the partisan zeal of the court below" had placed "too heavy a burden on the defendant in her endeavor to meet the evidence which the Government produced against her."[54] No such recourse, needless to say, was available to Stokes against the *Star* and its overzealous managing editor.

The Stokes trial had the incidental effect of focusing Wilson's attention on the *Star,* which had been a thorn in his side ever since Roosevelt started writing for it. The opposition *Kansas City Post* urged Attorney General Thomas Gregory to prosecute its competitor for publishing a letter that had had a demoralizing effect on the war effort. The paper ridiculed Stokes as a "former cigar girl, now millionaire socialist" and one of its reporters testified against her at the trial.[55] Even so, the flap might have blown over without further repercussions for the *Star* if George Creel hadn't sent the president a clipping of the *Post* editorial demanding Stout's indictment.

As head of the euphemistically named Committee on Public Information, the former Kansas City newsman was Wilson's propaganda czar and hence one of the most powerful figures in Washington. One of the "original Woodrow Wilson men," Creel had been appointed to the post eight days after the nation went to war. Both the new agency and its self-promoting chairman sparked controversy from the get-go. Robert Lansing, Wilson's conservative secretary of state, bridled at Creel's "Socialistic tendencies" and refused to cooperate with the CPI. Journalist Mark Sullivan observed that Creel's background as "the most violent of muckrakers" (Sullivan had once been one himself, but had since moved appreciably to the right) made him unfit for the top censor's job. "President Wilson might just as appropriately have appointed Billy Sunday. Indeed, George Creel and Billy Sunday have much in common. What Sunday is to religion Creel is to politics. Creel is a crusader, a bearer of the fiery cross. His ten years as a newspaper man in Kansas City and five in Denver were devoted to the championship of one form after another of idealism."[56]

The CPI was nothing if not an idealistic enterprise. Convinced that a system of "voluntary censorship" would keep the news media in line during the war, Creel persuaded Wilson that it could be slipped in under the innocuous guise of a wide-ranging program of information and education. The CPI quickly mushroomed into a gigantic bureaucracy with a news division that published an official government newspaper, an education division that employed well-known scholars and supplied a semimonthly newsletter to public school teachers, and a battalion of speakers known as "Four-Minute Men" who traveled the country spreading the administration gospel. To Wilson, who stopped holding press conferences in his second term because he considered them a "waste of time," Creel's ambitious scheme seemed sure to solve many of his public relations problems.[57]

Creel saw his job as disseminating "not propaganda as the Germans defined it, but propaganda in the true sense of the word, meaning the 'propagation of faith.'"[58] But Wilson's military chiefs, less susceptible to such inspirational pep talk than their commander, continued to press for stiffer controls, particularly over news out of Europe. When Wilson capitulated to their demands and created a separate Censorship Board in October 1917, Creel's "voluntary" regime was exposed for what it was. War correspondents complained bitterly about the heavy hand of the military censors but distrusted Washington bureaucrats still more. Creel added to his woes by shamelessly using the CPI's resources to glorify Wilson, insulating the prickly chief executive further than ever from the press. Congress, too, was growing resentful of Creel's ever-expanding authority, an attitude that he did nothing to alleviate by referring to his excursions to Capitol Hill as "slumming." In 1919 legislators would finally pull the plug on the CPI, refusing even to appropriate funds for publishing Creel's final report.

Creel never lost the president's confidence, however, and when Wilson received his note in June 1918, with the *Post* editorial enclosed, he immediately instructed his attorney general to look into the matter. "I have had a good many people speak to me recently about the fact of the (very just) conviction of Rose Pastor Stokes and at the same time the apparent injustice of convicting her when the [managing] editor of the *Kansas City Star* seems to be, to say the least, a direct participant in her offense. Don't you think that there is some way in which we could bring this editor to book?" Gregory gave his opinion that it was difficult to impute "disloyal intent or purpose" to Stout, since he had merely done his patriotic duty by showing Stokes's letter to the proper authorities. "My Department," he added, "has repeatedly received complaints against the *Kansas City Star* with suggestion of prosecution. These have had their source partly in the fact that the managing editor [*sic*] of the paper, one August F. Seested, is a German who secured his citizenship papers as late as July 2, 1917, almost four months after the declaration of war, and partly in the paper's persistent criticism of your administration. My Department has carefully examined all issues that have been sent in, but has not found anything on which to base a hope for successful prosecution."[59]

Seested's tardy application for American citizenship and his purported German sympathies made him a sitting target for the *Star*'s enemies. But it was

Roosevelt who took the brunt of the abuse from friends and members of the administration. In a political speech in Indianapolis, Vice President Thomas Marshall taunted the sidelined Rough Rider with blistering sarcasm. "Lady Theodora, being left at home, concluded to take a hand in the war by writing letters in derogation and criticism of its management to a newspaper, which newspaper had as its general manager a man who was, at the declaration of hostilities against the Imperial German Government, an alien enemy of the United States, and which newspaper had published the Rose Pastor Stokes letter and other seditious documents. Some men at least are going to object if she is the Republican Party and if she is going to fight the war in this way—through the columns of the *Kansas City Star*—and notwithstanding her great desire to take charge of everything, they are going to insist that she shall not be permitted to do so earlier than March 4, 1921, and not then, if God and the right prevail."[60]

Although the Justice Department declined to take action, the Post Office's none-too-subtle monitoring of the *Star* had a chilling effect. According to Stout, a "post-office inspector" visited Kansas City "with the idea of denying the *Star* admission to the mails, but the Administration made no further move in this direction." Nevertheless, the paper's executives were watching their backs. They even took the extraordinary step of censoring Roosevelt, declining to run two of his more incendiary editorials in the spring of 1918. Congress's debate of the Sedition Act, expanding the government's powers to clamp down on dissent, finally pushed Roosevelt over the edge. The idea that he, of all people, could be prosecuted for using "contemptuous and slurring language about the President" was unthinkable. The proposed law, he fumed, was "sheer treason to the United States" and almost certainly unconstitutional. The Wilson administration had "shown itself anxious to punish" newspapers that loyally and lawfully criticized its conduct of the war while failing "to proceed against various powerful newspapers" that unpatriotically opposed the war and supported Germany. Therefore, he concluded, "no additional power should be given the Administration to deal with papers for criticizing the Administration."[61]

Postmaster General Burleson called Roosevelt's bluff, challenging him to identify specific papers that had given aid and comfort to the enemy with impunity. "If true," press reports quoted him as saying, "I am utterly unworthy of trust and I should be scourged from office in disgrace. If false, right-thinking men and women will form their own opinion of the man who uttered them." Stout pressed Roosevelt to reply at once, advising Kirkwood that Burleson had given him "a very fine opening which I am sure he will take advantage of." Roosevelt was clearly unprepared to name names but finally came up with three: the *New York Tribune*, *Collier's*, and the *Metropolitan* magazine. Burleson promptly issued a press release denying that any had been subjected to official sanctions. "The Post Office Department has received possibly more complaints from the public alleging that Mr. Roosevelt's articles were in violation of the Espionage Act than it has against the Hearst newspapers. No matter published by either Mr. Roosevelt or Mr. Hearst has come to my attention which, in my opinion, warranted action by the Post Office Department under the Espionage Act against either of them."[62]

For the time being, the administration was holding its fire. Meanwhile, President Wilson signed the Sedition Act into law on May 21.

Wilson's intolerance of dissent alarmed civil libertarians on both left and right. In July 1917 Walsh, Stedman, Clarence Darrow, and Morris Hillquit had gone to Washington on behalf of the Socialist Party to protest the wholesale suppression of left-wing publications. The president flatly refused to meet with the distinguished delegation and Burleson declined to explain his justification for suspending postal privileges for the staunchly pacifist *Masses*. A frustrated Walsh reported to Emma Goldman, editor of *Mother Earth*, that the group had spent an entire day "laying the matter" before Burleson and an assistant attorney general. "We received assurances from all the officials that they intended to 'act fairly' in their interpretation of the law, but so far as any definite result is concerned I am afraid that our efforts were nil."[63]

Apparently confident that his direct line to the White House was still open, Walsh followed up with a personal letter to Burleson, pointing out, in carefully legalistic language, that the "ultra-bureaucratic methods" adopted by the Post Office Department had made it impossible for "ordinary citizens to locate the definite source of the power which is exercised in the suppression of publications." This bureaucratic smokescreen had created an "intolerable and dangerous" situation. In the interest of ensuring accountability, Walsh asked for reassurance that Burleson's subordinates would take no action without his "direct personal" approval. "If, in your opinion, the exigencies of the time preclude your giving these matters your personal attention, will you be good enough to so indicate, in order that appeal may be made to the President for what I deem some very necessary check upon the potential abuse of the vast powers over the press exercised by your Department . . . ."[64] Walsh's politely veiled threat seems to have had little effect. The *Masses* never recovered from the loss of its mailing privileges and folded that November.

No publication, it seemed, was too insignificant to elude the clutches of

Wilson's thought police. In the spring of 1918 suspicion fell on the *Missouri Staats Zeitung*, a German-language weekly published out of Kansas City with a paid circulation of 1,068. An employee of the paper, one Jacob Frohwerk, was charged under the Espionage Act for writing "seditious" editorials asserting that the United States had entered the war for mercenary reasons and had violated the terms of its neutrality and international law by supplying armaments to England before the declaration of war. An all-male and mainly rural jury, a mirror image of the one that had convicted Stokes a month earlier, deliberated barely three minutes before returning a guilty verdict. The hapless newsman was sentenced to ten years in the federal penitentiary at Leavenworth but was released two years later—no thanks to the *Star*, which was busy fanning the flames of war hysteria and keeping the government's watchdogs at bay.

Even all-out support for the war didn't shield the venerable *Appeal to Reason* from harassment. Along with Stokes and many others, the socialist weekly had flip-flopped on the issue, first endorsing the antiwar plank adopted at the Socialist Party's stormy 1917 convention in St. Louis, then joining the converts on the Wilson bandwagon. When Burleson moved to ban the *Appeal* from the mails in July 1917, Emanuel Haldeman-Julius, who had recently bought a controlling interest in the paper, responded by restyling it the *New Appeal* in a bid to underscore the change of editorial policy and boost its sagging circulation. Although thousands of card-carrying Socialists canceled their subscriptions in protest, the facelift may have helped convince Burleson to back off. In his newfound patriotic zeal, Haldeman-Julius ignored the wartime plight of prominent Socialist dissidents like Stokes and Debs.[65]

Another radical voice conspicuous for its silence during Stokes's ordeal was that of Walsh. Like many left-wingers, he found it necessary to trim his sails to the prevailing winds. A few days after Stokes's trial he quietly shelved the manuscript he had been working on with the late Dante Barton, even though its forthcoming publication had already been announced. *Downfall or Democracy* was billed as "a consideration of the industrial situation in the United States . . . based in part upon the findings of the Industrial Relations Commission." Walsh, who was doing his best to placate the employer representatives on the War Labor Board, offered a lame excuse to Barton's widow. "The entry of this country into the war has made such rapid and radical changes that I really feel that a posthumous work of this kind would not do justice to Dante's memory."[66] It seems more likely that Walsh saw nothing to gain, and much to lose, by stirring up old controversies in the turbulent political atmosphere of mid-1918.

Walsh's dilemma was shared by many liberals, who believed they could go only so far in challenging the increasingly illiberal "progressive" in the White House without sacrificing whatever influence they had. A committed Democrat, however irregular, Walsh had never considered himself more than a fellow traveler in the socialist movement. Philosophically, he had parted company with Debs, Stokes, and other pacifists by early 1917. Disclosure of the "Zimmerman telegram," proposing a secret alliance between Germany and Mexico in the event the United States entered the war, convinced him that Wilson's policy of "peace without victory" was justified. Out of the public eye, however, Walsh continued to aid his fellow radicals in distress. He corresponded with Goldman while she was serving time in Jefferson City and intervened with his friend Francis Wilson to ensure that her mail wasn't censored. He readily complied with "Big Bill" Haywood's request that he investigate the harassment of Wobblies in Kansas City, who had been repeatedly beaten by militiamen and arrested by local police. After the war, he even took up Tom Mooney's apparently hopeless case, defending the West Coast labor leader in the courts for nearly two decades and eventually winning his pardon.

On balance, the record shows, Walsh did what he could, when he could, for his embattled friends on the left. Like Nelson, he was a pragmatic activist who picked his fights and believed that consistency was the hobgoblin of timid souls. "Philosophies," he reflected in an interview with a socialist newspaper in 1918, "impose limitations. They also have a habit of getting under your feet. Those who have philosophies invariably waste effort in being consistent. No man, considering the film of life as it flickers by, can be both consistent and truthful. Events shape and reshape themselves so fast and reactions gained from them are so changeful and even inconsistent with each other, that the man with a philosophy would carry mental bruises all the time."[67]

In December 1917 August Seested presented himself at the Federal Courthouse in Kansas City and took the oath of American citizenship before Judge Van Valkenburgh. It was an embarrassing situation for the *Star*'s powerful general manager, who had always taken it for granted that he *was* an American citizen. Not until he registered to vote for Charles Evans Hughes in 1916 did he discover that his Danish father had failed to fill out the necessary naturalization forms decades before. The whole thing had been a silly misunderstanding. At any other time it would have been laughable, but not now, not when the United States and Germany were at war. Seested hoped to keep the incident quiet, but the *Post* picked up the story and ran with it, and in no time the retiring businessman found his name in the headlines nationwide.

August Seested, the *Star*'s powerful and secretive general manager, was frequently targeted by the paper's enemies.

The *Star*'s critics made hay of the revelation that Seested had been a German citizen when the United States declared war. Even Roosevelt's vicious attacks on the "shadow Huns" in the domestic German-American Alliance failed to immunize the paper against charges of disloyalty. The *Post* chastised Roosevelt for choosing the *Star*, "a paper whose general manager was so lately a subject of the kaiser that the ink is scarcely dry upon his naturalization papers," as the "organ to spread his propaganda." In line with Nelson's practice, the *Star* refused to dignify such calumnies with a response, and privately Haskell dismissed the episode as a tempest in a teapot. Seested, he remarked to White, had "never visited Germany or even had a letter from anybody in Germany—except from Mr. Nelson when he was visiting there."[68]

Xenophobic lightning struck closer to home when government officials tagged Haskell's own brother as a German agent. Edward Haskell returned from Bulgaria in early 1918 on a secret mission to dissuade Congress from declaring war on the ally of the Central Powers. Well known for his pro-

Bulgarian sympathies, Edward had been stationed in Bulgaria since the beginning of the war. Neither the State Department nor the Turks had forgotten his role in the Ellen Stone affair sixteen years earlier. The State Department viewed the entire American Near East mission as amateurish meddlers in Balkan geopolitics. Given the inflamed state of American public opinion, Edward's trip was sensitive enough in itself. To make matters worse, the tiny delegation traveled as guests of the Bulgarian government, which paid for Edward, his Swiss wife and six children, and a missionary colleague to return to the United States via neutral Switzerland.

With the full knowledge and support of the missionary board in Boston, Edward went to Washington to meet with the chief of the State Department's Near East Division. Albert Putney's "attitude was browbeating from the start," he recorded. When the missionary argued that reports of Bulgarian atrocities were grossly exaggerated, Putney flew into a rage and threatened him with prosecution under the Espionage Act "even before it had been passed." Edward's superior in Boston, convinced that Putney was "practically committed to war with Bulgaria," offered cautious encouragement but admonished him to "work very quietly, avoiding publicity to the last possible degree."[69] Edward, however, ignored the friendly warning and approached Colonel House, who arranged for him to present his unpopular views to members of the Senate Foreign Relations Committee.

At the end of May, Putney's boss formally notified the board that two missionaries "recently returned from Bulgaria" had been observed making "bitter attacks upon countries associated with the United States in the war" and apparently "engaging in a pro-Bulgarian propaganda." Unless they desisted, the official hinted ominously, the State Department might be forced to invoke the Trading with the Enemy Act and shut down all missionary activities in the Balkans. Putney waited another year—long after the armistice had made the Bulgarian issue moot—to play his trump card. Somehow he had stumbled onto Edward's dirty secret about accepting funds from the Bulgarians. In the spring of 1919 he sent an envoy to Boston to remind the board that the department had received information that its missionaries had engaged in "political or propaganda activities on behalf of Bulgaria" during the war and regarded it as a "very serious matter."[70]

Edward, who had been delivering innocuous speeches around the country and trying to keep out of trouble, was now summoned to Boston to defend himself. In an impassioned statement, he characterized Putney as "narrow, vindictive and reactionary" and said it was "unthinkable that this great Board with its glorious history can withdraw its hand from the outstretched hands of an enslaved people pleading for deliverance from bondage."[71] At the end of a lengthy interrogation, Edward emerged with a formal reprimand and renewed instructions to abstain from political activity. To ensure that Putney couldn't raise the matter again, the board quietly compensated the Bulgarian government for the missionary's travel "advance."

Edward's spirited defense of Germany's wartime ally and his outspoken pacifist views estranged him from his brother and sister-in-law in Kansas City. Isabel Haskell threw him out of the house when he came to stay with them in February 1919. Unrepentant, Edward chided Henry for making an "unnatural alliance with the forces of reaction" and referred to the *Star*, behind his brother's back, as "that sheet which 'like the sheep hath gone astray' into Rooseveltism and other things which make the angels weep!"[72] As far as Washington was concerned, however, Edward's case was closed. In the summer and fall of 1919, America's attention was diverted from domestic squabbles to the momentous debate over President Wilson's new world order.

Henry Haskell would look back on the *Star*'s fight against American membership in the League of Nations as "perhaps its most important achievement in the period of its management by the Nelson trustees."[73] An achievement it certainly was, but hardly a constructive one, not one in the best Nelsonian tradition of "building things up." It put the *Star* in league with its ancient enemy, Jim Reed, and its new bête noire, Frank Walsh, and pitted it against traditional allies like William Allen White, Burris Jenkins, and the *St. Louis Post-Dispatch*. The debate over America's postwar role in world affairs fractured the already weakened progressive coalition, antagonized the country's European allies, broke Wilson's health and spirit, and ultimately his presidency, and threw open the door to the lurking forces of reaction, complacency, and isolationism.

Haskell, internationalist to the core, tried to believe in the League's idealistic covenant but found it impossible. Wilson's plan to bring pressure on the Paris peace conference to adopt his Fourteen Points by appealing to the people of Europe over the heads of their leaders impressed him as "daring and brilliant" but doomed to failure. Haskell's concept of realpolitik, conditioned by his family's long experience of the Balkans, taught that human nature couldn't be changed overnight. If the world ever came around to a new political order, he was convinced, it would do so only incrementally and after cautiously testing the waters of international cooperation. Still, the United States could never again withdraw into its shell. "When a Balkan murder can touch off a war eventually involving the United States," he wrote to Roosevelt in November 1918, "isn't it essential that we sit in, in the European conferences hereafter, as we did in your administration at Algeciras, in order to obtain just settlements that will not lead toward war? Won't the present alliances have to look after the German border states for years to make sure they are not brought under German domination? Isn't a continuance of the present alliance in some form essential?"[74]

Roosevelt incorporated several of Haskell's observations in his next *Star* editorial. While acknowledging that the war had made isolationism impossible, he argued that "any declaration or peace league which represents the high-flown sentimentality of pacifists and doctrinaires" would be "worse than useless." In the short term, membership in such a body should be limited to the United States and its allies, whose national sovereignty and interests would be strictly protected. Haskell proposed that Henry Allen, then in Paris, be commissioned to serve as "liaison officer" in formulating a workable program for an international organization that Roosevelt, as the presumptive Republican presidential nominee in 1920, could get behind. With Roosevelt's blessing, the *Star* instructed its special correspondent to remain abroad long enough to solicit the views of Prime Minister David Lloyd George and other British and French leaders on the "sort of League of Nations they favor[,] not for immediate publication but for future reference."[75] At the same time, Stout belatedly bit the bullet and subscribed to the outstanding foreign service syndicated by Victor Lawson's *Chicago Daily News.*

Meanwhile, opposition to the "Wilson league" was slowly building on the home front. The well-publicized defection in September of diplomat William Bullitt, who charged that the great powers had "simply gone ahead and arranged the world to suit themselves," had exposed deep fissures within the administration.[76] Secretary of State Robert Lansing and others were rumored to share Bullitt's views. Party lines were breaking down in the Senate as well, in no small part thanks to Reed's fire-and-brimstone oratory. A crucial preliminary vote on the peace treaty held on November 19, two weeks after congressional Republicans seized power in midterm elections, showed sixty-three senators for and thirty-two against ratification with appropriate "reservations." This close call, just one vote shy of the necessary two-thirds majority, stiffened Wilson's resolve to stand pat and drum enemies like the gentleman from Missouri, whom he famously branded a "marplot," out of the Democratic Party.

But Reed was no more susceptible to intimidation than Roosevelt, who attacked Wilson's decision to attend the peace conference despite his party's setback at the polls. "In no other free country in the world to-day would Mr. Wilson be in office," Roosevelt observed. "He would simply be a private citizen like the rest of us. Under these circumstances our allies and our enemies, and Mr. Wilson himself, should all understand that Mr. Wilson has no authority whatever to speak for the American people at this time. His leadership has just been emphatically repudiated by them."[77] By what authority Roosevelt presumed to speak for the American people was unclear, inasmuch as the League continued to enjoy widespread popular support. Even the new Republican chairman of the Senate Foreign Relations Committee, Roosevelt's close friend Henry Cabot Lodge, believed the treaty could be made acceptable provided the United States obtained appropriate safeguards.

Haskell urged Roosevelt to emphasize that Lodge and other "reservationists" were not just naysaying obstructionists. "The point is in regard to the League-of-Nations question we hold the liberal position, our opponents the reactionary," he wrote to the columnist on Christmas Eve. "The President is apparently ready to sacrifice the real substance of a practical peace arrangement for a Utopia which would inevitably produce a recrudescence of imperialistic nationalism. Yet he has to a degree succeeded in creating the impression that his plan is the product of liberal thought, and I think it is up to us pretty vigorously to correct this impression." Roosevelt's vigor, however, had been sapped by a recent illness. In any case, he didn't share Haskell's enthusiasm for the wartime alliance and questioned whether the United States would want to fight alongside France, England, and Italy in future wars. Wilson was a "conscienceless rhetorician," he declared, and "anything he says about the World League is in the domain of empty and windy eloquence."[78]

Still trying to nudge Roosevelt in a constructive direction, Haskell suggested that he revive his old idea of a European-American "posse comitatus" empowered to keep the peace. Such an "entente" or "gentleman's agreement," he argued, was more realistic than the unworkable "superstate" favored by the naive "visionaries" on the other side of the League debate. As Haskell was typing his letter in Kansas City, Roosevelt in Oyster Bay was dictating his valedictory editorial on the League of Nations for the *Star*. Three days letter, the mighty Bull Moose was dead. "I suppose I was one of the last persons outside his family to see him," Haskell wrote to his brother, recalling a visit to Roosevelt's hospital bed in early December. "With my distrust of the gentleman who is ready to substitute rhetoric for action, I feel a sense of irreparable loss."[79]

Roosevelt had restored some of the vitality and spark that the "Twilight Twinkler" had lacked since its founder's death. It was easy to "keep the *Star* respectable," Haskell confided to White, but "a harder job to keep it clever."[80] All the same, Nelson had been right when he decided against inviting Roosevelt to be his partner. The Rough Rider, Haskell had learned, couldn't help running roughshod over everyone around him. In subcontracting the *Star's* editorial policy to Roosevelt, Kirkwood and Stout had fallen into a trap of their own making. No one, least of all the top managers, any longer thought of the paper as politically independent. For the next four decades and more, it would be seen as a reliable mouthpiece of the Republican Party.

The day after Roosevelt's death, Bonfils and Tammen—who had tried to woo him away from the *Star* with the promise of doubling his salary—pulled another surprise by naming the "two-fisted fighting parson" of Linwood Boulevard Christian Church editor of the *Post*. Burris Jenkins had collected his wartime dispatches for the *Star* in a pair of books that enhanced his national reputation as a journalist, lecturer, novelist, and religious philosopher. "He wanted to be an editor and we wanted him," Tammen explained to Walsh. "Of course it remains to be seen how milk and vinegar will mix and we will also see how the church and the devil get along together."[81]

A blunt-spoken, hard-living man who drove to work in a bright red sports car, Jenkins was as addicted to the limelight as Walsh. In his autobiography he recalled that he "was fully aware of the motives of the two owners, of their desire to put up a front of respectability for what had hitherto been looked upon in the community as a sort of outlaw paper. I was aware that they would regard me as a figurehead, but I flattered myself that once the figurehead got seated in its place it would do a considerable job of leading."[82] The clergyman's "Unholy Alliance" with his roguish employers gave him a new bully pulpit from which to preach the gospel of the League of Nations.

In his punchy, down-home style, Jenkins warned the "little two-by-four, hide-bound envious and self-seeking politicians of both parties, as well as the purblind newspapers, who cannot see through the grime of their cobwebbed brains" that they should "either get into the band wagon or get out of the way before they are run over. The League of Nations is a-coming." Bon and Tam were no more committed to the League than to the battle of ideas, but it was the best weapon the *Post* had to use against the *Star*. And, win or lose, the spry, husky-voiced Jenkins was a man after their own hearts. By his own account, the novice editor recognized that the odds were overwhelmingly against the pro-Leaguers, but he boasted that the *Post* "quickly became known east and west as one of the die-hards, the forlorn hopes, and even the President took notice and wrote his appreciation."[83]

Events had reached a critical stage for Wilson in the winter of 1918–1919. Having presented his draft covenant to the peace conference in Paris in mid-February, he sailed back to the United States to find Congress in open rebellion. During his absence, White wrote, "the American jingoes joined the world jingoes, and took charge of things."[84] Roosevelt's death had made Senator Lodge the recognized kingpin of the GOP opposition. But as vexatious as they could be, it wasn't the Republicans who gave Wilson conniption fits so much as the obstreperous "irreconcilables" in his own party—most particularly, Senator James Alexander Reed, commander in chief of the "Battalion of Death." His red-hot antipathy to the League was stoked by Wilson's flagrant disregard for senatorial prerogative in denying the Kansas City postmastership to Reed's pal R. Emmett O'Malley—the same O'Malley, it should be noted, whom Reed's patron, Tom Pendergast, had previously backed for the mayoralty, with similarly disappointing results.

With his chiseled features, powder-white hair, and courtly demeanor, Reed was often likened to a Roman senator, a resemblance heightened by his trademark white linen suit and panama hat. As an orator, he was conceded by friend and foe alike to be in a class with Patrick Henry and William Jennings Bryan. His objections to the League of Nations comprised a catalogue of sins, from violating U.S. sovereignty to threatening the American way of life. Reed argued eloquently, and at almost superhuman length, that the international body would be hugely expensive to maintain and do little more than maintain the status quo. It would be powerless to restrain the arms race that the Great Powers were sure to revive as soon as their exhausted economies permitted. And it would be composed disproportionately of countries populated by the "black, yellow, brown, and red races," who, in Reed's steely gray eyes, represented "the very dregs of ignorance, superstition, and barbarism."[85] He reserved special contempt for the British, whose far-flung empire ensured that they would dominate the League, and for Wilson's war-relief czar, whom Reed twitted on the Senate floor as "Sir Herbert Hoover."

Lodge proposed to address the most serious of these objections in a series of amendments to the covenant, and for some time the Massachusetts senator and his fellow reservationists held the upper hand. Had the White House shown the slightest willingness to compromise, the United States could have joined the League on terms acceptable to the vast majority of legislators. But Wilson refused to bend and positions on both sides quickly became carved in

Senator James A. Reed hurled his prosecutorial thunderbolts against the League of Nations. The Missouri Democrat denounced the League as an "international conspiracy" to "destroy our country and take from it its independence."

stone. Missourians held prominent positions on both sides of the debate. Assistant Secretary of State Breckenridge Long served as Wilson's point man, while Walsh, who attended the Paris peace conference as head of a delegation seeking self-determination for Ireland, was resolved to strangle the League at birth. O'Malley warned that 95 percent of Irish-American voters would bolt the Democratic Party if it adopted a pro-League stand, and Pendergast for once found himself in accord with the *Star*. "I don't know anything about the League of Nations," the Irish boss said. "But if Jim Reed says it is wrong, it's wrong."[86]

The spectacle of a senior Democratic senator repudiating the president of his own party created a sensation. The state party organization threatened to blackball Reed, but the *Star* found much to praise in his remarks and began according its favorite bogeyman greater respect. Reed reciprocated by sending a page boy to the Senate press gallery one day with an invitation for the *Star*'s Washington correspondent. Roy Roberts found the senator in the marbled chamber downstairs "pacing the floor like a lion in a cage," while passersby stopped and stared. "I notice from your preliminary editorials on this infamous scheme to betray America that your paper is going to be American in this greatest of all crises before our country," the old prosecutor began. "I have spent weeks studying this dastardly document which would destroy our country and take from it its independence. I know my motives will be misconstrued both here and at home. I know they will destroy me. I know my name will become a hissing and a byword on the street corners of Missouri when I oppose President Wilson on this covenant. I know it means the end of my political career. But a man must sleep with his own conscience. It matters not a whit what happens to me if I can help save America from this international conspiracy."[87]

Wilson carried his appeal to the American people on a grueling cross-country tour that brought him to Kansas City on September 6, 1919. The League covenant, he told an audience of twenty thousand in Convention Hall, was "one of the greatest documents of human history" and "little groups of selfish men" must not be allowed to prevent the country from reaping its benefits. If any of his opponents had a better scheme for keeping the peace, he would gladly support it. But mere "negation" would not "save the world," he declared. "Opposition constructs nothing. Opposition is the specialty of those who are Bolshevistically inclined." The president closed with his customary peroration: "My ancestors were troublesome Scotchmen, and among them were some of that famous group that were known as the Covenanters. Very well, here is the Covenant of the League of Nations. I am a Covenanter!"[88]

Wilson's oratory lit a fire under Reed, and on September 22 he unleashed his Olympian contumely in a four-hour speech on the Senate floor that many considered the climax of his career. Wilson, he sarcastically declared, "hears the echo of his own voice and the next day proclaims [it] the voice of God." The president had misled the American people by failing to acknowledge that the League would be dominated by the "backward nations of the world." It was unconscionable that "the half-civilized peoples of black states like Liberia and the wandering Arabs of Hedjaz" would be "given a voice in shaping America's destiny." The whole scheme was a sinister plot to subjugate the

United States to a tribunal that was accountable to no one but itself. "Senators," the Great Roman declaimed, "I know not what you will do, but as for me I decline to set up any government greater than that established by the Fathers, baptized in the blood of patriots from the lanes of Lexington to the forests of the Argonne, sanctified by the tears of all the mothers whose heroic sons went down to death to sustain its glory and independence—the government of the United States of America."[89]

As Reed's words hung in the air, the Senate chamber erupted in a scene of bedlam. "By God, you are right, Senator!" a crippled soldier yelled from the gallery, shattering his wooden crutch on the rail in his excitement. Doughboys tossed helmets in the air and boisterously banged them together. Vice President Marshall pounded his gavel but soon gave up trying to call the crowd to order. "Personally," he wrote later, "if I had my choice of running up against Jim Reed or a buzz saw, I should choose the buzz saw."[90]

Ten days after Reed's speech, Wilson fell victim to a massive stroke. His tragic incapacitation effectively ruled out American participation in the world body. Nor was he the only casualty of the League fight. What was left of the old progressive movement, the proud band who had rallied behind Wilson and Roosevelt before the war, went down in action as well. They would never forgive Wilson for affixing his name to the vindictive Treaty of Versailles, a peace, as Oswald Garrison Villard acidly observed, based on "intrigue, selfish aggression, and naked imperialism." A cynical Edward Haskell wrote to his brother in Kansas City, "I thought we had another Lincoln in the president's chair, and it was a hollow plaster cast." The "new Europe," White ruefully opined, stood exposed as the old Europe.[91]

Bereft of their cause célèbre, Jenkins resumed his churchly pulpit and the *Post* fell back into its old sensationalist ways. As for the *Star*, hadn't it warned that Wilson's fatally flawed Covenant was a pale reflection of the Bull Moosers' idealistic "Covenant with the People"? Stout was only too glad to get back to the local news that had always been the *Star*'s bread and butter. When he dropped the *Chicago Daily News* foreign service in early October, on the grounds of declining reader interest, Victor Lawson was disappointed but not surprised. "We have assumed that, with the world in the remaking, news from abroad would from this time on take on an interest for the average American reader unknown before the war," he wrote to the *Star*'s managing editor. "If, however, you are right it argues that we may be wrong."[92]

Isolationists and disgruntled progressives were already queuing up behind General Leonard Wood, a conservative law-and-order fanatic whose opposition to the League of Nations was exceeded only by his visceral hatred of communism. With Nelson and Roosevelt in their graves and Wilson a wasting shell, the glory days of the progressive movement were fast fading from memory. The *Star* had lost its heroes but found a new purpose. For Haskell and his colleagues, the millennium remained just around the corner. Unlike Nelson, though, they were determined to transcend their insurgency.

CHAPTER 6

❖

Main Street Paper

The 1920 Republican convention was coming down to the wire. All night long, Henry Haskell had been prowling the corridors of Chicago's Blackstone Hotel. Somewhere behind closed doors, he knew, party leaders were holding a conclave in hopes of breaking the deadlock between Leonard Wood, the controversial commander of the Army's Department of the East, and Governor Frank Lowden of Illinois. Shortly after midnight, he ran into George Harvey, the politically influential editor of the *North American Review.* The parley was taking place in his suite, Harvey confided to the *Star*'s representative. "Go up there. They's ready to talk." Haskell corralled his boss, Irwin Kirkwood, and together they dashed up to the fourth floor. "Kirkwood, tell us whom to nominate," a voice cried out as they entered the crowded sitting room. "That's your job, thank God!" the publisher returned good-naturedly.[1]

> *"A glorified organ of Main Street—thus one is tempted to describe the* **Kansas City Star,** *probably the most influential daily to be found west of Chicago. . . . Kansas City regards it as much an institution to be proud of as the new Union Station, or the Elks Club, or the splendid boulevard system."*
>
> —Oswald Garrison Villard

In years to come, Haskell would often reminisce about the legendary smoke-filled room where Warren Harding's dark-horse candidacy burst out of the starting gate. Senators Reed Smoot of Utah and Frank Brandegee of Connecticut pulled him and Kirkwood aside into Harvey's bedroom. The Republican elders were eager to tell the press why neither of the two front-runners stood a chance of garnering a majority of delegates. Wood, they explained, was widely seen as a career military man who lacked political experience and sensitivity. He would try to run the country by fiat, without consulting Congress, just as Wilson had done. Smoot conceded that Lowden "belonged to the lodge," but his campaign had been fatally compromised by a fund-raising scandal. What the country needed, the party leaders agreed, was a clean, seasoned, clubbable politician, one who would "seek advice and counsel" and eschew Wilson's autocratic tendencies. Senator Harding of Ohio was their man.[2]

Haskell could scarcely believe his ears. Politics was the art of compromise, but this was going too far. Not only was Harding practically unknown outside his home state and the Senate chamber, the newsman protested, he had studiously avoided taking positions on most major issues of the day. Did the Republican leadership seriously expect the American people to vote for a man whose record was a virtual cipher? Brandegee didn't mince words. "Gentlemen, we might as well be frank. This ain't a convention of 1880 when the party had a Blaine, a Sherman, an Edmunds, a Grant and a Garfield to choose among. We've got a lot of second raters. This man Harding isn't a world beater, but we think he's the best of the bunch." Party scouts had already been sent out to lobby the heads of the state delegations. Harding's nomination was sewn up in a night of no-holds-barred horse trading that left veteran Progressives shaking their heads. "Nineteen hundred twelve was a Sunday-school convention compared with this," one declared.[3]

If the Bull Moose campaign had initiated Haskell's education in practical politics, the 1920 convention season was his finishing school. No one in Chicago that summer was belting out "Onward, Christian Soldiers," standing defiantly at Armageddon, or electrifying the armies of disaffected with calls to insurgency. Nor did the Democrats set many souls on fire two weeks later when they conferred their nomination upon Governor James Cox of Ohio, a decent, centrist politician not known for rocking boats. Evangelical idealism was out of fashion. Reformers were reluctantly coming to the conclusion that old-fashioned pork-barrel politics was their best hope. For all their lofty rhetoric and militant ardor, the Bull Moosers of 1912 had in the final analysis been politically inept. An efficient, well-oiled party organization was a prerequisite for any serious reform movement, Haskell reflected in his wrap-up of the Republican convention for the *Outlook* magazine.

It is futile to rush out every four years, as many of us are inclined to do, and exclaim: "Let us have a new third party. The old parties do not express our aspirations. They have lost their meaning. We must organize a new party and nominate a leader who stands for what we believe." Futile, that is, except as a protest. . . . In general, if the reformer or the idealist is to get anywhere in politics, he must come up through the ranks, as Roosevelt did. . . . We must understand the importance of the political organization and the essential nature of the work it does. If we are to make ourselves an effective force, we must make up our minds to join a local party organization and have something to say before the issues are made up. We have no particular license to complain of the results if we take no hand in making them.[4]

Eager to share his political epiphany, Haskell sent tearsheets of the article to Brandegee, Harvey, Herbert Hadley, Will Hays, and other GOP notables. Not surprisingly, most of them warmly applauded his plea for a revival of partisan spirit. Kirkwood did too. A dyed-in-the-wool Republican, he had never seen much point in the *Star*'s vaunted mugwumpery. Although he considered himself a lower-case progressive, Kirkwood was happy to see his chief editorial writer atone for Nelson's incomprehensible rapprochement with the Wilsonian Democrats. Only William Allen White, who had helped draft the Republican platform in Chicago and fought with mixed success to salvage its liberal planks, welcomed Haskell's paean to party regularity with less than open arms. "I suppose we might as well get down to that basis; but it is rather hard for long-horned, free-ranging natives to come in and be stall-fed," he quipped.[5]

As usual, White's congenital optimism was tempered by a keen awareness of human imperfections. The Harding he had encountered at the Chicago convention, pitifully dejected, disheveled, and visibly the worse for drink, inspired neither confidence nor affection. The Republican Party, he later observed, had fallen under the influence of "sinister predatory economic forces" and bidden "farewell to the twenty years of liberalism which had grown up under the leadership of Theodore Roosevelt." In White's normally forgiving eyes, Harding was a "poor dub who had made his reputation running with the political machine in Ohio," spouting "resounding platitudes" and "saying nothing because he knew nothing."[6] He possessed neither the political skill nor the intellectual vision to address the formidable problems that confronted America at home and abroad.

"What a God-damned world!" an exasperated White exclaimed in the wake of Harding's victory that November. "Starvation on the one hand, and indifference on the other, pessimism rampant, faith quiescent, murder met with indifference; the lowered standard of civilization faced with universal complaisance, and the whole story so sad that nobody can tell it. If anyone had told me ten years ago that our country would be what it is today, and that the world would be what it is today, I should have questioned his reason."[7]

Both White and the *Star* had been beating the Wood-for-president drum ever since Roosevelt's untimely demise in early 1919. Among old Bull Moosers it was taken for granted that the virile, spit-and-polish officer would have been Roosevelt's choice in the unlikely event that he himself decided not to run. Even Wood's admirers, however, conceded that he was no substitute for the charismatic Rough Rider. In a military career that took him from tracking down Apaches in the wild West to battling entrenched bureaucrats as Army chief of staff in Washington, Wood had built a reputation as a bare-knuckled disciplinarian who met crises swiftly and efficiently. In the summer of 1919 he had put down race riots in Omaha with a ruthless military operation that raised the hackles of civil libertarians. That fall, when Wilson's hard-line attorney general, A. Mitchell Palmer, launched the infamous "Palmer raids" in response to a spate of radical unrest, Wood threw himself heart and soul into the communist witch-hunt. After observing him in action at a *Star* editorial conference, Haskell was convinced that the general's reasonable, articulate private persona was at odds with his public image as a rabid red-baiter. "When I hear Wood make a public speech I always get cold feet," he told a friend. "When I talk to him I am strong for him."[8]

White and Henry Allen, now governor of Kansas, pressed Wood to tone down his anticommunist bombast. "This crazy notion to hunt 'em down and shoot 'em and see Red, and all that sort of thing is going to pass during the Spring, and leave you high and dry unless you definitely appeal to the Progressives," White advised the headstrong general, to no apparent effect.[9] Allen, whose strong-armed reaction to a massive Kansas coal strike in 1919 had demonstrated his own law-and-order credentials, loyally placed Wood's name in nomination in Chicago, unaware that party chieftains regarded his candidacy as the kiss of death. Their backstage machinations ensured that Wood's momentum quickly dissipated once balloting got under way. At a decisive juncture, the Kansas delegation, hoping to secure the vice-presidential spot for Allen, switched their votes to Harding. Missouri and other key states joined the stampede, and by the tenth ballot the genial nonentity from the Buckeye State was on the road to the White House.

Thwarted in his ambition to serve as Harding's secretary of war, Wood accepted the governorship of the Philippines as a consolation prize. The sena-

E. Mont Reily (left) and President Warren Harding. The Kansas Citian foresaw
Harding's election in a dream, but later came in for a rude awakening.

torial cabal had rightly judged him too stiff-necked and militaristic for a nation sated with war, sacrifice, and cerebral proselytizing. Americans, White
diagnosed, were suffering from a sort of "moral shell-shock." They yearned
for a respite from the insatiable demands of patriotic duty, a return to easygoing "normalcy" in which they could get on with the country's business free

from undue government interference. Harding, liked by many, envied by none, was the man of the hour. Even his harshest critics admitted that he looked re-assuringly presidential, comported himself well on ceremonial occasions, and was capable of genuinely statesmanlike behavior. He did his best to stuff the genie of labor strife and social discord back in the bottle. Among other acts of clemency, he pardoned the aging Eugene Debs, who had polled nearly a million votes for the Socialist Party while languishing in the prison cell to which Wilson and Palmer had vindictively consigned him. In November 1921 Harding's Justice Department would quietly drop its sedition case against Rose Pastor Stokes. The era of good feelings had arrived.

Harding's elevation to the nation's highest office was due in no small mea-sure to the unstinting efforts of Kansas Citian E. Mont Reily. A minor Re-publican functionary who crossed the aisle from time to time to cut deals with the Pendergast crowd, Reily claimed credit for launching every successful Re-publican presidential bandwagon since Benjamin Harrison's. One night, by his own account, it was revealed to him in a dream that the unprepossessing lawmaker from Ohio was destined for greatness. Harding modestly derogat-ed any attempt to promote his candidacy, assuring Reily that he did "not pos-sess the elements of leadership or the widespread acquaintances which are es-sential to the ideal leadership of our Party in 1920."[10] But Harry Daugherty had different ideas. With Reily's connivance, Harding's chief political advis-er (and later attorney general) was secretly lining up delegates in Missouri—then as later a bellwether swing state—and talking his man up to the party's conservative leadership and their friends in the oil industry.

Democrats, too, were in the market for new faces. At the party's San Fran-cisco convention in late June, both the venerable William Jennings Bryan and Wilson's ambitious son-in-law, William McAdoo, were passed over in favor of Governor Cox, thus offering the American people a Hobson's choice be-tween two relatively obscure Ohio newspaper publishers who had ingratiated themselves with the party faithful mainly by avoiding giving offense. The stand-out figure in Missouri's delegation was Senator James Reed, fresh from his oratorical inquisition against the League of Nations. The credentials com-mittee, controlled by unforgiving Wilsonians, refused to seat the turncoat who had made common cause with the Republican irreconcilables. Amid a barrage of vilification, Reed stormed out of the convention and returned to a hero's welcome in Kansas City. Shortly thereafter, he reprised his attack on Wilson in a vintage oration at the Convention Hall that some said swayed many Mis-souri voters to Harding. Rehabilitated after Wilson's death in 1924, Reed would emerge as a strong contender for his party's nomination in each of the next three presidential elections.

The 1920 campaign proved beyond doubt that Wilsonian idealism was on the wane. Burris Jenkins, having placed McAdoo's name before the San Francisco convention "in the shortest nominating speech ever spoken, a single sentence," soon abandoned his quixotic crusade for the League of Nations, and with it the editorship of the *Kansas City Post*. Frank Walsh, a vociferous opponent of the League, refused to endorse the Democratic nominee, complaining that Cox's managers had turned the election into a referendum on the world body. Outraged by Wilson's continuing persecution of dissidents after the war, he vigorously protested Attorney General Palmer's draconian deportation policies and nearly allowed himself to be drafted on a third-party ticket with Robert La Follette. (The Wisconsin senator read the political tea leaves and concluded that a decorous withdrawal was the better part of valor.) Cast adrift from their political moorings, old-guard progressives of both major parties looked on in bewildered dismay as the "gaudy, bawdy, hell-roaring" twenties got under way.[11]

State politics presented a more edifying picture, with bona fide reformers installed in the executive mansions in both Jefferson City and Topeka. For only the second time since Reconstruction, Missourians in 1920 elected a Republican governor, Arthur M. Hyde, and awarded his party control of both legislative houses. "We have great hopes now of a cleanup from Hyde and the new prosecuting attorney," Haskell enthused to a friend. The *Star*, he added, "had quite a bit to do with getting Hyde into the race and getting him nominated. We have a hunch he will listen to some good advice as to his appointments."[12] Although Hyde's moderate progressivism was virtually indistinguishable from Harding's moderate conservatism—he ran on a platform calling for lower taxes, a businesslike administration, and strict enforcement of the new prohibition laws—he earned the affection of the *Star*'s managers by waging a notably immoderate feud with their archenemy, whom he taunted as "Bridlewise Jim" Reed of Tom Pendergast's stable of political hacks.

Across the state line, Governor Allen displayed an equally combative streak in responding to a wave of strikes in Kansas coal fields. When a work stoppage at Pittsburg almost succeeded in shutting off the region's energy supplies in November 1919, he induced legislators to create a special court empowered to prevent strikes in the fuel, food, transportation, and clothing industries. Like Wilson's National War Labor Board, the Kansas Court of Industrial Relations was ostensibly set up to arbitrate labor disputes in an impartial manner. But there was no mistaking the anti-union thrust of the governor's proposal. Intended to protect the public from being "victimized" by what Allen described as "industrial warfare," the three-member tribunal served largely as an instrument for keeping organized labor in line. Allen openly welcomed union threats to boycott the state. "We shall lose some radicals, but, for every radical, two conservatives will come in and we shall establish a mecca of well-ordered, contented commercial relationship," he boasted to a sympathetic audience in Boston.[13]

Labor leaders rose up in arms against legislation that would drastically curtail rights workers thought they had secured during the war. Walsh, whom the *Star* dubbed "attorney general for labor in the middle West," hastened to Topeka to plead their case. In a five-hour-long speech before a joint session of the legislature, he subjected the pending bill to a scathing critique. Calling the proposed court "state socialism in its most odious form," he warned that passage of the measure would mean "the striking down of labor unions as they are known in the nation today." Walsh charged that the court's authoritarian regime struck "at the heart of industrial freedom" and was both insidious and unconstitutional, a judgment in which the U.S. Supreme Court would concur when it invalidated the industrial court law six years later.[14]

The *Star*, having long taken the position that the public interest was better served by compulsory arbitration than by adversarial bargaining, applauded Allen's determination to impose industrial peace by force majeure. Calling the court "an experiment station for the nation in the matter of industrial legislation," the paper predicted that if it proved successful in Kansas, every state would soon enact similar legislation in the interest of "preventing the wasteful, baneful methods of the strike." (Privately, Haskell acknowledged that legislation so hostile to organized labor would never have gotten off the ground in a more industrialized state.) Rumors that a *Star* editor had helped draft the bill pointed to Lacy Haynes, the politically savvy correspondent who looked after the newspaper's interests in Kansas. Like his brother-in-law, William Allen White, Haynes had his finger in political pies throughout the state. After the industrial court law was enacted, he wrote a magazine article praising its sponsor and "emphasizing forward progress in Kansas," which he brazenly asked Governor Allen to help him peddle to *Collier's*.[15]

Resistance to Allen's tactics came from an unexpected quarter. White had been moving steadily to the left in politics, having come to agree with William Rockhill Nelson that the country had more to fear from reactionaries than from radicals. When railway workers in Emporia walked off the job in the summer of 1922, the editor mounted a civil-disobedience campaign by posting a placard in the *Gazette*'s office window supporting their right to strike. In so doing, he flouted both the antipicketing provision of the industrial court law and Allen's executive order forbidding such signs on the bizarre grounds that they might intimidate people who disagreed with the strikers. The governor had no choice but to order the state's best-known writer arrested. White decried the action as "an infamous infraction of the right of free press and free speech," to which Allen facetiously replied that only "a general epidemic of lockjaw" could prevent the irrepressible Sage of Emporia from freely speaking his mind. On cue, White sat down at his cluttered desk and spun out a classic defense of free speech in 345 well-chosen words. "To an Anxious Friend" would win a Pulitzer Prize and establish the editor's reputation as a champion of civil liberties in an increasingly uncivil and illiberal age.[16]

If White counted on the *Star*'s support in his one-man crusade, however, he was disappointed. Haskell's gut reaction was to side with his old friend and rebuke Allen for overreacting. But a month later he reversed himself, explaining in a somewhat tortured letter to White that in his view speech was constitutionally protected only when it called for laws to be changed, not broken. In essence, this was the same majoritarian reasoning the *Star* had followed when it denounced Rose Pastor Stokes and her fellow dissidents during the war. To liberals like White, it was one more sign that the paper was back-pedaling from its longstanding commitment to protecting the rights of minorities. To Edward Haskell, it was painfully clear that his younger sibling had sold his soul. "My brother Harry used to be a moderate Single-Taxer," he wrote to a mutual friend, "but I fear that his position as practically editor-in-chief of a successful, money-making daily is transforming him unconsciously into a conservative on industry and economics."[17]

Haskell's career as a political commentator blossomed during the Republican ascendancy of the 1920s. The cynical maneuvering he witnessed in George Harvey's smoky suite in Chicago had convinced him that reformers needed to get their hands dirty in grassroots politics, but postwar Kansas City offered little encouragement to disturbers of the status quo. After their brief flirtation with charter reform in the late teens, party bosses got back to business as usual in the 1920 municipal election, united as never before in their determination to stop the good-government brigade in its tracks. The "move for righteousness" was getting out of hand, Boss Joe Shannon warned Walsh. Unless something was done about it, the only people likely to escape unblemished were newspaper editors, police commissioners, and court officials, as they would be "the only ones who are *free* from all sin and thoughts thereof."[18]

The *Star* and its fellow "sin hounds"—as Atchison editor Ed Howe nicknamed the censorious crusaders for civic morality—reposed their battered faith in Matt Foster, the straitlaced Republican police commissioner who was running for mayor under the antiboss banner. Democrats dubbed him the *Star*'s "silk-underwear" candidate and charged that the paper's covert agenda was to assert its control over local politics and advance its campaign for Hyde and Wood in the state and national contests. When the votes were counted, though, neither side had much to crow about. Kansas Citians returned the incumbent mayor, a Democrat, to office by a narrow margin. Whereupon the *Star*, in the best Nelsonian tradition, declared victory and turned its attention to Governor Hyde's promised crackdown on crime and corruption.

Haskell, putting on a brave face, looked forward to the "smashing of the old Democratic machine crowd that was in alliance with crime in Kansas City." But his use of the past tense was premature. By any reasonably objective standard, the city was rapidly descending into chaos. Prohibition, the sin hounds' panacea for all social ills, paradoxically fostered a climate of unprecedented lawlessness. By the early twenties Kansas City had the dubious distinction of leading the nation in homicides, with a per capita murder rate five times higher than New York's and almost triple that of Chicago at the dawn of Al Capone's reign of terror. Even Conrad Mann, the relentlessly upbeat head of the Chamber of Commerce, warned apocalyptically about a breakdown of law and order. "Conditions are so intolerable that it is almost impossible for people to drive about with any degree of safety in their automobiles," he advised Governor Hyde. Daylight robbery was commonplace and "pimps and crooks of all kinds" went about their business openly, unmolested by the police. "Personally I could hardly be accused of being bigoted or narrow minded, neither have I ever had the earmarks of wanting to be a reformer," Mann wrote, "but if something is not done and done quickly, in order to straighten some of the things out, it will be a sorry day for Kansas City and the Republican Party."[19]

Police corruption and brutality moved up a notch on the *Star*'s agenda when two notoriously abusive members of the force beat a young reporter investigating a case of murder and suicide. Never known for its decorum, Kansas City journalism became markedly more rough-and-tumble after sewer-pipe magnate Walter Dickey purchased the *Star*'s two surviving daily competitors, the morning *Kansas City Journal* in April 1921 and the afternoon *Post* a year later. A pillar of the commercial aristocracy, Dickey was reputed to be the city's de facto Republican boss. Despite lavish expenditures on behalf of numerous GOP candidates, however, his own political ambitions had thus far gone conspicuously unrewarded. Like Nelson, Dickey discovered that his zest for local politics cooled after he began playing in the big leagues: he too had hitched his star to Roosevelt's wagon, though he declined to follow the Bull Moose into political exile. He emulated Baron Bill in other ways as well, erecting a white-columned limestone mansion on a prominent hillside just south of Oak Hall and breeding prize Herefords on his Kansas farm.

Apparently convinced that his political alliance with E. Mont Reily entitled him to membership in Harding's inner circle, Dickey acted as if his day had at last arrived with the Ohioan's election to the presidency. Scuttlebutt had it that he was under consideration for a cabinet appointment, but someone—possibly the obsequiously obliging Reily—had briefed Harding on the delicacy of the political situation in Kansas City, and Harding sensibly steered clear of that particular hornet's nest. Undaunted, Dickey decided to use his newspapers to jump-start his stalled political career and redress the catalogue of grievances he had chalked up against the *Star* over the years. Installing his younger son as publisher of the *Journal* and *Post*, he proceeded to sink millions of dollars into the newspapers without gratifying his desire for elected office or making a perceptible dent in the *Star*'s ironclad monopoly. In 1928 he combined the two failing papers in a desperate bid to salvage his investment and reputation. Successful in neither attempt, he died, bankrupt, three years later.

The *Post*'s metamorphosis under Dickey into a Republican house organ not only silenced the city's principal Democratic voice but also deprived readers of the scurrilous irreverence they had come to enjoy during the thirteen years of the Bonfils and Tammen regime. Journalistically speaking, Kansas City was now a one-party town. To be sure, the *Star* continued to back the occasional maverick Democrat in local campaigns and earnestly strove to rise above the partisan fray. But the managers' efforts to follow in Nelson's footsteps while charting a course of their own were increasingly erratic and unconvincing. On Ida Nelson's death in October 1921, Laura Kirkwood became sole trustee of her father's entailed estate. As such, she controlled the paper's purse strings, adjudicated its editorial policy, and held the destiny of Nelson's devoted "helpers" in her hands. They were uncomfortably aware that the sale of the paper couldn't be postponed indefinitely. Those privy to Laura's dark secret— her growing addiction to alcohol—couldn't help wondering how much longer their reprieve would last.

At the weekly Saturday night suppers she gave for the senior staff at Oak Hall, Laura was inquisitive and deferential, but firmly in charge. The paper's old guard was slowly shuffling off stage; the no-longer-young Turks—Haskell, Roy Roberts, George Longan—stood impatiently in the wings. When longtime managing editor Ralph Stout wrote a fawning biography of Nelson, his colleagues discreetly prevailed on him to suppress it, even though the publisher had already set the book in proof. Roberts later explained that the executives in waiting considered the book uncritical, as indeed it was. It also threatened to embarrass the new regime in another way. The managers were trying to put a new face on the staid-looking old paper by instituting such modest innovations as half-tone photographs and syndicated comic strips, both of which Nelson had banned. In 1922 they set up a small radio studio at Eighteenth and Grand, making the *Star* one of the first newspapers in the country to embrace the new medium. At such a pivotal time in the paper's history, it wouldn't do to be too closely identified with Baron Bill.

Irwin Kirkwood, the scapegrace son-in-law no longer, now wielded authority in his own right. He had been named editor of the paper after Mrs. Nelson died and would shortly step into the Old Man's shoes as a director of the Associated Press. But even he deferred to the all-powerful Gus Seested, who received a monthly stipend of five hundred dollars from the estate in addition to his on-the-books salary. Fortunately for in-house harmony, the general manager and the Kirkwoods saw eye to eye with Haskell in steering the *Star* along the path of Rotarian respectability. When Laura announced her impulsive decision to publish a full-color Sunday magazine devoted largely to art and literature, Kirkwood warned that it would break the bank. But Seested and his colleagues were inured to her champagne tastes and waited until the bills grew exorbitant to abandon the experiment. Fond of travel and high society, the Kirkwoods exchanged Nelson's summer "cottage" in Massachusetts for a luxurious mountain "camp" in the Adirondacks. There they indulged their love of fishing, horse racing, and partying—a far cry from the rarefied political atmosphere of Boston's exclusive North Shore.

The *Star*, ostracized by Washington officialdom during the second Wilson administration, had come in from the cold as well. Flexing his political muscles, Kirkwood tried on his father-in-law's mantle as spokesman for the western "progressives." It soon became apparent, however, that he and Nelson were cut from different cloth. Kirkwood's bred-in-the-bone conservatism had been fortified by his journalistic apprenticeship under Stout, Seested, and Haskell. Calvin Coolidge, the tight-lipped apostle of minimalist government, was his ideal of a far-sighted political leader. When the vice president came to Kansas City in the fall of 1921 to address an American Legion convention and dedicate the site for the new war memorial, the Kirkwoods billeted General John J. Pershing and Marshal Ferdinand Foch of the Allied high command at Oak Hall, while Coolidge, perhaps mindful that the *Star* had refrained from en-

An American Legion parade passes a reviewing stand in front of the *Star,* November 1, 1921. Irwin Kirkwood's public-relations coup infuriated Walter Dickey of the rival *Kansas City Journal.*

dorsing Harding the previous year, accepted an invitation to stay at Dickey's suburban home.

On the final day of the convention, the *Journal*'s new proprietor belatedly discovered that the reviewing stand for the grand parade had been erected in front of the *Star*'s headquarters at Eighteenth and Grand. The *Post* naturally attributed this public-relations coup to its rival's insatiable lust for power and self-promotion. The patriotic solemnity of the occasion was further spoiled when the Bonfils and Tammen paper dredged up the old canard about the supposed pro-German sympathies of the *Star*'s general manager during the war. Seested, the *Post* contended, had not only waited until the last possible moment to take out his naturalization papers in 1917 but had actually "contributed" thousands of dollars to the "imperial German government" while he was legally a subject of the kaiser.[20] Shop-worn though these allegations were, they got under Seested's skin so effectively that he persuaded his brother, the *Star*'s circulation manager, to sue the *Post* for libel.

Why hadn't Seested fought to clear his name four years earlier, when the *Post* first circulated its defamatory innuendos? The explanation seems clear: For the *Star*'s top executive to have flaunted his German heritage while America was at war and the Wilson administration was gunning for the paper might have had serious repercussions. Better to wait until the wind shifted and public opinion was more on his and the paper's side. In the end, the *Post*'s hard-slugging managing editor was jailed for refusing to divulge his paper's sources,

The *Star*'s high command as caricatured by the *Kansas City Post* in 1921: August Seested, Irwin Kirkwood, and Ralph Stout. Seested's failure to take out naturalization papers years before had come back to haunt him.

Bonfils and Tammen cut their losses and unloaded the *Post* to Dickey a few months later, and by the time Seested was posthumously vindicated by the courts, in 1935, the dream of peace and brotherhood symbolized by the Liberty Memorial had been shattered by another imperialistic German dictator.

The spring 1922 election was uneventful by Kansas City standards. With the vote fixers and plug-uglies mostly on holiday, the contest pitted Governor Hyde's bulldog police commissioner, Matt Foster, against an easygoing butter-and-egg merchant named Frank Cromwell whom the Democratic factions had put forward in a rare show of party unity. Having identified police oppression as the central issue of the campaign, the Rabbits and Goats tapped into the resentment sparked by the police board's overzealous clean-up campaign, in which thousands of otherwise law-abiding citizens were hauled in for minor traffic violations. When Democrats howled that the Republican-controlled force had unleashed a reign of terror, the *Star* countered that the machine bosses were up to their old tricks of protecting their "underworld allies" in the gambling racket and pandering to "the lowest elements in the community." But the *Star*'s bona fides were no longer taken for granted, even by its traditional friends. In St. Louis, the *Post-Dispatch* railed that "the daily press, led by the *Kansas City Star*," had "practically suppressed the news of the Cromwell campaign" in its eagerness to defend the "lawless and brutal methods of Gov. Hyde's police satraps." The only solution to the problem, the Pulitzer paper argued, was to restore "home rule," transferring authority over metropolitan police forces from the state house back to the city halls.[21]

In the throes of the mayoral contest, Frank Walsh leaped into the fray on Cromwell's behalf, delivering a fiercely partisan speech at a community hall in the heart of the Country Club district, a Republican stronghold. Commissioner Foster's "cruelty," the lawyer told his mostly middle-class audience, was on a par with that "of the czars or of Nero or of the ancient depredators of old." The *Star* would have voters believe that Foster "is a surly sort of a fellow but means well," that his clean-up campaign unfortunately "became a little rough and occasionally an innocent citizen was brought in," with the regrettable result that "the rights of 50,000 people were trampled upon." In an ironic twist to the story, the mother of the newspaper's city editor, a well-respected club woman, was running for a council seat on the Democratic ticket. When she and Cromwell were both swept into office, the *Star* accurately interpreted the election results as both "a repudiation of law enforcement as undertaken by the Foster police administration" and "a vote of confidence in the boss system."[22]

This backhanded compliment to Pendergast and his ilk betrayed a subtle change in Haskell's own attitude toward boss politics. Shortly after the city election, he wrote a long letter to Herbert Hadley, soliciting the former governor's advice about creating a new kind of political machine, one dedicated to reform instead of pork. The question he posed to Hadley was whether it was possible to "build an effective party machine in competition with a thoroughly unscrupulous one by using patronage to reward party workers, but at the same time keeping clear of graft and dishonesty." Such an organization, in order to compete successfully against the entrenched machines, would have to be

> a combined employment agency, philanthropic institution, and friend to the people generally. If it captures the City Hall it should give the jobs to party workers. It must not try to enforce ideal conditions. It must not enforce ordinances which would make all contractors mad by compelling them to take their material off the streets. It must be very lenient with traffic violators and close its eyes to a good deal that goes on, at least until public opinion is aroused on the subject. Its government must be made human and good natured, not stern and severe. Unless it has some dramatic political genius to put forward as its candidate for mayor, like Tom Johnson in Cleveland or [James] Couzens in Detroit, it must be content to nominate the typical "good fellow," depending on making him perform by the influences back of him. It must sacrifice efficiency very often to expediency. It must realize that people are bundles of prejudices and only a small percentage are open to reason. . . .
>
> We tried a non-Partisan movement here and it got no where. Our anti-boss movement was much more promising, but went to smash because of defective management. Our tendency always is to count too much on reason and not enough on prejudice. From experience else where I judge non-partisan movements will not work. It seems to me that hope lies in developing such movements as the anti-boss movement along practical lines.[23]

In suggesting that the reformers should concentrate on beating the crooks at their own game, the *Star*'s chief editorial writer was ringing a variation on the theme he had sounded in the wake of Harding's nomination two years earlier. Progressives and boss-busters could no longer afford the luxury of standing aloof from party politics. It was time to come down from their ivory towers, slog through the muck of local politics, and lower their unrealistic expectations. The millennium wasn't just around the corner, and no amount of good intentions or wishful thinking would bring it any closer.

Whether Haskell was urging the reformers to fight fire with fire, or merely issuing a counsel of despair, only the future would tell. As for the present,
one eminent critic had already reached a verdict. Writing in the December
1922 issue of the *Nation,* Oswald Garrison Villard criticized the post-Nelson
Star as a "waning luminary" and a "glorified organ of Main Street." Years before, the great liberal editor had tried to hire Haskell away to the *New York
Evening Post.* Now he heaped scorn on the *Star's* editorial page as timid, lackluster, trivial, and provincial. There was, he observed, "extraordinarily little to
suggest to the reader that American labor is desperately unhappy or that the
plight of the farmer, so distressing to himself, is keeping the *Star's* editors
awake at night." The paper's coverage of foreign affairs was little better. The
Star, Villard opined, "knows nothing of the profounder economic issues, and
by its inherited tradition it is compelled to treat the United States of today
just as if the world had not been turned over and stood upon its head since
1914." In short, a paper that "once had a nation-wide reputation for force and
vigor of utterance" had degenerated into a "mouthpiece of narrow and medi-
ocre respectability."[24]

Months before Villard published his acid critique, the *Star* had undertak-
en a quaint crusade that laid its bourgeois principles on the line. The episode
was known as the "Kansas City milk war," and at issue was the safety of the
city's milk supply. For years, milk produced by local dairies, most of which
were tiny, mom-and-pop operations, had been subjected to cursory or no inspection before being brought to market. Small dairy farmers resisted the
growing pressure for mandatory pasteurization, claiming that a centralized
system would favor large-scale producers and distributors and eventually drive
them out of business. Nonetheless, scattered outbreaks of typhoid, tuberculosis, and other bacterial diseases across the country convinced the municipal
authorities that sanitary regulations needed to be tightened, and in the summer of 1921 they hired a nationally known public health expert to advise them
how to go about it.

Having come to town under the auspices of a Democratic administration,
Dr. Charles E. North naturally looked to the *Post* to publicize his controversial campaign for clean milk. Bonfils and Tammen took up the cause with gusto, inasmuch as the *Star* had lined up with the small dairymen in their increasingly sour-tasting squabble with Big Milk. Both sides in the ensuing
journalistic donnybrook resorted to the time-honored tactics of sensationalism and caricature. The *Post* accused its competitor of slanting the news, pandering to its free-market Republican constituency, and turning a blind eye to
the plight of sick and dying babies. In return, the *Star* branded North an

alarmist, cast doubt on his scientific credentials and infant-mortality statistics, and even challenged him to milk a cow in public at a downtown hotel.
The upshot of this undignified mudslinging was a stringent new milk-
pasteurization ordinance, which the *Post* hailed as a victory for the city's babies, while the *Star* assailed it as a victory for the "big dealers."[25]

Although Kansas City's "milk war" generated more heat than light, it made
one thing crystal clear. Less than a decade earlier, the *Star* had supported Helen Keller's controversial fight to eradicate the venereal disease that caused
blindness in newborns. Now, it seemed, economic considerations took precedence over the rights of the weak and defenseless.

The fall of 1922 witnessed the political debuts of two men destined to occupy special niches in the *Star*'s gallery of rogues. Harry Truman and Henry
McElroy made an oddly matched pair. Both were country bred and plain spoken. Both had wiry physiques, leathery complexions, and notoriously short
fuses. There, however, the resemblance ended. Truman, a dirt farmer and
failed haberdasher from Independence, was head over heels in debt when the
Democrats nominated him for office on the strength of his wartime camaraderie with Tom Pendergast's nephew. The Iowa-born McElroy, by contrast,
had made a tidy fortune in real estate and enjoyed a reputation as a shrewd
businessman. He was a safe choice to run alongside Truman in the race for
the administrative judgeships of eastern and western Jackson County.

Both McElroy and Truman owed their careers to Pendergast and remained
loyal to him to the bitter end. But in the *Star*'s estimation Truman would always be a small-time machine politician, a kept man, not quite up to the important jobs he undertook, while McElroy would reap the benefit of the doubt
as a successful realtor, a privileged class in a city that revered its builders.
McElroy had attracted the *Star*'s notice in 1919, when he and J. C. Nichols
formed a partnership for the purpose of acquiring land quietly, hence cheap-
ly, for the future Liberty Memorial. His reputation for thrift, financial sagacity, and managerial competence never quite deserted him, even after he was
exposed as one of the biggest crooks ever to operate out of City Hall. "Listen," McElroy assured reporters on becoming western county judge, "I've got
$500,000 all my own. I'm going into this court job and give a real business ad-
ministration."[26] In years to come he and Truman would build deluxe hard-
surfaced county roads at rock-bottom prices and generally run a tight ship.
That both men were strong Democrats was a fact the *Star* chose not to dwell
upon. Exemplary public servants were always in short supply and it was
enough to hold Truman and McElroy up as paragons of honesty and efficiency.

Unfortunately, honesty and efficiency were not hallmarks of Warren Harding's administration. The whiff of scandal that perfumed the nation's capital in early 1921 soon thickened into a heavy stench. He could take care of his enemies, Harding muttered; it was his friends who gave him headaches. Conspicuous among the troublemakers was E. Mont Reily, the original Harding go-getter from Kansas City. During his brief, inglorious stint as governor of Puerto Rico—a post with which the president had rewarded him under the mistaken impression that he could do no harm there—Reily's insufferably regal pretensions and ham-fisted treatment of local politicians drove the islanders to open rebellion. At length, a Puerto Rican official was dispatched to Washington to demand his recall. "The administration of Governor Reily has been a succession of insults to the people," the official complained. "When he went to the island he found a land of peace and happiness, and almost overnight he transformed it into a hotbed of dissension and despair."[27]

After Reily's forced resignation, a correspondent for Villard's *Nation* observed that a fiasco had been inevitable in light of Harding's "quaint idea of sending as Governor of what is in fact, if not in law, a foreign country in a time of acute political tension a provincial politician unversed in foreign affairs, unacquainted with Latin-American life, temperament, or ideas, ignorant of the Spanish language, whose idea was to 'clean up' Porto Rico as they 'mopped up' the trenches in France during the war. Beyond the fact that he had been trained for the American colonial service by a term as park commissioner and later as assistant postmaster in his home town on the Big Muddy, nobody seemed to know much of Mr. Reily." Even the city's leading paper had ridiculed him from the outset, the reporter noted. "When the Kansas City *Star* fails to support a Republican appointment in its own town the man must be either a mighty poor stick or a remarkably good one. There had been nothing in Mr. Reily's career to suggest the latter contingency."[28]

Back home in Kansas City, Reily nursed his wounded pride, abjured presidential politics, and devoted himself to building his working relationship with Boss Pendergast. No such course was available to the hapless Harding. As one member of his administration after another came under suspicion or indictment for various forms of corruption, he struggled to focus attention on his fight for America's participation in the World Court, a cause only marginally less odious to Republican isolationists than the League of Nations. In the summer of 1923 he took his campaign on the road, just as his predecessor had done when the fate of the League was hanging in the balance. Arriving at Kansas City's Union Station on June 22, Harding looked confident and relaxed. Photographers captured him beaming at the camera as he and his wife departed for a tour of the city in an open motor car. Florence Harding, affectionately known as the "Duchess," sported a brightly printed gown, wide-brimmed hat, and long white gloves. Balancing a decorative parasol on her shoulder, she looked for all the world as if she were setting out to a lawn party.

Rain would soon fall on the presidential parade, however. Such, at least, was the testimony of William Allen White, who called on Harding in Kansas City that evening and accompanied him on the train across Kansas the next day. White was in the Hardings' suite at the Muehlebach Hotel when a woman he didn't recognize was ushered in. The president, "obviously aghast," whisked his visitor away into an adjoining room, without making introductions. Subsequently, White learned that she was Mrs. Albert Fall, the wife of Harding's former secretary of the interior. Fall's name would become a byword for corruption a few weeks later when congressional investigators pried the lid off the Teapot Dome oil scandal. Harding, White recalled, looked "perturbed and anxious" as he left to give a speech at the Convention Hall. Whatever Emma Fall had told him, the newsman deduced, must have been "a wallop on the jaw."[29]

In some mysterious way, White believed, the president's private interview with Mrs. Fall in Kansas City was connected to his collapse in Alaska a few weeks later and his death in San Francisco in early August. The legend that the well-meaning Harding died of a broken heart, betrayed by his friends, was compelling enough to survive later disclosures that appeared to refute White's recollections.[30] Nevertheless, the image of an ordinary, decent man who was tragically out of his depth, surrounded by scheming deceivers and overwhelmed by the office of president, lodged itself in the popular imagination. Two decades later, it would resurface when another common man from the Midwest moved into the executive mansion under similar circumstances, having had greatness suddenly thrust upon him.

The *Star*'s posthumous assessment of President Harding was judicious but charitable. With all his faults, the paper opined, the late president deserved to be remembered fondly for his "great human qualities," his "solidity, his caution and his sanity," and above all his "practical idealism." The latter phrase is one that Haskell had taken to using repeatedly since his baptism in the chilly waters of political pragmatism at the Chicago convention. It encompassed everything from Harding's veto of the budget-busting soldiers' bonus bill to his achievement in negotiating a modest reduction in world armaments. Given the choice between an intellectual giant, a man of sterling character and principle, and a plodding politician who was willing and able to compromise, voters would do well to remember who was likely to be more successful at getting things done. While critics depicted Harding as, at best, a big-hearted bumbler with feet of clay, the *Star* chose to memorialize the twenty-ninth president as a prudent leader who had "kept his feet on the ground and refused to permit the government to be led off in any moonbeam chasing."[31] In short, Harding was not Woodrow Wilson, for which the country could be eternally grateful.

What sort of chief executive Vice President Coolidge would make remained to be seen, as far as Haskell was concerned. The inscrutable Vermonter's brief stopover in Kansas City in 1921 had yielded few clues as to his leadership abilities. In any case, Haskell's mind was on other matters in the fall of 1923. His beloved wife died that September after a long bout with cancer. Try as he might to emulate Roosevelt's "ruthless stoicism," Haskell was devastated by his bereavement. Family members described him as uncharacteristically "intolerant and gloomy."[32] Brooding over the cosmic forces of darkness, he lost interest in mundane politics. When the Kirkwoods offered him a leave of absence from the *Star*, he jumped at the opportunity to take a busman's holiday in Europe. Armed with letters of introduction to politicians, journalists, writers, and academics, he sailed for England in mid-October. It was his first trip abroad since his boyhood in Bulgaria and he meant to make the most of it. For years he had been waging a rearguard action to make the *Star* more internationalist in its outlook. Now was his chance.

From provincial editorial writer to cosmopolitan pundit—the distance Haskell traveled over the next four months would not be measured in miles alone. Suddenly, the world was his oyster. In London, he met such luminaries as the novelist H. G. Wells, the economist Francis Hirst, and Geoffrey Dawson, the legendary editor of the *Times*. Archibald Henderson, disciple of Einstein and biographer of Mark Twain and Bernard Shaw, squired him around the English countryside. In Paris, he held an "old settlers' reunion" with American ambassador Myron Herrick, exchanging memories of their childhoods in the now-defunct hamlet of Huntington, Ohio. (Unbeknownst to Haskell, Reily, eager to curry favor with the *Star*, had urged Harding to send him to Paris in Herrick's place.)[33] Touring the troubled Ruhr Valley, still occupied by French troops, he concluded that reports of French brutality were exaggerated and that the Germans were largely to blame for their postwar economic crisis. Christmas found him at the home of the violinist Fritz Kreisler in Berlin. In Rome, he attended a papal audience and renewed his acquaintance with a favorite classics professor from Oberlin. All of this and more he chronicled in a series of highly personal dispatches billed as "Notes from a Kansas City Traveler." Part travelogue, part political and social commentary, the articles proved so popular with the *Star*'s readers that Haskell toyed with the idea of gathering them into a book.

A widower in his late forties, Haskell was belatedly coming into his own as a writer and thinker. Summing up his grand tour in a letter to his expatriate brother, he remarked that conversing with Europeans had taught him that "you can't believe much of anything anybody with a cause says." Of all the people he encountered on his travels, "only the British come half way near telling you the truth, and they don't tell it all."[34] Though no one would have mistaken him for a hardened cynic, Haskell's newfound skepticism made him less susceptible than ever to the consolations of philosophy and religion. Sooner or later, he was convinced, the deep-rooted distrust between the French, Germans, and British was sure to bear fruit in another cataclysm. If twentieth-century Americans couldn't avoid foreign entanglements altogether, they could at least see the world through clear, unsentimental eyes and repress their penchant for political and economic quick fixes. The era of postwar reconstruction was no time for airy-fairy promises or moralistic posturing. Both politicians and journalists had more serious work to do.

Making landfall in Boston in early February 1924, Haskell stopped off in Dayton, Ohio, to see his old friends Katharine and Orville Wright. He had known Katharine since the early 1890s, when they were fellow undergraduates at Oberlin, and through her had learned about the "boys," Wilbur and Orville, long before they became household names. Over the years, he had kept in touch with America's first family of flight. Since Wilbur's death in 1912, he had become increasingly active on Orville's behalf in the brothers' dispute with the Smithsonian Institution over Samuel Langley's competing claim to be the inventor of the airplane. Katharine, unflinchingly devoted to her surviving brother, had never fully acknowledged her feelings for the studious, considerate man she knew in college. Yet even before his wife died she had nurtured Haskell's interest in foreign affairs, encouraging him to overcome his feeling of inferiority toward "eastern journalists" and win the "personal recognition" that he deserved by branching out into "a different field." Their budding epistolary courtship would finally blossom into love and they would be married in October 1926, over Orville's sullen and implacable protest.[35]

Buoyed by Katharine's selfless devotion, Haskell felt like a new man. In the summer of 1924, he dutifully made the rounds of the national conventions—the Democrats in New York, the Republicans in Cleveland—in harness with Washington correspondent Roy Roberts. But his heart was no longer in the game of politics. Coolidge stood only marginally higher in his estimation than Harding, chiefly on account of his negative virtues. "I can't think of any other President except perhaps Grover Cleveland, who would have dared risk his political life by vetoing the bonus, the G.A.R. pension bill and the postal clerks salary bill," he commented to a friend. Yet even as he praised "Silent Cal" with faint damns, Haskell offered enough hosannas to the new administration's bedrock conservative values to remain a Republican in good standing. Shortly before the fall election, the president dropped him a line to express his "appreciation of the work you are doing for our party."[36] Flattered in spite of himself, Haskell tucked the note away for posterity. The GOP hadn't covered itself in glory of late, but there was always hope. Besides, Coolidge didn't look quite so bad when one considered the alternatives.

The Democrats, fractious as ever, had thrilled to the spectacle of McAdoo and Reed wrestling each other to a draw in a virtual replay of their 1920 match-up. When Al Smith's short-lived boom fizzled out—the popular New York governor would resurge to capture his party's nomination four years later—Robert La Follette was left as the only certified progressive in contention. The Wisconsin senator had once again bolted the Republican Party and Kirkwood was positively livid, calling him a "fake Progressive" who was "utterly selfish" and "without principles on any subject except La Follette." Haskell's more nuanced criticism previewed the objections progressives would raise to the New Deal. La Follette's "whole scheme of things," he wrote to a friend, "is to have the government dip into business on every hand. I believe real liberalism lays far more stress on individual development than LaFollette does." Kirkwood joined the publisher of the Philadelphia *North American* in urging the original Bull Moosers to take steps "to prevent La Follette, through the misuse of the name 'Progressive,' from destroying the identity of the great group of Progressives of 1912."[37] By the mid-twenties, however, the Progressives' identity crisis was already in its terminal stage. Soon after leading his party to glorious defeat, polling nearly five million votes, "Fighting Bob" faded from national politics.

The outcome of the election had been a foregone conclusion. Coolidge carried Missouri by just under half the popular vote, and Kansans preferred him to his conservative opponent, Democrat John Davis, by a margin of almost three to two. Hoping to gain an inside track in the new administration, the *Star* had promoted Arthur Hyde for vice president, largely on the strength of his opposition to the League of Nations and the World Court. (Kirkwood, whose views were even more right-wing than Hyde's, praised the Missouri governor for making a "splendid stand for American Ideals and against this

sentimental International slush.") When the convention picked financier
Charles G. Dawes instead, the paper smoothly transferred its favoritism to
Herbert Hoover, the smart, pug-faced dynamo of a commerce secretary.
Haskell rated Hoover as "one of the great constructive minds of this generation" and warmly applauded his efforts to revamp the federal bureaucracy
along business lines.[38] As the *Star*'s newest hero, assiduously cultivated by both
Kirkwood and Roberts, Hoover would become the embodiment of progressive Republican efficiency, the can-doers' answer to Coolidge's policy of doing as little as possible.

Although the *Star*'s influence in Washington was slowly rebounding from
its wartime nadir, the home front was a different story. The election of reform
Republican Albert Beach in the spring 1924 mayoral contest briefly put wind
in the paper's sagging sails. But Beach, having run afoul of powerful forces in
both Democratic and Republican headquarters, had little to show for his
earnest efforts to root out bossism and eliminate a whopping $5 million deficit
inherited from the previous administration. Stymied by bipartisan opposition,
Beach endeavored to dissuade his allies from reviving the issue of charter reform. After all, Kansas Citians had decisively rejected a new charter as recently
as 1922. More important, the reformers were still gathering strength and
needed more time to build a workable consensus for a genuinely nonpartisan
city administration. But Beach's prescient advice was swept aside in the head-
long rush toward civic renewal. In an election marked by an unusually low
turnout—barely a third of the city's registered voters came to the polls in February 1925—a new charter passed by a margin of more than four to one.

The public's apparent apathy suggested to some that the machines were not
highly motivated to get out the vote. This inference, however, is flatly contra-
dicted by the lopsided tally in favor of the charter in the Pendergast-controlled
wards. After his own fashion, Boss Tom was a practical idealist too. Calculat-
ing that the charter was almost certain to pass, he figured he stood a better
chance of working the system to his advantage by going with the flow. "It
ought to be as easy to get along with nine men as thirty-two," he reasoned in
an interview with the *Star*, alluding to the proposal to replace the unwieldy
bicameral city legislature with a streamlined nine-member council. A major
selling point of the charter was a provision to insulate city government from
politics by selecting candidates in a nonpartisan primary, thereby masking
their party affiliations. But this procedural fig leaf didn't deter the Democratic and Republican organizations from running straight party-line tickets.
When the *Star* struck a blow for nonpartisanship by endorsing candidates
from both slates, the mayor's wife complained that the paper was sticking its

head in the sand. "Its attitude was such that one would have thought Pendergast was out of the picture," wrote Mrs. Beach.[39] That Pendergast was still very much in the picture was a fact that the *Star* belatedly acknowledged in an editorial crediting the crafty boss with an enlightened public spirit for which he had not heretofore been known.

> In the charter election Mayor Beach with the Republican organization and T. J. Pendergast with the Democratic organization were on the side of the progressive movement. This had been expected of Mayor Beach because he had been identified with the progressive wing of his party. It was a surprise to many persons so far as the Pendergast organization was concerned, because that organization in the past has been largely preoccupied with political spoils.
>
> But, after all, why should not political machines identify themselves with enterprises for the benefit of the city? That would be the farsighted policy. Those that take pains to make themselves instruments for city progress will get popular backing and popular respect that have been lacking under the old regime.[40]

The city's new "model" charter reflected the thinking of the leading experts on government efficiency. It had been drafted in the office of the Civic Research Institute, an independent data-gathering agency cum think tank funded largely by philanthropist William Volker. For the institute's director, an earnest young economist named Walter Matscheck, nonpartisan government was as much an article of faith as it was for Nelson and his successors at the *Star*. Things didn't work out quite the way they expected, however. In the first election held under the charter, in November 1925, Mayor Beach squeaked back into office, but machine Democrats seized power on the nominally nonpartisan council, with a five-to-four majority. Ironically, the measure the reformers had touted as the end to boss rule produced a city government that was more boss-ridden than ever. Pendergast had not only legitimized his own power but effectively sidelined Joseph Shannon, who had unwisely refrained from endorsing the charter. In a few short years, "Uncle Joe" would be on his way to Washington as a freshman in Congress, with Pendergast's blessing, and Kansas City would become known far and wide as "Tom's Town."

All of which suggested that Haskell had been right when he told Beach's cousin, Herbert Hadley, that nonpartisan government ran contrary to human nature and could never be made to work. In light of recent events, his idea of a viable reform machine seemed equally impractical. Nor, discouragingly, was the now proverbial smoke-filled room a thing of the past. Four days after the city election, Pendergast and his cronies caucused in the office of banker W. T. Kemper. Then and there they decreed that the council's choice for the key post of city manager in the new "reform" administration would be none other than Judge Henry McElroy. Nobody seems to have thought it necessary to consult the four Republican councilmen. Probably they would have gone along in any case. McElroy, after all, was a valued public servant who pledged to run the city like a business, just as he and Judge Truman had managed the county's affairs. Main Street welcomed his appointment as warmly as the *Star*.

McElroy proceeded to justify these high expectations by waving the city's crippling deficit out of existence. This disappearing trick was accomplished by means of "country bookkeeping," an idiosyncratic method of accounting that McElroy had perfected in his previous career as an Iowa storekeeper. Matscheck criticized it as voodoo economics, but his fellow citizens were in no hurry to abandon their illusions. In a more ominous departure from the spirit of the new charter, McElroy declared open season on Republicans. His administration, he announced, would be conducted strictly on the old-fashioned spoils system. In short order, he replaced half the employees on the city payroll with party workers. The city manager left no doubt as to who was in charge. There would be no nonsense from bleeding-heart reformers or overly conscientious elected officials. He took special pleasure in upstaging Beach, whose role under the new charter was largely ceremonial. At meetings where the mayor was speaking, Mrs. Beach recalled, McElroy "would come up and slip his arm through my husband's. He was always talking about what the Mayor and he were doing at city hall. My husband would withdraw the arm and step aside, but McElroy would follow him right up."[41] Beach suffered a crowning indignity when McElroy commandeered his corner office and even took away his official car.

All in all, the new era for Kansas City was beginning to look more like a bonanza for T. J. Pendergast Inc.

That Christmas season of 1925, the Country Club Plaza blazed with colored electric lights for the first time. It was a modest display, for J. C. Nichols had declared his suburban shopping center open for business only a couple of years earlier. But the lighting ceremony instantly became a popular tradition. As a promotional stunt, the Plaza lights rivaled even Pendergast's annual holiday banquets for the needy. Torn between his progressive principles and his pragmatic alliance with Boss Tom, Nichols had nearly capitulated to a draft in the fall mayoral race. His decision to stick to real estate was made easier by the fact that the city had embarked on another giddy home-building spree.

Thanks in part to the *Star*'s cheerleading, the master builder of the Country Club district was nationally recognized as a real estate guru. Writing in the *World's Work,* Haskell portrayed Nichols as Nelson's heir, a "practical dreamer" who dared to dream on a far grander scale than his mentor.[42] The two thousand acres that Nichols controlled were protected from undesirable encroachments more securely than ever, now that the City Council had heeded his call to enact a zoning ordinance. As a member of the National Capital Park and Planning Commission—an appointment he owed in part to Kirkwood's intercession with Hoover and Coolidge—Nichols would soon be following in Nelson's footsteps in Washington as well.

To the world at large, the Country Club district had come to stand for Kansas City in much the same way as the *Star* did. Nichols was second to none as a booster. In a speech to a national group of realtors, he asserted that "the City Practical, the City Orderly, the City of Economy, the City of Efficiency, the City of Health, the City of Wise Plan—yes, the City of Culture and Beauty . . . is one that will stand the competition of time, is the one that will win its race for commercial supremacy, and hand down to future generations a heritage of unconquerable spirit, of imperishable human values, of undying influence for better life among its citizenry."[43] But this glowing vision of progressive paradise wasn't all sweetness and light. The Country Club district, walled off by racial and other restrictions and with its own privatized municipal services, was rapidly turning into a city apart. Nichols marketed his new Armour Hills subdivision, on the Missouri side, to middle-class whites who were fleeing the inner city in growing numbers after the war. With the complicity of the police and antivice crusaders, including the *Star,* prostitution, gambling, and bootlegging were effectively quarantined between Twelfth and Eighteenth streets, mostly on the east side. The white business establishment had ignored the proposal advanced by Delbert Haff, the former Park Board attorney, to create a Country Club–like ghetto for the city's disadvantaged African Americans, where they too could taste the character-building fruits of home ownership. Isolated in their well-kept south-side enclave, the reformers devoted their energies to creating a "city of culture and beauty," as exemplified by the magnificent seahorse fountain that Nichols had recently brought home from Europe and donated to the city. Anchoring a new European-style traffic circle named in honor of August Meyer, the fountain far outshone the simple memorial to the revered Park Board president that overlooked Kessler's neglected sunken gardens on the lower Paseo. What better way to proclaim Ward Parkway's status as the grandest of the city's grand boulevards, the cynosure of the City Beautiful?

Meyer Circle—a prestigious address that Haskell and fellow *Star* executive George Longan would soon call home—neatly symbolized the crossroads that the progressive movement had reached in the mid-1920s. As a chronicler of that giddy, self-indulgent decade observed, "In 1915 the word reformer had been generally a complimentary term; in 1925 it had become—among the intellectuals, at least—a term of contempt." William Allen White complained that "the spirit of democracy" had "turned away from the things of the spirit . . . gone out and lived riotously and ended by feeding among the swine." The materialistic, money-worshipping temper of the times made Haskell equally despondent. Kansas City's achievements in art, literature, politics, and religion lagged far behind its impressive track record in providing for its citizens' physical welfare, he told White. "I have been inclined to be optimistic and to think this cultural life would follow. But thinking it over I don't know that there is ground for this optimism. Haven't we created a powerful industrial machine and given it such momentum that it is going to continue to grind on and absorb us in the material side of life without giving the cultural side a chance to develop?"[44] Significantly, it was the industrial, not the political, "machine" that drove Haskell to despair. Like many another frustrated boss-buster, he had come to accept Pendergast and his kind as a necessary evil.

Ironically, the *Star*'s chief editorial writer felt more pessimistic than ever in the wake of the 1925 charter election. On White's recommendation, he had been invited to write a chapter on Kansas City for a book called *The Taming of the Frontier.* Its theme—the demise of old-fashioned American individualism and the wholesale standardization of western cities as they morphed into blandly conformist "Boosterburgs"—was a favorite subject among the Jazz Age smart set. (Two of the other essays in the book first appeared in H. L. Mencken's irreverent *American Mercury.*) Haskell glossed over the city's political notoriety, alluding only in passing to a shadowy "informal government of a few powerful interests." Instead, he characterized the city's identity crisis in cultural terms as a conflict between low-brows and high-brows—or, as he put it, between the "houn' dawg" tradition of the old West and the "civilization of beauty." The latter he attributed primarily to the influence of Nelson, who "regarded the industrialism of his day with the same abhorrence that France feels toward the monstrous industrial organization that is Germany." Although Haskell told White that he "tried to treat Mr. Nelson as a human being," the figure described in his essay was part Renaissance prince and part robber baron, "a combination of Lorenzo the Magnificent and Jim Hill, with a dash of St. Francis, Nietzsche, and Oliver Cromwell." It was this superhuman colossus who had saved Kansas City from turning into just another river town of the "commonplace commercial type." But it remained to be seen whether "Kansas City of to-day, tamed, domesticated, Kiwanized, Chamber-of-Commerced, Heart-of-Americaed as it is," would develop into a genuinely civilized community or "simply continue to grind out the same material comforts to the exclusion of the culture and the appreciation of beauty that make the comforts worth while."[45]

In his indictment of Kansas City's redneck heritage, religious fundamentalism, and Mammon worship, Haskell anticipated themes that Sinclair Lewis would reprise when he came to town the following year to write his novel *Elmer Gantry*. But Haskell's finger-wagging made little impression on Kansas Citians, most of whom were enjoying their fair share of the Coolidge prosperity. Not surprisingly, the Chamber of Commerce didn't go out of its way to publicize the findings of the blue-ribbon commission that was studying the soaring crime rates in Missouri cities. Written by a team of experts including former Governor Hadley and Professor Raymond Moley of Columbia, Roosevelt's future brain truster, the *Missouri Crime Survey* adduced alarming statistics showing that "the homicide rate of Missouri cities is twice that which obtains in American cities as a whole." Urban police departments, the study found, were rife with corruption, inefficiency, and incompetence. Screening of applicants was a farce, many officers having criminal records themselves. As a result of political patronage, police service in Kansas City had "seldom been viewed as anything more than casual employment." Hadley conceded that "the measures of social, economic, and political reform which many earnest men and women urge for reducing the amount of crime" had done some good. But in the long run, he warned, only "a stern sense of justice and a respect for law upon the part of the general public" would deter hardened criminals.[46]

This sobering analysis was at odds with such expressions of the "Kansas City spirit" as the prize-winning poem in a contest sponsored by the *Star*, which culminated in the inspirational lines:

North and South and East and West land, mighty spirits, all were gone,
With the Kansas City Spirit, all were blended into one,
And, within the spirit-dwelling, throbbed America's greatest heart,
Radiating cheer and courage to the land's remotest part.[47]

No one radiated more cheer than Conrad Mann, the jowly, bulbous-nosed president of the Chamber of Commerce. A political naif, Mann held the ineffectual Republican reformers at arm's length and applied himself to the more rewarding task of fostering friendly relations with the ruling Democratic machine. In his tireless efforts to promote Kansas City as the "Heart of America," he found it expedient to keep Boss Pendergast's name out of the news. Over the years, the Chamber had distilled its booster message to a handful of reassuring platitudes. A 1924 pamphlet entitled "Kansas City Offers Unusual Advantages to Industry," for example, noted that only 8 percent of the population was foreign-born. "This," the Chamber boasted, "accounts largely for the absence of labor controversies, from which the city has been exceptionally free throughout its history." Like most of his fellow businessmen, Mann had suppressed memories of the city's devastating general strike in 1918, the widely publicized trial of Wobblies the following year, and other distasteful episodes.

With bulging coffers and one of the largest memberships in the country, the Chamber could afford to expend vast sums of money to burnish the city's image. A pioneer in municipal advertising, Mann hired a public relations firm to place articles favorable to the city in national magazines. (Hitherto, this function had been performed, gratis, by writers for the *Star.*) After an abortive attempt to revive the annual Priests of Pallas parade, a mythological extravaganza that the old Commercial Club had instituted in the 1880s to foster civic pride, the Chamber sponsored a more conventionally religious pageant celebrating the city's triumphal march to civilization and sent it on tour around the country in 1926. When the *American Mercury* ridiculed "The Miracle" as an overblown civic status symbol, Mann and his colleagues were mortally offended. "Evidently," huffed the Chamber's official newsletter, the magazine's correspondent had been "snooping around when we weren't looking."[48]

The flood stage of the booster campaign reached its high-water mark that November with the long-anticipated dedication of the Liberty Memorial. Although the monument was still a work in progress, the "eternal flame" that billowed from its two-hundred-foot shaft (in reality, an illusion concocted with steam and mirrors) awaited ignition at the presidential command. Months earlier, Kirkwood had invited Coolidge to deliver the keynote address at the ceremony. Not put off by the president's laconic refusal, the *Star*'s editor offered the Coolidges his rustic compound in the Adirondacks for their use as a summer White House. That apparently sealed the deal.

Asked to supply a list of talking points for the president, Haskell suggested that he stress "the aspirations of this Mid-Western country for ideals, for beauty, for patriotism" and comment on "America's peace service to the world" as a "stable and prosperous country, whose influence steadies finance and trade." Coolidge, who found speech-making onerous, took the advice to heart

**Calvin Coolidge at the dedication of the Liberty Memorial on Armistice Day 1926.
The *Star* lauded the president as "a straightforward, plain American, with no frills
but with abundant common sense."**

and devoted his remarks largely to a recitation of America's efforts to stabilize the world economy and secure international peace. The latter point was somewhat undercut by his headline-grabbing announcement that the United States would not be joining the World Court, owing to "reservations" imposed by senators still smarting from the League of Nations debacle. Kirkwood, who made no secret of his opposition to the court, praised Coolidge to the assembled multitude as a "level headed practical idealist" (that phrase again!) who had "made America a great and helpful force in international relations."[49]

After considerable pomp and ceremony, including a twenty-one-gun salute and an ode to fallen heroes specially composed for the occasion to a text by Mayor Beach's wife, the Coolidges boarded an afternoon train and returned to Washington. Their stay in Kansas City had lasted a mere seven hours, every minute of which had been a trial for Silent Cal. In paying tribute to the publicity-shy president the next day, the *Star* demonstrated how far its expectations for the office had fallen since the days of Roosevelt's barnstorming administration. Kansas Citians, the paper editorialized, had marked the occasion

The Liberty Memorial shaft soars above a sea of some 175,000 spectators: a monument to the City Beautiful that might have been.

with a display of popular admiration "for Coolidge the man; the straightforward, plain American, with no frills but with abundant common sense; with a passion for the homely virtues; with an honest belief that public office is an opportunity for public service."[50]

Although the *Star* didn't actually claim credit for proposing the war memorial (the idea had originated with the *Kansas City Journal*), it seized on the grassroots fund-raising campaign as a symbol of everything that was pure and noble: patriotism, civic-mindedness, local initiative, urban beautification, and nonpartisan spirit. The latter was reflected in the composition of the memorial's board of governors, on which Haskell sat, somewhat uneasily, alongside Dickey, Nichols, Kemper, Volker, and other civic worthies. In lauding the memorial as an expression of the community's highest aspirations, the *Star* epitomized the Main Street newspaper that Oswald Garrison Villard had described four years earlier. But there was one crucial difference. In the fall of 1926 the *Star* was no longer a "trusteed" newspaper basking in the reflected glory of its departed founder. Kirkwood and a handful of executives had bought it. For the next half-century, they and their successors would be calling the shots.

PART 3

THE SAGE AND THE COUNTRY BOY

Editor Henry J. Haskell (left) and managing editor Roy Roberts as drawn by *Star* artist Dale Beronius.

CHAPTER 7

———— ◆ ————

Changing of the Guard

On April 21, 1926, Tom Pendergast received an unexpected caller in his spartan office downtown. Fred Bonfils, swashbuckling publisher of the *Denver Post* and late proprietor of its Kansas City namesake, had come to ask the Democratic boss to carry a message to Irwin Kirkwood. To Pendergast's astonishment, Bonfils proposed to go in with Kirkwood in purchasing the *Star* from the Nelson estate. He said he had reliable information that Kirkwood couldn't buy the paper on his own. He wanted Pendergast "to relate that he had the money and if there was any doubt for Mr. Stout or others to call the First National Bank of Denver and inquire if his check for 20 million dollars was good." Should Kirkwood be so rash as to spurn his offer, Bonfils threatened to bid the price of the newspaper up "so high that it would not be a good investment."

> *"At every change at the* Star *the ravens on the ridgepole begin to caw disaster. But somehow the* Star *shines on even with the giants of the old days mostly gone to their reward."*
>
> —Marvin Creager

Later that day, Pendergast phoned the *Star's* political reporter, George Wallace, and asked him to relay the offer to his superiors. He professed to have no idea why Bonfils had approached him. He wouldn't know Kirkwood if he laid eyes on him, had never crossed the *Star's* threshold in his life, and "could not understand why Bonfils should make such a proposal or what might be behind it." Wallace dutifully typed out a confidential office memo, but he wasn't taken in by Pendergast's clumsy attempt at playing dumb.[1] Rumors that an outsider might conspire with the machine in an attempt to gain control of the paper had been circulating for months. The prospect of discomfiting Nelson's successors was by no means distasteful to Pendergast. At the same time, having reached an accommodation with the *Star* in the big charter election a year before, he saw no compelling reason to upset the status quo.

Pendergast had recently moved his political headquarters from the old north side to a second-story walk-up in a small, nondescript brick building at 1908 Main, the better to serve his growing south-side constituency and keep a watchful eye on his neighbor at Eighteenth and Grand. In a small way, Tom was in the newspaper business himself. The machine's new house organ, the *Missouri Democrat*, touted him as a model businessman, devoted to city, family, church, and country. But he and Kirkwood had something more in common. Pendergast, too, was fond of the finer things in life—a prestigious home address, smartly tailored clothes, resort vacations, foreign travel, the aristocratic pastime of horse racing. About the only creature comfort the two men didn't share was drink: though Pendergast had made a fortune in the wholesale liquor business, he switched to producing soft drinks during prohibition and seldom touched a drop of alcohol.

Kirkwood, by contrast, was addicted to the lush life. So was his wife, Laura Nelson Kirkwood. Their drinking had been an open secret, and a source of growing concern, around the office for years. One editor, visiting the Kirkwoods' retreat in upstate New York, found a plentiful supply of prohibition-era scotch and bourbon thoughtfully laid on in his guest cabin. Laura, "nervous, frail-looking and frequently under a physician's care," had never held her liquor as well as her robustly athletic husband.[2] Since the death of her domineering father, with whom she had an intense and troubled relationship, she had been in and out of treatment, her condition discreetly hushed up even when she nearly died from an alcohol-induced hemorrhage. But two months before Bonfils marched into Pendergast's office, her affliction had touched the *Star* "family" in a most dramatic fashion.

In early February 1926 Laura's personal physician took Haskell aside and told him, in confidence, that she was gravely ill and could die at any time. Strictly speaking, it was a violation of professional ethics, but Haskell was as close to the Nelsons as any outsider could be—closer in some ways, indeed, than Irwin Kirkwood himself. He interpreted the doctor's indiscretion as a hint that he and his colleagues should prepare themselves for the worst.[3] Haskell was at first inclined to think his informant was being alarmist. But when Nelson's forty-three-year-old daughter died alone in a Baltimore hotel room, where she had fled to dry out away from prying eyes, he realized with a jolt that the day of reckoning had finally arrived.

At midmorning on Saturday, February 27, assistant managing editor George Longan took the telephone call from Baltimore. Sunday editor Ruby Garnett watched him and general manager Gus Seested jump up from their desks and follow Kirkwood into his private office off the corner of the newsroom. Moments later Longan emerged, tense and ashen-faced, returned to his desk, and picked up the phone. "Why so solemn?" Garnett asked a colleague. "It's a report that Mrs. Kirkwood is dead," came the reply. "Mr. Longan is trying to verify it—and get more details."[4] Reporters huddled around the city desk, speaking in muted tones. Everyone knew this wasn't just another news story. Laura's death affected each of them personally. Under the familiar terms of Nelson's will, it triggered the sale of the *Star*.

In Dayton, Katharine Wright read Haskell's telegram and instantly grasped its significance. "The dreaded thing has actually happened," she wrote back. Katharine knew how attached her fiancé was to the Kirkwoods. After his wife's death in 1923, they had not only sent him to Europe but invited him to move in with them at Oak Hall. Laura had even tried to match him up with a string of eligible women—"the widders," Katharine called them. Haskell surmised that Laura had deliberately drunk herself to death, convinced her husband no longer loved her.[5] Yet his own bereavement quickened his sympathy for the *Star*'s publisher. Kirkwood, he saw, was in a tough spot too. He owed his wealth and position to the Nelson family, as surely as Haskell owed his career to the Old Man. As Laura's consort, Irwin had a purpose in life, was treated like royalty. As her widower, he would be just another supernumerary member of the leisure class. It was unlikely that the paper's new owner would require his services, much less support him in the princely lifestyle to which he had grown accustomed.

Lately, Haskell had become increasingly despondent about the paper. He had confided his unhappiness to Katharine—his intense loneliness, his bitterness about the injustice of the world, his feeling that Laura didn't appreciate him, his resentment at the appearance of Irwin's name at the top of *his* editorial page. Restless and dissatisfied, he considered cutting his ties to Kansas City and moving east, or possibly abroad. He and Roy Roberts, the *Star*'s ambitious Washington correspondent, had toyed with the idea of forming a news syndicate. Katharine discreetly fanned the flames of his discontent, while acknowledging how wrenching it would be to uproot himself. For almost three decades, the *Star* had been his life. Suddenly, he felt cast adrift. Katharine was in the same boat. She dreaded deserting Orville, who still thought of Haskell only as a close family friend and not as his spinster sister's lover.

The mood in the newsroom was grim. On Longan's desk lay a copy of Nelson's will, whose terms every *Star* employee knew by heart. "Older heads," recalled Garnett, "left all other news of the day to subordinates" while they examined the document "from every angle, trying to read into its meticulously legal phraseology some sentence that would give them the right to carry on the newspaper to which they had given their journalistic souls."[6] Kirkwood and Seested closeted themselves together, drawing up plans to buy the paper. The executives shielded Ralph Stout from the news of Laura's death. Now old and infirm, the veteran managing editor was on holiday in the Far East. Other senior staff members suspected that they were being kept out of the loop as well. In frustration, Haskell and Roberts consulted their old comrades in arms William Allen White of the *Emporia Gazette* and Henry Allen of the *Wichita Beacon*. Still smarting from his betrayal at Nelson's hands a dozen years earlier, Haskell half hoped that Kirkwood and Seested would come up short. It would serve them right, he felt, if the *Star* fell under the control of the Old Man's enemies.

Nelson, a college dropout, had designated the presidents of the state universities of Missouri, Kansas, and Oklahoma to execute his will. They, in turn, would appoint trustees to auction the paper off and use the proceeds to establish a top-notch art collection. In the eyes of the paper's employees, everything hinged on the choice of the three so-called university trustees. It was vital that they be sympathetic to the staff's interests. Early signs were not altogether reassuring. One of the university presidents called at the *Star* office and pointedly sat down in Seested's chair, as if to signal that his days in authority were numbered. But it was a false alarm. On March 3, one day after Laura's funeral at Oak Hall, the staff learned that their fate was in good hands. Of the three merchant princes who had been elected trustees, two—J. C. Nichols and William Volker—were longstanding members of the *Star*'s inner circle. The third trustee, realtor Herbert V. Jones, chairman of the city plan commission, was also presumed to favor a continuation of local ownership.

Haskell and his associates had left nothing to chance. On their instructions, White had pressured President E. H. Lindley of the University of Kansas to vote for Nichols. "I am glad Lindley played ball," White wrote to Haskell after making his pitch. "I had wanted him to do just one thing: go to the last ditch to refuse a compromise on Nichols. I knew then they had Volker and with Nichols and Volker I knew the situation was cinched." Haskell himself traveled to Norman to seek reassurance from President William B. Bizzell of the University of Oklahoma.[7] Nelson's will stipulated that the paper be "sold at the best price and on the best terms available." Did this mean, he wanted to know, that the trustees were obliged to accept the highest bid? Or could they take other factors, such as Nelson's intentions or the public welfare, into account as well? In the latter case, the staff felt reasonably confident of winning the bidding war.

To be sure, Nelson's intentions had always been unfathomable. To suggest that his mind could be read posthumously was sheer wishful thinking. Equally wishful was Haskell's hypothesis, advanced in a letter to White, that the will "did not express the real Nelson" and that the great editor's "naturally strong egotism simply ran away with him" when he mandated the sale of the paper. At the same time, Haskell grumbled to Katharine about the selfishness of the Nelson clan. In bequeathing Oak Hall to her husband, Laura stipulated that the huge house be razed after his death and the contents sold to "strangers" residing at least 250 miles from Kansas City. This was further proof, according to Walter Dickey's *Kansas City Post,* that the Nelsons had no desire to be identified with the *Star* in perpetuity. "There is nothing in any one of the wills to indicate that the members of the family desired that the paper be continued in a manner in effect a continuance of the Nelson regime or control. On the contrary, there is every reason to believe that Colonel Nelson desired that the family name be relieved of responsibility for the conduct of the paper after the death of his wife and daughter." Dickey pointed out that Laura and her mother could have sold the *Star* to the employees at any time, "if they had felt Colonel Nelson so wished."[8]

Not surprisingly, Dickey was at the head of the line when the trustees officially opened the bidding on May 14. The *Star* was one of the richest prizes in American journalism, netting close to a million dollars a year free and clear, and hungry bidders swooped down on it like birds of prey. In addition to Dickey and Bonfils, Frank Gannett and Roy Howard were rubbing their hands over the prospect of adding it to their journalistic dominions. Publishers from St. Louis, Detroit, Minneapolis, Nashville, and several other cities expressed interest. In Girard, Kansas, Emmanuel Haldeman-Julius of the old socialist *Appeal to Reason* (now scarcely recognizable as the *Haldeman-Julius Weekly*) announced his intention to bid $8 million. There was even an inquiry from a broker representing Governor Al Smith of New York. All told, seventeen prospective purchasers contacted the trustees for information. Some were out for prestige, some for profit, and some, like Bonfils and Dickey, were looking to settle old scores.[9]

From the start, the home team of "I. R. Kirkwood, A. F. Seested and Associates" were the local favorites. Kirkwood, never known to put in long hours at the office, was in the newsroom constantly delivering pep talks to the staff. With all his wealth, he didn't have enough cash on hand to outbid corporate moguls. But he did have friends, investors in the East and in Kansas City too, who reportedly stood ready to pitch in. Volker himself quietly offered to help finance the deal (something that, as a trustee, he could hardly do openly). Meanwhile, Roberts pulled strings in Washington, securing a pledge of support from Commerce Secretary Herbert Hoover. Katharine urged Haskell to invest as much as he could afford and proposed to put some of her own savings into the paper.[10] Other employees scrounged around, begging and borrowing whatever they could. Together, Kirkwood kept assuring them, they would pull the rabbit out of the hat.

The *Star*'s editor and publisher had a plan. If things worked out, not only would the paper remain in local hands but the employees themselves would become part owners. Naturally, Kirkwood would be the majority shareholder—not for nothing was he Nelson's son-in-law. At the same time, he would spread the wealth by loaning carefully selected staff members money to buy stock in the new company. It was a farsighted scheme, this bold experiment in socialized capitalism, all but unprecedented in American journalism and decidedly out of keeping with Kansas City's conservative business traditions. Yet there was method in Kirkwood's apparent madness. Nelson had treated him contemptuously as a charity case, a black sheep who was neither good enough to marry Laura nor clever enough to run the *Star*. Now Kirkwood saw his chance to get even. He would dust off the staff-ownership scheme that Nelson had projected before his mysterious change of heart in 1914. In effect, he would nullify Baron Bill's last will and testament.

The instrument of his revenge would be known as the Irwin R. Kirkwood Employee Ownership Plan. At its heart was a "stock trust indenture," a legal instrument designed to prevent stock in the Kansas City Star Company from falling into the hands of anyone who wasn't an active employee of the newspaper. In theory, the plan guaranteed that outside interests would never be able to seize control of the *Star* and hobble its independence. In practice, employee ownership would prove only slightly more durable than the flawed treaty that had concluded the "war to end wars." Even the term *indenture* had an ironic twist. During the nerve-racking days of early 1926, the senior staff fretted incessantly about being "sold down the river" by the trustees, like indentured servants or slaves. Haskell complained to Katharine that he felt chained to the newspaper and couldn't afford to leave even if he wished to.[11] The heavy burden of debt, both collective and individual, that the employees would shoulder if their bid for the paper succeeded ensured that they would not be wholly their own masters any time soon.

On Friday, July 9—the deadline set by the university trustees—a succession of bidders began filing in and out of a suite at the Muehlebach Hotel, dodging the cordon of *Star* reporters stationed in the hallways and lobby. Nichols, Volker, and Jones justified their refusal to divulge specific offers on the grounds that some bidders had insisted on confidentiality. Furthermore, they explained, any information released while interviews were in progress could be misinterpreted or maliciously distorted by one of the other bidders. Deliberately or otherwise, this silent-bid policy placed outsiders at a disadvantage. The trustees were accused of withholding information, undervaluing the *Star*'s assets, and giving the employees an unfair edge. The editor of the *Minneapolis Journal* complained to Nichols about "a constant flow of rumors" that the trustees had made up their minds to do business only with Kirkwood and Seested, using outside bids as a "basis" to establish a fair market price. Nichols replied, disarmingly, that he too had heard the rumors, but insisted that there was no truth to them and that the sale would be handled "on a fair, business-like basis."[12] Nevertheless, reports persisted that the *Star* group had received preferential treatment and even been permitted to submit a revised bid.

Plainly, *something* was going on outside of public view. On April 15, six days before Bonfils called on Pendergast, the *Star*'s afternoon Associated Press franchise was quietly transferred from Laura Kirkwood's name to August Seested's, thus putting one of the paper's major assets safely out of an unfriendly proprietor's reach.[13] (A year later the franchise would be transferred back to Irwin Kirkwood.) Dickey, whose *Kansas City Journal* held the morning AP franchise, reckoned it was worth $1 million. Overall, the *Star*'s "goodwill value" was reported to be in the neighborhood of $5.5 million, but estimates of its market value ranged as high as $18 million. In fact, how much the paper might fetch was anybody's guess. A few months earlier, a management-led group had bought the *Daily News* in Chicago—a city six times as large as Kansas City—for a record-breaking $13.6 million. Nichols, Volker, and Jones had gone to the Windy City to meet the new proprietors and pick up some tips. In their effort to appear businesslike and impartial, the trustees had also sought advice from newspaper officials in New York, Philadelphia, Baltimore, and Washington.

When the trustees interviewed Bonfils on the morning of July 9, the employees could only speculate as to what transpired. The Denver sharpshooter had made it known that he would bid at least $10 million, possibly more. Haskell, putting on a show of confidence for White's benefit, reported that Bonfils was "threatening to bid the price sky high, as he well might, knowing the trustees wouldn't sell to him." How Bonfils—or Haskell, for that matter— could have known what the trustees would or wouldn't do isn't clear. In any case, the bluster wasn't confined to one side. Roberts put out the word that Gannett was a front man for the hated "power trust," and Seested told Gannett to his face that if their bid failed, the entire staff would walk out and start a new paper. Meanwhile, White warned readers of the *Gazette* that a St. Louis "wolf pack" was scheming to attack Kansas City and "make it a vassal of St. Louis financially and politically" by taking over the *Star*.[14]

There was no dearth of targets for the prophets of doom. But it was chiefly "that blackmailer" Bonfils, Nelson's ancient nemesis, who gave Haskell and his colleagues the jitters. Compared to him, Dickey and Gannett were paragons of journalistic rectitude. "It would be a pretty little blow pipe of hell if [Bonfils] should buy the Star," White declared; "not only for the Star but all its satellites, rings, moons and nebular wreaths, one of which I am such."[15] As it turned out, they needn't have worried. The $7 million bid that Bonfils finally submitted to the trustees wasn't even in the ballpark. He had been bluffing all along. Did he seriously believe that Kirkwood detested Nelson enough to be tempted by his ham-fisted offer of partnership? Or had he simply been gambling on his ability to intimidate Kirkwood and pick up a valuable property on the cheap? Either way, he emerged from the contest with his reputation as a troublemaker somewhat diminished.

Of the other seven bids that materialized, the highest—$13 million—carried the name of Clyde Reed, the pugnacious proprietor of the *Parsons Sun* and a familiar figure in Kansas politics. The trustees felt there were too many strings attached to his offer, however, and so rejected it. That left the spotlight on Dickey as the only other local contender. The *Journal* and *Post*, which he had been subsidizing heavily in an effort to capture some of the *Star*'s advertising, were hemorrhaging cash. Already perilously overextended, he risked the shop by bidding $8 million. Neither he nor Bonfils proposed to buy the *Star*'s real estate, both having newspaper plants of their own to maintain. This may have accounted in part for their lower-than-expected offers. The employee group led by Kirkwood and Seested bid $11 million—$2.5 million in cash, from Kirkwood's personal fortune, and $8.5 million in the form of a bank loan secured by the paper's future earnings. The trustees deemed it the best offer and so announced on July 12.

Bonfils conceded gracefully, calling it "a rattling good price," and other bidders let it be known that they felt they had been treated fair and square. Dickey alone cried foul and sued to have the sale set aside, alleging that the trustees had failed to satisfy his requests for information in a timely manner and that, in any case, the current management should have been disqualified from bidding on the paper.[16] Other local businessmen heaved a sigh of relief. In the weeks before the sale, they had been under intense pressure to speak out in favor of the employees. In a "spontaneous" show of support that bore all the hallmarks of a well-orchestrated *Star* campaign, the trustees had been barraged with letters and petitions from business and civic groups, warning of dire consequences if the paper fell into the wrong hands. The decision in favor of the employees elicited a flowery panegyric from Conrad Mann, Kansas City's silver-tongued promoter par excellence. "Children unborn will call you blessed," he told the trustees, for delivering "this great influential newspaper" into the hands of those who had made it a "weapon for all of those things that mean a greater city, a finer trade territory and a happier people." For his part, Kirkwood made it clear that the community's support would not go unrewarded. "If we have been courteous in the past, let us be more courteous in the future," he wrote in a memo to the staff. "That we classify a man as a crank or a nut does not justify us in offending him. Kansas City has several thousand cranks and nuts, and we simply can't afford to lose their subscriptions and good will if we intend to maintain a 100% circulation."[17]

Tom Pendergast's reaction to the sale is unrecorded, but he had every reason to be as satisfied with the trustees' action as Main Street.

Mann and his fellow Babbitts were still reeling from the good-humored savaging they had suffered that spring at the hands of Sinclair Lewis. The celebrated debunker of Main Street values and midwestern provincialism took up residence in Kansas City to work on what he called his "preacher novel." He minced no words in telling members of the Chamber and Rotary Club what he thought of their boosterish complacency. Lewis took unerring aim at the proud city's icons, notably the soon-to-be-dedicated Liberty Memorial, which he described with discomfiting acuity as "Teutonic architecture that would look well in Munich."[18] Lewis took the Heart of America to task for its mindless flag waving, materialism, and ersatz culture. He even had the temerity to scoff at the gracious houses in the Country Club district as architectural hand-me-downs from Europe.

The broadside at J. C. Nichols was fired during the writer's standing-room-only appearance on January 24 at William L. Stidger's Linwood Boulevard

Sinclair Lewis in Kansas City, January 1926. The celebrated author of *Elmer Gantry* scandalized local burghers by daring God to strike him dead and thumbing his nose at the Pulitzer Prize board.

Methodist Church. Stidger, a brawny showman who had invented the revolving electric cross mounted on church steeples across the country, was something of a celebrity in his own right. The two men had met several years earlier in Indiana, where "Red" Lewis was visiting his friend Eugene Debs, and got along famously. Upon hearing of Lewis's plans for a "literary vivisection of the ministry," Stidger invited him to Kansas City and furnished introductions to local clergy.[19] Whatever visions of artistic immortality Stidger may have entertained were soon dashed, however, when Lewis cast him aside in favor of Leon Birkhead, the charismatic, liberal-tempered minister of All Souls Unitarian Church. Equal parts social activist and religious nonconformist, Birkhead had recently attended the Scopes "monkey" trial as attorney Clarence Darrow's adjutant. He was just the sort of skeptic Lewis was looking for to steer him through the maze of fundamentalist theology.

"I met a dozen preachers in Kansas City who form a liberal preacher-group and are as violently opposed to fundamentalism as you," the novelist reported to H. L. Mencken. It was "astonishing how many read the *Mercury* and quote Mencken—sometimes with delight and sometimes with fury," Lewis added, referring to Mencken's much talked-about new magazine. After a brief excursion out west, Lewis returned to Kansas City and checked into the Ambassador Hotel to begin serious research. Assisting him was a group of more or less freethinking men of the cloth, who forgathered weekly in the writer's suite over the lunch hour. A brief invocation by Lewis—typically along the lines of "This damned Sunday School Class will now come to order"—set the tone for a notably unrefined debate about matters religious, irreligious, and occasionally sacrilegious.[20] These philosophical free-for-alls were "often couched in Rabelaisian language" and well lubricated with booze. Word quickly got around and invitations to Lewis's weekly sessions were eagerly sought after by the local smart set.

Among the ministers who welcomed Lewis to their pulpits was Kirkwood's "two-fisted fighting parson," Burris Jenkins. It was at his Linwood Boulevard Christian Church that Lewis made national headlines on April 18 by challenging God to strike him dead within a quarter of an hour. (Birkhead, seated in the congregation, ostentatiously checked his watch every few minutes until the deadline passed.) True believers were duly scandalized. "Has the man lost his head completely? So conceited, so brazen, so vulgar!" Katharine Wright harrumphed to Haskell. In what was arguably an even more flagrant act of lèse majesté, Lewis declined the Pulitzer Prize for his novel *Arrowsmith*. "Between Pulitzer Prizes, the American Academy of Arts and Letters, amateur boards of censorship, and the inquisition of earnest literary ladies, every compulsion is put upon writers to become safe, polite, obedient, and sterile," he wrote to the Pulitzer board on May 5, on Ambassador Hotel stationery. The *Star* chose to interpret Lewis's protest as that of a literary and religious "modernist," commenting that his "epistle to the Pulitzer committee will be incorporated into the agnostic Bible."[21]

In fact, Haskell wasn't quite sure what to make of America's premier contemporary novelist. Part of him agreed with Katharine that Lewis was an intellectual exhibitionist, a self-centered smart aleck who worshipped only the god of success. Yet another part of him approved of Lewis's sassy send-up of middle-class Babbittry and Bible Belt hypocrisy. After all, he himself had lambasted his hometown's "houn' dawg" tendencies in a similar vein and was flattered when Lewis complimented him on the essay he had published a year earlier in *The Taming of the Frontier*. Despite Katharine's warning that he was falling in with the wrong crowd, Haskell couldn't resist sitting in on Lewis's Sunday School Class, seeking solace for what White called his own "grouch on God."[22] Nor did Birkhead's well-reasoned agnosticism cause him any particular offense. As chairman of the Unitarian church's board of trustees, he had been instrumental in bringing the minister to Kansas City in 1917. In years to come, Birkhead's outspoken advocacy of "companionate" marriage and other liberal fashions would alienate the newspaperman, but at the time of Lewis's visit he was still an admirer of the "free-love parson" and shared Birkhead's disdain for Bible-thumping fundamentalists.[23]

In a notebook he kept in Kansas City, Lewis characterized the fictional metropolis of his novel-in-progress in terms that Haskell might have approved: "a cosmos, good and bad, flat-mindedness and curve-mindedness; mystery and banality and some reason to believe in its inherent greatness." Late that spring, he deposited a preliminary draft of his manuscript in a local vault and, accompanied by Birkhead—whom he had taken to calling "comrade"—and his family, headed north to spend the summer writing. "Boys," he announced to his last class, "I'm going up to Minnesota, and write a novel about you. I'm going to give you hell, but I love every one of you." En route, writer and adviser stopped off to visit Debs in Terre Haute. The socialist patriarch cheered Lewis on as feistily as he had defended Rose Pastor Stokes eight years earlier. Lewis's novel, Debs predicted, would "make the gentry of the 'cloth' see red and shake their pulpits throughout the country. They are all followers of the Prince of Peace until Wall street sounds the tocsin of war and then they all wrap the flag about the pulpit with patriotic unction and join in the howl of the pack for blood and slaughter."[24]

When *Elmer Gantry* came out ten months later, Lewis's portrait of a hard-drinking, hard-swearing, hard-loving preacher became a sensation overnight. So many preachers took it as the lesson of the day that one minister in Kansas City advertised his services for people who preferred to "hear about Jesus Christ instead of Elmer Gantry." Pastor I. M. Hargett of the Grand Avenue Temple, who flattered himself on being the real-life model for Gantry, attacked Lewis's portrait as "overdrawn" and "preposterous." Many of his fellow brethren were equally indignant. Stidger felt the sting of betrayal despite Lewis's forewarning that he wouldn't recognize himself in the book. "We were looking for some criticism of the fundamental problems of the church—of its capitalistic ways, of its attitude toward peace," he told reporters. "Instead we got this story of a little, perverted minister, an altogether impossible picture, entirely unreal, not even a good caricature."[25]

Reviewing *Gantry* for the *Star*, White impishly suggested that God had taken Lewis at his word in Jenkins's church. "Sinclair Lewis, the artist, is dead. He may rise again; probably he will. But in this book he got so excited in making faces at God that he forgot his craftsmanship." Although White counted himself among Lewis's and Stidger's friends, he complained that Gantry's womanizing went over the top. "Seventy-two seductions in one book are too many," he observed to the Methodist minister. Birkhead, a lapsed Methodist, rejoined that "there is no such God as Mr. White writes about. The only kind of a God that this modern scientific age believes in is not going about whacking artists over the head because they are out of line with Main Street religious opinions."[26]

In some respects, Haskell may have reflected, Gantry was less representative of the "modern scientific age" than the protagonist of another popular "preacher novel" published in 1927. *God and the Groceryman*, by bestselling author Harold Bell Wright, struck equally close to home. Its hero—or antihero, depending on one's point of view—is a disillusioned preacher who renounces his pulpit to seek his salvation as a millionaire businessman in Kansas City. Convinced that the church's biggest problem is not godlessness or decadence but sectarianism and inefficiency, Dan Matthews helps set up a model "supradenominational" church to demonstrate that religion can still be a powerful force in Americans' everyday lives. A combination of Babbitt and Billy Sunday, with a dash of the progressive reformer thrown in for good measure, Wright's spiritual entrepreneur would have been equally at home on Lewis's Main Street and in the columns of the "new" employee-owned *Star*.[27]

On January 18, 1927, the Star Company held its second annual stockholders meeting. In a pro forma election, Kirkwood and Seested were unanimously reappointed. Also reelected to the board were Haskell, Longan, and Roberts from the news side and assistant general manager Earl McCollum and advertising manager John T. Barrons from the business side. Of the eighty-odd other employees whom the senior directors had singled out for the privilege of going into debt to finance the paper's future, fewer than half had bothered to attend the meeting. They were not surprised to learn that no dividend would be declared that year, despite the paper's record profits. Instead, the directors had decided to catch up on deferred maintenance, spending liberally on new presses and linotype machines, delivery trucks, water coolers, sewage upgrades, and fire sprinklers. Although Haskell and Longan had prevailed on the tightfisted Seested to grant a modest raise in rank-and-file salaries, most employees were feeling the pinch. They didn't need to be reminded of Kirkwood's veiled warning about falling behind in the circulation war with the Dickey papers.

One familiar name wasn't recorded in the minutes of the January meeting: Ralph Stout had suffered a fatal heart attack the previous October, forcing the other employee-owners to ante up the money to purchase his thousand shares of stock. As a precaution, the directors took out a $625,000 life insurance policy on Kirkwood, who owned a bare majority (12,501) of the 25,000 outstanding shares of common stock. The *Star*'s president was only forty-seven and there seemed every reason to expect that he would remain at the helm for many years. That May, as a newly elected director of the Associated Press, he was photographed in New York, standing sheepishly in the shadow of Colonel Robert McCormick of the *Chicago Tribune* and looking distinctly out of his element among the high and mighty of the Fourth Estate. Four months later, Kirkwood would unexpectedly drop dead in the more congenial surroundings of Saratoga Springs, where he had gone to sell some of his thoroughbred horses. Alcohol may have been a contributing factor: it was noted that he had been partying the night before his death.

Irwin and Laura's long, losing struggle with alcohol was as symptomatic of Jazz Age prosperity as their reflexive Republican politics and self-indulgent lifestyle. In Haskell's eyes, the couple had had everything to live for, not least the *Star* itself, but frivolously threw it all away. He had never understood what drove people to drink. Since his marriage to Katharine, a bishop's daughter with decidedly traditional views on morality, in November 1926, he had become less tolerant of such willfully self-destructive behavior. Officially, the *Star* supported prohibition and had refused to accept liquor advertising for nearly two decades. But the policy was increasingly difficult to explain in light of the staff's unconcealed bibulousness. At a dinner party one night, the hostess asked Haskell over cocktails why the *Star* was so "dry" when so many of its editors were so "wet." Caught off guard, he could only stammer, "Why, Gertrude, that's a long story."[28]

With Kirkwood's demise on August 29, 1927, Seested more or less automatically took over as the *Star*'s sole chief executive. His life was promptly insured for $500,000, in consideration of his advanced age and 20 percent stake in the paper. At the same time, the board announced that no editor would be named to replace Kirkwood. Henceforth, an executive committee consisting of Seested, Longan, and Haskell would manage the company's day-to-day operation. "This means," commented the trade magazine *Editor and Publisher*, "that the *Star* will be an impersonal newspaper."[29] In formalizing the ascendancy of the paper's business side, Seested's elevation drove the final nail into the coffin of old-style "personal" journalism. The *Star* had narrowly escaped corporate takeover in 1926 only to embrace the very market forces that were inexorably hastening the era of corporate journalism.

At sixty-three, Seested was no longer the vital force he had been during Nelson's lifetime. The editorial staff viewed him with a certain wariness, even though one of his first acts as president was to raise Haskell's and Longan's salaries. Deep down, they understood that Seested was the architect of their success, but they didn't want to know too much about how he had pulled it off. In the spring of 1927, however, they caught an unexpected glimpse of the tactics he had long employed to sustain the *Star*'s monopoly of local advertising. Walter Dickey, smarting from the rejection he had suffered at the hands of the university trustees, commissioned an exposé of his powerful rival. He brought in a hired gun from the East in the person of Jason Rogers, a onetime Nelson associate who billed himself as a troubleshooter for ailing newspapers. Officially, Rogers's assignment was to examine the operation of the *Journal* and *Post* and recommend how they could be made more competitive. Unofficially, his mission was to dig up any dirt he could find on the *Star*.[30]

Rogers set out to prove that Seested's business department had inflated the newspaper's reported circulation in the months leading up to the sale in order to command a premium price. With Dickey's wholehearted approval, he hired a team of private investigators to snoop around and interview past and present *Star* distributors. They obtained dozens of sworn affidavits to the effect that distributors, who were not employees of the *Star* but independent contractors, had been routinely threatened with the loss of their routes if they refused to certify the paper's own circulation figures—figures that, in some cases, showed more papers being delivered on a street than the number of residents. After the employees bought the *Star*, one carrier testified that the management was riding them harder than ever. "They are going to pay for that paper just as soon as they can pay for it, and they are going to make the carriers help pay for it," he told Dickey's men.[31]

To cap their investigation, Rogers's sleuths discovered a boxcar loaded with unfolded issues of the *Star* and *Times*, most dating from the four months preceding the sale. The papers were on their way to Omaha to be pulped, but Rogers had the car sidetracked in Lawrence, Kansas, and hauled back to the Union Station yards in Kansas City, where he and Dickey could keep an eye on it from their offices on nearby Hospital Hill. Rogers contended the unread papers were prima facie evidence that the *Star* had been systematically padding its circulation to justify its premium advertising rates. At Dickey's request, the Audit Bureau of Circulation sent a team to Kansas City to look into the allegations. When their report exonerated the *Star*, no one was more relieved than Haskell. Rogers, he told White, was an itinerant agitator who "bribes, steals, makes false affidavits and generally raises hell for six months, at the end of which time he is blown up by the ABC audit and then moves to another town."[32]

But Rogers showed no inclination to move on. Instead, he claimed the auditors had been bamboozled and ratcheted up the pressure on the *Star*. His next target was Seested's requirement that all advertisers buy space in both the morning and afternoon papers. Rogers charged that the combination-rate policy was "monopolistic and arbitrary," a judgment in which a federal grand jury would concur thirty years later. He confidently assured Dickey that "when we get things started our way, and it will not be long before we do so, we will gradually make it increasingly difficult for the *Star* to club in the dollars to maintain its highly unnatural position." But Rogers's relations with his temperamental employer soured as the promised results failed to materialize. Amid mutual recriminations and threats of legal action, he stormed back to New York in September 1928, abandoning Dickey to his fate. Three days later, the Missouri Supreme Court threw out the rival publisher's suit to overturn the sale of the *Star*. A relieved Haskell wrote to his son that things were finally "coming our way."[33]

As fortune continued to smile on the *Star,* the directors declared a 10 percent dividend for 1927. The following year, shareholders divvied up a whopping $500,000 profit, even after paying down their mortgage. Politically, too, 1928 would be a banner year for the paper. Herbert Hoover's presidential candidacy promised to give the *Star* the kind of insider status at the White House it hadn't enjoyed since the Taft administration. As president of the Chamber of Commerce, the indefatigable Conrad Mann fought tooth and nail to bring the Republican convention to Kansas City. Facing an uphill battle in the rural hinterlands, party leaders were eager to plant their flag in a city that was once again a focal point of agrarian discontent. Nor was it overlooked that the *Star* had been a stalwart friend to the Coolidge administration and studiously cultivated its backroom ties to Silent Cal's anointed successor.

"Civic pride is almost a religion with Kansas Cityans," the *New York Times*'s chief political correspondent observed in a preconvention profile of the host city. Richard Oulahan painted a glowing portrait of the economic and industrial gateway to the West, while Haskell dutifully recited the official trade and industry statistics in a lengthy puff piece for the *American Review of Reviews*. Kansas City, it would seem, was no longer torn between backwardness and civilization. According to Haskell, the city that rolled out the red carpet for Republican delegates was a model of efficient government, gracious neigh-

Chamber of Commerce president Conrad Mann (center, front) leads the cheerleading for Herbert Hoover at the 1928 Republican national convention. "Civic pride is almost a religion with Kansas Cityans," observed the *New York Times*.

borhoods, and enlightened commerce. The Chamber's handouts made less of an impression on the correspondent for the *New Republic*, who described a city of "prim ideals and prim homes" peopled by "the backwash of the westward impulse." In the relentless pursuit of middle-class domesticity, Shaemas O'Sheel wrote, "the progress of the successful Kansas Citian will be marked by a train of homes, each one newer and more pretentious than the last, and each one farther south."[34]

The image of old-fashioned southern hospitality that boosters were at pains to convey to their visitors was somewhat tarnished by evidence of old-fashioned southern racism. Turned away from downtown hotels, African American delegates were compelled to seek lodging in private homes and in the black YMCA on the east side. "We wish to accord the visiting Negro delegates the same courteous treatment we always give our own Negro population," Mann announced, with unconscious irony. A vote to unseat black delegates from southern states elicited an outraged protest from the black-owned *Kansas City Call*, whose managing editor, Roy Wilkins—later head of the

NAACP—dismissed the city's "Heart of America" image as "a concoction of boosterism and Babbittry." Mencken, who covered the convention for the *Baltimore Sun,* grumbled that the city was overrun by "third-rate rabble-rousers" and "white morons." After going slumming in the black district, he patronizingly concluded that two "Aframerican" delegates he met there were the smartest men in Kansas City.[35]

Although the *Star* featured Mencken and White as special correspondents during the convention, their mildly iconoclastic commentaries barely concealed the paper's high-powered partisanship. For the past decade it had been doing its utmost to stoke the Hoover boom. Roberts, one of a handful of newsmen who had managed to get on intimate terms with Hoover, helped mastermind a tendentious campaign that cast the ultracosmopolitan secretary as an Iowa farm boy, the better to distinguish his "traditional" midwestern values from the urbane sophistication of the well-liked Democratic challenger, Governor Al Smith of New York. Not taken in by this charade were the farmers themselves. During the convention some two thousand of them, angered by Coolidge's veto of a bill that would have facilitated the sale of surplus crops abroad at subsidized prices, paraded through the city streets chanting, "We won't vote for Hoover."[36] Their suspicions were confirmed when the convention picked Kansas senator Charles Curtis, an archconservative opponent of the farm lobby, as Hoover's running mate.

Haskell considered that the fall campaign was shaping up to be "the most interesting since 1912." In pitting Hoover, the dour, industrious Quaker, against Smith, the outgoing "Happy Warrior" of the Roman church, the 1928 election foretold a political watershed as significant as the conflict between progressives and "standpatters" sixteen years earlier. In terms of sheer human drama, however, a battle between Hoover and Jim Reed would undoubtedly have generated even more excitement. The prospect of a knock-down fight with his old sparring partner appealed to Missouri's senior senator as a fitting climax to his long crusade against progressive busybodies and unpatriotic internationalists. Reed seemed to hold Hoover personally accountable for the erosion of individual freedom, states' rights, and American independence that had begun under Wilson. Hoover had shown that he could be just as "irreconcilable." While he was abroad during the war, agents acting in his name had visited the *Star* office in search of compromising material on the Missouri lawmaker. Ralph Stout granted them free access to the paper's files, declaring it "a labor of love to furnish any information" that could conceivably discredit Reed.[37] Thereafter the *Star* was firmly in the Hoover column.

In many ways, an election contest between the internationalist Hoover, the quintessential technocrat and Main Street organization man, and the isolationist Reed, a machine pol who pined for "the days of unlimited individualism" and opposed anything that smacked of governmental paternalism, would have been more indicative of the country's divisions than one between Hoover and Smith, which centered largely on the peripheral issues of prohibition and Catholicism. But it was not to be. After losing out to Smith at the Democratic convention in Houston, Reed decided he had had his fill of political hypocrisy and returned to Kansas City to practice law. Paradoxically, the "gruff old warrior" would be lauded as a reformer in his retirement. "They will be remembering him in Washington as a Killer, and shuddering over the memory long after they have forgotten what mountebanks he fought and laid low," wrote Mencken.[38] Even the *Star,* deeming it finally safe to bury the hatchet, joined in the tumultuous ovation that greeted the Stormy Petrel when his train pulled into Union Station one winter day in early 1929.

By then Hoover was safely ensconced in the White House, having outpolled Smith by a decisive margin in both Kansas City and Missouri. The *Star* reflected that the election had indeed marked a turning point. Confronted with a choice between tradition and modernity, American voters had chosen to stay the course. "Smith," the paper astutely editorialized after the election, "represented the big city, its cosmopolitanism, its impatience with . . . 'the moral yearnings of the rural communities,' its absorption in itself, its failure to think nationally. Hoover was the embodiment of the qualities and the standards of the older rural and small city America. In the election . . . the newer, urban life clashed with the older tradition, and the older America swept to victory."[39]

Nothing was more emblematic of the clash of cultures than the widely perceived breakdown of morality. And few episodes dramatized the mixed-up mores of the Jazz Age more vividly than the scandal that erupted in early 1929 on the normally placid Columbia campus of the University of Missouri. That March, students enrolled in a class on the family received a clinically worded questionnaire inquiring about their views on marriage and sex, both inside and outside the sacred institution. When this precursor of the Kinsey Report was revealed in the local press, a hue and cry arose throughout Missouri's conservative hinterland. Amid rumors that innocent undergraduates were being instructed in the techniques of sexual intercourse, the university president denounced "sewer sociology" and demanded that the board of curators take disciplinary action against the offenders.[40] In no time the controversy snowballed into a major confrontation with the fledgling Association of American University Professors over the issue of academic freedom.

The *Star* virtuously refrained from reprinting the offensive questionnaire and reacted to the furor with bewildered soul-searching. While conceding that "the age of liberal thought and action" had come to stay, the paper took issue with "those who are so enamored of our franker attitude toward many things of life that they have become obsessed with sex and sex discussion." Such "abnormal" individuals, the editorial went on, "are our prurients, and to some extent they must be tolerated; but they should not be permitted to insult or viciously influence our student bodies." In keeping its own hands clean, the *Star* cast aside the progressive social attitudes that it had so boldly championed when it invited Helen Keller to broach the forbidden topic of venereal disease on its front page fifteen years earlier. It was left to liberal clergymen like Leon Birkhead and Burris Jenkins to speak out on behalf of the beleaguered teachers. Joining them was Samuel Mayerberg, newly appointed rabbi of Temple B'nai Jehudah, who chastised the curators for violating the fundamental tenets of religious faith and deplored the "mental terror" visited on the faculty by the university administration.[41]

Despite the ministers' protests, two instructors were summarily fired and a third, Professor Max Meyer, an internationally renowned psychologist who served as course adviser, was suspended for a year. In the ensuing storm of criticism, an AAUP investigatory committee returned a report condemning the administration. Other critics drew parallels to the Scopes "monkey" trial and likened Meyer to Socrates as an unjustly persecuted "corrupter" of youth. The *Star* mildly opined that although it might have been wiser to censure the misguided instructors, public confidence in the university must be maintained at all costs. Meyer, disgusted by the small-mindedness of the cultural fundamentalists, told a friend that he "could make up for mutual misunderstandings," but "to remove the University from a town of Babbitts" was "impossible." In due course, MU's president was sacked and amends made to the wronged faculty. But recriminations continued to fly and the broader issues raised by the "sex questionnaire scandal" showed no signs of fading away.[42]

For further evidence that the "prurients" were at the gates, Haskell and his colleagues had only to look in the opposite direction. John Brinkley, M.D., the "goat gland doctor" of Milford, Kansas, presented an irresistible target for demonization in the *Star*, even though his unconventional methods of sexual rejuvenation were as unmentionable in a family newspaper as the indelicate questions posed to MU undergraduates. Professionally speaking, Brinkley's credentials were decidedly dubious; the American Medical Association had been trying for years to get his license revoked. But what really rankled the guardians of public morality at Eighteenth and Grand was the doctor's masterful use of the airwaves to promote his clinical services. Brinkley's KFKB, "the Sunshine Station from the Heart of the Nation," trespassed on the territory of the *Star's* WDAF—whose twin antennas soared above the paper's Italianate water tower—and horned in on its advertising. Matters came to a head in 1927, when both stations applied to increase their wattage. The *Star's* application was denied while Brinkley's was granted, instantly turning KFKB into one of the most powerful radio outlets in the country.

Soon thereafter, the *Star* began receiving complaints from patent medicine companies that Brinkley's high-powered promotion of glandular treatments for male sexual disfunction was driving away their customers. Their business also being the *Star's* business, A. B. Macdonald, the paper's ace investigative reporter, was assigned to check out the story. Brinkley, a flamboyant individual who sported a reddish goatee and diamond-studded rings, was subsequently subjected to "one of the most intense newspaper attacks ever waged against a single individual in the history of American journalism." The editors allowed Macdonald, a born-again disciple of Billy Sunday, to sermonize freely, embellishing his front-page articles with lurid allegations of Brinkley's surgical incompetence, professional quackery, and general moral turpitude. As one commentator noted, the reporter's harrowing verbal crucifixion "would have been effective as a description of the head-devil from a Fundamentalist hell."[43]

A reporter for the recently combined *Kansas City Journal-Post* took a cynical view of the motives behind the *Star's* crusading debut under employee ownership. In addition to building reader interest, W. G. Clugston noted, Macdonald's sensational exposé was calculated not only to "crush Brinkley" and his radio station but also to "win the undying gratitude of all the ethical doctors in every town and village throughout the land."[44] From the *Star's* perspective, the campaign proved singularly successful on all counts. Despite an impressive parade of witnesses who testified on his behalf before the state medical board, Brinkley was stripped of both his radio and medical licenses, while the *Star* emerged with both its circulation and its reputation for public service magnified.

Whether the "superquack of Milford" was an unscrupulous demagogue or a bona fide prairie populist depended on the eye of the beholder. The *Star* had declared him "finished," but others were less sure. Five days after losing his medical license in June 1930, Brinkley entered the Kansas governor's race as

a write-in candidate and garnered strong support among the state's financially distressed farmers. That fall he came in third in what even the *Star* conceded was an uncomfortably close race. White warned in the *Emporia Gazette*
that Brinkley's appeal to the downtrodden masses should be a wake-up call to
the "smug, well-fed group" that "there must be a more equitable distribution
of the common wealth."[45] Brinkley's campaign precipitated a shake-up in
Kansas politics that would lead to Alf Landon's election as governor in 1932
and his quixotic run for the White House four years afterwards—a story in
which the *Star* would play a not inconsiderable part.

Haskell had another reason for feeling that things were "coming our way"
in 1928. On October 2 Seested, the last of the *Star*'s old guard, passed away
in his sixty-fourth year. The directors immediately appointed Haskell editor
of the paper, formalizing the position he had held since Nelson's death. Two
years of marriage to Katharine Wright had given him a new lease on life. It
was she who pressed him to stand up for himself and hold out for more recognition (and money), suggesting he consider leaving the *Star* if he didn't receive
his just deserts. With Seested, Stout, and Kirkwood out of the way, the
younger generation was free at last to run the paper as they saw fit. Roy Roberts was recalled from Washington to become managing editor and George
Longan succeeded Seested as president of the Star Company. Echoing Kirkwood's call for good corporate citizenship, Longan put the staff on notice that
"the public will keep a critical eye on our performances. Even the most friendly observers will be interested to see in what manner and to what degree we
will live up to our opportunities and obligations."[46] Some things, clearly, were
not going to change under the new regime.

Longan, Haskell, and Roberts formed a tightly knit triumvirate, working
together in a "continuous conference," their desks placed within twenty feet
of one another in the open-plan newsroom. Both the new modus operandi
and the managers' not-so-new priorities were dramatized in a short promotional film shot at the paper late in 1929. In one obviously staged scene, Longan, wearing a three-piece suit with a white kerchief poking out of his breast
pocket, saunters up to the telegraph desk and inquires about the latest bulletins. Informed that "they just tried another ex-king in Afghanistan," the
Star's chief executive officer waves his cigar in the air and says, "Well, put it
with the cookie recipes on page four, the women's page. Anything closer to
home?" Moments later, a stick-up at a downtown bank fortuitously answers
Longan's prayer. Reporters and editors scurry to their stations. Roberts rushes
into the picture, exclaiming, "Say, that's a hell of a story. George! Harry!" Hud-

Roy Roberts (left) and George Longan (center) huddle with Henry J. Haskell at the editor's desk in a 1929 *Star* promotional film: the young Turks were finally calling the shots.

dled around Haskell's paper-strewn desk, the three men discuss what to bump from page one to make room for the fast-breaking news.

Although the film portrays Haskell as the final arbiter of newsroom policy, his heart wasn't in the performance. Katharine's sudden death of pneumonia in March 1929 had deprived him of the partner he called "the most vital, radiant spirit I ever knew." Stricken with grief, he plunged into such a tailspin that concerned colleagues persuaded his twenty-six-year-old son to give up a fast-track job on the *Baltimore Sun* and join the *Star*'s editorial staff. Henry C. Haskell quickly made his mark with a series of editorials warning of an impending stock market crash. Published in early September 1929, the prescient alarm elicited a snide reprimand from the *Wall Street Journal,* which demanded to know "who is to start liquidating? And what is a normal basis for stocks, not in the opinion of the *Star,* but in the opinion of those who really understand it?" The *Star* confidently stood its ground, for, as Haskell *père* wrote to a friend, "there is nothing that does a westerner so much good as to be attacked by Wall Street."[47] Heeding their own advice, the paper's managers invested excess earnings not in ballooning stocks but in Liberty Bonds, which continued to appreciate dramatically even after the market collapsed.

That the seed for the *Star*'s editorials had been planted by none other than President Hoover himself was not widely known, nor were the new managers eager to publicize it. Like most of the cautious initiatives that would characterize his administration, Hoover's covert bid to dampen the stock market frenzy was too little and came too late to have any appreciable effect. Nevertheless, the *Star* gave him full marks for trying. In return, the grateful president used the *Star* as a sounding board to gauge how his economic and agricultural policies would be received in the nation's heartland. On Roberts's recommendation, he named former Missouri governor Arthur Hyde his secretary of agriculture. (Hyde's appointment, Roberts counseled gleefully, "would probably give Jim Reed a stroke of apoplexy.")[48] Like William Jardine, his predecessor from the Sunflower State, Hyde swore by the old-fashioned virtue of self-reliance. When his program to stabilize depression-era farm prices and stimulate international trade foundered, Hoover caved in to congressional demands for a sharply regressive tariff—a bill that Haskell had urged him to veto. Instead of shielding American farmers from cheap imports, the protectionist measure merely added to their woes by making it harder to sell surplus crops abroad.

As one of Hoover's principal apologists, the *Star* was at pains to point out that although his policies didn't always work out the way they were intended to, he nevertheless deserved credit for putting in superhuman hours and doing *something* to alleviate the nation's suffering. Editorial after editorial praised the president as a great humanitarian and activist whose administration accomplished as much in its first six months as most did in four years. Between 1929 and 1933, Roberts, Haskell, and Ted Alford, Roberts's successor in the Washington bureau, were in and out of the White House on a regular basis. From his desk in Kansas City, Roberts showered Hoover and his aides with advice on agricultural policy, the unemployment crisis, political appointments, and campaign strategy. Haskell, more attuned to the administration's foreign and economic policies, praised such initiatives as a world disarmament conference and a moratorium on European debt. As an ad hoc member of Hoover's kitchen cabinet, the *Star*'s editor was regularly debriefed by the White House after the fact-finding trips he took to Europe every year or two, beginning in 1929.

Haskell's third marriage in 1931 to the widow of Herbert Hadley, the former Missouri governor whom Republican progressives had nearly nominated for president in 1912, opened more doors in the nation's capital. Bright, gregarious, and politically well connected—she counted the president's wife, Lou Henry Hoover, among her friends—Agnes Hadley served as Haskell's ambassador to Washington officialdom. Under her influence, the diffident, re-tiring editor would emerge from his shell and come to be regarded as more than a sympathetic observer of the administration. On a tour of European capitals in the spring of 1932, Haskell wrote a letter to the London *Times* sug-gesting that the United States might agree to renegotiate Britain's war debt after the forthcoming election. Such was his reputation that the comment was widely interpreted as reflecting Hoover's own views. The president's testy re-lationship with the Washington press corps made him more dependent on loyal critics like Haskell. On his return, Haskell lunched alone with Hoover at the White House and cautioned that although many Americans regarded him warily as a dyed-in-the-wool internationalist, Europeans on the whole considered him "an exceedingly stiff and hard boiled American nationalist."[49]

The *Star*'s coziness with the Hoover administration put paid to whatever lingering claim it had to political independence. At the same time, the tie en-hanced both Roberts's stature as a political savant and Haskell's renown as a commentator on economic and foreign affairs. In the early 1930s a heaven-sent opportunity to test their political mettle and burnish their credentials as public ombudsmen presented itself in the person of Henry L. Doherty, the egotistical, acerbic president of Cities Service Gas Company. The latest in a long line of sore losers who demonstrated the truth of Nelson's dictum that the *Star*'s enemies were its greatest asset, Doherty took exception to the pa-per's vigorous campaign for lower natural gas rates. In July 1931 he brought the first of several suits against the *Star* for libel and conspiracy, seeking a grand total of $54 million in damages. To prosecute his case outside the court-room, he bought a half interest in the faltering *Journal-Post*, prompting William Allen White to quip that it was "an expensive form of medical treat-ment to use a newspaper as a mustard plaster for a private bellyache."[50]

"It seems like old days in the *Star* office to be in the thick of a fight like this," Roberts crowed to the Emporia editor. "I can almost imagine the old man still sitting over in the corner thumping and growling for us to go to it and hit harder." In a rambling, paranoid letter to Hoover, Doherty complained about rumors that Roberts—allegedly appointed managing editor on the president's personal intervention—had received private assurances of admin-istration support in fending him off. He accused the *Star* of "color[ing] the news to its own evil purposes," recklessly slandering his good name in a way tending to "shake business confidence" and possibly precipitate a "nation-wide panic." In communications with the university trustees, Doherty went still far-ther out on a limb, demanding that they dismiss the *Star*'s managers outright (something they had no authority to do) and hinting broadly that he might take legal action to "pull" the paper's "poisonous fangs" by having the sale set aside.[51]

Diplomatically rebuffed by Hoover and infuriatingly ignored by the *Star*, Doherty eventually dropped his suits and, on orders of the state utility commission, grudgingly cut the price Kansans paid for natural gas. In the end, the widely publicized joust with the unpopular proprietor of "the Gas House News" did more for the *Star*'s image than any promotional film. Some went so far as to suggest that the paper must have secretly put Doherty on its payroll. "Without the pied piper of Wall Street July and August of this dreary year of grace would only have been a couple of blanks in the annals of the fourth estate," commented *Editor and Publisher*, adding that the *Star* could well afford to lose the libel suit "and charge it up to good will."[52]

As the *Star*'s fiftieth birthday approached, Roberts asked University of Missouri president Walter Williams to write an article for a special anniversary edition in September 1930. Williams, who had founded the university's famous School of Journalism, accepted the assignment in a spirit of objectivity. Balancing the paper's commitment to public service against its often disappointingly timid editorial stands, he told the *Star*'s readers: "Although one has at times to take antidote for its views by the reading of another and more venturesome journal, or even an emetic to rid oneself of social, political or economic theories against which his intellectual stomach protests, yet with all he must pay tribute to the *Star*'s general excellence as a newspaper and to its great influence in making Kansas City a better place to live in, Missouri a better commonwealth of which to be a citizen."[53]

Under the new employee managers, Nelson's philosophy of using the newspaper "to build things up" converged ever more seamlessly with the Chamber of Commerce's bricks-and-mortar agenda. It did indeed seem almost like the old days when, in the early thirties, the *Star* and the Chamber pooled their resources to promote a massive public works program that would both prime the city's sluggish economy and impart a sleek, modernist profile to the skyline. Spearheaded by Conrad Mann, the city's ever-smiling public face, the so-called Ten-Year Plan was the most ambitious project the city had undertaken since the construction of the parks and boulevards. More than two hundred community groups took part in the seven-month planning effort. Haskell and Longan, no longer bound by Nelson's injunction against community involvement, served on the Civic Improvement Committee. In May 1931 voters overwhelmingly approved $40 million in bonding for city and county proj-

Flanked by City Manager Henry McElroy (left) and Jackson County Judge Harry Truman, Conrad Mann appraises the *Star*'s coverage of the Ten-Year Plan: a godsend for the jobless and a windfall for the Pendergast machine.

ects, making it a red-letter day for Main Street progressives and pork-barrel politicians alike.

Conspicuous among the latter were City Manager Henry McElroy and Jackson County Judge Harry Truman, both of whom were firm believers in patronage, despite their hard-earned reputations for fiscal prudence. Citizens of all political persuasions agreed that the Ten-Year Plan—which mandated preferential treatment for local workers and businesses—would help insulate the city from the depression. "How much better it all is than the expensive soup kitchens maintained for idle men by private charity, or an equally demoralizing government dole!" declared White. The *St. Louis Post-Dispatch* held the plan up as an example to the do-nothing Hooverites: "While the administration is coasting along puerilely hoping the depression will solve itself, a middle-western city is shrewd and progressive enough to launch an offensive against it."[54] That winter, an army of some twenty thousand men wield-

Downtown Kansas City in 1929, with the site of Henry McElroy's municipal airport in the distance. Soon the skyline would acquire a sleek, modernist profile in the biggest building spree in the city's history.

ing mostly picks and shovels (the object of the program being to make work, labor-saving tools were shunned) dug the foundation for a new municipal auditorium, installed sewers and water mains, laid trafficways, and spruced up parks. Mann boasted to Hoover's unemployment relief committee—on which he sat, at Roberts's recommendation—that Kansas City could take care of its own, without government handouts.

If the Ten-Year Plan was a godsend to the jobless, it was a positive windfall for Tom Pendergast. His Ready-Mixed Concrete Company supplied the bulk of the cement used in the civic improvement spree, including an extensive system of concrete roads and the cosmetic (and, as the great flood of 1977 would prove, disastrously misguided) paving of the Brush Creek bed, a controversial amenity that McElroy had inserted into the bond proposal at the last minute. Thanks to his free-flowing pipeline to City Hall, Boss Tom was living on a grander scale than ever. On his return from a three-month European vacation in 1927, he decided the time had come to take his place among the Country Club elite. When Nichols quoted him a price for an undeveloped lot, Pendergast pulled out his wallet and fingered five crisp thousand-dollar bills. (The developer, unaccustomed to conducting business on a cash basis, persuaded him to get a money order.) Two years later, he sold his big house on Fifty-Fourth Street to the Nichols Company for $33,500 and moved into an even more imposing French Regency–style mansion at 5650 Ward Parkway, for which he shelled out another $48,000 (also in cash). Weeks later, burglars broke in and stole more than $100,000 worth of jewelry and clothing, prompting Mayor Beach to observe that "the Republican party is no longer the silk stocking party. The Democratic party now is."[55]

As the line of supplicants lengthened outside Democratic machine headquarters downtown, the boss was raking in enough to cross the Atlantic first class, send his children to expensive private schools, maintain a suite at the Waldorf-Astoria in New York, take out memberships in swank clubs, and keep a stable of racehorses. One thing his money couldn't buy, however, was social acceptance. Pendergast was good enough to do business with the likes of Nichols and Kemper, but they refused to eat with him at the same table. The boss wanted the best for his family and it pained him to feel rejected. Still, his power was such that he could afford to turn the other cheek. His forgiving nature was displayed on one occasion when a prominent Republican blackballed him at the most exclusive club in town. Subsequently, the man ran for office and his opponents threatened to dredge up details of a crime he had committed years before. In desperation, his attorney appealed to Pendergast. To the lawyer's surprise, Tom declared that he held no grudge and instructed his subordinates to see that the exposé was suppressed. Character assassination was beneath the dignity of a gentleman.[56]

Not that Pendergast balked at more conventional methods of assassination, especially after his expanding business and political empire bumped up against the underworld territory that Johnny Lazia ruled with a velvet-gloved iron fist. A novice to big-time organized crime, Pendergast found it prudent to maintain cordial relations with the dapper, charming north-end racketeer. In a spirit of amity, they banded together to keep the lid on gang violence and other "rough stuff," which they invariably attributed to outside elements. In their effort to promote Kansas City as a clean, well-ordered town, they found willing accomplices in Mann's Chamber of Commerce and the *Star*. One of Haskell's first actions as editor, in the fall of 1928, had been to announce that the paper would take run-of-the-mill crime stories off the front page and add a full page of wholesome church news.[57] If the new managers hoped by ignoring the crime problem to make it go away, they were soon disabused. Law and order continued to disintegrate, with the city's homicide rate stuck at the stratospheric height to which it had shot up at the outset of the Roaring Twenties.

The Pendergast prosperity, backed up by Lazia's bare-knuckled enforcement at the polls, produced yet another Democratic landslide in the spring 1930 municipal election. The new mayor, a millionaire baking executive named Bryce Smith, provided what the organization had hitherto lacked: a popular, socially respectable front man. Far from wringing its hands as of old, Haskell's editorial page expressed admiration for the machine's vote-getting ability, comparing it with New York's legendary Tammany Hall. Even the Democrats' monopoly of seats in the "nonpartisan" City Council didn't perturb the *Star* unduly. The editors declared themselves well satisfied with the first four years of Judge McElroy's administration. They viewed the lanky city manager as a financial wizard who made ends meet by some form of hocus-pocus inscrutable to ordinary citizens.[58] What did it matter if he had loaned his copy of the city charter to an acquaintance and never bothered to replace it? Other aspects of the Democratic ascendancy were less palatable to the *Star*. That fall, for example, it felt compelled to oppose Joe Shannon's candidacy for the U.S. House of Representatives—a campaign that enjoyed Pendergast's unstinting and wholly self-interested support—despite the fact that one of its own editorial writers was instrumental in engineering the chief Rabbit's late-life metamorphosis from second-tier political boss to Jeffersonian statesman. John Gilday, the token liberal on the editorial staff, was credited with ghost-writing many of Shannon's speeches, a service similar to the one he performed for Mayor Smith and, later, Senator Harry Truman.

With Shannon grazing greener pastures in Washington, the Rabbits fell on lean times and the Goats had the field pretty much to themselves. In March 1932 Missouri's Supreme Court inadvertently greased the machine's wheels by tossing control of the police department—a perennial political football—back into the hands of McElroy and his cronies. Police-protected gambling and boozing, long a significant source of machine revenue, were now more lucrative than ever. Although the gaming industry had become a mainstay of the local economy, it paled in comparison to City Hall's patronage-bloated payroll, which by McElroy's calculations numbered some 3,750 full-time and 5,000 part-time employees. (Most of the latter were day-laborers employed on Ten-Year Plan projects.) Pendergast reaped another unexpected bonus that year when Republican governor Henry S. Caulfield vetoed a statewide redistricting bill, forcing congressional candidates to run at large. Instantly, the Goat leader became a force to be reckoned with in state and national politics as well.

Thus it was only a minor irritation to Boss Tom when, on May 21, 1932, Samuel Mayerberg blew the whistle on the machine. Speaking to members of a women's government study club at the Muehlebach Hotel, the intrepid rabbi fulminated that McElroy had delivered the city into the hands of "gangsters and racketeers." The "iniquitous alliance" between the underworld and the machine had to be stamped out, starting with McElroy's immediate removal from office. As reported in that afternoon's *Star,* Mayerberg's vow to wage a "war to the death against corruption and iniquity" stirred up a hornet's nest. In the ensuing days, he repeated his inflammatory allegations to a group of fellow clergymen, the state attorney general, and anyone else who would listen. The response was discouraging. Mann's Chamber of Commerce for once had nothing to say. After the City Council sent the rabbi packing, having granted him ten minutes to present his case, the *Star* took the opportunity to affirm its faith in the city manager's "ability and personal integrity."[59]

Undaunted, Mayerberg organized a nonpartisan pressure group in hopes of forcing an election to recall the City Council, as provided for in the 1925 charter. In mid-June, a day after the Charter League held its first rally, he slipped away to attend a Rotary convention in Seattle, where he collapsed in exhaustion. Advised by a doctor to rest up on a voyage to Alaska, he was about to board the ship when he received a telegram from Haskell. Was there any truth, the editor wanted to know, to the rumor that the rabbi had either been fired by his congregation or run out of town by Lazia? Mayerberg replied reassuringly that he would return to Kansas City in July "to take up the war and relentlessly to wage it against Pendergast and his gang."[60]

Sensational as they were, Mayerberg's dire warnings were hardly new. For years Walter Matscheck's Civic Research Institute (a spinoff, ironically enough, of the Chamber of Commerce) had been painstakingly documenting McElroy's malfeasance and issuing regular bulletins questioning the veracity of his claims to have cleaned up the city's financial mess. Nevertheless, the *Star,* taking its cue from the business community, refused to believe the emperor had no clothes and persisted in giving the smooth-talking "country bookkeeper" the benefit of the doubt. McElroy himself was cool as a cucumber under fire. Deftly combining condescension with menace, he likened Matscheck to a neighbor's dog that used to bark at him every day as he went out his front door. "The more I ignored it, the more it barked. One day I missed it and asked what had become of it. It was explained to me that the little fellow had simply barked himself to death." Less subtly, Police Chief Eugene C. Reppert attacked Mayerberg as "a yipping, howling, reforming, mudslinging personage." Mann, ever the soul of compassion, urged his fellow citizens to remember that "after all McElroy is but human. He has a heart of gold but he makes mistakes now and then. Fortunately they have not been destructive; they have been more annoying and even that term is possibly a little harsh."[61]

Tolerance of the city manager's mistakes wore thin as racketeers and hoodlums muscled in on Pendergast's turf, vying for a slice of the action, and Kansas City began to attract less favorable attention as the nation's putative crime capital. But in mid-1932 Mayerberg's was a voice crying in the wilderness. Only two members of the business elite, William Volker and Sig Harzfeld, had permitted their names to appear in connection with the Charter League. Even the *Star*, hesitant to burn its bridges with Main Street, gave him tepid support. The rabbi persevered, despite finding himself on the receiving end of threats, an assassination attempt, and even unsolicited tips on Lazia's operation from an underworld "Deep Throat." As the months dragged on, he tired of beating his head against the wall and gave up the fight—but not before his message had gotten through to Washington. That September Hoover apprized his attorney general of reports that Kansas City and Chicago were so rife with "political rings and corruption" that only federal intervention to protect voters could ensure the "proper election of federal officials" in the fall election.[62] The Justice Department dragged its feet, however, leaving Pendergast and Lazia to their own nefarious devices.

Boss Tom had already flexed his political muscles as a powerbroker at the Democratic convention that summer. Skillfully playing the odds, he had manipulated the Missouri delegation in Chicago so as to pay lip service to Jim Reed's favorite-son candidacy while maneuvering behind the scenes to throw the nomination to Franklin D. Roosevelt. In addition to possessing what Pendergast called "the most magnetic personality of any individual I have ever met," the New York governor had pledged to give the machine a free hand in dispensing Kansas City patronage. Pendergast's subsequent boast that he delivered Missouri into the Roosevelt column is open to question, but the episode did nothing to deflate his reputation for political omnipotence. His stature was further enhanced when he plucked a country lawyer named Guy Park out of well-deserved obscurity and got him elected governor of Missouri after the untimely death of his first choice, Francis Wilson. The latter had been in the *Star*'s good books ever since his patriotic prosecution of Rose Pastor Stokes in 1918. Notwithstanding the boss's endorsement, Haskell was inclined to believe that Wilson was a man of principle who would not "let P. run his administration."[63] Park, as events would show, had no such redeeming virtues.

Haskell contemplated the prospect of a Roosevelt administration with a mixture of alarm and guarded optimism. Many things about the genial New

Yorker troubled him—his ties to Tammany and other big-city machines, his lack of gravitas, his tendency to improvise rather than set policy. In common with many former Bull Moosers, he regarded Teddy Roosevelt's cousin as a lightweight, cocky, insincere, and largely untested, especially in the international sphere, despite his impressive political resumé. FDR, downplaying his image as an eastern aristocrat, cheekily launched his presidential campaign in Topeka. Standing in his shirt sleeves in front of the state capital, he accused the Republicans of ignoring the farm crisis. Haskell rode on the candidate's train from Kansas City and informed White that "the correspondents on board think he has the election in the bag, unless he makes a frightful blunder." While conceding that Roosevelt's attack was "vigorous and forceful," he thought it inferior to Hoover's acceptance speech, "which seemed to come from the heart of a man who had been forced down to brass tacks through the bitter impact of events." Roosevelt, he added, "hasn't been through the fiery furnace—yet."[64]

In 1932, however, Hoover was damaged goods. In private, White judged him a "grand administrator" but a poor politician. "I am very fond of him but he is not for this hour," he had written to a friend a year earlier. The Emporia editor was resigned to Hoover's defeat. So was Haskell. After taking soundings in Washington in January 1932, he alerted the Star's readers that stock in the Republican Party, "which might have been listed three short years ago at around 5000, is quoted today at perhaps 50." At the end of October, he wrote to his brother in Bulgaria, "So far as I can see the election was over before the campaign started. The country is going to vote its deep-seated grouch and throw out the ins." Hoover was not wholly to blame for his plummeting popularity, Haskell argued. The president's eminently sensible policies had been sabotaged by "a series of bad breaks." After all, the economic crisis and most of the other problems he had had to contend with hardly dated from his watch. He had tackled them in good faith, with unflagging energy and supreme competence, but his blind spots as a practical politician and the limitations of his philosophy of economic nationalism had done him in. Hoover's gravest mistake, in Haskell's eyes, had been to support the Smoot-Hawley Tariff against his better judgment. "He was outjockeyed, as Taft was, by the high tariff people in congress," he observed to White.[65]

Nevertheless, both Haskell and White publicly kept faith with Hoover, denying in the face of the facts that his presidency had been a failure. In July the Star gave prominent play to White's editorial "Hail Genius of Hoover," lauding the president's unparalleled capacity for leadership. (The GOP circulated White's paean during the campaign, just as they had done with "What's the Matter with Kansas?" in 1896.) A few days later, Haskell catalogued

Hoover's achievements in stabilizing prices, channeling capital to farmers and home owners, spending prudently on public works, and forestalling the wholesale collapse of the country's financial institutions. The administration's bias in favor of big business, the editor argued, was both necessary and far-sighted. "It happens that most modern business is done through the instru-mentality of great corporations. The most effective way to help the Forgotten Man is to save these corporations and get them to operating normally, while at the same time promoting public and semipublic works that provide em-ployment. In his whole program the President has kept steadfastly in view, not the few stockholders, but the 25 million families dependent on these institu-tions."[66]

Most of the country's struggling blue-collar families, however, had reached a very different conclusion. Whatever faith they may have had in old-fashioned trickle-down economics during the fat days of the Coolidge prosperity van-ished in the aftermath of Black Tuesday. Even Kansas Citians, comparative-ly unscathed by the depression, took the *Star*'s last-ditch appeals with a grain of salt. "The country knows Hoover through and through," Haskell wrote in an election-eve editorial. "It knows where he stands and what he will do. It has every reason to feel confidence in the results of his extraordinary experi-ence as applied to future problems." Although Roosevelt had "sought to cap-italize the depression as the paramount issue" in the campaign, "his speeches have indicated that he fails to recognize the nature of the complicated causes that have produced it and his definite proposals for recovery have had slight substance." Few Americans questioned Hoover's intellectual ability; it was his philosophy of severely limited government that they found wanting. The peo-ple knew the president through and through all right. That was why they de-cided it was time for him to go. As Haskell would later observe, the election was a struggle between Hoover and the depression, and the depression won.[67]

In what the *Star* termed "the most violent reversal of political sentiment in American history," voters overwhelmingly rejected Hoover's business-friendly, go-slow approach to the country's economic crisis in favor of Roosevelt's promise of "bold, persistent experimentation." Yet the decisiveness of FDR's victory camouflaged a profound ambivalence in the electorate. Was Hoover a genuine progressive in the mold of Teddy Roosevelt, as he appeared to ad-mirers like Haskell and White? Or was he a reactionary Luddite masquerad-ing as an up-to-date technocrat, a man who spoke the language of the mod-ern corporate executive but in reality wanted to turn back the clock? As Haskell's friend Anne O'Hare McCormick wrote in the *New York Times*, "The contradictions in his struggle to keep to the old course while tacking with the

A sour-faced Herbert Hoover escorts Franklin D. Roosevelt to the Capitol for FDR's inauguration in March 1933. "I am very fond of him but he is not for this hour," William Allen White wrote of the outgoing president.

winds, to reconcile a Jeffersonian philosophy with finance corporations, Federal farm boards and railroad regulation, is [*sic*] typical of the inner conflict of America."[68]

Hoover seemed as bewildered as anyone by his stunning reversal of fortune. A few days after the election, Roy Roberts boarded the train carrying the lame-duck president back to Washington from California. Hoover, uncharacteristically subdued, gazed into his old friend's eyes and asked, forlornly, "Why?"[69]

CHAPTER 8

Tom's Town

Tom Pendergast was all charm and affability as he greeted the reporter from the *American Magazine* in his office at the Ready-Mixed Concrete Company. "Hello there! Have a seat," he boomed from behind a battered oak desk, easing his 232-pound frame back into the chair. Boss Tom was in an unusually loquacious mood that winter's day in early 1933. He talked freely about his job as "political leader" of a typical American city. The key to his success, he explained, lay in his brother Jim's adage that politics is the art of making friends and in the corollary proposition that all politics is local. The big man brushed aside questions about war debts, the tariff, and other national issues. "I don't know anything about those things. My interest is only in Kansas City—and in my family." His organization, he boasted, had turned the city "from a hick town into a metropolitan city. Look at our streets and our parks and public buildings and everything! This is a metropolis—one of the greatest in the world!"

> *"The man who makes the organization possible is the man who delivers the votes, and he doesn't deliver them by oratory. Politics is a business, just like anything else."*
>
> —Tom Pendergast

Clearly captivated, the interviewer glossed over Pendergast's peccadilloes and presented him as a pillar of the community—a civic-minded businessman, good Catholic, devoted husband and father, and model public servant. "Newspapers, churches, reformers, or

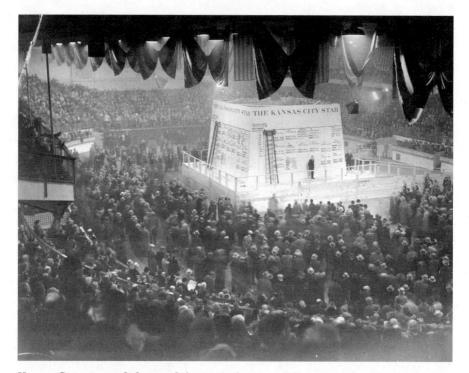

Kansas Citians crowded around the *Star*'s election-night scorecard at Convention Hall on November 8, 1932. The paper called it "the most violent reversal of political sentiment in American history."

narrow-minded fellows—they can't bulldoze me," the boss declared. "I have never changed my mind when I knew I was right and I have never broken my word." City Manager Henry McElroy vouched for Tom's bona fides. Pendergast, he told the reporter, "insists that all the men he appoints shall be honest and do their work. He says to them, 'Don't take a chance. Don't do anything you shouldn't.' When we find a man in the organization is being tempted to take easy money, we get him in and reason with him. We show him that if every man in the organization took graft, the party would soon be out of office."[1]

Pendergast's recent exertions on behalf of the national Democratic Party had spread his renown far beyond the Missouri border. His ability to get out the vote had been attested by the overwhelming majorities Roosevelt racked up both in Jackson County and statewide in November 1932. ("Thus does practical politics again run counter to private virtue," the boss's sometime ally Frank Walsh wryly observed to Jacob Billikopf.) Tom anticipated a productive relationship with the incoming administration. Shortly after the election, he reminded Roosevelt's campaign manager, James Farley, that he expected to be consulted on federal appointments. "My predictions, when I saw you in New York and here, as to the majority we would give Governor Roosevelt have been more than realized," he wrote. "Our County of Jackson gave him a majority of about ninety thousand. We had a great candidate and, if I do say it, we did a good job. . . . I cannot believe Governor Roosevelt would fail to recognize those who laid the ground-work for him in Missouri."[2]

It was Farley's job to see that FDR didn't neglect his obligations to the big-city bosses who had helped put him in the White House. In Pendergast's case, however, his task was complicated by the machine's increasingly hard-to-ignore ties to organized crime. A Justice Department report issued in 1933 would conclude that "the whole town is under the control of a racket—composed of bankers and business men working with exconvicts and gangsters."[3] Heading the list was Johnny Lazia, the cool-headed kingpin of the mostly Italian north side. Having muscled in on Pendergast's turf some years previously, Lazia made himself indispensable to the boss and his allies when a rash of high-profile kidnappings and gangland shootings broke out in the city in the early thirties. The machine availed itself of his good offices in securing the release of Nell Donnelly when the wealthy dress manufacturer was abducted for ransom in 1931. And when renegade hoodlums nabbed McElroy's twenty-five-year-old daughter a year and a half later, the city manager knew better than to call in the police. Instead, he turned the rescue operation over to Lazia, with eminently satisfactory results.

Mary McElroy's ordeal contributed to the upwelling of sympathy for Lazia in his dispute with the U.S. Treasury Department concerning an overdue income tax bill. This time, it was Pendergast's turn to go to bat for him. On May 13, 1933, Tom asked Farley, now Roosevelt's postmaster general, to "use your utmost endeavor to bring about a settlement of this matter." Lazia, he added, "is one of my chief lieutenants and I am more sincerely interested in his welfare than in anything you might be able to do for me now or in the future." When the *St. Louis Post-Dispatch* belatedly published Pendergast's letter nineteen months later, the boss immediately fessed up, explaining matter-of-factly that he had "tried to intercede for Lazia" just as he "would speak for any other active Democrat under similar circumstances."[4] Farley, however, claimed he couldn't recall seeing any such letter and Attorney General Homer Cummings backed him up, insisting that Lazia had never received special treatment from his department. Subsequently, it was revealed that the district attorney in charge of Lazia's case had backed off on orders from Washington. Only when a member of the grand jury cried foul was the prosecution resumed.

Lazia made news again that summer in connection with a dramatic event that put Kansas City on the crime map big time. On June 17, 1933, three gunmen attempted to spring Frank Nash, convicted train and bank robber, when he arrived at Union Station flanked by a phalanx of lawmen escorting him to Leavenworth Penitentiary. Lazia had declined to take part in the rescue himself. Instead, he put the desperadoes in touch with "Pretty Boy" Floyd, who happened to be passing through town. The operation was not a success. Nash and four officers, including one FBI agent, were mowed down in an early-morning gunfight in front of the station. J. Edgar Hoover swooped into Kansas City and pledged that the bureau would "never stop until we get our men, if it takes ages to accomplish it."[5] Meanwhile, Lazia quietly spirited the killers out of town. The case was never solved, although Congress soon acceded to Hoover's demand that his G-men be authorized to carry guns.

The Union Station Massacre opened a new chapter in the federal government's escalating "war on crime." For shell-shocked Kansas Citians, it offered a preview of coming attractions attendant on the repeal of prohibition the following December, when Tom's Town would become wider open than ever.

The editor of the *Star* learned about the excitement back home from reports in the British press. That June found Henry Haskell in London attending a major international economic conference, a parley that promised to be almost as fractious and exasperating as a Kansas City political campaign. But Haskell was feeling on top of the world: a month earlier, his editorial page had won a Pulitzer Prize for its "compelling demonstration of editorial responsibility and leadership." The jury cited a group of editorials, mostly written by Haskell, dealing with efficiency in government, foreign trade, and the European debt problem. For Haskell, the coveted prize vindicated the more tolerant, evenhanded, analytical editorial policy the paper had pursued during the seven years of staff ownership. "If the newspaper cannot command public sentiment by mere vehemence as in the old days, it must depend on moving it by a rational interpretation of events, both through editorial correspondence and straight editorials," he told journalism students in accepting a public-service award from the University of Missouri in Columbia on May 3.[6]

National recognition, which Haskell had hoped for but never sought, had belatedly arrived in the fifty-ninth year of his life. Anonymity was still the rule on the tradition-bound *Star,* but for the past ten months the unassuming editor had contributed a signed column of travel notes, biographical and histor-ical vignettes, and behind-the-news commentary that quickly became a pop-ular staple of the Sunday paper. The North American Newspaper Alliance gave wide distribution to his analyses of political and economic trends, the kind of "interpretive reporting" associated with syndicated columnists like Mark Sullivan, Walter Lippmann, and Frank Kent. Haskell had too much missionary blood in his veins to seek public-figure status in his own right. But he was eager to make his voice heard in policymaking circles and prove him-self more than Hoover's apostle. In a series of articles published in December 1932, he had outlined a moderately liberal program for economic recovery based on "vigorous and effective action to restore the farm market as a pre-liminary to any real prosperity." Noting that Wall Street was increasingly re-ceptive to the idea of centralized economic planning, he reported that Roo-sevelt was widely pictured in the East "as a man of abounding vitality, with a fresh and open mind, willing to listen to a multitude of counselors, with enough common sense to distinguish good from bad advice, and a sufficient-ly shrewd politician to make the most of his opportunities." FDR, he reas-sured his midwestern audience, was "expected to be progressive, but not wild or visionary."[7]

As had been his habit with Hoover, Haskell sent tearsheets of his articles to the president-elect and was gratified to learn that Roosevelt passed them along to his senior advisers. An opportunity to influence government policy more overtly presented itself in February 1933, when the editor traveled to Washington to testify before the Senate Finance Committee. As reported in the *New York Times*, Haskell "presented a four-point program containing de-tailed recommendations for economic readjustment" to address the problem of farm indebtedness. In an exchange with Senator Reed Smoot, cosponsor of the tariff bill that had alienated many of Hoover's supporters, he argued that healthy industries had little to fear from foreign competition, while American farmers urgently needed lower tariffs to facilitate access to foreign markets. In calling for increased government intervention to combat the deep-ening depression and giving the president "almost dictatorial powers to bal-ance the budget," Haskell served notice that he was no doctrinaire advocate of small, efficient government, locked in a pre-1929 time warp.[8] Unlike many in the progressive old guard, he recognized that the United States was under-going a profound social and political revolution, one that required a new phi-losophy of activist government along the lines of Theodore Roosevelt's New Nationalism.

Within days of the Senate hearings, a newly energized Congress pushed through the Emergency Banking Act, Agricultural Adjustment Act, and other landmarks of FDR's fabled Hundred Days of legislative hyperactivity. "The President's course so far has brought an immense lift in spirit to our part of the country," Haskell wrote to Assistant Secretary of State Ray Moley at the end of Roosevelt's first week in office. "His handling of the banking and budget situations has rallied public sentiment behind him to an amazing degree." Like many "Roosevelt Republicans," the *Star's* editor admired FDR's boldness in addressing the economic crisis. William Allen White was equally bedazzled. "The old timers are sitting around rubbing their eyes and wondering what is happening, talking about Franklin wandering in Wonderland and all the while we are making major social moves from which there will be no turning back," he told Roy Roberts after a trip to Washington that spring. To Harold Ickes, the crusty Bull Mooser whom Roosevelt had roped into his cabinet as secretary of the interior, White exclaimed: "Your Big Boss is doing a splendid job. I am scared stiff about him. Every day, as he handsprings lightly over the first page, tossing the world on his toes, I am jostled by a fear that he will fall down. But he has not fallen down so far."[9]

In many ways, Roosevelt's New Deal coalition of business and labor, reformers and machine politicians, urban liberals and small-town conservatives mirrored the motley progressive confederation of the prewar years. And, as time would show, it was almost as fissile. The moralists and uplifters clustered around Teddy Roosevelt's bully pulpit would have found little in common with the policy wonks and wheeler-dealers who descended on Washington in the spring and summer of 1933. Characteristically, Haskell was of two minds, applauding FDR's progressive goals and can-do spirit while deprecating his autocratic methods, casual disregard for individual liberties, lack of financial discipline, and intellectual fuzziness. Despite his friendly relations with Moley and other administration officials, he remained more a wary onlooker than an insider, an attitude encapsulated by his remark to a friend that he had been in Washington "studying the New Deal in its lair."[10] Most of Roosevelt's idealistic brain trusters, in turn, instinctively regarded any confidant of Hoover as a closet reactionary and potential foe.

As early as the summer of 1933, some old-line reformers had begun to peel away from the New Deal. The National Industrial Recovery Act, with its controversial provisions for collective bargaining and a guaranteed minimum wage, was perceived in some quarters as pandering to labor militants and "special interests." Haskell's editorial page, however, emphasized that compliance was purely voluntary and welcomed the NRA regime as "an extraordinary and inspiring spectacle" infused with the "spirit of willing sacrifice" that was "the true test of patriotism." Its praise for Roosevelt's agricultural policy was more restrained. Although the AAA incorporated some measures that the *Star* had long advocated, several of its more radical components—notably the domestic allotment plan, designed to stabilize commodity prices and production—struck Haskell as unwise and unworkable. "The stream of letters coming to our farm weekly is overwhelmingly against" the plan, he informed Moley. What the farmer needed most, the *Star* continued to insist, was "the expansion of the consuming power at home through business recovery and an unblocking of the foreign market, so that he can dispose of his surplus abroad."[11]

However welcome FDR's initial moves had been to Main Street, his decision in the spring of 1933 to abandon the gold standard alarmed conservative proponents of "sound money." Among the blue-chip bankers and economists to whom Haskell looked for advice—men like Thomas Lamont of the Morgan Bank, E. W. Kemmerer of Princeton, Benjamin Anderson of Chase National, and Eugene Meyer of the Federal Reserve—it was an article of faith that the stabilization of exchange rates was prerequisite to setting the world's economic house in order. Their hopes had been dashed even before Haskell sailed for England at the end of May in the company of White and Secretary of State Cordell Hull, a staunch internationalist. On the eve of the economic conference, Roosevelt jettisoned plans to stabilize the dollar and showed a distinct lack of enthusiasm for the lower tariff barriers that Hull considered the most realistic path to world peace. René Pleven, the French diplomat and future premier, predicted that nothing would come of the meeting. The United States, he told Haskell, "had started on a program of devaluing its currency and trying to raise domestic prices, which ran directly counter to the proposed principles and aims" of the conference.[12] Yet despite his misgivings about the administration's inflationary strategy, Haskell remained optimistic that reciprocal trade agreements with individual countries would open foreign markets to American goods.

Back home, fresh from the Europe of Hitler and Mussolini, Haskell wrote that Roosevelt promised to be a "dictator" of a different stripe, one who ruled with the consent of the governed. En route to Kansas City, he lunched at the White House on July 25 and came away convinced that the president possessed "the same quality of boyish enthusiasm, of restless, eager curiosity, that characterized Theodore Roosevelt." Haskell was heartened by FDR's resolve to stand up to ultraconservative central bankers, economic nationalists, and unregenerate plutocrats. He even dared to hope that the New Deal might mark the dawn of the millennium for which he and his fellow progressives had long been waiting. "Alone, the profit incentive, the motive for gain, for the piling up of wealth as the aim and end of life no longer will obtain," he lectured the *Star*'s readers. "The new order which it is sought to institute will, and should, mean less profits for some and more economic security for all. It should bring, accordingly, a transformation of success standards, a broader, a more equitable and just procedure looking to that equality of opportunity which is, and ought to be, the right of every individual."[13]

Many disillusioned Hooverites were having second thoughts about laissez-faire liberalism and pined for a dose of Teddy Roosevelt's big-stick theory of governance. But the *Star*'s editorial page moved farther to the left than most, advocating the establishment of formal diplomatic ties with the Soviet Union and even expressing cautious admiration for Lenin's New Economic Policy. For a few brief months in early 1933, Haskell felt almost as euphoric as he had in the throes of the great Bull Moose adventure two decades earlier, when a wholesale transformation of the American political system appeared to be in the cards. All too soon, however, the irreconcilable tension between the administration's collectivist mentality and the individualistic philosophy of the conservative libertarians would sunder the fragile ties that held the First New Deal coalition together.

On April 1, 1933, *Star* readers learned that Hitler, Germany's newly appointed chancellor, had undertaken a "program of extermination" against Jews that threatened to exceed even the bloodbath of the Spanish Inquisition. This apocalyptic warning was issued by Rabbi Samuel Mayerberg in a sermon at Temple B'nai Jehudah and backed up by dispatches out of Germany from respected foreign correspondents like H. R. Knickerbocker. Haskell knew and trusted Knickerbocker and Mayerberg. Yet he was loath to believe that the prostrate, demoralized, and virtually bankrupt republic he had visited barely a year earlier could have succumbed so abruptly to a plague of intolerance and vitriolic nationalism. He decided to investigate for himself.

At the close of the London conference, he and his wife boarded a train for Berlin and checked into their favorite hotel on Unter den Linden, where they had stayed on their honeymoon in 1931. At first glance, the German capital seemed unchanged. The hotel staff greeted them warmly and, despite hard times, the streets of the posh commercial district were thronged with shoppers. Milling about among them, however, were groups of armed soldiers and police, as well as processions of young men wearing brown breeches, shirts, and caps. Troubled, Haskell sought out Knickerbocker, Edgar Ansel Mowrer of the *Chicago Daily News*, and other journalistic acquaintances. Several told him they had received threats from Brown Shirts and Nazi officials. The

British ambassador said he had warned His Majesty's government that Germany's only program under Hitler was militarism. Louis Lochner, the Associated Press's Berlin bureau chief, supplied details of the Nazis' efforts to intimidate Jewish citizens and prevent them from leaving the country. Several men Haskell had met in 1932 had mysteriously disappeared; others refused to see him or agreed to talk only where they couldn't be overheard. After a sumptuous performance of Wagner's *Fliegende Holländer*, the Haskells stepped out onto the square where, just weeks before, Goebbels's henchmen had built a bonfire of proscribed books. The atmosphere was pathological, surreal, reminding Haskell of "an asylum where the abnormal is the accepted thing."[14]

Seared by his experience, the editor returned home determined to help spread the alarm about the true nature of the "Nazi revolution." In a series of sixteen nationally syndicated articles, he warned that it was no longer possible to dismiss Hitler as a tin-pot demagogue and the Germans as a weak, oppressed people suffering under the boot of the vindictive French and British. The Nazis' persecution of Jews, intellectuals, and radicals, their regressive economic policies and aggressive militarism—the classic symptoms of a revolution's "terror" phase—proved that Hitler was deadly serious. The chancellor had cynically exploited the discontent of Germany's unemployed and dispossessed masses. Most ominously, the Nazi police state appeared to enjoy near universal popular support. Such government-sponsored bestiality was unparalleled in modern European history. "Germany has virtually split off from western civilization," Haskell wrote in the *Oberlin Alumni Magazine*. "We have had a glimpse through a half opened door into the dark caves of human conduct; a glimpse of the brute that skulks therein."[15]

The impact of Haskell's wake-up call is difficult to gauge, but as one of the first American journalists to visit Germany after the Nazis' rise to power, he received dozens of invitations to lecture about the German crisis. The *Kansas City Jewish Chronicle* praised him for speaking out about "the conditions he observed in Nazi-dom," adding that "what he saw there must have moved this quiet, reserved, scholarly man to his depths." Haskell told his old friend Jacob Billikopf that he had never "had such a profoundly depressing experience" as his visit to Germany. "Billie" had also toured Germany that summer and needed no convincing that the Nazis had embarked on the systematic annihilation of European Jewry. He drafted a harrowing, twelve-page memorandum of his trip and sent it to Roosevelt through Governor Herbert Lehman of New York.[16] To both Billikopf's and Haskell's keen disappointment, however, the new administration lacked the political will to press Congress to relax the restrictive immigration quotas that made it all but impossible for most European Jews to seek asylum in the United States.

That spring, Kansas City synagogues had contributed sixteen thousand dollars to support Jewish immigration and resettlement—a drop in the bucket in light of the generosity the city had shown in throwing its doors open to eastern European Jews in the Galveston Movement a quarter-century earlier. Billikopf, who had spearheaded the resettlement effort in Kansas City before moving to New York and then Philadelphia, had singlehandedly raised some $30 million for Jewish relief during the war. But times had changed. In Kansas City, as elsewhere, economic hardship and isolationism fanned the embers of anti-Semitism. Since returning from Europe, Haskell told Billikopf, he had been alarmed by "the number of intelligent persons" he had met who weren't "particularly disturbed about the Jewish persecutions because of their anti-Jewish prejudice." In his analysis, the Nazis' seizure of power signified the growing influence of what White called the "moronic underworld." Like the Ku Klux Klan, such barbarism was something that no civilized nation could tolerate. Just as the Klan fever of the 1920s had subsided, he was inclined to believe that "the thuggery aspect of the anti-Jewish movement" in Germany had played itself out by mid-1933.[17]

Oswald Garrison Villard was less sanguine. The Nazi outrages were "continuing if anything with greater refinement and cruelty," he wrote to Haskell in September. The *Nation*'s editor asserted that Hitler was "merely sparring for time" before going to war. "The question is whether there shall be preventive measures now, or the world shall calmly await the inevitable." (Despite his seeming belligerence, Villard was a lifelong pacifist and would sharply criticize Roosevelt for leading America into war.) Haskell remained hopeful that the German people would come to their senses. In the meantime, like his friend Charles Nagel, a prominent St. Louis lawyer of German extraction who had served in Taft's cabinet, he was anxious to prevent a recurrence of the rabid anti-German prejudice to which Americans had fallen prey during the war. Nagel was torn between sympathy for Germany's withdrawal from the League of Nations, which he saw as a justifiable protest against the punitive terms of the Versailles Treaty, and revulsion at the Nazis' domestic policies, which he described to Haskell as "lacking in ordinary wisdom." Eager to avoid "stirring up extremists on both sides," both men pointed out that the Jews weren't Hitler's only victims. The "Jewish brutalities," Haskell wrote to Billikopf, were "merely one striking symptom of the disease, which is essentially a revolt against civilization."[18]

Such scrupulous evenhandedness made it all the easier for Haskell, and the

Star, to discount Rabbi Mayerberg's prescient alarms about thuggery on their own doorstep.

The *Star's* attitude toward Tom Pendergast exemplified the practical idealism Haskell had so often preached. At election time the paper could usually be counted on to give the machine a sharp tongue-lashing; between elections, like most of Main Street, it muted its criticism and occasionally did business with the big boss. In the early thirties the paper used Ready-Mixed concrete for a renovation project. "Did I coerce the *Kansas City Star* when they bought cement from my firm?" Pendergast not unreasonably asked. No one, of course, could avoid doing business with Henry McElroy. If Boss Tom looked like he had stepped out of a cartoon by Thomas Nast, the lanky, irascible city manager was blessed with the features of a country parson, sea-green incorruptible. Even J. C. Nichols, the *Star's* poster child for civic virtue and business efficiency, thought highly enough of McElroy to admit him as a shareholder of the Nichols Company.[19]

The newspaper's loyal support of McElroy in his unstinting efforts to "put the government on a business basis" highlighted the old progressive paradox: If business culture was rife with corruption, government run on business principles was bound to be corrupt as well. This home truth was confirmed in December 1932, when the ebullient president of the Chamber of Commerce, the unfortunately named Con Mann, was convicted in New York City for violating federal lottery laws. It was an awkward moment: the city's chief mover and shaker, idol of the *Star* set, stalwart ally of Pendergast and McElroy, and member of President Hoover's unemployment commission had been caught with his hand in the till. As a high-ranking officer of the Fraternal Order of Eagles, Mann had helped organize a charitable lottery that netted him and an associate $460,000, a healthy rake-off even by Pendergast's standards.

Vowing to reclaim his good name, Mann returned to a cheering crowd at Union Station, McElroy standing at his side while a brass band intoned "Let Me Call You Sweetheart." Dozens of upstanding businessmen, judges, labor leaders, and politicians appealed for a presidential pardon, but FDR refused to act, even when Pendergast presented his formidable personage at the White House in October 1933. Miffed, the boss proceeded to New York and called on his friend Jim Farley. The president finally relented, but only after subjecting Mann to the indignity of being fingerprinted and glimpsing the inside of a jail cell. When the reprieved prisoner returned to Kansas City shortly before Thanksgiving, only a handful of newsmen and supporters braved the chill winds to greet him at the new downtown airport built by his friend McElroy.

Conrad Mann and his wife arrive at the Kansas City airport after his pardon by President Roosevelt, November 17, 1933. The city's chief mover and shaker had been caught with his hand in the till.

Still, most Kansas Citians seemed to agree with the *Star* that "the verdict of the New York court will not affect the esteem in which Conrad Mann is held by his fellow citizens for what he is and for his great services to the city."[20]

Although a registered Republican, Mann performed his greatest service to the city as middleman between Main Street and the Democratic machine. These credentials made him the natural choice to chair the bipartisan committee that oversaw the expenditure of $40 million in bond funds that voters had approved for the Ten-Year Plan. Mann's blithe assurances that Kansas City could take care of its own during the depression were music to the ears of the laissez-faire ideologues in the Hoover administration. He changed his tune only when it became apparent that FDR's people were committed to a different approach to public welfare, one that, in the long run, would prove considerably more advantageous to Mann's patron at 1908 Main.

Long years of commanding an army of ward heelers had given Pendergast a keen appreciation of the importance of charity work. "My organization, all by itself, sees to it that not a family goes hungry in the city," he boasted. "Every one of my ward workers has a fund to buy food, coal, shoes, and clothing for the poverty-stricken. When a poor man comes to old Tom's boys for help, we don't make one of those investigations like these city charities. We feed 'em and we vote 'em."[21] The machine specialized in cutting red tape, a service it also provided for hard-pressed businessmen, irrespective of political affiliation. The beauty of the scheme was that it was independently funded through an elaborate system of kickbacks, lugs, payoffs, and bribes. There was no need for a cumbersome municipal bureaucracy; the machine already had its precinct captains in the field, ready to respond to any distress call. Their needs thus provided for at apparently minimal expense, few Kansas Citians heeded Walter Matscheck's Cassandra-like warnings that the machine's padding and log rolling were in fact costing the city millions of dollars a year.

So it was entirely understandable that, midway through FDR's first year in office, Harry Hopkins, the smart, abrasive head of the new federal Emergency Relief Administration, approached McElroy for details of Kansas City's highly touted work-relief program. "In the past three years," the city manager informed him, "Kansas City, out of its own resources, expended something like $4,000,000.00 to produce 'emergency' or 'day' work, which gave part-time employment to several thousand men each winter." This sounded too good to be true, and at the end of October 1933 Hopkins came to Kansas City to discuss the program with McElroy and County Judge Harry Truman, Missouri's federal reemployment director. Shortly thereafter, FDR created the Civil Works Administration—precursor to the Works Progress Administration—and placed Hopkins in charge. McElroy was quick to lay claim to being godfather to Roosevelt's signature relief effort, although critics accused the city manager of turning the make-work program into an unwieldy patronage machine and "play[ing] politics with human misery and want."[22]

Pendergast had received FDR's private assurances of patronage long before the 1932 election and the president had reiterated his promise publicly just after his inauguration. Now it was payback time. To the chagrin of Senator Bennett Champ Clark, who insisted that federal appointments were a senatorial prerogative, the Kansas City boss remained firmly in charge of patronage on his own turf. In 1935 he would secure Clark's assent to the appointment of Matthew S. Murray as Missouri's relief czar. Murray was a Pendergast crony and Kansas City's director of public works, in which capacity he played a significant part in carrying out the Ten-Year Plan. This experience proved excellent preparation for doling out the eighty thousand jobs he controlled as state WPA director. Although Hopkins stoutly denied that Pendergast was the shadow-boss behind the agency's operations in Missouri, it was not lost on observers that the vast majority of men and women on Missouri's federal work-relief rolls were employed in and around Tom's Town.

Farley, who doubled as Roosevelt's chief political operative and patronage dispenser, was eager to keep peace with Pendergast. His "private file" records frequent consultations with the boss and his agents concerning appointments and political matters, as well as Pendergast's repeated complaints that the administration wasn't giving him the consideration he deserved. At the same time, Farley took pains to stay on good terms with the *Star,* meeting regularly with managing editor Roy Roberts and Washington correspondents Ted Alford and Duke Shoop, as well as monitoring the paper's daily coverage of the administration. By late 1934 he noted with satisfaction that even Haskell appeared to have been won over. Calling one of the editor's signed reports from Washington to the attention of Louis Howe, he told the president's confidential adviser that "as he understands it, Mr. Haskell is a real 'New Dealer' now."[23]

Haskell's favorable midterm report card took the form of a series of articles on the New Deal published in late November and early December. After a rocky start in which radicals had been in the driver's seat, he observed, the president had taken the wheel and demonstrated his goodwill toward Wall Street. "It seems evident that Franklin Roosevelt, like his great predecessor, Theodore, is apt to follow a friendly gesture to business with a strong statement of criticisms which reassures his popular following. The timing seems studied to produce the best political results." FDR's programs, Haskell opined, were no more revolutionary in contemporary terms than TR's, and certainly far from socialistic. His prudent goal was to correct the abuses of the capitalist system and "bridge the gap" until business had time to recover. Even the administration's controversial embrace of massive deficit spending, with its concomitant inflation, was a gamble worth taking. "To sum up," Haskell wrote, "the record shows the President as a liberal experimentalist, but not a radical, who is anxious to see the capitalistic system work better and more fairly in the future than it has in the past."[24]

This remarkably sympathetic assessment of the Democratic administration echoed the "Olympian tolerance" that the Republican *Star* had traditionally accorded to the Pendergast machine.[25] But all that had changed nine months earlier, in the bloody city election of 1934.

Pendergast, enjoying the perks of national celebrity, had pitched the election as a referendum on boss rule. Although his ward workers outdid themselves, boosting voter registration to an all-time high, he took out insurance in the form of some fifty thousand votes later discovered to be "ghosts," "repeaters," or otherwise fraudulent. These ballots partly compensated for the more than eighty-eight thousand names that had been struck from the rolls at the instigation of the boss-busters. Since Mayerberg's short-lived Charter League shut down in late 1932, the reformers' ranks had been replenished by a cadre of twenty-something businessmen calling themselves the National Youth Movement. Former Senator James Reed was not overly impressed. "Evidently in despair of getting anywhere under its own name, the Republican party now comes forward disguised in the knickers of youth, with a children's organization apparently for the purpose of rejuvenating Kansas City. Few voters will be deceived by the masquerade," he told the press.[26]

Playing to its well-heeled south-side constituency, the NYM put together a "Citizens Fusion" ticket heavy on socialites and headed by a former University of Missouri president. On the eve of the election, they gained a well-placed ally in FDR's assistant secretary of commerce. Ewing Y. Mitchell hailed from Springfield, Missouri, and was sorely distressed by conditions in the big city to the north. Kansas Citians, he declared, "live in a state of coercion and terror from the heartless exactions and atrocities of the Pendergast machine." He went on to suggest that the fight against "corruption and racketeering" was a cornerstone of the New Deal, which was undoubtedly news to Roosevelt and Farley. Boss Tom, at any rate, was less than overwhelmed by Mitchell's credentials. "I've got more friends in Kansas City than he ever will have, as will be shown March 27," he retorted.[27]

The *Star* had been gearing up for another of its biennial tussles with the machine. It was "a very muscular paper" in the thirties, recalls one newsroom veteran. "They had big guys. Reporters often had to fight their way out of meetings. It was like a bunch of dock workers writing that newspaper."[28] But on election day the *Star*'s muscle-men were no match for the plug-uglies deployed by the machine and its north-side allies. One reporter, checking out a report of irregularities at a downtown polling place, was set upon by thugs who chased him to the side entrance of the *Star* building, riddling his car with bullets. Editor Haskell's African American chauffeur had a narrower escape. Kidnapped by two gangsters while driving Fusion workers to the polls, he was pistol-whipped in a midtown alley and heard one of the hoodlums say, "Let's finish him now." Fleeing in a storm of bullets, he took refuge in a nearby mortuary. All day long suspicious-looking black cars, shorn of license plates, patrolled the streets, unmolested by police. Tom's "friends" were out in force.

When the smoke cleared, the machine had racked up one of its biggest victories, retaining the mayor's office and a solid majority of council seats at a toll of four dead, eleven severely injured, and hundreds roughed up. The final tally showed 223,866 ballots cast out of some 244,000 registered voters, a rate of participation that would have done credit to Mussolini or Hitler. In the wake of the debacle, Police Chief Reppert offered himself up as a scapegoat, to be replaced, in one of City Manager McElroy's cheekier maneuvers, by a member in good standing of the *Star* family. Veterans at Eighteenth and Grand fondly recalled Otto Higgins's colorful escapades as the paper's war correspondent. Having lost fifteen hundred dollars in a dice game and sold his typewriter to pay for his return passage from France, Higgins briefly practiced law before enlisting for duty as one of Pendergast's junior lieutenants. The *Star* tactfully refrained from criticizing his appointment, but it soon became apparent that Higgins didn't run a noticeably tighter ship than his predecessor. When Johnny Lazia was gunned down on the steps of his midtown apartment hotel on July 10, police experts determined that the bullet had come from one of the guns fired in the Union Station Massacre a year earlier. Beyond that, they were clueless. The sight of Higgins, Pendergast, and McElroy paying their respects at the gangster's funeral suggested that the forces of law and order had yet to find a home in City Hall.

At the time of his death, Lazia was free on appeal from the jail sentence he had drawn five months earlier for neglecting to file tax returns in 1929 and 1930. Frank Walsh, now one of the country's leading labor attorneys, prominent New Dealer, and chairman of the New York State Power Authority, had returned from New York to assist in his defense. Despite the mayhem on the streets, Walsh thought things were looking up in the old town. After spending ten days in Kansas City that July, he reported to Billikopf that "the Irish and Jewish boys, who formerly gave the uplifters, such as you, and the courts, so much trouble, have been shunted into the background. Italy rules the older further downtown neighborhood." Walsh had always gotten along with Pendergast, whom he credited with delivering Missouri for Roosevelt in 1932. As a good Catholic, moreover, he believed in redemption from sin. In September 1933 he had held a reunion with the boss in New York and found him "very much broadened and with quite a progressive outlook, political and otherwise."[29]

"Progressive" is probably not an adjective that many Kansas Citians would have applied to Pendergast, least of all in the thirteen tumultuous months between June 1933 and July 1934, when Tom's Town was rocked by the so-called Holy Trinity of crimes. The *Star* found some consolation in balancing the Union Station Massacre, election-day violence, and Lazia's murder against the

Attorney Frank P. Walsh (left) confers with Johnny Lazia during the racketeer's income tax trial in early 1934. Lazia's gangland assassination a few weeks later capped the Holy Trinity of crimes that rocked Kansas City in the early thirties.

three-pronged cultural renaissance symbolized by the Kansas City Philharmonic, the University of Kansas City, and the Nelson Gallery of Art, all of which opened their doors in the fall of 1933. Yet the stark truth was that half a century of progressive crusading had left the city more disunited than ever. Nelson and Pendergast, both bosses, both builders, had offered competing visions of the city of the future. In the mid-1930s, that future was still hanging precariously in the balance.

The outcome of the 1934 municipal election put Pendergast in a strong position to name his own man to the U.S. Senate. After one or two other candidates declined the honor, the boss unexpectedly gave the nod to his hard-working protégé, Judge Harry S. Truman. "The *Star*'s been hammering Tom hard and he naturally wants to make sure his man's all right," Congressman Joe Shannon explained to the press. (Shannon was rumored to have taken himself out of contention for the post.) Truman was indeed squeaky clean. He had spent $8 million in Ten-Year Plan bond funds on county roads and ended up with a tidy surplus, with which he threw a grand barbecue for taxpayers on the grounds of Sni-a-Bar Farms in suburban Grain Valley. As a later historian would write, "the Nelson farm and Democratic judge combined to furnish the nonpartisan love of fun."[30] Pendergast's confidence in Truman wasn't shared by McElroy, who viewed his former colleague on the County Court as a dangerously independent-minded rival. In years to come, visitors to the city manager's grand office on the twenty-ninth floor of City Hall would be treated to ill-tempered diatribes about the shoddy construction across the street, where the county courthouse had thrust its twenty-two stories skyward under Truman's supervision.

Truman, however, had few illusions about independence, even after winning the August Democratic primary by a comfortable forty-thousand-vote margin and trouncing his Republican opponent in the fall. He had made his feelings clear to an off-duty *Star* reporter as they downed the boss's vintage prohibition-era bourbon a few months earlier. "I owe my political life to the Pendergast organization," Truman reflected. "They have been loyal friends. I know that the organization has countenanced some things which I believe are wrong. But I do believe this, and that is that you can get further cleaning up a political organization from the inside than you can from the out. At least, I can in the position I am in. If I came out against the organization and tried to wreck it, people would say I was a yellow dog, and they'd be right." Publicly, Truman seemed unconflicted about his relationship with Pendergast. Privately, however, he agonized over his obligation to "the Big Boss." Pendergast, he wrote, was "a man of his word; but he gives it very seldom and usually on a sure thing. But he's not a trimmer. He in times past owned a bawdy house, a saloon and gambling establishment, was raised in that environment but he's all man. I wonder who is worth more in the sight of the Lord?"[31]

By the early 1930s Pendergast had put his unsavory past far behind him—so far, indeed, that he could keep a straight face in assuring a *Star* reporter that the prevalence of gambling and racketeering in Kansas City was vastly overstated. He had visited New York, Philadelphia, and Chicago, he said, and all of them were much wider open than Kansas City. "So far as rackets are concerned, I can say advisedly that Kansas City is freer from racketeering than any city its size in the country. Outside of the gambling and slot-machine complaints, I say that Kansas City is the standout city of the country so far as the protection of its city by the police is concerned." The *St. Louis Post-Dispatch*, ever alert to its sister city's travails, begged to differ. In December 1934 the

Pulitzer paper devoted several columns to a trenchant exposé of "the moral and civic destitution of Kansas City." An "irresponsible political machine," in league with the lawless underworld, had seized control and threatened to expand its suzerainty. "It is no exaggeration to say that the shadow of Tom Pendergast now falls across the whole length and breadth of Missouri. His nod makes governors and United States Senators, by the puissance of his Kansas City machine that produces votes in whatever quantity desired. Pendergast has enslaved Kansas City."[32]

Whether power-crazed despot or enlightened progressive, Pendergast stood at the peak of his powers during the first Roosevelt administration. Granted, he had let things get out of hand in the 1934 election. That was regrettable and wouldn't happen again. The *Star* had burned its bridges with him and the business community was growing restive. But he had weathered such storms in the past. With its friends in high places, there seemed no reason to believe that Pendergast Inc. shouldn't continue to pay dividends for years to come. So invincible did the boss appear that for quite a while neither he nor his friends noticed the fatal chink in his armour: he was a compulsive gambler. Even the country bookkeeper in City Hall would have been hard-pressed to cover Pendergast's traces as he ran up horse-racing debts estimated as high as a million dollars a year. The man whose sneer of cold command brought the high and mighty to their knees was known from coast to coast as one of the biggest suckers in the game. Some speculated that hubris drove him on. Or greed. Or perhaps he was betting on finding another Climax, the horse with which his brother Jim had struck it lucky all those years ago.

In 1936, at the apex of his fame and fortune, Pendergast consented to have his portrait painted. The Missouri legislature had commissioned Thomas Hart Benton to decorate the lounge of the state capitol with a mural, and the outspoken artist was determined to show Missouri's history warts and all. Enthroned in a sturdy office chair, cigar in hand, Pendergast dominates the foreground of Benton's Kansas City panel, exuding an air of studied nonchalance while gazing haughtily over two pint-sized figures identifiable as J. C. Nichols and W. T. Kemper, in the vague direction of two show dancers on a far-off stage. It was Kemper who persuaded Pendergast to sit for Benton, somewhat against Tom's better judgment, for he was a genuinely private man. Benton refused to sugarcoat either the Show Me State's inglorious past or its checkered present, of which the bald-pated boss was the universally recognized symbol. Besides, he had a soft spot for Pendergast. When Benton's father, a state congressman and nephew of the famous Missouri senator, lay dying in 1924, Tom had brought his political friends to his sick bed, passed the hat, and pressed into the struggling artist's hand an envelope containing a charitable donation of eight hundred dollars.[33]

Yes, Tom Pendergast was all man. If anything, as time would tell, he was all too human.

Under Haskell, the *Star* had greeted Roosevelt with an unfeigned enthusiasm redolent of Nelson's late-life embrace of Wilson. FDR was a politician after Baron Bill's heart: a nose-to-the-front man, big-natured, flexible, resilient, fearlessly progressive, classy but down to earth. The "old" *Star* almost certainly would have cut its ties and run with him, just as Nelson had with Wilson after the election of 1912. But by 1935 many Bull Moose progressives were growing disenchanted with the Democratic Roosevelt. They had gone along with the reasonable, business-friendly policies he had adopted in his first two years, which were essentially an updated version of TR's New Nationalism. But when the First New Deal floundered, FDR shifted gears and bolted on a radical new course, signposted by the Social Security Act, the Wagner Act, and the Works Progress Administration, that left many of his followers trailing in the dust.

Organized business opposition to the New Deal crystallized after the fiercely partisan 1934 midterm elections and over the next two years the Supreme Court confirmed conservatives' fears by invalidating key pieces of New Deal legislation. For Haskell, who had never quite overcome his misgivings about Roosevelt's impetuousness and political promiscuity, the prospect of a benevolent dictatorship guided by socialistic principles gradually lost its luster. More and more he identified himself with fiscal conservatives inside and outside the administration. In the spring of 1935 he wrote that many businessmen remained sympathetic to FDR's goals but faulted him for rushing into action without thinking things through. As he now saw it, "the president's spectacular achievements, the ending of the banking crisis, the relief to debtors, the war on child labor and sweat shops, the restoration of the nation's shattered morale, [and] the jarring of the country out of bad ruts" had "faded into the past."[34]

As they contemplated the deteriorating international situation, old-line reformers saw red flags in Europe's drift toward economic nationalism and totalitarian government. On a trip to England and the Continent in the summer of 1935, Haskell discussed Germany's lurch to the right with Fred Howe in Paris and was dismayed to find the old progressive warrior "taking the attitude of so many of the young New Dealers that personal liberty is of slight

Herbert Hoover (center) flanked by newspaper friends in Emporia, Kansas, February 17, 1935: from left, Henry J. Allen, William Allen White, Charles F. Scott (owner of the *Iola Register*), and Henry J. Haskell. "A curiously spotted mind he has, with extensive dumb spots and some brilliant flashes," Haskell wrote to White.

importance." Over tea with the American ambassador in Berlin, the editor told William Dodd that Roosevelt would almost certainly win reelection, since he was "the only man who can hold liberal groups together and thwart the extremists of left and right." As much as he deplored Farley's influence in the administration, Haskell predicted that in years to come the United States would be unable to "get on without chiefs tied in with city politicians, almost American Fascists." Dodd noted in his diary that he found this a "sad comment" coming from "the one independent, liberal paper in the West."[35]

All the same, Haskell was under no illusion that a revival of Hoover's laissez-faire doctrine would solve any of the nation's problems. Publicly, both he and Roy Roberts praised the conservative manifesto that Hoover published in 1934 under the title *The Challenge to Liberty*, in a transparent bid to launch a political comeback. Privately, however, he shared Roberts's opinion that the book was an embarrassing relic of eighteenth-century political thought. Two years of Roosevelt's dizzying innovation had shown how inept the former president's stewardship of the economy had been. "Men who worked with him tell me he thought himself a great economist and financier, whereas he was neither. Also that if he once got a wrong idea in his head you couldn't dislodge it," he wrote to White from Washington. "A curiously spotted mind he has, with extensive dumb spots and some brilliant flashes."[36]

White, temperamentally disposed to play both ends against the middle, was markedly more sympathetic toward both Hoover and Roosevelt, but warned Farley that his boss faced a tough fight in the upcoming election. In what he coyly described as "a confidential letter from the Republican Precinct man in the Fourth Ward, Emporia, Kansas swapping a chaw of tobacco across the line," White advised the Democratic National Committee chairman that "Roosevelt is slipping because he is running against the ideal Roosevelt of March 4, 1933. People compare the inevitably battered figure of today with the knight who had fresh stove polish on his armor in early 1933." In the spring of 1935, Haskell returned from Washington convinced that Roosevelt's missteps had "reinvigorated" the Republicans. A few months earlier, he wrote in the *Star*, the party had been looking not for a presidential candidate but for a "sacrificial bull" to offer up in 1936. Now, in an unexpected echo of 1912, the GOP was actively searching for a "lusty bull moose to lead what it hopes will prove a growing and formidable herd."[37]

By early fall both Haskell and White had a pretty fair idea who the next Republican standard-bearer would be. Governor Alf Landon of Kansas was the coming man in Republican politics. A veteran Bull Mooser who had struck it rich as an independent oil producer before entering politics, Landon had come to the attention of party elders that summer as the "Great Budget Balancer." Skeptics pointed out that state law mandated a balanced budget and that he could hardly have succeeded in running the government on a pay-as-you-go basis without healthy injections of federal relief aid. Nevertheless, Landon was the sole Republican governor who had withstood the Democratic landslide of 1934, a distinction he enjoyed largely thanks to the savvy promotion of Lacy Haynes, the *Star*'s shrewd and dandified Kansas correspondent. Haynes set the Landon bandwagon in motion late in 1934, but it was Roberts, a classmate of the governor's at the University of Kansas, who put him on the fast track to national celebrity. According to one account, Roberts ran into Kansas newspaper publisher Oscar Stauffer on the street in Kansas City early in the fall of 1935. "Look here, Roy," Stauffer said, "when are we going to do something about getting Alf nominated for president?"[38] Not long after that chance encounter, Roberts, Haynes, Stauffer, and a fellow Kansas newspaperman named Fred Brinkerhoff chipped in five hundred dollars apiece and opened a two-room campaign headquarters in Kansas City's Muehlebach Hotel, a few blocks down from the *Star.*

White, who preferred to remain an ex officio member of Landon's "Kansas Gang," testified that Roberts ran the office as if it were an extension of the newsroom. Despite Landon's personal wealth, the campaign started off on a shoestring. His self-appointed managers didn't even print letterhead; instead, they economized by using the stationery of Stauffer's *Arkansas City Daily Traveler.* As one national magazine commented, "in big-league politics" the Landon organization "was a sand-lot team." The governor, who cut an appealingly folksy figure with his square shoulders, tousled gray hair, rimless spectacles, and twangy voice, was cast as the latest in a long line of Great Commoners from the flat and dusty hinterland. Roosevelt's point men quickly swung into action in an effort to deflate the Landon balloon. Federal relief administrator Harry Hopkins fired the first salvo during a Washington press conference at which a *Star* correspondent taunted him by broaching the topic of the Sunflower State. "The state of Kansas has not put up a thin dime for relief," Hopkins exploded, adding that "the last I heard, the Governor was trying to get enough from me to keep his schools going." He admitted that Landon had balanced the state budget, but only by "taking it out of the hides of the people."[39]

Hopkins's apparently impromptu attack in early November was Landon's first lucky break. Another soon followed in the form of an unsolicited, and wholly unforeseen, endorsement from William Randolph Hearst. A visceral foe of the New Deal, the Democratic press magnate had sent his minions around the country that summer and fall to scope Landon out. Their glowing reports induced him to take a look for himself. In what a writer for *Fortune* magazine described as "a spectacle not soon to be forgotten," two private railroad cars and a chartered Pullman rolled into Topeka on December 10, 1935, for a state visit. On board were Hearst, movie star Marion Davies, and a retinue of journalists not known for their allegiance to the party of Lincoln. All except Hearst's girlfriend repaired to the governor's home for a get-acquainted session, along with Haskell, *Star* president George Longan, and Senator Arthur Capper, a leader of the powerful farm bloc in Congress. After lunch, the Lord of San Simeon emerged to announce to reporters that "if the Republicans and those opposed to the New Deal united on a man like Governor Landon—a man who is a doer and not a promiser—the New Deal can be defeated."[40]

Although Haskell and Longan, in *Fortune*'s words, "tried valiantly to conceal their embarrassment" at being forced to break bread with Nelson's bête noire, Hearst's well-publicized stopover in Topeka confirmed what most people already knew: that the *Star* had never really strayed from the Republican fold. Banker W. T. Kemper reminded Farley in mid-January 1936 that "the *Star,* just as I told you many, many moons ago, when the time comes will do everything they can to beat the Democratic ticket." Longan's feelings toward Roosevelt were no secret: at shareholders' meetings he regularly railed against the NRA and other New Deal programs for reducing the paper's profit margin. Haskell, meanwhile, had joined the elite group of writers, economists, and industrialists featured in the "Voice of Business" section put out by the elitist and rabidly anti-Roosevelt *New York Sun.* Not surprisingly, he soon found the door to the White House shut in his face. That March FDR's press secretary advised that "the *Kansas City Star,* and Henry Haskell in particular, according to reliable informers, is promoting Governor Landon's candidacy." Unless the president had some "special reason" to grant the editor an interview, Steve Early wrote in a memo, "my judgment is that the time otherwise would avail little."[41]

To Erwin Canham of the *Christian Science Monitor* it appeared that the *Star,* which had "fairly liberal views and the most conservative format of any newspaper in the country," had a good deal in common with Landon, the "Kansas Coolidge." Like Silent Cal, Landon had been schooled by his handlers to say as little as possible, in the hope that Roosevelt would self-destruct. Having entered the race as a dark horse, Landon seemed content to run as a stealth candidate, one who "sat back and kept his mouth shut and let the Press of the country work for him." Beyond suggesting "that it would be nice to attain many New Deal goals without New Deal spending and experiment," *Time* magazine complained later that spring, Landon had taken no forthright positions on most of the pressing issues of the day. The governor's calculated evasiveness galled White. Once again, as in campaigns past, he found himself compelled to stand up for progressive principles against the doctrinaire conservatives who dominated the GOP platform committee. Pointedly referring to Landon as "your candidate," White wrote to Haynes in late February: "I realize it is wise strategy for him to be innocuous. But God, think of getting the Presidency at that price."[42]

Nevertheless, White consented to write the introduction to a slender campaign biography by *Star* reporter Richard B. Fowler. *Deeds Not Deficits* portrayed Landon as a smart, practical, commonsense progressive—a "doer" rather than a "promiser"—whose outstanding gubernatorial record proved that "good business can be good politics." If it wasn't yet clear precisely what the candidate stood for, there could no longer be any doubt who was feeding him his ideas and strategies. Not since 1912 had the *Star* been so heavily invested in a national political campaign, and never before had it openly attempted to run one. In its analysis of the "Landon boom," *Fortune* characterized the paper as "part of the folk culture of Kansas. It is plump, provincial, moral, homely, somewhat self-righteous, and consciously rustic. And enormously profitable." Roberts and Haynes were "the stars of the *Star's* political backfield," with the former "calling the signals" and the latter "carrying the ball." Although *Fortune* omitted Longan and Haskell from its roster of the Kansas Gang (the official membership seemed to vary from one account to another), a *Time* cover story identified them as the brains behind the campaign, senior advisers who "nursed the Landon candidacy along with quiet talk and sage advice."[43]

That Landon's bid for the presidency was at best a long shot didn't discourage Haskell unduly. Writing in the April number of the *Review of Reviews,* he guardedly predicted that "the present outlook in Missouri would be regarded by most unprejudiced observers as still Democratic. Yet there are many who believe the nomination of Landon at the Republican national convention would bring the state into the doubtful column and lay the foundation of possible Republican success." Sensing that White was wavering, Haskell tried to rope his friend onto the governor's publicity team, urging him to help "establish Landon as a real personality—the man who only a few years ago was stubbing around oil wells in lace boots and a leather coat, whose progressivism flowers naturally from his experiences and his point of view as a man of the people, representing the feelings of the great mass of Republicans (and Democrats, too) of the Valley states." White, however, remained resolute in his ambivalence. "I don't see very well how Roosevelt can be beaten unless he beats himself, which is not at all impossible," he told Villard. For Landon he had words of praise so faint as to be all but damning: "barring the fact that he is a Pennsylvania Dutchman and stubborn as a mule when he gets his head set, he is pretty much all right barring his limitations."[44]

White was deeply offended by the governor's shotgun marriage to Hearst, whom he considered "a hitch-hiker on the Landon bandwagon." Haskell's argument that candidates should be entitled to take support wherever they could find it cut little ice with the Emporia editor. Neither did his assurance that there had been no quid pro quo. He had been "present throughout the whole conversation in Topeka," Haskell said, "and Hearst hardly spoke unless he was spoken to and certainly asked nothing." Unappeased, White told Haskell and Roberts that the "whole difference" between them was that they wanted to keep Hearst on Landon's side at all costs, whereas he "felt it was vital to back away from Hearst even if we lost his support." Both privately and publicly, White continued to hold the Landon organization at arm's length. In May he told a *Time* reporter he was "inclined to believe" that Landon would rise to the "overwhelming responsibility" of the presidency, then undercut his feeble endorsement by sighing, "I don't know. No man knows. I don't think he knows." Several weeks before the election, White published a breezy recap of the campaign, focusing on issues rather than personalities and carefully masking his own advisory role.[45] So skittish was he about being associated with the Kansas Gang that he didn't even mention the book to his friends at the *Star* until it was already in the shops.

Farley, whose sensitive political antennae soon picked up the signals of disharmony in the Republican ranks, deemed Landon a gift to Roosevelt, not least because of his lameness in front of the microphone. "The Republicans," he recorded in his diary that April, "are now within six weeks of their national Convention and the only candidate who has any support is Governor Landon and they will have to take him whether or not they want to. His managers are afraid to have him appear on a movie screen and the radio; he doesn't make a speech and his personality is bad. They can't elect a candidate they can't bring out and show—they will have to have movie shots taken and when they do Landon will fare badly; he will have to go on the radio—and against Roosevelt who is at his best not only on the stump but on the screen as well."[46]

In the event, Landon had as much to fear from his fellow Republicans as from the Democrats. Although he sailed to the nomination in June with apparent ease, his even-keeled candidacy was buffeted by a gale of criticism from the party's left and right wings. Senator George Norris of Nebraska, one of Roosevelt's key Republican allies, thundered that "representatives of special interests" operating "behind the smokescreen" at the Cleveland convention had "nominated a man for President whose greatest asset is that nobody knows him and nobody knows what he stands for." Roberts, putting in eighteen-hour days in his dual role as reporter and campaign manager, struggled to placate Norris and other disgruntled progressives, with disappointing results. White, meanwhile, had drawn the unenviable assignment of mending fences with Hoover, who had come to Cleveland half hoping to win a third nomination. Irrationally and irreconcilably hostile to the Kansas governor, Hoover agreed to put his name to a joint statement declaring Landon unfit for the office of president, but the scheme fell through when Senator William Borah of Idaho refused to sign. In a huff, Hoover gave White the impression that he intended to quit politics if Landon won.[47] The choice of Frank Knox, conser-

Governor Alf Landon (right) gets the lowdown from Roy Roberts in the home stretch of the 1936 presidential contest. Roberts and his "Kansas Gang" ran the Republican candidate's campaign office as if it were an extension of the *Star* newsroom.

vative publisher of the *Chicago Daily News,* as the party's vice presidential nominee did little to smooth the troubled waters.

In light of the turmoil behind the scenes, Haskell had good reason to feel, as he told Landon after the convention, "more sober than jubilant." Press reports from Cleveland had described the *Star*'s editor as a "one-man 'brain trust'" whose "analytical experience and familiarity with a wide range of national and world issues put the Landon campaign on solid ground." As the

summer wore on, however, Haskell's misgivings about the governor's "popular appeal" and grasp of economic issues intensified. He was uncomfortable
having to defend the oil man against charges that he was under the thumb of
big business and thought Landon had been ill advised to send a last-minute
telegram to the convention pledging to put the economy back on a gold basis. In effect, Landon had unilaterally amended the carefully worded currency plank in the party platform, which Haskell had helped hammer out in
Cleveland and which deliberately omitted any reference to gold. When
Arthur Krock pointed out that the telegram provided fodder for the candidate's liberal critics, Haskell took it upon himself to respond. "So far as I
know," he wrote the *New York Times*'s influential political correspondent,
"Landon was interested only in getting a sound currency plank, that did not
pussyfoot." He added that "in all these negotiations in which I took part there
was never the slightest intimation, direct or indirect, that the governor was
thinking of any financial group in New York."[48]

The fight was uphill all the way, however. H. L. Mencken, who grumbled
that "the snake-charmers now operating at Washington have been disgracing
the party and harassing the country long enough," placed little stock in Landon's chances. If Roosevelt won reelection, he wrote Haskell, "I can only con-
sole myself with the thought that the American people will deserve it. Whenever they have a choice between an honest man and a quack they almost
invariably choose the quack." Nevertheless, there were signs that Landon was
picking up eleventh-hour support from conservative Democrats like Newton
Baker and John W. Davis. Haskell saw Ray Moley in New York in late September and found him "all full of suggestions for the Landon campaign. If he's
not for Landon," Haskell reported gleefully to White, "like Marion Pinkham,
he gets a great kick out of telling the story." Even Jim Reed, disappointed in
his hope of returning to Washington as attorney general, announced that he
would have to hold his nose while casting his ballot for FDR.[49]

There was nose-holding in the Landon camp at the end of September, when
the governor, speaking in Minneapolis, lashed out against the administration's
program of reciprocal international trade pacts as damaging to the interests of
American farmers and livestock men. The address, with its unfortunate echoes
of Taft's high-tariff speech at Winona, Minnesota, that had sparked the Republican insurgency twenty-six years earlier, infuriated many of Landon's progressive supporters. Haskell, summoned to Topeka to go over the speech in
advance, discovered that the governor had already made up his mind and
would agree to only minor revisions. At the end of a frustrating late-night bargaining session at the executive mansion, Landon asked what his adviser

thought of the speech. "I am not happy over it," Haskell sighed, "but I am much less unhappy than I had feared I might be."[50]

Others found the governor's sop to the protectionists a bitter pill to swallow. Called in to do damage control with key figures like Baker, banker James Warburg, and columnist Walter Lippmann, Haskell halfheartedly defended Landon's position as a tactical concession to Republican conservatives. In reply, Lippmann insisted that the speech may have been "fatal to the moral integrity" of the campaign. Landon couldn't "possibly lose the votes of the old-fashioned, high tariff, reactionary Republicans," but he desperately needed to win the confidence of "the moderate tariff people, and particularly the peace people who know the effect of economic nationalism in provoking a war." This was precisely the argument that Nelson had made to Taft in 1910, and Landon's response—essentially, that political considerations trumped economic arguments in a close-run election—had an all-too-familiar ring to Haskell's ear. "I'm glad I'm not in politics," he wrote to White in exasperation. "Well, the *Star* will have to dissent and keep its self respect; tho it isn't necessary for us to be violent about it."[51]

At Farley's behest, FDR seized the advantage and swung through Landon country early in October, passing through Kansas City just long enough to show the flag for Pendergast, who was convalescing in New York after surgery for an intestinal ailment. At a whistle stop in Emporia, the president impishly put his friend White on the spot. "I was standing in the station as far back as I could get in the crowd in that direction," the editor related to Roberts. "He called for me. I made no response. Somewhere in his speech he referred to me and asked if I were there, and I said nothing and tried to duck back into the doorway, but couldn't. Then the crowd told him where I was and he beckoned me up to the train, and I grinned and shook my head. Finally, after he had finished speaking, he said to the guards, 'Make a gangway there for Mr. White.' Then he said again 'Come on up. I want to see you a minute.' And there was nothing for me to do but to come unless I had been conspicuously rude to the President of the United States."[52]

Landon was known as "The Fox," in tribute to his wiliness as a businessman, but he and his rookie country-kitchen cabinet were clearly outfoxed by the battle-hardened Roosevelt team in the closing weeks of the campaign. Farley liked to tell how he lengthened his candidate's odds in the Sunflower State by adding twenty-seven thousand workers to the WPA payroll on the eve of the election.[53] Such get-out-the-vote tactics may have made a crucial difference, for the Kansas race remained too close to call until the wee hours of election night. The final tally showed Landon the loser in his home state by more than sixty-six thousand votes. In Tom's Town, FDR's margin of victory (later shown to have been inflated by the usual methods) was better than three to one, and nationwide he outdistanced the Kansas governor by nearly eleven million popular votes (27,478,945 to 16,674,665). The electoral vote was a crushing 523 to 8. In the end, only Maine and Vermont kept faith with the Kansas Coolidge.

At 9:30 p.m. on November 3, a wire-service flash announced that the *Star* had conceded the election, and four hours later Landon made it official in a telephone call to Roosevelt. "I was prepared for defeat, but not for catastrophe," a chastened Haskell wrote White the next day. (Roberts would later confess to Farley that he realized the campaign was a lost cause as early as September.) In retrospect, it was obvious that "an angel from heaven couldn't have won against" FDR, Haskell said. He had "no apologies or regrets," but recognized "that in this fight we evidently were far away from our readers. We have got to swallow some economically unsound things to keep in touch with them. I've been convinced that we have got to go along so far as we possibly can and put up with quackery at times—unless it is too evidently catastrophic, like inflation."[54]

Salving their bruised pride, Landon's campaign managers and boosters quickly got back down to business as usual. "You made a great fight, old fellow, and we are all proud of you!" J. C. Nichols wrote consolingly as a prelude to trying to interest the governor in purchasing a home in his Mission Hills subdivision. Haskell, feeling "like an old and seasoned campaigner—especially old" after two weeks on the hustings, was relieved to return to editorial writing full time. Longan, whose zest for politicking had waned long before the election, ordered the *Star*'s campaign clipping files purged, muttering that "we won't need this stuff any more." Lacy Haynes was already gearing up for future presidential contests—he had his eye on New York's crime-busting prosecutor Thomas E. Dewey—but Roberts told Farley he was "all through trying to make Presidents" and was "going to remain as a newspaper publisher."[55] Time would show that the "fat country boy from Kansas" was no more capable than Nelson of sticking to his vow of political abstinence.

Local affairs in 1936 gave the *Star* more cause for celebration. Soon after the machine racked up another crushing victory in the fall election, a six-month-long investigation sparked by a suspicious spike in voter registration finally hit pay dirt. So cocksure, or careless, had Pendergast and McElroy become that they scarcely bothered to conceal incriminating evidence. Reporters discovered lists of "ghost" voters' names on the walls of vacant boardinghouses and storerooms around the city, where they had presumably been posted to help precinct workers keep their records straight. Deeming himself all but invincible and determined to avoid a repetition of the 1934 bloodbath, the boss even provided bodyguards for the newsmen.

A week before polling day, the *Star* estimated that at least 40,000 of the city's 263,000 registered voters were fraudulent. An "honest election" was an "impossibility," the paper declared. Not a single public official had "made so much as a genuine effort toward enforcement of the law." The machine's power rested upon "a foundation of public indifference, coupled with a system of business and political racketeering that permeates the community." The *Star* had fulminated against election fraud times beyond number, but never before had it so clearly implicated the business community. If Pendergast's monolithic support on Main Street was beginning to crack that fall, he still had plenty of defenders, even in the reformers' ranks. Frank Walsh was moved to send the boss a personal letter deploring the "undeserved criticism" to which he and his family had been subjected "throughout the years—years mainly devoted to the public welfare and helping the underprivileged."[56]

Of late, it seemed, Pendergast had been rather more attentive to his own welfare, having taken steps to boost his "take" from his well-oiled cash machine in order to pay down his soaring gambling debts and hospital bills. However, the public good was arguably served to the extent that the election took place in an almost unprecedentedly law-abiding atmosphere. Only those in the know, which may or may not have included Pendergast himself, could have foreseen that the boss's deceptively peaceable kingdom was soon to be shaken to its foundations. As the *Star*'s bloodhounds pursued the scent of corruption and estimates of illegal votes cast in the election soared toward the 60,000 mark, pressure for a grand jury investigation intensified. District Attorney Maurice Milligan, an antimachine Democrat, was champing at the bit to take Pendergast on, but held back for want of evidence that federal laws had been violated. Finally, in early December, federal district court Judge Albert Reeves, a ramrod-straight Republican, set a jury to work with a ringing charge to "reach for all, even if you find them in high authority." In New York, Pendergast shrugged it off. "I have been investigated for forty years," he told reporters. "If Reeves and Milligan can find anything wrong I'll not squawk."[57]

Shortly thereafter the judiciary gained an unexpected ally in Governor Lloyd Stark, a well-to-do apple grower whom Pendergast had installed in Jefferson City in November against his better judgment and largely as a favor to Harry Truman. Stark may have nursed a grudge against his reluctant patron for having passed him over in 1932. Possibly, too, the ambitious governor already had his eye on Truman's Senate seat, or even higher office. In any event, that fall and winter Stark rounded on Pendergast with a righteous zeal that put old-timers in mind of "Holy Joe" Folk in his prime. Meanwhile, the *St. Louis Post-Dispatch,* hitherto preoccupied with a vote-fraud investigation in its own backyard, dispatched a team of reporters to Kansas City to get the lowdown on Pendergast. The ensuing months almost turned back the clock to the days of Nelson and Pulitzer, the two great boss-busting papers crusading in tandem against corruption, hard-digging reporters competing for a "beat" as the full picture of the machine's perfidy slowly unfolded, revelation by shocking revelation, and a flood of indictments and trials emanated from Milligan's relentless prosecution.

Pendergast, seemingly heedless of the gathering storm, took his customary vacation the following summer at the posh Broadmoor Hotel in Colorado Springs, where he offered a homily on civics to Spencer McCulloch of the *Post-Dispatch:*

> Give the people good major officials, give them a good government, see that things that touch their daily lives, like good sanitation, efficient fire and police protection, run efficiently, and they should be satisfied. . . . Reform must be brought about through training in the home and church. You cannot write it in statute books. You can't make a man good by passing a law saying that he must be good. It's against human nature. The public doesn't care for reformers—certainly not the Kansas City and St. Louis public. Why, there's not one in a hundred that's sincere and there are mighty few sincere ones that are practical. William Jennings Bryan was the only sincere practical reformer that I ever knew in my 45 years of politics.[58]

A month later Governor Stark called on Pendergast on his way home from vacation in Alaska. The boss had extended the invitation partly as an olive branch and partly because he wanted to ask Stark for a favor. The governor rejected Pendergast's request that he reappoint R. Emmet O'Malley as state insurance commissioner, but agreed to let Tom's crony stay on for another year while he looked for a replacement. At the time, Stark didn't grasp the full import of the request. Not until some six months later did he learn that O'Malley and Pendergast had conspired to bilk Missouri policy holders out of nearly half a million dollars. In October, Stark fired the commissioner for insubordination. Subsequently, Duke Shoop of the *Star'*s Washington bureau made an appointment to talk with Roosevelt about the governor's clean-up campaign. The president still had no thought of breaking with Pendergast; in the fall of 1937 he needed the boss's support more than ever. But the *Star* had at last found a responsible public official who was prepared to buck the machine. However belatedly, the stage was set for a showdown.

Despite these positive signs, the reformers were in no rush to count their chickens. As they saw things, they were waging a war of attrition against the Pendergast machine. Experience had taught them that it was futile to mount a frontal attack on the organization. It merely kept bouncing back, like a hydra, entrenching itself deeper and deeper with the help of its friends and accomplices in City Hall, Jefferson City, and Washington. The enemy, the reformers believed, was not just a nefarious political machine but a whole system riddled with corruption, from police headquarters and courthouses to council chambers and boardrooms. The odds against the boss-busters seemed overwhelming. They had no alternative but to adopt a long-term strategy. In their code of "practical idealism," compromise was not just a necessity but a virtue.

Haskell took an equally dim view of the international situation. "I have been pretty low in my mind over the prospects for the world in general and our beloved country in particular," he wrote to White as he prepared to sail for Europe in March 1937. "We have developed a complex industrial system, and I don't know but what the moronic underworld will insist on running it. . . . We have brought a vast submerged mass of people to an active interest in government thro the radio. Every American thinks he is competent to run the government, and I don't know whether the country will be willing in the long run to trust its destinies to competent men or not."[59] Like most Bull Moose progressives, Haskell was at heart an elitist. It was one thing for the *Star*'s reporters to seek out the opinions of the man on the street and muck about in White's "moronic underworld." The editor considered his time better spent with financiers, statesmen, and the other "important people" whose thinking informed and guided the paper's editorial policy.

In London that May, Haskell attended the coronation of King George VI. The Westminster Abbey ceremony reinforced his conviction that Great Britain and the United States were the principal guarantors of democratic values and international peace. In a letter to the *Times* of London, he urged the adoption of reciprocal trade agreements between the two countries as a step toward world unity. Secretary of State Hull had made such agreements the cornerstone of the administration's foreign policy, but now they were under attack from isolationists in Congress. The editor was equally scornful of Prime Minister Neville Chamberlain's insularity; Chamberlain's background, he told Newton Baker, was "that of Republican high protectionism." In Haskell's view, Britain's swift rearmament—if necessary, with American support—was key to stabilizing Europe and preventing another war that could be disastrous to the United States. "If the British empire should fall," he wrote in an editorial enclosed with his letter to Baker, "a heavy blow would be dealt to those fundamental ideals of liberty which are at the foundation of American life and institutions. The autocratic system would be left supreme in Europe."[60]

Baker, now a successful corporate lawyer in Cleveland, was one of the conservative Democrats who had parted company with Roosevelt with the advent of the Second New Deal. He saw eye to eye with Haskell about the strength of the Atlantic alliance and the importance of reducing tariff barriers, while sharing the editor's misgivings about the administration's collectivist mind-set. "I can think of nothing spiritually more barren than a world divided into dictatorships, the continued existence of which depended upon a complete merger of the interest and opportunities of the individual into the dominant pretensions of nationalistic states," he wrote.[61] Despite their free-market libertarianism, however, both men recognized that the survival of democracy depended on leveling the playing field, ensuring equality of opportunity, and reducing the economic disparities between both nations and social classes.

A high-level colloquy on "public opinion in a democracy," held in August at Williams College in Massachusetts, gave Haskell an opportunity to elaborate on his ideas. Reflecting on his travels that spring in England, Italy, and southern France, he said he had been moved to ponder why the Roman Empire had disintegrated while the English monarchy remained "a going concern." Haskell's reading of history, and his observation of modern societies, convinced him that three major factors had brought about Rome's fall: lack of education and the consequent pandering to the "moronic underworld," the extreme centralization of government, and the growing gap between rich and poor. England, in contrast, had prospered because of its willingness to compromise and its sense of decency, moderation, justice, and tolerance—qualities that had once flourished in the Roman Republic but later died out. Americans, he suggested, stood to learn as much from the Roman experience as from the British. "We have made progress in limiting the accumulation of menacingly great fortunes and using taxation to give the under-privileged a share of the gains of civilization." But it remained to be seen "how far this leveling process" could go "without stopping progress and lowering the standard of living."[62]

Whether FDR was an emperor in the making or a lower-case republican in disguise was an open question in Haskell's mind. A more urgent issue, one that came to haunt him during the dispiriting months when things seemed to be falling apart both at home and abroad, was whether the United States stood any chance of succeeding where Rome had failed. The parallels were too glaring to be ignored. Rome, too, had had its "New Deals," from "the back-to-the-land movement of Tiberius Gracchus, and the PWA and ever-normal granary of his brother Gaius in the second century before Christ, down to the price-fixing, wage-regulating NRA of Diocletian 400 years later." These initiatives represented attempts to solve the same sorts of social and economic problems that confronted governments in the twentieth century, Haskell told the *Star*'s readers at the end of October. But all were doomed to fail because the Roman emperors neglected to provide a "decent standard of living for the masses" and to develop an "enlightened, intelligent and aggressive business leadership." It was a familiar story:

> The centralization of power in a paternalistic government sapped the feeling of social responsibility and blunted initiative. The pauperization of large numbers of people through indiscriminate relief was destructive. Rome educated its citizens to believe they could get something for nothing. A continuously unbalanced budget called for mounting taxes that strangled business and produced an inflation ruinous to property owners, both large and small. Finally under the government's last desperate attempt to save a disintegrating economic system through universal control and regimentation the whole social structure of the empire collapsed.[63]

Syndicated nationally, Haskell's essay "The New Deal in Old Rome" elicited praise from politicians, financiers, scholars, and public figures across the ideological spectrum. One friend, an enthusiastic New Dealer, couldn't resist gently parodying his exercise in comparative economic history: "You will recall they were able to prevent the institution of slavery ever entering the Roman Empire and that it continued a democracy clear up to the Barbarian invasion. It was just like today in America. It is terrible to think too that in Great Britain the inflation of the pound by its devaluation and its housing program leaves only half a millennium ahead for the British Empire. I was afraid that the centralized paternalism of Mussolini and Hitler might destroy it sooner."[64] Although his interpretation of Roman history as a "struggle between the Haves and the Have-nots" was hardly new, Haskell had sounded a theme that resonated from Wall Street to the corridors of power in Washington. With its emphasis on fiscal restraint, self-reliance, and individual liberty, it was a deeply and unmistakably conservative theme. At the same time, Haskell's thesis reflected the values of social equity and civic morality that had been central to

progressive philosophy from Teddy Roosevelt to Franklin. Whether that philosophy remained relevant in the age of mass unemployment and totalitarian
regimes was a question to which Haskell soon turned his mind as, encouraged
by publisher Alfred A. Knopf, he began expanding his article into a book.

One day in February 1938 Westbrook Pegler was sitting in Bryce Smith's
office, chatting with the mayor, City Manager Henry McElroy, and Police
Chief Otto Higgins. The well-known columnist had just toured the city's
hopping red-light district and was amused to hear McElroy enunciate the official policy of leaving the "boys and girls" alone, so long as they behaved themselves. McElroy freely admitted that Kansas City was a machine town and intimated that any time voters wanted a change, they were free to vote it out of
office. He further explained that the machine took no graft from gambling
houses and brothels, at which statement, according to Pegler, "Mr. Higgins
coughed politely, blinked behind his glasses and looked at the ceiling."[65]

McElroy's business practices were squarely in the spotlight in the city election a month later. The *Star* gave his administration credit for achieving "good
results in spite of the constant demands of political interests." The major issue was whether Kansas City was "paying too much for too little." The *Star*
clearly thought it was but voters just as clearly disagreed, awarding eight of
the nine council seats to Pendergast candidates who promptly named the
prickly city manager to a fourth term. When Farley phoned to congratulate
Pendergast, the boss responded coolly "that the argument had been used that
the President and the Attorney General were against him, and in view of the
fact that the argument was unanswered, he was satisfied with the results received." Governor Stark's terse announcement that he was "always pleased
when the Democrats win" likewise impressed Pendergast as rank ingratitude.
"I have never done a thing in my life except support Democratic officehold-
ers to the best of my ability," he fumed. "I have not received that kind of consideration from Governor Stark."[66]

Tension between the party and the machine had recently bubbled to the
surface, when FDR reappointed District Attorney Milligan over Truman's angry protest. Milligan's fraud squad had been joined by Treasury Department
investigators on the trail of a big insurance scandal that seemed likely to lead
to Pendergast's door. But the boss was fighting back, pulling strings in Washington to instigate an FBI investigation of Milligan and the two Republican
judges involved in the vote-fraud trials. At the same time, Pendergast was
smarting from the defection of his two most prominent allies in the business

Tom Pendergast (right) and his protégé, Senator Harry S. Truman, at the 1936 Democratic national convention. The *St. Louis Post-Dispatch* warned that the Democratic boss had "enslaved Kansas City," but by early 1938 his friends were deserting him.

community. J. C. Nichols and W. T. Kemper had soured on the machine as a result of a building trades strike in the summer of 1937, when McElroy had failed to take what they viewed as appropriate action to put down "flying squads" of union organizers. The city manager, never one to take things lying down, responded by threatening to construct a viaduct bypassing Nichols's Country Club Plaza.

As brickbats flew back and forth, the Chamber of Commerce stepped forward to assist the machine in its hour of need. Why Con Mann's outfit chose

1938 to celebrate the legacy of the seven-year-old Ten-Year Plan was never explained, but the Chamber's glossy commemorative book—the text written with "fact-checking assistance" from the *Star*—had all the earmarks of a whitewash job on McElroy, Mann, and Matt Murray.[67] (In keeping with settled Chamber policy, Pendergast himself was nowhere mentioned.) Yet even as the boss in October bowed his head to accept the Italian government's Order of the Crown, Mussolini's valentine from one *duce* to another, the noose around the machine's neck was drawing tight. By year's end, juries had convicted 259 machine workers named in thirty-nine separate indictments for conspiracy to interfere with the right of citizens to vote.

Pendergast was beginning to wonder where all his friends had gone. In March 1939 he dispatched Higgins to Washington, where the police chief cooled his heels for a week and Roosevelt, tipped off by Stark, refused to see him. Thereupon Truman and Jim Pendergast, the boss's nephew and heir apparent, appealed to Farley, with equally unsatisfactory results. On April 4 J. Edgar Hoover and Attorney General Frank Murphy flew to Kansas City and announced that government investigators now had all the evidence they needed. Three days later, on Good Friday, Pendergast was summoned to the U.S. marshal's office and indicted for income tax fraud. A *Star* reporter overheard him mutter to one of his lawyers that "they persecuted Christ on Good Friday, and nailed him to the Cross."[68] No doubt Pendergast's Christlike qualities were more apparent in 1939 than in years past, for he had always been less inclined to turn the other cheek than to deal opponents a firm right to the jaw.

At a press conference on April 11, Roosevelt denied taking an "active interest" in the Kansas City investigation. In fact, the president had finally decided Pendergast was a liability, a conclusion he reached somewhat earlier than Farley, who was contemplating a run for the presidency in 1940 and still counted on the machine's support. Two days later, amid allegations of graft, McElroy tendered his resignation to Mayor Smith with as much dignity as he could muster under the circumstances. "Things seem to be breaking up pretty fast," Higgins remarked to a conclave of his top officers shortly before he too turned in his badge.[69] Subsequently, the Bureau of Internal Revenue determined that McElroy owed $62,000 in taxes on unreported income of $274,000. But that sum was dwarfed by the millions of dollars the resourceful country bookkeeper had diverted from the city treasury over the years, much of which—including $6 million deposited in something called the City Manager's Emergency Fund—would never be adequately accounted for.

McElroy's ignominious departure and other disquieting portents—even the Chamber of Commerce had belatedly joined the clean-up brigade—took the wind out of Boss Tom's sails. On May 22 he threw himself on the mercy of the court with such a convincing show of contrition that Judge Merrill Otis was moved to observe from the bench, "I can understand the feeling that has been expressed for him here by his friends. I believe that if I had known him, I too might have been one of his friends." (Otis seems to have had a similar effect on Johnny Lazia, who, in the midst of his own tribulations, was heard to exclaim, "That sonofabitch almost makes me respect the law.") Pendergast was sentenced to fifteen months in prison followed by five years' probation and ordered to pay a $10,000 fine plus $350,000 in back taxes, a penalty that Haskell and other critics dismissed as a slap on the wrist. "Most people, I think, were rather jolted by the mildness of Judge Otis's sentence yesterday," the editor wrote Governor Stark. "I believe it was a serious mistake. At the same time I think the final reaction will be to stir people to greater efforts in the cleanup." Pendergast continued to read the *Star* every day in Leavenworth Penitentiary, where he was joined by O'Malley, Higgins, Murray, and numerous lesser apparatchiks of the machine. Others would serve time in the county jail, among them E. Mont Reily, who was convicted of obtaining money under false pretenses from the city's public works department. When a policeman served him with a subpoena, the former governor of Puerto Rico and confidant of presidents drew himself up and protested, "Would a man of my intelligence do these things?"[70]

Evidently, many intelligent men and women *had* gone along with the machine, at least as long as the going was good. For whatever reason—convenience, venality, ignorance, poor judgment, wishful thinking—many citizens had come to think of Tom's Town, almost with pride, as a city both beautiful and efficient. Haskell contritely admitted to a friend that he had been "very mistaken in both Pendergast and McElroy. I thought P. was satisfied with selling his stuff to the city and didn't suppose he went out as a gangster and strong-armed people. As for McElroy I thought he was a competent business man who made necessary concessions to the machine. None of us knew that he had turned it over to the machine to loot." Plenty of people had known, of course, but Haskell and others had chosen not to listen to them. Nevertheless, Haskell took pleasure in regaling his fellow editors at a convention in Washington that spring with stories of the *Star*'s valiant fight to bring the machine down. H. L. Mencken, for one, wasn't buying it. "I was tempted to ask him why, if Pendergast was really so corrupt, the *Star* had not exposed and wrecked him long ago," the Sage of Baltimore inscribed in his diary. "As a matter of fact, the *Star* is a very timorous paper, and I doubt that it had anything to do with Pendergast's final scotching. The war was carried on by other and more courageous heroes."[71]

Even observers less incorrigibly skeptical than Mencken conceded that the paper had been hamstrung in its fight by the managers' commitment to even-handedness—a virtue to which Nelson had never subscribed—and consequent reluctance to rock the boat. White argued that the *Star* could only go so far until the community as a whole rose up against the machine. "Pendergast controlled the courts absolutely," he told Villard in 1942, "and the Pendergast crowd encouraged people to file libel suits against the *Star* which were withheld from trial as a gun in the ribs. But if the *Star* had ever gone all out hell bent against Pendergast on its own, it would have been wiped out with judgments."[72] There may have been some truth in this: Henry Doherty's lawsuits, now totaling some $400 million, were dismissed immediately after Pendergast's conviction. But it's not at all apparent that Pendergast controlled the courts, absolutely or otherwise, and in any case the *Star* had little to fear financially from adverse judgments. The paper remained almost phenomenally profitable throughout the depression, enabling the employee owners to pay off their bank loan in February 1939, four years ahead of schedule.

Neither White nor Haskell nor anyone else close to the *Star* seems to have acknowledged one salient factor that long immunized Pendergast from criticism: his hard-earned reputation as a "city builder" in the mold of Nelson and Nichols. Some even likened him to that other civic icon, William Volker, as a philanthropist and public servant. In a city that had a soft spot for Jesse James and prided itself on being a wide-open land of opportunity, Pendergast was not an altogether unlikely candidate for folk hero. When Darrell Garwood was collecting material for a book on Kansas City in the late 1940s, Milligan, who claimed credit for "smashing" the machine all by himself, advised him that "there's no use talking to these people around here. They're all Old Tom's friends."[73]

Even in disgrace, Pendergast retained an impressive circle of friends, of whom Senator Truman was the most famously loyal. After the boss's fall, the *Star,* practicing the fine art of guilt by association, published an old photo of Harry standing beside Tom's portrait above the mantel in his Washington office. The "senator from Pendergast," his critics called him. *Star* executives had choicer names for that other notable Pendergast apologist, Frank Walsh. When the labor attorney dropped dead of a heart attack on a New York sidewalk, three weeks before Pendergast pled guilty in Judge Otis's courtroom, the newspaper's obituary made no mention of his intimate relationship with Nelson. It chose instead to reprint a photograph of Walsh conferring with Johnny Lazia at the latter's trial in 1934. Truman and Walsh, it seemed, were to be judged by the company they kept. The *Star* was not.

On May 15, 1939, Knopf brought out Haskell's *New Deal in Old Rome* and within weeks the book appeared (briefly) on bestseller lists in Washington, Chicago, and Kansas City. The publisher's ads featured a blurb by the distinguished historian Charles A. Beard, praising the book as "a mighty jar and a sheer delight for people who enjoy trying to use their brains." Despite the author's protest that the book was "neither a criticism nor a defense of the New Deal," it was inevitably received in some quarters as a sophisticated dig at the Democratic administration. Typical was Mencken's review in the *Baltimore Sun*, whose title, "The Downhill Road," said it all. The *Wall Street Journal* was equally unsubtle. Noting that Haskell's "deceitfully unpretentious style of presentation" masked impressive scholarship, Thomas F. Woodcock judged the book "stimulating, suggestive and well worth reading, but the parlor pinks won't like it."[74]

White, reviewing the volume for the *Star* at Roberts's invitation, warned New Dealers that they "should not be misled by the title . . . into thinking that here is a polemic intended to discredit their cherished experiments. But they may go to this book and learn that certain fundamentals in human nature work about the same in the machine age and in the stone and iron and copper ages of man's progress." Whether or not he meant "machine age" as a double entendre, White's implicit linkage of the New Deal with boss politics was echoed in a passage from the book that several other reviewers singled out for quotation. The problem that governments both ancient and modern had failed to solve, Haskell wrote, was that of "building a unified yet free society, with decent minimum standards of living. A society so intelligently and justly organized that there is no menacing, submerged class. A society that provides reasonable incentives for the free rise of a general staff of competent managers whose ranks are always open to new recruits. A society that develops a social pressure under which leaders accept an enlightened and far-sighted view of their responsibilities."[75] It was the credo of an unrepentant progressive.

At the end of June Haskell sailed for Europe, accompanied by his wife, to fill himself in on the security situation and gather material for a biography of Cicero that Knopf had invited him to write. He hoped, he told the publisher, to "round" the Roman orator "into a human being—a real pillar of society, as he felt he was, and the greatest wishful thinker before the Baldwin-Chamberlain governments." In an interview in New York with *Editor and*

Publisher before embarking, Haskell joked that he hoped the fighting would hold off until he got back, because he had no desire to become a war correspondent. In the event, he deemed it unsafe to stay abroad longer than three weeks and confined his visit to London and Paris, where he found the French "realistically apprehensive" about the efficacy of the Maginot line. In an interview with the *Petit Parisien,* he cautioned Hitler not to interpret Roosevelt's dispute with Congress over neutrality as a sign of American indifference to the fate of the European democracies. The United States didn't want to fight another war, he said, but resistance to lifting the arms embargo would vanish overnight if France or England were directly threatened.[76]

"It looks as if the world is in for it," he wrote to Billikopf after his return. "The only faint cheer I see in this immense tragedy is that it may result in destroying the lunatic and the regime that caused it. But I am under no illusions about the suffering and destruction that may be involved."[77] Haskell's letter was dated September 1, 1939. News of the Nazi invasion of Poland dominated the paper two weeks later when Henry McElroy died quietly at his home, a day after the once mighty city manager had been subpoenaed by a grand jury. Later that month, Pendergast's two attorneys, a Democrat and a Republican, approached Farley in Washington about arranging a parole. The postmaster general put them off.

Tom's friends would remain active on his behalf even after his early release from prison the following May. In 1943 a delegation of leading citizens—including Nichols, minister Burris Jenkins, and banker James M. Kemper—unsuccessfully petitioned the attorney general to relax the terms of his probation and allow him to return to politics. Some would claim they acted only after Pendergast threatened to expose their complicity with the machine. But others, Milligan among them, credited the boss with pleading guilty to spare his friends the embarrassing revelations that would have come out in open-court testimony.[78]

When death finally came calling for Pendergast in January 1945, Vice President Harry Truman flew out to Kansas City for the funeral and was spotted hobnobbing with the late boss's nephew. The hydra had risen again.

CHAPTER 9

◆

Voice of Middle America

Back home in Kansas City, safe and sound, Mrs. Bridge counted her blessings. She and her husband, a successful attorney, had been vacationing in Rome when the Nazis invaded Poland in September 1939. Fortunately, Mr. Bridge had had the presence of mind to book a return passage immediately. Over lunch at a comfortable residence in her Country Club neighborhood, Mrs. Bridge tried to sort out her somewhat disjointed impressions of the Italians and French. "The poverty of the Europeans must be simply appalling," one of her friends remarked. "They say there's no middle class at all, just the rich and the poor. I suppose they're all dying to emigrate to this country." Yes, Mrs. Bridge agreed, politely asking her neighbor to pass the cream. And after all, who could blame them for wanting to live in America?[1]

To the feckless heroine of Evan S. Connell's classic novel about upper-class life in Kansas City, the outside world was a menacing and incomprehensible place. The news of blitzkriegs, civil wars, and social unrest that she read in the *Star* hardly encouraged her to broaden her horizons. Insular by nature, the Mrs. Bridges of Middle America had grown accustomed to sweeping unpleasantness, whether foreign or domestic, safely under the carpet. The typical midwesterner, Henry Haskell told an interviewer on the eve of his de-

> *"With God's help, we will lift Shanghai up and up, ever up, until it is just like Kansas City!"*
>
> —U.S. Senator Kenneth Wherry

parture for Europe that July, took an interest in foreign affairs only when her own economic welfare was demonstrably affected. The *Star*'s old-fashioned typography and layout catered to the region's conservative populace. "We feel that most of our readers would object to any change to modern typographical dress as a man would object to his wife having her face lifted. We have discussed typographical changes in the office and with carriers but the verdict has always been heavily against it because the readers have been brought up on the *Star*'s conservatism and they don't regard the *Star* any more old fashioned than the weather."[2]

With the apparent victory of Kansas City's boss-busters in 1939, moral uplifters and "sin hounds" seized the banner of reform, determined to root out the last traces of Pendergastism. The new Kansas City, purified and prettified, was no wicked, wide-open town but a haven of wholesome middle-class values. A vigilant legislator even called for Pendergast to be expunged from Thomas Hart Benton's statehouse mural in Jefferson City. In the end, however, the deposed boss's likeness was left in place, just as the statue of his brother, Jim, stood surveying the West Bottoms—figurative memorials to the late, unlamented machine. Toward Benton himself Kansas Citians showed less forgiveness. The controversial artist would soon be ejected from the Art Institute faculty after spouting off to reporters in New York that "the typical museum is a graveyard run by a pretty boy with delicate curving wrists and a swing in his gait."[3] By the time the musical *Oklahoma!* reached Broadway in 1943, the city's storied red-light district, whose burlesque houses and jazz clubs had long been a badge of the "up-to-date" metropolis, was on its last legs.

In the spring of 1940 the good-government forces stormed the bastion of Henry McElroy's sleekly modernist City Hall, their ranks swollen by hordes of newly converted businessmen and a brigade of affluent south-side women brandishing symbolic clean-up brooms. "Let the wires carry to the nation the message that Kansas City has been redeemed!" proclaimed Mayor John Gage. As City Manager L. P. Cookingham attempted to straighten out the city's tangled finances, Police Chief Lear B. Reed, an ex-FBI agent brought in to repair the damage done by Pendergast's cronies, threw the book at gangsters, radicals, and other undesirables. Reed's highhanded zeal made him widely unpopular and he stepped down in the summer of 1941, shortly after the *Star* found it necessary to rebuke him for harassing a visiting Communist who had been invited to address a local women's club. "It was wholly wrong and we said so editorially," Haskell told William Allen White, adding that he had taken the matter up privately with the president of the police board, a lawyer who understood "the importance of preserving civil liberties."[4]

Discreet intervention, Haskell had found, often produced better results than noisy crusading. No longer hampered by outdated notions of independence, *Star* editors and reporters were increasingly open about their ties to the establishment. Nelson's ideal editor, one who had "absolutely no financial or social interest in his community," was a dusty relic. Under staff ownership, the *Star* redoubled its efforts to identify itself with the city. Senior managers set an example by serving as officers of the Art Institute, Philharmonic, Liberty Memorial Association, and other cultural groups. Even the *Star*'s music critic sat on the orchestra's board of trustees. "We try not to let personal opinions interfere with editorial policy," explained Haskell, "but we do keep in touch with movements going on in our city by having our executives mingle with those in public affairs." By the late 1930s, editor Haskell, president George Longan, and managing editor Roy Roberts all lived in spacious Country Club mansions, the better to mingle with their fellow movers and shakers. *Life* magazine, in a 1939 feature spread on the Nelson Gallery, pictured the paper's three top news executives as preeminent representatives of the power elite.[5]

The alliance between the *Star* and Main Street, which had taken a beating during the Pendergast years, rebounded swiftly after the boss's downfall. As the United States belatedly shored up its defenses, hoping to escape being drawn into another European conflict, Roberts and developer J. C. Nichols spearheaded a campaign to ensure that the area got its share of the spoils. Recently Nichols had been instrumental in founding the Urban Land Institute to propagate his ideas about sustaining neighborhoods and land values. In 1939 the nation's leading real estate journal devoted an entire issue to the Kansas Citian, hailing him as "America's foremost subdivider and realtor-builder."[6] In the era of Roosevelt's common man, the Nichols Company concentrated on building starter homes for upwardly mobile members of the middle class. As a trustee of the Nelson estate, Nichols oversaw the maintenance of the Rockhill residential district, still attractive if slightly déclassé, and pushed for the installation of a gigantic reflecting pool south of the Art Gallery. The time for such grandiose Beaux Arts schemes had passed, however, and the Nichols Company would seek other means of buffering the Country Club Plaza from unwelcome encroachments.

Meanwhile, Nichols had begun commuting to Washington, where he held down a dollar-a-year job with the Advisory Council for National Defense. The Roosevelt administration, he soon discovered, had no plans to site defense plants between the Mississippi River and the Rocky Mountains. Here was an opportunity for Nichols to serve both his country and his own interests. Working closely with Roberts and other community leaders, he started knocking on doors in the capital, pitching his vision of a greater Kansas City: workers in defense-related factories in the area would buy medium-priced homes in his new Armour Hills Gardens, Fairway, and Prairie Village subdivisions, the better to strengthen Fortress America. Industrialization of the nation's heartland, he argued, would not only bolster the country's defenses but also help preserve the "resident farm ownership" that all patriotic citizens recognized as "essential to safe Americanism." In a speech that was part Madison Avenue spiel and part civics lesson, Nichols declared that "the daily, happy employment of increasing thousands in our industry will be our trusty safeguard against communism and nazism, as well as the blessed assurance of the continuance of our American institutions."[7]

Among the institutions in need of patriotic patronage were the real estate and newspaper industries, both of which were still coping with the aftereffects of the depression. Although the *Star* had squeaked through the thirties without laying off any employees, by early 1940 unemployed blue-collar workers in other industries were fleeing Missouri and Kansas in droves. The announcements later that year that the government would build a major munitions plant in rural Jackson County and a mammoth bomber factory in the Fairfax district stemmed the exodus. Over the next three years, factories turning out everything from parachutes and bunk frames to naval landing craft and gun stocks attracted some forty thousand workers to the area, creating a pent-up demand for housing that would prove a gold mine for Nichols and his fellow developers after the war. Meanwhile, notwithstanding the wartime shortage of newsprint, a deluge of want ads and space advertising sent the *Star*'s revenues soaring, making 1943 the second most profitable year in the paper's history.

Unlike Nichols, a lifelong Democrat, Roberts had no special "in" with the Roosevelt administration. But he was a past master at pulling strings in Washington. His appeal to Steve Early in July 1940 that "the government should do everything possible in allocating long-time defense orders to plants and industries in these [midwestern] states—to keep the boys at home" achieved gratifying results. Roosevelt instructed his press secretary to sound out members of his cabinet and other administration officials. If they were in favor of Roberts's proposition, he wouldn't stand in the way. FDR further suggested that Early "might intimate to Roy" that if the *Star* stayed neutral in the upcoming presidential campaign, "we will put some new plants right next to his own house in Kansas City."[8]

Where Roosevelt was concerned, the *Star* was anything but neutral in the summer of 1940. Haskell's enthusiasm for the New Deal had long since soured. As for Roberts, although his days as a front-office campaign manager were behind him, he was closely linked with Wendell Willkie in the public eye as a senior "adviser" to the Republican challenger. "Willkie at heart is a genuine liberal," the newsman opined, "more so even than President Roosevelt."[9] Willkie did indeed stand well to the left of his erstwhile rivals for the nomination, Senator Charles Taft of Ohio and Thomas Dewey, New York's hard-hitting district attorney. A registered Democrat only months before, Willkie supported much of the New Deal social legislation and refused to truckle to the GOP's isolationist wing. Where he parted company with Roosevelt was in his belief that the private sector was better equipped than government agencies to put the country back on the track to prosperity and social justice.

Roosevelt's publicity-savvy attorney general had warmly acknowledged the *Star*'s help in the Pendergast probe, writing to Haskell in January that "it has long been my conviction that there can be no finer contribution to the work of public servants who regard office as a public trust than the support of an honest, courageous press." If Frank Murphy hoped thereby to curry favor for the administration, the president himself had drawn the inescapable conclusion that the *Star* was unalterably in the Willkie camp. Even former brain trusters like Ray Moley were gravitating toward the personable and articulate utilities executive. Willkie "would make a great campaigner and a great President," Moley wrote Haskell early in May, as the editor was drafting a position paper on the party's economic platform for the Republican National Committee. When Willkie, still trailing behind Dewey and Taft, made a campaign swing through the *Star*'s territory later that month, Roscoe Drummond of the *Christian Science Monitor* noted that the *Star* was particularly "generous in its attention to the Willkie movement." Willkie's refrain that the New Deal had merely substituted big government for big business, he wrote, was music to midwesterners' ears.[10]

Haskell looked on with satisfaction as economic internationalism and civil liberties emerged as major themes of the Willkie campaign. He remained ambivalent about Dewey, who had drawn criticism for his aggressive use of wiretaps and lavish payouts for evidence in building his case against New York racketeers. The *Star*'s Washington correspondent had gotten the low-down on Dewey from none other than J. Edgar Hoover, who predicted the Democrats wouldn't hesitate to raise the wiretap issue to embarrass the prosecutor in a presidential race.[11] Haskell forwarded this confidential intelligence to Alf Landon, but the GOP's titular head was more worked up over what he saw as Roosevelt's assault on civil liberties. Although Haskell and Roberts shared his concerns, they protested when Landon equated the New Dealers with Hitler's Brown Shirts. The editor was equally disappointed in the work of the Republican platform subcommittee on foreign affairs, which Landon chaired, feeling that too many compromises had been made with the isolationists.

As the summer convention season drew nigh, Haskell had little hope that any Republican, however progressive, could overcome Roosevelt's formidable popularity. Although he predicted Willkie would stand up "under the stress of the campaign" better than any other candidate, he doubted he was electable. Roberts took a more upbeat view, writing after the Republican convention in Philadelphia that "the Willkie thing sprouted and grew like Kansas corn after a 2-inch rain in July." White had declared himself for Willkie at the eleventh hour, admonishing party elders not to adopt a knee-jerk anti-Roosevelt stance or indeed to take any firm position at all on the crucial question of aid for England. In light of the unstable situation in Europe, he advised Henry Stimson, it would be rash to hobble the candidate by making "any specific pledge, promise, or declaration" that would "rise to damn us" later. Although White protested that he was "not pleading for any let up on the strafing of Roosevelt in the national platform," his intimacy with the Democratic incumbent was no secret.[12] Whatever they said in public, neither White nor Haskell was unduly distressed by the prospect of a third Roosevelt administration at a time when continuity of leadership was of overriding concern.

White's record as a political chameleon—his readiness to change his stripes according to circumstance, often subordinating abstract principles to personal feelings—stood in sharp contrast to Haskell's principled consistency. When Roosevelt startled the country on the eve of the Republican convention by inviting Stimson and Frank Knox to join his administration in a national unity cabinet, the *Star* attacked it as a political ploy intended to forestall "criticism by the Republican members of the cabinet without imposing the slightest obligation on the President to give attention to their advice." Haskell's harsh reaction wasn't motivated by partisanship—he was as relieved as anyone to see former Kansas governor Harry Woodring, an avowed noninterventionist, replaced as secretary of war by a man of Stimson's temperament and experience. Rather, he objected to the arrangement as a "one-way coalition" that would stifle the free "give and take among divergent policies."[13] National Committee Chairman John Hamilton's threat to drum Knox and Stimson out of the Republican Party struck him as sheer partisan posturing.

White, true to form, was slower to impugn the president's motives. Roosevelt felt confident enough of the Emporia editor's sympathy to commission him to serve as go-between with Willkie that summer in a bid to take the issue of American logistical support for Britain off the table during the campaign. White conferred with Willkie in early August at Colorado Springs, where the candidate was preparing his formal acceptance speech, and succeeded in gaining his tacit endorsement of the administration's controversial destroyers-for-bases deal. A week later, it was announced that Willkie would make the Democrats' unseemly dalliance with political bosses the centerpiece of his fall campaign, with Dewey barnstorming the Midwest to drive the lesson home. Inasmuch as the announcement followed close on the heels of Haskell's own visit with Willkie in Colorado, it seems likely that he too had a hand in shaping the Republican strategy.

Willkie kicked off the campaign on September 16 with a series of speeches in the *Star*'s backyard, beginning in Coffeeville, Kansas, where he had taught high school as a young man. Characterizing the New Deal as government by an arrogant East Coast "intelligentsia" who scoffed at the "simple virtues which you and I learned here in the Mid-West," he chided Roosevelt for failing to address the root causes of the depression by stimulating business recovery. It was alarming to think that at a time of crisis in Europe, Americans had vouchsafed their security to a man who had sabotaged American industry and "in seven years of peace could not get factories producing even the peacetime needs." Speaking later that day in Butler and Nevada, Missouri, the candidate called on Show Me Staters to clean house and "get rid of the last remnants of the Pendergast machine." (His listeners didn't need to be reminded that Boss Tom was again at large, having been paroled from prison in May on condition that he abstain from politics.) In seeking an unprecedented third term, Willkie suggested, FDR was following in the dictatorial footsteps of Hitler, Mussolini, and Stalin.[14]

For a while, the Republicans' cautious strategy of feint and attack appeared to be working. In September polls showed the two candidates running neck and neck. But as Willkie trimmed his sails to placate Republican conservatives, sounding more and more like an old-school isolationist, and abandoned his moderate rhetoric for increasingly partisan attacks on FDR, the incumbent steadily pulled ahead. During the final weeks of the campaign, Willkie called Roberts in to help him analyze Roosevelt's campaign speeches and radio "fireside chats," desperately searching for weak spots in his opponent's armor. But it was no use. Eight years in office had made FDR almost as invincible as Pendergast in his heyday. When the final vote was tallied, Willkie carried Kansas and seven other midwestern states, but lost Missouri. "We are truly disappointed," Haskell's wife recorded in her diary.[15]

While the *Star* was otherwise engaged, Senator Harry Truman coasted to reelection after a hard-fought primary, small thanks either to his next-door newspaper or to his party's president.

   The *Star* continued to support the administration's efforts to make America the arsenal of democracy while attacking its spendthrift domestic programs. Haskell's persistent emphasis on war preparedness echoed the unpopular editorial stand the paper had taken during the last war. If his articles and speeches lacked the white-hot passion with which Teddy Roosevelt had fulminated from his bully pulpit at the *Star*, they were equally free of the Bull Moose's myopic vindictiveness. Reporting from Washington in February 1941, Haskell devoted a week-long series of articles to the thesis that a robust defense was America's best hope of keeping out of war. The traditional concept of neutrality was obsolete, he argued. If the Nazis had built a military machine capable of invading the British Isles, Americans could no longer rest easy in their beds. A negotiated peace was a vain hope, for Hitler couldn't be bargained with. By lending material aid to the British, the Roosevelt administration was effectively buying time for the United States to upgrade its own defensive capability. The country was inevitably being sucked into the conflict on Britain's side, Haskell advised; the only question was how far it was prepared to go.

   Haskell's mantra that the *Star* couldn't get too far ahead of its readers without losing its influence over them—a policy whose limitations had been exposed in the on-again, off-again fight against Pendergast—was resoundingly vindicated in the protracted struggle against isolationism. Since the early 1930s the editor had been harping on the theme that the country's vital interests were directly affected by events overseas. While it's impossible to quantify the impact of the sustained campaign waged by journalists like Haskell and White, the daily and weekly editions of the *Star*, with a combined circulation of nearly three-quarters of a million, were beyond question a significant factor in overcoming the smug complacency of Mrs. Bridge and her ilk. It was not the internationalist press but Republican isolationists like Senators Vandenberg and Taft who were out of touch with their midwestern constituents, Roberts believed. "We have tried our damnedest to support the President's [foreign] policy, even though we have much distrust of him, and certainly do not accept all of the new deal," he wrote White in early 1941.[16] Willkie likewise insisted that Republicans couldn't afford to stand on the sidelines lobbing potshots at Roosevelt. During the war, he would undertake several special missions for the Democratic president, most notably a two-month tour of allied capitals that served as the basis for his bestselling book *One World*.

Like Willkie, White was caught on the horns of the bipartisan dilemma as the nation sidled toward war. Convinced that the president needed full authority to assist Britain, he led the effort to overhaul the country's anachronistic neutrality laws as head of the influential Committee to Defend America by Aiding the Allies. Upon taking office in May 1940, White soon found himself pinned down in the crossfire between antiwar activists—both isolationists and pacifists—and interventionists for whom the country couldn't jettison its neutrality fast enough. It was a no-win position, and White made matters worse by warning, in response to criticism from newspaper publisher Roy Howard, that the pro-British eastern establishment was moving too fast for public opinion in the Midwest. When the executive committee insisted that he make it clear he was speaking only for himself, White stepped down, convinced, he told Haskell, that many of his colleagues "were hellbent for war." In an uncharacteristically labored, handwritten announcement, drafted for the *Star* but never used, White attributed his resignation to the pressure of overwork.[17] It seems likelier that the prospect of Americans dying in another foreign war was more than he could stomach.

With London still smoldering from the German blitz, Haskell had reached a different conclusion. "It was disconcerting that the British weren't able to defend London from the air," he wrote to White in April 1941. "Looks very much as if we would have to get in. I wish I could figure how Hitler can be beaten even with our help. Don't see how we can get a large expeditionary force to England and keep the enormous amount of supplies necessary going forward; and even if we got there don't see any chance to land a force on the Continent with Hitler able to strike rapidly in any direction. The idea that German morale will break under bombing after all these enormous successes seems to me wishful thinking." All the same, the *Star* continued to wave the Union Jack and rolled out the red carpet for Lord Halifax when he visited Kansas City that May. Roberts spent two and a half days squiring the British ambassador around. "It was highly important that that side of the story be told out here," he wrote Willkie. "If there ever was a time when we needed national unity and a cessation as far as possible of domestic fights it is now."[18]

In that spirit, Haskell demurred when Alf Landon sent him a draft speech referring to Roosevelt and "his fellow conspirators." "It won't sit well with a lot of people. It doesn't sit at all well with me. And I am no fanatic for the President, as you know!" the editor shot back. While critics charged war production had been stymied by FDR's refusal to delegate authority, Haskell was inclined to give him the benefit of the doubt. "From information that comes about our deficiencies in equipment—partly due perhaps to what we are sending overseas—I suspect the President is stalling about getting us involved directly in order to give us more time," he wrote to White in July. The Kansan agreed that spurring Americans to think globally was an uphill struggle. "When I think of how hard it is to convince a Flint Hills cattleman that we have some national obligations to buy at least some beef from Argentina in order to hold the commercial magnetic needle to us as the North star of their trade, I just want to throw the ashes over my head like Job and curse God and die. But I suppose when a good rain washes off the ashes, I am still just a starry-eyed damn fool waiting wistfully for the rainbow."[19]

For Haskell, as for many supporters of Roosevelt's preparedness policies, Pearl Harbor came as a blessing in disguise. "The Japanese didn't know what a service they were doing in uniting the country," he wrote to White on December 8, 1941. In Haskell's opinion, the United States had been drawn into the war just in time. His military sources feared that the British had lost their nerve and were determined "to fight the present War on the pattern of Waterloo with the battles won on the cricket fields of Eton and Harrow." As the conflict in the eastern theater intensified, Haskell heaped sarcasm on the same United Kingdom that he had lately extolled as the bulwark of democracy. In Moscow, he observed to White in early 1942, "the whole civilian population went out to build fortifications against the Nazis" and succeeded in repelling the invaders. At Singapore, by contrast, "the civilians had tea every afternoon and the council didn't even consider building airraid shelters until last Saturday." Sometimes it seemed the British army was being led by Colonel Blimp. "I don't like to think of the reaction when the American people generally realize that the British aren't willing to fight. There is already a strong feeling that England expects every American to do his duty."[20]

Although the difficulties of wartime travel conspired with heart and eye problems to keep Haskell close to home, his intellectual horizons continued to expand. Early in the summer of 1942 he put the finishing touches on a political biography of Cicero, which Knopf published that fall to wide acclaim. *This Was Cicero* depicted the great Roman orator and philosopher as a flawed statesman who idealized the Roman Republic and was unable, or unwilling, to adapt to the harsh realities of the empire. In surveying the existing literature on Cicero, Haskell had come to the realization that none of his previous biographers had any experience of practical politics. "I was horrified to find them taking political speeches seriously," he commented to Mencken. Like many modern politicians, including more than a few of his fellow Republicans, Haskell's Cicero stubbornly adhered to "political institutions adapted to a simpler time but now outworn." In the final analysis, the ancient Roman's brilliant but unsuccessful political career served as a reminder of what can happen when "blind conservatism" resists change "in the hope of reconstructing the vanished past."[21]

The primary contemporary exemplar of unreconstructed conservatism was of course Herbert Hoover, and, not surprisingly, the former president's critics—men like Willkie and Landon—responded enthusiastically to Haskell's latest exercise in comparative history. "I find myself something in a position of Cicero and I find a great many old Bull Moosers in the same situation," Landon reflected in a long letter to the author. "We favored an extension of Democratic control. Later what we had come to regard as excess of this control has alarmed us." After reading *This Was Cicero*, Associate Justice Robert Jackson of the U.S. Supreme Court, Roosevelt's former attorney general, told Haskell that lawyers generally failed to make good statesmen because they were too bound by precedent, which was "a little like driving by one's own tail lights." Commentators on both ends of the political spectrum found food for thought in Haskell's biography, as they had in *The New Deal in Old Rome*. Mark Ethridge of the *Louisville Courier-Journal*, seeking to convince FDR that the press was behind him in prosecuting the war, called his attention to the fact that "the *Kansas City Star*, whose editor wrote a book to prove that New Deal relief was on a par with what the Grachii did in ancient Rome, is nevertheless withholding no conceivable lick to speed along the war."[22]

Roosevelt's advisers took the *Star* seriously, even if he himself did not. In the 1940s it was, by almost any measure, among the most powerful newspapers in the country. Through its hugely successful weekly farm edition, the *Star* had become the unofficial mouthpiece of the agricultural heartland, the voice of that wide swath of Middle America, stretching from the Mississippi to the Rocky Mountains, so trenchantly chronicled by novelists like Connell, Lewis, and Dreiser. The *Star*'s hegemony over this inland empire was unchallenged now that the *Kansas City Journal*, tattered remnant of the pugnacious *Journal-Post*, had bitten the dust. Inept management and wartime newsprint shortages had hastened its demise, but there was no question that the *Star* had fought tooth and nail to rid itself of its last real competitor. After the *Journal* published its final edition, on March 31, 1942, *Star* president George Longan admonished his staff not to gloat or slack off now that they had the field to themselves. A month later the paper hiked its subscription rates, confident that readers had nowhere else to turn. Haskell's pat explanation that the *Journal* "just ran out of funds and folded" was far from the full or unvarnished truth.[23]

Although as editor Haskell was nominally in overall charge of the *Star*'s news operation, he gave most of his attention to the editorial page. It was Roberts who ran the newsroom on a day-to-day basis, deliberately or otherwise blurring the lines of authority to such an extent that outsiders often identified him as the paper's editor, or even its publisher. With Longan's death in October 1942, the presidency passed to a man from the business side, Haskell and Roberts becoming next in the line of succession as, respectively, first and second vice president of the Star Company. While outwardly deferential, Roberts had no qualms about upstaging his senior colleague behind the scenes. On occasion he even contrived to convey the impression that he, not Haskell, was responsible for setting the *Star*'s editorial policy. Roberts's ego could be as insatiable as his appetite. When Hoover sent a copy of his latest book with a request that Roberts pass it along to Haskell, the managing editor acted for all the world as if he were top dog. "As soon as I am through with it," he replied, "I will pass it along to Haskell and have him do our editorial and review."[24]

Roberts's personal star rose rapidly during the war, which he seemed to enjoy nearly as much as political wrangling. In 1943 he was elected president of the American Society of Newspaper Editors, the plummiest job in the profession, and articulated a policy of toeing the government line. "Keeping the home front unbroken, as I see it, is the newspapers' first function in war," he told a gathering of journalists at the University of Missouri. In resisting calls that he step down from the advisory committee of the Office of War Information, the government's official censorship agency, the *Star*'s managing editor brusquely dismissed the suggestion that his two assignments posed a potential conflict of interest. "If," he said, "the time ever comes when giving all possible service to the war effort is incompatible with the presidency of the A.S.N.E., then the God-given right of every American to resign, tell why and raise hell remains."[25]

Later that same year Roberts took his seat on the AP's board of directors, a position previously held by Nelson and Kirkwood, and one that signaled his elevation into the ranks of the journalistic elite. Roberts took pleasure in stepping into Baron Bill's capacious shoes. The physical resemblance between the two tubby gourmands—at nearly three hundred pounds, both had plenty of weight to throw around—was impossible to overlook. With his ever-present cigar wedged between pudgy fingers, his voice booming through the newsroom, Roberts inspired both camaraderie and fear. But the contrast between him and the *Star*'s legendary cofounder was equally obvious. Universally known as just plain Roy, the managing editor played a mean game of poker, drank like a fish, and had no aversion to being photographed, preferably in the company of the rich and famous. If these attributes clashed with Nelson's regal, abstemious, publicity-shy image, they were even more incongruous when set alongside Haskell's old-world courtesy and unassuming, scholarly demeanor. W. W. Baker, a future *Star* editor, became aware of the two men's closeness as soon as he joined the staff in 1947. "I always thought they were an improbable pair," he recalled, "the lion lying down with the lamb."[26]

By the early forties Roberts and Haskell were virtually inseparable, socializing with their wives as often as two or three times a week. Trim, bespectacled, and impeccably tailored, Haskell projected a persona that was patrician, intellectual, detached, and apolitical. On top of his voluminous writing for the *Star,* he contributed elegantly crafted essays to publications like the *Saturday Review* and the *New York Herald Tribune.* Roberts, in keeping with the principle that opposites attract, was an old-fashioned news hound with keen political instincts. An indifferent writer, he had few intellectual pretensions and little gift for analysis. Like Nelson, he was a doer, not a thinker. Haskell recoiled from the smoke-filled rooms of political legend; Roberts thrived in them. Whether despite or because of these differences, the dapper editor and his roly-poly sidekick were bracketed together in the public eye. Often they seemed to play off each other, like a musical duo. When Vice President Henry Wallace encountered them at a reception in Washington early in 1943, Roberts warned him that "the people of the Midwest were going to continue to raise hell about gasoline rationing and farm labor shortage" and faulted the administration for being "awfully slow in waking up to the manpower problem." A short time later, *Look* magazine featured Haskell as one of five Pulitzer Prize–winning editors who faulted FDR for mismanaging the war effort. "Poor administration is what is wrong on the home front," he wrote, adding that "there is a widespread sense that things have been allowed to run at loose ends in Washington, that the President has been slow to pick first-string men and give them the necessary authority, and that there has been too much disposition to use the emergency to promote controversial New Deal policies."[27]

Over the years Roberts and Haskell had become adept at delivering the journalistic one-two-three punch they had picked up from Nelson and Pulitzer, coordinating news stories, features, and editorials to maximum effect. If Roberts was the *Star's* public face, Haskell was its private editorial conscience and arbiter of style. A collage presented by admiring colleagues pictured him in the guise of a Confucian sage, an honor previously bestowed on his friends White (the "Sage of Emporia") and Ed Howe (the "Sage of Potato Hill"). Yet the man Nelson had characterized as a "walking dictionary" never flaunted his sagacity and seldom put himself forward. Even the announcement in May 1944 that he had won a Pulitzer Prize for editorial writing—his second, counting the 1933 prize awarded to the *Star's* editorial page under his direction—caught him completely by surprise. Only later did he learn that Arthur Krock of the *New York Times*, a member of the Pulitzer nominating committee, had been dissatisfied with the entries that year, rung up his friends at the *Star*, and submitted a portfolio of Haskell's editorials without his knowledge or consent.[28] A telegram from New York was the first the editor heard about the award.

Missionary to the last, Haskell looked upon editorial writing as a kind of higher journalism. While others fought in the trenches, he waged a loftier battle for hearts and minds. "It is not the function of editorials to win elections," he told a *Star* reporter who interviewed him after the Pulitzer award was announced. "It is their function to bring readers information and intelligent comment based on sound principles; to stimulate people to think intelligently on the problems of common life; to help them appreciate and value the long run view over short sighted selfishness. In short, editorials should be made one of the vital educational influences in a democracy. If they are, in time they will bear fruit in promoting social progress."[29] The *Star's* editor seemed unconcerned that the influence of the old, oracular editorial page had waned. To him, it would always remain at once the soul of the newspaper and a repository of society's deepest communal values.

While Roberts's signature campaigns were invariably political in nature, Haskell's legacy would be a quietly determined effort to lead Americans toward an enlightened awareness of their common humanity and global responsibilities. His editorial voice was neither polemical nor folksy, but rational, dignified, and dispassionate. Unlike White, who addressed his readers as friends, conversing with them as if over a cup of coffee at the corner cafe, Haskell treated his readers like the eager student of human affairs that he was himself. At his death, White would leave an unfinished autobiography, a dazzling blend of self-revelation and self-justification that was destined to become an American classic. Haskell had no such gift, nor, in truth, any such desire to bare his soul. At Alfred Knopf's prodding, he began dictating a memoir in 1945, but quickly laid it aside. His life, after all, was an open book, printed in the pages of the *Star*. Beyond that, what remained to be said?

Perhaps only White could truly see Haskell whole, balancing the idealistic progressive he had known at the turn of the century with the practical idealist who guided the *Star* through the roaring twenties, turbulent thirties, and heroic forties. In a letter to Oswald Garrison Villard, written in 1942, the Sage

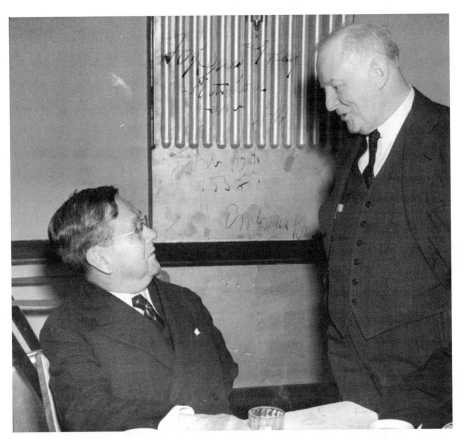

Henry J. Haskell (left) and William Allen White, 1938. Fast friends and lifelong progressives, the two midwestern editors never lost their faith in the essential sanity of the human race.

of Emporia offered a candid but affectionate appraisal of his oldest and closest friend. "The *Star*'s editorial page does lack punch," he admitted to Villard, who was updating his chapter on the paper for a book titled *The Disappearing Daily*. "But it isn't cowardice. It is Haskell's temperament. He is likely to see both sides and he is not cocksure in his mental attitudes. He is more of a scholar than a crusader. If the *Star* had Walter Millis or Herbert Agar in the editorial chair, it would be much stronger. But I should hope that always they would keep Henry Haskell around and follow his judgment if not his judicial methods."[30]

It was a characteristically charitable summing up. In passing judgment on Haskell, White was also passing judgment on himself. As Bull Moose progressives struggling to come to terms with a less than ideal world, both men had embraced a succession of heroes, from Teddy Roosevelt to Herbert Hoover to Alf Landon, who upon closer inspection were shown to have feet of clay. Believing personal liberty and private enterprise to be society's greatest good, they viewed the rise of big government, interest-group politics, and self-governing nation-states with grave misgivings. Seeing an enlightened governing class as the surest bulwark against the "moronic underworld," they nevertheless accepted the necessity for capitalist societies to reorganize themselves on a more equitable and sustainable basis, to forestall another disastrous slide into totalitarianism or complacency. Crusaders for decency and tolerance at a time when both were increasingly endangered, they never lost their faith in the essential sanity of the human race or their humane compassion for its folly and suffering.

White's death in January 1944 marked the end of a journalistic era. Few newspapermen before him, and fewer since, brought the virtues and values of small-town journalism to play on the national stage. The Sage of Emporia, Haskell said in his funeral oration, had written his own epitaph as "a great interpreter of life," a "preacher of righteousness, of sane and wholesome and unselfish living." On a more personal note, Haskell recalled his friend's "exuberance, his humor, his quaint ways of expression, his kindness, his sympathy, his independence, his courage."[31]

In 1944 the United States needed those qualities more than ever. Resentment toward Roosevelt, among both Republicans and conservative Democrats, had created an ominously polarized political climate. The upcoming presidential campaign promised to be exceptionally nasty. Shortly before he died, White confided to Haskell that he was "scared to death about the country. The President is finding that in these terrible times the country needs a forthright man who will speak the truth to his own hurt. For ten years and more he has been functioning on technique rather than on conviction, and technique does not go any more." For once, Haskell found himself defending Roosevelt against White's doubts. "FDR has developed into a fine war leader," he replied, "and I don't know whether we can afford to dispense with him if the war is still on. At the same time, I don't know that we can afford to have four more years of phony domestic policies. His crowd, I am convinced, is trying to make it impossible to operate the American system and they are making a darn lot of headway."[32]

Like White, Haskell was laying odds on Willkie, hoping the Republicans would have the common sense to give him a second shot at the presidency. Instead, Dewey emerged as the party's standard bearer. Although Haskell still hadn't warmed to him, White and Roberts thought Dewey had what it took to defeat FDR, especially after the stiff-necked prosecutor renewed his attack on the president for coddling machine bosses in Kansas City and Chicago. Roberts was momentarily thrown for a loop when Roosevelt picked Truman as his running mate, but by the time the Democrats convened in Chicago in July, the joke was going around that the *Star* was promoting a bipartisan Dewey-Truman ticket. Undeterred by Truman's protests that he didn't want the nomination, Roberts introduced himself to one of the senator's friends as "Harry's campaign manager for Vice President." "The hell you are," came the reply. "You're nothing but a lousy Republican." To those who derided Roosevelt's choice of the diligently self-effacing man from Independence as the "Missouri Compromise," Roberts offered reassurance that "the Senator's friends, and especially his colleagues" knew him to be "an old-fashioned Missourian—not a pink or a reformer."[33]

As late as October 1944 Lacy Haynes, by grace of the *Star* boss of Kansas and political operator par excellence, confidently predicted that the Sunflower State would end up in the Dewey column. "Missouri is close as the devil," he advised the paper's Washington correspondent, "but I think right at this time Dewey has a decided advantage . . . . With the Pendergast machine making a stand to get back, but without its control of election machinery in Kansas City, Jackson County Missouri can't be expected to carry the whole load this time." Haynes told Ted Alford he couldn't understand why Roosevelt's handlers were so pugnacious. "They knew and everybody else knows Dewey's strength and his training enables him to be one of the best prosecutors in the United States. When they stepped off and started slugging at him they gave him an opportunity to turn prosecutor and just present the New Dealers' own words to his jury, the American people." By this time in 1936 and 1940, Haynes wrote, FDR had the election sewn up, but Dewey was still running strong. The governor faced "a hell of a fight," but Haynes reckoned that things were "going his way."[34]

When the ballots were counted, Dewey had bested both of his opponents on their home turf, in Hyde Park, New York, and Independence, Missouri. Nationwide, however, Roosevelt had squeaked by to the tune of some three million votes, making it the closest-run race since Wilson's wartime victory in 1916. After the dust settled, representatives of Roosevelt and Willkie tentatively explored the possibility of launching a new third party, drawing progressive internationalists from both ends of the political spectrum into a grand coalition reminiscent of the Bull Moosers of 1912. But White House leaks angered Willkie and he died of a heart attack before the initiative got off the ground. The nonpartisan ideal, it seemed, remained as elusive in Washington as in Kansas City.

If Cicero, in Haskell's estimation, was cut from the same cloth as the modern political boss, Roosevelt more nearly resembled his formidable antagonist, Julius Caesar, the fearless war leader and proponent of a new order who "won supremacy at the cost of alienating vital elements in the state." Haskell had been toying with the idea of writing a life of the "noblest Roman of them all." The eminent Oxford historian Hugh Last had urged him on. So had André Maurois, the acclaimed biographer of Disraeli, Byron, and Châteaubriand. Although the editor's failing eyesight made another project of that magnitude all but impossible, he continued to ruminate on the lessons of antiquity, apprehensive that the modern planned economy would inevitably lead to dictatorship. "I go back to the fact that Rome got on well so long as it was a simple agricul[tural] economy," he observed to a friend. "When it reached a more complicated economic structure it became unmanageable and crashed."[35]

In his opinion, the international outlook was equally bleak. Plans for a postwar "United Nations" evoked memories of the *Star*'s fight against the League of Nations a quarter-century earlier. Haskell's attitude toward such utopian projects hadn't changed. "At the present stage of world affairs," he believed, it was simply out of the question to "set up every little nation as a sovereign state." Those who "think they can accomplish something worthwhile by getting every nation to promise to be good" were equally fatuous. The parallels between Hitler's Germany and Stalin's Russia boded ill for efforts to integrate either country into the community of western democracies. The Germans, he believed, were incurably militaristic and would have to be collectively "re-educated to become part of the modern world." He feared the Allies would lack the political will to disarm Germany after the war, forgetting the lessons of World War I. "I think there is great danger that in a few years we will say, After all the Germans are a nice people and it's too bad not to give them liberty of action. Whereupon I would expect another Pied Piper to come along behind whom the German people would enthusiastically goosestep," he wrote to Dorothy Thompson, the distinguished foreign correspondent.[36]

Truman's sudden elevation to the presidency on April 12, 1945, occasioned more hand-wringing than celebration at Eighteenth and Grand. The *Star*'s reservations about the vice president had been deepened by his conspicuous attendance at Tom Pendergast's funeral two and a half months earlier. Unabashed, Truman had chatted amiably with his World War I buddy Jim Pendergast, who as the boss's nephew had inherited the keys to the Jackson Dem-

Jim Pendergast (left) and President Harry S. Truman hobnob in Independence, 1946. "I owe my political life to the Pendergast organization," Truman confided to a *Star* reporter.

ocratic Club and was doing his best to resurrect the machine. All of this had been duly noted—and deplored—at the time by the managers of the *Star*. Now, however, was a time to pull together. Two days after Truman's swearing in, Roberts called at the White House, where the new president—grudgingly, one supposes—granted him a half-hour interview. "I think President Truman will do a fine, commonsense job and that the country will rally behind him. I've got confidence in him," Roberts told reporters afterwards. He assured the *Star*'s readers that "the sheer fact he is the average man, understands the average man and his quality, is probably Truman's greatest asset." Haskell too was impressed, almost in spite of himself, by the accidental president's unsuspected skill as an alliance builder. In late August, after the surrender of Germany and Japan, he wrote to a friend that "Truman seems to me to be doing exceptionally well—better in the circumstances than FDR would have done. We heard from Potsdam that Stalin liked Truman's simplicity and directness."[37]

If Roberts's credentials as a "friend of Harry" were somewhat spurious, Haskell's sympathetic regard for the much maligned former "senator from Pendergast" was genuine. Truman, after all, exemplified many of the same qualities he admired in Willkie. Anyway, the older he got, the less political labels meant to Haskell. He was neither narrowly partisan nor, as White observed, "cocksure in his mental attitudes." Instinctively, he searched for common ground with people of different backgrounds and persuasions. His marriage to Agnes Hadley had broadened his range of social contacts appreciably, for few doors in Missouri or Washington, D.C., were closed to the widow of Governor Hadley. Her death in February 1946 was a bitter blow. Haskell had now outlived three wives, each a vivid personality, strong-willed and keenly intelligent, and each devoted to furthering his career while pursuing her own interests in the public sphere. Cataract surgery later that year restored some of his sight, but, like Nelson, he was increasingly reduced to being read aloud to. In 1948 he declined the Wright family's invitation to edit Wilbur and Orville's papers for publication, wistfully telling one of the brothers' nieces, "I have a feeling that Katharine would have liked me to do it if I could."[38]

Haskell did, however, undertake one last project: a memorial for William Volker, the city's iconic benefactor, who died in November 1947 at age eighty-eight. Having given some $10 million away during his lifetime, Volker left another $15 million to a charitable foundation. A man of deep convictions but few words, he had been quietly instrumental in almost every major civic reform of the past half-century. Despite his selfless devotion to the public welfare, he had eyed the growth of the welfare state with alarm, for it offended his sense of individual responsibility and dignity. Volker's spontaneous, man-to-man style of philanthropy—it was his habit to hand his checks personally and privately to those in need—put Haskell in mind of Saint Martin, the legendary Roman soldier who shared his cloak with a roadside beggar. As chairman of the memorial committee, the editor not only steered the commission for a Saint Martin fountain to Carl Milles but handled the negotiations with the temperamental Swedish sculptor with such tact and aplomb that the two men soon became fast friends.[39] Installed on the banks of Brush Creek, in close proximity to both Nelson's Rockhill neighborhood and Nichols's Country Club, the Volker Fountain would symbolically link the city's progressive past with its mercantilist future.

Having given the best years of his life to a paper that doled out bylines sparingly, Haskell instinctively shared Volker's penchant for anonymity. But the fiftieth anniversary of his arrival at the *Star* was no time for hiding his light under a bushel. In February 1948 Roberts threw a small party for him at the Muehlebach Hotel—Haskell's doctors had cautioned that a big shindig might be too much for his heart—and solicited messages from well-wishers far and wide. President Truman set political differences aside and dictated a warmly appreciative telegram: "Henry Haskell deserves all the tributes his friends can pay him. Few men have his wide knowledge of world affairs—a knowledge gained not in an ivory tower but by on-the-spot observation and talks with leaders, and just plain people, all over the world." The president asked Roberts to "wish for him, please, on my behalf, health and happiness in what I trust will be a large addition to the years of his life. In the discussion of our relationships with the rest of this troubled and complex world, we need his clear and reasonable voice as never before." Haskell sent Truman an autographed copy of the second edition of *The New Deal in Old Rome*, which Knopf had issued the previous autumn. "I wonder," the president wrote back, "if there will be a Henry Haskell Two Thousand years from now to write up The New Deal of this age."[40]

In keeping with the bipartisan spirit of the occasion, former President Hoover saluted Haskell as "one of the few editors of sense in the United States." Herbert Bayard Swope, the renowned editor of the old *New York World*, called his career "an example of steadfastness and resultfulness," adding, "I am proud to belong to a profession which is honored by his membership." Praise from peers and presidents was sweet, but sweeter still, because so completely unforeseen, was a note from a man whose name was synonymous with civil liberties. "I can't refrain," Roger Baldwin wrote, "from adding my word of satisfaction in your long and distinguished service to the best in our traditions. I've kept up with you these years far more than you could know. It is a comfort in desperate days to feel a moral personality reacting as you do to our problems."[41] Baldwin chose his words with care, aware that the *Star*'s "service to the best in our traditions" hadn't always been so exemplary. Three decades earlier, shortly before founding the American Civil Liberties Union, he had been jailed as one of the conscientious objectors whom Haskell's ultrachauvinistic editorial page had branded unpatriotic slackers and worse.

Times and attitudes had changed, in many ways clearly for the better. Yet from the perspective of veteran progressives like Baldwin and Haskell, the United States in 1948 offered no cause for complacency. When the Pendergast machine reared its head in Kansas City's primary election that summer, this time in league with an Italian gangster of a far more sinister stripe than Johnny Lazia, Haskell was assailed by something close to despair. "We have been fighting against this sort of mercenary and unscrupulous politics for many years—in my case for nearly fifty years. And where have we got? I ask you," he complained to Jacob Billikopf.[42] In a long letter to his friend Wiley Rutledge, associate justice of the U.S. Supreme Court and an ardent New Dealer, the editor reflected balefully on the "progress" the nation had made in the past half-century:

> One of our first crusades after I came on the *Star* was against election crookedness. We are still crusading. We favored all sorts of social progress measures on the ground that they would cure glaring evils. An immense number of things have been done to do away with juvenile delinquency —a boys hotel, the juvenile courts, recreation centers, etc. But juvenile delinquency remains one of our big problems. I recall so vividly the years just before World War one. There seemed to be growing tolerance, spreading democracy, the duma arriving in Russia, the reichstag gaining more and more power—the world definitely on the forward path. And now![43]

Despondent though he was, Haskell's melioristic belief in the moral redemption of humankind never deserted him. As progressive fellow travelers like Mark Sullivan, George Creel, and Isaac Don Levine veered sharply to the right, bitterly disillusioned by Roosevelt's policies and the rising menace of world communism, he remained true to the bedrock values that had sustained him all his life. If anything, Haskell, like White and Nelson, became more broadminded and tolerant as he aged, his moderate mugwumpery increasingly out of step with Roberts's in-your-face partisanship. Some of his best friends on the federal bench—men like Rutledge, Supreme Court Chief Justice Harlan Fiske Stone, and William Denman of the Ninth Circuit Court in San Francisco—were prominent civil libertarians who regarded him as a staunch ally. A conservative of the old school, neither cynical nor reactionary, he remained in all things a practical and practicing idealist. In hindsight, he saw that the progressives' grandiose dreams of political reform and social justice had been impractical from the start. Ensconced in his Georgian-style mansion on Meyer Circle, framed by the graceful jets of water spewing from the

majestic fountain across the way, Haskell reflected that even the City Beautiful had been a splendid illusion, a vision no less worth pursuing for being un-
attainable. By all rights, he mused to Billikopf, "Kansas City ought to be a
Heaven-on-earth today. Curious how human nature keeps getting in the way
of Utopia."[44]

As Haskell scaled back his active role in the *Star's* management, fifty-nine-
year-old Roberts sashayed onto center stage, burnishing his reputation as a
newsmaker and presidential counselor. In early 1947 *Time* and *Newsweek* ran
copycat feature stories on "Big Roy," characterizing the "fat and florid ex-
travert" as "the driving force behind the strongest newspaper monopoly in the
U.S." Since becoming managing editor in 1928, *Time* reported, Roberts had
"been the man to see in Kansas City, to build a hospital, to get things into the
paper or to keep them out." That March *Reader's Digest* published a fulsome
profile of "Kansas City's boss-busting editor," drawing attention to his skill-
ful generalship in the battle with the resurgent Pendergast machine. "We
Kansas City people have learned the lesson that clean government requires
constant watchfulness from the people," the article quoted him as saying.[45]
Later that year, John Gunther, in his book *Inside U.S.A.*, identified Roberts as
the city's number-one citizen.

Not all the publicity Roberts attracted was so favorable. Emmanuel Haldeman-Julius, the armchair socialist who presided over what was left of the *Appeal to Reason* empire in tiny Girard, Kansas, published a jeremiad pillorying
the newsman as the city's "reigning poobah," an "all-powerful deity who must
constantly be appeased and flattered," and, unkindest cut of all, a "reverse edition of the late Tom Pendergast." (As reported in *Fortune* magazine, Roberts
was particularly sensitive to being called the boss's successor, protesting that
he was for the people at all times. "That's what Tom Pendergast used to say,"
former Mayor Bryce Smith joshed.) Ex-*Kansas City Journal-Post* reporter
W. G. Clugston borrowed a leaf from Lincoln Steffens's muckraking classic
when he accused Roberts of conspiring "behind a facade of sanctimonious respectability" with J. C. Nichols and W. T. Kemper to impose on the city "a
crushing and reprehensible business hegemony" that had ceded to the *Star*
control over "every form of civic activity from the Chamber of Commerce to
the City Hall."[46]

Roberts's national notoriety was sparked by the resolution of a strike that
had shut the newspaper down for the first time in its sixty-six-year history.
Although Nelson and his successors prided themselves on running a "paper
for the people," the *Star* had never been notably hospitable to organized la-

"Big Roy" Roberts, Kansas City's number-one citizen, takes to the airwaves over the *Star*'s WDAF radio station in the late 1940s.

bor. A wildcat pressmen's strike in 1919, an aftertremor of Kansas City's crippling general strike, had jolted the paper's top executives and convinced them that labor leaders couldn't be trusted. In January 1947 it was the carriers who walked out, demanding employee status and recognition as a union. Management refused to submit the dispute to arbitration under the New Deal Wagner Act, arguing that the carriers were independent contractors and thus not covered by its collective-bargaining provisions. When pressmen refused to cross the picket line, the paper was forced to suspend publication for more than two weeks, while Roberts negotiated with the International Printing Pressmen's Union. Fearing that a lengthy strike would lead to unionization of the newsroom, he struck a shrewd bargain, promising the pressmen a pay raise but making no concessions to the carriers. Shortly thereafter, *Star* president

Earl McCollum died and his fellow directors showed their appreciation of Roberts's toughness by electing him the company's new CEO, Haskell having taken himself out of the running for reasons of health.

Fourteen months later Roberts achieved his highest accolade. On April 12, 1948, *Time* magazine pictured the cigar-chomping newsman on its cover, his jowly face superimposed on a silhouette of the Kansas City skyline. "I'm just a big, fat country boy," read the legend below. Qualifying its previous description, *Time* declared that "Roberts is No. 1 citizen, but he is by no means Kansas City's boss. His position is unique in big-town journalism and politics. He never gives an order, has asked only one favor of the city administration in eight years (one of 'the Senator's' friends needed a job). His great power is the *Star*. He can sit back, dictate an editorial or work up a story that will get things done." Illustrated with photos of Nelson and Pendergast, the article portrayed Roberts as a man of gargantuan appetite who routinely downed four large scotch highballs before dinner. On top of his fifty-thousand-dollar salary, he reportedly owned stock in the company worth close to a million dollars.[47]

It was neither wealth nor power, however, that landed Roberts on the cover of *Time,* but rather his latest political coup. In a page-one story headlined "Ike Means 'No,'" he had recently scuttled reports that another country boy from Kansas, Dwight D. Eisenhower, would allow himself to be a candidate for president that year. No matter that Ike had already emphatically declared himself out of the running. It was well known that Roberts was the ultimate authority on the popular general's political future. Convinced that Eisenhower's sense of duty would compel him to accept his party's call (the party in question being the GOP, as Roberts had revealed some months previously), the newsman had been busy for the past year whipping up enthusiasm for a draft. Eisenhower, whose political instincts were as yet untested, was almost abjectly grateful for his expert advice. After definitively withdrawing from the race in January, he wrote to Roberts: "In all your talks, on every subject, you have always shown to me such a broad and common sense attitude toward intricate problems that I should have liked very much to have had the benefit of your counsel."[48]

Roberts would have a great deal to do with putting Ike in the White House in 1952. For the time being, though, he was hedging his bets. Still professing "confidence" in Truman, he was laying the groundwork for a future Eisenhower candidacy, carrying a sentimental torch for Senator Arthur Vandenberg, and cultivating his ties to Dewey, now the presumptive Republican nominee. The New York governor had tested the waters on a visit to Kansas City the preceding summer and later commended Roberts for the "shrewd politi-cal judgment" he had shown in making the arrangements. By early 1948 the two men were acting like old chums, and at the Republican convention that summer Roberts reportedly "did some politicking" on Dewey's behalf, advis-ing delegates that Eisenhower's recusal had freed them to pass over the con-servative Robert Taft. (Apparently done in by his exertions, he sat out the eventful Democratic convention at which Truman staved off challenges by southern "Dixiecrat" segregationists and liberals rallying around Wallace.) In October, the *Star* hosted a buffet supper for Dewey's campaign entourage, warming up for the anticipated postelection bash. Roberts told the candidate's manager in Minnesota that his speech in Kansas City "went over big," but ad-vised that the governor looked tired and needed more rest.[49]

Like everyone else, Roberts and his colleagues had seen the polls and as-sumed that Dewey was a shoo-in. Truman's upset victory not only came as a rude shock but wounded their journalistic pride. Haskell, who had never un-derestimated Truman's resilience, considered the press's miscall of the election "the greatest professional failure in my recollection." He told Billikopf that he was "organizing a Go Jump in the Lake Club for all newspaper editors and correspondents, pollsters and commentators. Only there is no lake around here big enough to hold us all." Roberts defended press coverage of the cam-paign as fair and objective (a view not universally shared), but admitted that most newspapers had neglected to "do the job of old-fashioned reporting" that would have alerted them to late swings among the millions of undecided vot-ers. The Republicans had been so cocksure that "there was entirely too much golfing and sitting around the club and telling how better times were coming and too little getting of the voters to the polls." It wasn't so much that Tru-man had won the election, Roberts hinted, as that Dewey had defeated him-self. "The sheer, smug confidence of the Dewey campaign drove a lot of peo-ple to Truman out of sympathy."[50]

Haskell too was disappointed in the governor's performance, regretting that he hadn't "made a fighting campaign as Truman did." But in the final analysis, he felt, voters had repudiated the GOP as much as Dewey. The orig-inal party of progressive reform had fallen behind the times. Roosevelt, the editor observed, had "made over the Democratic party," turning it into "the party to which the people under the middle class bracket look for help." For his part, Dewey took umbrage at Roberts's suggestion that he had run a smug campaign. "Whatever it was," he wrote, "we followed the best advice we could get and the best information available, and now we are stuck with four more years of Democrats. Maybe this country is so great it can survive anything."

Lacy Haynes was less sanguine. "I just want you to know how deeply I feel about the failure of the American people to take advantage of having you in the national service the next four years. A lot of things could have been done," he consoled Dewey after the returns were in. "And now," he added, "I am fearful of the tides which fan the waves and what will happen in steering us through the stormy times ahead."[51]

The day after Christmas 1948, the *Star* belatedly made amends to Truman by publishing (and later reprinting in pamphlet form) a long, laudatory article by Henry A. Bundschu about the president's boyhood, family, and military and political career. Bundschu, a friend and neighbor of the Trumans and a certified Republican, diplomatically glossed over the Pendergast connection and other touchy subjects. Truman accepted the olive branch warily, telling Roberts that Bundschu's expurgated account came "more nearly being the truth of the facts with regard to my political career than has been written lately."[52]

Although Truman and the *Star* would never bury the hatchet, the president had earned the paper's grudging respect in his Senate years through his dogged exposure of wartime production inefficiency and profiteering. At the height of the Truman Committee's investigation, he was unsettled by the praise bestowed upon him by his long-time nemesis. "It is funny, sure enough, to have Haskell sending me special letters with his editorials. The world will probably stop going around if that keeps up," he joked to his wife.[53] In line with Roberts's policy of maintaining a united home front, the *Star* had rallied behind Truman in the early months of his presidency, but he quickly fell back out of grace during the 1946 congressional campaign, when he publicly called on young Jim Pendergast to help block the reelection of Roger Slaughter, a two-term Democratic representative from Missouri's Fifth District who had butted heads with Truman in opposing the Fair Labor Employment Practices Act.

At a press conference in Washington on July 18, the president made it known that he was throwing his support to a political newcomer named Enos Axtell. Although impartial observers rated Axtell's chances as slim, he won the August 6 primary handily, largely on the strength of voting in wards under machine control. Roberts smelled a rat and two days later assigned a pair of seasoned war veterans on his staff to ferret out evidence of fraud. By the end of September they had enough to file a complaint with U.S. District Attorney Sam Wear. Wear promptly dumped the political hot potato in the lap of Truman's attorney general, Tom Clark. And there it sat, much to the consternation of the state's Republican senator, James Kem. From his soapbox on the Senate Judiciary Committee, Kem raised such a stink that Clark finally authorized a limited investigation by his department, on the basis of which a panel of federal judges in Kansas City concluded that there was insufficient evidence to warrant empaneling a grand jury.

The attorney general, no doubt heaving a sigh of relief, ordered the case closed on January 6, 1947. But Pandora's box had already been prized open. A diligent Jackson County prosecutor had convened his own grand jury, which eventually returned indictments against eighty-one defendants. The ballots and other documents the jurors had weighed in reaching their decision were returned to local authorities for safekeeping. In the meantime Kem, faced with what he regarded as stonewalling by Clark and FBI director J. Edgar Hoover, tabled a Senate resolution proposing a full-scale investigation by the Judiciary Committee. On May 27, as Clark was testifying before the committee in Washington, news arrived that thieves had blown open the vault in the county courthouse in Kansas City and absconded with the incriminating evidence. The circumstances were suspicious, to say the least, and a number of conflicting theories quickly emerged as to who was behind the dastardly deed. Truman, however, declined to speculate. "No comment" was his response to reporters who questioned him at his hotel a short distance from the crime scene.[54]

By the first of June, Hoover decided he had no choice but to order his agents back into the field to investigate both the theft and the *Star*'s original allegations of vote fraud. But in the absence of hard evidence (the stolen ballots would never be recovered), they came up empty-handed. Truman, who was keeping as far away from the spreading scandal as possible, wrote to his sister that "the Congress, the *Post Dispatch* and the *Star* seem to be having spasms over the K.C. vote situation. I am reliably informed that as many Republicans as Democrats are expected to end up in the jug before it's over. All I hope is that they get that fat no good can of lard named Roberts of the *Star*. They may do it too." It seems probable that the president's informant was a Justice Department official dispatched to Kansas City by Attorney General Clark. H. Graham Morison later claimed to have discovered that "the business manager of the *Kansas City Star*, through an emissary, had employed a safecracker from out of town to get into the Jackson County Courthouse and steal those ballots from a flimsy safe," ostensibly in hopes of discrediting the Pendergast machine.[55] Morison's unsubstantiated charge spoke volumes about the Truman administration's almost paranoid distrust of the *Star*, and Roberts in particular—an attitude that was cordially reciprocated.

Publicly, the president and the newspaper's executives maintained a semblance of decorum, but behind the scenes brickbats flew thick and fast. During the 1946 primary, Roberts had posted a reporter to spy on the Trumans' home in Independence, binoculars in hand. (This was a refinement of a form of harassment Roberts had devised years earlier in assigning a reporter to rouse Truman by telephone at three o'clock every morning with an urgent question about his duties as county judge.) After the safecracking episode, the *Star* continued to feed damaging information to Senator Kem on the quiet. One of the paper's attorneys passed along supposedly confidential intelligence Roberts had received to the effect that the FBI had shown less than due diligence in investigating vote fraud in Jackson County. It was further rumored that Henry Ess, a principal in the *Star*'s law firm, assisted the Republicans in digging up dirt on Truman for use in the 1948 campaign. At one point, Roberts boasted to a newspaper colleague that he had spent three months trying to prove Truman had joined the Ku Klux Klan early in his political career, only to conclude feebly that "he came very goddamn close."[56]

The Star Company's newly enthroned president was doing his best to keep up the heat on Truman and his cronies. But the tables would soon be turned.

A second, unrelated development forcefully brought Kansas City to the attention of federal authorities in 1947. Even as vote fraud stories grabbed the headlines, a new threat to Roberts's peace of mind emerged in the person of Garrett Smalley, publisher of the *Kansas City News-Press,* a small north-side weekly allied with the Democratic machine. Previously, Smalley had served as Truman's publicity manager in his county judgeship contests. For several months, he had quietly been leading a group of the *Star*'s competitors in an investigation of his own into the paper's business practices. Armed with affidavits from sixty aggrieved parties, Smalley and another man descended on Washington and presented their evidence to Truman and Clark. The attorney general replied that they had a strong case, but, apparently deeming it inopportune to antagonize the *Star,* advised that he would take no action until after the 1948 election. He promised the Justice Department would set up a field office in Kansas City to search for more evidence of antitrust violations.[57]

The *Star,* which had hitherto belittled Smalley as the "Town Crier for Pendergast," sat up and took notice. As premonitions of trouble filtered through the newsroom, Roberts decided it was a good time to remind the paper's 360,000 subscribers of their debt to Nelson and his anointed successors. Two editorial writers were detailed to write a large-scale history of Kansas City to be published in conjunction with the forthcoming centennial of its founding,

City manager L. P. Cookingham tries on a Navajo headdress during the 1950 centennial celebration, as *Star* writer Bill Vaughan looks on. After a decade of "reform" government, Kansas City was still struggling to put on a new face.

in 1950. The celebration itself would be organized by the Native Sons, a Waspish club of middle-aged males, and had all the trappings of a Boy Scout jamboree. A pageant titled "Thrills of a Century" took the stage at the open-air Starlight Theater in Swope Park. Historical markers sprouted up around the city. A cohort of Hopi and Navajo Indians pitched camp in a vacant lot downtown. Other festivities included a fiesta, a fashion show, a circus, a rodeo, water follies, and an ice show. Two centennial parades attracted crowds estimated at 350,000. Not since the Century Ball of 1900 had the city seen such unconstrained hoopla.

Haskell's son, Henry C. Haskell, and Richard Fowler, a future *Star* editor, collaborated on the *Star*'s literary commemoration. *City of the Future* captured both the town and the newspaper at the zenith of their fortunes. Serialized in early 1950 and brought out soon thereafter as a bestselling book, the saga of Kansas City was dramatized for radio on CBS's *Hallmark Playhouse* and broadcast nationwide from the Music Hall in June, with Robert Young and Jane Wyman in the starring roles. The publicity generated by this flurry of civic-minded breast-beating was a welcome fillip for the Chamber of Commerce, for even after a decade of "reform" government, the city's progressive image remained in dire need of refurbishment. Only that spring, *Holiday* magazine had run a feature on the "rowdy, prosperous city noted for its meat, mills and sin," likening Kansas City to "a middle-aged reprobate come into the arms of the Lord" and still unsure of salvation. As usual, the *Post-Dispatch* was doing its part to show its rival city in a true light as a "sink of iniquity," prompting the senior Haskell to snort that "I believe in general, except for some spot murders, the St. Louis criminal record is worse than Kansas City's."[58]

City of the Future, Roberts wrote in a foreword to the book,

> furnishes a refreshing antidote to the so-called story of Kansas City. . . . The period of boss rule and gangster sin was so colorful, so dramatic, writers invariably have turned to it as their conception of Kansas City. Yet that period was only a chapter, and far from the most significant one, in the annals of a century. The progress of more than a decade as a city freed from political bondage has been almost ignored in the scores of magazine stories depicting Kansas City in a fashion its own citizenry does not recognize today, except as a memory. Kansas City, the City of the Future, is not an apology! Far from it. It is a factual account of the inspiring growth of a great city built with many ups and down and lapses and falls from grace, but with its sights set eternally toward the promise of the future.[59]

The *Star's* triumphalist portrait pictured a raw-edged but eternally progressive City Beautiful as seen from the vantage of Eighteenth and Grand. The authors might have taken as their subtext the paper's old advertising slogan: "The *Star* is Kansas City and Kansas City is the *Star.*" Lively and authoritative, *City of the Future* would become a standard history of the River City, a stirring master narrative of progress and manifest destiny. The timing of its appearance, however, left something to be desired, coming as it did on the heels of a fresh spate of mob bloodletting. When gambling kingpin Charles Binaggio was assassinated in a gangland slaying on April 6, Ray Moley tut-tutted in his *Newsweek* column that "Kansas City politics is a national disgrace." James Reston of the *New York Times* acknowledged Roberts's gift of the *Star's* new history with a pungent jab: "I was mildly disturbed to find that even you cannot control affairs in your own home town well enough to keep the local plug-uglies from getting in the news just at the time your book was coming out." Reviewing the volume in the *Washington Post,* Roscoe Fleming wondered "how a city with a self-appraised Great Newspaper could ever have drifted into the fix from which the *Star* admittedly did a fine and courageous job in rescuing it. With a really Great Newspaper on the job, would a rescue have been necessary?"[60]

That June Jerome Walsh, Frank Walsh's lawyer son and no friend of the *Star,* presented an autographed copy of *City of the Future* to the occupant of the White House. "You know," Truman told him, "I know a little about the history of Kansas City and am anxious to read what others have written." A week or so later, having apparently perused the volume with some care, Truman fired off (but refrained from mailing) a peppery letter to Roberts ripping it to shreds. He was particularly galled by the unflattering portrait of Tom Pendergast, whom he called "a gentleman" compared to "Pigface Bill" Nelson. The lengthy diatribe was signed "Harry S. Truman, President of the United States in spite of you, Bertie McCormick and Willie Hearst." Letting off steam in another unsent letter, this time addressed to Jim Pendergast, Truman mused a few months later: "It certainly would be a fine thing if we could get Kansas City back into the picture once more as a progressive Democratic town. I don't think the so-called 'clean-up' boys have made one step that has improved conditions of the city. It seems since they have been in power about all they do is kowtow to the *Kansas City Star* and then let the river take its course. It seems to me that the Kansas City spirit is dead, buried and forgotten."[61]

In July 1951 the Kaw River did take its course, once more inundating low-lying sections of the city and dealing the old industrial district a mortal blow from which it would never recover. As the flood waters slowly receded, the *Star* took out full-page ads in major papers around the country proclaiming that "you can't lick Kansas City." Roberts defiantly vowed that the city would bounce back, with a little help from its friends in Washington. "While the bulwarks of democracy must be strengthened abroad, America must be kept strong at home," he wrote in pleading for increased federal spending on flood-prevention measures. "The great industrial heart of a great industrial and agricultural empire is entitled to protection from flood, which in its way is as disastrous as war. We know America will provide it because it makes sense. . . . The courage, the unbeatable spirit of the people out here have made us more proud than ever that *The Star* is serving such a community and trade territory. We are going ahead, bigger than ever. Just watch."[62]

When the *Star* won its fourth Pulitzer Prize for coverage of the disaster,

Roberts was more than ever king of the mountain—or so it appeared. J. C. Nichols's death in 1950 had left no other serious claimants for the title of Mr. Kansas City. In his mid-sixties, Big Roy was still vital and energetic and had no thought of retiring. When his time came, he blustered, he would "have the biggest damn funeral Kansas City has ever seen. They'll all come out to see their old master laid away." The *Star* was more powerful, prestigious, and profitable than at any time in its history. After a quarter-century of staff ownership, the paper's future seemed as bright with promise as the city's. In the general euphoria, no one, Roberts least of all, gave more than a passing thought to Garrett Smalley and his wild allegations.

CHAPTER 10

❖

Busted Trust

Roy Roberts could hardly believe his eyes. There it was, in black and white, for the whole world to see: the U.S. government had accused the *Star* of being an illegal monopoly. On January 6, 1953, a federal grand jury returned an indictment charging that the newspaper had systematically violated the Sherman Antitrust Act for decades by monopolizing advertising and stifling competition. Since the previous summer, a team of Justice Department investigators in an air-conditioned office on the third floor of the *Star* building had been combing through business records dating back to the turn of the century, while anxious editors and reporters in the newsroom below waited for the ax to fall.

> *"The only monopoly I recognize as legitimate is the monopoly of excellence."*
>
> —William Rockhill Nelson

For seven months the *Star* had held its fire as the grand jury heard secret testimony from some 250 witnesses. No sooner was the indictment made public than Roberts—who was named as a defendant in the government's suit, together with advertising director Emil A. Sees—took to newspaper columns and air waves to denounce the outgoing Truman administration for conducting an "inquisition." In a half-page ad placed in the *New York Times, Washington Post,* and other major papers, the *Star's* president noted "the remarkable contrast in the zeal of the Department of Justice in this proceeding against *The Star* and their strange lack of zeal when an election fraud scandal was before them back in 1946." The president of the United States, Roberts hinted, was retaliating against the paper for exposing the Pendergast machine's wholesale ballot-box stuffing. He was confident that the *Star*'s business practices—which, he said, "conform to the law and good morals"—would be vindicated in court. "We are either right or wrong," he told the paper's jittery employee shareholders. "There is no room for consent decrees or compromises."[1]

Thus began the biggest, widest-ranging, and most publicized antitrust action ever instituted against an American newspaper. Whether the *Star* was the victim of a political witch-hunt was a question on which the jury would remain out indefinitely. Despite Garrett Smalley's representations to no fewer than three Democratic attorneys general since 1947, Truman claimed he had been kept in the dark. "Roy Roberts blames me for indicting him," he told columnist Drew Pearson, "but the fact is I didn't know about it until well after the Justice Department had begun the case." Beyond a shadow of a doubt, however, the incubus of politics hung heavily over the legal proceedings. Senator Frank Carlson, a Kansas Republican, rose to the *Star*'s defense, declaring that anyone familiar with its campaign against the local Democratic machine "could well anticipate this vindictive action on the part of the President."[2] For years Roberts and his colleagues had tiptoed around Pendergast lest they provoke him to seek retribution through the courts. Now their worst nightmare seemed to be coming true. The federal district court judge assigned to the case, Richard M. Duncan, was a former Democratic congressman whom *Star* executives regarded as beholden to the machine for his appointment to the bench.

Legal problems aside, 1953 was a banner year for the *Star*. Circulation soared to all-time highs in the postwar economic boom. The paper claimed to be read in 96 percent of Kansas City households and Roberts's peers rated it among the top five or ten most influential dailies in the country. Fundamental to this position, in the managers' eyes, was the forced combination-rate plan that had drawn the Justice Department's ire. Originally formulated by Nelson and August Seested, the plan had been in place practically since the evening *Star* absorbed the morning *Times* in 1901. Reasoning that the *Star* and *Times* were effectively a single paper operating on two continuous twelve-hour news cycles, they decreed that customers could take the whole thirteen-paper package or nothing. The *Star*'s unit rate not only compelled many advertisers to buy more space, and subscribers more papers, than they really wanted, the government argued; it also prevented competing papers from gaining a toehold. This was one Nelson policy that the employee owners had not seen fit to change with the times. After all, they reasoned, the *Star* was legitimately entitled to reap the rewards of its "monopoly of excellence."

Of more immediate relevance to the *Star's* flourishing fortunes was Roberts's success in placing his man in the White House. Dwight Eisenhower's election was widely seen as the high-water mark of the paper's prestige. For Roberts, who had cut his political teeth in the epic Bull Moose crusade, the 1952 campaign had strong echoes of 1912, with another valorous soldier holding the progressive line against a conservative standpatter named Taft.[3] He and Eisenhower had known each other since the war, and when the Army's chief of staff passed through Kansas City in June 1945 on his way home to Abilene, Kansas, Roberts hailed the conquering hero in words strikingly reminiscent of those the *Star* had applied to Teddy Roosevelt in 1900. "There is nothing synthetic or phony about General Ike," the newsman wrote; he was "utterly unspoiled and modest." Like Nelson, Roberts saw his own image in the mirror when he described Eisenhower as a "country boy from Kansas, of poor parents, starting with nothing and rising to great eminence." The general's career, he added, symbolized "what democracy in America really means."[4]

After the Republicans seized control of Congress in 1946, Roberts observed that in eighteen months President Truman had "plummeted from the top of popularity to the most severe verdict pronounced by the American electorate in a generation." Pegging Thomas Dewey as the "No. 1 contender" for his party's presidential nomination, he predicted that voters would throw Truman out of office in 1948. By early 1947 Roberts let it be known that Eisenhower would be his "personal choice" for the presidency, although he doubted the general would consent to run. Mimicking the Roosevelt of 1912, Ike dithered while Roberts pressed his suit until, finally, he lit on an argument he knew the general couldn't resist. If, he suggested that September in the *Star*, "there was an honest-to-God draft," Eisenhower's "sheer sense of duty" would compel him to answer his country's call. When Roberts sent a copy of his article accompanied by a note asking the reluctant candidate for "some explanation of the general picture," Ike responded by unequivocally disavowing any thought of a political career, thereby proving himself a better politician than even Roberts had given him credit for being.[5]

The fact that Eisenhower was still in uniform inhibited for the time being any expression of his political views, not to mention presidential aspirations. Speculation was fueled by his return to civilian life in early 1948, and Roberts, as a member of the Republican Advance, a political action group dedicated to electing a "liberal" to the nation's highest office, was only too glad to fan the flames. His increasingly open politicking provoked another feeble denial from Eisenhower, this time in a letter to Leonard Finder, the politically influential publisher of the Manchester, New Hampshire, *Union-Leader*. Undeterred, Finder telephoned Roberts and suggested it was time to initiate a draft, only to be politely rebuffed. As Finder recorded their conversation, Roberts "felt keenly that any effort on his part individually, considering how close a friend he was to the General, would be misinterpreted so as to reflect upon Eisenhower's integrity. Likewise, he did not want to embark upon any venture which he feared might be 'humiliating' to the General, especially if it should end in failure."[6]

Thwarted but not discouraged, Roberts stepped up his back-door lobbying efforts after Truman's hairbreadth election. Soon Eisenhower was back in uniform and back in Europe, laying the groundwork for a transatlantic collective-security regime. Prior to the election, Truman had offered the general his full support should he decide to run as a Democrat, in the interest of keeping the isolationists at bay. But when Roberts visited NATO headquarters in September 1951, Eisenhower confirmed that he was "a good Kansas Republican." Later that fall, alarmed that Senator Robert Taft was already lining up support in Kansas, Roberts helped young Bill White of the *Emporia Gazette* draft a telegram urging Eisenhower to send his home-state delegates a clear signal of his intentions. This plea elicited a confidential letter from Paris in which Ike at last agreed to give serious consideration to running for president.[7]

Roberts lay low and waited for his seed to germinate. In February 1952 Eisenhower dispatched his top political adviser to Kansas City, where he spent two hours with Roberts and Kansas industrialist Harry Darby. General Lucius Clay, concerned that the Eisenhower bandwagon was "developing too much of an eastern tinge," pressed them to shift their operation into high gear. The two men, Clay reported to his chief, "agreed to go all out, and to quickly set up a working organization below them which can spread out from Kansas through the Middle West." In late March, Roberts notified Eisenhower (who was still abroad) that Taft's forces were "on the run." Eisenhower's campaign had gotten off to a slow start in Kansas and Missouri, a consequence of having "too many generals and not enough active workers," but now "we are organized in every district and we are not letting them go by default." Roberts implored Eisenhower to return to the United States as soon as possible. "But for God's sake, don't do what I suggest, do what Ike thinks is right.

Dwight D. Eisenhower
listens approvingly to
Roy Roberts, his fellow
"country boy from
Kansas," during the 1952
presidential campaign.

After all, that is the important thing—more important than the presidency
or anything else."[8]

Evidently, Roberts pushed the right buttons. Within weeks Eisenhower's
hat was in the ring and Truman's was out, clearing the path for Adlai Stevenson to lead the Democratic ticket. As the Republicans set up campaign headquarters in Topeka, Roberts cautioned Eisenhower not to make the same mistake Wendell Willkie and Charles Evans Hughes had made, of listening to
too much well-intentioned advice. "The people are hunting for a leader now,
not a politician," he counseled. Shortly after the Republican convention in
Chicago—at which one national news magazine assigned a reporter just to
tail Roberts—the editor proudly informed the candidate that his mission was
accomplished. "We are closing the Missouri for Eisenhower headquarters and
turning them over to the Republican state and county committees," he wrote,
along with "tens of thousands of names of Democrats and Independents" that
campaign workers had "gathered up in the delegate fights." Everyone was hap-

py, Roberts said, adding, "I believe we will have a smooth working organization going soon."[9]

This time, for a change, Roberts had backed a winning horse. Eisenhower cantered to an easy victory in November, carrying all but nine of the forty-eight states, including Missouri and Kansas. Truman let off steam in his diary: "My good for nothing, highjacking, blackmailing *Kansas City Star* has decided that 'Truman was a Drag' to Stevenson," he grumbled. But Eisenhower had glowing words for Roberts, whom he considered "one of the principal architects of the movement to bring new leadership" to the GOP. For his part, the newsman was beginning to feel somewhat less fretful about the Justice Department investigators beavering away overhead. "My love to you and Mamie," he wrote the president-elect. "It was the greatest vote of confidence any president has ever received. We want nothing for ourselves but a successful administration and will try to help you make it that. Get away and get some rest. God bless you both."[10]

"We want nothing for ourselves": Was Roberts using the royal "we"? Or was he speaking institutionally? Like Nelson, he had come to regard the *Star* as an extension of himself, almost his sovereign domain. As of the fall of 1952, he no longer had to share his oversized throne in the far corner of the newsroom. Henry Haskell, his longtime mentor and latterly coregent, had died on August 20. At seventy-eight, the *Star*'s editor was the last surviving member of Nelson's privy council. He had been around so long that most people on staff had never known the *Star* without him. Many considered him the paper's editorial conscience, the wise philosopher-king to Roberts's scrappy field marshal.

In the *Star*'s lengthy front-page obituary, Haskell's soft, owlish countenance was sandwiched between accounts of American casualties in Korea and an assault on U.S. servicemen by "Red-inspired Iranians" in Tehran. In the ensuing days he would be remembered as a man of reason and unfailing courtesy, a gentleman and a scholar, imbued with resilient optimism and a lifelong spirit of discovery. The values he had lived by—tolerance, moderation, respect for human dignity—were under siege in the age of the Bomb and Senator Joseph McCarthy. Taking the long view, as he instinctively did, the chauvinistic tirades of United Nations ambassadors were no different from delegates' antics at American political conventions or, for that matter, the craven demagoguery of Cicero's contemporaries. He had seen it all so often before. Human nature didn't change. That knowledge had made him alternately hopeful and despondent. A speaker at his funeral summed him up as "provincial in the best sense and international in the best sense; intellectual in the best sense, and democratic in the best sense; interested in the lessons of history, busy with problems of the present, working out the dreams of the future."[11]

Oddly enough, many of the same sentiments would figure in Truman's political obituaries. A history buff who seldom minced words, the unpretentious man from Independence admired the patrician editor's ability to impart his wide learning in "clear, readable English." A fiercely partisan Democrat who reached across the aisle to men like Senator Arthur Vandenberg and brought Herbert Hoover out of retirement, Truman put Haskell's centrist, bridge-building politics into practice. A conservative midwesterner who helped inaugurate a new world order, Truman exemplified Haskell's practical idealism. In his last "Random Thoughts" columns, the editor had recapped the benchmarks of his political education: William Jennings Bryan's "Cross of Gold" speech in 1896, the spontaneous stampede to Teddy Roosevelt in 1912, the smoke-filled room where the country's fate was sealed in 1920, the Democratic horse-trading at the 1932 convention that nominated FDR. Adept at putting current events in perspective, he had met victory and defeat alike with equal composure. Now, as Truman had once said, the world needed "his clear and reasonable voice" more than ever.

Haskell had stayed aloof from the 1952 campaign, holding his opinions of Eisenhower and Stevenson close to his chest. His strong convictions about the importance of preserving civil liberties and respectful political discourse must surely have been offended by the Republican candidate's cynical wooing of the junior senator from Wisconsin. As a "progressive," moreover, Eisenhower inevitably stood in the shadow of giants like Teddy Roosevelt and William Rockhill Nelson. He was not a statesman of deep and abiding principles, as Haskell understood them, but a political tactician, inclined by instinct and training to gauge his opponent's strengths, probe his weaknesses, and strike when the time was right. Lacking Roberts's partisan fervor, it's unlikely that the editor considered Eisenhower in every way preferable to the thoughtful, articulate, and unimpeachably progressive Stevenson. What he thought of Roberts's compulsive politicking and grandstanding can only be imagined.

So, too, one can only speculate about Haskell's reaction to the *Star*'s legal predicament. The government subpoenaed the *Star*'s business records just two months before he died. Had he foreseen the antitrust suit and, like Roberts, ignored or misjudged the warning signs? Had he spoken out and been overruled by his fellow directors? That the editor was well aware of the business practices at issue can scarcely be doubted. Even cub reporters knew about them. As the resident financial expert on the company's board, Haskell kept a close eye on the steadily rising profits and stock dividends. He may have excused the newspaper's bullying, anticompetitive behavior on the grounds that it was just hard-nosed business practice. Or perhaps he hid behind the traditional curtain separating the news and business sides. Neither explanation is easy to square with Haskell's exacting standards of personal and public morality. Whatever the reason, he had never regretted turning down the presidency of the Star Company in 1947. The job, as Roberts would soon come to realize, was a "graveyard."[12]

Haskell was buried beneath an inconspicuous headstone beside his first wife in Mount Washington Cemetery, on a grassy knoll overlooking Nelson's white-marble mausoleum. He owed more to the *Star*'s legendary proprietor, he said, than to any other person. Nelson had filled a void in his life, taking the place of his largely absent missionary father and furnishing the sense of journalistic mission that he craved. Although Haskell had long since pushed the Old Man off his pedestal, Nelson in his eyes towered over his puny epigones like a mighty volcano. In the end, the editor had more than realized the modest ambition he had expressed to his parents five decades earlier, to "help a little in the building of Kansas City." Unlike Nelson's bricks and mortar, his building blocks were ideas, and he had stacked them up, course by course, with the unflagging patience of a man who knows that a well-built edifice will stand for the ages.

Upon Haskell's death, Roberts became editor of the *Star* as well as president and general manager. He now exercised direct control over every aspect of the paper's business and editorial operation. Not since August Seested's ascendancy in the 1920s had any one man wielded so much authority. Indeed, backed by a compliant board stocked with his handpicked appointees, Roberts was arguably more powerful than anyone at the *Star* since Nelson. No longer a mere kingmaker, he was now a king in his own right. Only the skeletons rattling in the Justice Department's makeshift office overhead troubled the head that wore the crown.

The federal antitrust suit would monopolize Roberts's time and energy for much of the ensuing decade. The climactic set piece of a drama that had begun half a century before, it would unfold with the grim inexorability of a Greek tragedy. Roberts's hubris was far from unique. Newspaper publishers had long held that they were exceptions to the rules governing other big businesses. The National Industrial Recovery Act and other New Deal legislation didn't apply in their case, they argued, because they infringed the freedom of the press. When Nelson and Pulitzer had fended off libel attacks four decades earlier, the *Star* hadn't been unduly alarmed—press lords, after all, carried even bigger sticks than presidents. But government had grown bigger and more threatening. Business ethics had changed as well. Cutthroat practices that might have been acceptable at a time when the newspaper industry was fiercely competitive, and the federal antitrust regime in its infancy, stood in a different light when more than 90 percent of daily newspapers enjoyed effective monopolies in their communities.

After the indictments came down in January 1953, Roberts vigorously defended the *Star*'s unit subscription rate of forty cents a week for the morning, evening, and Sunday papers—four times the rate in Nelson's day, but still the best newspaper bargain in the country, he boasted. To hold the *Star* guilty of restraint of trade was preposterous; in fact, the paper was simply run more efficiently than its competitors and provided a better product. As for the combination rates the *Star* imposed on advertisers, Roberts was confident the company was on firm ground. A few months earlier, members of the *Star*'s law firm had participated in a case involving the *New Orleans Times-Picayune,* in which the U.S. Supreme Court had overturned a lower-court ruling that that paper's unit-rate plan violated the Sherman Act.

As attorneys for both sides prepared for the trial, life at the *Star* returned to something like normal. The criminal indictment didn't diminish Roberts's welcome at the White House. Shortly after meeting privately with Eisenhower on April 10, he underwent surgery for a stomach ulcer and was out of commission for several months. Back on his feet, he wrote Ike in July that he wanted to come east soon and "have a real visit," as he had "some ideas that might be helpful." In the event, Roberts didn't return to Washington until December. "I just stopped by to say howdy," he called to reporters as he emerged from the White House, looking perceptibly slimmer. The president recorded in his diary that Roberts offered advice on the Taft-Hartley labor-relations law, which he was considering asking Congress to amend. The editor further said he hoped the Republicans would make a special effort to field "young, dynamic candidates" in the forthcoming midterm election. The party had "a lot of inertia to overcome in this regard," but Roberts regarded an infusion of fresh blood as essential.[13]

A month later Roberts made a shakeup of his own at the *Star.* Now sixty-six, he told stockholders he wanted to make way for younger men and return to his first love, writing. Among other changes, he put his protégé Richard Fowler in charge of the editorial page and promoted Pete Wellington, the demanding but well-liked managing editor, to the newly created post of executive editor. "I have been in the process of tightening up and freshening up our organization for some time and this was just a move in the more or less top levels," he explained to Joseph Pulitzer II of the *Post-Dispatch*. "Frankly, I have felt for a long time that I was carrying too much of a load, but I was putting some of our men through a testing period before I took final action."[14]

In a postscript to his letter, Roberts mentioned that the *Star* was nominating Alvin McCoy for a Pulitzer Prize. No one could have been more surprised by this news than McCoy himself. In 1953 the reporter had written a long series of investigative articles showing that the chairman of the Republican National Committee had accepted kickbacks from lobbyists. When the official was forced to resign, McCoy became a national celebrity, but there had been no kudos from the paper's chief executive. Roberts, the consummate insider, seemed almost put out that he hadn't uncovered the story. McCoy shrugged it off and submitted the articles to the Pulitzer committee himself, but only after doing an end-run around Roberts, who had ordered the clipping files impounded in the *Star* library. After the cat was out of the bag, Roberts boasted to Pulitzer that the reporter's investigation was "one of the greatest pieces of work, done under the most trying circumstances, a man has done in a long time." Yet when McCoy won the award in May 1954, the *Star* gave the announcement just four paragraphs.[15]

As if to make amends for McCoy's politically inconvenient exposé, Roberts stepped up his efforts on behalf of Eisenhower's agricultural policy. On March 1, 1954, he attended one of the president's famous stag dinners at the White House, having previously instructed the *Star*'s Washington office to send Eisenhower a copy of an editorial "going all-out" for the administration's farm program. As congressional elections approached, the publisher conferred regularly with the president and his advisers, urging them to go on the offensive and accentuate the positive in selling their policies to the country. Subsequently, Ike tapped Roberts for a high-level advisory committee charged with keeping tabs on local issues and identifying new recruits for the party. On a trip to Washington accompanied by the *Star*'s lead attorney in the antitrust case, the publisher met with Eisenhower "off the record," and eleven days later, on December 20, he was among the guests at another stag dinner at which his new committee assignment was discussed.[16] Not since the heady days of the Hoover administration had Roberts felt so at home in the White House.

On Tuesday, January 11, 1955, some 250 *Star* employees gathered in the third-floor meeting room to hear Roberts make his annual report to the stockholders. The outlook was mixed, the publisher said. On the one hand, the company was coming off its all-time best year, with more than forty-six million lines of advertising pumping the bottom line. On the other hand, the looming antitrust suit wasn't to be taken lightly. It would, he warned, be "the most critical battle in our paper's history."[17]

That Friday, three days before the attorneys were scheduled to make their opening arguments in Judge Duncan's courtroom, the Eisenhower administration unexpectedly dropped its criminal indictment against Roberts. Emil Sees and the Star Company still stood accused, and they and Roberts would eventually have to answer the government's concurrent civil lawsuit. But for now, at least, the big fish had been let off the hook.

The government action came as a "complete surprise" to Roberts, who told reporters he had been unjustly "smeared" by the indictment. Garrett Smalley denounced the move as a "damnable outrage" that "stinks to high heaven." Several weeks later the Justice Department's antitrust chief, a California Republican, admitted that the order to drop the charges had come from him. He had reviewed the case on the eve of the trial and concluded that the evidence wasn't strong enough to prove criminal intent on the publisher's part beyond the shadow of a doubt. Most, though not all, of his staff concurred in the decision, he added, as did Attorney General Herbert Brownell. The columnist who broke the story noted that Roberts and Eisenhower had dined together shortly before the trial.[18]

Whoever was ultimately responsible for Roberts's last-minute reprieve, and for whatever legal or political motives, there could be no question that the Justice Department was determined to make an example of the *Star*. Although since 1940 the government had prosecuted five daily newspapers and the Associated Press for violating antitrust laws, the case against the *Star* was by far the biggest and the most far-reaching in its implications for the newspaper industry. Significantly, however, none of the 185 other papers that had similar combination-rate plans in place in the early 1950s jumped to the *Star*'s defense. Not until the case reached the Supreme Court did the AP's New York law firm associate itself with the *Star* in its appeal. No doubt Roberts's fellow publishers were reluctant to call attention to their own possibly illegal practices, many of which would continue unchallenged for decades after the *Star* had its day in court.

Unseen by the public, two years of intense strategizing and jockeying for position preceded the highly publicized criminal trial. Roberts and his top lieutenants had spent countless hours closeted with the *Star*'s attorneys, poring over the indictments point by point, searching for loopholes in the government's case and plotting their defense. The publisher bombarded the lawyers with long memos assailing his persecutors and defending his own and the paper's integrity. The government had left the door open to an out-of-court settlement without formal admission of guilt, but Roberts would accept nothing less than complete vindication. On the witness stand, neither he nor Sees would give an inch under the government's aggressive examination. "You couldn't talk to Roberts," one participant in the case recalled. "He blustered. Hearing him, the *Star*'s lawyers blustered, too, all reinforcing the feeling they were going to whip the government."[19]

A battery of fourteen lawyers confronted Judge Duncan when he entered the courtroom at ten o'clock Monday morning on January 17, 1955. Representing the Justice Department were Earl Jinkinson, an experienced litigator and soon to be head of the department's Midwest antitrust division, and five junior attorneys. The *Star* fielded a team of eight lawyers—six from the old-line Kansas City firm of Watson, Ess, which had looked after the paper's legal affairs for decades, and two senior attorneys whom Roberts, in a surprise move, had brought in for reasons both tactical and sentimental. James Aylward and his father were well connected in Democratic circles. A former law partner of Frank Walsh, and a key ally of Tom Pendergast, Aylward had assisted Walsh in Nelson's contempt trial back in 1913 and defended the *Star* against Henry Doherty's libel suits two decades later. Roberts had no more love for Aylward's politics than Seested had. But in a trial taking place before a Democratic judge and a jury drawn from an overwhelmingly Democratic populace, he was taking no chances.

In his opening remarks, Jinkinson previewed the prosecution's case, telling the jury the government would prove that the "elimination" of the *Kansas City Journal-Post* and other competing dailies "did not happen as a mere accident." The *Star*, he said, had routinely "coerced and threatened advertisers" who took out ads in competing print and broadcast media, thereby becoming so powerful that it had been able to "starve out all other publications" and prevent potential competitors from gaining a foothold. "The proof of existence of such a condition, I submit, is a monopoly," the attorney said. "It is directly contrary to the Sherman Act." The defense's main arguments were succinctly summarized in a two-page in-house memorandum. "Emphasize the difference between hard-hitting salesmanship and anti-trust violations," read one of the eighteen talking points. "Being the only newspaper in a community is not an offense" was another. And again: "The *Star* is a private enterprise which is entitled to seek as much business as possible—it is not a public utility."[20]

Despite its carefully planned counterattack, however, the *Star* was on the defensive from the outset of the trial. A parade of government witnesses—

Star president Roy Roberts (right) and advertising director Emil Sees arrive for their day in court in this rare photo published in January 1955. "We are either right or wrong," Roberts told the paper's employees. "There is no room for consent decrees or compromises."

ninety-one in all, including advertisers, former *Star* solicitors, and past and current competitors—attested the strong-arm treatment meted out by Sees and his staff. Advertisers complained that they had repeatedly been threatened with loss of space or position in the paper unless they toed the line. Many had difficulty getting into the *Star;* others had to buy more ads than they needed; all were forced to sign contracts containing an "equal-space" clause that enjoined them from buying more ads in any competing medium than in the *Star.* These requirements were backed up by rebates, special discounts for heavy advertisers, and preferential extension of credit. Sees mercilessly browbeat his own salesmen, bombarding them with notes demanding to know why so-and-so's ad had run in another publication. "The more you squeeze" an advertiser, one witness heard Sees say, "the more you get out of" him.[21]

The *Journal-Post* was the prosecution's exhibit A. Although Jinkinson eventually admitted he couldn't prove the *Star* had been directly responsible for the Democratic paper's demise in 1942, he skillfully tied it to the government's case as evidence of a long-established pattern of monopolistic conduct.

Whether the *Star* had run its last remaining daily competitor out of business was immaterial, he stated; the evidence clearly showed that it had purchased the *Journal-Post*'s name and assets to prevent a competitor from getting hold of them and immediately raised its own subscription rates. The defense countered that Doherty had purchased the *Journal-Post* with the avowed intention of running the *Star* out of business. The *Star* had been "compelled to use defensive measures, such as combination rates for space and subscriptions, to preserve its own life." The judge listened to the lawyers' sparring with mounting impatience and finally cut it short. "Now why go out here, gentlemen, and dig up all the dead horses in town and try to skin them again?" Even if it could be proved that the *Star* had killed off its competitor, he observed, the statute of limitations had long since expired.[22]

Judge Duncan's folksy interjections and evenhandedness in holding both sides' feet to the fire helped keep a lid on the simmering caldron. At the close of the government's presentation he seemed briefly to side with the *Star*, ruling that combination advertising and subscription rates were not illegal per se absent clear proof of monopolistic intent. However, the trial soon took a less promising turn for the defense. The frustrations the paper's attorneys experienced in presenting their side of the case were illustrated when one of their star witnesses took the stand. Frank Luther Mott, a distinguished journalism historian at the University of Missouri, had been expected to provide crucial evidence about the highly competitive nature of the Kansas City newspaper market. But when the attorneys asked him whether in his opinion a monopoly of news was possible, Judge Duncan barred him from answering, saying that was for the jury to decide. Nor did he allow Mott to testify that the national trend toward newspaper monopolies was due to economic and technological factors rather than criminal intent. When the defense tried to present Mott's scholarly account of the *Journal-Post*'s life and death, the judge again ruled the testimony irrelevant.

Stymied, defense lawyers argued that the *Star* didn't dominate the local market nearly as completely as the government alleged, despite its own promotional boast that it had 96 percent coverage of Kansas City homes. When they attempted to define the market as the twenty-five-county "retail trading zone" used by the Audit Bureau of Circulation, Judge Duncan refused to adopt a definition that would prolong the trial "until Doom's day." They claimed the *Star* faced genuine competition not only from radio and television but from eight other daily newspapers, forty-five weeklies, nine shopping journals, and no fewer than 132 other "publications," including billboards and concert programs. Time after time, the judge sustained Jinkinson's objections.

When a *Star* executive extended the putative list of competitors to skywriting, the courtroom erupted in laughter.[23]

Such moments of levity were, however, few. Roberts took his seat in the courtroom day after day, outwardly impassive but inwardly seething. This wasn't the way it was supposed to be. "The *Star* is Kansas City and Kansas City is the *Star*": that was the mantra the employees had chanted when they bought the paper in 1926, and it had held true ever since. What had gone wrong? What had turned all these people against the paper—against *him*? When Roberts finally took the stand, he proved a weak witness, asking Jinkinson to repeat questions, giving evasive answers, and generally putting up an unconvincing front. The defense had called only sixteen other witnesses, almost all of whom had close ties to the paper and its top managers. Lead attorney Elton Marshall and his colleagues raised so many objections about the admissibility of testimony and evidence that at one point an exasperated Judge Duncan blurted out that if they persisted in that line of defense, "we might just as well begin to think about eating Christmas dinner here."[24]

In the end, the trial lasted twenty-seven days, far fewer than the seventy to eighty the judge had predicted. It might have been over sooner, in the opinion of some, had Roberts listened to reason. At least one member of the defense team believed the *Star* should have pleaded nolo contendere—no contest—in the criminal trial and negotiated a consent decree with the Justice Department. It was obvious to Colvin Peterson that the newspaper had been violating the Sherman Act for many years. But neither he nor his senior colleagues at Watson, Ess would have presumed to propose that Roberts cut a deal with Jinkinson. The publisher, he recalled decades later, was "determined to have his day in court." Nor did the *Star*'s lawyers discuss requesting a change of venue, even though they knew the odds were stacked heavily against them in Kansas City. "We wanted to try it locally," Peterson said. "If we couldn't win in our own town, how could we win somewhere else?"[25]

"And remember," a newspaper editor in a popular novel of the day instructed his correspondent overseas, "you are writing international politics so it can be understood by the Kansas City Milkman. If the Kansas City Milkman can't understand it, the dispatch is badly written."[26]

On February 22, 1955, an all-male, blue-collar jury composed almost entirely of "Kansas City milkmen" found the *Star* and Emil Sees guilty of violating federal antitrust laws. It had taken them four hours and twenty-five minutes to reach a verdict. During the jury selection process, Judge Duncan

had asked the pool of jurors whether any of them was affiliated with "a political group which had been the subject of attack in the public press and had
formed any political prejudice against the newspaper." No one spoke up. Roberts, however, remained convinced that the prosecution was a political vendetta. "Oh, my God!" he groaned when Judge Duncan read out the verdict.[27]

Nelson had frequently boasted that "the *Star* never loses," but this time its
luck seemed to have run out. "We feel low, but will appeal," Sunday editor
Ruby Garnett recorded laconically in his diary.[28] The fines Judge Duncan imposed six months later—$5,000 on the *Star* and $2,500 on Sees—were nominal. Even the million or so dollars the paper had spent on its defense would
have been little enough to preserve its good name. Before the ordeal was over,
fines, court costs, attorneys' fees, and out-of-court settlements would cost the
paper nearly $2 million more. In the late 1940s, when the *Star* had invested
$4 million in a couple of paper mills, the economic outlook for newspapers
looked rosy. Now, suddenly, Roberts and his colleagues felt uneasy, especially
in light of the government's impending civil suit.

Significant as the paper's financial outlay was, the intangible cost of the trial in terms of prestige and goodwill was infinitely greater. Supremely confident of their standing in the court of public opinion, the *Star*'s executives had
suffered a devastating repudiation. Roberts would look back on the trial as "a
sorry, expensive, frustrating, and in some respects, humiliating experience."
Nelson, it was recalled, had refused on principle to answer attacks on his character, reasoning that if his "neighbors" in Kansas City, who knew him, thought
he was "a rascal, a court decision wouldn't alter their opinion."[29] Roberts's fellow citizens had just indicated in the clearest possible way that they considered him a rascal. No matter how the fine print in the government's bill of
particulars read, Roberts, not Sees, was the real target of the public's ire, just
as Nelson had always been.

Angry and hurt, the publisher lashed out on the offensive. In a belligerent
statement published on the *Times*'s front page the morning after the trial ended, Roberts vowed to appeal the verdict and charged that the Justice Department's real objective had been to destroy the *Star*'s successful circulation plan
of thirteen papers a week for one low price. That program, he wrote, had "been
in effect more than half a century" and gave subscribers "the greatest newspaper bargain in the United States—morning, afternoon and Sunday for 40
cents, and, we believe, a good decent paper at that." The government "apparently was more concerned over theoretical competition than economies and
service to the reading public." The *Star* would "never be a willing party to sell-

ing its readers down the river," he declared. "If the highest court says our system of cheap, efficient service is wrong, of course as good citizens we will obey. Until then, we will continue to get out the best paper possible and to give subscribers and advertisers the best service at the lowest price in the country. Above all, we shall continue to strive in every way to aid in the growth and building of this great community, and making it a better place in which to live."[30]

But the ritual appeal to civic pride that had been so effective in 1926 had lost its potency. This time, there would be no rising up en masse to the *Star*'s defense, no ringing testimonials from businessmen and community leaders. Somehow over the past three decades, the organic ties between the newspaper and the city seemed to have weakened, or possibly dissolved. In the eyes of many, the managers had crossed the line between strong leadership and arrogance and, like the robber barons of yore, confused their private interests with the public interest. In so doing, they had shown contempt for the landmark antitrust act that Nelson and his fellow progressives had fought to uphold and strengthen. Like the National Industrial Recovery Act, they seemed to believe, the Sherman Act simply didn't apply to them.

Still hot under the collar, Roberts wrote a revealing personal letter to Eisenhower on May 3. After some preliminary chitchat about his forthcoming second marriage, he segued into the subject that was really on his mind:

> I very much regret the existence of the anti-trust suit against the *Star* has prevented me from keeping as close touch with you as would have been the case otherwise. Probably you have had a surfeit of free advice, anyhow, and you've been lucky to be spared my two bits worth. There were three ways such a suit could have been handled. Fight it out in the paper and on TV. Seek some kind of a settlement along the political route. Handle it at arm's length in a strictly legal fashion.
>
> The honor and integrity of our newspaper, I sincerely feel, is its greatest asset and I didn't have a bit of doubt in reaching the decision that the *Star* should handle this case the latter way so that when the whole unpleasant episode was over the honor of our great institution would be unstained. For that reason, I gave flat orders to all of our people that they must keep out, not talk the case with anyone, including yourself, and let the lawyers handle it. You know and I think everyone around you knows that I have never at any time discussed the anti-trust case with any of you. Sometimes the situation has been tough but we will fight it out ourselves. It is our honor that is at stake. I strictly enforced that rule, even though many senators and political friends volunteered to try to reach an adjustment.

I might as well be frank and say that we received mighty shabby, if not shocking, treatment in some quarters—not that we expected favors but certainly where we had a right to expect fair play. But that is neither here nor there, and certainly nothing to concern you. Until the stigma of what I believe an utterly unjustified verdict has been erased, as I confidently feel it will be on appeal, there can be not even talks for the honor and integrity of our institution is at stake. And I'm going to live long enough to hand the *Star* down unbesmirched.

However, I did want you to know why I have not come to the White House or even written to you more often. I'm not mad at anyone and certainly not sulking. There are sewer rats in our profession as there are vultures in politics who do not hesitate to stoop to unjustified charges of attempted political or friendship pressure. I would not have you subjected to such assumptions nor do I care for them myself. And for that reason I have carefully avoided as far as possible any visits to the White House or contacts that might be misconstrued.

I have done my best in a quiet way, mostly through the paper, to uphold your efforts to the best of my ability and interpret what you are trying to achieve. I think you have made a great President. I feel deeply the outstanding question before the whole world, as well as our nation, is peace and maintenance of peace, but peace with honor. You probably more than anybody else in the world have this passion for peace. For anyone who has sent by his personal orders millions of young men into battle could not help but have seared on conscience and heart what war means. So, despite anti-trust suits and anything else, I am for you 1000 per cent. And I hope when this horrible anti-trust episode is behind, I can be much more useful in my small way.[31]

The president declined to rise to Roberts's clumsily dangled bait. When a White House aide asked if he wanted to talk to anyone about the trial, particularly with regard to "that 'shabby, if not shocking treatment' charge," Eisenhower answered in the negative by blandly congratulating Roberts on his approaching nuptials, without so much as mentioning the controversy.[32] Nor, the official record shows, did he take the matter up with Attorney General Brownell in any of the conversations they had in the months after the trial. Advisedly or otherwise, Eisenhower preserved his "deniability" and belatedly backed off from his association with Roberts. Not until March 1959 would the publisher darken the door of the White House again, as one of hundreds of guests at a state dinner. Nor would Eisenhower return to Kansas City until after he left office.

Although the *Star* supported Ike's reelection in 1956, there were signs that

Roberts's ardor had cooled. In May 1955, around the time he complained to Eisenhower about the trial, the publisher speculated in a public speech that the President might decide not to seek a second term. On the eve of the election, Eisenhower's brother, a vice chairman of the Commerce Trust Company in Kansas City, noted Roberts's apparent lack of enthusiasm to a White House staffer. Arthur Eisenhower reported that he had sat next to the publisher at a dinner and heard Roberts make disparaging remarks about Vice President Richard Nixon.[33]

In the end, there would be no "smoking gun" to prove political interference in Roberts's case on the part of Eisenhower or Brownell, any more than there was proof that Truman had instigated the lawsuit out of spite. But the circumstantial evidence is strong. Roberts and the attorney general were old friends from the first Dewey campaign in 1944, when Brownell had been chairman of the Republican National Committee. As the nation's chief law-enforcement officer, Brownell showed no apparent reluctance to see and be seen with Roberts while the publisher was under criminal indictment. He attended a reception Roberts threw at Washington's Statler Hotel on December 9, 1954, only hours after the *Star*'s president met privately with Eisenhower. Roberts's presence at the White House stag party on December 20 had not gone unnoticed. Moreover, two fellow newspaper publishers and close friends—Paul Block of the *Toledo Blade* and Eugene Pulliam of the *Indianapolis Star*—were invited to the White House four days before the administration dropped its charges against Roberts. The other guests at the stag dinner on January 10, 1955, were Eisenhower, Brownell, Dewey, and current RNC chairman Leonard Hall.

Politics or no politics, and notwithstanding Roberts's indignant protestations of innocence, the paper's conviction came as no surprise to the *Star* reporters who had covered the trial exhaustively from gavel to gavel. Roberts won no popularity contests in the newsroom, and among the paper's rank and file it was widely assumed that he and Sees were both "guilty as hell." Many years after his death, one writer would recall the scotch-swigging CEO as "a man of brutal habits" who was "terribly defined by his pleasure in power." The jury's verdict hadn't diminished that power, but it had diminished the awe that Roberts had heretofore commanded in his staff. One day after the trial, as he was making his customary early-morning rounds of the newsroom, boorishly slapping employees on the back, one nearsighted reporter peered up at Roberts and remarked, "Hi, Boss, I thought you were in jail."[34]

If Jinkinson had had his way, Roberts and Sees both would have been in jail. Instead, Big Roy would never suffer so much as a slap on the wrist from the judicial system for his part in the *Star*'s misdemeanors. Nonetheless, he paid a heavy price, both mentally and physically. In 1955 he was sixty-eight and still looked solid and energetic. Soon his hair would turn snow-white, his choirboy face would be creased with lines and folds, and his beefy frame would start to shrivel up. Before the trial he had looked like a jovial Falstaff; now he was beginning to resemble a battle-scarred Don Quixote. The *Star* had tilted at many windmills in years gone by, but taking on the U.S. government was a different matter. Not since World War I, when Woodrow Wilson and his postmaster general were on the rampage, had the paper faced such a serious existential threat. Then it had been targeted by a hostile Democratic administration. Now it had been hung out to dry by an unresponsive Republican president whom Roberts had been instrumental in putting in office.

In their appeal, the *Star*'s lawyers switched tactics and focused on freedom of the press, an issue they had hardly raised at all during the trial. They attempted to show that the government was seeking to impose unconstitutional restraints on the paper's freedom. The Justice Department, in return, contended that the *Star* had denied freedom to others by monopolizing the dissemination of news and advertising. Roberts went a step farther. In a speech delivered at the University of Kansas in February 1956, he defended newspaper monopolies on principle and argued that publishers in one-newspaper towns were more responsive than ever to their customers. The legal restrictions the Justice Department was seeking to impose on the industry, he hinted, smacked of the tactics employed by totalitarian regimes. In a free-market society, Roberts declared, "prime and first responsibility must always be in the individual ownership of newspapers with the final judgment lodged with the readers."[35] In Roberts's view, it was the public that had passed judgment on the *Journal-Post*. In Jinkinson's eyes, the *Star* had been a far from innocent bystander.

On January 23, 1957, the federal appellate court in St. Louis unanimously upheld the district court's verdict. The *Star*'s attorneys promptly filed another appeal with the Supreme Court, where they may have hoped to receive a more sympathetic hearing. Charles Whittaker, a former partner in the paper's law firm, would be confirmed as an associate justice a few weeks later. Whittaker, however, took no part in the high court's decision not to review the case.

Finally conceding defeat, the *Star*'s counsel signaled to the Justice Department that they were ready to talk. For all intents and purposes, the impending civil antitrust trial promised to be a replay of the criminal trial, with the same evidence, the same legal arguments, and the same cast of characters.

Even Roberts could see that there was nothing to be gained by prolonging the paper's agony. On November 15, 1957, officials signed a consent decree stipulating that the company divest itself of its WDAF radio and television stations, refrain from acquiring publishing or broadcasting interests in the Kansas City area without prior court approval, discontinue its forced combination rates for both advertisers and subscribers, and publicize the decree in its own pages for the next six months.

William Rockhill Nelson's great trust-busting newspaper had become a busted trust.

All of a sudden, it was open season on the *Star*. In the wake of the federal action, forty-nine private suits would be filed by aggrieved competitors, advertisers, and distributors claiming a grand total of $43 million in damages. Roberts had set aside less than a third of that amount, $13 million, in a contingency fund. By the time the last of the suits was settled, in 1964, the company would pay out just $2,237,032 in fines and settlements. All but nine of the disputes would be resolved out of court, thereby avoiding the trebled damages mandatory in antitrust cases. Smalley, the little man who had set the legal avalanche in motion, was quietly bought off for a reported $600,000. His case was settled quickly, even before the consent decree was announced, on condition that the terms remain secret. The *Star* had moved from defiance into damage-limitation mode.

In retrospect, it was clear that resentment against the paper had been building ever since forced combination rates were established in 1903. Roberts's assertion that that policy had never before been challenged was true only in the narrowest legalistic sense, as he was well aware. The "m" word had been flung at the *Star* many times in the past. In 1914, five years after Roberts joined the staff, the *Kansas City Post* filed suit against its competitor, charging that advertisers had been "intimidated and coerced by Mr. Nelson through the columns of *The Star*" and seeking $200,000 in damages. Although the case was dismissed for lack of evidence, the *Post*'s proprietors, Fred Bonfils and Harry Tammen, broached the possibility of suing the *Star* for "unfair competition" with Frank Walsh as late as 1916.[36] Ten years later, Walter Dickey's apparently well-substantiated allegations of circulation padding briefly threatened to derail the employees' purchase of the *Star* and strengthened their resolve to prevent the paper from falling into his hands.

More recent history provided abundant warning as well. As radio became more and more profitable, newspapers like the *Star* fought hard to maintain their privileged market position. The president of a competing station testified at the criminal trial that in the late 1930s, when KCMO applied to the

Federal Communications Commission for an increase in power, then *Star* president Earl McCollum hauled him down to Eighteenth and Grand and threatened to drive KCMO out of business. The Roosevelt administration, which had its own bone to pick with publishers it considered unsympathetic to the New Deal, soon began making noises about clamping down on newspaper-owned radio outlets. In December 1940 FCC chairman James Fly noted in a memo to FDR that newspaper publishers controlled more than 300 of the nation's 825 licensed radio stations. He warned that "the present status of the newspaper industry in many respects approximates a monopoly condition" and proposed to conduct an investigation into "the business practices of newspaper-owned radio stations" aimed at "uncovering instances of unfair competition, discrimination between advertisers, advertising rates based on what the traffic will bear, and denial of facilities to certain groups."[37]

Roosevelt backed off after Fly, an alumnus of the Justice Department's Antitrust Division, advised him that newspaper chains were "prepared to seek the destruction" of the FCC if any "substantial" regulation was imposed on their radio networks. Stalling for time, he appointed newspaper executive Mark Ethridge, past president of the National Association of Broadcasters, head of a commission to study the problem. Not surprisingly, Ethridge concurred in advising the president against picking a fight with the radio industry at a time when all energies should be directed toward fighting Hitler. A few weeks later, Ethridge resigned in a huff when the FCC jumped the gun by issuing a proposed set of new regulations for radio station ownership, with FDR's approval. Presidential adviser James Rowe wasn't sorry to see the newsman go. He regarded Ethridge as a front man for the newspaper publishers and accused him of trying to blackmail FDR by implying that the radio industry would "swing over to the support of the isolationists" if it didn't get its way.[38]

The spat between Fly and Ethridge flared into public view at the NAB's annual convention in May 1941. Roberts, alerted by the *Star's* radio writer that something big was afoot, rushed to St. Louis, learned about the FCC's proposed regulations, and promptly hit the ceiling. Fortified by a couple of stiff drinks, he fired off a hot-tempered letter to the paper's Washington correspondent. Unless the president brought Fly to heel, he warned, "a lot of us who have been trying to give everything we have in us to handling the international situation" would have to "peel off our coats and dig in on this utterly unnecessary domestic war." Two days later he wrote in a similar vein to Wendell Willkie, warning that if it came to an "all-out fight," there was "going to be a lot of dirty linen washed in public." Willkie forwarded the letter to the White House without comment and FDR answered with a retort courteous. "You can tell Roy, if you will, that I have read his letter with care and have given serious consideration to his suggestions." FDR said he had complete confidence in Fly and in any case had no authority to interfere with the work of a congressional commission. He was sure "Roy would be one of the last to propose that I engage in such action."[39]

The crisis soon blew over, but the threat of government regulation, direct or indirect, continued to haunt Roberts after the *Star* branched out into television in 1949. A couple of years later, Truman remonstrated with Fly's successor about the FCC's decision to deny a license for a second television channel in Kansas City. It was "rank discrimination," the president charged, "probably brought about by my good friends at the *Kansas City Star* who are now in complete control of nearly every means of distribution of information."[40] Clearly, divestiture was a major objective in the government's antitrust suit. Although Jinkinson requested that the *Star*'s broadcasting licenses be revoked, the court gave the paper the option of selling its broadcast outlets. Roberts and the other top executives didn't think twice. Their hearts were in print journalism; better writing and more aggressive reporting were the best way to fend off competition from radio and television. Besides, they badly needed cash to meet the obligations they expected to incur in the forthcoming flood of private lawsuits.

Less than two weeks after the court rendered its final judgment, the *Star* disposed of its highly profitable WDAF stations for $7.6 million. One member of its legal team speculated that the paper's managers "thought if they gave in, they would get the government off their back."[41] In coming years, the decision to divest would be criticized as shortsighted. Had the *Star* continued to diversify beyond print journalism, as many other newspapers did, it might have been in a stronger position to weather the economic storms that lay ahead. Roberts was right about one thing, though. By the late 1950s the question of opening Kansas City's newspaper market to effective competition was academic. The *Star*'s monopoly was a fait accompli. Nothing could stop the inexorable trend toward concentration of ownership in the news industry. The government's antitrust squad had slammed the barn door shut after the cows had escaped.

Roberts kept up a brave front throughout the *Star*'s long and excruciatingly public ordeal. In the spring of 1956 he spent six weeks in Europe reporting on economic recovery, cold war tensions, and prospects for world peace. The *Star*'s reputation in the coverage of foreign affairs rested on the kind of thoughtful, interpretive reporting that Haskell had instituted in the twenties.

But Roberts's thirteen-part series relied on general impressions, with little evidence of either in-depth reporting or sustained analysis. The self-styled "country-boy reporter" seemed interested mainly in political and ideological conflicts, Commie bashing, and flag waving. "Getting home possibly makes it in order to go Texas a bit and do a bit of bragging about our own great country," he gushed in his final peroration. "We were coming up New York harbor and the famed Statue of Liberty loomed. Next to me a fellow passenger, tears streaming down his cheeks, said, 'It's all right over there. But my land here, my home is best of all in the world.'"[42]

Such pious platitudes could have come straight out of the mouth of the fictional Mrs. Bridge. Even the average "Kansas City milkman" was more sophisticated than Roberts appeared to give him credit for. In reprinting his European correspondence as a pamphlet, the *Star* may have hoped to buff its tarnished image. Instead, the articles illustrated a marked decline in intellectual, literary, and journalistic standards. Gone were the principled internationalism and boss-busting zeal that had characterized the paper in years past. Under Roberts, the *Star* was once again a "Main Street paper," its values scarcely distinguishable from those of the Chamber of Commerce. The more embattled Roberts was, the more determined he became to prove that the *Star* was a loyal team player. Instead of serving as an independent catalyst for reform, it sought consensus. Instead of shaping public opinion and challenging its readers, it wrote down to them. Slowly but surely, bottom-line journalism "lite" was taking the place of enterprise reporting and informed comment.

In the final analysis, Roberts was more corporate chief than natural insurgent, more J. C. Nichols than William Rockhill Nelson. After all, he had risen to power through the corporate system, sitting on the company's board of directors almost since the beginning, playing his cards skillfully at every juncture, patiently gathering the reins of authority into his own hands. By the late fifties, however, he was no longer the journalistic dynamo who knew Washington inside-out, orchestrated the *Star*'s coverage of vote-fraud scandals, and managed political campaigns in his spare time. Increasingly, he was cut off from Washington, from Kansas City, and, as some thought, from reality. One staff member, shaking his head over Roberts's apparently sincere belief that the *Star* was universally beloved, faulted the publisher for spending too much time at the Kansas City Club "with people sitting around and kissing his ass."[43] Nelson, for all his shortcomings, had never succumbed to the lure of the country club, wrote William Allen White. Pet causes he had in spades, but when push came to shove, he never hesitated to sacrifice one of his sacred cows on the altar of public-service journalism.

To be sure, even if Roberts had been cut out of the same cloth as Nelson, it was manifestly impossible to run a newspaper in the 1950s the way it had been run fifty years earlier. Roberts was hardly the only big-city publisher who found himself groping his way through the brave new world of broadcast news, media conglomerates, and government regulators. The consent decree ensured that the *Star* would have no part in the rapid growth of radio and television, though it would benefit from the supercharged economy of the fifties and sixties, which helped transform newspapers into bigger businesses than ever before. Yet even as newspapers were expanding, *Fortune* magazine observed, profit margins in the industry were shrinking due to steeply rising labor and newsprint costs.

> It is no wonder, therefore, that publishers linger around the countinghouse. In a short period the newspaper "game" has matured into a business—a big, hardheaded business with tough problems in labor and supply—and where it was once easy for a newspaper to net 15 per cent or more on its gross revenues, it takes an effort to make 5 per cent today. Hence the passing of the plunger publisher who blew his opposition off the streets with talent raids and flamboyant editorial safaris. In his place is the prudent publisher. As much as he may love the "game," he is first of all a businessman, as he damn well has to be if he would remain a publisher.[44]

It was equally true that the Kansas City Roberts lorded over in the 1950s was no longer the city in which Nelson had exercised his benevolent "government by newspaper." The overgrown cow town was undergoing a painful and awkward transition to a more diversified economy. Kansas City remained an important freight and distribution center, but the "heart of America" was no longer a major crossroads. Rail passenger traffic fell off precipitately and the old municipal airport, once the very symbol of civic pride and up-to-dateness, was showing signs of age. River commerce, touted by a succession of civic leaders from Nelson to Nichols, became steadily less important after the great flood of 1951. Construction of Eisenhower's interstate highways fueled the explosive growth of suburbs and hastened the decline of the old central city— both, ironically, trends that had their roots in the 1893 parks-and-boulevards plan. The city's racial divide—institutionalized on the *Star*, as in most local businesses—remained as intractable as ever. City government had been "cleaned up," but imported organized crime had filled the vacuum left by the collapse of the home-grown Pendergast machine.

As "Mr. Kansas City," an accolade officially bestowed by the Chamber of Commerce in 1960, Roberts even long past his prime appeared to bestride the "city of the future" like a Colossus. A magazine profile published the year before painted an upbeat picture of a youthful, "pink-faced" seventy-one-year-old in his fiftieth year at the *Star,* "ambling across the big, bright, unpartitioned newsroom like a jovial panda." Declaring he would "rather be a reporter than anything else," Roberts told *Newsweek* he was still putting in six days a week at the office and expected to be carried out feet first. Another news weekly described the publisher as "rumpled and jowly, the very image of a ward politician—a role he loves to play." The reporter noted that a *Star* editorial writer had recently left his "ivory tower" to lead a successful crusade for stricter enforcement of city traffic laws. "Through their public-service crusades," *Time* observed, "the Kansas City papers hope to erase the taint of monopoly." The *Star* had hung up its hair shirt for good, Roberts suggested. "Our job is to be the hair shirt of the community."[45]

Appearances notwithstanding, the past few years had taken their toll on the publisher. One reporter who joined the paper in 1961 perceived Roberts as a "broken man." After a series of stomach ulcers and mild heart attacks, doctors had ordered him to rein in his voracious appetite for food, drink, and tobacco. As a result, he had cut his weight from 300 to around 220 pounds. The paper's circulation was shrinking too, though less dramatically, *Time* reported at the end of 1959. "Together, the *Star* and *Times* have 671,181 subscribers today, down some 40,000 since 1949. Staffers wonder, too, who will take over when Roy Roberts decides to retire. His key editors have worked long years in his shadow; behind him stands no one groomed to take his place."[46]

In fact, Roberts had given the succession considerable thought. Since the early fifties he had been keeping his eye on the staff, "putting some of our men through a testing period," as he told Joseph Pulitzer II. By 1963 he felt ready to step aside—not all the way, but far enough to give some of the fifty-somethings below him on the corporate ladder a taste of real power. As chairman of the board, a new position created especially for him, Roberts moved into a private office on the third floor, a few steps from the room in which federal investigators, a decade earlier, had raked over the *Star*'s past. One of his last acts as company president was to institute a pension plan that paid sixty dollars a month for employees starting at age sixty-five. Minuscule as it was, the income was welcome to the paper's notoriously underpaid workers. Roberts himself had long since provided for his own retirement. Over the past decade alone, despite the company's financial turmoil, he had increased his stockholdings from about 40,000 to more than 130,000 shares, now worth some $4 million.

Departing on a ten-week Pacific cruise that January, Roberts promised that he'd be back soon and "just ooze in the back door to keep an eye on things." This uneasy interregnum lasted until January 1, 1965, when Roberts finally relinquished his command. At seventy-seven, he was well past the mandatory retirement age of sixty-five that the board had recently enacted at his instigation. Many considered his retirement long overdue, not least his soft-spoken successor, Richard Fowler, who had borne the brunt of Roberts's hectoring memos for the past two years. *Time* called it "the end of one-man rule," and when the *Star* celebrated its eighty-fifth anniversary that fall, Big Roy took the opportunity to salute his autocratic role model. "Nelson could be mean as hell," he told a reporter for the magazine. "But he inspired loyalty. He loved a fight, and if there wasn't one going, he would go out and pick one." Roberts had created himself in Nelson's image, from his regal, capricious personality to the corpulence that prevented him from tying his own shoelaces. There was one crucial difference between them, however, Roberts claimed. Baron Bill "ran the *Star* as his personal paper," whereas the paper he was bequeathing to the new regime was "run as the readers' paper."[47]

Fowler, who had been in charge of the editorial page since 1954, had grown up on a farm in western Missouri and joined the *Star* as a reporter in 1930, cutting his teeth on the anti-Pendergast campaign under Roberts's direction. Trim, scholarly-looking, and slightly stooped, he observed the corporate ritual of insisting on continuity of leadership. "Hell," he told reporters, "I was hand-raised by Roy. I don't think I could separate my own ideas from his."[48] But Fowler soon showed that he was a clone of neither Roberts nor Nelson. In 1964, for the first time in nearly seven decades, the *Star* endorsed a Democrat, Lyndon Johnson, for president. Fowler pumped more money into the news operation, beefing up the paper's coverage of the civil rights struggle, the emerging nations of Africa, and innovations in science and technology. In addition to improving salaries and benefits, he took steps to attract younger talent and minorities to the newsroom staff.

Roberts scowled at the sight of his paternalistic edifice being dismantled, piece by piece, and particularly disapproved of Fowler's free-spending ways. But there was no longer anything he could do about it. Nelson had clung to power to his dying breath, unable, finally, to hand his creation over to the men who had served it—and him—so faithfully. Roberts, it seemed, was both

more self-serving and less selfish than Nelson. When he kicked himself upstairs, the new board chairman posted the traditional valedictory letter in the
newsroom. Addressed to his "fellow workers and associates on the *Star*," it
stressed that building the paper was a "team job" for which credit was due
to the entire "*Star* family." With a parting nod to Edward R. Murrow, he
signed off "Good-bye and good luck" before affixing his shaky signature to
the note.[49]

Newspaper of the Future

"The *Star* is just at the foothills of its success. The mountain peaks are ahead." Irwin Kirkwood's words to the staff in 1926, a few days after they assumed ownership, proved prophetic in more ways than one. The paper's greatest days, some of them, did indeed lie ahead. Under the new regime, it would continue to be a notable "champion for justice and human rights." At the same time, Kirkwood called for the employee owners to draw on "latent wells of inspiration and service" in making the *Star* greater than ever. "If we do not feel this thing stirring us and rousing us and broadening our horizons," he warned, "then the new plan of management is foredoomed to failure and it was a grievous mistake to have entered upon a policy of staff control."[1]

Almost exactly fifty years later, on February 15, 1977, Kirkwood's successor, W. W. Baker, signed the death certificate of the Irwin R. Kirkwood Employee Ownership Plan. Capital Cities Communications, a fast-growing New York–based media conglomerate with little experience in newspaper publishing, had made the company's board of directors an offer they couldn't refuse. The $125 million purchase price was more than ten times what Kirkwood and his associates had paid for the paper and roughly twice the company's book value of $62 million. Best of all, the payment would be made in cash, with no strings—at least, no financial ones—attached.

Baker, who didn't relish going down in history as the last president of the independent Kansas City Star Company, consoled himself with the thought that "any form of ownership eventually loses its vitality." But was the staff regime really foredoomed to failure? Was there some fatal flaw in the Kirkwood plan? No one seemed able to put a finger on what precisely had finished off the *Star*'s pathbreaking scheme. Was it want of dedication and idealism on the part of the employees? Lack of foresight, nerve, or just plain competence on the part of management? Was the real cause of death, as Baker and others contended, economic forces beyond anyone's control? Or did the legacy that Nelson bequeathed to his successors harbor the seeds of its own destruction? Had he, as was said of Joseph Pulitzer, forced them "to be dependent on him; to depend on his independence, so that they must automatically have been robbed of any great independence of their own"?[2]

The official post mortems focused on the inherent weaknesses of staff control and the insular, inbred management culture it engendered. It was pointed out that employee ownership, a laudably progressive principle in the abstract, in practice deprived the *Star* of access to capital at a critical time. In the 1970s the company's long-range outlook was deeply problematic. Recent stock offerings had found few takers, suggesting that many employees either regarded the newspaper as a poor investment or lacked confidence in the board. Kirkwood had considered company stock a managerial incentive to reward "conspicuous service"—and, incidentally, deter newsroom employees from unionizing—rather than as a share-the-wealth entitlement.[3] Not until the 1960s did the board abandon the "ritual secrecy" that surrounded the stock-sale program. Moreover, a large percentage of shares were in the hands of retired employees. In 1977–1978 alone, the board estimated it would have to shell out $4 million in buybacks—a stiff price to pay for avoiding a public stock offering and keeping the paper in the *Star* "family."

In the late sixties and early seventies, a combination of factors brought the crisis to a head. Chief among them were the urgent need for new investment in computer technology and other upgrades, an impending bill for bringing the *Star*'s paper mill in Wisconsin into compliance with federal environmental regulations, and the difficulty of distributing the newspaper efficiently throughout the rapidly expanding Kansas City metropolitan area. Despite its healthy balance sheet, these obligations and liabilities hung over the paper's future like a dark cloud. In the eyes of Capital Cities' executives, however, the cloud had a silver lining. The *Star* had always been a healthy money maker. Undercapitalized it might be; it was also an undervalued and underexploited property, ripe for corporate picking.

It was that "counting-room" mentality, some would say, that really drove the nails into the coffin of the Kirkwood plan. After Roy Roberts died in 1967, there was no one left of the original group of directors who had bought into Kirkwood's vision by putting their own cash on the line. When a senior exec-

utive went around after the antitrust trial telling people the *Star* was on the
market, Roberts fired him; his successors, in critics' eyes, had all but hung out
the "for sale" sign. Some argued, debatably, that Nelson had intended the paper to remain a public trust in perpetuity. The board, they said, had been seduced by Capital Cities' record-breaking offer, which amounted to $139 per
share, enough to make fifteen employees instant millionaires and dozens more
rich beyond their wildest dreams. The fact that among the biggest winners
were directors who had lobbied hard for the deal added to the widespread feeling inside the paper that the staff had at long last been sold down the river by
their masters.

Outside the *Star* building, the transaction occasioned strangely little com-
motion or interest, in sharp contrast to the business community's "spontaneous" uprising on the employees' behalf in 1926. "I can't recall getting many
telephone calls or letters from leaders in Kansas City. It was as though they
were spectators watching what was going on," Baker said in 2004.[4] Rumors
about a consortium being formed to keep the paper in local hands came to
naught. Nor was there any public outcry when it was revealed that the son of
the *Star*'s treasurer and financial editor, who worked in the Kansas City office
of E. R. Hutton, would receive a share of the 1 percent broker's commission
for arranging the deal. Together, the treasurer and the other six board members controlled nearly half the company's outstanding stock, leaving the five
hundred rank-and-file shareholders little choice but to rubber-stamp the sale.

Whatever the proximate causes, the *Star* in 1977 was no longer independent, in either name or fact. Ironically, its corporate reincarnation came about
on the eve of the centennial of William Rockhill Nelson's spunky declaration
of journalistic independence. In the midst of the antitrust litigation in the
1950s, the old managers—distracted or possibly abashed—had neglected to
celebrate the paper's seventy-fifth anniversary with the customary pomp.
Capital Cities, however, was not about to let another such opportunity slip by.
A full-dress history of the *Star*, a thorough and thoroughly professional job,
would be published in a special centennial issue in September 1980. The new
masters were happy to tell the whole story, warts and all, not just because it
was a ripping good yarn but because it was history. The *Star* of the future, their
Star, was just at the foothills of success.

As the company's "flagship" newspaper, the *Star* benefited from a sorely
needed infusion of capital and top-level decisiveness. Capital Cities swiftly
sold off the unprofitable paper mill and plant, replaced virtually all the senior
management, and reduced the board of directors to figureheads. In the old

days the directors had conferred informally, as the need arose, in the big open newsroom; now they met only rarely and at the CEO's pleasure. "We don't have meetings where everybody sits down and chats," said the new publisher Capital Cities brought in from Fort Worth, Texas.[5] In exercising the publisher's traditional prerogative over political endorsements and the like, the new head man was behaving exactly like Nelson and Roberts, but with one crucial difference: he was handing down orders from a private office on the third floor, not from a desk in the newsroom.

More realists than idealists, the new breed of corporate executives ran a tight ship. Subsequent sales to Disney (which absorbed Capital Cities in 1996) and Knight Ridder confirmed the *Star*'s value as a gilt-edged corporate asset, a value that bore only a tangential relation to the quality of its journalism. By one estimate, the Star Company in 2006 was worth $750 million, the result, in large part, of economy measures imposed by its successive corporate overlords.[6] In contrast to the employee-owned *Star*, which took pride in never laying anyone off, the new proprietors downsized the news operation with often ruthless efficiency. As editorial policy became increasingly market-driven, the paper had less and less room for in-depth reporting, penetrating analysis, or even the human interest stories that Nelson prized. In its emphasis on "soft" features, lifestyle and consumer-oriented news, celebrities, entertainment, and sports, the new *Star* would have been virtually unrecognizable to its cofounder.

After a brief period of hot-house competition between the "day-side" and "night-side" staffs, the *Star* and *Times* (long billed as "The Morning *Kansas City Star*") were folded together into a single morning publication. As in many other American cities, the once-dominant afternoon paper had fallen victim to readers' changing work schedules and habits. There was no more time, it seemed, for the leisurely, thoughtful commentaries traditionally associated with the newspaper delivered at the end of the day. The editorial page suffered further loss of prestige as the "op-ed" phenomenon caught on, substituting a smorgasbord of opinions and sound-bite polemics for oracular essays so magisterial in tone that editors used to speak of the *Star*'s "foreign policy," almost as if the newspaper were a sovereign state. The protracted time scale of the paper's legendary campaigns for social and political reform bespoke a journalistic philosophy at odds with the quick-turnaround mentality of the modern corporate world.

In any case, by the late twentieth century the *Star*'s influence in either national politics or international affairs was negligible. Locally, it still spoke with authority and its shrunken staff continued to win accolades for special investigations and spot news coverage. But there was little doubt that the paper no longer had the resources, or perhaps the will, to cover even its own community as comprehensively as it once had. Veterans complained that the paper had become so cut off from its immediate environs that many reporters and editors knew little about the city's history and inner workings. Yet corporate executives demonstrated their civic boosterism in other ways, such as building an eye-catching, state-of-the-art, $200 million printing plant on the edge of downtown and opening the *Star*'s pages to news of the city's far-flung neighborhoods and communities.

At the *Star,* as in most other newspaper offices, CEOs no longer aspired to be city bosses or political kingmakers, but rather good corporate citizens. Unlike Nelson and Roberts, they were answerable to higher authority in distant places and considered themselves primarily responsible not for selling more papers or improving the product but for boosting the company's bottom line. Many newsmen grumbled that their leaders had sold out or lost their sense of journalistic values, even when one of their own was sitting in the publisher's chair. They recalled that Nelson and other successful publishers of his generation had been businessmen first and always kept one eye on the balance sheet. For them, however, making money had been essentially a byproduct of printing the news; for their successors, the situation was almost completely reversed.

The cumulative effect of these changes was to magnify what William Allen White long ago identified as the newspaper industry's "innate conservatism."[7] It was no coincidence that press critics in the 1980s and 1990s stepped up their lamentations about the demise of the skeptical, crusading spirit in American newsrooms. Reporters, they charged, had fallen into the trap of complacency and "pack journalism." Lulled by the specter of objectivity, spoon-fed by political spin-masters, and neutralized by editors acting more and more like harried midlevel corporate executives, too many had become "bland purveyors of fact, polite packagers of bureaucratic news." Nelson, even as he raked in profits hand over fist, had boasted that he was no mere "merchant of news." A century on, the news merchants sitting in corporate boardrooms had a very different take on both journalism and business.

The *Star*'s change of ownership in 1977 marked the culmination of the gradual shift from entrepreneurial to corporate culture that had begun at Nelson's death in 1915. In broader journalistic terms, the process was already under way when Henry Haskell joined the paper in 1898 and was substantially complete by the time he died fifty-four years later. The line from Nelson to

Roy Roberts—from the crusading "personal" editors of American journalism's Golden Age to what *Fortune* magazine called the "prudent publishers" of the mid-twentieth century—leads through Haskell's moderate progressivism, consensus politics, and old-fashioned social and economic liberalism. Each in his different way, the three men exemplified the strengths and weaknesses of the journalistic enterprise as it was practiced in the heyday of the American daily newspaper, a period that just happened to coincide with the extraordinarily newsworthy period of history known as the Progressive Era.

It may be, as has been said, that the United States is on the threshold of a new progressive era in the early twenty-first century, with cities and states once again becoming incubators of reform, stalemated politicians groping toward a new consensus, and public-service journalism receiving a new lease on life. Yet for most big-city newspapers the future remains murky at best. Readership for print editions continues to fall, online editions have yet reliably to turn a profit, and ad revenues are stagnant or worse. The profession doesn't lack for talent and idealism, but the organic bonds that historically made many newspapers key players in their local communities have weakened or dissolved. Profit margins in the industry are still roughly twice that of the Standard and Poor 500 companies, but little of that money flows back into newsrooms. Only a few papers are known for consistently plowing profits back into the news operation. Employee ownership is an idea whose time seems to have come and gone. In all but a handful of companies, dividends are paid not to those who make the papers but to stockholders who treat news much as they do any other commodity. One well-regarded paper, the *St. Petersburg Times* in Florida, operates under a trust set up by its last owner, Nelson Poynter. Another, the Boston-based *Christian Science Monitor,* is subsidized by a church. Neither provides a business model that can readily be copied elsewhere.

Modification of the *Star*'s consent decree in 1999, freeing it to buy smaller local newspapers (though not other media outlets) without Justice Department approval, strengthened the paper's competitive position somewhat. But it couldn't rewrite history. Earnest efforts to restore vitality to the industry in recent decades have produced disappointing results. Media conglomerates continue to grow, big fish eating little ones in a relentless fight for the survival of the fittest and fattest. Today, freedom of the press is arguably a less worrisome issue than freedom of information. Concentration of ownership in the newspaper industry remains a red flag for government regulators, despite the current Republican administration's generally permissive attitude toward mergers. In some dozen major cities, formerly competing newspapers survive partly by virtue of congressionally mandated exemptions from antitrust law known as "joint operating agreements," which allow rivals to combine certain business functions while, in theory at least, preserving editorial competition. Vanished are the great newspaper circulation wars of the past, together with the crusades that sustained them.

Pulitzer Inc.'s decision to put the *Post-Dispatch* up for sale in 2004 marked another industry milestone. St. Louis and Kansas City, with their strong traditions of local ownership, eluded the chain juggernaut longer than any other big cities in the country. Joseph Pulitzer's descendants had long fought off the day of reckoning; as Joseph Pulitzer II observed in 1938, "There were never many Wattersons, Bowlses, Nelsons, even in my father's time and there are not many of them today." But once Pulitzer Inc. went public in 1986, its fate was sealed. In 2005 the company was swallowed by Lee Enterprises, a small newspaper chain operating mainly in the Midwest. One can only speculate how differently things might have worked out if Pulitzer's grandson had followed through on his impulse to put in a bid for the *Star* in 1976.[8] In the event, neither he nor other prospective suitors—among them the Times Mirror Company in Los Angeles, the Tribune Company in Chicago, and the Gannett Company—seriously attempted to match Capital Cities' preemptive offer. Since then, Disney has taken over Capital Cities, the Tribune and Times Mirror companies have entered into a rocky corporate marriage, and the once-mighty Knight Ridder name has been consigned to corporate Valhalla.

In this endless round-robin of buy-ins and buy-outs, consolidations and mergers, continuity of leadership, let alone editorial policy, has become an increasingly impossible dream. The *Star* may, in fact, have been luckier than most. In 2006 it was acquired by the McClatchy Company as part of a $6.5 billion deal for Knight Ridder's thirty-two papers. A public company headquartered in Sacramento, California, that traces its roots back to Gold Rush days, McClatchy enjoys an enviable reputation among both journalists and investors. Exuding a bullishness rare among his fellow CEOs, McClatchy's Gary Pruitt says his board viewed the decision to triple the company's newspaper holdings at one stroke as prudent business strategy. Despite declining circulation, readership, and ad revenues, he maintains reports of the industry's imminent demise are exaggerated. "No competitor in local markets has held onto audience as well as newspapers have," he points out. "Others proliferate—more TV channels, more radio stations, infinitely more Web sites—but the number of papers stays steady. While we rarely face direct competition, our competitors see more all the time."[9]

Pruitt argues that well-run newspapers are in a unique position to capitalize on the opportunities presented by emerging technologies. "While it may seem counterintuitive to suppose that a company founded before the advent of electric lights would be a media leader in the age of blogs, podcasts and text messaging, that's exactly what has happened. We certainly have competition from Google and others. But in each of the communities where we compete, almost every newspaper has the largest news staff, largest sales force, biggest audience and greatest share of advertising in its market." McClatchy's success, according to Pruitt, proves that "good journalism is good business." But his definition of journalism extends far beyond anything Nelson or Pulitzer could have imagined. As newspapers morph into diversified media concerns, he says, "we're fast becoming multiplatform, 24/7 news companies—and it's working."[10]

One example of such a futuristic newspaper exists right down the road from Kansas City, in the small state-university town of Lawrence, Kansas. Owned by the Simons family for more than a century, the highly profitable *Lawrence Journal-World* is the very model of an innovative, plugged-in, 24/7 news operation. An early investor in cable technology, the company began publishing on the Internet in 1995. The same reporters cover stories not only for the newspaper's print and online editions but for the company-owned television station as well. The *Journal-World* has long treated its core product as information, a philosophy that has guided its transformation into a combined newspaper, community bulletin board, public-record repository, and interactive Web site. Industry analysts caution that the business strategy of the *Journal-World*, which has a mere twenty thousand subscribers, may be of limited relevance to newspapers in larger markets. Still, one wonders whether the *Star*'s board of directors didn't miss the boat thirty years ago, when they fended off overtures from the Times Mirror Company in part because they feared its chairman would install his friend Dolph Simons as publisher in Kansas City.[11]

The "multiplatform" news company that Simons and Pruitt are working to create is light-years away from the newspaper Irwin Kirkwood foresaw when he told the staff in 1926: "The *Star* of the future, as I vision it, will be an organization fired by an individual zeal and a collective enthusiasm that will beggar all past standards of loyalty and performance."[12] Inside the entrance to the *Star* building at Eighteenth and Grand—a designated historic site in journalism—visitors encounter a poster display tracing the paper's history back to its humble beginnings. If Nelson were to walk through the front doors today, he would have no trouble finding his way to the second-floor newsroom, though he would undoubtedly be taken aback by the ubiquitous computer terminals, subdued lighting, and partitioned cubicles. The newspaper, though many times redesigned, still carries his name on the editorial page.

In other respects, however, the daily *Star* delivered to some 270,000 subscribers today bears little resemblance to the densely packed newssheet of the 1940s, much less the brash "Twilight Twinkler" that burst into the Kansas City skies in 1880. At the start of the twenty-first century, the *Star* is no longer the voice of Middle America, or even of Kansas City. Like newspapers everywhere, it is one of many voices clamoring for attention and patronage amid the cacophony of the Information Age. Perhaps Nelson, Haskell, and Roberts can best be understood as what Michael Janeway calls "information brokers," members of a quasi-official governing class that administered the communications pipeline in what they deemed the public interest. Their power and influence, Janeway argues, derived from long-established networks of local elites that disintegrated in the late twentieth century, much like the cadre of upper-class reformers and journalistic missionaries who provided the impetus for the original progressive movement.[13]

In consequence, the top-down concept of journalism that inspired Nelson to focus on the thirty thousand "best people" in the city has gradually given way to a grassroots philosophy in which "news" is defined as much by the consumer as by the producer. "Big media," writes one student of this phenomenon, "treated the news as a lecture. We told you what the news was. You bought it, or you didn't." According to this observer, the old system "bred complacency and arrogance on our part. It was a gravy train while it lasted, but it was unsustainable. Tomorrow's news reporting and production will be more of a conversation or a seminar. The lines will blur between producers and consumers, changing the role of both in ways we're only beginning to grasp. The communication network itself will be a medium for everyone's voice, not just the few who can afford to buy multimillion-dollar printing presses, launch satellites, or win the government's permission to squat on the public airways."[14]

Flash back a century or more, to a time when journalists like Nelson and White could purchase a press for a few hundred dollars and with it the power to change the world. Can "big-media" companies like McClatchy replicate the blend of rugged individualism and communal values that typified small-town newspapers? Can they embrace the unmediated egalitarianism of blogs and interactive Web sites without sacrificing the authority and sense of high purpose that old-model journalism represented at its best? Can they reconnect with their readers and take their place again "at the heart of the national conversation"? McClatchy's Pruitt believes they can and must. "Self-government," he says, "depends on continuous civic conversation, which in turn depends on people having a common vocabulary. Without a shared sense of what the problems are, there's little hope of finding solutions."[15]

To the new flock of newsroom missionaries, this updated concept of public-service journalism leaves little room for companies that see themselves as mere packagers and purveyors of information or entertainment. "Newspapers" of the future, like those of the not-so-distant past, will go beyond reporting, digesting, and interpreting the news. They will provide a vitally needed forum for exchanging views, defining issues, setting priorities, building consensus, and effecting change, both locally and farther afield. Pulitzer's description of the reporter as the "lookout on the bridge of the ship of state" is as meaningful today as it was a century ago. But for the crusading journalist, he maintained, "almost every reform would fall stillborn. He holds officials to their duty. He exposes secret schemes of plunder. He promotes every hopeful plan of progress. Without him public opinion would be shapeless and dumb. He brings all classes, all professions together, and teaches them to act in concert on the basis of their common citizenship."[16]

Are such lofty ideals hopelessly impractical in our increasingly polarized, globalized, plugged-in and tuned-out society? No more so, surely, than when the first progressive crusaders set out to reconstruct American society from its foundation. Journalism schools like the one Pulitzer founded at Columbia University still turn out legions of journalists no less infused with a sense of mission than twenty-two-year-old Henry Haskell was when he first laid eyes on the industrial squalor of Kansas City's West Bottoms. Few will have the opportunities he did to change the face of a city with parks, boulevards, and residential districts; to help bring down a mighty political machine, install presidents in the White House, lead the country out of isolationism, or enact sweeping social and political reforms. But there will be other crusades, just as momentous and just as rewarding. In Nelson's words, "The only institution whose peculiar privilege, if not obligation, it is to survey the whole field and act for the whole community is the free, progressive, vigorous newspaper, acting with all the intelligence, foresight and courage that its concentrated energies can exert."[17]

ENDNOTES

Abbreviations

Bell William Jackson Bell, "A Historical Study of The Kansas City Star since the Death of William Rockhill Nelson, 1915–1949" (diss., University of Missouri, 1949)

Blackmore Charles P. Blackmore, "Joseph B. Shannon: Political Boss and Twentieth Century 'Jeffersonian'" (diss., Columbia University, 1954)

HJH, "Houn' Dawg" Henry J. Haskell, "Kansas City: Houn' Dawg vs. Art," in Duncan Aikman, ed., *The Taming of the Frontier* (New York: Minton, Balch, 1925)

HJH memoir Henry J. Haskell, untitled memoir (unpaginated TS, n.d.), author's collection

KCS *Kansas City Star*

KCT *Kansas City Times*

McCorkle William Littleton McCorkle, "Nelson's *Star* and Kansas City, 1880–1898" (diss., University of Texas, 1968)

Rogers Charles Elkins Rogers, "William Rockhill Nelson: Independent Editor and Crusading Liberal" (diss., University of Minnesota, 1948)

Rollins Robert J. Rollins, "Roy A. Roberts: Newspaperman-Politician" (thesis, University of Kansas, 1967)

Rytting Lorry Elbon Rytting, "United States of America, et al., v. The Kansas City Star Company, et al.: An Antitrust Case Study" (diss., University of Wisconsin, 1969)

Star history	*"The Kansas City Star": The First 100 Years* (Kansas City: Kansas City Star, 1980)
Stout, *Nelson*	Ralph Stout, "Nelson of 'The Star'" (unpublished account, ca. 1926, that reached the page-proof stage), author's collection
Stout, *Roosevelt*	Ralph Stout, ed., *Roosevelt in the "Kansas City Star": Wartime Editorials by Theodore Roosevelt* (Boston: Houghton Mifflin, 1921)
WAW, *Auto*	*The Autobiography of William Allen White* (New York: Macmillan, 1946)
WAW, "Early"	William Allen White, "An Early Autobiography" (TS, ca. 1927–1928), William Allen White Collection, Emporia State University
WRN	Members of the Staff of the *Kansas City Star, William Rockhill Nelson: The Story of a Man, a Newspaper, and a City* (Cambridge, Mass.: Riverside Press, 1915)

Epigraph: Stanley Walker, *City Editor* (New York: Frederick A. Stokes, 1934), 20. Walker was a legendary city editor of the *New York Herald Tribune*.

Prologue: A Puritan in River City

1. Henry J. Haskell [hereafter, HJH] to Edward B. Haskell, 9 July 1896, Edward B. Haskell Papers, Houghton Library, Harvard University. Citations of these papers will reference either the originals at Harvard or the photocopies at the Hilandar Research Library, Ohio State University, Columbus, according to where the material was consulted.

2. Julian B. Hymer, "As I Remember Kansas City from My Boyhood and Its Townhood Days," Kansas State Historical Society, MS 371.06.

3. Edward Dahlberg, "Kansas City Revisited," in *The Leafless American* ([Sausalito, Calif.]: R. Beacham, 1967), 23; WAW, *Auto,* 205.

4. "Street Scene in Kansas City," *Harper's Weekly,* 7 June 1890: 451–52.

5. HJH memoir; *KCS,* 17 July 1896: 1 and 9 July 1896: 4. Whenever possible, page numbers are given for newspaper citations. This information was not always available, however, for clippings consulted in scrapbooks, correspondence, and other collections.

6. George Creel, *Rebel at Large* (New York: Putnam, 1947), 13–14; HJH memoir.

7. HJH, "Random Thoughts," *KCS,* 21 December 1947; Creel, *Rebel at Large,* 35.

8. HJH to Edward B. Haskell, 30 January 1898, Haskell Papers.

9. *KCS,* 29 February 1898: 1.

10. HJH memoir; George Creel to Roy Roberts, 3 February 1948, Jacob Billikopf Papers, box 5, f. 7, American Jewish Archives; *Star* history, 14.

11. WAW, "Early," chap. 4, p. 25.

12. HJH memoir. To the end of his life, Carter fought unsuccessfully to have his conviction set aside.

13. HJH to his parents, 9 July 1900, author's collection.

14. HJH to his parents, summer 1901, author's collection.

Chapter 1. The Daily W. R. Nelson

Epigraph: "Fifty Years of the Star," *KCS*, 18 September 1930.

1. Julian Street, *Abroad at Home* (New York: Century Co., 1914), 303–4.

2. WAW, *Auto*, 230; William Allen White [henceforth, WAW], "The Man Who Made the 'Star,'" *Collier's* 55 (26 June 1915): 13.

3. *KCS*, 7 December 1893; Oswald Garrison Villard, "The Kansas City *Star*—A Waning Luminary," *Nation* 115 (20 December 1922): 684.

4. Stout, *Nelson*, 235.

5. Reproduced in Carrie Westlake Whitney, *Kansas City, Missouri: Its History and Its People, 1808–1908* (Chicago: S. J. Clarke, 1908), 667.

6. Willis J. Abbot, *Watching the World Go By* (Boston: Little, Brown, 1933), 46–47.

7. *WRN*, 48.

8. Stout, *Nelson*, 250; Joseph Pulitzer, "The College of Journalism," *North American Review* 178 (May 1904): 656, 679; Will Irwin, *The Making of a Reporter* (New York: Putnam, 1942), 165.

9. Charles Dudley Warner, *The American Newspaper* (Boston: J. R. Osgood, 1881), 5; Stout, *Nelson*, 235; Pulitzer, "College of Journalism," 659.

10. William Rockhill Nelson [henceforth, WRN] to Father John Cavanaugh, 13 June 1911, repr. in *Notre Dame Scholastic* 44 (June 1911): 602.

11. *WRN*, 87.

12. Ibid., 13.

13. *KCS*, 13 April 1915, cited in Rogers, 25.

14. *WRN*, 190.

15. Charles Grasty, "The Best Newspaper in America," *World's Work* 18, no. 2 (June 1909): 11730. See also WRN to Samuel J. Tilden, 29 November 1879, Tilden Papers, New York Public Library.

16. *KCS*, 18 September 1880.

17. HJH, "Houn' Dawg," 212.

18. WAW, "Man Who Made the 'Star,'" 13; HJH, "Houn' Dawg," 217.

19. Charles S. Gleed, "The Central City of the West," *Cosmopolitan* 29 (July 1900): 299; HJH, "Houn' Dawg," 217.

20. WAW, "Man Who Made the 'Star,'" 25.

21. Stout, *Nelson*, 248–49.

22. *KCS*, 19 October 1891, cited in McCorkle, 104; Stout, *Nelson*, 234; "Fifty Years of the Star," *KCS*, 18 September 1930.

23. HJH, "Random Thoughts," *KCS*, 9 July 1944; A. B. Macdonald, "William Rockhill Nelson Dead," *Editor and Publisher*, 17 April 1915: 924.

24. Rogers, 7; "Fifty Years of the Star"; Darrell Garwood, *Crossroads of America: The Story of Kansas City* (New York: Norton, 1948), 162.

25. Frank Luther Mott, *American Journalism* (New York: Macmillan, 1941), 471.

26. WRN to William Howard Taft, 18 February 1911, Taft Papers, Library of Congress; Stout, *Nelson*, 105.

27. WAW, "Man Who Made the 'Star,'" 13.

28. *E. W. Howe's Monthly*, February 1915: 2; McCorkle, 523; Rogers, 129.

29. Rogers, 86; Stout, *Nelson*, 22; WRN, "A Word for the Reporter," *University of Missouri Bulletin* 15, no. 20 (July 1914): 5.

30. Icie F. Johnson, *William Rockhill Nelson and "The Kansas City Star"* (Kansas City: Burton, 1935), 183; WRN, "The Reporter as an Editorial Writer," *Quill* 3, no. 1 (Oct 1914): 8.

31. HJH, "The Newspaper as a Personality," *University of Missouri Bulletin*, Journalism Series 1, no. 2 (May 1912): 9; Icie F. Johnson, *Nelson*, 131.

32. Grasty, "Best Newspaper in America," 11729; Irwin, *Making of a Reporter*, 165; WRN, "Word for the Reporter," 7.

33. Charles Austin Bates, ed., *American Journalism from the Practical Side* (New York: Holmes, 1897), 257; *WRN*, 50; Rogers, 304–7.

34. WAW, "Early," chap. 4; WAW, *Auto*, 247.

35. HJH memoir; WAW, "Early," chap. 4.

36. Garwood, *Crossroads of America*, 162.

37. Stout, *Nelson*, 100–101.

38. Arthur Krock to Jacob Billikopf, 30 August 1948, Billikopf Papers, American Jewish Archives; *KCS*, 16 October 1901: 6; WRN to Henry Watterson, 12 February 1913, Watterson Papers, Library of Congress.

39. "The American Newspaper as Seen by Henry Watterson in 1873," *KCS*, 30 March 1908; *New York World*, 2 October 1886, cited in W. A. Swanberg, *Pulitzer* (New York: Scribner, 1967), 96.

40. Walter B. Stevens, "The New Journalism in Missouri," *Missouri Historical Review* 19, no. 2 (1924–1925): 331.

41. "Fifty Years of the Star"; "Who Being Dead Yet Speaketh," *KCS*, 13 April 1916.

42. *Journalist* 7 (16 February 1889): 4, cited in McCorkle, 75; Abbot, *Watching the World Go By*, 79.

43. Bates, *American Journalism*, 256.

44. *Atchison Globe*, 2 March 1897, cited in Calder M. Pickett, *Ed Howe: Country Town Philosopher* (Lawrence: University Press of Kansas, 1968), 188–89.

45. HJH, "Houn' Dawg," 206.

46. Ibid., 219.

47. WAW, "Man Who Made the 'Star,'" 12.

48. Stout, *Nelson*, 176.

49. WAW, *Auto,* 238.

50. *WRN,* 89.

51. *KCS,* 7 March 1890, cited in McCorkle, 531; WAW, *Auto,* 230; *Brann, the Iconoclast* (Waco, Tex.: Herz Brothers, 1911), 2: 96.

52. Sherry Piland, "Henry Van Brunt of the Architectural Firm of Van Brunt and Howe: The Kansas City Years" (thesis, University of Missouri, 1976), 4.

53. Repr. in William A. Coles, ed., *Architecture and Society: Selected Essays of Henry Van Brunt* (Cambridge, Mass.: Harvard University Press, 1969), 307–8.

54. Lyle Dorsett, ed., *The Challenge of the City* (Lexington, Ky., 1968), 76.

Chapter 2. City Beautiful

Epigraph: Charles Moore, *Daniel H. Burnham* (Boston: Houghton Mifflin, 1921), 2: 102.

1. Henry Schott, "A City's Fight for Beauty," *World's Work* 11, no. 4 (February 1906): 7204–5.

2. Ibid.

3. Alfred Henry Lewis, "The Confessions of a Newspaper Man," *Human Life,* August 1906: 7.

4. H. L. Mencken, *Heathen Days* (New York: Knopf, 1943), 109.

5. *WRN,* 35.

6. HJH, "Houn' Dawg," 217.

7. Austin Latchaw, "W. R. Nelson's Model Development, Rockhill, Still Remains Unique," *KCS,* 10 October 1943: 14C.

8. Stout, *Nelson,* 136.

9. Latchaw, "Nelson's Model Development."

10. Lewis, "Confessions," 7.

11. I am obliged to Marilyn Siegel for bringing this transaction to my attention and to Ann McFerrin, archivist of the Kansas City Parks and Recreation Department, for supplying a photocopy of the deed dated 29 May 1891, transferring the Southmoreland property to the town of Westport.

12. Lewis, "Confessions," 8.

13. *KCS,* 17 February 1892.

14. Edwin D. Schutt, "The Saga of the Armour Family in Kansas City, 1870–1900," *Heritage of the Great Plains* 23 (1990): 25–42.

15. "The Packers' Side of It," *New York Times,* 11 September 1889: 1.

16. F. L. Olmsted & Co. to August R. Meyer, 28 April 1892, Frederick Law Olmsted Papers, container 29, f. "Parks: Kansas [City], Mo., 1892," Library of Congress.

17. George Kessler, "On Public Parks at Kansas City" (MS, May 1892), Kessler Papers, box 7, f. 1, Missouri Historical Society.

18. *KCS,* 4 October 1892: 1.

19. *KCS,* 14 October 1892: 1; Erik Larson, *The Devil in the White City* (New York:

Vintage, 2003), 179; *KCT,* 15 October 1892. The *Times* reported that Codman accompanied Olmsted from Chicago, but this was clearly an error, as Codman had already been laid low by the illness that would kill him three months later.

20. *KCS,* 28 March 1893: 1.

21. *Report of the Board of Park and Boulevard Commissioners of Kansas City, Mo., Embracing Recommendations for the Establishment of a Park and Boulevard System for Kansas City, Resolution of October 12, 1893* (Kansas City, 1893).

22. HJH, "Houn' Dawg," 221.

23. "Fifty Years of the Star," *KCS,* 18 September 1930.

24. HJH, "The Star and Kansas City," *KCS,* 4 June 1950.

25. Whitney, *Kansas City, Missouri: Its History and Its People,* 262.

26. George E. Kessler, "The Kansas City Park System and Its Effect on the City Plan," *Good Roads,* 2 June 1917: 324.

27. HJH, "Houn' Dawg," 223.

28. *WRN,* 92, 177; Stout, *Nelson,* 172–73.

29. Charles Cowdrick, "The Robust Beginning and Fateful End of the Western Gallery of Art," *Pitch Weekly,* 29 January 1997: 10–13; Louis W. Shouse, "W. R. Nelson First Gave Art to the Public in 1897," *KCS,* 4 April 1948.

30. Lyle Kennedy, "The House at 420 East 44th Street and William R. Nelson, Real Estate Developer of the Area" (TS, 1976), 17, MS File, Kansas City Public Library.

31. [U. S. Epperson], "As He Knew W. R. Nelson," *KCT,* 27 April 1915: 3.

32. "Laura Nelson-Kirkwood," *KCS,* 28 February 1926: 1; Stout, *Nelson,* 265.

33. *KCS,* 22 April 1900: 4.

34. August Meyer to George Kessler, 27 April 1901, Kessler Papers, box 7.

35. *Olathe Mirror,* n.d., cited in Robert Pearson and Brad Pearson, *The J. C. Nichols Chronicle: The Authorized Story of the Man, His Company, and His Legacy* (Kansas City: Country Club Plaza Press, 1994), 20.

36. James H. McCullough, "He Makes Homes Grow in Waste Places," *American Magazine,* March 1923: 157.

37. *WRN,* 8.

38. Latchaw, "Nelson's Model Development."

39. Lyle Kennedy Papers, f. 18, Western Historical Manuscript Collection, University of Missouri–Kansas City.

40. *Star* history, 19; *WRN,* 94.

41. Latchaw, "Nelson's Model Development."

42. William S. Worley, *J. C. Nichols and the Shaping of Kansas City: Innovation in Planned Residential Communities* (Columbia: University of Missouri Press, 1990), 68–69.

43. "Jesse Clyde Nichols 1880–1950" (TS, n.d.), 29, J. C. Nichols Company Records, Western Historical Manuscript Collection, University of Missouri–Kansas City.

44. Pearson and Pearson, *Nichols Chronicle,* 39.

45. Worley, *Nichols,* 60; A. Theodore Brown and Lyle Dorset, *K.C.: A History of Kansas City, Missouri* (Boulder, Colo.: Pruett, 1978), 174; *Report of the Board of Park and Boulevard Commissioners,* 14.

46. *KCS,* 6 February 1904: 6.

47. HJH, "Houn' Dawg," 224.

48. William S. Worley, "Street Names," www.hydeparkkansascity.retrosites.com.

49. *Kansas City As It Is* (Kansas City: Union Bank Note Co., [1903?]).

50. The extensive correspondence between Kessler [GK] and Nichols [JCN] documents their symbiotic relationship. See, for example, JCN to GK, 3 December 1910, 24 January and 25 November 1914, and 20 May 1915; and GK to JCN, 21 and 24 January 1914, and 7 December 1914, Kessler Papers.

51. JCN to GK, 21 May 1914, Kessler Papers.

52. Mel Scott, *American City Planning since 1890* (Berkeley: University of California Press, 1971), 75; Nichols in *KCS,* 28 April 1913.

53. Giles Carroll Mitchell, *There Is No Limit: Architecture and Sculpture in Kansas City* (Kansas City: Brown-White Co., 1934), 85; Mark H. Rose, "'There Is Less Smoke in the District': J. C. Nichols, Urban Change, and Technological Systems," *Journal of the West* 25 (January–February 1986): 48.

54. On Grasty, Bouton, and Roland Park, see Worley, *Nichols,* 28–36; and Carl H. Nightingale, "The Transnational Contexts of Early Twentieth-Century American Urban Segregation," *Journal of Social History* 39, no. 3 (2006): 58 pars. 13 November 2006 http://www.historycooperative.org/journal/jsh/39.3/nightingale.html.

55. JCN to Seward H. Mott, 17 May 1949, Nichols Company Records, f. 19.

56. See Sherry Lamb Schirmer, *A City Divided: The Racial Landscape of Kansas City, 1900–1960* (Columbia: University of Missouri Press, 2002); and Kevin Fox Gotham, *Race, Real Estate and Uneven Development: The Kansas City Experience, 1900–2000* (Buffalo: State University of New York Press, 2002).

57. D. J. Haff, "Where May Kansas City Negroes Build Homes?" *Citizen's League Bulletin* no. 95 (8 April 1922): 1; Kessler, draft report to Board of Park and Boulevard Commissioners, 1910, Kessler Papers, box 7, f. 8.

58. Scott, *American City Planning,* 108; Kessler, "Kansas City Park System," 324; JCN interviewed in *KCS,* 2 April 1928.

59. *America's Most Beautiful City* (Kansas City: Commercial Club, 1910); *Between Trains in Kansas City* (Kansas City: Lechtman Printing Co., 1913).

60. Rogers, 353.

61. Rogers, 355; Kennedy Papers, f. 18.

62. HJH, "Random Thoughts," *KCS,* 26 June 1949.

63. Jeffrey Spivak, *Union Station Kansas City* (Kansas City: Star Books, 1999), 37; *KCS,* 21 February 1906: 1, cited in William H. Wilson, *The City Beautiful Movement in Kansas City* (Columbia: University of Missouri Press, 1964), 110.

64. *Kansas City Journal,* 21 July 1912, cited in Wilson, *City Beautiful Movement,* 114–15; Gerald A. Motsinger, "The Development of Main Street, Kansas City, Missouri" (thesis, University of Missouri, 1985), 90ff; *Kansas City Post,* 16 December 1914.

Chapter 3. Progressive Decade

Epigraph: WRN to Theodore Roosevelt [henceforth, TR], 7 September 1910, Roosevelt Papers, Library of Congress.

1. *KCS,* 28 December 1930; 1 January 1901: 4. If documentation concerning Nelson's public life is sparse, firsthand evidence of his private life is virtually nonexistent. Even his letters to his daughter, Laura, which Henry J. Haskell consulted at the *Star* as late as the 1950s, seem to have vanished without trace.

2. "Smelting for the World," *KCS,* 7 May 1899: 24.

3. *Kansas City Post,* 27 March 1908.

4. Rick Montgomery and Shirl Kasper, *Kansas City: An American Story* (Kansas City: Star Books, 1999), 149.

5. *WRN,* 207.

6. WAW, "The Two of Us—Boy and Man" (TS, 1930), William Allen White Collection, Emporia State University.

7. Harper Leech and John Charles Carroll, *Armour and His Times* (New York: Appleton-Century, 1938), 292.

8. Stout, *Roosevelt,* xv–xvi.

9. WRN to TR, 27 June 1913, Roosevelt Papers, Library of Congress.

10. TR to WRN, 1 October 1900, Roosevelt Papers, William L. Clements Library, University of Michigan; "A Strenuous Personality," *KCS,* 1 October 1900: 6.

11. "Maggio's Kansas City Record," *New York Times,* 11 September 1901: 2.

12. Rogers, 179–80; Stout, *Roosevelt,* xvii.

13. "30 Days for the Ransom," *KCS,* 28 September 1901: 1; Teresa Carpenter, *The Miss Stone Affair: America's First Modern Hostage Crisis* (New York: Simon and Schuster, 2003), 58.

14. "30 Days"; "Can't Ransom Miss Stone," *KCS,* 29 September 1901: 1; Carpenter, *Miss Stone Affair,* 30.

15. Carpenter, *Miss Stone Affair,* 44; "How Brigands Send Their Mail," *KCS,* 18 October 1901: 1.

16. Edward B. Haskell to J. L. Barton, 20 January 1902, American Board of Commissioners of Foreign Missions Papers, reel 579 (ABC 16.9, 1900–1909), Houghton Library, Harvard University; Edward B. Haskell to Martha Bell Haskell, 22 October 1922, Haskell Family Papers, box A/1, Hilandar Research Library, Ohio State University.

17. Willa Cather, ed., *The Autobiography of S. S. McClure* (Lincoln: University of Nebraska Press, 1997), 241.

18. WRN to Edward Mandel House, 18 March 1914, House Papers, box 83, f. 2842, Yale University Manuscripts and Archives.

19. HJH, "Houn' Dawg," 222; Channing Folsom in *KCT,* 2 March 1940.

20. *KCS,* 22 June 1904, cited in Rogers, 183; Rogers, 186.

21. *KCS,* 9 November 1904, cited in Blackmore, 141.

22. Creel, *Rebel at Large,* 57; *KCT,* 5 July 1906, cited in Rogers, 274–75.

23. *KCS,* 8 April 1909, cited in Blackmore, 156; Willard Grosvenor Bleyer, *Main Currents in the History of American Journalism* (Boston: Houghton Mifflin, 1927), 319.

24. *Appeal to Reason,* 11 November 1905: 1.

25. Eliot Shore, *Talkin' Socialism: J. A. Wayland and the Role of the Press in American Radicalism, 1890–1912* (Lawrence: University Press of Kansas, 1988), 168.

26. *KCT,* 1 April 1905, cited in Rogers, 273–74.

27. Ray Ginger, *The Bending Cross: A Biography of Eugene Victor Debs* (New Brunswick, N.J.: Rutgers University Press, 1949), 252.

28. August Meyer to C. F. Adams, 22 May 1895, Meyer Papers, box 1, f. 2, Colorado Historical Society; "Smelting for the World."

29. Bernard Corrigan, "An Answer to His Critics, Frank Walsh and the Kansas City Star," *National Motorman Conductor* 1, no. 3 (August 1909): 7.

30. William Kittle, "The Making of Public Opinion," *Arena* 41 (1909): 436, 439; "Fifty Years of the Star," *KCS,* 18 September 1930.

31. Denis Brian, *Pulitzer: A Life* (New York: Wiley, 2001), 292.

32. WRN to William Loeb, 20 December 1907, encl. with WRN to William Howard Taft [henceforth, WHT], 23 December 1907, Taft Papers, Library of Congress.

33. WRN to WHT, 16 June 1906, Taft Papers; WRN to TR, 24 August and 22 September 1906, Roosevelt Papers, University of Michigan.

34. WAW, "Two of Us"; WRN to WHT, 16 June 1906, Taft Papers.

35. Stout, *Nelson,* 291; William Loeb to WRN, 6 January 1909, Taft Papers.

36. *Taft and Roosevelt: The Intimate Letters of Archie Butt, Military Aide* (New York: Doubleday, 1930), 135; HJH, "Random Thoughts," *KCS,* 24 February 1952; "The Baron of Kansas City," *Saturday Evening Post,* 26 November 1910: 21.

37. WHT to WRN, 25 December 1907, Taft Papers.

38. WRN to WHT, 17 June 1908, Taft Papers.

39. WRN to WHT, 2 and 21 July 1908, Taft Papers; *Washington Post,* 20 June 1908.

40. Ralph Stout to R. H. Lindsay, ca. June 1908, Taft Papers; *KCS,* 8 August 1908, cited in Rogers, 196; WRN to WHT, 14 July 1908, Taft Papers.

41. Oscar King Davis, *Released for Publication: Some Inside Political History of Theodore Roosevelt and His Times, 1898–1918* (Boston: Houghton Mifflin, 1925), 102; Ray Stannard Baker, *American Chronicle* (New York: Scribner, 1945), 201.

42. WRN to WHT, 3 and 31 August 1908, Taft Papers.

43. WRN to WHT, 11 September 1908, Taft Papers.

44. WHT to WRN, 8 November 1908, Taft Papers; *KCT,* 1 December 1908: 1.

45. Joseph L. Bristow to WRN, 30 August 1909, and Bristow to Fred Trigg, 21 June 1909, Bristow Papers, boxes 20 and 21, Kansas State Historical Society.

46. Stout, *Nelson*, 240–41.

47. *KCS*, 8 March 1908; HJH to Jacob Billikopf, 11 April 1922, Billikopf Papers, American Jewish Archives.

48. *KCT*, 8 November 1907; *Harper's Weekly*, 28 October 1905: 1570.

49. Mary Lou Fenberg, "History of Board of Public Welfare, Kansas City, Missouri, 1910–1918" (diss., Washington University, 1942), 24.

50. Board of Public Welfare, *Report on Housing Conditions . . .* (Kansas City, 1912), 5, cited in Wilson, *City Beautiful Movement*, 128–29; *KCS*, 19 April 1913.

51. Wilson, *City Beautiful Movement*, 123.

52. Jacob Billikopf to William Volker, 8 November 1944, Billikopf Papers, box 30, f. 23; George Creel, "The Power of Purpose: The Illuminating Story of Wm. R. Nelson and The Star," *Advertisers Magazine* 2 (1909), George Creel Papers, box OV4, Library of Congress.

53. Brian, *Pulitzer*, 292.

54. TR to Henry L. Stimson, 9 December 1908, Stimson Papers, reel 17, Yale University Manuscripts and Archives; John Tebbel and Sarah Miles Watts, *The Press and the Presidency* (New York: Oxford University Press, 1985), 345.

55. *KCT*, 16 December 1908.

56. TR to Henry L. Stimson, 10 February 1909, Stimson Papers, reel 17.

57. *New York Times*, 30 October 1911.

58. Stout, *Roosevelt*, xix; Charles Grasty, "The Best Newspaper in America," *World's Work* 18, no. 2 (June 1909): 11730.

59. WRN to WHT, 29 December 1908, and WHT to WRN, 5 January 1909, Taft Papers.

60. WHT to WRN, 23 February 1909, Taft Papers; Joseph Bristow to Fred Trigg, 21 June 1909, and WRN to Bristow, 26 August 1909, Bristow Papers, boxes 20 and 21.

61. *Taft and Roosevelt*, 135.

62. WRN to WAW, 17 August 1909, White Papers, box 2, Library of Congress.

63. *Taft and Roosevelt*, 201–2; *Chicago Tribune*, 19 September 1909.

64. "Baron of Kansas City."

65. WRN to Mabel Boardman, 7 February 1912, Roosevelt Papers, Library of Congress; B. P. Cheney to Charles Sumner Gleed, 18 December 1909, Gleed Papers, box 28, Kansas State Historical Society; *KCS*, 8 January 1910, cited in Rogers, 203.

66. *Washington Post*, 5 August 1910.

67. WRN to TR, 7 April 1910, Roosevelt Papers, Library of Congress.

68. Stout, *Nelson*, 303–4; TR to WRN, 24 August 1910, Roosevelt Papers, University of Michigan.

69. *New York Times*, 1 September 1910; HJH, "Random Thoughts," *KCS*, 16 December 1951.

70. Robert S. La Forte, "Theodore Roosevelt's Osawatomie Speech," *Kansas Historical Quarterly* 32, no. 2 (summer 1966): 187–200.

71. Davis, *Released for Publication*, 215; Herbert S. Hadley, "A Day with Colonel Roosevelt" (TS, October 1910), Hadley Papers, Western Historical Manuscript Collection, University of Missouri–Columbia.

72. WRN to TR, 7 September 1910, Roosevelt Papers, Library of Congress.

73. TR to WRN, 15 September 1910, Roosevelt Papers, University of Michigan.

74. *Chicago Tribune*, 18 November 1910.

75. WAW, *Auto*, 442.

Chapter 4. Insurgents

Epigraph: Ray Stannard Baker, *American Chronicle* (New York: Scribner, 1945), 253. This apothegm has also been attributed to Herbert Hadley; see Peter Clarke Macfarlane, "What Happened to Hadley?" *Metropolitan Magazine* 36, no. 5 (September 1912): 37–39.

1. Henry J. Allen, "What Happened at Chicago" (TS, n.d.), 3, Herbert S. Hadley Papers, Western Historical Manuscript Collection, University of Missouri–Columbia.

2. WAW, *Auto*, 467.

3. Agnes Hadley Haskell Daybooks, 19 June 1912, Western Historical Manuscript Collection, University of Missouri–Columbia.

4. TR to WRN, 28 May 1912, Roosevelt Papers, University of Michigan (original) and Library of Congress (letterbook copy); Allen, "What Happened at Chicago," 8.

5. Herbert S. Hadley, "A Day with Colonel Roosevelt" (TS, October 1910), 4–5, Hadley Papers; Hadley to TR, 16 January 1912, cited in Harlan Hahn, "The Republican Party Convention of 1912 and the Role of Herbert S. Hadley in National Politics," *Missouri Historical Review* 59–60 (1964–1966): 409; Allen, "What Happened at Chicago," 10.

6. Allen, "What Happened at Chicago," 12–13; William T. Miller, "The Progressive Movement in Missouri," *Missouri Historical Review* 22 (1927–1928): 490–91; James Chace, *1912: Wilson, Roosevelt, Taft and Debs: The Election that Changed the Country* (New York: Simon and Schuster, 2004), 118.

7. Stout, *Nelson*, 322.

8. Ibid., 323, 316.

9. WAW, *Auto*, 473, 467; Hadley to TR, 1 December 1917, cited in Hahn, "Republican Party Convention," 422; WRN to TR, 5(?) July 1912, Roosevelt Papers, Library of Congress.

10. WRN to TR, 3 July and 5(?) July 1912, Roosevelt Papers, Library of Congress; *KCT*, 5 July 1912: 1.

11. Stout, *Nelson*, 324–25.

12. WRN to TR, 24 July 1912, Roosevelt Papers, Library of Congress.

13. Herbert Hadley to TR, 18 July 1912, Hadley Papers, f. 343; Hadley to WAW, 14 August 1912, White Papers, box 12.

14. Republican State Press Bureau, release dated 16 March 1912, Charles Nagel Papers, ser. 2, box 62, f. 81, Yale University Manuscripts and Archives.

15. WRN to HJH, 1 September 1911, author's collection.

16. WRN to TR, 22 May 1912, Roosevelt Papers, Library of Congress.

17. WRN to TR, 11 March 1912, Roosevelt Papers, Library of Congress; TR to WRN, 15 March 1912, Roosevelt Papers, University of Michigan (original) and Library of Congress (letterbook copy).

18. WRN to TR, 9 July 1912, Roosevelt Papers, Library of Congress.

19. Miller, "Progressive Movement," 493; *KCT,* 30 July 1912: 1.

20. *Chillicothe Constitution,* 31 July 1912.

21. WRN to TR, 22 May 1912, Roosevelt Papers, Library of Congress; TR to WRN, 28 May 1912, Roosevelt Papers, University of Michigan (original) and Library of Congress (letterbook copy).

22. Haskell waited until after the election to disclose their conversation in a *Star* editorial: *KCS,* 6 November 1912: 8.

23. *KCS,* 5 May 1911: 1.

24. *KCT,* 6 May 1911: 1.

25. WRN to Henry Watterson, 20 May 1911, Watterson Papers, Library of Congress.

26. *New York Sun,* 16 February 1912; *Philadelphia Bulletin* story repr. in *KCT,* 27 February 1912.

27. WRN to TR, 24 July 1912, Roosevelt Papers, Library of Congress; TR to WRN, 30 July 1912, Roosevelt Papers, University of Michigan.

28. Davis, *Released for Publication,* 262. Nelson had an emended version of his letter to Roosevelt posted in the *Star* newsroom as notice of a "permanent assignment" for editors and reporters. Correspondence between the two men broke off—or at least none survives—until after the November election, suggesting that Roosevelt deliberately distanced himself from Nelson in the final three months of the campaign.

29. WAW, *Auto,* 484; HJH, "Nelson, the Editor and the Man," *KCS,* 18 September 1930.

30. Stout, *Nelson,* 324; *New York Times,* 5 August 1912: 1.

31. Chace, *1912,* 165; *KCS,* 7 August 1912; Fred Warren to Eugene Debs, 8 August 1912, in J. Robert Constantine, ed., *Letters of Eugene V. Debs* (Urbana: University of Illinois Press, 1990), 1: 535.

32. *Boston Herald,* 8 August 1912.

33. *KCT,* 9 August 1912.

34. Davis, *Released for Publication,* 327; Page Smith, *America Enters the World* (New York: McGraw-Hill, 1985), 346.

35. Stout, *Nelson,* 326; WRN to Henry Watterson, 18 November 1912, Watterson Papers.

36. Shore, *Talkin' Socialism,* 217; Ginger, *The Bending Cross,* 313.

37. *KCS,* 1 September 1911; *KCT,* 8 September 1911.

38. *KCS,* 23 April 1912.

39. *KCS,* 15 October 1912, cited in Blackmore, 205.

40. Joseph Pulitzer II to Joseph Pulitzer, 3 April 1911, cited in Daniel W. Pfaff, *Joseph Pulitzer II and the "Post-Dispatch"* (University Park: Pennsylvania State University Press, 1991), 121.

41. Charles Grasty, "The Best Newspaper in America," *World's Work* 18, no. 2 (June 1909): 11729; Will Irwin, "The American Newspaper," part 13, "The New Era," *Collier's* 47, no. 16 (8 July 1911): 16.

42. HJH to WAW, 26 November 1930, White Papers; Will Irwin to Inez Haynes Irwin, 11 April 1910, Inez Haynes Irwin and William Irwin Papers, box 5, Beinecke Rare Book and Manuscript Library, Yale University.

43. Garwood, *Crossroads of America,* 248; *WRN,* 157.

44. WRN to Henry Watterson, 12 February 1913, Watterson Papers.

45. Garwood, *Crossroads of America,* 253; William M. Reddig, *Tom's Town: Kansas City and the Pendergast Legend* (Philadelphia: Lippincott, 1947), 75.

46. *Washington Post,* 2 February 1913: 3; *KCS,* 2 February 1913.

47. *KCT,* 3 February 1913; Lucia Slavens to WRN, cited in A. B. Macdonald, "From the Personal Correspondence of William Rockhill Nelson," *KCS,* 14 August 1932.

48. L. V. B. Rucker to Frank Walsh, 26 April 1913, Walsh Papers, box 1, New York Public Library.

49. August Seested to Frank Walsh, 8 July 1913, Walsh Papers, box 1.

50. Street, *Abroad at Home,* 305.

51. *KCT,* 4 October 1913: 1.

52. TR to WRN, 17 June 1913, Roosevelt Papers, University of Michigan (original) and Library of Congress (letterbook copy); WRN to TR, 27 and 28 June 1913, Roosevelt Papers, Library of Congress; WRN to WAW, 28 June 1913, White Papers.

53. Henry J. Allen to WAW, 6 June 1913, White Papers.

54. Edward Mandel House Diaries, p. 28 (28 August 1913), House Papers, Yale University Manuscripts and Archives.

55. House Diaries, p. 256 (25 July 1913); Stout, *Nelson,* 226–27.

56. "One Man's Influence," *KCS,* 7 November 1913; *KCS,* 9 November 1913; Frank Walsh to E. M. House, 10 November 1913, House Papers, box 114, f. 4007; House to Walsh, 15 November 1913, Walsh Papers, box 1.

57. WRN to Walsh, 15 December 1913, Walsh Papers, box 1; *KCS,* 20 and 19 December 1913.

58. WRN to House, 7 January 1914, House Papers, box 83, f. 2842; Stout, *Nelson,* 206.

59. WRN to House, 18 March 1914, and House to WRN, 26 March 1914, House Papers, box 83, f. 2842; Stout, *Nelson*, 205–6.

60. Emma Goldman, *Living My Life* (New York: Knopf, 1931), 2: 585.

61. Dante Barton, "Frank P. Walsh," *Harper's Weekly,* 27 September 1913: 24; George Creel, "Why Industrial War?" *Collier's,* 18 October 1913.

62. Dante Barton to Frank Walsh, 14 December 1913, Walsh Papers, box 1.

63. Smith, *America Enters the World,* 395.

64. Ibid., 396; *KCS,* 17 December 1914.

65. Graham Adams, Jr., *Age of Industrial Violence, 1910–15: The Activities and Findings of the United States Commission on Industrial Relations* (New York: Columbia University Press, 1966), 162ff.

66. Joe Popper, "Frank Walsh: Attorney at Law," *KCS Magazine,* 30 August 1987: 11; Walsh to Dante Barton, 24 May 1915, cited in Adams, *Age of Industrial Violence,* 171.

67. Smith, *America Enters the World,* 400.

68. Mrs. J. Borden Harriman, *From Pinafores to Politics* (New York: Holt, 1923), 139.

69. *KCT,* 27 December 1913; *Kansas City Post,* 27 December 1913 and 5 April 1914; *KCS,* 8 April 1914.

70. *KCS,* 2 July 1914.

71. Jacob Billikopf to Frank Walsh, 2 July 1914, Walsh Papers, box 2; *KCT* and *KCS,* 1–7 July 1914; William B. Henderson to Henry C. Haskell, 1 September 1952, author's collection.

72. *WRN,* 144, 155, 148–49.

73. Stout, *Nelson,* 252–54; *KCS,* 23 August 1914, cited in Rogers, 295; A. B. Macdonald, "From the Personal Correspondence of William Rockhill Nelson," *KCS,* 31 July 1932.

74. WRN to Helen Keller, 29 April 1914, Keller Papers, American Federation for the Blind.

75. Keller speech to Anglo-American Association (TS, ca. 1946), Keller Papers.

76. WRN to Keller, 29 April 1914; Keller letter dated 4 December 1910 published in *Appeal to Reason,* 21 December 1910 and Kansas City *Independent,* 31 December 1910.

77. *KCT,* 7 November 1912: 2; *KCS,* 8 November 1912: 6B; *KCS,* 19 October 1913, cited in Rogers, 249.

78. Isaac Don Levine, *Eyewitness to History* (New York: Hawthorn, 1973), 20–24.

79. *KCS,* 12 and 19 July, 13 and 27 September 1914; Levine, *Eyewitness,* 23.

80. Levine, *Eyewitness,* 23.

81. Davis, *Released for Publication,* 427.

82. Stout, *Nelson,* 329; WRN to Ralph Stout, summer 1914, cited in Macdonald, "Correspondence of Nelson," *KCS,* 31 July 1932; WRN to TR, 16 May 1914, Roosevelt Papers, Library of Congress.

83. TR to WAW, 7 November 1914, TS copy attached to WAW to WRN, 23 November 1914, author's collection.

84. Ibid.

85. HJH to WAW, 24 November 1914, White Papers.

86. *WRN*, 79.

87. *WRN*, 148; *Star* history, 51.

88. Frank Walsh to Jacob Billikopf, 2 January 1914, Walsh Papers, box 2.

89. WRN to HJH, 19 July 1914, author's collection.

90. *WRN*, 155; Icie F. Johnson, *Nelson*, 113.

91. *WRN*, 140–41.

92. Frank Walsh to the *Star*, 13 April 1915, Walsh Papers, box 2.

Chapter 5. Bully Pulpits

Epigraph: HJH, "Houn' Dawg," 214.

1. Stout, *Nelson*, 338; Henry Van Brunt in *KCS*, 10 April 1955: E1.

2. *KCT*, 17 April 1915; *WRN*, 166; *KCT*, 20 April 1915.

3. *KCT*, 26 April 1915: 2.

4. Logan Clendening letter, cited in Rogers, 352. Information about Laura Kirkwood's and Ida Nelson's income, as well as other financial records relating to Nelson's family and businesses, can be found in the Nelson Trust Records housed at the Nelson-Atkins Museum of Art.

5. Bell, 179.

6. *New York Times*, 29 August 1915: 4; Maria Eucharia Meehan, "Frank P. Walsh and the American Labor Movement" (diss., New York University, 1962), 76.

7. Harry Tammen to Frank Walsh, 13 September 1915, Walsh Papers, box 2, New York Public Library.

8. Walsh to Bert St. Clair, 2 November 1915, Walsh Papers, box 2.

9. Ibid.

10. E. M. House to Woodrow Wilson, 8 November 1915, Wilson Papers, Library of Congress.

11. WAW to HJH, 4 January 1916, White Papers, Library of Congress.

12. Walsh to Basil Manley, 6 May 1916, Walsh Papers, box 3; *Reedy's Mirror*, 5 May 1916.

13. J. M. Shook to Walsh, 16 March 1916, Walsh Papers, box 3; J. I. Sheppard to Eugene Debs, 13 July 1916, in Constantine, ed., *Letters of Eugene V. Debs*, 2: 247; Walsh to E. M. House, 15 July 1916, House Papers, box 114a, Yale University Manuscripts and Archives; Harry Tammen to Walsh, 1 July 1916, Walsh Papers, box 3. House's and Debs's responses to Sheppard's overtures, if any, have been lost.

14. *Kansas City Post*, 3 May 1915, cited in Lawrence H. Larsen and Nancy J. Hulston, *Pendergast!* (Columbia: University of Missouri Press, 1997), 55.

15. J. C. Nichols Company promotional booklet, 1916, Nichols Company Scrapbooks, p. 181, Western Historical Manuscript Collection, University of Missouri–Kansas City.

16. WRN to E. M. House, 28 April 1914, House Papers, box 83, f. 2842.

17. *Kansas City Post,* 16 March 1916, cited in Blackmore, 219.

18. *Kansas City Post,* 4 April 1916 and *KCT,* 5 April 1916, cited in Blackmore, 224–25.

19. "An Address on Preparedness in Kansas City," *The Papers of Woodrow Wilson,* ed. Arthur S. Link et al. (Princeton, N.J.: Princeton University Press, 1966–1993), 36: 100–110.

20. WAW, *Auto,* 521.

21. *KCT,* 31 May 1916: 1.

22. WAW, *Auto,* 526–27; Oswald Garrison Villard, *Fighting Years: Memoirs of a Liberal Editor* (New York: Harcourt, Brace, 1940), 316.

23. WAW, *Auto,* 530.

24. *New York Times,* 17 October 1916: 3; WAW to HJH, 27 September 1916, White Papers; WAW, *Auto,* 532; Smith, *America Enters the World,* 497.

25. Arthur Krock to Henry Watterson, 21 April 1915, Watterson Papers, Library of Congress; Stout, *Roosevelt,* xxxvi; *Star* history, 55.

26. HJH to WAW, 1917 (n.d.), White Papers.

27. E. B. Garnett, "Life on the *Star*" (TS, n.d.), 99, 103–4, Kansas City Star Library.

28. HJH, "Houn' Dawg," 218; Emmet Crozier, *American Reporters on the Western Front, 1914–1918* (New York: Oxford University Press, 1959), 202.

29. Stout, *Roosevelt,* xxvii-xxix.

30. Ibid., xxxii. A facsimile of Roosevelt's manuscript is reproduced on p. 2.

31. Ibid., 2–5.

32. "Laura Nelson-Kirkwood," *KCS,* 28 February 1926: 1.

33. HJH to WAW, 5 June 1917, White Papers; E. David Cronon, ed., *The Cabinet Diaries of Josephus Daniels, 1913–1921* (Lincoln: University of Nebraska Press, 1963), 216 (entry for 5 October 1917).

34. Ralph Stout to TR, 15 December 1917, Roosevelt Papers, Library of Congress.

35. Stout, *Roosevelt,* 113, 142.

36. HJH, "Random Thoughts," *KCS,* 1 May 1949.

37. Stout, *Roosevelt,* xxxvi.

38. M. Wright to Hemingway biographer Charles Fenton, 27 April 1952, Fenton Papers, f. 10, Beinecke Rare Book and Manuscript Library, Yale University.

39. HJH to WAW, 26 June 1917, White Papers.

40. Upton Sinclair, *The Brass Check: A Study of American Journalism* (Pasadena, Calif.: The Author, [1919]), 304.

41. Alice Godfrey to Frank Walsh, 30 March 1918, and Sarah Green to Walsh, 13 March 1918, Walsh Papers, box 5.

42. *KCT*, 25 March 1918: 1; *KCS*, 28 March 1918: 10.

43. Henry F. Pringle, *The Life and Times of William Howard Taft* (New York: Farrar and Rinehart, 1939), 917.

44. Maria Eucharia Meehan, "Frank P. Walsh and the American Labor Movement" (diss., New York University, 1962), 96; Pringle, *Taft*, 920; Walsh to Taft, 18 July 1918, Walsh Papers, box 6.

45. William E. Lyons to Walsh, 27 December 1918, Walsh Papers, box 6; Meehan, "Frank P. Walsh," 101.

46. *KCS*, 17 March 1918: 1.

47. *KCT*, 18 March 1918: 1; *KCS*, 20 March 1918: 1S.

48. Sinclair, *Brass Check*, 395; *KCS*, 18 March 1918: 1; *KCT*, 20 March 1918: 1.

49. *KCS*, 23 March 1918; HJH to Orville Wright, 22 November 1918, Wilbur and Orville Wright Papers, box 34, Library of Congress.

50. Rose Pastor Stokes to Jane Mayer Sugar, 1918 (n.d.), Rose Pastor Stokes Papers, ser. I, f. 95A, Yale University Manuscripts and Archives; Lawrence H. Larsen, *Federal Justice in Western Missouri: The Judges, the Cases, the Times* (Columbia: University of Missouri Press, 1994), 139.

51. Testimony quoted from the legal record of Stokes's appeal, Stokes Papers, box 9, f. 12.

52. Arthur Zipser and Pearl Zipser, *Fire and Grace: The Life of Rose Pastor Stokes* (Athens: University of Georgia Press, 1989), 190; Miss J. M. Stricker to TR, 25 May 1918, Roosevelt Papers, Library of Congress.

53. Scott Nearing, *The Debs Decision* (New York: Rand School of Social Science, 1919), 11; Seymour Stedman to Stokes, 29 August 1918, Stokes Papers, ser. I, f. 94; Stokes to Harriet N. Viets, 18 June 1918, Stokes Papers, ser. I, f. 100.

54. Larsen, *Federal Justice*, 124.

55. *Kansas City Post*, 17 March 1918, cited in Michael P. Donnelly, "Capital Crime and Federal Justice in Western Missouri: Four Cases" (thesis, University of Missouri, 2001), 9.

56. Creel, *Rebel at Large*, 153, 148; *War Memoirs of Robert Lansing, Secretary of State* (Indianapolis: Bobbs-Merrill, 1935), 322–24.

57. George Creel, *How We Advertised America* (New York: Arno, 1920), 24; George Juergens, *News from the White House: The Presidential Press Relationship in the Progressive Era* (Chicago: University of Chicago Press, 1981), 150–51.

58. Creel, *Rebel at Large*, 158.

59. Wilson to Thomas Watt Gregory, 24 June 1918, and Gregory to Wilson, ca. 25 June 1918, *Papers of Woodrow Wilson*, 48: 420–24.

60. *New York Times*, 20 June 1918: 1.

61. Stout, *Roosevelt*, xxxix, 149–50.

62. Stout to Kirkwood, 8 May 1918 (quoting Burleson), Theodore Roosevelt Papers, Library of Congress; press release dated 13 May 1918, Albert Burleson Papers, container 20, Library of Congress.

63. Clarence Darrow to Frank Walsh, 12 July 1917, and Walsh to Emma Goldman, 16 July 1917, Walsh Papers, box 4.

64. Walsh to Albert Burleson, 24 July 1917, Walsh Papers, box 4.

65. Haldeman-Julius married a wealthy niece of Jane Addams. His socialist convictions were considerably shallower than his wife's pocketbook. In the early 1920s he abandoned the newspaper and began publishing mass-market "Little Blue Books," becoming the father of paperback publishing in America.

66. Publisher's ad enclosed in B. W. Huebsch to Walsh, 7 June 1918; Walsh to Ruth Barton, 6 June 1918, Walsh Papers, box 5.

67. *New York Call,* 20 July 1918.

68. Stout, *Roosevelt,* 7; *Kansas City Post,* 27 December 1917, cited in Francis F. Shoemaker, *"The Kansas City Post:* Its Founding, Growth, and Decline" (thesis, University of Missouri, 1958), 132; HJH to WAW, 7 February 1918, White Papers.

69. Edward B. Haskell to American Board of Commissioners for Foreign Missions (ABCFM), 29 April 1918, Haskell Family Papers, box A/8; James Barton to Haskell, 9 May 1918, ibid., box A/9, Hilandar Research Library, Ohio State University.

70. Haskell to ABCFM, 29 April 1918.

71. Ibid.

72. Edward B. Haskell to HJH, 6 March 1919, Haskell Family Papers, box A/7; Haskell to Jane Addams, 8 September 1919, ibid., box A/8.

73. *KCS,* 18 September 1930.

74. HJH to Orville Wright, 22 November 1918, Wright Papers; HJH to TR, 9 November 1918, Roosevelt Papers, Library of Congress.

75. Stout, *Roosevelt,* 261–65; HJH to TR, 9 November 1918; Fred Trigg to Henry J. Allen, 16 November 1918, Allen Papers, Library of Congress.

76. John Milton Cooper, Jr., *Breaking the Heart of the World: Woodrow Wilson and the Fight for the League of Nations* (Cambridge: Cambridge University Press, 2001), 170.

77. Stout, *Roosevelt,* 273–74.

78. HJH to TR, 24 December 1918, Roosevelt Papers, Library of Congress; TR to HJH, 28 December 1918, author's collection.

79. HJH to TR, 3 January 1919, Roosevelt Papers, Library of Congress; HJH to Edward B. Haskell, 11 January 1919, Haskell Family Papers, box A/7.

80. HJH to WAW, 26 June 1917, White Papers.

81. Irwin Kirkwood to TR, 7 December 1917, Roosevelt Papers, Library of Congress; Harry Tammen to Frank Walsh, 11 January 1919, Walsh Papers, box 7.

82. Burris Jenkins, *Where My Caravan Has Rested* (Chicago: Willett, Clark, 1939), 198.

83. *Kansas City Post,* 9 January 1919, cited in Shoemaker, *"Kansas City Post,"* 126; Jenkins, *Caravan,* 200.

84. WAW, *Masks in a Pageant* (New York: Macmillan, 1930), 383.

85. James A. Reed, "Race Equality and the League of Nations," speech delivered

to U.S. Senate, 26 May 1919 (Washington, 1919), Reed Papers, box 49, Western Historical Manuscript Collection, University of Missouri–Kansas City.

86. Franklin D. Mitchell, *Embattled Democracy: Missouri Democratic Politics, 1919–1932* (Columbia: University of Missouri Press, 1968), 27; Reddig, *Tom's Town*, 208.

87. Roy Roberts, "A Giant in the Senate," *KCT*, 9 September 1944.

88. "An Address in Convention Hall in Kansas City," *Papers of Woodrow Wilson*, 63: 66–75.

89. Cooper, *Breaking the Heart*, 192; Lee Meriwether, *Jim Reed: "Senatorial Immortal"* (Webster Groves, Mo.: International Mark Twain Society, 1948), 85; Thomas F. Eagleton, "James A. Reed and the League of Nations" (thesis, Amherst College, 1950), 40; Meriwether, *Jim Reed*, 89.

90. Eagleton, "Reed and League of Nations," 40, 14.

91. *Nation*, 26 April 1919, cited in Cooper, *Breaking the Heart*, 85; Edward B. Haskell to HJH, 15 July 1919, Haskell Family Papers, box A/7; WAW, *Masks in a Pageant*, 384.

92. Victor F. Lawson to Ralph Stout, 5 September 1919, Lawson Papers, Outgoing Letters, Regular Series, Newberry Library, Chicago.

Chapter 6. Main Street Paper

Epigraph: Oswald Garrison Villard, "The Kansas City *Star*—A Waning Luminary," *Nation* 115 (20 December 1922): 684.

1. HJH, "Random Thoughts," *KCS*, 20 July 1952; Hermann Hagedorn, *Leonard Wood: A Biography* (New York: Harper, 1931), 2: 360.

2. HJH, "Random Thoughts," 20 July 1952. American playwright David Greenspan has dramatized incidents from Harding's life in a one-man play titled *The Myopia*, including a scene in the famous "smoke-filled room" in which he portrays both Haskell and Kirkwood.

3. Ibid.; Hagedorn, *Leonard Wood*, 363.

4. HJH, "Politics as a Going Concern," *Outlook*, 4 August 1920.

5. WAW to HJH, 3 September 1920, White Papers.

6. WAW, *Auto*, 584, 587, 596.

7. WAW to Ray Stannard Baker, 8 December 1920, in Walter Johnson, ed., *Selected Letters of William Allen White, 1899–1943* (New York: Holt, 1947), 213.

8. HJH to Orville Wright, Sunday [1920], Wilbur and Orville Wright Papers, Library of Congress.

9. WAW to Leonard Wood, 26 December 1919, Wood Papers, Library of Congress.

10. Francis Russell, *The Shadow of Blooming Grove: Warren G. Harding and His Times* (New York: McGraw-Hill, 1968), 313.

11. Jenkins, *Caravan*, 20; WAW, *Auto*, 597.

12. HJH to Orville Wright, 13 November 1920, Wright Papers.

13. *Boston Transcript,* 10 March 1920.

14. *KCS,* 8 January 1920; *Topeka Daily Capital,* 9 January 1920; *Hutchinson Gazette,* 9 January 1920; Maria Eucharia Meehan, "Frank P. Walsh and the American Labor Movement" (diss., New York University, 1962), 110.

15. *KCT,* 19 January 1920; HJH to Jacob Billikopf, Saturday [1920], Billikopf Papers, American Jewish Archives; Lacy Haynes to Henry J. Allen, 10 March 1920, Allen Papers, Kansas State Historical Society.

16. *Los Angeles Times,* 21 July 1922; *Philadelphia North American,* 9 December 1919; WAW, "To an Anxious Friend," *Emporia Gazette,* 27 July 1922, repr. in WAW, *Auto,* 613.

17. WAW to HJH, 27 July 1922, and HJH to WAW, 25 August 1922, White Papers; Edward B. Haskell to Maynard Metcalf, 1 December 1921, Haskell Family Papers, box A/9, Hilandar Research Library, Ohio State University.

18. Joseph Shannon to Frank Walsh, 27 September 1921, cited in Blackmore, 277.

19. HJH to Edward B. Haskell, 16 November 1920, Haskell Family Papers, box A/4; Conrad Mann to Arthur M. Hyde, 5 May 1923, Hyde Papers, Western Historical Manuscript Collection, University of Missouri–Columbia.

20. *Kansas City Post,* 2 November 1921, cited by Francis Shoemaker, *"The Kansas City Post:* Its Founding, Growth, and Decline" (thesis, University of Missouri, 1958), 135.

21. *KCS,* 13 March 1922; *St. Louis Post-Dispatch,* 5 May 1922.

22. Transcript of Walsh speech dated 30 March 1922, Hyde Papers, f. 358; *KCT,* 5 April 1922, cited in Blackmore, 284.

23. HJH to Herbert S. Hadley, June 1922, Hadley Papers, Western Historical Manuscript Collection, University of Missouri–Columbia.

24. Villard, "Waning Luminary."

25. Bill Kovarik, "Dr. North and the Kansas City Milk War," paper presented to the Association for Education in Journalism and Mass Communications, Washington, D.C., August 1989, www.radford.edu/~wkovarik/papers/north.html.

26. Robert H. Ferrell, *Truman and Pendergast* (Columbia: University of Missouri Press, 1999), 11.

27. *KCS,* 2 March 1922: 1.

28. Arthur Warner, "The Pot and the Kettle in Porto Rico," *Nation* 116 (31 January 1923): 117–18.

29. WAW, *Masks in a Pageant* (New York: Macmillan, 1930), 432; WAW to Roy Roberts, 2 July 1931, White Papers.

30. David H. Stratton, "Behind Teapot Dome," *Business History Review* 31, no. 4 (winter 1957): 399–402, concludes that "it seems fairly certain that Albert B. Fall and Teapot Dome had no part in Harding's death." White was never the most reliable of witnesses, but in this case he stuck by his story to the end of his life. At his suggestion, Roy Roberts, then the *Star*'s managing editor, sent his ace investigative reporter, A. B. Macdonald, to Texas to interview Mrs. Fall in 1931. She told him that her meet-

ing with Harding had been purely a social call and that the subject of naval oil leases never came up.

31. Cited in E. Mont Reily, "The Years of Confusion," 456–58, MSS 61, Ohio Historical Society, Columbus.

32. Martha B. Haskell to Edward B. Haskell, 12 November 1922, Haskell Family Papers, box A/1.

33. Reily, "Years of Confusion," 109–10.

34. HJH to Edward B. Haskell, 22 December 1923, Haskell Family Papers, box A/6.

35. Katharine Wright to HJH, 24 May 1923, Katharine Wright Haskell Papers, Western Historical Manuscript Collection, University of Missouri–Kansas City. Katharine's engagement to Haskell prompted Orville to break off relations with his sister. He saw her only one more time, minutes before her death in 1929.

36. HJH to C. W. Alvord, 7 February 1924, Alvord Collection, f. 776, Western Historical Manuscript Collection, University of Missouri–Columbia; Calvin Coolidge to HJH, 13 August 1924, author's collection.

37. Irwin Kirkwood to Edwin Van Valkenburg, 30 July 1924, Van Valkenburg Papers, f. 157, Theodore Roosevelt Collection, Houghton Library, Harvard University; HJH to Jacob Billikopf, 13 August 1924, Billikopf Papers; E. Van Valkenburg to Kirkwood, 5 August 1924, Van Valkenburg Papers, f. 394.

38. Irwin Kirkwood to Arthur M. Hyde, 29 April 1923, Hyde Papers, f. 793; HJH to Edward B. Haskell, 23 December [1922], Haskell Family Papers, box A/4.

39. Reddig, *Tom's Town,* 117; Marjorie M. Beach, *The Mayor's Wife: Crusade in Kansas City* (New York: Vantage, 1935), 150.

40. *KCS,* 25 February 1925, cited in Blackmore, 338.

41. Beach, *Mayor's Wife,* 189.

42. HJH, "What Kind of Pittsburgh Is Kansas City?" *World's Work* 41 (January 1921): 295. See also A. B. Macdonald, "Home District Beautiful," *Ladies' Home Journal* 38 (February 1921): 12–13, 80, 82.

43. Pearson and Pearson, *Nichols Chronicle,* 70.

44. Frederick Lewis Allen, *Only Yesterday* (New York: Harper, 1931), 235; WAW, *Auto,* 632; HJH to WAW, 26 March 1925, White Papers.

45. HJH, "Houn' Dawg."

46. Missouri Association for Criminal Justice, *The Missouri Crime Survey* (New York: Macmillan, 1926), 19, 39, 350, 374.

47. Clara Virginia Townsend, "The Spirit of Kansas City," cited in Donald Bright Oster, "Community Image in the History of Saint Louis and Kansas City" (diss., University of Missouri, 1969), 258.

48. Samuel W. Tait, Jr., "Missouri," *American Mercury* 8, no. 32 (August 1926): 481–88, cited in Oster, "Community Image," 153–54.

49. HJH to Everett Sanders, 26 October 1926, Calvin Coolidge Papers, Library of Congress; *KCS,* 11 November 1926, cited in Jerry L. Wallace, "Calvin Coolidge and

the Liberty Memorial," in *The Real Calvin Coolidge,* Calvin Coolidge Memorial Foundation no. 18 (Plymouth Notch, Vt., 2005), 26.

50. *KCS,* 12 November 1926, cited in Wallace, "Calvin Coolidge," 35.

Chapter 7. Changing of the Guard

Epigraph: Marvin Creager to Jacob Billikopf, 22 February 1947, Billikopf Papers, American Jewish Archives. Creager was a writer and editor for the *Star* before becoming editor of the *Milwaukee Journal.*

1. [George] Wallace, "Confidential Office Report," Nelson Trust Records, RG 80/15, series VII (John E. Wilson Files), box 6, Nelson-Atkins Museum of Art.

2. E. B. Garnett, "Life on the *Star*" (TS, n.d.), 200, Kansas City Star Library.

3. Katharine Wright to HJH, 16 February 1926, Katharine Wright Haskell Papers, Western Historical Manuscript Collection, University of Missouri–Kansas City.

4. Garnett, "Life on the *Star,*" 224.

5. Katharine Wright to HJH, 27 February 1926, 8 May 1925, and 3 March 1926, Katharine Wright Haskell Papers.

6. Garnett, "Life on the *Star,*" 222–23.

7. WAW to HJH, 6 March 1926, White Papers, Library of Congress; Katharine Wright to HJH, 15 March 1926, Katharine Wright Haskell Papers.

8. HJH to WAW, 8 March 1926, White Papers; *Kansas City Post,* 21 June 1926.

9. Notably absent from the list of bidders was William Randolph Hearst. In 1930 Henry Allen told Roy Roberts that Hearst had considered entering the "Kansas City field" but decided against it. There is no evidence that Frank Walsh renewed his bid for the *Star* in 1926.

10. HJH to Jacob Billikopf, 7 December 1947, Billikopf Papers, American Jewish Archives; Katharine Wright to HJH, 4 March and 7 July 1926, Katharine Wright Haskell Papers.

11. Katharine Wright to HJH, 18 February 1926, Katharine Wright Haskell Papers.

12. H. V. Jones to JCN, 24 June 1926, Nelson Trust Records, RG 80/15, series VII (John E. Wilson Files), box 6.

13. *Star* history, 59.

14. HJH to WAW, 6 July 1926, and WAW to Frank Gannett, 10 May 1929, White Papers; Bell, 191; White editorial repr. in *Kansas Citian,* 15 June 1926.

15. HJH to Jacob Billikopf, 15 June 1926, Billikopf Papers; WAW to HJH, 27 March 1926, White Papers.

16. *New York Times,* 13 July 1926. After the sale was announced, Kirkwood's attorney, John E. Wilson, took an affidavit from Nichols, who stated that "while we were taking bids we had no association with any member of the Star Organization except when they came in and put in their bid and there were at least three bids received af-

ter the Star bid." Jim Fisher, one of the authors of the official *Star* history, believes Kirkwood and his associates misled the university trustees, and "flummoxed" potential buyers, by "saying the paper was a wreck when in truth it was in damn good shape" (email to author, 25 November 2003).

17. Conrad Mann to H. V. Jones, 14 July 1926, Nelson Trust Records, RG 80/05, series I, box 3, f. 26; Irwin Kirkwood to E. B. Garnett, 2 August 1926, photocopy supplied by Jim Fisher.

18. Richard Lingeman, *Sinclair Lewis: America's Angry Man* (New York: Random House, 2002), 270.

19. *KCS*, undated clipping in Kansas City Public Library vertical file "Lewis, Sinclair."

20. Sinclair Lewis to H. L. Mencken, 7 February 1926, Mencken Papers, New York Public Library; John C. Moffitt, "A Lion in the Daniels' Den," *McNaught's Monthly* 7, no. 5 (May 1927): 134. Moffitt was an editorial writer for the *Star*.

21. Katharine Wright to HJH, 22 April 1926, Katharine Wright Haskell Papers; Mark Schorer, *Sinclair Lewis: An American Life* (New York: McGraw-Hill, 1961), 453; *KCS*, 14 May 1926.

22. Sinclair Lewis to HJH, 5 April 1926, author's collection; WAW to HJH, 4 July 1927, White Papers.

23. In 1939 Birkhead would move to New York and found the Friends of Democracy to combat indigenous fascists and hate groups. As such, he was deemed worthy of a three-part *New Yorker* profile.

24. Sinclair Lewis Papers, f. 156, Beinecke Rare Book and Manuscript Library, Yale University; Schorer, *Sinclair Lewis*, 454; Eugene Debs to Lewis, 13 May 1926, in Constantine, ed., *Letters of Eugene V. Debs*, 3: 571.

25. E. J. Kahn, Jr., "Democracy's Friend," *New Yorker*, 9 August 1947; *KCS*, 10 March 1927.

26. *KCT*, 10 March 1927; William L. Stidger, "A Preacher Tells the Inside Story," *Dearborn Independent*, 19 March 1927: 22; *KCT*, 11 March 1927.

27. Wright, pastor of Kansas City's Forest Avenue Christian Church at the turn of the century, lived on the same block of Tracy as Henry Haskell's family. The young editorial writer read proofs on Wright's first book, *That Printer of Udell's*.

28. Leland Hazard, *Attorney for the Situation* (Pittsburgh: Carnegie-Mellon University Press, 1975), 16.

29. "A. F. Seested Is New KC Star President," *Editor and Publisher*, 24 September 1927: 4.

30. The university trustees had approached Rogers about evaluating the *Star* before the sale, apparently unaware that he was simultaneously negotiating with Dickey.

31. Report of interview with R. B. Pollard, 15 October 1926, Jason Rogers Papers, box 2, f. 2, Kansas City Public Library.

32. HJH to WAW, 27 January 1927, White Papers.

33. Jason Rogers to C. C. Peters, 20 February 1928, Rogers Papers, box 1, f. 9; Rogers to Walter Dickey, 2 August 1927, Rogers Papers, box 1, f. 7; HJH to Henry C. Haskell, 29 September 1928, author's collection.

34. *New York Times,* 27 May 1928: 74; HJH, "Kansas City: Where the Frontier Lingers," *American Review of Reviews,* June 1928: 616–24; Shaemas O'Sheel, "Kansas City: The Crossroads of the Continent," *New Republic,* 16 May 1928.

35. Schirmer, *A City Divided,* 156; Roy Wilkins, with Tom Matthews, *Standing Fast: The Autobiography of Roy Wilkins* (New York: Viking, 1982), 60; "Just Too Bad—Mencken," *KCS,* 11 June 1928: A10.

36. Abbot, *Watching the World Go By,* 343.

37. HJH to Jacob Billikopf, 22 August 1928, Billikopf Papers; "Report on R[eed]" (TS, 20 April 1918), Herbert Hoover Papers, Pre-Commerce Period, box 13, Hoover Library.

38. Oswald Garrison Villard, *Prophets True and False* (New York: Knopf, 1928), 94; James A. Farley, *Behind the Ballots: The Personal History of a Politician* (New York: Harcourt, Brace, 1938), 86; Meriwether, *Jim Reed: "Senatorial Immortal,"* 185.

39. *KCS,* 8 November 1928, cited in Mitchell, *Embattled Democracy,* 121–22.

40. Hazard, *Attorney for the Situation,* 97, 102.

41. *KCS,* 14 March 1929, cited in Lawrence J. Nelson, *Rumors of Indiscretion: The University of Missouri "Sex Questionnaire" Scandal in the Jazz Age* (Columbia: University of Missouri Press, 2003), 4; Frank J. Adler, *Roots in a Moving Stream: The Centennial History of Congregation B'nai Jehudah of Kansas City, 1870–1970* (Kansas City: The Temple, Congregation B'nai Jehudah, 1972), 163.

42. Nelson, *Rumors of Indiscretion,* 119, 253.

43. Maurice E. Shelby, "John R. Brinkley and the *Kansas City Star,*" *Journal of Broadcasting* 22 (1978): 33; Ernest A. Dewey, "The Kansas City Star and Brinkley," *Debunker,* April 1931: 86.

44. W. G. Clugston, *Rascals in Democracy* (New York: R. R. Smith, 1940), 151.

45. R. Alton Lee, *The Bizarre Careers of John R. Brinkley* (Lexington: University Press of Kentucky, 2002), 131.

46. George Longan to E. B. Garnett, 11 October 1928, photocopy supplied by Jim Fisher.

47. HJH to Edward B. Haskell, 9 April 1929, Haskell Family Papers, box A/7, Hilandar Research Library, Ohio State University; *Wall Street Journal,* 24 September 1929; HJH to Griffith Brewer, 25 September 1929, Charles Gibbs-Smith Papers, Museum of Science and Industry, London.

48. Roy Roberts to Lawrence Richey, 15 February 1929, Herbert Hoover Presidential Papers, Campaign and Transition Period, box 58.

49. [HJH], "An American Comment," London *Times,* 23 March 1932: 15; HJH to Theodore Joslin, 2 May 1932, Hoover Presidential Papers, PSF box 611.

50. Icie F. Johnson, *Nelson,* 176.

51. Roy Roberts to WAW, 17 July 1931, White Papers; Henry L. Doherty to Her-

bert Hoover, 5 September 1931, Hoover Presidential Papers, PPF box 79; Icie F. Johnson, *Nelson*, 176.

52. Icie F. Johnson, *Nelson*, 176–77.

53. "50 Years of The Star," *KCS*, 18 September 1930.

54. Kansas City Chamber of Commerce, *Where These Rocky Bluffs Meet: Including the Story of the Kansas City Ten-Year Plan* (Kansas City: Chamber of Commerce, 1938), 173, 174.

55. *KCS*, 8 September 1929, cited in Maurice M. Milligan, *Missouri Waltz: The Inside Story of the Pendergast Machine by the Man Who Smashed It* (New York: Scribner, 1948), 91.

56. Samuel S. Mayerberg, *Chronicle of an American Crusader* (New York: Block, 1944), 112.

57. *Christian Science Monitor*, 25 October 1928; Bell, 267.

58. *KCS*, 23 March 1930, cited in Blackmore, 356; *KCS*, 13 March 1930, cited in M. N. Munroe, "Political Opposition to Pendergast, 1926–34" (thesis, Georgetown University, 1954), 29.

59. *KCS*, 21 May 1932: 1; Mayerberg, *Chronicle*, 119–20; *KCS*, 18 June 1932.

60. Mayerberg, *Chronicle*, 138–39.

61. *KCS*, 22 March 1933, cited in Munroe, "Political Opposition," 41; *KCT*, 7 June 1932; *KCS*, 7 June 1932, cited in Munroe, "Political Opposition," 68.

62. Memo dated 12 September 1932, Herbert Hoover Presidential Papers, PSF box 660, f. "Kansas City, 1929–1932."

63. Arthur Schlesinger, Jr., *The Crisis of the Old Order* (Boston: Houghton Mifflin, 1957), 376; HJH to WAW, 7 August 1932, White Papers.

64. HJH to WAW, 15 September 1932, White Papers.

65. HJH to WAW, 15 June 1931, White Papers; WAW to Julian Street, 29 September 1931, Street Papers, box 48, f. 11, Firestone Library, Princeton University; *KCS*, 29 January 1932; HJH to Edward B. Haskell, 28 October 1932, Haskell Family Papers, box A/6; *KCT*, 13 December 1931; HJH to WAW, 16 July 1932, White Papers.

66. WAW, "Hail Genius of Hoover," transcript attached to Theodore Joslin to Mrs. Hoover, 25 July 1932, Hoover Presidential Papers, box 993; "'Forgotten Man' not Forgotten," *KCS*, 13 August 1932.

67. *KCS*, 6 and 10 November 1932.

68. *KCS*, 12 November 1932; *New York Times*, 5 February 1933.

69. Richard Norton Smith, *An Uncommon Man: The Triumph of Herbert Hoover* (New York: Simon and Schuster, 1984), 149.

Chapter 8. Tom's Town

Epigraph: Ralph Coghlan, "Boss Pendergast: King of Kansas City, Emperor of Missouri," *Forum and Century*, February 1937: 70.

1. Jerome Beatty, "A Political Boss Talks about His Job," *American Magazine,* February 1933: 31ff.

2. Frank Walsh to Jacob Billikopf, 26 July 1932, Billikopf Papers, American Jewish Archives; T. J. Pendergast to James Farley, 22 November 1932, Farley Papers, Library of Congress.

3. Patrick McClear, "'Gentlemen, Reach for All': Toppling the Pendergast Machine," *Missouri Historical Review* 95 (2000–2001): 46–67.

4. *St. Louis Post-Dispatch,* 1 December 1934: 1; *Missouri Democrat,* 7 December 1934.

5. Bryan Burrough, *Public Enemies: America's Greatest Crime Wave and the Birth of the FBI, 1933–34* (New York: Penguin, 2004), 58.

6. "Missouri's Honor Awards—1933," *University of Missouri Bulletin* 34, no. 25 (1 September 1933): 13.

7. *KCS,* 27 November and 4 December 1932.

8. *New York Times,* 22 February 1933: 31.

9. HJH to Raymond Moley, 13 March 1933, Moley Papers, box 71, f. 4, Hoover Institution Archives, Stanford, Calif.; WAW to Roy Roberts, 3 May 1933, and WAW to Harold Ickes, 23 May 1933, White Papers, Library of Congress.

10. HJH to Ernest H. Wilkins, 18 February 1934, Oberlin College Archives.

11. *KCS,* 13 August 1933, cited in Dilip Sengupta, "A Study of the Editorial Policies of the New York *Times,* Kansas City *Star,* and the St. Louis *Post-Dispatch* with Regard to the NRA and AAA" (thesis, University of Missouri, 1938); HJH to Raymond Moley, 13 March 1933.

12. HJH, "Random Thoughts," *KCS,* 31 December 1944.

13. *KCS,* 28 July 1933: 1; 30 July 1933: 6D.

14. HJH, "The Nazi Revolution—Whither Bound?" *Oberlin Alumni Magazine,* November 1933: 38–40.

15. *KCS,* 12–28 July 1933; HJH, "Nazi Revolution."

16. *Kansas City Jewish Chronicle,* 15 September 1933: 1; HJH to Jacob Billikopf, 10 September 1933, Billikopf Papers; copy of Billikopf memo attached to Billikopf to Walter Lippmann, 13 October 1933, Lippmann Papers, box 56, f. 224, Yale University Manuscripts and Archives.

17. HJH to Billikopf, 10 September 1933; *KCS,* 15 July 1933.

18. O. G. Villard to HJH, 15 September 1933, author's collection; Charles Nagel to HJH, 19 October 1933, Nagel Papers, series I, box 46, f. 545, Yale University Manuscripts and Archives; HJH to Billikopf, 10 September 1933.

19. *KCS,* 2 March 1934, cited in Larsen and Hulston, *Pendergast!* 87; see correspondence in J. C. Nichols Company Records, box 23, f. "McElroy, H. F.," Western Historical Manuscript Collection, University of Missouri–Kansas City.

20. *KCT,* 5 December 1932.

21. Robert B. Dishman, "Machine Politics—Kansas City Model" (thesis, University of Missouri, 1940), 62.

22. H. F. McElroy to Harry Hopkins, 23 October 1933, Bryce Smith Papers, box 9, f. 160, Kansas City Museum Archives; *KCS,* 25 March 1934.

23. Private File, 1918–76, James A. Farley Papers, Library of Congress; Farley to Louis Howe, 14 December 1934, Franklin D. Roosevelt Presidential Papers, PPF 3368, Roosevelt Library.

24. *KCS,* 7 and 9 December 1934.

25. Hazard, *Attorney for the Situation,* 120.

26. *KCT,* 21 March 1934, cited in A. Theodore Brown, *The Politics of Reform: Kansas City's Municipal Government, 1925–1950* (Kansas City: Community Studies, 1958), 114.

27. *KCS,* 2 March 1934.

28. Jim Fisher interview, 3 April 2004.

29. Frank Walsh to Jacob Billikopf, 27 July 1934, Billikopf Papers; Blackmore, 449.

30. Blackmore, 455; Henry C. Haskell, Jr., and Richard B. Fowler, *City of the Future* (Kansas City: Frank Glenn, 1950), 146–47.

31. Alfred Steinberg, *The Man from Missouri: The Life and Times of Harry S. Truman* (New York: Putnam, 1962), 107–8; Ferrell, *Truman and Pendergast,* 18.

32. Reddig, *Tom's Town,* 219; *St. Louis Post-Dispatch,* 9 December 1934: 2B.

33. Garwood, *Crossroads of America,* 312.

34. *KCS,* 2 April 1935: 1.

35. HJH to Jacob Billikopf, 21 August 1935, Billikopf Papers; William Dodd, Jr., and Martha Dodd, eds., *Ambassador Dodd's Diary, 1933–38* (New York: Harcourt, Brace, 1941), 261 (entry of 23 July 1935).

36. HJH to WAW, 1935 [n.d.], White Papers.

37. WAW to James Farley, 7 September 1935, Farley Papers; *KCS,* 31 March 1935:1.

38. "The Kansas Gang," *American Magazine,* October 1936: 17.

39. "The Landon Boom," *Fortune,* March 1936: 79, 119.

40. Ibid., 79; *New York Times,* 11 December 1935: 6.

41. "Landon Boom," 79; W. T. Kemper to James Farley, 18 January 1936, Farley Papers; Stephen Early memo, Franklin D. Roosevelt Presidential Papers, PPF 3368.

42. *Christian Science Monitor,* 3 February 1936: 18; "Landon Boom," 76; *Time,* 18 May 1936; WAW to Lacy Haynes, 27 February 1936, Haynes Collection, Kansas State Historical Society.

43. Richard B. Fowler, *Deeds not Deficits: The Story of Alfred M. Landon* (Kansas City: Punton Printing Co., 1936), 56–57; "Landon Boom," 77; *Time,* 18 May 1936.

44. HJH, "Missouri Democratic, Unless . . . ," *Review of Reviews* 93 (April 1936): 54; HJH to WAW, 12 April 1936, and WAW to O. G. Villard 7 April 1936, White Papers.

45. *Time,* 18 May 1936; HJH to WAW, 28 April 1936, and WAW to HJH and Roy Roberts, 29 April 1936, White Papers; WAW, *What It's All About* (New York: Macmillan, 1936).

46. James Farley, Private File, diary entry for 20 April 1936, Farley Papers.

47. Geoffrey Kabaservice, *Guardians: Kingman Brewster, His Circle, and the Rise of the Liberal Establishment* (New York: Holt, 2004), 29; O. G. Villard to Franklin D. Roosevelt, 16 June 1936, Roosevelt Presidential Papers, PPF 2178; Donald R. McCoy, *Landon of Kansas* (Lincoln: University of Nebraska Press, 1966), 236.

48. HJH to Alfred Landon, 15 June 1936, Landon Papers, box 45, Kansas State Historical Society; *Christian Science Monitor,* 12 June 1936: 4; HJH to Arthur Krock, 8 July 1936, Krock Papers, Seeley G. Mudd Manuscript Library, Princeton University.

49. H. L. Mencken statement attached to Dorothy Russell to Mencken, 15 September 1936; Mencken to HJH, 16 October 1936, Mencken Papers, New York Public Library; HJH to WAW, 22 September 1936, White Papers; Meriwether, *Jim Reed: "Senatorial Immortal,"* 247.

50. HJH to James Warburg, 10 October 1936, enclosed with HJH to Walter Lippmann, 10 October 1936, Lippmann Papers, Yale University Manuscripts and Archives.

51. Walter Lippmann to HJH, 13 October 1936, Lippmann Papers; HJH to WAW, 22 September 1936, White Papers.

52. White to Roy Roberts, 14 October 1936, White Papers.

53. Richard Norton Smith, *Thomas E. Dewey and His Times* (New York: Simon and Schuster, 1982), 219.

54. HJH to WAW, 4 November 1936, White Papers; James Farley, Private File, diary entry for 16 January 1937, Farley Papers.

55. JCN to Alfred M. Landon, 5 November 1936, Landon Papers; HJH to WAW, 2 November 1936, White Papers; Rollins, 50; James Farley, Private File, diary entry for 16 January 1937, Farley Papers.

56. *KCS,* 1 November 1936; Frank Walsh to T. J. Pendergast, 9 October 1936, cited in Blackmore, 449.

57. Milligan, *Missouri Waltz,* 150.

58. *St. Louis Post-Dispatch,* 6 June 1937.

59. HJH to WAW, 19 March 1937, White Papers.

60. HJH to Newton Baker, 1 June 1937, Baker Papers, box 113, Library of Congress; "America and Britain," *KCS,* 30 May 1937: 8D.

61. Newton Baker to HJH, 3 June 1937, author's collection.

62. Hugh O'Connor, "'Right to Work' Hit in Institute Talks," *New York Times,* 2 September 1937: 22.

63. HJH, "The New Deal in Old Rome," *KCS,* 31 October 1937: C1.

64. William Denman to HJH, 13 November 1937, author's collection.

65. "Machine Defends 'Night Life,'" *Citizens' League Bulletin,* 26 February 1938: 460.

66. *KCS,* 4 March 1938; James Farley, Private File, diary entry for 30 March 1938, Farley Papers; Reddig, *Tom's Town,* 304.

67. Kansas City Chamber of Commerce, *Where These Rocky Bluffs Meet.*

68. Reddig, *Tom's Town,* 327.

69. *Complete Presidential Conferences of Franklin D. Roosevelt* (New York: Da Capo, 1972), 13: 264–65; *KCT,* 15 June 1965.

70. Steinberg, *Man from Missouri,* 164; Hazard, *Attorney for the Situation,* 86; HJH to Lloyd Stark, 23 May 1939, Stark Papers, Western Historical Manuscript Collection, University of Missouri–Columbia; *KCS,* 20 June 1939.

71. HJH to Jacob Billikopf, 6 June 1939, Billikopf Papers; Charles A. Fecher, ed., *The Diary of H. L. Mencken* (New York: Knopf, 1989), 121–22 (entry for 21 April 1939).

72. WAW to O. G. Villard, 2 October 1942, Villard Papers, Houghton Library, Harvard University.

73. Garwood, *Crossroads of America,* 310.

74. HJH author's summary, 28 December 1938, Alfred A. Knopf Inc. Records, New York Public Library; Mencken in *Baltimore Sun,* 30 May 1939; Woodcock in *Wall Street Journal,* 17 May 1939.

75. White in *KCS,* 11 May 1939; HJH, *The New Deal in Old Rome: How Government in the Ancient World Tried to Deal with Modern Problems* (New York: Knopf, 1939), 234–35.

76. HJH to Alfred Knopf, 20 June 1939, Knopf Records; *Editor and Publisher,* 8 July 1939: 5; HJH to Thomas W. Lamont, 10 August 1939, Lamont Papers, Baker Library, Harvard Business School; *Le Petit Parisien,* 22 July 1939.

77. HJH to Jacob Billikopf, 1 September 1939, Billikopf Papers.

78. John Lofflin, "Burke, Pendergast, and J. C. Nichols," *Corporate Report Kansas City,* August 1981: 37; Milligan, *Missouri Waltz,* 199.

Chapter 9. Voice of Middle America

Epigraph: Eric Goldman, *The Crucial Decade—and After, 1945–1960* (New York: Vintage, 1960), 116.

1. Evan S. Connell, *Mrs. Bridge* (New York: Viking, 1959), 170.

2. *Editor and Publisher,* 8 July 1939: 5.

3. Garwood, *Crossroads of America,* 294.

4. Haskell and Fowler, *City of the Future,* 161; HJH to WAW, 15 May 1941, White Papers, Library of Congress.

5. Stout, *Nelson,* 176; *Editor and Publisher,* 8 July 1939: 5; "A Great Newspaper Builds a Great Art Museum," *Life,* October 1939: 52.

6. *National Real Estate Journal,* February 1939.

7. *Kansas City Journal-Post,* 3 January 1942.

8. Stephen Early to Franklin D. Roosevelt, 2 July 1940, and FDR to Early, 3 July 1940, Stephen T. Early Papers, box 15, Roosevelt Library.

9. Steve Neal, *Dark Horse: A Biography of Wendell Willkie* (Garden City, N.Y.: Doubleday, 1984), 307.

10. Frank Murphy to HJH, 1 January 1940, author's collection; Raymond Moley to HJH, 4 May 1940, Moley Papers, box 22, Hoover Institution Archives, Stanford, Calif.; *Christian Science Monitor,* 24 May 1940: 3.

11. "Summary of Duke Shoop's memo on Dewey cases in New York," HJH to Alfred M. Landon, n.d. [1940], Landon Papers, box 98, Kansas State Historical Society.

12. HJH to Landon, 13 June 1940, Landon Papers, box 98; *KCS,* 28 June 1940, cited in Rollins, 54; WAW, "Memorandum for the Honorable Henry L. Stimson," 1 May 1940, Stimson Papers, Yale University Manuscripts and Archives.

13. "The Knox-Stimson Move," *KCS,* 21 June 1940.

14. TSS of speeches in Wendell Willkie Presidential Campaign Papers, box 1, Yale University Manuscripts and Archives.

15. Agnes Hadley Haskell Daybooks, entry for 5 November 1940, Western Historical Manuscript Collection, University of Missouri–Columbia.

16. Roy Roberts to WAW, 25 February 1941, White Papers.

17. Walter Johnson, *The Battle against Isolation* (Chicago: University of Chicago Press, 1944), 192; WAW to "Star Kansas City Mo Nite Press Collect," n.d. [1940], White Collection, Emporia State University.

18. HJH to WAW, 17 April 1941, White Papers; Roy Roberts to Wendell Willkie, 17 May 1941, Willkie Papers, Lilly Library, Indiana University–Bloomington.

19. HJH to Alfred M. Landon, 18 July 1941, Landon Papers, box 111; HJH to WAW, 8 July 1941, and WAW to HJH, 15 August 1941, White Papers.

20. HJH to WAW, 8 December 1941, 25 and 11 February 1942, White Papers.

21. HJH to H. L. Mencken, 1 May 1942, Mencken Papers, New York Public Library; HJH, *This Was Cicero: Modern Politics in a Roman Toga* (New York: Knopf, 1942), 5, iv.

22. Alfred M. Landon to HJH, 3 November 1942, Landon Papers, box 111; HJH to Jacob Billikopf, 5 January 1943, Billikopf Papers, American Jewish Archives; Mark Ethridge memo, 19 October 1942, Franklin D. Roosevelt Presidential Papers, POF 4403, box 3.

23. Longan letter repr. in *Newsweek,* 20 April 1942: 70; HJH to Charles E. Rogers, 17 March 1948, cited in Rogers, 115.

24. Roy Roberts to Herbert Hoover, 8 June 1942, Herbert Hoover Papers, Post-Presidential Personal File, box 192, Hoover Library.

25. Roy Roberts, "Report from the Home Front," in American Council on Foreign Affairs, *Journalism in Wartime* (Washington, D.C., 1943), 10; *Christian Science Monitor,* 9 July 1943: 7.

26. W. W. Baker interview, 12 April 2004.

27. John Morton Blum, ed., *The Price of Vision: The Diary of Henry A. Wallace, 1942–1946* (Boston: Houghton Mifflin, 1973), 187 (entry for 11 February 1943); "What's Wrong with the Home Front?" *Look,* 1943 [n.d.], photostatic copy in author's collection.

28. Arthur Krock to HJH, 11 May 1944, Krock Papers, Seeley G. Mudd Manuscript Library, Princeton University; HJH to Jacob Billikopf, 13 May 1944, Billikopf Papers.

29. Paul I. Wellman, "Periscope on the World Front," *KCS,* 7 May 1944: C1.

30. WAW to O. G. Villard, 2 October 1942, Villard Papers, Houghton Library, Harvard University.

31. HJH, "Delivered at funeral of Wm. Allen White" (TS, n.d.), author's collection; repr. in *Congressional Record* 90, no. 25 (9 February 1944): 1455–56.

32. WAW to HJH, 12 July 1943, and HJH to WAW, 7 August 1943, White Papers.

33. Tom L. Evans Oral History Interview, Harry S. Truman Library; Reddig, *Tom's Town,* 383.

34. Lacy Haynes to Theodore C. Alford, 9 October 1944, Haynes Collection, Kansas State Historical Society.

35. HJH, *This Was Cicero,* 5; HJH to Jacob Billikopf, 30 March 1945, Billikopf Papers.

36. HJH to Billikopf, 30 March 1945; HJH to Thomas W. Lamont, 11 May 1944, Lamont Papers, Baker Library, Harvard Business School; HJH, "How the Germans Got That Way" (TS, 27 April 1943), author's collection; HJH to Dorothy Thompson, 4 January 1944, Thompson Papers, Arents Research Library, Syracuse University.

37. Rollins, 62; Steinberg, *Man from Missouri,* 238; HJH to Billikopf, 24 August 1945, Billikopf Papers.

38. HJH to Ivonette Wright Miller, 16 April 1948, Wright Collection, Wright State University.

39. Haskell's letters to Carl Milles are in the Milles Papers, National Library, Stockholm. The sculptor's letters to Haskell are in the author's collection, with photocopies on deposit in Stockholm.

40. *KCT,* 9 February 1948; Harry Truman to HJH, 20 February 1948, Truman Presidential Papers PPF 3639, Truman Library.

41. Letters from Hoover, Swope, Baldwin, and others are pasted in a scrapbook commemorating the anniversary dinner, author's collection.

42. HJH to Jacob Billikopf, 7 August 1948, Billikopf Papers.

43. HJH to Wiley Rutledge, 21 September 1948, Rutledge Papers, Library of Congress.

44. HJH to Billikopf, 22 October 1949, Billikopf Papers.

45. "Big Roy," *Time,* 24 February 1947: 64–65; "Top of the Star," *Newsweek,* 24 February 1947; O. K. Armstrong, "Kansas City's Boss-Busting Editor," *Reader's Digest,* March 1947: 119–23.

46. Charles H. Hogan, *The Kansas City Star: A Literary Cat-House that Parades Its Benign, Pontifical Purity and Saintliness* (Girard, Kans.: Haldeman-Julius, 1946), 7–8; "The State of Missouri," *Fortune* 32, no. 1 (July 1945): 215; W. G. Clugston, "Kansas City: Gateway to What?" in Robert S. Allen, ed., *Our Fair City* (New York: Vanguard, 1949), 274.

47. "K.C.'s Sun," *Time,* 12 April 1948: 24–26.

48. Dwight Eisenhower to Roy Roberts, 30 January 1948, cited in Rollins, 71.

49. Thomas E. Dewey to Roy Roberts, 2 August 1947, Dewey Papers, University of Rochester Library; *Time,* 21 July 1948: 63; Roberts to Paul Lockwood, 15 October 1948, Dewey Papers.

50. HJH to Jacob Billikopf, 12 November 1948, Billikopf Papers; Roberts, "Let Hardboiled Reporters Search for Vote Trends," *Editor and Publisher,* 13 November 1948: 74; *U.S. News and World Report,* 3 December 1948: 35.

51. HJH to Jacob Billikopf, 22 January 1949, Billikopf Papers; Thomas E. Dewey to Roy Roberts, 23 December 1948, Dewey Papers; Lacy Haynes to Dewey, 4 November 1948, Haynes Collection, Kansas State Historical Society.

52. Henry A. Bundschu, "Harry S. Truman: The Missourian," *KCS,* 26 December 1948; Truman to Roberts, 21 March 1949, Truman Presidential Papers, PPF 366.

53. Harry S. Truman to Bess Truman, 9 August 1942, in Robert H. Ferrell, ed., *Dear Bess: The Letters from Harry to Bess Truman, 1910–1958* (New York: Norton, 1983), 485.

54. Milligan, *Missouri Waltz,* 267.

55. Harry Truman to Mary Jane Truman, 25 July 1947, in Robert H. Ferrell, ed., *Off the Record: The Private Papers of Harry S. Truman* (New York: Harper and Row, 1980), 115; H. Graham Morison Oral History Interview, Truman Library.

56. David McCullough, *Truman* (New York: Simon and Schuster, 1992), 508; Harry Truman to Bess Truman, 7 August 1946, in Ferrell, *Dear Bess,* 529; Frank Mason, *Truman and the Pendergasts* (Evanston, Ill.: Regency, 1963), 52; James C. Logan to James P. Kem, 29 May 1947, Kem Papers, Western Historical Manuscript Collection, University of Missouri–Columbia; Tom L. Evans Oral History Interview and Frank Holeman Oral History Interview, Truman Library.

57. Rytting, 154–58.

58. Debs Meyers, "Kansas City," *Holiday* 7 (March 1950): 46–47; HJH to Jacob Billikopf, 13 January 1950, Billikopf Papers.

59. Haskell and Fowler, *City of the Future,* 7.

60. *Newsweek,* 22 May 1950; James Reston to Roy Roberts, 12 April 1950, author's collection; *Washington Post,* 3 September 1950: B7.

61. *KCS,* 5 June 1950; Harry Truman to Roy Roberts, 12 June 1950, in Ferrell, ed., *Off the Record,* 180–82; Truman to Jim Pendergast, [late March] 1951, in Monte M. Poen, ed., *Strictly Personal and Confidential: The Letters Harry Truman Never Mailed* (Boston: Little, Brown, 1982), 112.

62. Rollins, 77.

Chapter 10. Busted Trust

Epigraph: "50 Years of the *Star,*" *KCS,* 18 September 1930.

1. *New York Times,* 9 January 1953: 22; *Star* history, 77.

2. Drew Pearson, "Truman Pays Tribute to Hoover," *Washington Post,* 8 January 1954: 47; *Time,* 19 January 1953.

3. The parallels extended to the delegate fight. Republican National Committee chairman Herbert Brownell studied the record of the 1912 Republican convention and based his strategy for 1952 on it. Brownell Oral History Interview, Columbia Oral History Project.

4. *KCS,* 24 June 1945, cited in Rollins, 67.

5. *KCT,* 7 November 1946, cited in Rollins, 65; Rollins, 68.

6. "Conversation with Roy Roberts," Leonard V. Finder Papers, box 2, Dwight D. Eisenhower Library.

7. Smith, *Dewey and His Times,* 578; E. Jay Jernigan, *William Lindsay White, 1900– 1973: In the Shadow of His Father* (Norman: University of Oklahoma Press, 1997), 233–34.

8. Lucius Clay to Dwight Eisenhower, 1 February 1952, *The Papers of Dwight David Eisenhower* (Baltimore: Johns Hopkins University Press, 1989), 12–13: 965; Roy Roberts to Eisenhower, 22 March 1952, Rollins, Appendix.

9. Roberts to Eisenhower, 5 May 1952, Eisenhower Pre-Presidential Papers, box 99; and 7 July 1952, Campaign Series, box 24, Eisenhower Library.

10. Ferrell, ed., *Off the Record,* 273; Roberts to Eisenhower, 5 November 1952, Eisenhower Papers Central Files, PPF 510 (box 951), Eisenhower Library.

11. Obituary, *KCS,* 20 August 1952: 1; "A Long Life of Service," ibid., undated clipping in author's collection.

12. *Star* history, 88.

13. Roberts to Eisenhower, 15 July 1953, Eisenhower Papers Central Files, PPF 510 (box 951), Eisenhower Library; Rollins, 86; Diary Series, box 4 (October– December 1953), Eisenhower Library.

14. Roberts to Joseph Pulitzer II, 23 January 1954, Charles G. Ross Papers, box 20, Truman Library.

15. *Star* history, 82.

16. Cross-reference File, 4 February 1954, Eisenhower Library; Eisenhower to Roberts, 24 September and 9 October 1954, in *Papers of Dwight David Eisenhower,* 15: 1304 and 1342; Rytting, 178; reference cards to appointments calendar, Eisenhower Library.

17. E. B. Garnett Diaries, 1955, Kansas City Star; *Star* history, 79.

18. Rytting, 179–80; Drew Pearson, "Barnes Balked Publisher's Trial," *Washington Post,* 8 May 1955: E5.

19. *Star* history, 79.

20. *Editor and Publisher,* 22 January 1955: 7; Rytting, 183–84; photocopy of memorandum supplied by Jim Fisher.

21. "Case against the *Star,*" *Time,* 14 February 1955: 75.

22. *Editor and Publisher,* 29 January 1955: 61.

23. Rytting, 203–4.

24. *Editor and Publisher,* 29 January 1955: 55.

25. Colvin Peterson interview, 7 August 2003.

26. Reynolds Packard, *The Kansas City Milkman* (New York: Dutton, 1950), 16.

27. *Editor and Publisher,* 22 January 1955: 62; Rytting, 218.

28. E. B. Garnett Diaries, Kansas City Star.

29. *Star* history, 76; *WRN,* 192.

30. *KCT,* 23 February 1955: 1.

31. Roberts to Eisenhower, 3 May 1955, Name Series, box 28, Eisenhower Library.

32. Eisenhower to Roberts, 10 May 1955, Name Series, box 28, Eisenhower Library.

33. "Duty Seen If Ike Runs," *Washington Post and Times Herald,* 12 May 1955: 2; Roy A. Roberts cross-reference file, Eisenhower Library.

34. Giles Fowler telephone interview, 21 October 2003; *Star* history, 80.

35. Roy A. Roberts, *Responsibility of Newspapers* (Lawrence: University of Kansas, 1956).

36. Francis F. Shoemaker, *"The Kansas City Post:* Its Founding, Growth, and Decline" (thesis, University of Missouri, 1958), 100–101; Frederick G. Bonfils to Frank Walsh, 16 October 1916, Walsh Papers, New York Public Library.

37. "Kansas City Star Criminal Case," Tom L. Evans Papers, box 3, Truman Library; "Memorandum of Newspaper Ownership of Radio Stations," attached to James Lawrence Fly to Franklin D. Roosevelt, 23 December 1940, Roosevelt Presidential Papers, POF 1059, box 2, f. "FCC 1941," Roosevelt Library.

38. "Memorandum of Ownership"; James Rowe to Roosevelt, 5 May 1941, James Rowe, Jr. Papers, box 13, f. "FCC (2)," Roosevelt Library.

39. Roberts to Theodore C. Alford, 15 May 1941, Roosevelt Presidential Papers, POF 1059; Roberts to Wendell Willkie, 17 May 1941, Willkie MSS, Lilly Library, Indiana University; Willkie to Roosevelt, 19 May 1941, and Roosevelt to Willkie, 23 May 1941, Roosevelt Presidential Papers, POF 1059.

40. Harry S. Truman to Wayne Coy, 24 April 1951, cited in Franklin D. Mitchell, *Harry S. Truman and the News Media* (Columbia: University of Missouri Press, 1990), 171.

41. Colvin Peterson interview, 7 August 2003.

42. *It's Peace or Else! Roy A. Roberts Reports from Europe* (Kansas City: Kansas City Star, 1956).

43. *Star* history, 79.

44. "The Prudent Publishers," *Fortune,* August 1950: 83–84, 86–87.

45. "A Big 50 in Kansas City," *Newsweek,* 8 June 1959: 98–100; "Good for Kansas City," *Time,* 28 December 1959: 41–42.

46. Jim Fisher interview, 3 April 2004; "Good for Kansas City," 41–42.

47. "Succession in Kansas City," *Time,* 18 January 1963: 68; "End of One-Man Rule," *Time,* 1 October 1965: 68.

48. "Succession in Kansas City."

49. Roberts to "Fellow Workers and Associates on The Star," 31 December 1964, Charles G. Ross Papers, box 20, Truman Library.

Epilogue: Newspaper of the Future

1. Irwin Kirkwood to E. B. Garnett, 2 August 1926, photocopy supplied by Jim Fisher.

2. *Star* history, 143; Franklin P. Adams in *The End of the "World,"* cited in Walker, *City Editor,* 74.

3. Kirkwood to Garnett, 2 August 1926.

4. W. W. Baker interview, 8 April 2004.

5. *Star* history, 155.

6. C. W. Gusewelle, "Rumblings of Change," *KCS,* 1 January 2006.

7. George Seldes, *Lords of the Press* (New York: J. Messner, 1938), 278.

8. Pfaff, *Joseph Pulizter II and the "Post-Dispatch,"* 326; *Star* history, 144.

9. Gary Pruitt, "Newspapers Are Still the Center of the Media Galaxy," *KCS,* 18 March 2006: B7.

10. Pruitt, "Newspapers"; Chris Lester, "Melding Journalism, Business," *KCS,* 21 March 2006: D11.

11. Timothy L. O'Brien, "The Newspaper of the Future," *New York Times* online edition, 26 June 2005; *Star* history, 152.

12. Kirkwood to Garnett, 2 August 1926.

13. Michael Janeway, *The Fall of the House of Roosevelt* (New York: Columbia University Press, 2004).

14. Dan Gillmor, *We the People: Grassroots Journalism by the People for the People,* cited in *Manchester Guardian Weekly,* 26 November–2 December 2004: 25.

15. Howard Kurtz, *Media Circus: The Trouble with America's Newspapers* (New York: Times Books, 1993), 6–7; Pruitt, "Newspapers."

16. Joseph Pulitzer, "The College of Journalism," *North American Review* 178 (May 1904): 656, 679.

17. Stout, *Nelson,* 250–51.

A Note on Sources

———————◆———————

A newspaper's history is, by its very nature, highly perishable. If journalism is history written on the fly, journalism history is doubly elusive. As anyone who has worked on a newspaper knows, only a tiny portion of the real news ever makes it into print. The rest—the stories behind the stories, as it were—must be read between the lines or teased out of whatever company records, personal letters, memos, and other documents may have been fortuitously preserved in the daily race against deadlines.

The genesis of this book was a dozen or so typed and handwritten notes signed by William Rockhill Nelson that my grandfather, Henry J. Haskell, lovingly preserved. I had no idea how rare these artifacts were until I began research in earnest. Three years of assiduous hunting in archives around the country yielded just enough of Nelson's private correspondence to fill one five-inch-thick archival box. The bulk of it consists of letters to and from two U.S. presidents, Theodore Roosevelt and William Howard Taft. Their papers in the Library of Congress, supplemented by a smaller collection of Roosevelt-Nelson correspondence in the William L. Clements Library at the University of Michigan in Ann Arbor, provided much of the grist for my early chapters. The editor's letters to his daughter, Laura, which seem to have been housed on the *Star* premises as late as 1950, have apparently vanished (though substantial excerpts have been published over the years). Nelson is one of the few authentic giants of American journalism who still lacks a proper biography. Whether enough primary source material for such a book survives remains an open question.

Fortunately, Haskell, like most newspaper editors of his generation, was a prolific letter writer. Among the letters he kept are several dozen from men and women in public life, in addition to eighty or a hundred letters from his longtime friend William Allen White. Using this small sample as a guide, I tracked down as much of my grandfather's correspondence as possible in archives around the United States. Much more undoubtedly remains to be ferreted out, particularly in Europe. Four collections proved particularly fruitful inasmuch as they document extended periods of his (and the *Star*'s) life: the William Allen White Papers at the Library of Congress; the Jacob Billikopf Papers at the American Jewish Archives in Cincinnati; the Edward B. Haskell Papers at Houghton Library, Harvard University; and the Katharine Wright Haskell Papers at the Western Historical Manuscript Collection, University of Missouri at Kansas City. At this writing, Katharine Wright's original letters remain in our family's possession, but microfilms are available through UMKC, Wright State University in Dayton, Ohio, and other research libraries. Photocopies of the Edward B. Haskell Papers are at the Hilandar Research Library, Ohio State University in Columbus, where they were temporarily deposited before coming to Harvard as part of the American Board of Commissioners of Foreign Missions (ABCFM) Papers. Both the originals and copies of Haskell's correspondence, together with the bulk of my research collection, will eventually be donated to UMKC.

Roy A. Roberts's vast outgoing correspondence is similarly scattered. (He seems to have left no private papers.) Among the major collections from which I've drawn are the Henry J. Allen Papers (Library of Congress), Thomas E. Dewey Papers (University of Rochester), Dwight D. Eisenhower Presidential Library, James A. Farley Papers (Library of Congress), James V. Forrestal Papers (Princeton University), Herbert Hoover Presidential Library, H. L. Mencken Papers (New York Public Library), Eugene Meyer Papers (Library of Congress), Franklin D. Roosevelt Presidential Library, Harry S. Truman Presidential Library (including the papers of Truman's press secretary, Charles G. Ross, whose widow Roberts married), William Allen White Papers (Library of Congress), and Wendell Willkie Papers (Lilly Library, Indiana University).

Frank P. Walsh's papers at the New York Public Library are a mine of information about Kansas City history and politics, the *Star*, the Bonfils-Tammen *Kansas City Post*, the labor movement, and the Progressive Era in general. Unfortunately, almost all of Walsh's pre-1913 correspondence was destroyed in a house fire, leaving the period of his closest association with Nelson largely undocumented. Walsh, whose legal career stretched from the early 1890s to his death in 1939, played a more significant role in the history of Kansas City, the American labor movement, and national Democratic politics than scholars have generally realized. His papers have yet to receive the attention they deserve.

William Allen White has long been recognized as a shining light of both American journalism and letters. Understandably, historians have gravitated toward the irresistibly quotable autobiography that he left unfinished at his death in 1943. (His son, the journalist William L. White, added a postscript on the last two decades of his life when the autobiography was published in 1946.) But the "Sage of Emporia" was a notoriously unreliable witness and on many matters his testimony must be handled with caution. In his letters—which constitute two voluminous collections, at the Library of Congress and Emporia State University in Kansas—he blithely contradicts himself time and again, even from one day to the next. No one could accuse White of prevaricating intentionally, for he wore his sincerity and integrity on his sleeve. Like Walt Whitman, however, he was large and contained multitudes. His vivid and intensely human correspondence provides an invaluable perspective on Nelson, Theodore Roosevelt, Haskell, Roberts, and many others.

In the course of my research, I mined the papers and libraries of every U.S. president from Grover Cleveland to Dwight Eisenhower. All yielded nuggets of information and insight into the story I was trying to flesh out, as the citations in my endnotes attest. But the *Star*'s on-again, off-again involvement in national politics is only one facet of its contribution to the progressive movement. Of equal importance is evidence of its pervasive presence in state and local politics. In this regard, the wide-ranging holdings of the University of Missouri's Western Historical Manuscript Collection are exceptionally fruitful. The Kansas City campus houses the papers of Senator James A. Reed as well as records of the J. C. Nichols Company, including a small chunk of the developer's private correspondence. On the Columbia campus, I made many an eye-opening discovery in the papers of Governor Herbert S. Hadley, Agnes Hadley Haskell, Governor Arthur M. Hyde, Senator James P. Kem, and Governor Lloyd C. Stark. The collections of the Kansas State Historical Society in Topeka are equally rich, in particular the papers of Governor Henry J. Allen, Senator Joseph L. Bristow, Charles S. Gleed, E. W. Howe, Governor Alfred M. Landon, and Governor Walter R. Stubbs. The correspondence in the George E. Kessler Papers at the Missouri Historical Society in St. Louis speaks volumes about the evolution of Kansas City's parks-and-boulevards system, as well as the crucial connection between Nelson, Kessler, and Nichols.

The *Star*'s institutional history, like that of most newspapers, is very sketchily documented. Apart from a single "daybook" dated 1880–1881, no financial records are known to survive from the paper's first two decades. Indeed, a few photographs of the *Star* offices at the turn of the last century, portraits and snapshots of the Nelson family and friends, and some isolated payroll sheets are virtually the only contemporary documentation of this period. Luckily, the evidence for later periods is much fuller. Some years ago, the records of the William Rockhill Nelson Trust were transferred to the library of the Nelson-Atkins Museum of Art, where they were meticulously catalogued and invite the scrutiny of researchers. These records include not only account books for Nelson's journalistic and real estate enterprises but also auditors' statements, attorneys' files, and correspondence and other documents relating to the sale of the paper in 1926, libel actions against the *Star,* the building of the art gallery and its collections, and management of the Rockhill properties by the university trustees under J. C. Nichols's supervision. Recently, the Kansas City Public Library acquired a small but highly revealing collection of Jason Rogers's papers concerning the investigation of the *Star* that he undertook in the mid-1920s at the behest of rival publisher Walter Dickey.

Back issues of the *Kansas City Star* and *Times* (available, alas, only on microfilm) were of course a vital source of information, though any student of history soon learns that newspapers, produced by men and women who are both actors in and observers of the historical pageant, belong in a class by themselves somewhere between primary and secondary sources. Many of the books, articles, and dissertations I've consulted are referenced in the notes. But the wide scope of my study made it impractical to cite an authority for every statement of fact. For the most part, therefore, I have confined myself to acknowledging sources for direct quotations, paraphrases, and new or controversial interpretations. The principal secondary sources on which I've drawn are listed at the beginning of the notes section.

ACKNOWLEDGMENTS

———————◆———————

My father and mother, he a newspaperman and playwright, she a social activist and professional volunteer, taught me to believe in newspapers without believing everything I read in them. But for them, the questions I needed to ask in telling this story never would have occurred to me. I owe much, too, to my friends and former colleagues at the *Star*, among them Bill Baker, Brian Burnes, Monroe Dodd, Derek Donovan, Jim Fisher, Giles Fowler, Charles Gusewelle, Don Hoffmann, Repps Hudson, Bill McCorkle, and Steve Paul. Craig Whitney of the *New York Times* and Richard Mooney, former editor of the *Hartford Courant*, allowed me to pick their brains about the future of print journalism. Selwyn Pepper shed light on the rivalry between the *Star* and the *St. Louis Post-Dispatch*. Christopher White Walker of the *Emporia Gazette* welcomed me to the office in which his grandfather and mine spent many hours discussing politics, philosophy, and life.

Ian Mackersey and Richard Maurer offered valuable perspectives on Henry J. Haskell's courtship of Katharine Wright and his relationship with her brother Orville. Roland Baumann, archivist of Oberlin College, helped me understand my grandfather's educational and missionary background. The late Jane Flynn, doyenne of Kansas City preservationists, and sociologist Richard Coleman set me right on matters of Kansas City history and society. Jim Scott, student as well as practitioner of urban planning, took me on a guided tour of Kansas City's parks and boulevards and elucidated their significance. William Worley shared his vast knowledge of J. C. Nichols and Kansas City real estate development, as well as offering valuable comments on my manuscript. Jerry Wallace put his painstaking research on Calvin Coolidge and the Liberty Memorial at my disposal. Jerome Walsh and Mary Walsh Abbott offered memories of their grandfather, Frank P. Walsh. Colvin Peterson, the last surviving member of the *Star's* legal defense team, gave me a firsthand account of the antitrust trial in the 1950s.

Theresa Taylor and Richard Moore cast expert eyes over the byzantine account books in the Nelson Trust Records at the Nelson-Atkins Museum of Art. Irene Hummel recalled her parents' experiences as members of William R. Nelson's domestic staff, and Frances Hines of the Magnolia Historical Society illuminated the editor's role in the Massachusetts summer colony. Randal J. Loy and Mary Byrne shed light on the Nelson family's involvement with Grace and Holy Trinity Cathedral. Marilyn Siegel and Ann McFerrin alerted me to a previously overlooked Nelson deed in the Kansas City Parks and Recreation Department archives. O. J. Nelson supplied photocopies of Nelson-era documents relating to the *Star's* Associated Press franchises. Winnie Crapson and Howard Sims gamely volunteered to do legwork on my behalf.

The helpful staff and rich collections of the Yale University Libraries provided an invaluable home base for my research. Of the many other librarians and archivists who gave generously of their time and expertise over the years, I would like to acknowledge in particular Mary Beveridge of the Missouri Valley Room, Kansas City Public Library; David Boutros of the Western Historical Manuscript Collection, University of Missouri–Kansas City; Dawne Dewey of the Wright State University Libraries; Bob Knecht of the Kansas State Historical Society; Max Krause of the Anderson Memorial Library, Emporia State University; Predrag Matejic of the Hilandar Research Library, Ohio State University; Denise Morison of the Kansas City Museum; Randy Roberts of the Leonard H. Axe Library, Pittsburg State University; Randy Sowell of the Harry S. Truman Library; Alison Stankrauff, formerly of the American Jewish Archives; Bill Stolz of the Western Historical Manuscript Collection, University of Missouri–Columbia; and Holly Wright of the Helen F. Spencer Library, Nelson-Atkins Museum of Art.

Robert Ferrell and John Dizikes, two of my all-time favorite historians and writers, read the manuscript and gently steered me away from many a pitfall. Jonathan Kemper, Bill Frohlich, and Willis Regier took an early interest in the project, and Sam Bennett facilitated a grant from the William T. Kemper Foundation that provided crucial support for my travel and research. The good people at the University of Missouri Press extended me every consideration and produced a handsome book.

My debt to Ellen and Lucy goes beyond words.

ILLUSTRATION CREDITS

———————◆———————

Numbers refer to the pages on which the illustrations appear.

Author's collection: 17, 94, 107, 242, 265, 299, 335
Jackson County Historical Society: 220
Kansas City Star: 8, 27, 35, 38, 78, 86, 162, 184, 196, 252, 269, 290, 295, 305, 344, 358
Library of Congress: 101, 133, 219, 237, 270, 277, 339
Special Collections, Kansas City Public Library: 2, 12, 21, 43, 57, 61, 138, 153, 203, 238
Special Collections Department, University of Missouri–Kansas City Libraries: 350
State Historical Society of Missouri, Columbia: 117
Harry S. Truman Library: 315
Union Station/Kansas City Museum Archives: 211
Western Historical Manuscript Collection, University of Missouri–Kansas City: 57, 69, 127, 175, 259, 280
Yale University Libraries: 147, 366

INDEX

Page references in italics refer to illustrations.